The Medieval Origins of the Legal Profession

THE MEDIEVAL ORIGINS OF THE LEGAL PROFESSION

Canonists, Civilians, and Courts

James A. Brundage

The University of Chicago Press   Chicago and London

The University of Chicago Press, Chicago 60637
The University of Chicago Press, Ltd., London
© 2008 by The University of Chicago
All rights reserved. Published 2008
Paperback edition 2010
Printed in the United States of America

19 18 17 16 15 14 13 12 11 10   2 3 4 5 6

ISBN-13: 978-0-226-07759-8 (cloth)
ISBN-13: 978-0-226-07760-4 (paper)
ISBN-10: 0-226-07759-4 (cloth)
ISBN-10: 0-226-07760-8 (paper)

Frontispiece: A cardinal sitting as judge. On his right, a solider and his proctor put forward their case, while an advocate kneels at his left, holding a plea for his client. At the cardinal's feet sit three notaries, one of whom is taking notes on the proceedings. Italian, ca. 1355–60; attributed to Bartolomeo dei Baroli. Fitzwilliam Museum, Cambridge, MS 331, 1r. Reproduced by permission.

Library of Congress Cataloging-in-Publication Data

Brundage, James A.
The medieval origins of the legal profession : canonists, civilians, and courts / James A. Brundage.
p. cm.
Includes bibliographical references and index.
ISBN-13: 978-0-226-07759-8 (cloth : alk. paper)
ISBN-10: 0-226-07759-4 (cloth : alk. paper) 1. Law, Medieval. 2. Law—Europe—History. I. Title.
KJ147.B78 2008
340.5'5—dc22
2007036086

♾ The paper used in this publication meets the minimum requirements of the American National Standard for Information Sciences—Permanence of Paper for Printed Library Materials, ANSI Z39.48-1992.

*For Mike and Karen
and Ken and Marlene
in gratitude*

Contents

List of Abbreviations	ix
Preface	xv
Introduction	1
1 The Foundation: The Roman Legal Profession	9
2 Law without Lawyers: The Early Middle Ages	46
3 The Legal Revival of the Twelfth Century	75
4 Church Courts, Civil Procedure, and the Professionalization of Law	126
5 Pre-Professional Lawyers in Twelfth-Century Church Courts	164
6 The Formation of an Educated Elite: Law Schools and Universities	219
7 Attaining Professional Status	283
8 Professional Canon Lawyers: Advocates and Proctors	344
9 Judges and Notaries	371
10 The Practice of Canon Law	407
11 Rewards and Hazards of the Legal Profession	466
Conclusion: The Tradition of the Legal Profession	488
Bibliography	493
Index	579
Citations Index	601

Abbreviations

AKKR	*Archiv für katholisches Kirchenrecht*
Angelica Statutes	Angelica Statutes, in M. B. Hackett, *The Original Statutes of Cambridge University: The Text and Its History* (Cambridge: Cambridge University Press, 1970).
ANRW	*Aufstieg und Niedergang der römischen Welt: Geschichte und Kultur Roms im Spiegel der neueren Forschung*, ed. Hilldegard Temporini and Wolfgang Haase, 22 vols. to date (Berlin: Walter De Gruyter, 1972–).
BAV	Biblioteca Apostolica Vaticana
BL	British Library, London
BMCL	*Bulletin of Medieval Canon Law*
BN	Bibliothèque Nationale, Paris
Bologna University Statutes, ed. Denifle	Heinrich Denifle, "Die Statuten der Juristen-Universität Bologna vom J. 1317–1347 und deren Verhältnis zu jenen Paduas, Perugias, Florenz," *Archiv für Literatur- und Kirchengeschichte des Mittelalters* 3 (1887) 196–397.
Bologna University Statutes, ed. Maffei	Domenico Maffei, "Un trattato di Bonaccorso degli Elisei e i più antichi statuti dello Studio di Bologna nel manoscritto 22 della Robbins Collection," *BMCL* 5 (1975) 73–101.

BRUC	A. B. Emden, *A Biographical Register of the University of Cambridge to 1500* (Cambridge: Cambridge University Press, 1963).
BRUO	A. B. Emden, *A Biographical Register of the University of Oxford to 1500*, 3 vols. (Oxford: Clarendon Press, 1957–59).
Caius glosses	Cambridge, Gonville and Caius College, MS 283/676
CCL	Corpus Christianorum, series Latina
CCM	Corpus Christianorum, continuatio mediaevalia
Clm.	Codex latinus Monacensis
Cod. Theod.	Codex Theodosianus, in *Codex Theodosianus, cum constitutionibus Sirmondinis*, ed. Paul Krueger and Theodor Mommsen, 2 vols. in 3 (Berlin: Weidmann, 1905; repr., 1990).
Coing, *Handbuch*	*Handbuch der Quellen und Literatur der neueren europäischen Privatrechtsgeschichte*, ed. Helmut Coing, vol. 1, *Mittelalter, 1100–1500: Die gelehrten Rechte und die Gesetzgebung* (Munich: C. H. Beck, 1973).
Compilationes antiquae	*Quinque compilationes antiquae necnon collectio canonum Lipsiensis*, ed. Emil Friedberg (Leipzig: Bernhard Tauchnitz, 1882; repr., Graz: Akademische Druck- u. Verlagsanstalt, 1956).
1 Comp.	Bernard of Pavia, *Compilatio prima* (*Breviarium extravagantium*)
2 Comp.	John of Wales, *Compilatio secunda*
3 Comp.	Petrus Beneventanus, *Compilatio tertia*
4 Comp.	Johannes Teutonicus, *Compilatio quarta*
5 Comp.	Tancred, *Compilatio quinta*
Const. Sirmond.	Constitutiones Sirmondianae, in *Codex Theodosianus, cum constitutionibus Sirmondinis*, ed. Paul Krueger and Theodor Mommsen, 2 vols. in 3 (Berlin: Weidmann, 1905; repr., 1990).

Corpus iuris canonici	*Corpus iuris canonici*, ed. Emil Friedberg, 2 vols. (Leipzig: Bernhard Tauchnitz, 1879; repr., Graz: Akademische Druck- u. Verlagsanstalt, 1959).
Gratian	*Decretum Gratiani*
X	Liber Extra (= *Decretales Gregorii IX*)
VI	Liber Sextus Decretalium
Clem.	Constitutiones Clementinae
Extrav. Jo. XXII	Extravagantes Johannis XXII
Extrav. comm.	Extravagantes communes
Corpus iuris civilis	*Corpus iuris civilis*, ed. Paul Krueger et al., 3 vols. (Berlin: Weidmann, 1872–95; repr., 1963–65).
Auth.	Authenticum
Cod.	Codex Iustinianus
Dig.	Digesta (= *Pandekta*)
Nov.	Novellae leges
CSB	*Chartularium studii Bononiensis: Documenti per la storia dell'Università di Bologna dalle origini fino al secolo XV*, 14 vols. to date (Bologna: Commissione per la storia dell'Università di Bologna, 1909–).
CSEL	Corpus scriptorum ecclesiasticorum latinorum
CUL	Cambridge University Library
CUP	*Chartularium Universitatis Parisiensis*, ed. Heinrich Denifle and Émile Chatelain, 4 vols. (Paris: Delalain Frères, 1889–97; repr., Brussels: Culture & Civilisation, 1964).
DA	*Deutsches Archiv für Erforschung des Mittelalters*
DDC	*Dictionnaire de droit canonique*, ed. R. Naz, 7 vols. (Paris: Letouzey & Ané, 1935–65).
DEC	*Decrees of the Ecumenical Councils*, ed. Giuseppe Alberigo et al., trans. Norman P. Tanner et al., 2 vols. (London: Sheed & Ward; Washington, DC: Georgetown University Press, 1990).

DMA	*Dictionary of the Middle Ages*, ed. Joseph R. Strayer et al., 13 vols. (New York: Scribner, 1982–89).
EDR	Ely Diocesan Records
Gaius, *Inst.*	*The Institutes of Gaius*, ed. E. Seckel and B. Kuebler, trans. W. M. Gordon and O. F. Robinson (Ithaca: Cornell University Press, 1988).
Glos. ord.	*Glossa ordinaria*
HUE	*A History of the University in Europe*, ed. Walter Rüegg, vol. 1, *Universities in the Middle Ages*, ed. Hilde de Ridder-Symoens (Cambridge: Cambridge University Press, 1992).
HUO	*The History of the University of Oxford*, ed. T. H. Aston, vol. 1, *The Early Oxford Schools*, ed. J. I. Catto (Oxford: Clarendon Press, 1984).
IRMÆ	Ius Romanum medii aevi
JEH	*Journal of Ecclesiastical History*
JE, JK, JL	Philip Jaffé, *Regesta pontificum romanorum ab condita ecclesia ad annum post Christum natum MCXCVIII*, 2nd ed., revised by S. Loewenfeld (JL = AD 882–1198), F. Kaltenbrunner (JK = AD ?–590), and P. Ewald (JE = AD 590–882), 2 vols. (Leipzig: Veit, 1885–88; repr., Graz: Akademische Druck- u. Verlagsanstalt, 1956).
JMH	*Journal of Medieval History*
JTS	*Journal of Theological Studies*
Mansi	Giovanni Domenico Mansi, *Sacrorum conciliorum nova et amplissima collectio*, 53 vols. in 60 (Paris: H. Welter, 1901–27).
Markaunt Statutes	Markaunt Statutes, in M. B. Hackett, *The Original Statutes of Cambridge University: The Text and Its History* (Cambridge: Cambridge University Press, 1970).
MGH	Monumenta Germaniae Historica
SS	Scriptores
SSRG	Scriptores rerum Germanicarum

MIC	Monumenta iuris canonici
NCMH	*The New Cambridge Medieval History*, 7 vols. in 8 (Cambridge: Cambridge University Press, 1995–2005).
Nov. Theod. Nov. Val.	Novellae Thedosiani and Novellae Valentiniani, in *Codex Theodosianus, cum constitutionibus Sirmondinis*, ed. Paul Krueger and Theodor Mommsen, 2 vols. in 3 (Berlin: Weidmann, 1905; repr., 1990).
PL	*Patrologiae cursus completus . . . series Latina*, ed. J.-P. Migne, 221 vols. (Paris: J.-P. Migne, 1841–64).
Po	*Regesta pontificum romanorum inde ab a. post Christum natum MCXCVIII ad a. MCCCIV*, ed. August Potthast, 2 vols. (Berlin: R. de Decker, 1874–75).
Proceedings II–X	*Proceedings of the International Congress of Canon Law*. MIC, Subsidia (Vatican City: BAV, 1965–2001).
Powicke & Cheney	*Councils and Synods with Other Documents Relating to the English Church, II, A.D. 1205–1313*, ed. Frederick M. Powicke and Christopher R. Cheney, 2 vols. (Oxford: Clarendon Press, 1964).
QFIAB	*Quellen und Forschungen aus italienischen Archiven und Bibliotheken*
QGRKP	Quellen zur Geschichte des römisch-canonischen Processes im Mittelalter
RDC	*Revue de droit canonique*
RHDF	*Revue historique de droit français et étranger*
RHE	*Revue d'histoire ecclésiastique*
RIDC	*Rivista internazionale di diritto comune*
Sarti-Fattorini	Mauro Sarti and Mauro Fattorini, *De claris archigymnasii Bononiensis professoribus a saeculo XI usque ad saeculm XIV*, ed. C. Albacino and C. Malagola, 2 vols. (Bologna: Merlani, 1888–96; repr., Turin: Bottega d'Erasmo, 1962).
Schulte, *QL*	Johann Friedrich von Schulte, *Die Geschichte der Quellen und Literatur des canonischen Rechts*, 3 vols.

	(Stuttgart: Ferdinand Enke, 1875–80; repr., Graz: Akademische Druck- u. Verlagsanstalt, 1956).
SDHI	*Studia et documenta historiae et iuris*
SG	*Studia Gratiana*
TRG	*Tijdschrift voor Rechtsgeschiedenis*
TUJ	*Tractatus universi juris*, 22 vols. in 28 (Venice: Franciscus Zilettus, 1584–86).
VCH, Cambs.	*Victoria History of the County of Cambridgeshire and the Isle of Ely*, ed. L. F. Salzman et al., 10 vols. to date (London, 1938–).
Whitelock, Brett & Brooke	*Councils and Synods with Other Documents Relating to the English Church I, A.D. 871–1204*, ed. Dorothy Whitelock, Martin Brett, and Christopher N. L. Brooke, 2 vols. (Oxford: Clarendon Press, 1981).
ZRG	*Zeitschrift der Savigny-Stiftung für Rechtsgeschichte*
KA	Kanonistische Abteilung
RA	Romanistische Abteilung
GA	Germanistische Abteilung

Preface

This book has been close to forty years in the making. It began with questions that occurred to me while searching the glosses, commentaries, and legal opinions written by canon lawyers who lived in the twelfth, thirteenth, and fourteenth centuries for evidence about the regulation of crusades and the efforts of medieval churchmen to formulate and implement rules for Christian sexual behavior. I began to wonder about the authors of the works I was reading, about where they studied law and with whom. I wondered, too, about their social and economic backgrounds and the careers they pursued. Most of the authors I was reading taught law and many of their writings were by-products of teaching, but was law teaching their only, or even their principal, occupation throughout their adult lives? Did they practice as well as teach? Did their legal training provide a stepping-stone to high office in church or state?

As I thought about these questions and began accumulating notes on the evidence that might help answer them, I began to realize that subtle changes in the ways these jurists thought and acted were gradually occurring during the decades between the middle of the twelfth century and the middle of the thirteenth. The notion of what it meant to be a jurist slowly altered during that period. Roman and canon lawyers who wrote during the second half of the twelfth century and the opening decades of the thirteenth seemed primarily, if not exclusively, interested in the intellectual problems that the law presented. By the middle of the thirteenth century, however, their successors seemed far more preoccupied than their predecessors had been with the details of legal practice and procedure, both in the courts and in providing clients with legal advice. In the process, legal writers' approach to the law seemed to be shifting. What had been an academic occupation was becoming a learned profession. This book embodies what I have been able to discover and infer about what that entailed and how the process worked.

During the years that I have wrestled with these problems I have accumulated intellectual and personal obligations beyond counting. Several of those to whom I am deeply indebted, although no longer among the living, still live in my memory. They include Robert L. Benson, Leonard Boyle, O.P., Christopher Cheney, Geoffrey Elton, John Gilchrist, Philip Grierson, Edgar N. Johnson, Stephan Kuttner, Charles Loughran, S.J., Jack McGovern, Jeremiah O'Sullivan, Dorothy Owen, Gaines Post, Robert Reynolds, Michael Sheehan, C.S.B., and Schafer Williams. My gratitude to them remains undimmed.

Happily, many more of those who have helped me remain very much alive. Martin Brett, Elizabeth A. R. Brown, Marjorie Chibnall, Giles Constable, Gero Dolezalek, Charles Donahue, Jr., Linda Fowler-Magerl, Richard Fraher, André Gouron, Richard Helmholz, Michael Hoeflich, Mia Korpiola, Peter Linehan, Elizabeth Makowski, Laurent Mayali, Jasonne Grabher, Kenneth Pennington, Olivia Robinson, Jonathan Rose, Barbara Seater, Carole Shammas, Tim Sistrunk, Jacques Verger, and Patrick Zutshi, among others, have patiently answered questions and shared their insights with me. I am grateful to Ernest Metzger, Michael Hoeflich, and especially to Paul Brand and Kenneth Pennington, for generously taking time from their own work to read my drafts. They have saved me from countless errors both of omission and commission. I am indebted to the research assistants who have helped me over the years, including Clay Barker, Robert Berberich, Charles Harbaugh, Mark Munzinger, and Kristine Utterback. I am grateful as well to Randolph Petilos, Carlisle Rex-Waller, and the editorial staff at the University of Chicago Press for their care and efficiency in bringing this book into being. Despite the best efforts of all these kind people, the errors and misjudgments that remain are inescapably my own.

I could not have written this book without access to the riches of numerous libraries and the help that members of their staffs have provided over many years. Among them are the Bayerische Staatsbibliothek, the Biblioteca Apostolica Vaticana, the British Library, the Cambridge University Library, the Golda Meier Library at the University of Wisconsin–Milwaukee, the Memorial Library at the University of Wisconsin–Madison, the Newberry Library, the Robbins Collection at Boalt Hall in the University of California at Berkeley, and the Watson, Anschutz, Law, and Spencer Research Libraries of the University of Kansas, as well as the libraries of several Cambridge colleges, notably Gonville and Caius, Pembroke, Peterhouse, Trinity College, and Trinity Hall. To all of them my warmest thanks.

I have resorted to a number of strategies in order to keep this long and complicated book within a moderate compass and at a reasonably affordable price. To economize on space, I have provided only the author's name, title, and page references in my notes, so that readers who want complete bibliographical details on the works cited will need to turn to the bibliography to find them.

Introduction

Around the year 1150, a small number of jurists were teaching Roman or canon law and practicing in ecclesiastical courts in a handful of cities, but there is no evidence that a legal profession in the rigorous sense of that term existed at that point anywhere in western Europe. Roughly a century later, by around 1250, professional lawyers had set up shop in every European city of any consequence and in some smaller towns as well.

Trained lawyers by the late twelfth century represented and argued on behalf of clients with some regularity in courts that functioned according to new procedural rules that were emerging in the medieval *ius commune*, the European general law, during that period.[1] Lawyers were usually rewarded for performing these services, and the fees they received apparently provided at least some of them with a livelihood. They differed significantly, however, from their thirteenth-century successors. For one thing, thirteenth-century lawyers learned their law by systematic study that followed a curriculum prescribed by a university law faculty, whereas neither universities, law faculties, nor curricula existed before the end of the twelfth century. By the mid-thirteenth century, many lawyers held academic degrees in law. Their degrees certified that they had performed well enough in rigorous examinations that their examiners deemed them competent to teach the subject. Credentials of this sort likewise did not exist

---

1. The medieval *ius commune* drew upon both Roman and canon law to adjudicate disputes; see Calasso, *Medio evo del diritto*, 377–86; Bellomo, *Common Legal Past*, 55–77; Pennington, "Learned Law, Droit Savant, Gelehrtes Recht"; Lange, *Römisches Recht im Mittelalter*, 461–62; and Brundage, "Universities and the 'ius commune.'"

in the twelfth century. Beyond that, lawyers by the mid-thirteenth century were professionals in the sense that they had been formally admitted to practice in one or more courts and at the time of their admission had pledged themselves to observe the rules of a special body of ethics peculiar to their calling. This, too, was something that twelfth-century lawyers were not required to do.[2]

Opinions vary concerning what constitutes a profession and how it differs, if indeed it differs at all, from other kinds of occupation.[3] In my view, the term "profession" properly speaking involves something more than simply a body of workers who do a particular kind of job on which they depend for support. A profession in the rigorous sense applies to a line of work that is not only useful, but that also claims to promote the interests of the whole community as well as the individual worker. A profession in addition requires mastery of a substantial body of esoteric knowledge through a lengthy period of study and carries with it a high degree of social prestige. When individuals enter a profession, moreover, they pledge that they will observe a body of ethical rules different from and more demanding than those incumbent on all respectable members of the community in which they live.

Professional lawyers were doing all of those things by the mid-thirteenth century. They often occupied positions of considerable authority as well, and their influence grew more pervasive with each passing generation during the next two hundred years. The study of law, to the dismay of philosophers and theologians, attracted a great many of the most original and talented minds in the generations that flourished during the centuries that followed 1150. Members of the legal profession were crucial players in the social and intellectual revolutions that began with the so-called renaissance of the twelfth century and continued to unfold well into the later Middle Ages.

All of this raises questions. Where did these lawyers come from? What kind of social background produced them? What career prospects faced a medieval lawyer once he had finished his studies? Would he even have thought in terms of a career? What did lawyers who practiced in the courts

2. For a different reading of the evidence, however, see Reynolds, "Emergence of Professional Law in the Long Twelfth Century," as well as "Medieval Law," 494, and *Fiefs and Vassals*, 231 and passim.

3. See, e.g., among many others, Kultgen, *Ethics and Professionalism*, 60; Turner and Hodge, "Occupations and Professions," 27–30; Kronman, "Law as a Profession," 31–34; Ridder-Symoens, "Training and Professionalization," 149; Royal Commission on Legal Services, *Final Report* 1:28–30; Burrage, "Professions in Sociology and History."

of the medieval *ius commune* actually do? What kind of demand existed for their services, and why did clients consider those services important enough to justify their cost?

The suddenness with which an organized legal profession sprang up, especially in church courts, during the early 1230s seems as puzzling as it is remarkable. What circumstances led this to happen at that particular time? Did legal practitioners organize professional associations in order to secure a monopoly on the practice of their trade, as artisans and craftsmen had been doing for generations? Or did judges and higher authorities take the initiative in order to exert greater control over the actions and behavior of the lawyers who appeared in their courts?

The evidence that I have explored suggests that professional lawyers first emerged in the courts of the medieval church. Practitioners in civil courts that employed the procedural system of the *ius commune* quickly followed suit and adopted procedures that resembled those already introduced in the ecclesiastical courts. Development of a professional identity among the canonists thus seems to have supplied a model that other professional groups, such as English common lawyers and university-trained physicians, adapted to their own needs and purposes.

The prestige attached to professions, like the word "profession" itself, has religious roots connected with making a solemn promise or undertaking. Theologians, pastors, and homilists, both medieval and modern, describe recitation of the Nicene Creed as making a "profession of faith" and speak of monks or nuns who have taken solemn religious vows as "professed members" of monastic communities. Medieval lawyers were undoubtedly aware of these religious connotations of "profession" when they used the term *professio advocatorum*, familiar to them from Roman legal sources, to describe themselves and their colleagues. Medieval lawyers used related terms as well, such as *ordo* (assemblage, band, or class), *officium* (duty, office, or function), *vocatio* (calling), and *militia* (military service, employment), to describe the group to which they belonged.[4] They regarded themselves and their colleagues with pride (frequently mixed with self-righteousness) as an intellectual elite who deserved to enjoy power, wealth, and other privileges because what they did was difficult, demanding, and vital to the

---

4. See, e.g., Cod. 2.6.5, 2.6.8, 2.7.3, 2.7.4 (= Cod. Theod. 2.10.6), 2.7.14, 2.7.18, 2.7.20, 2.7.24 pr., and 3.13.7; Azo, *Summa super Codicem*, proem., 1; Gratian, Decretum C. 3 q. 7 c. 2 §8; Bonaguida de Arezzo, *Summa introductoria*, proem., 133; William Durand, *Speculum iudiciale*, proem. §8, at 1:2; Antonio de Butrio, *In quinque libros decretalium commentaria* to X 1.37.2 §2, vol. 1, pt. 2, at 102vb, among many others.

well-being of society. Advocates and doctors of law, they insisted, were every bit as essential to a community as the soldiers who protected it from its enemies. Hence lawyers claimed that they were entitled to the same rights and respect that knights enjoyed.[5]

The legal professionals who became visible in growing numbers from the second quarter of the thirteenth century onward performed four different kinds of functions. Advocates were university-trained legal experts who furnished clients with knowledgeable legal advice and argued points of law on their behalf in the courts. Professionally qualified judges were often appointed from the ranks of the advocates, and by the end of the thirteenth century they, too, frequently held university law degrees. Proctors were agents who literally represented their clients during litigation in the sense that they could and frequently did appear not only on the client's behalf but in his place. Their statements and actions carried the same force and effect as if the client had said or done them in person. Proctors were experienced in dealing with the practical details of litigation. They saw to it that the cases they handled proceeded as smoothly as possible. A close familiarity with the working habits, preferences, and foibles of staff members at the courts in which they practiced formed part of their stock in trade, and this enabled them to smooth the way for their client's business. Notaries produced legal instruments of all kinds, including the reams of documents that litigation entailed. Notaries public, commissioned by high-ranking authorities such as the emperor or the pope, prepared contracts, testaments, and other documents that were often critical for a successful outcome in contested matters. Courts operated on the assumption that notarial documents were authentic reports of the transactions that they recorded. Over the course of time, it became increasingly common for notaries to boast advanced academic credentials. The dividing lines between these subgroups within the legal profession were not watertight. It was not unknown, at least by the fourteenth century, for individuals to begin their careers as notaries, then to move up into the ranks of proctors, and occasionally to become advocates or judges.

The jurisdiction of medieval church courts, despite variations in practice between different regions of Western Christendom, transcended the political boundaries between kingdoms, principalities, duchies, and city-states. A properly trained judge, advocate, proctor, or notary consequently

---

5. Thus, e.g., Johannes Teutonicus, *Glos. ord.* to C. 23 q. 1 c. 5 v. *militiae*; Bernard of Parma, *Glos. ord.* to X 3.34.9 v. *maturitate tamen consilio*; Johannes Andreae, *Glos. ord.* to VI 3.12.4 v. *castrense*.

might be able to ply his trade just as well at Riga, Rouen, or Regensburg as at Rome. Mobility, both geographical and social, was common among members of the legal profession who practiced in the ecclesiastical courts. As the courts of lay rulers, especially on the Continent, gradually adopted romano-canonical judicial procedures, it became increasingly possible for lawyers trained in Roman and canon law to find work in those courts as well.

I have based my account of the development of a medieval legal profession in part on the normative sources of the *ius commune*. I have read and reread the law books that medieval law students studied, as well as many of the glosses, commentaries, and treatises that tell us how their teachers interpreted the legal texts. In addition, I have drawn heavily on procedural guides written for practicing lawyers for evidence about what lawyers were supposed to do in the church courts. Although these manuals were not part of the formal curriculum of most medieval law faculties, there is no doubt that law students and practitioners read them. Copies of these books formed part of every lawyer's working library. In addition, I have made use of some medieval how-to-do-it books that offered lawyers tips about the tricks of the trade and advised them about how they were expected to behave. I have also searched for information about the professional activities of medieval lawyers in some records of actual practice.

A comprehensive account of the appearance of a legal profession within the medieval *ius commune* tradition should in principle deal with developments across the whole width and breadth of Western Christendom. For practical reasons, however, I have used records from some regions much more extensively than those from others. This reflects variations both in availability and accessibility. Relevant records simply do not survive in equal abundance from all parts of medieval Christendom. The records I have used come principally from regions where archival holdings are particularly rich and especially from record material that has been studied, analyzed, and published, at least in part, by earlier scholars. Medieval ecclesiastical court records and other documents of practice, such as bishops' registers, survive from England in relative abundance, and they have also been more fully surveyed and published than is commonly true elsewhere.[6] As a result, English evidence features prominently in this book. I have naturally paid attention as well to records concerning practices at the papal curia and have in addition examined some published evidence from north-

---

6. The indispensable survey of what is known to be available is *Records of the Medieval Ecclesiastical Courts*.

ern Italy, the French kingdom and the Midi, and to a lesser extent from Aragon, Catalonia, Germany, and eastern Europe. In addition to official records, I have also made use of a handful of narrative accounts in which practicing medieval lawyers described some of their professional activities.

Law is a learned profession, and its members, especially those who frequented the higher-level courts, almost invariably received their legal training at one or more universities. The ideas of law professors about how law should be practiced and how its practitioners should behave clearly influenced the formation of the profession. University records yield important information about the activities of law teachers as well as their students. Law professors frequently supplemented their academic income in numerous ways. Many of them regularly practiced in the courts as advocates, they often furnished judges and litigants with formal legal opinions on specific matters, and they frequently engaged in profitable nonlegal enterprises as well. Evidence from Bologna, Paris, Oxford, Cambridge, and other university cities accordingly furnishes important evidence both about the legal profession's origins and about the activities of its members.

The two opening chapters of this book aim to provide background information for understanding the context within which medieval legal professions took shape. Chapter 1 sketches the way in which a legal profession arose in Roman antiquity. Medieval lawyers learned much about the organization of Roman legal practice and the ways that Roman lawyers were expected to behave from the same late ancient legal texts that furnished them with rules and arguments they could use in court. They could also learn a good deal more about Roman advocates from such writers as Cicero, Quintilian, Aulus Gellius, Tacitus, and the younger Pliny. Popes, bishops, and councils played a leading role in adapting the Roman model of a legal profession to fit the distinctive needs and problems of legal practice in medieval society. The aspirations and ideals that Roman jurists aimed for, together with the rights and privileges that Roman emperors conceded to legal practitioners, provided the ideological framework within which medieval legal professions developed. Chapter 2 sketches the circumstances under which the Roman legal profession faded away in the aftermath of the barbarian invasions and briefly outlines the workings of the legal institutions that supplanted or supplemented Roman law throughout most parts of western Europe between the fifth and twelfth centuries.

Chapter 3 explains the circumstances that surrounded the renewed interest in Roman law and the radical reordering of the canon law of the Western Church that commenced in the late eleventh century and continued through the two centuries that followed. Chapter 4 examines some practical consequences of these developments, especially the restructuring of church courts and the emergence of the new legal procedures of the *ius commune* during the second half of the twelfth and the opening decades of the thirteenth century. Chapter 5 then takes a closer look at the advocates and proctors who advised, represented, and argued on behalf of litigants in those courts under the emerging romano-canonical procedural system. Chapter 6 examines the role of legal education in these developments, especially the appearance of the earliest European universities. Their years of study in university law faculties equipped advocates, and somewhat less frequently judges, proctors, and notaries, with the conceptual tools they needed to function effectively in the new legal environment. At the same time, systematic study of the Roman legal sources imbued students with admiration for the ideals and practices of their Roman predecessors. University law faculties thus played a crucial role in creating a common legal culture among their alumni. That in turn was a necessary precondition for the appearance of a medieval legal profession.

Chapter 7 deals with developments during the second quarter of the thirteenth century that transformed lawyers trained in the *ius commune* into full-fledged professionals. A key element in this transformation appeared when judges began to require that those who regularly appeared before them to represent clients and argue on their behalf be formally admitted to practice. When advocates and proctors were admitted, they solemnly promised to observe a set of ethical prescriptions concerning their relationships with their clients and with the court. Church authorities asserted their power to deprive those who failed to obey those behavioral rules of the right to be heard in court. They also established for the first time minimum educational requirements for admission to practice. Chapter 8 considers various kinds of career patterns open to professional lawyers between about 1250 and 1500. As it became increasingly common during that period to expect men appointed as judges to have some formal legal training, and very frequently to have some experience working as advocates as well, judges themselves (at least in the major church courts) likewise became assimilated to the profession. Notaries public, too, were more and more expected to have some formal academic training in law before they could qualify for appointment. Chapter 9 deals with those developments. Chapter 10 shows how professional advocates and proctors established and conducted their legal practices, and chapter 11 examines some of the interactions between medieval lawyers and the larger society in which they lived and worked.

This book aims to set out what is known or can reasonably be inferred about the rebirth of European legal professions in the High Middle Ages based on the scattered evidence that I have used. I cannot claim that what follows is anything like the whole story. Much evidence has yet to be made readily accessible, and much more of it almost certainly still remains to be discovered in archives dispersed far and wide. This provisional account attempts to demonstrate how a recognizable legal profession in the rigor of the term came into existence in the courts of the medieval church, just before the middle of the thirteenth century.

The evidence I have examined plainly shows that many features that still characterize modern legal professions were in place by about 1250. I hope that this study may persuade other scholars to investigate aspects of the topic that remain unresolved.

* ONE *

The Foundation
The Roman Legal Profession

Roman orators and jurists during the last two centuries of the Republic created the earliest recognizable legal profession.[1] Laws and legal systems, of course, existed long before that in the ancient Near East and the Mediterranean basin. One medieval jurist asserted that the first trial occurred in Paradise, when God found Adam and Eve guilty of disobeying his command not to eat the fruit of the tree of the knowledge of good and evil.[2] A modern writer has asserted that the earliest recorded European trial occurs in Homer's description of a dispute over compensation for damages in the *Iliad*.[3] Neither episode, however, involved anyone we might reasonably describe as a professional lawyer.

Lawyers never secured a stable foothold in the societies of ancient Greece.[4] Athenians showed little enthusiasm for the practice of law, al-

---

1. The Roman Republic is traditionally deemed to have begun with the expulsion of the last of the city's Etruscan kings, Tarquinius Superbus, in an aristocratic coup in or about 509 BCE. It lasted until Augustus Caesar's triumph at the battle of Actium in 31 BCE brought him to power as *princeps* (effectively, emperor).

2. Stephen of Tournai, *Summa*, praef., 2. Stephen was referring to Gen. 3:1–24. For an English translation, see Somerville and Brasington, *Prefaces to Canon Law Books*, 195.

3. Forbes, "Early Stages in European Law," 40–41, referring to *Iliad* 18.496–508. Citations to Greek and Latin classical writers and to standard legal texts refer to internal divisions of the texts. Unless otherwise stated, I have used the texts of classical authors published in the Loeb Classical Library, although I have frequently modified the Loeb translations in the interest of idiom or emphasis.

4. Todd, *Shape of Athenian Law*, 94–96. Specialists in advocacy were also apparently unknown in ancient Egypt until after its conquest by Alexander the Great in 332 BCE (Taubenschlag, "Legal Profession in Graeco-Roman Egypt," 188–89).

though they enthusiastically indulged in philosophical speculations about the nature of legal systems. Indeed, they sought to discourage the formation of a legal profession. The Stoic philosopher Zeno (335–263 BCE) even advocated that the courts should be abolished altogether.[5] Among the charges levied against Socrates (469–399 BCE) was the accusation that he encouraged friends who were involved in lawsuits to secure the services of advocates.[6] Litigants in ancient Athens required permission from the jury to call in an orator to speak on their behalf, and although such requests were rarely refused, the advocate could not be paid for his services and was forbidden to appear in that capacity more than once.[7]

Despite these obstacles, advocates did manage to practice before Athenian courts, and by the middle of the fourth century BCE litigants regularly employed them. By that time, formal restrictions on legal practice had relaxed to the point that they were routinely ignored. Athenian advocates, however, never showed great interest in legal analysis. They concentrated instead on rhetorical skills, which they cultivated with considerable success. They apparently considered legal expertise a shade undemocratic.[8] Not surprisingly, they failed to develop distinctive standards of professional conduct, professional organizations, or disciplinary sanctions.[9]

Forensic proficiency and legal learning thus enjoyed scant prestige in Athenian society. As Cicero (106–43 BCE) observed, "Among the Greeks the humblest persons, *pragmatikoi* as they are called, are induced for a pittance to proffer their assistance to orators in the courts, whereas among us the most honorable and illustrious men engage in this sort of thing."[10]

The College of Pontiffs

Matters were indeed different at Rome. Legal prowess was highly prized there, and faint foreshadowings of a distinctive and prestigious legal profession began to appear early in the Roman Republic's history. During the early generations of the Republic, expert knowledge of its laws was confined to the select group of aristocratic priests who made up the college of

---

5. According to Diogenes Laertius, in *Stoicorum veterum fragmenta* 1:267.

6. Xenophon, *Memorabilia* 1.2.51; Bonner, *Lawyers and Litigants*, 217.

7. Bonner, *Lawyers and Litigants*, 202–3, 206–7.

8. Legal speech writers (*logographoi*) did, however, develop a specialized technical vocabulary for dealing with legal topics (Todd, "Language of Law in Classical Athens," 35–36).

9. Chroust, "Emergence of Professional Standards," 588–89; Bonner, *Lawyers and Litigants*, 208–09.

10. Cicero, *De oratore* 1.45.198 and 2.13.55.

pontiffs.[11] The pontiffs kept archives, not open to outsiders, that contained records of many kinds. Religious and ceremonial matters probably made up the bulk of them, but they also included material that was essential for the conduct of legal business. These included the official calendar (which, among other things, designated the days on which judicial business could be conducted), records of early laws, and books that contained the formulas required for initiating lawsuits under the archaic procedural system of the *legis actiones*, as well as the formal legal opinions, or *responsa*, that the pontiffs themselves provided from time to time in answer to applications from magistrates and private citizens.[12] This arrangement, while wonderfully convenient for those in the know, was unsatisfactory for others, especially the plebeians, or commoners, who made up the vast majority of Rome's citizens.[13] Ordinary citizens who wished to discover what legal recourse was available to remedy wrongs they felt had been done to them needed to secure advice from one of the pontiffs, something that might be difficult or impractical for humbler members of society.

The Law of the Twelve Tables

Discontent arose about this and other situations that left ordinary citizens disadvantaged politically, socially, economically, and legally. Plebeian dissatisfaction, according to the traditional version of events, culminated in popular demonstrations in or around 451 BCE that threatened to bring down the government.[14] In response to this constitutional crisis, the Senate and the magistrates suspended elections and appointed a Commission

---

11. Livy, *Ab urbe condita* 1.20.5; Watson, *State, Law and Religion*, 4–13; Mitchell, "Roman History, Roman Law, and Roman Priests," 541–60. Schulz, *History of Roman Legal Science*, 6–14, and Kunkel, *Römischen Juristen*, 45–49, provide lists of members of the college.

12. Kaser, *Römische Zivilprozessrecht*, 34–37, 81–113; Thomas, *Textbook of Roman Law*, 73–81; Robinson, *Sources of Roman Law*, 80–84; Livy, *Ab urbe condita* 9.46.5; North, "Books of the Pontifices," 45–63. The Roman Senate maintained its own archive (*aerarium*) of legislative records (Coudry, "Sénatus-consultes et *Acta Senatus*," 65–102).

13. Roman citizens, in turn, comprised only a small fraction of the total population. Slaves, who by definition were not citizens, accounted for a substantial part of the population, while citizenship was extended only gradually to the inhabitants of conquered territories.

14. Livy, *Ab urbe condita* 3.9.1–7. This traditional version of events has often been challenged, perhaps most radically by Westbrook, "Nature and Origins of the Twelve Tables," 74–121. Westbrook argues among other things that the Twelve Tables were not legislation at all, but rather an academic treatise on law. My thanks to Ernest Metzger for bringing this article to my attention.

of Ten (the *decemviri*) to take charge of the government for a year and commanded them to put the laws into written form. At the end of their year in office, the commissioners published a written statement of the Roman law, which they had inscribed on ten bronze tablets and put up in the Forum, the city's principal marketplace.[15] The leaders of the insurrection that led to the appointment of the commissioners, however, were still not satisfied. The commission's term of office was extended for a further year, at the end of which they added two further bronze tablets to the original ten. Despite further strife and a threat that the plebeians might secede from the Republic, an uneasy peace was patched up, the commission was dissolved, and the normal processes of government resumed.[16]

The Law of the Twelve Tables furnished the foundation for all subsequent Roman law. The original bronze tables disappeared during a Gallic invasion of the city in 387 BCE, but copies were in circulation long before then, and knowledge of their contents was common among all educated Romans. Schoolboys had to memorize the Twelve Tables as part of their basic education and continued to do so at least as late as Cicero's childhood.[17]

The publication of the Twelve Tables marked the beginning of a gradual erosion of the pontiffs' monopoly on knowledge of the law. The Twelve Tables did not of course contain the whole of Rome's existing law, which, even in the mid-fifth century BCE, was already copious and complex. Instead, the tables provided a series of general legal rules, mixed with some procedural guidelines. The commissioners apparently omitted any topics treated by statutes, since those were already matters of public knowledge. The Twelve Tables dealt mainly with agrarian matters and only occasionally touched on commercial or urban concerns. The statements of the law in the tables, moreover, were brief and often enigmatic.[18] Unfortunately, from a potential litigant's viewpoint, this left judges and magistrates free to

---

15. Livy, *Ab urbe condita* 3.34.2–8, as well as Dig. 1.2.2.4. The Twelve Tables were based primarily upon Roman customary law, although they may have incorporated a few rules adopted from Greek law as well (Buckland, *Text-Book of Roman Law*, 1–2; Stein, *Roman Law in European History*, 3–4; Thomas, *Textbook of Roman Law*, 32–34).

16. Livy, *Ab urbe condita* 3.34.6–7, 3.37.4

17. Livy, *Ab urbe condita* 3.34.6, 6.1.10–12; Cicero, *De oratore* 1.44.195, 157.246, and *De legibus* 2.23.59.

18. See Watson, *State, Law and Religion*, 14–20, and *Rome of the XII Tables*, 3–4. Only fragments of the Twelve Tables have survived. For a reconstructed text, together with an English translation and commentary, see *Roman Statutes* 2:555–721. Different reconstructions and translations also appear in *Ancient Roman Statutes*, 9–18, and *Remains of Old Latin* 3:424–515.

interpret the law in varying ways. Litigants, then as now, wanted to be certain, or as nearly so as possible, about the likely outcome of legal actions. In order to feel secure either in bringing or defending an action, a prudent litigant still needed legal advice, even after the publication of the Twelve Tables. The pontiffs thus retained effective control over the furnishing of expert legal counsel for several generations more.

Their monopoly began to crumble around the beginning of the third century BCE, when, according to the traditional account, one Appius Claudius Caecus (fl. 312–280 BCE) published a book on *usucapio*, a type of transaction whereby property could legally change hands as a result of peaceful possession for a prescribed period of time. The publication of further law books soon followed. Then, in the mid-third century, according to the same account, Tiberius Coruncanius (d. 243 BCE), the first plebeian to become Pontifex Maximus, or chief priest of the college of pontiffs (between 255 and 252 BCE), began to teach law to anyone who wished to learn.[19]

Although many details in the traditional account are dubious, and some may be downright fabrications, it does point up an important reality: early Roman law developed in three different branches. The pontiffs were first and foremost masters of legal procedure and sacral law, the body of regulations for conduct that involved sacred matters.[20] They probably never had a total monopoly on knowledge of the customary practices that underlay much of archaic Roman private law, which dealt with transactions between private individuals and constituted a separate category from sacral law. Early Roman private law dealt mainly with family relationships, personal status, inheritance, and property issues. In addition, magistrates and senators were certainly familiar with the elements of public law, which concerned the machinery of government and public administration, since after all they created and ran it.[21]

Once the contents of the pontiffs' archives started to become public knowledge, lay jurists who were not members of the priestly college soon emerged as legal advisers, in direct competition with the pontiffs. Although this weakened traditional links between law and religion, Roman jurists never completely forgot that theirs originated as a sacred calling. Ulpian (d. 223 CE), one of the preeminent jurists of the classical period, for example, referred to jurists as priests and still thought it appropriate to de-

---

19. Dig. 1.2.2.35, 36, 38; Bauman, *Lawyers in Roman Republican Politics*, 2, 71–72; Schulz, *History of Roman Legal Science*, 9; Kunkel, *Römischen Juristen*, 6, 7–8, 45.

20. Gaius, *Inst.* 2.2–8.

21. Watson, *Rome of the XII Tables*, furnishes a helpful content analysis of private law. On public law, see Gaius, *Inst.* 2.10–11.

clare more than half a millennium after pontifical control over knowledge of the law had ended that "knowledge of the civil law is a most sacred thing, not to be valued in terms of money."[22]

These events coincided with other basic changes in Roman government and society. By the beginning of the third century BCE, Rome's armies had brought the greater part of the Italian peninsula under Roman control. In the mid-third century, the legions began to reach out beyond the peninsula to subject other parts of the Mediterranean world to Roman rule. By the beginning of the second century, they had secured control of Spain, much of North Africa, and substantial areas in the Balkans. Expansion continued through the two following centuries, so that by the middle of the first century BCE, Rome's frontiers stretched from Britain in the northwest to the borders of Persia in the southeast. Between those extremities, Roman governors ruled all of Europe west of the Rhine and south of the Danube, as well as the Anatolian peninsula, Syria, Egypt, and much of the North African coast.

Military expansion brought new problems and opportunities. Commercial expansion went hand-in-hand with the advance of Roman armies. Personal wealth increased massively, not only among the elite families who had traditionally dominated Roman society and politics, but also among new entrepreneurial families who found ample opportunities for profit in the wake of Roman conquests.

Rome's legal system, originally fashioned to deal with the problems of a relatively homogenous population living in the city and surrounding regions, necessarily had to adjust to accommodate this vast expansion of Roman power. The need became acute early in the first century BCE when two laws extended Roman citizenship to virtually all free adults living in the Italian peninsula and thus brought them for the first time under Roman civil law.[23]

Procedural Law

The ancient procedural system of the *legis actiones*, under which success in litigation depended upon the performance of customary rituals, was

---

22. Dig. 1.1.1 and 50.13.1.5. The classical period of Roman law comprised the period from the reign of Augustus to that of Diocletian (Schulz, *History of Roman Legal Science*, 99–101; Honoré, *Ulpian*, 1–46).

23. These were the *Lex Iulia de civitate* (90 BCE) and the *Lex Plautia Papiria de civitate* (89 BCE); see Rotondi, *Leges publicae populi Romani*, 338–41. The problem became even more pressing after 212 CE, when the *Constitutio Antoniniana* of Caracalla (211–17) extended citizenship to most free inhabitants of the empire, no matter where they lived. Justinian extended it even further in 531 (Gaius, *Inst.* 1.28–34; Cod. 7.6.1; see also Buckland, *Text-Book of Roman Law*, 94–96).

poorly suited to the new conditions. The old procedural system gradually began to fall into disuse during the second century BCE. The *Lex Aebutia* (between 145 and 120 BCE) commenced the process of replacing the *legis actiones* with a new procedure that came to be known as the formulary system. Augustus (r. 31 BCE–14 CE) completed the process with two further statutes, the *leges Iuliae iudiciorum*. The formulary system remained in use until the latter part of the second century CE, when it was in turn superseded by a third type of procedure known as *cognitio extra ordinem*.[24]

FORMULARY PROCEDURE

These procedural changes were critical for the development of the Roman legal profession. Under the *legis actiones*, parties in litigation, with few exceptions, had to conduct their cases in person. Under the formulary and *cognitio* procedures, however, litigants enjoyed the option of appearing, acting, and arguing in court through one or more third parties. This opened the way for the routine use (at least by those who could afford it) of a litigation agent (*cognitor, procurator, defensor*) who literally took the place of the party he represented. The actions and statements of such an agent bound his principal just as if the principal had done them in person. In addition, litigants increasingly began to seek advice about the law from jurists and to employ an orator or advocate to argue cases on their behalf.[25]

Another feature of the judiciary system gave further impetus to the professionalization of Roman law. Roman judges, both under the *legis actiones* and the formulary system, were not career judges. Instead, they were selected on an ad hoc basis in each individual lawsuit and did not necessarily have legal training.[26] Men who had studied law might occasionally be named as judges, and we know that eminent jurists were chosen in a handful of cases, but there is no reason to think that most judges could boast of any great expertise in dealing with complex questions of law. They were much like members of a common law jury, whose primary task was to evaluate the facts of the case before them. They were expected to bring ordinary common sense to bear upon the issues and to determine them in the light of their general experience of the world and its working, using whatever bits of legal knowledge they might have acquired along the

---

24. Gaius, *Inst.* 4.30; Aulus Gellius, *Noctes Atticae* 16.10.8; Robinson, *Sources of Roman Law*, 84–85; Kaser, *Römische Zivilprozessrecht*, 4–6, 151–53.

25. Gaius, *Inst.* 4.82 and 97; Kaser, *Römische Zivilprozessrecht*, 219, 360.

26. Crook, *Legal Advocacy in the Roman World*, 174–75 and n. 18.

way.[27] They often functioned as mediators between the parties, seeking an amicable solution to the dispute. Jurists could be called in when needed as impartial experts to explain the law to the judges. Orators and advocates also attempted to interpret the law for the benefit of judges, although they, of course, did so in ways calculated to favor the interests of their clients.

Formulary procedure prescribed a two-stage process in civil cases. The first stage was a preliminary hearing (technically called *in iure*) that took place before an elected magistrate, the praetor, who was not required to have formal legal training, but who could seek advice from trained jurists when necessary.[28] The plaintiff began the case by bringing his complaint to the praetor and was responsible for persuading the defendant to appear in order to answer it.[29] During *in iure* proceedings, the parties described their respective versions of their dispute to the magistrate. The praetor then selected a judge from a list of male citizens eligible to serve and dictated a formula, or set of directions, for the judge to follow.[30] The causes for which the praetor would take action, and sometimes the actual terms of the appropriate formula, were described in the edict that each praetor published at the beginning of his year in office.[31] The formula in an action concerning a contested sale might, for example, say something on this order:

> Aulus Agerius claims that he agreed to sell a hunting dog to Numerius Negidius for 1,000 *sesterces* and that Numerius Negidius has failed to pay this by the agreed time.[32] Numerius denies that he ever contracted to buy a

---

27. Dawson, *A History of Lay Judges*, 21–30; Tellegen-Couperus, "Role of the Judge in the Formulary Procedure," 1–13. My thanks to Ernest Metzger for calling my attention to the latter article.

28. See Brennan, *Praetorship in the Roman Republic*.

29. This might understandably be no easy task. For details, see Metzger, *Litigation in Roman Law*, 4–5, 15–16.

30. In practice, it was usual for the magistrate to allow the parties an opportunity to agree on the judges they would prefer (*Lex Irnitana* c. 87, in González, "Lex Irnitana," 177; Metzger, *A New Outline of the Roman Civil Trial*, 61–66; but cf. Kelly, *Roman Litigation*).

31. This eventually became standardized and was reissued with minor changes annually; Robinson, *Sources of Roman Law*, 39–42. For the reconstituted text see Bruns, *Fontes iuris Romani antiqui* 1:211–37.

32. Aulus Agerius and Numerius Negidius were conventional names that Roman jurists used to designate the plaintiff (*actor*) and defendant (*reus*) in hypothetical cases. They are analogous to the fictitious names John Doe and Richard Roe that lawyers in the common law tradition use for similar purposes.

hunting dog from Aulus and denies that he owes him 1,000 *sesterces*. If you find that Aulus has proved his case, award him 1,000 *sesterces*. If you find that Aulus has failed to prove his claim, absolve Numerius.[33]

The formula thus defined the issues of law and fact that the judge had to decide and told him what remedy to impose, depending on the outcome of his deliberations.

The second (technically, *apud iudicem*) stage of proceedings, which comprised the trial proper, took place before the judge, or in some situations, arbitrators (*arbitri*). The judge's tasks were to examine the evidence and arguments that the parties or their spokesmen produced, to determine what the evidence indicated had occurred, and to give judgment according to the terms prescribed in the formula.

The formulary system and its successor, *cognitio* procedure, created a situation that fostered the growth of the Roman legal profession.[34] Unlike proceedings under the *legis actiones*, the legal representatives (*procuratores ad litem*, or proctors) and spokesmen (orators or advocates) of the parties under formulary procedures played central roles in the trial.[35] Although they were seldom as deeply learned in the law as jurists (*iurisperiti*) were, advocates had to know at least enough about the relevant law and procedures to be able to present a client's case efficiently and effectively.[36] If a case presented difficult and sophisticated legal issues, they might secure a written opinion (*responsum*) on the problem from a jurist. Cicero described the jurist as the oracle of the community. His mastery of the laws and customs of the commonwealth enabled him to advise, guide, and caution those involved in litigation.[37] Praetors themselves often sought guidance from jurists before adding a formula to their edicts, and the formula might

---

33. Gaius, *Inst.* 4.39–52 describes, with examples, the structure of the formula. See also Mantovani, *Le formule del processo privato romano*.

34. Frier, *Rise of the Roman Jurists*, 272–73.

35. Inst. 4.10; Cod. Theod. 2.12.7; Dig. 3.3.1 pr., 1–2; Kaser, *Römische Zivilprozessrecht*, 213–17; Mecke, "Die Entwicklung des 'Procurator ad litem.'" In the classical period, the functions of the advocate and the *procurator ad litem* were not rigidly separated from one another. In the postclassical period, they became more clearly distinguished (Kaser, *Römische Zivilprozessrecht*, 563; Landau, "Erteilung des Anwaltsmandats," 414).

36. Frier, *Rise of the Roman Jurists*, 134–35.

37. Cicero, *De oratore* 1.45.200, 1.48.212, 3.133–35. Elsewhere Cicero was considerably less laudatory and claimed that he could, if he wished, turn himself into a jurist in three days (*Pro Murena* 13.28; cf. *De oratore* 1.41.185). Quintilian likewise compared jurists unfavorably with advocates (*Institutio oratoriae* 8.3.79, 12.3.9 and 11).

even take the name of the jurist who devised it.[38] Judges, since they were seldom well versed in law, might also seek guidance from a jurist when they encountered difficulty in fitting the formula they had been given to the facts that emerged during *apud iudicem* proceedings.[39] The prestige of the jurists was augmented by the introduction under Augustus of the *ius respondendi*, which put the weight of imperial authority behind the replies (*responsa*) that a few designated jurists wrote on questions of law raised in private lawsuits. Although the selected jurists were technically private citizens, their opinions acquired the force of law.[40] The emperor's power to choose the jurists who enjoyed the *ius respondendi* did not, however, enable Rome's rulers to dictate the interpretations that the jurists arrived at, a fact that considerably annoyed the more autocratic members of the Julio-Claudian dynasty. Suetonius (ca. 70–130) related among the other symptoms of madness in Caligula (r. 37–41) that he often expressed the wish to control the jurists so that they would produce no *responsa* of which he did not approve.[41]

COGNITIO PROCEDURE

The formulary system encouraged both jurists and orators to develop a more technical style of forensic reasoning and argument than their predecessors had employed.[42] This became still more marked under *cognitio* procedure, in which lay judges were replaced by permanent government officials, who often had legal training.[43] *Cognitio* procedure was highly bureaucratized. Plaintiffs initiated an action through a formal written complaint (*libellus*), rather than an oral statement. No longer did the plaintiff have to see that the defendant showed up in court, as had been true earlier: defendants were now summoned by government order. Written sub-

---

38. Thus the *iudicium Cascellianum* (Gaius, *Inst.* 4.166a, 169) was named after the late republican jurist Aulus Cascellius (Kunkel *Römischen Juristen*, 25–27; Schulz, *History of Roman Legal Science*, 51 n. 8; Kaser, *Römische Zivilprozessrecht*, 418 n. 16).

39. Aulus Gellius (*Noctes Atticae* 14.2) recounts such an episode from his own experience as a judge.

40. Gaius, *Inst.* 1.7; Dig. 1.2.2.49; Frier, *Rise of the Roman Jurists*, 284; Kunkel, *Römischen Juristen*, 281–85; Schulz, *History of Roman Legal Science*, 112–13. Gaius (fl. 160–78 CE), the author of a standard legal textbook long used in the schools, counted the *responsa* of the jurists as an acknowledged source of law, along with statutes, edicts, and resolutions of the Senate (Gaius, *Inst.* 1.2; Kunkel, *Römischen Juristen*, 186–213).

41. Suetonius, *De vita caesarum* 4.34 (Caligula).

42. Lewis, "Autonomy of Roman Law," 40; Frier, *Rise of the Roman Jurists*, 157–71.

43. Schulz, *History of Roman Legal Science*, 118.

missions and depositions largely displaced oral testimony, and greater emphasis throughout proceedings was placed on written documents than had previously been common.[44] All of this encouraged parties in litigation to secure expert advice, assistance, and representation.

The Training of Roman Lawyers

The history of the training of lawyers in the Roman world is shrouded in obscurity. Pomponius (second century CE) referred to two schools, the Sabinian and the Proculian, in which law was taught together with rhetoric. He also mentioned lectures given by law teachers and reports that their students paid fees, but his account is far from clear and parts of the surviving fragments of his text seem garbled.[45]

The training that advocates received during the Republic and the Principate began with the study of rhetoric and the skills of persuasion.[46] Only later did they proceed to study law, and for many the legal training was minimal.[47] Cicero described the distinguished advocate Marcus Antonius (fl. 102–87 BCE) as spokesman for the view that an advocate rarely needed more than a slight knowledge of law. The outcome of litigation rarely hinged on points of law, he observed, and should any abstruse legal issues arise in a case, the orator could always look it up in books or consult a jurist on the matter.[48] While Cicero acknowledged that orators who could fortify their eloquence with sound knowledge of the law deserved high marks, he considered legal skills far less important for winning cases than the capacity to play effectively on the feelings and prejudices of judges.[49]

Lucius Licinius Crassus (140–91 BCE), Cicero's own master, however, saw things differently. He maintained that the study of law ought to be cen-

---

44. Kaser, *Römische Zivilprozessrecht*, 442–45; Robinson, *Sources of Roman Law*, 90–96; Wieacker, *Allgemeine Zustände und Rechtszustände*, 27–29, 32–34.

45. Dig. 1.2.2.47–48, 50–53. The surviving fragments of Pomponius's work derive apparently from student notes of lectures delivered before 131 CE (Nörr, "Pomponius oder 'Zum Geschichtsverständnis der römischen Juristen'").

46. Principate conventionally describes the early generations of imperial rule at Rome, from the reign of Augustus (31 BCE–14 CE) to the beginning of the reign of Diocletian in 284. The period after 284 is sometimes called the Dominate.

47. Kodrębski, "Rechtsunterricht am Ausgang der Republik," 177–96; Liebs, "Rechtsschulen und Rechtsunterricht," 288–462; Kaser, *Römische Zivilprozessrecht*, 564; Bonner, *Education in Ancient Rome*, 288–327; Humfress, "Law Schools"; and Stein, "Two Schools of Jurists."

48. Cicero, *De oratore* 1.48.208, 1.56.24, 1.57.241, 1.58.248 and 250.

49. Cicero, *Brutus* 26.98, 39.145, 41.152, 44.164–65, 47.175.

tral to the education not only of an advocate, but also of every responsible citizen.[50] Quintilian (ca. 35–90 CE), an eminent authority on the training of advocates, emphatically agreed that an adequately trained advocate needed a thorough grounding in law:

> How can he be persuasive either in public or private if he is ignorant of so many matters central to the state? How, pray tell, can he truthfully hold himself out as an advocate if he needs to consult others to discover what is most important in a lawsuit? He would be something like the men who recite the words of poets.[51]

Law teachers sought to develop their students' proficiency in analyzing the legal issues that common situations presented by framing hypothetical questions designed to explore their juristic ramifications.[52] Quintilian also advised advocates in training to acquire some experience in actual courtroom practice while they were still at school. Although students of advocacy had for generations routinely participated in mock trials about hypothetical situations, Quintilian maintained that exposure to the real thing was essential.[53]

By the mid-third century CE, law students and teachers faced the daunting task of familiarizing themselves not only with the statutory law (including edicts, decrees, and resolutions of the Senate, in addition to statutes in the strict sense), but also with the enormous mountain of juristic opinion that had acquired the force of law.[54] The jurist Paul, for example, was credited with writing no fewer than 296 books, and Ulpian with 242, while Gaius was responsible for 86, Modestinus for 64, and Papinian for a mere 61, to name only five especially important authorities.[55]

---

50. Cicero, *De oratore* 2.44.195 and 197, 2.45.198.

51. Quintilian, *Inst. orat.* 12.3.1; note also 12.3.8–10. On Quintilian as an authority on the practice as well as the theory of advocacy, see Crook, *Legal Advocacy*, 167–71, and Tellegen-Couperous, "Quintilian and Roman Law."

52. E.g., Aulus Gellius, *Noctes Atticae* 13.13.1–6; Quintilian, *Inst. orat.* 3.5.17–18 and 3.6. See also Frier, *Rise of the Roman Jurists*, 157–71, and the lists of controverted topics in Liebs, "Rechtsschulen und Rechtsunterricht," 244–75.

53. Quintilian, *Inst. orat.* 12.11.16, Cicero, *De oratore* 1.67.244; Watson, "Tricks of Advocacy."

54. Gaius, *Inst.* 1.7.

55. Harries, *Law and Empire*, 17–18. An ancient book was often just long enough to fill a single papyrus scroll. Although scrolls varied in size, they commonly measured roughly twenty to twenty-six feet in length. Other variables that affected the length of an ancient "book" included the width of its margins, the numbers of lines per sheet,

Codification of Roman Law

The teaching and practice of Roman law were transformed during the fourth and fifth centuries CE by a vast increase in the numbers and importance of imperial statutes, edicts, and decrees. Some of these enacted ideas, doctrines, and interpretations of the classical jurists in the form of imperial constitutions, while other legislation embodied fresh policies and regulations. The volume of legislation, together with the huge mass of juristic opinion accumulated over the centuries had grown so formidable that law teachers and practitioners alike needed to make it manageable.

THE THEODOSIAN CODE

One approach was to compile collections of the current laws, edicts, decrees, and other statutory instruments organized by topic into a code. The earliest such codes of Roman statute law were the *Codex Gregorianus* and the *Codex Hermogenianus*, private collections put together with the encouragement of Diocletian (r. 284–305). Although these codes lacked official authority, teachers, law students, bureaucrats, and practitioners in the courts nonetheless found them useful.[56] They were eventually followed by an official code, the *Codex Theodosianus*, put together commencing in 429 at the command of the Eastern emperor Theodosius II (r. 408–50).[57] It was completed in 448 and promulgated jointly by Theodosius in the East and Valentinian III (r. 425–54) in the West.[58]

Theodosius had originally planned that in addition to imperial legisla-

---

and the size of the writing itself. The ancient "book" was thus something on the order of the length that we might expect in a chapter of a modern book. The fifty books of Justinian's Digest, e.g, run 969 pages in a modern printed edition, so that one book of this text occupies on average slightly more than 19 printed pages.

56. Neither collection survives intact, but their surviving fragments have been collected by modern scholars (*Fragmenta Vaticana*, 221–45; Schulz, *History of Roman Legal Science*, 308–10).

57. Cod. Theod. 1.1.5.

58. Matthews, *Laying Down the Law*, furnishes an account of the background of the Theodosian Code and the process of its composition, together with an analysis of its contents. See further the essays in *The Theodosian Code*, ed. Harries and Wood, as well as Harries, *Law and Empire*, 59–69; Honoré, *Law in the Crisis of Empire*, 97–153; and Wieacker, *Allgemeine Zustände*, 22–23. The Theodosian Code does not survive intact, although much of the text has been reconstructed by modern scholars. I cite the *Codex Theodosianus, cum constitutionibus Sirmondinis*, ed. Krueger and Mommsen; the English translation by Clyde Pharr and others is not always reliable.

tion, his code would also include excerpts from the authoritative opinions of the major jurists (*iurisprudentes*).[59] That part of the enterprise, however, failed to materialize. Lawyers, judges, and law teachers fell back instead on a cruder stratagem to cope with the enormous body of juristic opinion. That device was authorized by the Law of Citations of 426, which limited the use of juristic opinions in court to the works of just five major writers: Gaius, Paul, Ulpian, Papinian, and Modestinus. It also prescribed a rule of thumb to guide judges: where all five of these writers were in agreement, the judge must follow their opinion; where a majority took one view and a minority took another, the judge must accept the majority view; if they were equally divided, the judge should accept the position espoused by Papinian; and if there was an equal division but Papinian was silent on the matter, the judge could use his own discretion.[60]

Roman Law Schools

In the wake of these innovations, the curriculum of the empire's law schools became standardized, at least in the East, toward the end of the fifth century. It comprised a four-year course of study, and would-be practitioners had to show certificates from their professors as evidence that they had completed it. They also had to pass an oral examination before they were admitted to practice. Justinian I (r. 527–65) reorganized the course and extended it to five years.[61]

Quintilian, a Spaniard by birth, became one of the first professors of forensic oratory at Rome to be paid from the public treasury. Although he asserted that it was satisfaction enough to teach something that he knew well, Quintilian, like other law teachers, also expected material rewards. Had he not received them abundantly, he could not have retired after twenty years of teaching, in order to read and write.[62] The major product of Quintilian's retirement years was his book *Institutio oratoria*, which described what he considered the ideal education for a forensic orator.

The emperor Vespasian (r. 69–79) had placed professors of rhetoric on the public payroll,[63] but unlike official teachers of other subjects, profes-

59. Cod. Theod. 1.1.5; Dig. 1.2.2.49; Gaius, *Inst.* 1.7; Justinian, Inst. 1.2.8; Schulz, *History of Roman Legal Science*, 112–17; Kunkel, *Römischen Juristen*, 272–89.

60. Cod. Theod. 1.4.3; Wieacker, *Allgemeine Zustände*, 18–19.

61. On the oral examination, Cod. 2.7.11.1–2; Schulz, *History of Roman Legal Science*, 272–77; Jones, *Later Roman Empire* 2:1217 n. 99. On Justinian's reorganization, Dig. Const. Omnem §§1–5.

62. Quintilian, *Inst. orat.* 1, pr. 1, and 12.11.8.

63. Suetonius, *De vita caesarum* 8.18 (Vespasian).

sors of law apparently had to wait until 425 to receive direct public funding. Even earlier, however, law professors had enjoyed other favors from the imperial government. These took the form of exemptions from certain burdensome civic obligations, which amounted to indirect subsidies. This was especially useful because law teachers lacked legal recourse to recover unpaid fees (*honoraria*) from deadbeat students.[64]

In addition to the law school at Rome, the empire had a famous and influential law school at Beirut dating from the end of the second century CE. The "Museum" at Smyrna may have had one as well. In 425, the emperors Theodosius II and Valentinian III established a law faculty at Constantinople.[65]

Advocates and Jurists

The Roman legal profession during the late Republic and the Principate comprised two branches, although the division between them was never watertight.[66] Forensic orators or advocates, of whom Cicero and Hortensius (114–49 BCE) were the foremost exemplars, pleaded on behalf of clients in the courts, while jurists gave expert legal advice to clients who sought their counsel, although they did not usually appear personally in court.

Relationships between these two groups were ambivalent and varied over time. Jurists originally came from the ranks of the patrician aristocracy, but by the late Republic, this had ceased to be true and several highly regarded jurists were men of humble background.[67] As the golden age of Ciceronian advocacy began to fade during the early generations of the Principate, the volume of judicial business that Augustus and his successors needed to deal with increased enormously. By the reign of Claudius (r. 41–54), the empire's rulers found it necessary to rely upon a permanent group of legal advisers. As the influence of these jurists increased, the prestige of their occupation correspondingly grew at the expense of the advocates. Seneca (d. 65 CE) pictured a group of advocates lamenting the death of Claudius and the diminution of their own prestige. "Didn't I tell you?"

---

64. Cod. Theod. 6.21.1 (= Cod. 12.15.1); Dig. 27.1.6.8–12 and 50.13.1.5; Bernard, *Rémunération*, 50.

65. On Smyrna, Crook, *Legal Advocacy*, 194; Schulz, *History of Roman Legal Science*, 264 n. 1, 268–69, 273–74; on Constantinople, Cod. Theod. 14.9.3 (= Cod. 11.19.1); Bernard, *Rémunération*, 48 n. 27.

66. Crook, *Legal Advocacy*, 41; Neuhauser, *Patronus und Orator*, 176–77.

67. Cicero, *De oratore* 1.43.200, 3.133–35; Juvenal, *Satires* 8.47–50; Henriot, *Moeurs juridiques* 3:83, 95; Jones, *Later Roman Empire* 1:512; Visky, "Retribuzioni," 3.

one of them exclaimed, "the party couldn't last forever!"[68] Jurists gained still greater prestige when Hadrian (r. 117–38) and his successors added some eminent jurists to a body of officials known as the Consilium principis that met regularly to advise the emperor. This group had the power to give opinions that had the force of imperial law.[69]

Coupled with this was the gradual development of an esoteric legal vocabulary among jurists during the late Republic and the Principate. Jurists, said Quintilian, must take pains to find just the right words to express the precise shade of meaning they required. Their specialized vocabulary, in turn, contributed to an increasingly complex system of legal analysis that reached its apogee in the writings of the jurists of the classical period of Roman law. The elaboration of juristic subtlety further reinforced the separation of advocacy from jurisprudence that had been evident at least from Cicero's time.[70]

One concrete symptom of this separation was the fact that an advocate's fee was in theory an *honorarium*, that is, a free-will offering, which gave him no legal grounds to sue for payment, although it likewise gave his client no basis to sue him for defective performance. Jurists, by contrast, had the right to sue clients to recover the fees owed to them.[71]

Advocates, unlike jurists, represented clients in litigation.[72] Roman litigants always had the option of presenting their cases in person and some exercised that option regularly.[73] Most litigants who could afford the expense preferred to employ an advocate for this purpose. The fact that

---

68. Seneca, *Apocolocyntosis divi Claudii*, 12. See also Juvenal, *Satires* 4.78–79, 8.49–50; Martial, *Epigrams* 10.37.1–2; Henriot, *Moeurs juridiques* 3:85; Crook, *Consilium principis*, 51–55, 59–61.

69. Crook, *Consilium principis*, 56–65.

70. Quintilian, *Inst. orat.* 5.14.34; Dig. 1.22.1, 48.19.9.4, and 50.13.1.11; Crook, *Legal Advocacy*, 40, 197; Frier, *Rise of the Roman Jurists*, 140–41.

71. Dig. 50.13.4; this distinction between advocates and jurists later disappeared.

72. I use the generic term "advocate" to include orators and *causidici* as well as *advocati*; on the various shades of meaning, see Neuhauser, *Patronus und Orator*, 156–65, 170–71, and Bernard, *Rémuneration*, 88. Cod. 2.6 and Dig. 3.1 describe their activities. On the notion of the advocate as a "representative" of his client, see Crook, *Legal Advocacy*, 158–63.

73. See Cod. 2.7.13 pr.; Crook, *Legal Advocacy*, 64. Cato is said to have defended himself no less than forty-four times, but he was exceptional (Neuhauser, *Patronus und Orator*, 169–71). Certain classes of persons were required to employ proctors and advocates if they were involved in litigation because they were forbidden to make court appearances on their own behalf (Dig. 1.16.9.4–5; Crook, *Legal Advocacy*, 124).

the praetor eventually undertook to provide advocates for litigants who lacked them suggests that their services seemed essential to adequate presentation of a litigant's case.[74]

The advocate's function, according to Ulpian, was to plead cases before a judge or to oppose the cases put forward by an opponent.[75] His job, in other words, was to do for his client something that few clients could do adequately for themselves, namely, to present persuasive arguments that would bring out every point that could be made in favor of the client's case exhaustively and in detail. The advocate's goal was to secure victory for his client. Advocates also hoped to win admiration for their ingenuity, a glowing reputation for their skills, and, no doubt, a handsome reward for their efforts. To accomplish all of these successfully was, at least in Cicero's eyes, the most challenging of human enterprises.[76]

Roman advocates, even by Cicero's time, included a broad band of the social spectrum. While jurists generally came from the higher strata of the Roman social order, advocates were far more heterogeneous. Gentlemen from senatorial or equestrian families considered advocacy a necessary skill, compatible with their high social status and useful, too, in achieving celebrity and advancing their political ambitions, which benefited from the support of grateful clients. Men from less illustrious families, especially those of middling social rank, often saw advocacy as a means to enhance their economic position and, more problematically, to improve their social status.[77] The really poor, of course, could scarcely hope to enter the profession, since they were unlikely to enjoy the necessary educational preparation. Under the Principate, advocates and jurists of modest backgrounds almost certainly outnumbered their aristocratic colleagues by a considerable margin. Advocates were more numerous in the eastern provinces of the empire than they were in the western territories, where they sometimes seem to have been in short supply.[78]

Advocates had to meet some basic formal requirements. The minimum age for admission to practice was seventeen. The deaf and the blind were barred from advocacy, as were gladiators who fought wild beasts in the arena, men who took the passive role in homosexual acts, and those con-

---

74. Dig. 3.1.1.4 and 1.16.9.4–5.
75. Dig. 3.1.1.2 and 50.13.1.11. Lucretius (b. ca. 94, d. 55 or 51 BCE) would have us believe advocates even did it in their sleep (*De rerum natura* 4.966).
76. Cicero, *De oratore* 2.17.72; Crook, *Legal Advocacy*, 196–97.
77. Crook, *Legal Advocacy*, 44.
78. Jones, *Later Roman Empire* 1:508–9, 512–14, and 2:1216 n. 89, 1217 n. 98–102.

demned for capital crimes or who were for other reasons legally disreputable (*infames*).[79] Women could speak in court on their own behalf or that of their parents, but were barred from pleading for others, on the grounds that doing so was immodest and unbecoming. The prohibition allegedly arose because a shameless woman named Carfania had outraged the praetor by her brazen tactics during a case before him.[80]

PROFESSIONAL ORGANIZATIONS

The appearance of a professional organization signifies that an occupational group has assumed a corporate identity. Roman advocates from Constantine's reign (311–37) onward increasingly belonged to occupational associations (*collegia*) scattered throughout the empire.[81] Each *collegium* was attached to the courts in its own city or region, and its members were responsible to the judges of those courts.[82] Although no foundation documents or other internal records of these associations survive, their existence is attested by a constitution of the emperors Leo I and Anthemius in 468. Advocates' *collegia* on occasion also played a role in proposing or advising on legislation.[83]

Members of these associations enjoyed numerous privileges, but with privileges came governmental regulation.[84] Their central privilege was a monopoly on representing clients in court. By Constantine's time, advocates had to be enrolled on the list (*matricula*) of qualified practitioners maintained by the judges before whom they appeared.[85] Applicants first had to show that they were sufficiently learned by producing evidence that they had studied law and by passing an entrance examination.[86] Individual

---

79. Dig. 3.1.1.3, 5, 6, and 8; Cod. 12.1.2.

80. On women in the courts, see Dig. 3.1.1.5, 3.3.41, and 50.17.2. Carfania was perhaps the same person as Afrania, wife of the Senator Licinius Buccio, mentioned by Valerius Maximus, *Facta et dicta memorabilia* 8.3.2.

81. *Collegia* had to be licensed by the authorities (Dig. 3.4.1 and 47.22.3.1; Schulz, *Classical Roman Law*, 95–102). The earliest mention of an organized group of advocates appears in Cod. Theod. 2.10.4, a constitution of Constantine dated about 326 (Kaser, *Römische Zivilprozessrecht*, 564–65).

82. E.g., Cod. 2.7.13; Arias Ramos, "Advocati y collegia advocatorum," 49.

83. Cod. 2.6.8 (cf. 1.51.14.3); Travers, *Corporations d'avocats*, 5–6; Humfress, "Advocates," 277–78. Arias Ramos, "Advocati y collegia advocatorum," 55–61, cites examples of the advisory role of the *collegia*.

84. Cod. Theod. 12.1.152 (= Cod. 2.7.3); Nov. Theod. 10.1.4 (= Cod. 2.7.6); Cod. 2.7.11.

85. Cod. Theod. 2.10.2; Cod. 2.7.13 pr.

86. Cod. 2.7.11.1–2 and 2.7.22.4.

courts limited the numbers of advocates authorized to practice and also forbade individual advocates to practice for more than twenty years.[87] Any advocate who failed to engage in practice for a substantial period might be expelled from the *collegium*. From the mid-fifth century onward, the advocates' associations in the Eastern empire became closed corporations. Those who hoped to become members had first to be enrolled on a waiting list of *supernumerarii* and wait until a vacancy occurred in the ranks of active practitioners. In addition, existing members secured a preferential privilege for their sons, which placed them on the *matricula* ahead of other applicants. Advocates' sons were also exempted from the substantial admissions fee that other applicants had to pay. For practical purposes, the profession gradually became hereditary.[88]

THE SOCIAL STATUS OF ADVOCATES

Another indication of the professional status of an occupation is a widely held belief that its members perform an important, even vital, public function. Here, too, Roman advocates fit the professional mold. The Eastern emperor Anastasius (r. 491–518) explicitly designated their activities as a public duty (*officium*).[89] His predecessor, the emperor Leo (r. 457–74), had described them as *militia* and counted their work as no less important than that of soldiers who defended the realm. They became eligible for appointment as provincial governors.[90] Under the Dominate (the empire after 284), both jurists and advocates became government functionaries. As the practice of law became increasingly bureaucratized, the roles of jurists and advocates coalesced, and by the end of the fourth century the two branches of the legal profession had virtually fused into one.[91]

---

87. Nov. Theod. 10.2; Nov. Val. 2.2.2, and 2.2.4; Jones, *Later Roman Empire* 1:508 and 2:1216 n. 89. Constantine in 319 revoked earlier limits on the numbers of advocates (Cod. Theod. 2.10.1), but his successors reinstated the *numerus clausus* (Cod. 2.7.11 pr., 13 pr., and 17; *Constitutio Juliani de postulando*, 7, ll. 19, 23; Arias Ramos, "Advocati y collegia advocatorum," 49–50).

88. Cod. 2.7.11, 13, 15 pr., 22.5 and 6, 24.5 and 6, 26 pr., 26.2, 29 (ca. 531–34); Jones, *Later Roman Empire* 1:510, 514–15, 2.1216 n. 93, 1218 n. 103.

89. Cod. 2.7.22 pr.; the usage was not unknown in literature (e.g. Juvenal, *Satires* 7.107).

90. Cod. 2.7.9 and 14.

91. Kaser, *Römische Zivilprozessrecht*, 563; Crook, *Legal Advocacy*, 45, 196; Visky, "Retribuzioni" 3–4; Wieacker, *Allgemeine Zustände*, 29–30; Kunkel, *Römischen Juristen*, 300–304.

THE ETHICS OF ADVOCATES

Work-related ethical rules form a key element of professionalism, and Roman authorities prescribed strict behavioral standards that lawyers were held to observe toward the courts, toward their clients, and in their private conduct outside of court. Judges were empowered to penalize breaches of these norms, and clients had the right to bring legal action to recover damages that arose from a lawyer's violation of his ethical obligations. Other customary and usual practices of the profession were simply standard procedures that lacked formally prescribed enforcement mechanisms.

Rules of conduct among the small, homogenous group of patrician jurists in the early Republic were informal and left few traces in the surviving records. As the numbers of legal professionals began to rise during the late second century BCE, however, it became increasingly necessary to establish formal standards of conduct and to back them up with sanctions against violators.[92]

One clear expression of those standards appears in the calumny oath that Roman advocates were obliged to take at the beginning of each trial in which they participated. This oath was designed to discourage vexatious litigation and originally was required only of the parties to a lawsuit. By the classical period advocates, too, were obliged to swear the oath.[93] In its developed form, the oath outlined the basic elements of an advocate's professional responsibilities. He had to swear that he would faithfully and wholeheartedly strive to present his client's case justly and truthfully, that he would do so with all his strength and resources, that he would not present any case that he considered desperate, groundless, or based on untruths, and that, if approached to act in such a case, he would refuse. He also pledged that he would resign from any case that he discovered to be baseless after he had undertaken it and that he would see to it that no other advocate took it on.[94]

The terms of the calumny oath thus cast the advocate in the role of gatekeeper for the court. He was responsible for making a preliminary assessment of a case's merits and for deciding whether or not a prospective client

---

92. Chroust, "Emergence of Professional Standards," 595–96.

93. Gaius, *Inst.* 4.171, Cod. 2.58 (59), 2 pr.; *Inst.* 4.16.1; Dig. 50.16.233 pr.; Moriarty, *Oaths in Ecclesiastical Courts*, 9–10. The calumny oath had replaced an earlier form of action against litigants who brought groundless lawsuits to harass their opponents (Gaius, *Inst.* 1.174–81; Kaser, *Römische Zivilprozessrecht*, 284–85, 631).

94. Cod. 3.1.14.4

had a reasonable cause of action. The advocate also assumed responsibility for keeping his client honest during the course of an action. Should he discover that the evidence his client was presenting was fraudulent or untruthful, the advocate was obliged to withdraw his assistance publicly. Should he fail to do so, he could be disbarred.[95] The advocate thus became, in effect, his client's judge in first instance.

The Roman advocate's ethical responsibilities did not stop there. An advocate must avoid scheduling conflicts: he could not abandon one client's case in order to plead another client's case elsewhere.[96] Delays in legal processes were a perennial problem and advocates were supposed to move their cases along smartly so as not to waste the judge's time. Then as now, however, delays occurred routinely; some were inevitable, but it was not unknown for advocates, especially when acting for defendants, to contrive purposeful delays as part of their litigation strategy.[97] This was calculated not only to secure advantages in court—witnesses might die or fail to appear, the opponent might run out of patience or resources and either settle the case or abandon it—but also to arouse the opponent's anger and frustration, which he was likely to vent on his own advocates and legal advisers.[98] Imperial constitutions complained that lawsuits threatened to become immortal and imposed penalties upon advocates who deliberately prolonged lawsuits, especially if they did so in order to increase their fees.[99] While imperial law laid down the general rule that "mistakes of advocates in a court of law shall not prejudice the litigants," the injured party must take steps to correct the error within three days. Should he fail to do so, he had no further recourse.[100]

Advocates were admonished to keep their pleadings relevant to the issues before the court, although in practice irrelevant arguments were routine. They sometimes represented nothing more than simple incom-

---

95. Dig. 48.10.13.1.

96. Cod. Theod. 2.10.2.

97. Crook, *Legal Advocacy*, 72–73, 89–91, cites examples from the records of cases heard by Roman courts in Egypt.

98. Martial, *Epigrams* 7.65; Juvenal, *Satires* 16.42–50.

99. Cod. 3.1.13 pr., also 2.6.4; Cod. Theod. 2.10.3 (= Cod. 2.6.5); Cod. Theod. 2.7.2 (= Cod. 2.52 [53].6); Cod. 11.48.20. The penalties could be severe; in one egregious case, two lawyers were executed for having drawn out a case for thirty years (Jones, *Later Roman Empire* 1:494, 2:1210 n. 55).

100. Quotation from Cod. Theod. 2.11.1 (for the other side of the coin, see Martial, *Epigrams* 8.17); Cod. 2.9 (10).3. Crook, *Legal Advocacy*, 141–42, cites a case from Roman Egypt involving mistakes by the advocate.

petence, but clever advocates often deliberately introduced irrelevant matters as a diversion to draw the judge's attention away from inconvenient facts that might hurt their case.[101]

Conflict of interest between advocate and client, another perennial problem, also drew the ire of Roman authorities, who discouraged lawyers from accepting cases where such a situation might arise. An imperial constitution forbade an advocate to appear in a case brought by one client against another. A practicing advocate could not serve as a judge or as legal adviser to a judge in a case in which he was personally or professionally involved.[102] Similarly, proctors were forbidden to appear in cases where they were related to an opponent or to represent a party whom they strongly disliked.[103]

Roman magistrates had the power to discipline advocates for offenses against the rules of professional conduct. The primary sanction was disbarment, either for a fixed period or in perpetuity.[104] Disbarment might apply only to acting as an advocate; alternatively it could prohibit undertaking any type of legal practice. The latter was more serious and might be imposed on jurists or notaries as well as advocates. Men disbarred temporarily could be readmitted to practice after the expiration of the stipulated term, but those disbarred permanently were ineligible for reinstatement.[105]

Roman authorities came down especially hard on *praevaricatores*, that is, jurists, advocates, proctors, or notaries who betrayed clients by revealing confidential information.[106] A client whose proctor treacherously allowed his opponent to win could bring an action for fraud against his adversary. An advocate found guilty of secretly leaking information to his opponent or switching sides during a lawsuit became legally disreputable (*infamis*), which, among numerous unpleasant consequences, entailed disbarment.[107] Likewise, bribing the adversary's advocate was for obvious reasons forbidden, as was any other fraudulent or malicious behavior. Revealing docu-

---

101. Aulus Gellius, *Noctes Atticae* 1.22.6; Cicero, *De oratore* 1.36.166–67 and *Brutus* 23.89; Quintilian, *Inst. orat.* 6.1.14.

102. Dig. 3.1.11 pr., 5.2.32 pr.; Cod. 2.8 (9).1; Cod. Theod. 2.10.5 (= Cod. 2.6.6 pr.); Cod. 1.51.14 pr.

103. Dig. 3.3.8.3 and 3.3.22, 25.

104. Dig. 1.12.1.13, 1.16.9.2, 3.1.8, and 48.19.9 pr., 1–3; Kaser, *Römische Zivilprozessrecht*, 565.

105. Cod. 10.61(59).1; Dig. 48.19.9.4 and 50.2.3.1.

106. Dig. 3.2.4.4, 47.15.1, and 48.16.1.6. Justinian's Digest commissioners thought the subject so important that they devoted a whole title (Dig. 47.15) to it. See also Noonan, *Bribes*, 46–54.

107. Dig. 4.3.7.9, 47.15.4 and. 5; Cod. 2.7.1.

ments concerning a client's litigation to an unauthorized person was an extremely serious offense, equated with forgery. A lawyer who did so was liable (at least in theory) to be condemned to hard labor in the mines, which amounted to a particularly disagreeable version of the death penalty; even upper-class offenders stood to lose half of their property.[108]

None of these measures cured the problem. The younger Pliny (61 or 62–113 CE) observed, "Those of us who fritter away our energy on real lawsuits in the courts necessarily learn a good deal of sharp practice." Some advocates inevitably put that learning to use. "Nothing in the marketplace was cheaper," said Tacitus, "than an advocate's treachery,"[109] a statement that he illustrated by the story of a client named Samius, who after paying his advocate the enormous fee of 400,000 *sesterces* discovered that the advocate (a rogue named Suillius) was in collusion with the other side. Samius, distraught, rushed to Suillius's house, where he committed suicide by falling on his sword. The resulting scandal, although no doubt embarrassing, apparently did little to diminish Suillius's legal practice.

Courts handled *praevaricatio* actions in private. But even conviction of an advocate for this reason did not entitle his client to appeal the decision in the case, which may explain Samius's desperate deed.[110]

Praevaricatio was singled out for especially harsh treatment because it violated the client's trust and thus undermined the very foundation of the legal profession. Mutual trust between lawyer and client was as necessary in the Roman legal system as it is in our own. It was essential that a client be able to share sensitive details of his affairs with his legal adviser or representative with complete confidence that the lawyer would not reveal those secrets to anyone else, especially to his opponents. Concern to protect confidential information also lay behind the rule that barred advocates from giving testimony in cases in which a client was involved.[111] At the same time, the lawyer needed to be sure that his client was not holding back relevant information bearing upon the situation in which he had agreed to act, lest he be exposed to nasty surprises when advising, negotiating, or litigating.

The preliminary interview between an advocate and a prospective client was delicate but crucial in forming the lawyer-client relationship, and

108. Dig. 4.8.31, 48.10.1.6, and 48.19.38.8.
109. Pliny the Younger, *Epist.* 2.3.5; Tacitus, *Annales* 11.5.
110. Dig. 4.4.18.1 and 47.15.3.2.
111. The rule first appeared in the *Lex de repetundis* (sometimes known as the *Lex Acilia*) of 123 BCE; *Roman Statutes* 1:69, l. 33; Dig. 22.5.25. An example of the rule in practice appears in Cicero, *In C. Verrem* 2.2.8.24. See also Radin, "Privilege of Confidential Communication," 489.

Quintilian admonished the advocate never to rush through an interview or allow it to be interrupted. An advocate should never take a client's story at face value, he warned:

> Many of them lie and they talk as if they were speaking to a judge, rather than telling their advocate about the situation. For that reason a client should never be trusted; instead the advocate should test him in every way, get him confused, and so draw him out.[112]

The best advocate, he added, is a skeptical one: clients will promise anything, but making good on their promises was something else entirely. He must make the client go through his account more than once, not only to make sure that he understood the problem and all the issues that it might raise, but also to see if he could locate any inconsistencies in the client's story. The advocate should also be sure to take notes and to study the documents and other evidence in the case with great care, since prospective clients were prone to exaggerate their value in supporting his allegations. Quintilian cautioned the advocate to listen carefully during the interview and to try to identify what the client really wanted, as opposed to what he professed to want. Clients are often out for revenge, not justice, he warned, and the advocate must make sure that his prospective client does not intend to use him as a tool for some unworthy purpose.[113]

A prudent advocate needed to be cautious about choosing his cases. He should of course reject the dishonest ones, which were lamentably abundant, but even so he could not afford to take more legitimate ones than he could readily manage. An imperial constitution also warned advocates to be especially wary when accepting cases from female clients.[114] In general, Quintilian advised, it was better to act for the defense than for the prosecution, because it was easier to defend a client than to prove an accusation. Still, the advocate's public responsibility sometimes dictated that he appear for the prosecution. Whoever the client was, the advocate must be careful not build up false hopes, and he should never promise victory in litigation. Before deciding whether or not to accept a case, an advocate who cared for his reputation should also take into account who his adversary would be. When the advocate decided to take on a case, he should also try to persuade the client to engage a second advocate to assist him in presenting it.[115]

---

112. Quintilian, *Inst. orat.* 12.8.9.
113. Quintilian, *Inst. orat.* 12.8.7–12 and 12.9.10.
114. Quintilian, *Inst. orat.* 12.7.5, 12.9.15; Cod. Theod. 9.1.3.
115. Quintilian, *Inst. orat.* 6.4.7, 12.7.1 and 7, 12.9.19; Pliny, *Epist.* 6.23.

Advocates sometimes had no choice about the client they represented. Roman magistrates had the power to assign counsel in situations where one party had already engaged the services of all the older, more competent, or more experienced advocates locally available, leaving his adversary to make do with inexperienced or incompetent lawyers. Advocates thus assigned had to accept the case unless they were able to convince the judge that a conflict of interest or scheduling problem entitled them to be excused. Poor persons who would otherwise be unable to find an advocate to present their cases were also entitled to have counsel assigned to them.[116]

Clients could be fearfully demanding. They required attention at all hours. Ovid (43 BCE–18 CE) pictures the weary jurist roused from bed at daybreak by clients pounding on his door. The courts themselves were noisy and tumultuous, which strained the advocate's voice and made it difficult to maintain his concentration.[117] Horace (65–8 BCE) declared that an advocate had good reason to envy the calm and easy life of a farmer. The advocate's life, he maintained, was unhealthy: the stress it entailed brought on fevers and could lead to an early death.[118] Beyond that, advocates not only had to deal with judges, who were sometimes ignorant, lazy, and venal, but even worse with ungrateful clients, who were bound to blame their advocate should their case be lost. "The business," observed the younger Pliny in a morose moment, "is more fatiguing than pleasant."[119]

Criticism of Advocates

Both advocates and jurists, but especially advocates, had to deal with the fact that their profession inevitably attracted public criticism, and not infrequently outright vituperation. "Vultures in a toga," Apuleius (b. ca. 125, d. after 170) called them, while Juvenal (b. ca. 60, d. 100) opined that "they turn black into white" and accused them of practicing forensic piracy.[120] An advocate prostituted his voice, Ovid declared, while Quintilian derided the canine eloquence of lawyers who denigrated their oppo-

---

116. Cod. 2.6.7.1–2.; Dig. 1.16.9.4–5. Case records from Roman Egypt make it clear that people in humble circumstances often did have advocates to represent them in litigation (Crook, *Legal Advocacy*, 62–64, 124–25).

117. Ovid, *Amores* 1.13.21–22; *Constitutio Juliani de postulando*, 7, ll. 13–14; Suetonius, *De vita caesarum* 5.15 and 33 (Claudius); Crook, *Legal Advocacy*, 135–36.

118. Horace, *Satires* 1.1.9–10, and *Epist.* 1.7.8–9.

119. Ammianus Marcellinus, *Res gestae* 30.4.21–22; Pliny, *Epist.* 2.14.1.

120. Apuleius, *Metamorphoses* 10.33; Juvenal, *Satires* 3.29; Quintilian, *Inst. orat.* 12.7.11; cf. Ovid, *Metamorphoses* 11.314.

nents like snarling dogs.¹²¹ In the opinion of Ammianus Marcellinus (b. ca. 330, d. 395), advocates were a greedy and debased lot, who conspired with judges to rob the people of justice. In support of this position, he quoted Cicero as admitting that they corrupted judges, not with money, but with honeyed words.¹²²

Roman Advocates in Practice

Once he had taken a case, the conscientious advocate needed to study it, to plan his strategy, to determine what points he would make to the judge, and to anticipate the problems that his opponents might raise. Not all advocates, of course, were conscientious. Indeed, Quintilian thought that very few of them prepared sufficiently, and he scoffed at irresponsible ones who waited until the day of the trial to prepare a case or even tried to work it up while sitting in court.¹²³

When he got to court, the advocate needed to present a distinguished and prosperous appearance, so as to impress both his client and the judge. He had to pay close attention to the character of the judge, since different styles of advocacy appealed to different judges.¹²⁴ The judge, for his part, had to strive to be patient with advocates. He needed to make allowances for their limitations, Ulpian advised, since some were more clever and expert than others and it was important to see that everyone got his due. Still, the judge certainly should not coddle them.¹²⁵ People on each side of the bench had to cope with a difficult balancing act.

Only pettifoggers tried to knock down an adversary's case by jeering at the opponent and ridiculing his case. That sort of thing in Quintilian's opinion not only accomplished nothing, but was apt to be answered back in kind. Clients nevertheless enjoyed this sort of display and might encourage, or even expect, their advocates to engage in a bit of name-calling. Vicarious vituperation was in a sense one of the functions of litigation, and part of the advocate's job was, as John Crook puts it, "to let off your client's steam for him."¹²⁶ The advocate needed to be careful about this, however, and he was well advised to avoid abusing opposing counsel, since this

---

121. Ovid, *Amores* 1.15.5–6, at 53; Quintilian, *Inst. orat.* 12.9.9.

122. Ammianus Marcellinus, *Res gestae* 30.4.2–4, 10, preserves this quotation from a speech by Cicero that has not otherwise survived.

123. Quintilian, *Inst. orat.* 12.8.1–2.

124. Juvenal, *Satires* 7.135–38; Quintilian, *Inst. orat.* 11.1.45 and 11.3.137.

125. Dig. 1.16.9.2, 4.

126. Quintilian, *Inst. orat.* 12.9.8–9, quoting Appius; Crook, *Legal Advocacy*, 138.

might undermine his own credibility and diminish his client's chances of success. It was certain to do his own reputation no good.[127]

Advocates' Fees

Legal fees presented thorny issues for the Roman legal profession. During the early Republic, the lawyer's calling was ideally regarded as an honorable public service that right-thinking gentlemen ought to perform without thought of reward. Whether or not this ideal was ever consistently honored in practice must be a matter of conjecture. By the late third century, public authorities thought it necessary to buttress the ancient understanding by legislative action. The *Lex Cincia*, a plebiscite adopted in 204 BCE, forbade Roman advocates and legal advisers to accept payment for their services.[128] Even the most high-minded forensic orators in the early Republic, of course, expected other, nonmonetary rewards for their advocacy. Their legal services helped them to make friends, to enhance their reputations, and to enlist partisan supporters for their election to high office. Some ambitious advocates went so far as to hire claques of supporters to cheer their courtroom performances and thus build up their reputations and political visibility.[129]

The *Lex Cincia* was apparently easy to evade, and orators routinely made material profits from their legal work. Cicero openly boasted about the unsurpassed size of his earnings from advocacy. He and a few other outstanding forensic orators amassed considerable fortunes from their work in court, while lesser men, who were far more numerous, had to make do with less, often much less.[130]

Legislation, as usual, took a long time to catch up with life. Authorities continued to insist that advocates must not take fees, and advocates continued to take them anyway. Augustus persuaded the Senate to reenact the *Lex Cincia* and to attach a fourfold penalty for infringements.[131] This measure, too, failed to discourage advocates from demanding fees and clients from paying them. Tacitus ironically describes one notoriously greedy ad-

127. Quintilian, *Inst. orat.* 12.9.11.
128. Tacitus, *Annales* 11.5–6 and 13.42; Livy, *Ab urbe condita* 34.4.9; Visky, "Retribuzioni," 14–17.
129. Cicero, *Pro Murena* 34.71; Pliny, *Epist.* 1.18.4 and 2.14.4–6; Martial, *Epigrams* 6.48; Massol, "Des honoraires des avocats," 39–40.
130. Cicero, *Pro Murena* 4.8 (cf. Pliny, *Epist.* 5.13.6–7); Martial, *Epigrams* 4.46, 12.72; Juvenal, *Satires* 7.106–29; Crook, *Legal Advocacy*, 129–31 and *Law and Life of Rome*, 90–91; Henriot, *Moeurs juridiques* 3:152–54.
131. Cassius Dio, *Roman History* 54.18.2.

vocate as arguing, "All we ask is a reasonable amount, without which there will be no advocates to be had." Finally the emperor Claudius in 47 CE bowed to the inevitable. In the *Senatusconsultum Claudianum*, he conceded that thenceforth advocates could legally accept fees—but only up to a maximum of 10,000 *sesterces*.[132] That was not exactly a paltry sum: it works out to more than seven years' basic pay for a legionary. Any advocate who accepted more than that or who bargained for payment before the case was ended, Claudius decreed, should be considered guilty of extortion.[133] Advocates' fees were classed as *honoraria*, which in early Roman law differed from the wages of workmen in one important respect: while a worker for hire had a legal action to recover unpaid wages, there was no such recourse for an unpaid *honorarium*. A later addition to the praetorian edict changed this by creating a specific action for recovering a beneficial interest in an *honorarium*, which for practical purposes erased the distinction between the two kinds of compensation.[134] Once an advocate had accepted a case and received a fee, he was not obliged to repay the fee should the case not materialize, nor could the client reclaim fees paid to an advocate who died before the case was heard. The fee became the advocate's property on the order of a *peculium castrense*, even if he were still under the power of his paterfamilias.[135]

Later emperors continued to maintain Claudius's policy of allowing advocates to charge fees, while attempting to restrain their greed by fixing a ceiling on how much they could legally charge. Even so, advocates often demanded more and occasionally got in trouble for it.[136] The authorities

---

132. Tacitus, *Annales* 11.7; Pliny, *Epist.* 5.4.2; 5.9.3–4.

133. Tacitus, *Annales* 11.7; Pliny, *Epist.* 5.9.4; see also Crook, *Legal Advocacy*, 131. Claudius's cap on fees was renewed by the praetor in 105 CE, who specified that the advocate should receive his *honorarium* only after the case in which he acted had been decided (Pliny, *Epist.* 5.9.4). Clients customarily paid their advocates during the Saturnalia, a week-long festival that began on 17 December and which was a traditional time for gift giving (Martial, *Epigrams* 4.46).

134. Dig. 11.6.1 pr., 19.2.38, and 50.13.4; Cod. 3.1.13.9; Visky, "Retribuzioni," 2; Bernard, *Rémunération*, 100; Pescani, "Honorarium," 13.

135. Dig. 19.2.38.1 and 50.13.1.13; Visky, "Retribuzioni," 20; Cod. Theod. 2.10.6 (= Cod. 2.7.4).

136. Pliny, *Epist.* 5.9.4, and 5.13. Diocletian's Edict on Prices set advocates' maximum fees at 250 *denarii* for *postulatio* and 1,000 *denarii* for *cognitio*; *Corpus inscriptionum latinarum* 3/2:831, ll. 72–73. The maximum was later set at 100 *aurei*, which was virtually the same as the old maximum of 10,000 *sesterces* (Dig. 50.13.1.12; Visky, "Retribuzioni," 17–18, 30; Bernard, *Rémunération*, 94–95; Kaser, *Römische Zivilprozessrecht*, 565; Jones, *Later Roman Empire* 1:511 and 2:1217 n. 95).

quickly caught on to the most obvious ploys, such as attempts to disguise additional payment as a loan, reimbursement for court fees and costs (*sportula*), or as a bonus (*palmarium*) for victory, and ruled them out of order.[137]

Not all advocates, of course, were able to command anything approaching the maximum fee, and clients often paid in kind, rather than in money. The satirists, Martial (ca. 40–105) and Juvenal, poked painful fun at the payments lesser advocates collected: a sack of grain and beans, a handful of spices, a moldy ham, a wedge of cheese, a bag of aged onions, and five bottles of sub-ordinary wine.[138]

Even after the law permitted advocates to take fees for their work, some high-minded (and well-off) members of the profession continued to feel it inappropriate or even dishonorable to do so. Quintilian considered it still an open question whether advocates should take fees or not. He deemed it more honorable to refrain, because accepting a fee in some degree debased the advocate and made him beholden to his client. On the other hand, he conceded, many could ill afford to offer their services without compensation, and he was certainly not prepared to insist that they refuse fees. Quintilian's pupil, the younger Pliny, took his master's advice to heart and prided himself on never accepting money for advocacy. A century later Ulpian, as mentioned above, maintained that the jurist's profession was something holy that could not be valued in money terms. Although a jurist was within his rights to accept compensation if offered, Ulpian considered it inappropriate for him to demand payment.[139]

Self-denial of this sort was probably not feasible for most advocates and jurists. A more realistic view counseled that legal fees should vary depending on the situation. Ulpian defined four criteria that ought to determine the size of a fee: the amount at issue, the difficulty of the case, the skill and

137. On false loans, see Cod. 2.6.3 and 10.65 (63).2.1; Visky, "Retribuzioni," 21–22. On charges for expenses, see Cod. 3.2; for a mid-fourth-century schedule of fees in the province of Numidia, see Bruns, *Fontes iuris Romani antiqui* 1:280–81; Kaser, *Römische Zivilprozessrecht*, 557–58. On awards for a victorious outcome, see Dig. 50.13.1.12; Cod. Theod. 8.10.2 (= Cod. 12.61 [62].2); Bernard, *Rémunération*, 96; Emminghaus, "Vom Palmarium." The term *palmarium* presumably refers to the practice of decorating the staircase of a victorious advocate with palms (Juvenal, *Satires* 7.117–18).

138. Juvenal, *Satires* 7.118–23; Martial, *Epigrams* 4.46. Martial worked in the courts from time to time as an advocate and presumably knew what he was talking about. In *Epigrams* 8.17 he upbraided a client for paying him just 1,000 *sesterces*, which was only half of the fee they had agreed upon. If 2,000 *sesterces* represents even approximately his normal fee, Martial was doing significantly better than the advocates he satirized.

139. Quintilian, *Inst. orat.* 12.7.8, 10; Pliny, *Epist.* 5.13; Dig. 50.13.1.5.

reputation of the advocate, and the customary fee levels in the court where the case was heard.[140]

Authorities consistently agreed that it was immoral for an advocate to "buy an interest" in a case. By this they meant something much like what we now call a contingent fee arrangement, whereby the client agrees that if he wins the case his advocate will receive some stipulated part (typically one-third to one-half) of the award as his fee, while if the client loses the advocate will receive nothing. Imperial constitutions and juristic opinions repeatedly prohibited bargains of this kind, which Quintilian denounced as "a piratical practice."[141]

The modern argument in defense of contingent fees is that this arrangement makes it possible for clients who otherwise could not afford to do so to seek adjudication of their complaints by a court. Did the Roman prohibition of contingent fees in fact exclude poor litigants from the courts? Although some authorities have asserted that this was indeed the result, John Crook's examination of litigation records from Roman Egypt clearly indicates that in practice clients of meager means regularly appeared in the courts and often employed advocates to argue their cases.[142] Advocates who acted for these clients were often not very skilled and were miserably paid, to be sure, but their clients were able to get their cases into court and were represented there. In addition, as noted earlier, Roman law in some circumstances authorized judges to appoint advocates to act on behalf of litigants who could not otherwise secure legal counsel.

Tabelliones

Roman jurists and advocates relied on the skills and services of copyists to produce the documents that became increasingly important in legal practice during the late Republic and even more vital under the Principate and the Dominate. Private transactions in early Roman history were commonly executed orally, and proof of them depended on witnesses, not written records. As transactions came to be recorded more regularly, however, a class of specialized legal scribes or stenographers, sometimes described as *notarii*, emerged as a distinct occupational group. Bankers, merchants, businessmen, and government officials, along with advocates and jurists,

---

140. Dig. 50.13.1.10; cf. Quintilian, *Inst. orat.* 12.7.11.

141. Cod. 2.6.5 and 2.6.6.2; Dig. 2.14.53, 17.1.6.7 and 50.13.1.12; Quintilian, *Inst. orat* 12.7.11.

142. Crook, *Legal Advocacy*, 124, 131. For the counterargument, see Jones, *Later Roman Empire* 1:496, 498–99, and 2:1212–13.

grew to depend upon their services. Scribes employed by jurists and advocates inevitably became so familiar with the formulas appropriate to wills and other legal documents that they were able to compose as well as copy them. By the third century CE, these specialists in the redaction of legal documents formed a distinct occupational class whose members were known as *tabelliones* or *tabularii*.[143] They were often employed to produce public documents, such as the records of court proceedings, as well as legal documents for private transactions. By Constantine's reign, judges presumed that documents that *tabelliones* produced were authentic records of the transactions that they recorded unless the contrary could be proved.[144] By Justinian's time, they had become members of an officially recognized craft guild. The fees they charged for their services ultimately became subject to governmental regulation.[145] *Tabelliones* had to be licensed and typically worked out of private shops or offices (*stationes*). They were much more numerous than advocates and occupied a considerably lower status in the social hierarchy. They could be found even in quite small villages.[146]

The Christian Empire

Imperial power passed into Christian hands beginning in the early fourth century during the reign of Constantine, and the legal profession soon felt the effects of the new religious regime. Devotees of traditional Roman religions in the ranks of the profession gradually dwindled in number, and by the second half of the fifth century non-Christians were forbidden to practice as advocates. Justinian subsequently banned pagans from teaching law.[147]

Church fathers and early councils forbade clerics to practice as advocates in the civil courts, a prohibition that they justified by the scriptural admonition that Christians should avoid involving themselves in worldly affairs. Justinian later incorporated into imperial law the ban on legal practice by clerics.[148]

---

143. Dig. 43.5.3.3; Cod. 4.21.17; Amelotti and Costamagna, *Alle origini del notariato*, 5–16.

144. Cod. Theod. 9.19.1 (= Cod. 9.22.21); Nov. 44.2 pr.; Kaser *Römische Zivilprozessrecht*, 601.

145. Nov. 44.1.4 pr.; Cod. 12.21(22).8 and 12.29(30).3.2; Visky, "Retribuzioni," 26–27.

146. Nov. 44.1.1; Cod. Theod. 12.1.3 (= Cod. 10.32.15); Visky, "Retribuzioni," 24–25; Jones, *Later Roman Empire* 1:515 and 2:1218, n. 105–6.

147. Cod. 1.4.15, 1.11.10.2, and 2.6.8; Noonan, "Novel 22," 78.

148. 2 Tim. 2:4; Ambrose, *De officiis ministrorum* 3.9, in *PL* 16:162; Council of Chalcedon (451) c. 3, 7, 9, in *DEC* 1:88, 90–91; Charvet, "Accession des clercs aux fonctions d'avocat," 291; Nov. 123.6.

CANON LAW

At the same time, the church was developing its own legal system, separate from but related to the Roman civil law, and church officials naturally needed to know that law. That Christians should develop a legal system at all seems ironic, in view of the disparaging remarks about law, legalism, and lawyers scattered through the New Testament.[149] The process nevertheless began early in the church's history, as its leaders discovered that goodwill and brotherly love were not in themselves sufficient to create a viable community. Rules and regulations for the orderly conduct of worship, the administration of property, and the management of relationships among its members proved essential to the peaceful operation of the Christian community.

These rules, known as canons (from the Greek *kanon*, meaning a rule), appeared early in the church's history. The *Didache*, or *Doctrine of the Twelve Apostles*, which dates from the last years of the first or the opening years of the second century, is the earliest such collection to survive. The *Didache*, which is very brief, was soon followed by more lengthy and elaborate collections of rules for Christian communities, among them the *Pastor* of Hermas (ca. 140) and the *Traditio apostolica* (early third century), ascribed to Hippolytus (ca. 170–236). The *Didascalia apostolorum* (mid-third century) supplemented the *Traditio apostolica* with additional rules concerning the Christian community's support of widows and orphans, the functions and duties of the community's officials, Jewish-Christian relations, and fasting and penance.[150]

These early canons appeared during the formative centuries of the church's history, while Christianity was struggling to survive in a hostile environment. Jewish communities refused to accept the Christian belief that Jesus of Nazareth was the Messiah and were scandalized at the refusal of many Christians to observe the prescriptions of Mosaic law. Many gentiles, too, found the teachings of the new religion and the manners of its adherents repugnant. Pagan intellectuals considered Christian belief in di-

---

149. On the developing canonical system, see, e.g., the admonitions of Origen (ca. 185–254) and Pope Celestine I (r. 422–32) incorporated in numerous canonical collections, including Gratian's Decretum at D. 36 c. 3 and D. 38 c. 4. For scriptural disparagement of lawyers and law, see, e.g., Matt. 22:35 and 23:23; Luke 7:30, 10:25, 11:45–46, and 14:1–6; Rom. 4:15, Gal. 3:10–13; 1 Tim. 1:8–10.

150. Ferme, *Introduzione alla storia del diritto canonico*, 45–56.

vine revelation irrational, and government officials suspected Christians of criminal, even treasonous, activities. Ordinary Romans were put off by Christian ascetic practices and found Christian refusal to join in the festivals of the pagan religious calendar antisocial and inexplicable.

Since Christians constituted a tiny and unpopular religious minority within the Roman empire, the laws that the church developed during the first three centuries of its existence were primarily inward-looking. They dealt principally with the internal affairs of the community of believers and were much concerned to maintain a distance between Christians and their pagan or Jewish neighbors. Early Christian canons focused on matters of church discipline, the conduct of worship, and relations of Christians with one another. Bishops and other leaders formulated these rules, which presumably reflected a consensus among Christian communities scattered throughout the empire.

Relations between the imperial government and its Christian subjects long remained far from friendly. Although Roman governments tolerated numerous religious cults, some of them conspicuously exotic, Christianity aroused unusual antagonism among the empire's rulers. Christians attracted official displeasure from the time of Nero (r. 54–68), who made them scapegoats for the great fire that laid waste huge sections of the city of Rome in June 64.[151] For the next two-and-a-half centuries, Christians were subject to sporadic attacks by successive governments. The persecution was neither sustained nor systematic. Instead, periods of concerted attack were punctuated by months, sometimes years, of uneasy toleration, when Roman officials took little action, if any, against the Christians in their midst.[152] Unlike the devotees of other religions, Christians lived on the margins of Roman tolerance and could never be sure when or where the next wave of official persecution might strike. The most sustained and energetic efforts to wipe out their religion occurred during the reign of Diocletian, who blamed Christianity for many of the ills that afflicted the empire in his day.[153]

Imperial persecution of Christianity ended in 313, shortly after Constantine came to power. The so-called Edict of Milan in March of that year pro-

---

151. Tacitus, *Annales* 15.44; Suetonius, *De vita caesarum* 6.16 (Nero).

152. See, e.g., the well-known passages in the correspondence between the younger Pliny and the emperor Trajan in Pliny, *Epist.* 10.96–97.

153. Munier, *L'église dans l'empire romain*, 217–63, 274–84; Jones, *Later Roman Empire* 1:71–76.

claimed a policy of toleration toward Christians and, indeed, religions of every kind.[154] Constantine's subsequent enactments clearly favored Christianity above its competitors, and from his time forward it is customary to refer to the Roman state as a Christian empire. Constantine's successors, with the signal exception of the emperor Julian (r. 361–63), continued and augmented the favoritism that began during his reign.[155] Christianity's growing domination of Roman government reached its ultimate conclusion in 380, when the emperor Theodosius I (r. 379–95) proclaimed Christianity the official religion of the empire and penalized the practice of other religions.[156]

Canon Law and Roman Civil Law

This revolution in religious policy had enormous consequences for Roman civil law as well as for canon law, and those changes had an impact on legal practice and the legal profession. As Constantine himself observed, a changed religion entails a changed social order. The judicial functions of bishops expanded rapidly under the new regime, and Constantine obliged the civil courts to recognize and enforce the judgments of episcopal courts (*audientia episcopalis*).[157] The procedures employed in bishops' courts seem at first to have been relatively informal, but little by little they came to resemble those used in the civil courts. At length an imperial constitution of 376 required ecclesiastical courts to observe the same procedures that prevailed in the empire's civil courts.[158] This almost certainly meant that advocates were appearing in bishops' courts as well as in civil courts by the last quarter of the fourth century if not before.

Both imperial and canon law inevitably had to deal with relations be-

---

154. The document was technically not an edict and was published at Nicomedia, not Milan, although it does refer to a meeting between Constantine and his co-emperor, Licinius, at Milan. The text is preserved in Lactantius, *De mortibus persecutorum* 48.2–12.

155. Gaudemet, *L'église dans l'empire romain*, 7–14; Cochrane, *Christianity and Classical Culture*, 261–91; Jones, *Later Roman Empire* 1:77–137.

156. Cod. Theod. 16.1.2 (= Cod. 1.1.1), supplemented in the following year by Cod. Theod. 16.5.6 (= Cod. 1.1.2); Gaudemet, *L'église dans l'empire romain*, 13; Jones, *Later Roman Empire* 1:165.

157. Eusebius, *Life of Constantine* 2.65, at 116; Cod Theod. 1.27.1; Const. Sirmond. 1; Gaudemet, *L'église dans l'empire romain*, 229–40; Jones, *Later Roman Empire* 1:480–81; Humfress, "A New Legal Cosmos."

158. Cod. Theod. 16.2.23; Gaudemet, *L'église dans l'empire romain*, 246–52.

tween the church and civil government, particularly the jurisdictional boundaries between church authorities and their imperial counterparts. Church property and revenues, too, became the subject of a complex body of law governing their acquisition, management, tax status, and disposition. Marriage and family law comprised another area of mixed jurisdiction where both ecclesiastical and civil law were involved and sometimes clashed, especially over matters such as marriage across class boundaries, indissolubility, and divorce. Other contentious topics included sexual morality, theater and public entertainment, military service, slavery, commercial and financial law, and even contract law.[159]

The Sources of Canon Law

As ecclesiastical jurisdiction expanded, the church's law grew in volume and scope. Councils and synods accounted for much of that growth. These assemblies, composed largely, but not exclusively, of bishops and clerics, dealt with disciplinary and doctrinal problems of all kinds. Individual bishops and archbishops convened diocesan synods or provincial councils when critical problems arose in their region, while popes summoned churchmen from all parts to the Christian world to general or ecumenical councils to try to fashion solutions to grave problems that affected the church as a whole. Conciliar canons, which enunciated regulations agreed upon by these various assemblies, formed one principal source of new ecclesiastical law, while the Christian emperors also proved far from bashful about legislating on church affairs.[160]

The decisions that bishops, especially the pope, handed down concerning controversies referred to them for adjudication constituted another major source of new canon law, one that would become increasingly important over time. Papal decisions in cases appealed to the Roman Church were known as decretals. Decretal letters ultimately secured an authority equal to that of conciliar canons.[161] Decretals were routinely included in collections of canon law from the fifth and sixth centuries onward. The

---

159. Jones, *Later Roman Empire* 2:894–904; Gaudemet, *L'église dans l'empire romain*, 288–315, 515–61, 564–81, 703–9.

160. Gaudemet, *Sources*, 33–56; imperial constitutions dealing with ecclesiastical matters are collected in book 16 of Cod. Theod., which deals with religious law.

161. Gaudemet, *Sources*, 57–64; The earliest known decretal letter was written by Pope Siricius in 385; JK 255, trans. Somerville and Brasington, *Prefaces to Canon Law Books*, 36–46; Jasper and Fuhrmann, *Papal Letters*, 4, 16–17, 28–32; Hess, *Early Development of Canon Law*, 50, 58.

constitutions of the Christian emperors, too, were a source of canon law. In addition, the works of outstanding religious writers, the so-called fathers of the church, notably St. Jerome (b. ca. 345, d. 420), St. Ambrose (b. ca. 339, d. 397), and St. Augustine (354–430), were regarded as so authoritative that passages from their writings were often accorded the status of legal pronouncements.[162]

Canon Law Collections

These sources comprised such a vast and rapidly expanding body of rules and opinions that bishops and priests could scarcely be expected to scour them all when asked to decide or advise on a pressing problem that required speedy resolution. Instead, they or their assistants routinely turned for guidance to collections of canon law that presented decision makers with selected passages from the various canonical authorities and made it easier to discover the prevailing canon law.[163]

Canon Lawyers

Useful though they were, canonical collections were frequently not adequate to solve the problems that bishops and priests had to deal with. Few churchmen possessed the technical competence to deal with intricate legal analysis, especially when authoritative prescriptions themselves differed, as they often did. St. Augustine, for example, had to seek advice from a lawyer friend about the difficulties he encountered in coping with thorny issues in the law of personal status that arose when he was obliged to rule on the sale of a girl into slavery by her parents.[164] In so doing, Augustine was following a practice, common among bishops who lacked legal expertise, of relying upon assessors, often drawn from the ranks of advocates or jurists, to advise them on the law.[165]

Some ecclesiastical advocates, often described as *scholastici*, were clerics, whose practice tended to be confined to the bishops' courts, while others were laymen who worked in civil courts as well. In addition, churches in some parts of the empire could avail themselves of the services of lay advo-

---

162. Jasper and Fuhrmann, *Papal Letters*, 22–28; Gaudemet, *Sources*, 65–72, and *Formation du droit séculier*, 160–62.

163. See Kéry, *Canonical Collections*, Fowler-Magerl, *Clavis canonum*, and Ferme, *Introduzione alla storia del diritto canonico*.

164. Augustine, *Epist.* 24*, in *Epistolae ex duobus codicibus*, 127–28; Chadwick, "New Letters of St. Augustine," 433–34.

165. *Statuta ecclesiae antiqua*, 14, at 81.

cates (*defensores*) appointed to assist the bishop in his judicial functions and to protect church property from encroachment.[166]

By the fifth century CE, a legal profession had become an established part of the Roman social fabric. Both civil and ecclesiastical officials depended upon their lawyers in the conduct of public affairs, while private individuals could call upon them for advice and assistance in order to protect their interests, to settle their disputes, and to facilitate their transactions with others. This state of affairs, as it turned out, would not long endure, at least in the western half of the Roman empire.

---

166. On *scholastici*, see Jones, *Later Roman Empire* 1:480–81 and 2:1204 n. 22; on *defensores*, Cod. Theod. 2.4.7 (409) and 16.2.38 (407); *Registri ecclesiae Carthaginensis excerpta* 75 and 97, in *Concilia Africae*, 202, 215; Charvet, "L'accession des clercs," 289; Gaudemet, *L'église dans l'empire romain*, 367–68; Humfress, "Defensor ecclesiae."

* TWO *

Law without Lawyers
The Early Middle Ages

The early Middle Ages (ca. 500–1050) was a world without lawyers—or nearly so. The Roman legal system eroded drastically, at least in the Western empire, during the years that followed the turn of the sixth century. By the end of that century little more than its ghost remained, and the Roman legal profession faded away with it.[1]

The "Fall" of the Western Roman Empire

The eclipse of the Roman legal system and profession resulted from a series of events usually called "the fall of the Roman empire." That phrase is seriously misleading for three reasons. First, the eastern half of the empire remained reasonably intact throughout the early Middle Ages and indeed for nearly a millennium thereafter. The "fall," such as it was, directly affected only the western territories. Second, although Roman government eventually did crumble in the West, its demise was slow and chaotic, occurring at different rates and with different degrees of completeness in its various provinces. Third, the empire's fall was so silent that a great many of those who lived during the period either failed to notice that the empire was no longer there or continued to believe that it still survived, if not intact, at least in a transformed shape.[2] Inhabitants of western Europe around the year 800, for example, apparently

---

1. Bellomo, *Common Legal Past*, 34–35.
2. I owe the metaphor of the "silent fall" to Momigliano, "La caduta senza rumore." The sense of continuity was exemplified by Venantius Fortunatus (b. ca. 540, d. 609), in *Carmina* 7.8, addressed to Duke Lupus of Austrasia (Hoeflich, "Between Gothia and Romania," 127, citing *Carmina* 7.8.63).

saw nothing incongruous in acclaiming a German-speaking ruler who made his home on the banks of the Rhine as emperor of the Romans.[3]

They could do this because a significant part of the old empire's infrastructure, both physical and social, either remained largely intact or changed so gradually that the process was barely noticeable to contemporaries and became apparent only in hindsight. That so much of Roman administration either survived or adapted successfully to changing circumstances was due in considerable part to the leaders of the Western Church. The church's own organization helped to preserve numerous features of Roman administrative style. Some of its structural elements, such as provinces and dioceses, corresponded to administrative units of the late empire, while its reliance on written documents mirrored the routines of late imperial government and its officials long preserved the habits and practices of late Roman bureaucracy.

Barbarian Migrations and Settlement

Fundamental changes in government, politics, and society did occur, of course, during the years around and following 500 CE. The face of western Europe by the year 1000 certainly differed radically from what it had been a half-millennium earlier. For one thing, both the ethnic composition and the social structure of western Europe's population had changed markedly in the interim. This was a consequence of complex population movements across the old imperial frontiers that began late in the fourth century.

The boundary lines that we see on maps are inherently deceptive. They imply the existence of rigid barriers that sharply separate one polity from another. In real life, of course, all frontiers are to some degree permeable. People, goods, ideas, and cultural artifacts of all sorts pass to and fro across them, sometimes legally, sometimes not. The northern borders of Rome's reach, which during the imperial period lay for the most part along the Rhine and Danube valleys, were more permeable than most. For generations prior to the late fourth century, merchants, traders, adventurers, and military forces, both large and small, crossed those frontiers in both directions with considerable frequency and regularity.[4]

Romans and their central European neighbors, whom we conventionally call Germans or Germanic barbarians, interacted with and influenced one another in innumerable ways. Roman armies drew recruits from among Germanic warriors, and fashionable Romans adopted German garments

---

3. Nelson, "Kingship and Empire," 230–34.
4. Wheeler, *Rome beyond the Imperial Frontiers*, gives a lively account of this traffic.

and hairstyles, to the dismay of the empire's rulers.[5] Likewise, Germanic households, at least those that could afford such luxuries, became avid consumers of Roman textiles, jewelry, and tableware. Relations between Romans and Germans, while not invariably peaceful, were typically characterized by mutual interdependence rather than hostility.

During the last quarter of the fourth century, however, traffic across Rome's Rhine-Danube frontiers began to shift in volume and character. Groups of Germanic warlords and their followers commenced to cross the frontiers in sizable numbers.[6] They attacked Roman cities, towns, and estates, and plundered them successfully. Eventually Germanic warriors managed to wrest political control of whole provinces away from Roman authorities. Roman armies, many of them led by generals who were themselves of Germanic origin,[7] resisted, but gradually yielded control of one region after another to the invaders, who proceeded to settle and ultimately to establish Germanic kingdoms on formerly Roman soil.

The process of invasion and settlement that led to the eclipse of Roman rule was neither swift nor sudden. As early as the beginning of the last quarter of the fifth century, effective Roman government had virtually ceased to exist in the provinces north and west of the Adriatic Sea. Roman political control and civil administration gradually gave way in the Italian peninsula, Gaul, Britain, and Spain as decade by decade the regions under imperial control continued to shrink.

The Barbarian Kingdoms

The rulers of the new kingdoms that gradually supplanted Roman provinces in western Europe had no desire to destroy the society and econ-

---

5. Cod. Theod. 14.10.2–4. Note also the prohibition on marriage between Romans and barbarians in Cod. Theod. 3.14.1 (Sivan, "Why Not Marry a Barbarian?" 136–45). Both "Germanic" and "barbarian" present problems, but since they are long-established terms and do not seriously affect my argument, I shall continue to employ them. On the problems involved, see among others Goffart, *Barbarians and Romans*, 3–35, and *Rome's Fall and After*; as well as Wenskus, *Stammesbildung und Verfassung*; Geary, "Barbarians and Ethnicity"; and Lupoi, *Origins*, 47–52.

6. Conventional maps that purport to depict the movements of various Germanic peoples into and within the empire radically oversimplify an extremely complex situation and are both misleading and anachronistic. For an analysis of the problems involved, see Goffart, "What's Wrong with the Map?" 159–77.

7. Ammianus Marcellinus, writing of events in 378, expressed astonishment at encountering an army unit all of whose officers were Romans, "which rarely happens these days" (*Res gestae* 31.16.8).

omy that they now controlled. Barbarian settlers in most of those kingdoms comprised a fraction of the total population, the great majority of whom were either Roman, or at least thoroughly Romanized, in culture, economy, institutions, and law. The new rulers were eager to preserve as much as they could of the material and cultural fabric of the territories over which they had gained authority.[8] The surviving Roman population for its part was anxious to maintain as much of the social infrastructure of their society as they could under the new political and social regimes. Once the tumult of conquest died down, accommodation to the changed circumstances became a goal of both Romans and Germans in the newly established Germanic kingdoms that supplanted Roman government in what had been the Western empire.[9]

The church, especially its bishops, were key players in this process. As Roman civil administration began to fade away, bishops filled much of the vacuum that it left. They took over a host of functions previously performed by civil servants. Thus we find bishops proving wills and supervising the administration of decedents' estates, provisioning garrisons, supervising the maintenance of roads, bridges, and aqueducts, monitoring the performance of regional administrators, operating schools, and overseeing tax collection. Bishops, in short, stepped in to manage much of the day-to-day machinery of local government, in addition to their religious duties.[10]

Social changes inevitably accompanied these migrations and population changes. The total population of western Europe was apparently on the decline throughout the third and fourth centuries. The rate of decrease may have accelerated slightly during the sixth century, before it finally stabilized at a low level between about 600 and 1000 CE. Although reliable data are sparse and their interpretation poses problems, it seems reasonably clear that European population settlement patterns also shifted dramatically. Urban populations dwindled and some Roman cities vanished altogether, so that the proportion of the total population dwelling in the countryside increased greatly during this period.

8. Koschaker, *Europa und das römische Recht*, 11–12; Murray, "Pax et disciplina," 269–85.

9. Wallace-Hadrill, *The Barbarian West*, 31–32 and passim; Brown, *World of Late Antiquity*, 122–26; Goffart, *Barbarians and Romans*, 206–30.

10. Lupoi, *Origins*, 27–29. It was no coincidence that quite a few of these bishops belonged to Roman aristocratic houses and used their family fortunes to support both the civic and ecclesiastical enterprises in which they engaged (Brown, *Religion and Society*, 161–82). Pope Gregory the Great was an outstanding, but by no means an isolated, example (Llewellyn, *Rome in the Dark Ages*, 85–94).

By the beginning of the sixth century, only a handful of substantial cities remained in the West. In Italy these included Ravenna and a few other port cities, such as Rimini, Ancona, and Otranto. Inland cities were even sparser, although Pavia continued to be an important administrative center and Milan remained relatively populous. Rome, on the other hand, had ceased to be the principal center of imperial administration long ago, and its population had shrunk sharply. The city still remained a center of ecclesiastical administration, however, and the growth of papal power during and after the pontificate of Gregory the Great (r. 590–604) assured it of continuing importance.[11]

A few towns outside of the Italian peninsula continued, if not to prosper, at least to maintain an urban culture, notably in southern France (Marseilles, Arles, and Toulouse), and the Iberian peninsula (Toledo, Cordoba, Tarragona, and Seville), while Lyon in the former Roman province of Gaul had become the chief city of the Burgundian kingdom.[12]

Law in the Barbarian Kingdoms

Social change inevitably brought legal change in its train. One fundamental alteration that the migrations introduced was a shift in the concept of legal identity. In the modern world, we usually think of law (not altogether accurately in fact) in territorial terms and assume that everyone who enters a particular geographical region becomes subject to the laws of that region. Thus a Frenchman who crosses the border into Germany normally becomes subject to German law until he returns to France when he once again falls under French jurisdiction.

The situation in the early barbarian kingdoms was different, for the new rulers often treated jurisdiction in personal rather than territorial terms. Law was seen as central to a person's identity, a function of his or her ethnic heritage. Thus a Frank or a Burgundian, for example, retained the right (at least in principle) to be judged according to Frankish or Burgundian law no matter where he traveled or what he did while he was in foreign parts. Similarly, people of Roman heritage were entitled to conduct their affairs under the rules of Roman law, despite the fact that they had become subjects, say, of a Burgundian or perhaps a Visigothic, Frankish, or Bavarian

---

11. Wickham, *Early Medieval Italy*, 9–27, 80–92; Russell, *Late Ancient and Medieval Population*, 71–73.

12. Russell, *Late Ancient and Medieval Population*, 73–75, 83–85; O'Callaghan, *History of Medieval Spain*, 70–72.

king, while their Germanic neighbors conducted their business according to their own traditional laws. The obvious complications of this situation often made it clumsy to implement in practice.[13]

Matters became still more perplexing when a person of Roman stock became involved in a dispute with a person of Germanic heritage. In practice, it seems, judges usually tried to find some equitable compromise between the interests of the various parties and often applied rules taken from more than one of the laws involved. Ad hoc solutions that drew upon the rules of various bodies of law, however, meant that the legal consequences of a transaction became exceedingly difficult to predict. Uncertainty about the law pervaded early medieval societies.[14]

GERMANIC LAW CODES

Beginning in the late fifth century, the rulers of one barbarian kingdom after another undertook to record the laws of their peoples. We know virtually nothing about the laws of the various Germanic peoples prior to this time.[15] Few scholars now accept the premise that it should be possible to reconstruct some sort of primitive Germanic law from the common elements in the written versions of these laws. It seems unlikely that any such body of *germanisches Urrecht* ever existed, and in any event, the differences between the written versions of the laws in different Germanic kingdoms are at least as striking as the similarities.[16] Barbarian rulers entrusted the preparation of written versions of their laws to the notaries and clerks who worked in their chanceries. In the course of their normal duties, these officials drafted

---

13. Mathisen, "*Peregrini, Barbari,* and *Cives Romani*"; Ascheri, *Diritti del medioevo italiano*, 113–16. This situation persisted at Genoa among other places well into the eleventh century; Epstein, *Genoa and the Genoese*, 18. The term "personality of law," often used to describe this situation, can bear a variety of meanings (Guterman, *Principle of the Personality of Law*; Lupoi, *Origins*, 388–405).

14. Lupoi, *Origins*, 41–46, 390–91. For one example of the kinds of complications that might arise, see Manaresi, *Placiti del Regnum Italiae*, no. 236.

15. The *Germania* of Tacitus, written around 98 CE, does include statements about Germanic customs and dispute settlement, but their reliability remains dubious. To what extent the recording of customary laws actually constituted legislative innovation, rather than simply records of preexisting customs is much debated (see Dilcher, "Gesetzgebung als Rechtserneuerung"). Recent scholarly opinion has tended to deemphasize the differences between Germanic law and west Roman vulgar law (Murray, *Germanic Kinship Structure*, 116–18; Wormald, *Making of English Law*, 38).

16. Gilissen, *La coutume*, 42–44.

documents in Latin, and it is therefore no surprise to discover that they also produced law codes in Latin.[17] The drafters of the codes unquestionably knew some elementary Roman law, since they introduced technical words and concepts drawn from Roman law, as well as Roman analytical categories, into the laws that they redacted.[18]

The earliest Germanic law code from the Continent, the *Codex Euricianus* (also known as the *Leges Visigothorum*), was authorized by Euric, king of the Visigoths (r. ca. 466–85) about 476 or shortly thereafter. Only parts of Euric's code survive, although some missing sections can be reconstituted from closely related texts in the Bavarian laws (*Lex Baiuariorum*)[19] and from a reissue of the *Leges Visigothorum* in 654 by King Recceswinth. Not long after the appearance of the *Codex Euricianus*, other such collections began to appear. These include the *Edictum Theodorici*, promulgated by the Ostrogothic king of Italy, Theodoric II (r. 471–526); the *Leges Burgundionum*, issued by Gundobad, king of the Burgundians (r. 474–516); and the *Pactus legis Salicae*, probably promulgated shortly after 507 by Clovis, king of the Salian Franks (r. 481–511).[20] A century later the Lombard king Rothair (r. 636–52) followed suit with the *Leges Langobardorum* of 643. The rulers of other barbarian kingdoms would soon do likewise.[21]

17. By contrast, Irish and Welsh law books, as well as the laws of the Anglo-Saxons in England and the still later codes produced in Iceland and Scandinavia, were written in the vernacular.

18. A constitution issued in 727 by the Lombard king Liutprand directed that charters be written either according to Lombard law or Roman law (Liutprand 91 in *The Lombard Laws*, trans. Drew, 183–84). See also Vismara, "Leggi e dottrina nella prassi notarile italiana dell'alto medioevo"; Riché, *Écoles et enseignement dans la haut moyen âge*, 258; and Lupoi, *Origins*, 94–96.

19. *Leges Visigothorum*, in MGH, Leges §1, vol. 1; Buchner, *Rechtsquellen*, supplementary volume to Wattenbach and Levison, *Deutschlands Geschichtsquellen im Mittelalter*, 6–9; King, *Law and Society in the Visigothic Kingdom*, 6–9. On the *Lex Baiuuariorum*, see Buchner, *Rechtsquellen*, 26–29, as well as *Laws of the Alamans and Bavarians*, trans. Rivers, 107–80.

20. Vismara, *Edictum Theoderici*, 11–28; *Leges Burgundionum*, in MGH, Leges §1, vol. 2, pt. 1; Buchner, *Rechtsquellen*, 10–12 (see also the *Burgundian Code*, trans. Drew); *Pactus legis Salicae*, in MGH, Leges §1, vol. 4, pt. 1; Buchner, *Rechtsquellen*, 15–21; *Laws of the Salian and Ripuarian Franks*, trans. Rivers; and *Laws of the Salian Franks*, trans. Drew. See further McKitterick, *Carolingians and the Written Word*, 40–60, and Wormald, *Making of English Law*, 40–44.

21. *Leges Langobardorum*, in MGH, Leges §1, vol. 4; Buchner, *Rechtsquellen*, 33–37; *The Lombard Laws*, trans. Drew. Buchner, *Rechtsquellen*, 15–33, 37–44, describes the details of the process by which the various codes were established.

Although the various Germanic law codes differed from one another,[22] the contrast between the legal practices that they describe and those characteristic of Roman law are striking. The divergences are particularly apparent in the areas of personal injury and procedure. Restraining personal violence in order to preserve peace within the community was naturally a major goal of Roman as well as Germanic law, but the prominence of provisions regarding bodily harm in most Germanic codes is remarkable. The various codes include lengthy and detailed schedules of numerous kinds of physical injury that one person might inflict upon another, together with the sum of money required to make amends for each injury.[23] Roman law also prescribed compensation for injuries, but in Roman jurisprudence this formed a branch of the larger law of obligations, which also dealt with the legal consequences of contracts and other types of agreements that gave rise to duties.[24] Few of the Germanic codes, by contrast, said much about contracts and agreements. None of them linked what little they did say about these matters to their treatment of personal injuries. Sophisticated analyses of this type were uncommon in the culture in which the Germanic law codes took shape.

COURTS AND PROCEDURE

The procedural systems of Roman and Germanic law likewise differed, although not quite as radically as is sometimes maintained.[25] Roman procedural law, as we have seen, went through several stages in its development, but by the time of the barbarian invasions the prevailing system was *cognitio*. Under *cognitio* procedure, legally trained judges who were members of the imperial bureaucracy decided cases (at least in principle) on the basis of evidence contained in documents and the written depositions of witnesses.[26]

Courts in the barbarian kingdoms operated differently. Judges (called

22. Lupoi, *Origins*, 109–10.

23. E.g., *Pactus legis Salicae* 29; *Edictum Rotari* 45–127; and virtually the entire *Pactus legis Alamannorum*.

24. The Roman law of delict, a branch of the law of obligations, furnished civil remedies for personal injuries of numerous kinds. In addition, many delicts, such as assault, theft, kidnapping, forgery, and certain kinds of homicide, could be prosecuted criminally as well. See Frier, *Casebook on the Roman Law of Delict*; Zimmermann, *Law of Obligations*, 902; Robinson, *Criminal Law of Ancient Rome*.

25. Wood, "Disputes in Late Fifth- and Sixth-Century Gaul," 7–22.

26. Kaser, *Römische Zivilprozessrecht*, 435–71; Robinson, *Sources of Roman Law*, 90–101.

rachymburgi in Merovingian Gaul) were members of the community or later, under Carolingian rule, royal officials (*scabini, Schöffen*), selected for their maturity, social and political distinction, and reputation for honesty, reliability, and good sense. They need not have any particular legal expertise, although they could and did seek advice from others with greater experience in legal matters. The families of litigants usually provided whatever advice, counsel, and support the parties had available to them.[27]

Germanic procedure typically treated evidence and proof in ways much different from those employed in Roman law. Oral witness testimony played a relatively slight role in Germanic procedure, although written documents might be an important, and sometimes a crucial, type of evidence.[28] Germanic courts relied far more than Roman courts had ever done upon the sworn accusations and denials of the parties and, quite unlike Roman practice, often required that those oaths be supported by additional sworn statements by oath-helpers, or compurgators, who were prepared put their immortal souls at risk by calling upon God to witness that they believed the claims made by the party on whose behalf they appeared.[29]

If other forms of proof were lacking and the matter at issue was particularly serious, the court might also insist upon proof by ordeal, especially if the credibility of the party who bore the burden of proof seemed dubious. A party to a dispute also had the option of proposing to resolve the matter through an ordeal. An ordeal involved subjecting the party to a physical test, such as requiring him to carry a red-hot iron a prescribed distance or to immerse his forearm in boiling water for a stipulated period of time, and then observing the healing of the resulting wounds, on the theory that God would intervene to repair any damage to the innocent and would refuse to heal the guilty. Canny litigants could use the offer of an ordeal as a tactical device to put their opponent on the defensive in the hope of forcing a settlement. The ordeal thus became a bargaining tool. It was a peril-

27. Calasso, *Medio evo del diritto*, 133–37; Engelmann, *History of Continental Civil Procedure*, 85–87, 92–96; Wormald, *Making of English Law*, 89; Dawson, *Oracles of the Law*, 149–50; Lupoi, *Origins*, 207–11; Drew, "Peace and Security in the Early Middle Ages."

28. Caenegem, *History of European Civil Procedure*, 8–10; Fouracre, "'Placita' and the Settlement of Disputes"; Nelson, "Dispute Settlement"; Ourliac, "La pratique et la loi," 97–98; McKitterick, *Carolingians and the Written Word*, 60–75. Ascheri, *Diritti del medioevo italiano*, 105, notes that the testimony of witnesses and documentary evidence played a more central role in Italy under Lombard law than was true in Germanic kingdoms elsewhere.

29. Lupoi, *Origins*, 340–50; Engelmann, *History of Continental Civil Procedure*, 157–58.

ous one, however, for if the bluff failed to work, the opponent might refuse to back down and insist on going through with the test. Many litigants were clever enough to find ways of backing out of such an offer: at any rate litigation records show numerous cases in which an ordeal was proposed but never actually performed.[30]

As a result, the legal consequences of individual actions could be difficult or even impossible to predict. Not only was it hard to foretell, for example, what the outcome of an ordeal might be, but even the content of substantive law was not firmly fixed. A bench of Frankish *scabini* or *Schöffen* did not usually consult the written Salic laws as if they were a set of statutes and the final disposition of an action remained uncertain until a court gave judgment on it.[31]

ARBITRATION

Perhaps in consequence of such hurdles, disputes in the Germanic kingdoms were frequently resolved not by formal legal processes, but rather by arbitration. This certainly seems to have been usual in Languedoc and some parts of what is now western France; it was very likely common elsewhere as well. Early medieval arbitration practices differed considerably from the more formal kinds of arbitration proceedings found in classical Roman law.[32] The arbitrators themselves were often friends or relatives of the parties. Their authority depended on the fact that they were in a position to demand that the disputing parties agree to a settlement. Arbitrators were not bound by formal rules. Their aim was to devise a compromise that would leave each party at least partially satisfied. This often involved constraining them to divide the property at issue. When for some reason that would not work, the arbitrators might award the property to one contender, on condition that he pay appropriate compensation to his opponent. In any case, the arbitrators sought to avoid violence and to find a way

---

30. Bartlett, *Trial by Fire and Water*, 1–33; Hyams, "Trial by Ordeal"; Gaudemet, "Ordalies au moyen âge"; Engelmann, *History of Continental Civil Procedure*, 151–62; White, "Proposing the Ordeal and Avoiding It."

31. Landau, "Einfluß des kanonischen Rechts," 42–43. This is not to say that Germanic judges never consulted the written texts. The copying of law books and the reporting of litigation became a sizable industry by the Carolingian period, especially in the southern regions of the empire (McKitterick, *Carolingians and the Written Word*, 48–55; Wormald, *Making of English Law*, 56–58, 81, 91).

32. Cheyette, "Suum cuique tribuere," 289–91; White, "'Pactum . . . legem vincit et amor judicium.'" On Roman arbitration procedure (*compromissum*), see Stein, *Legal Institutions*, 51–53, and "Labeo's Reasoning on Arbitration."

to persuade, or if necessary to coerce, the adversaries to accept a peaceful solution to their differences.[33]

Some men doubtless became highly skilled in the rules of the Germanic law courts and proved unusually adept at manipulating their procedures, but it would be misleading to describe them as professional lawyers. Litigants sought out such men as experienced advisers who could suggest advantageous tactics and warn against pitfalls in the rigid formalities that characterized Germanic judicial procedures,[34] but there is little to suggest that they saw themselves, or were seen by others, as a distinct social group in early medieval communities.

ROMAN LAW IN THE EARLY MEDIEVAL KINGDOMS

In addition to written versions of their own laws, Visigothic and Burgundian monarchs also authorized the compilation of brief manuals of Roman law, the *Lex Romana Visigothorum* (ca. 506) and the *Lex Romana Burgundionum* (ca. 517). The *Lex Romana Visigothorum* was especially important because it remained in use much longer and over a far wider territory than the Burgundian compilation. The Visigothic manual—sometimes called the *Breviarium Alaricianum*, after King Alaric II (r. 485–507), who commissioned its compilation—drew much of its material from the *Codex Theodosianus*. Its redactors also provided explanatory *interpretationes* of many laws, presumably as guidance for judges who dealt with disputes among persons of Roman descent.[35]

Knowledge of Roman law certainly survived among descendants of the empire's former subjects throughout the period of barbarian invasions and settlement.[36] How, where, and under what circumstances knowledge of Roman law passed from one generation to the next in western Europe after the mid-fifth century is less clear. In 451 the emperor Valentinian III (r. 425–54) lamented that men knowledgeable in the law had become rare

---

33. Cheyette, "Suum cuique tribuere," 291–95.

34. E.g., the rules for the manumission of a slave in the *Lombard Laws*, Rothair 224, or for involving members of a kinship group in the payment of a judgment for homicide according to the *Pactus legis Salicae* 58.

35. Gaudemet, *Bréviaire d'Alaric*; Cortese, *Diritto nella storia* 1:55–68; King, *Law and Society*, 10–11; Buchner, *Rechtsquellen*, 9–10, 12–13. Alaric's *Breviarium* is one of the main sources for the reconstruction of the text of the Theodosian Code. See Wretschko, "De usu Breviarii Alariciani," in the *Prolegomena* to Cod. Theod., ed. Krueger and Mommsen, cccvii–ccclx.

36. A striking example is the persistence into the Carolingian period of elements of Roman procedures for proving wills (Taylor, "Testamentary Publication and Proof").

in Italy.[37] Roman law was still being taught at Rome a century later, and possibly at Ravenna as well: in a letter dating from around 533, Athalaric, the Ostrogothic king of Italy (r. 526–34), urged Rome's senators to provide funds to support law teaching in the city.[38] In 534, the Eastern emperor Justinian I (r. 527–65) ordered the suppression of most of the remaining law schools in the empire, but he exempted the one at Rome, together with those at Constantinople and Beirut.[39]

Justinian's Codification of Roman Law

Justinian's reign marked a watershed in the history of Roman law. Sweeping legal reforms ranked high among the emperor's priorities from the beginning.[40] The most successful of these projects involved a massive recasting of the sources of the law itself.

Shortly after he acceded to the throne of the Eastern empire, Justinian appointed the first of a series of commissions charged with the task of reducing to manageable size the unwieldy mass of enactments that had accumulated since the time of the Twelve Tables and the even greater abundance of juristic commentary on them. The key figure in realizing this goal was Justinian's protégé, the *quaestor* Tribonian (b. ca. 470, d. 543), who unrelentingly drove members of successive law reform commissions to complete their work within strict deadlines.[41] Justinian appointed the first of these commissions on 15 February 528 and assigned to it the responsibility

---

37. Nov. Val. 32.1.6.

38. Cassiodorus, *Variae* 9.21, ed. Fridh, 371–73; Justinian, *Constitutio pragmatica* (554) in Nov. App. 7.22; Riché, "Les Écoles en Italie," 11. The supposed law school at Pavia, on the other hand, was probably a myth (Riché, *Éducation et culture dans l'Occident barbare*, 66, 334–35, and "Les écoles en Italie," 6). Radding, *Origins of Medieval Jurisprudence*, argues unconvincingly for the existence of a school of Roman law at Pavia. As a note in *BMCL* 19 (1989) 79 put it: "The author's case for Pavia as the birthplace of jurisprudence in the Middle Ages bespeaks an *ignoratio elenchi*. It is unsupported by firsthand evidence, by any knowledge of MS texts and their transmission in both laws, and by a proper understanding of 20th-cent. scholarship." See also the reviews by André Gouron in *TRG* 57 (1989) 178–81; Johannes Fried in *DA* 45 (1989) 287–88; and Stanley Chodorow in *Speculum* 65 (1990) 743–45, among others.

39. Dig. Const. Omnem §7.

40. Barker, *Justinian and the Later Roman Empire*, 166–73; Moorhead, *Justinian*, 32–35.

41. Honoré, *Tribonian*, is the basic, although somewhat controversial, treatment of the whole enterprise; see the reservations about some of his arguments advanced by Waldstein, "Tribonianus," and Osler, "Compilation of Justinian's Digest."

for producing a new and enlarged code of Roman statutory law that would incorporate earlier laws that did not appear in the *Codex Theodosianus*, together with laws promulgated since 448. The commission completed its work with impressive speed, and on 7 April 529 Justinian promulgated the new code containing some 4,500 imperial constitutions in twelve books. This was the work known as the *Codex Justinianus*.[42]

Late in 530, Justinian appointed a new sixteen-member commission, again headed by Tribonian. The emperor charged these commissioners with the formidable task of bringing order to the vast accumulation of juristic opinions and treatises. Theodosius II had envisioned doing something of the sort a century earlier, when he informed the Senate at Constantinople in 429 about his grand design for what became the Theodosian Code.[43] This part of the plan proved overly ambitious and he finally abandoned it. Now Justinian took it up again, determined to succeed where his predecessor had failed.

By an extraordinary feat of compression, the commissioners managed to scale down some 3,000,000 lines of legal texts into approximately 150,000 lines. The commission completed this gigantic enterprise in three years, and on 16 December 533 Justinian promulgated the result of its labors as the Digest (also known in Greek as the *Pandekta*, or in English, the Pandects). Formal imperial approval gave the opinions included in the Digest quasi-legislative standing.[44]

While the Digest commission was still at work, Tribonian simultaneously headed a smaller committee whose task was to produce a basic textbook that would introduce beginning law students to the new legal codification. This group essentially refashioned the older institutes of Gaius into an introduction to the new law. The emperor promulgated this work, now known as Justinian's Institutes, in 533 as a required textbook for that all first-year law students.

Justinian's codification thus consisted of three parts, the Code, the Digest, and the Institutes. A compilation of new laws (*Novellae leges*, or the Novels) was later added to these. This collection, produced by private lawyers, comprised 168 of Justinian's constitutions that appeared after the

---

42. An enlarged edition of the *Codex Justinianus* was published in 534. The first edition immediately became outdated and no copies are known to survive (Honoré, *Tribonian*, 212; Buckland, *Text-Book of Roman Law*, 89, 46–47).

43. Cod. Theod. 1.1.5; Matthews, *Laying Down the Law*, 10–11.

44. Ascheri, *Diritti del medioevo italiano*, 34.

completion of the second edition of his Code. Later medieval writers came to refer to these four works collectively as the *Corpus iuris civilis*, or the *Body of the Civil Law*.[45]

Justinian's codification directly affected only the Eastern empire, which from his reign onward is usually styled the Byzantine empire. This change in terminology is symptomatic of the growing separation between the eastern portion of the old empire and the regions that had formerly constituted its western half. Save for a few isolated territories that remained under Byzantine rule, courts and judges in the Germanic kingdoms took no account of the new body of law. Even so, Justinian's codification was not completely unknown in the West.[46] The Venerable Bede (b. ca. 673, d. 735) mentioned it briefly in his chronicle of world history, for example, while Paul the Deacon (d. 797) presented a fuller account in his *History of the Lombards*.[47] Abbo, the father of Abbot Odo of Cluny (b. ca. 877, d. 944), was said to have memorized Justinian's Novels. Still, courts in the barbarian kingdoms made scant use of Justinian's codification, nor was it widely studied or taught there prior to the eleventh century.[48]

THE FATE OF ROMAN LAW IN THE WEST

The withering away of Roman law schools accounts in part for the failure of Justinian's codification to take hold in the West. By the late sixth century, systematic and detailed teaching of Roman law of the kind that a practicing lawyer needed had virtually vanished in the regions ruled by barbarian

---

45. Azo, *Summa super Codicem*, 9, to Cod. 1.14; Accursius, *Glos. ord.* to Cod. 5.13.1 pr. v. *corpore*. The ordinary gloss and *casus* are cited throughout from the 1584 Lyon edition of the *Corpus iuris civilis* (Kantorowicz, *Studies in the Glossators of the Roman Law*, 95; Savigny, *Geschichte des römischen Rechts* 3:516–17).

46. Weimar, "Corpus iuris civilis."

47. Bede, *Greater Chronicle*, s.a. 4518, in his *Ecclesiastical History of the English People*, at 329; Conrat, *Geschichte*, 99–102; Paul the Deacon, *Storia dei Longobardi* 1.25, 50; Conrat, *Geschichte*, 98–99; Zimmermann, "Römische und kanonische Rechtskentnis," 775. Ivo of Chartres at the end of the eleventh century incorporated this passage in his *Decretum* 4.171, in *PL* 161:304.

48. Johannes Cluniacensis, *Vita sancti Odonis* 1.5, in *PL* 133:46; Conrat, *Geschichte*, 40; Zimmermann, "Römische und kanonische Rechtskenntnis," 776. Copies of Justinian's Code were produced in the early medieval West, as was at least one surviving copy of the Digest, the so-called Codex Florentinus. See Lange, *Römisches Recht im Mittelalter*, 61–63, 71–76; Weimar, "Legistische Literatur der Glossatorenzeit," 158–64; see also, Dolezalek, *Repertorium Codicis* 1:61–81.

kings.[49] Knowledge of Roman law nevertheless did not entirely disappear. Notaries continued to function in at least some parts of early medieval Europe, much as they had done in late antiquity, and the legal documents that they produced often resembled late Roman instruments. Royal and papal notaries even continued to write formal documents on papyrus, long after parchment had come into general use for nearly all other kinds of writing.[50] These notaries probably received their training, as their predecessors had done, through an apprenticeship in a royal, papal, or episcopal chancery. Western scribes produced at least a few copies of the *Codex Theodosianus* and other Roman law texts as well.[51] Bishops continued to treat selected Roman law texts as part of canon law, and early medieval canon law collections contain hundreds of excerpts from Roman law. Church property, in particular, was still considered subject to Roman law in ninth-century Francia.[52] Although the Roman law tradition never quite vanished from the West, its presence there between the sixth and the eleventh centuries was tenuous.

People in the West who knew anything about Roman law during that period were likely to have encountered legal texts when they studied the liberal arts. Teachers of grammar and rhetoric mined laws and legal writings—Cicero's defense speeches, for example—for examples of effective oratory. When people of Roman descent were parties to litigation, attentive spectators in the law courts could doubtless pick up some bits and pieces of Roman law from observing the proceedings.[53] The Venerable Bede

49. Volterra, "Western Postclassical Schools." Some evidence suggests that Autun may have been a center of legal studies in the eighth century (Wormald, *Making of English Law*, 37, 44).

50. Amelotti and Costamagna, *Alle origini del notariato italiano*, 151–204; Ascheri, *Diritti del medioevo italiano*, 85–90; Ourliac, "La pratique et la loi," 108–11, and more generally Brown, "Origin and Early History of the Office of Notary." The Merovingian royal chancery produced documents on papyrus well into the eighth century. The even more conservative papal chancery continued to turn out papyrus documents occasionally as late as the eleventh century (Bishoff, *Latin Palaeography*, 8; Guyotjeannin, Pycke, and Tock, *Diplomatique médiévale*, 64).

51. McKitterick, "Some Carolingian Law-Books"; Noble, *Republic of St. Peter*, 218–22, and "Papacy in the Eighth and Ninth Centuries," 575–76; Petrucci, "An clerici artem notariae possint exercere," 561–63; Gouron, "Étapes de la pénétration du droit romain," 105, 113; Riché, *Éducation et culture*, 197–98, and *Écoles et enseignement*, 259–60.

52. Wormald, *Making of English Law*, 30–31.

53. Calasso, *Medio evo del diritto*, 278–79; Mor, "Un ipotesi sulle scuole superiori"; Bellomo, "Una nuova figura," 240–41; Ascheri, *Diritti del medioevo italiano*, 111–13; Riché,

claimed that the laws redacted in the opening years of the seventh century at the command of King Æthelberht of Kent (d. ca. 616) were modeled on the Roman style of lawgiving. However, no persuasive evidence suggests that professional legal training survived past the sixth century, much less that it continued to be available in the schools of the early Middle Ages.[54]

The presence or absence of law schools is critical for the history of legal systems. "Law schools make tough law," as Frederick William Maitland (1850–1906) observed. Without schools that taught law rigorously, the barbarian kingdoms could not produce lawyers who were truly professional. This is not to say that clever and tenacious legal advisers did not exist in the West during the early Middle Ages. Whether any of them made a living from their legal skills seems doubtful. They did not, in any case, constitute a profession in any proper sense of that term.[55]

LEGAL FUNCTIONARIES

Men described variously as *advocati, causidici, iurisperiti, legis docti, iurisprudentes, notarii,* and *iudices* occasionally appear in surviving records of lawsuits during the eighth, ninth, and tenth centuries. The precise meaning of these terms is difficult to determine. Different descriptions may be attached to the same individual, while the same term sometimes appears to describe individuals exercising quite different functions. Thus the *advocati* mentioned in court records from this period at times represented or argued on behalf of a party in litigation, but at other times they seem to have been witnesses or legal advisers to judges.[56] In other contexts, *advocatus* described the patron of a church, the holder of an advowson that carried the right to name a priest as rector of a church, or a champion who fought as the substitute for another in duels or ordeals. *Iudex* usually does mean a

---

Écoles et enseignement, 258; *Éducation et culture,* 65–66, 207–8; and *Enseignement du droit en Gaule*; Zimmermann, "Römische und kanonische Rechtskenntnis," 780–84.

54. Bede, *Ecclesiastical History of the English People* 2.5, ed. Colgrave and Mynors, 150; Kantorowicz, *Entstehung der Digestenvulgata,* 70–75, 93–110; Vaccari, *Diritto longobardo,* 4–7; Sorbelli, *Storia della Università di Bologna,* 49–50; Bruyning, "Lawcourt Proceedings," 194.

55. Maitland, "English Law and the Renaissance," 198. Scholarly views on how early the law became a profession nonetheless differ; compare, e. g., Bellomo, "Una nuova figura," 239–40, or Chroust, "Emergence of Professional Standards," 598, with Santini, "'Legis doctores' e 'Sapientes civitatis,'" 126–30, 132–36, 148–49, 167–68.

56. Ficker, *Forschungen* 3: 97–98, 124–25; *Leges Visigothorum* 2.2.2, at 80–81; Hirschfeld, "Gerichtswesen der Stadt Rom," 504, 517–18; Walther, "Anfänge des Rechtsstudiums," 129.

judge of some kind, although not necessarily one with much legal learning. Isidore of Seville (b. ca. 560, d. 636) cautioned that judges should not be stupid or wicked, but he never suggested that they need be learned in the law.[57] In some documents we find *iudices* who acted as *advocati* for litigants. In other places and different contexts, *iudex* simply seems to describe an official of any sort.[58] Civil authorities, such as counts, and church authorities, such as bishops and abbots, regularly employed notaries to prepare official documents, and *notarii* needed at least an elementary acquaintance with the legal terms and forms used in drafting formal documents. These notaries had almost certainly learned what they needed from practical experience.[59] References to men such as these (and they were, without exception, men) occur most frequently, but not exclusively, in records from Italian sources.

Some of these individuals acted at times very much like lawyers: they advised clients, spoke on their behalf before the courts, and argued points of law as well as fact.[60] Other men described as *advocati*, however, especially those who acted on behalf of women and children, were relatives of the parties they represented. They were, in all likelihood, family members who had some experience with the way the courts operated and were lending a helping hand to their less knowledgeable kinsfolk.[61] *Advocati* in other cases were often clerics who came to court primarily in a pastoral role, to help parishioners or persons who lacked influence and high connections to pursue their rights or to defend themselves against accusations.[62]

57. Isidore of Seville, *Sententiae* 52.2, 6, at 305, 306. See also Dawson, *History of Lay Judges*, 35–43, 94–102, and *Oracles of the Law*, 148–76; Engelmann, *History of Continental Civil Procedure*, 92–104.

58. Manaresi, *Placiti del Regnum Italiae*, nos. 108, 113, 122–23, 125–26, 128; Radding, *Origins of Medieval Jurisprudence*, 44, 47; Noble, *Republic of St. Peter*, 237.

59. *Capitulare missorum in Theodonis villa datum* (805) c. 4, in MGH, *Capitularia regum Francorum* 1:121; Amelotti and Costamagna, *Alle origini del notariato italiano*, 152–204.

60. E.g., Manaresi, *Placiti del Regnum Italiae*, nos. 6, 38, 76, 82, 110, 112, 119, etc. Radding, *Origins of Medieval Jurisprudence*, 189–244, provides a list of more than 450 such persons.

61. Bruyning, "Lawcourt Proceedings," 200–201; Davies, "Local Participation and Legal Ritual," 51.

62. Authorities discouraged the involvement of clerics in lawsuits in civil courts; Council of Chalcedon (451) c. 3 in *DEC* 1:88; *Capitularia ecclesiastica* (ca. 810–13) c. 13 in MGH, *Capitularia regum Francorum* 1:179. They made exceptions, however, for legal actions that involved widows, orphans, and other disadvantaged persons (Charvet, "Accession des clercs aux fonctions d'avocat," 295–96).

Clerics had to know something about canon law and occasionally picked up some bits of Roman law as well, since collections of canons almost invariably included passages taken from Roman sources.[63] The clergy thus constituted the principal reservoir of legal learning throughout the early Middle Ages. This is scarcely surprising since they were far more likely than most other people to have access to, and need for, advanced schooling. Virtually every school that we know much about in the West between the sixth century and the thirteenth aimed primarily, if not always exclusively, at training future priests, clerics, monks, or nuns. It was no accident that the Latin vocabulary of the early Middle Ages treated the words "cleric" and "literate" as synonyms.[64]

Canon Law

Canon law, unlike Roman law, was a constantly growing and developing body of written law. Ecclesiastical councils and synods formulated new regulations and modified old ones, popes and bishops handed down rulings that frequently changed or reinterpreted existing law, kings and other rulers repeatedly legislated on matters that involved church interests, while the teachings and opinions of authoritative writers on matters such as penance, church discipline, and behavior often came to enjoy the force of law. Customary practices that no authority had enacted produced still further binding norms.[65]

CANON LAW COLLECTIONS

Students and teachers, as well as bishops and priests, usually turned to collections that assembled selected passages from a welter of canonical sources for the legal information they required to deal with the questions they faced. Since canon law grew continually, older collections regularly became outdated, and new ones appeared in an attempt to keep pace with developments in the law. As a result, the early Middle Ages produced substantial numbers of canonical collections. Some enjoyed wide circulation, while others secured only a local readership; some were massive affairs that drew upon sources from far and wide throughout Christendom, others

---

63. E.g., Pope Celestine I (422–32), letter to the bishops of Apulia and Calabria, 21 July 419, JK 371; Lupoi, *Origins*, 249; and especially Gaudemet, *Formation du droit séculier*, 199–212, as well as "Survivances romaines," 163–77.

64. Riché, *Écoles et enseignement*, 189–220; Clanchy, *From Memory to Written Record*, 226–30; but cf. McKitterick, *Carolingians and the Written Word*, 211–70, for evidence about literacy among the Carolingian lay nobility.

65. Cortese, *Diritto nella storia* 1:209–25; Bellomo, *Common Legal Past*, 46–49.

were tiny compilations that contained little more than a handful of canons drawn from local authorities in the regions where they originated. Most of these collections were put together on the initiative of individual scholars or teachers, but a few secured the patronage of high officers of church or state and consequently achieved wide circulation.[66]

One of the earliest and most influential collections during the early Middle Ages was the *Collectio Dionysiana*, compiled around 500 by a Scythian monk, Dionysius Exiguus, who died sometime between 537 and 555.[67] Dionysius drew upon two principal types of sources: conciliar canons and papal decretals. He arranged material of each kind in chronological order and provided more accurate Latin translations of the Greek sources than those previously available. His collection enjoyed great prestige, especially at Rome. In 774, Pope Adrian I (r. 772–95) dispatched the *Dionysio-Hadriana*, an expanded version of Dionysius's work, to Charlemagne (r. 768–814), who encouraged its use throughout his realm.[68]

Another widely influential collection was the massive *Collectio Hispana*, of which numerous versions survive.[69] As the name implies, the core of this collection consisted of the canons of councils held in the Iberian peninsula, but it also included substantial numbers of conciliar canons from the Eastern empire, Africa, and Gaul. Like the *Dionysiana*, from which it borrowed, the *Hispana* contained papal decretals as well as conciliar texts arranged geographically and chronologically. It circulated and was copied not only in the Iberian peninsula, but elsewhere as well, particularly in the Frankish regions of the Carolingian empire and in Italy.

A group of industrious forgers who worked in the diocese of Reims, probably at the abbey of Corbie during the mid-ninth century, were responsible for several collections of spurious canons that achieved wide

---

66. The basic guides to these collections are Kéry, *Canonical Collections*; Fowler-Magerl, *Clavis canonum*; and Ferme, *Introduzione alla storia del diritto canonico*. Reynolds, "Organisation, Law and Liturgy," 613–17, presents a helpful overview.

67. Dionysius Exiguus also originated the practice of calculating dates from the year of Christ's birth, which has since become virtually universal, even among non-Christians. Unfortunately his calculations of the date of the incarnation were faulty. On him, see especially Jacqueline Rambaud-Buhot, "Denys le Petit."

68. Kéry, *Canonical Collections*, 9–21; Fowler-Magerl, *Clavis canonum*, 29–32, 44–45.

69. Kéry, *Canonical Collections*, 57–72; Fowler-Magerl, *Clavis canonum*, 39–42. Gonzalo Martínez Díez and Félix Rodríguez have been preparing a critical edition of the *Hispana* for nearly a half-century. Six volumes have appeared thus far under the title *La colección canónica hispana*.

circulation and exercised far-reaching influence throughout medieval Europe.[70] The largest and most important of their productions was what is now known as the *Pseudo-Isidorian Decretals*, so called because some manuscripts identified the maker of the collection as Isidore the Merchant (Isidore Mercator).[71] The work opens with a large cluster of counterfeit decretals attributed to a series of popes who held office between the late first and the early fourth centuries, intermingled in chronological order with a few authentic papal letters. The second part of the work comprises canons of fifty-four councils and synods, some genuine, some forged, together with the spurious Donation of Constantine and other documents. The third and final part of the collection interweaves still more bogus and genuine papal decretals with conciliar canons attributed to the period between the fifth and the eighth centuries.[72]

As with all frauds, the perpetrators of this one had an undeclared agenda. Unlike most such enterprises, however, personal gain was not their goal. The forgers sought to promote the independence and privileges of the clergy, to diminish the power of archbishops, and to strengthen the hand of bishops, including the pope, in the governance of the church. They apparently believed that the proper conduct of ecclesiastical affairs had been corrupted in recent times by lay authorities. Since the canonical collections then current failed to include genuine documents that would support their beliefs, the forgers undertook to produce the canons and decretals that they felt earlier popes and councils ought to have issued. They presumably regarded this as an appropriate way to restore the ninth-century church to what they viewed as its original and proper order.[73]

Suspicions about the authenticity of some of the forgeries began to ap-

---

70. Kéry, *Canonical Collections*, 100–124; Fowler-Magerl, *Clavis canonum*, 50–55; Cortese, *Diritto nella storia* 1:213–24. These collections include the *Collectio Hispana Gallica Augustodunensis*, the so-called *Capitula Angilramni*; the capitularies of Benedictus Levita, and what are now called the *Decretales Pseudo-Isidorianae*, or *Pseudo-Isidorian Decretals*. The Hinschius edition, *Decretales Pseudo-Isidorianae et Capitula Angilramni*, is faulty; a more reliable one is available on the Internet site of Projekt Pseudoisidor (http://www.pseudoisidor.mgh.de). See also Fuhrmann, *Einfluß und Verbreitung der pseudoisidorischen Fälschungen*, as well as Fuhrmann's chapter "The Pseudo-Isidorian Forgeries," in Jasper and Fuhrmann, *Papal Letters*, 137–95; and Williams, *Codices Pseudo-Isidoriani*.

71. Isidore Peccator and Isidore Mercatus occasionally appear as variants on the alleged compiler's name in some manuscripts.

72. Jasper and Fuhrmann, *Papal Letters*, 161–69.

73. Jasper and Fuhrmann, *Papal Letters*, 140–44.

pear within a few years after their composition. Pope Nicholas I (r. 858–67), the earliest pope to be aware of them, treated the Pseudo-Isidorian canons cautiously, although when it suited his purposes he was prepared to cite them as authorities. Most writers on church law, however, considered them genuine, and passages from the Pseudo-Isidorian collection regularly found their way into subsequent collections of canon law. The authenticity of the Pseudo-Isidorian material did not come under sustained attack until the fifteenth century, when Lorenzo Valla (1406–57) subjected the Donation of Constantine to close scrutiny and concluded on linguistic grounds that it must be bogus. Suspicions sharpened further during the religious controversies of the sixteenth century. Finally in the seventeenth century, a French Protestant scholar, David Blondel (1591–1655), showed conclusively that substantial portions of the texts must be spurious.[74]

Among the genuine canonical collections from Carolingian Francia, the most important was the one now called the *Vetus Gallica*, in all probability originally assembled by Bishop Etherius of Lyons between about 586 and 602, but considerably expanded by later hands.[75] The compilers of other canonical collections in the seventh and eighth century also pillaged it for their own collections.

The *Libri duo de synodalibus causis et disciplinis ecclesiasticis* by Regino, abbot of Prüm (d. 915), is unique in giving special attention to matters that affected the laity.[76] Regino compiled his collection about 906 in order to provide bishops with a guide to judicial procedure and the conduct of the periodic visitations that the law required them to make to the parishes

---

74. Jasper and Fuhrmann, *Papal Letters*, 186–95; Landau, "Gefälschtes Recht"; Valla, *De falso credito et ementita Constantini Donatione*; Maffei, *La donazione di Costantino*; Pfeiffer, *History of Classical Scholarship*, 34–41; *Pseudo-Isidorus et Turrianus vapulantes*. The Roman Inquisition placed Valla's treatise on the *Index librorum prohibitorum* in 1559 and Catholics were thereafter forbidden to read it under pain of excommunication (*Index auctorum et librorum*, at www.aloha.net/-mikesch/ILP-1559.html). The prohibition was still included in the thirty-second edition of the *Index* and apparently remained in effect, at least technically, until 1966, when canonical penalties for reading books on the *Index* were lifted, although the Congregation for the Doctrine of the Faith continues to insist that the *Index* still retains moral force. No mention of it appears in the 1993 *Codex iuris canonici*. Blondel's book, not surprisingly, joined Valla's on the *Index librorum prohibitorum* in 1661.

75. Kéry, *Canonical Collections*, 50–53; Fowler-Magerl, *Clavis canonum*, 36–38; and Mordek, *Kirchenrecht und Reform im Frankenreich*.

76. Kéry, *Canonical Collections*, 128–33; Fowler-Magerl, *Clavis canonum*, 77–29; and *Das Sendbuch des Regino von Prüm*, ed. and trans. Hartmann.

within their dioceses. The practical focus of his work no doubt accounts for its great popularity and wide circulation.

Early in the eleventh century, and certainly before 1023, Bishop Burchard of Worms (d. 1025) completed one of the most comprehensive and influential of all early canonical collections. Burchard's *Decretum* was the product of a collaborative effort between the bishop and his associates.[77] Burchard states in his preface that he compiled the *Decretum* specifically for teaching purposes, and the glosses in some manuscripts seem to indicate that it was in fact so used, possibly in Burchard's own cathedral school at Worms.[78] If so, the course in which it was used must have been demanding. Burchard's *Decretum* comprises nearly 1,800 canons, arranged in twenty books. Despite its size, the work was often copied and widely disseminated: at least seventy-seven manuscripts of the complete text still survive, in addition to numerous abbreviated or partial copies. Burchard's *Decretum*, like Regino's much shorter work, owed its popularity in part to its practical utility, not only for bishops, judges, and administrators, but also for confessors and parish priests, since it contained a helpful guide for hearing confessions, a short handbook of dogmatic theology, directions for holding synods, complete with sample sermons, and a host of other useful information.

Despite the numerous canonical rules and regulations enshrined in these and other collections, long-standing church policies discouraged clerics from serving as legal counselors and especially from representing parties in litigation. As early as the mid-third century St. Cyprian (d. 258), bishop of Carthage, had forbidden priests and deacons in his diocese to act as advocates in the courts, especially in civil cases.[79] Cyprian cited as authority for this position a statement ascribed to St. Paul that "No man, being a soldier to God, entangles himself in secular business" (2 Tim. 2:4). The general Council of Chalcedon (451), as well as local councils and popes, followed suit, usually citing the same biblical authority.[80]

---

77. *Vita Burchardi ep. Wormatiensis* 10, in MGH, SS 4:829–46, at 837. See also Kéry, *Canonical Collections*, 133–55; Fowler-Magerl, *Clavis canonum*, 85–90; and Hoffmann and Pokorny, *Dekret des Bischofs Burchard*. See also Dilcher, "Der Kanonist als Gesetzgeber."

78. Burchard, *Decretum*, praef., in *PL* 140:500, and the corrected version of this text in Hoffmann and Pokorny, *Dekret des Bischofs Burchard*, 67–68; a translation of this passage appears in Somerville and Brasington, *Prefaces to Canon Law Books*, 100. See also Brasington's "Prologues to Canonical Collections," 236.

79. Cyprian, *Epist.* 1.9 (249), quoted by Gratian C. 21 q. 3 c. 4–7.

80. Council of Chalcedon c. 3 in *DEC* 1:88–89; *Canones in causa Apiarii*, c. 16 and Council of Carthage (525) in *Concilia Africae*, 122, 138, 264; 2 Council of Nicaea (787)

Beginning in the sixth and seventh centuries, however, the compilers of canonical collections showed that some authorities admitted exceptions to this rule, and they incorporated those exceptions in their collections. The most common exception permitted clerics to represent widows and orphans as advocates or proctors in litigation.[81] Clerics also had a general obligation to serve poor and disadvantaged persons, and this could well include assisting them in legal proceedings. Similarly, a sixth-century council in Tarragona provided that monks might act in court on behalf of their monasteries, provided that their abbot directed them to do so.[82]

CANONICAL DISPUTE RESOLUTION

Christians ordinarily came into direct contact with canon law either when they sought to resolve disputes that fell under canonical jurisdiction or when they were accused of some infraction of canonical rules. Popes had long claimed legal jurisdiction as a court of last resort throughout Christendom. The Council of Serdica (343) had declared that the bishop of Rome constituted the final court of appeal from the decisions of other bishops. Pope Gelasius I spelled out the scope of the papacy's appellate jurisdiction more specifically in a letter of 495.[83]

The settlement of disputes and the prosecution of offenders against the canons in first instance, however, lay primarily in the hands of bishops, who were the ordinary judges of all such matters within their dioceses.[84] When faced with difficult or delicate cases for whose resolution they did not wish to assume sole responsibility, bishops might summon other members of

---

c. 10 in *DEC* 1:146–47; Council of Verno (755) c. 16 and Council of Mainz (847) c. 13 in MGH, Legum, *Capitularia regum Francorum* 1:36 and 2:179; Pope Gregory I, *Perlatum ad nos* in JE 1771 and Gratian D. 88 c. 4.

81. On the exception regarding representation of widows and orphans, see, e.g., Pope Gelasius I (492–96), letter to Bishops Gerontius and Peter, JK 707; Council of Mainz (847) c. 13, in MGH, Legum, *Capitularia regum Francorum* 2:179. See also more generally, Charvet, "L'accession des clercs," 295.

82. Pope Gelasius I, *Desolatis propriae* to Bishop Anastasius, 496, JK 726 and Gratian D. 87 c. 2; Pope Gregory I, letter to Anthony, subdeacon of Campania, March 603, JE 1894 and Gratian D. 84 c. 1; Council of Tarragona (516) c. 11, in Mansi 8:543.

83. Council of Serdica c. 3, c, 4, and 7; Hess, *Early Development of Canon Law*, 186–90, 213–16 (Gratian, C. 6 q. 4 c. 7, gives the *Hispana* version of canon 3, which also appears as c. 4 in Pseudo-Isidore, ed. Hinschius, 267); Pope Gelasius I, JK 664 (quoted by numerous canonists, including Gratian at C. 9 q. 3 c. 17).

84. Cod. Theod., Const. Sirmond. 3 (384); Roman synod (828) c. 12, in Mansi 18:221; Hartmann, "Die Briefe Fulberts von Chartres."

the clergy to sit with them as a synod and render collective judgment. Bishops, with or without a synod, thus constituted the principal courts for the adjudication of issues that arose under early medieval canon law.[85] Bishops were already complaining as early as the fifth century about the burden that this laid upon them, and the volume of their judicial business grew still more onerous under Germanic rule.[86]

The judicial procedures that episcopal synods employed resembled those used in the secular courts of the Germanic kingdoms. Defendants in less serious cases could clear themselves of an accusation through a solemn oath in which they affirmed their innocence. Those required to swear exculpatory oaths were also often required to produce compurgators as well. In more serious cases, synods sometimes resorted to trial by ordeal just as lay judges did. When proof by ordeal was required from a cleric, however, a less physically demanding kind of ordeal, the ordeal by the Eucharist, might be prescribed. This ordeal required that a priest place a consecrated host on the party's tongue. If he was able to swallow it, that proved his innocence; if he could not do so, he was adjudged guilty.[87]

This procedural system clearly did not require the services of highly trained lawyers. Bishops and their advisers could readily find what they needed to know from widely available reference works, especially from Regino of Prüm's *Libri duo de synodalibus causis*, as well as from an assortment of simplified handbooks produced specifically to guide bishops in fulfilling their judicial duties and in presiding over synods.[88]

Bishops and other clergymen, not surprisingly, developed special skill and expertise in dealing with canonical matters. Men who fit this description in the early Middle Ages can reasonably be styled canon lawyers, although it would be inappropriate to call them professionals. Some of them no doubt appeared as advocates in the courts and furnished legal advice to friends, relatives, and associates from time to time. They might even be re-

---

85. The emperor Valens, in a constitution issued at Trier in 376, had established the episcopal synod as the ordinary court for adjudicating ecclesiastical disputes (Cod. Theod. 16.2.23).

86. St. Augustine, Epist. 24*, ed. Divjak, 126–27. Complaints from bishops about being overworked are common; e.g., Regino of Prüm's preface to his *Libri duo de synodalibus causis*, ed. Hartmann, 20–22, and Burchard of Worms, *Decretum*, pr., in *PL* 140:500, 539. English translations of both passages appear in Somerville and Brasington, *Prefaces to Canon Law Books*, 93, 100.

87. Hartmann, "Probleme des geistlichen Gerichts," 659–65; Browe, "Die Abendmahlsprobe im Mittelalter."

88. Hartmann, "Probleme des geistlichen Gerichts," 632–37.

warded for doing so. But the other defining characteristics of professionalism were absent. These practitioners were not technically trained nor did any authority certify their legal knowledge and skills. Rather, these men learned their law as an incidental part of their general clerical education in monastic or cathedral schools, whose libraries often contained significant collections of legal texts.[89] Neither judges nor practitioners exercised systematic supervision, so far as one can tell, over admission to practice, nor did they formulate explicit standards of professional conduct; still less did they articulate disciplinary mechanisms for imposing sanctions on practitioners whose conduct they deemed inappropriate.

The Celtic Exception

The Celtic kingdoms of Ireland and Wales, where Roman rule had never penetrated and Roman legal institutions had never taken root, produced the most conspicuous exceptions to the generalization that western Europe lacked law schools and professional lawyers during the early Middle Ages. Early Irish customary law, often called Brehon law, was originally transmitted orally in verse, but beginning in the seventh century it began to be put down in writing. Even so, Irish lawyers and legal scholars differentiated themselves only slowly from the other poetic teachers of folk tradition in the Celtic world.

The Celtic kingdoms produced an extraordinary number and variety of legal texts between the seventh century and the beginning of the eleventh century. The legal culture of Wales and Ireland was also considerably more sophisticated than that found elsewhere in western Europe during that period. Seventy-seven Irish law tracts remain extant, the great majority of them written in the vernacular. Others once existed, but have apparently vanished.[90] The surviving texts include both civil and ecclesiastical laws, and canonical collections from the Continent probably provided models and incentives for their production. The material that appears in the ecclesiastical law tracts drew in part from the scriptures, church fathers, and other sources commonly found in Continental collections, but also from the numerous councils and synods that began to assemble in the Gaelic-

---

89. McKitterick, *Carolingians and the Written Word*, 46–57; Wood, "Administration, Law and Culture," 63–67; Noble, "Literacy and the Papal Government," 101–5; Contreni, "The Carolingian Renaissance," 748–50.

90. Kelly, *A Guide to Early Irish Law*, 264–82, provides a list. See also Breatnach, "Lawyers in Early Ireland," 1–3.

speaking regions of the British Isles from at least as early as 700 and perhaps even earlier.[91]

Glosses on the Irish law tracts strongly suggest that they were taught in law schools. The schools were probably located in monastic centers, and many, although not all, Irish lawyers were monks or clerics. While it is difficult to be certain which communities had law schools, a ninth-century text describes the monasteries of Cloyne, Cork, and Slane as centers of legal culture.[92] Legal writing in early Ireland shows considerable evidence of regional variation among the various kingdoms within the island. This is hardly unexpected, since no effective central government was available to impose legal uniformity throughout the island.[93] While some laws in these books clearly originated as royal enactments, the jurists themselves seem to have redacted much of the law that they contain from earlier traditions and customary practices. The early eighth-century compilation *Senchas Már* (Great Tradition) came to enjoy great authority in the northern part of the island and was probably produced at a law school located in north central Ireland, while a rival tradition known as *Nemed* prevailed in the south.[94]

Trained judges presided over early Irish courts and occupied a respected place in Irish society, as is clear from the honor price (*lóg n-enech*; similar to the wergild of the Germanic laws) assigned to them. Both kings and church authorities appointed judges, who might be either clerics or laymen. Judges were entitled to receive fees and expenses from the parties whose cases they heard.[95]

A ninth-century gloss on the *Senchas Már* distinguished three groups of advocates. "Fettering advocates" (*glasaigni*) constituted the lowest grade of lawyer and ranked socially among independent farmers. Still, even *glasaigni* were expected to have some formal training in the laws, since the gloss specifies the fees due to their teachers. "Court advocates" (*aigni airechta*) were more fully trained lawyers, who ranked among the lower levels of the nobility and were competent to plead in all courts, civil and ecclesiasti-

91. Dumville, *Councils and Synods*, provides a convenient introduction to the history of these assemblies.

92. Kelly, *Guide to Early Irish Law*, 242–50; Breatnach, "Lawyers in Early Ireland," 5.

93. The powers of the Irish high kings were extremely limited. See Byrne, *Irish Kings and High Kings*; Ó Corráin, "Ireland, Scotland and Wales," 43–46; Sheehy, "Influences of Ancient Irish Law," 32.

94. Kelly, *Guide to Early Irish Law*, 242–46.

95. Breatnach, "Lawyers in Early Ireland," 7–10.

cal. The highest-ranking Irish advocates were the "advocates whom judgment encounters" (*aigni fris-n-innle brith*). These lawyers were highly educated, greatly honored, and handsomely rewarded. They dealt with the most complicated disputes and represented litigants at the top levels of Irish society. They ranked, accordingly, with the highest nobility and received more generous fees that the two lesser types of lawyer.[96]

Invasions of Ireland from England, beginning with Henry II's expedition in 1169, gradually introduced English royal law into the regions where the invaders settled, but left Brehon law largely intact in regions where the native Irish predominated. The substantial body of fourteenth- and fifteenth-century glosses and commentaries on the legal texts testify to the continuation of systematic law teaching in the vernacular throughout the later Middle Ages. English common law did not finally displace Brehon law in Ireland until the seventeenth century.[97]

Wales, like Ireland, had an orally transmitted customary law prior to the Norman invasions that began in the late eleventh century.[98] Hywel Dda (Howel the Good, r. 942–ca. 950) was responsible for organizing the traditional customary law of Wales and putting it into written form. *Cyfraith Hywel* (*The Law of Hywel Dda*) retained many symptoms of its original oral transmission: its provisions are often repetitive, filled with alliteration, rhymes, and other mnemonic devices. Although the authors of later Welsh law tracts modified and supplemented Hywel's laws, his work remained at the core of Welsh law throughout the later Middle Ages. Between the twelfth and fourteenth centuries, a few elements of Roman and canon law found their way into Welsh law texts. About forty medieval manuscripts of Welsh law survive, six of them in Latin, the rest in Welsh. Little information survives about the pleaders (*cyngaws*) who practiced in medieval Welsh law courts, and still less is known about their training, save that at least by the thirteenth century it seems to have been centered in the principality of Gwynedd.[99]

The Icelandic Exception

Iceland, which like the Celtic kingdoms had never come under Roman rule, also developed a distinctive legal tradition that featured trained lawyers.

96. Breatnach, "Lawyers in Early Ireland," 10–13 furnishes the text and translation, as well as a commentary on this gloss.

97. Kelly, *Guide to Early Irish Law*, 250–63; Simms, "The Brehons"; Pawlisch, *Sir John Davies*.

98. Charles-Edwards, *The Welsh Laws*, 6–9.

99. See Walters, "Roman and Romano-Canonical Law"; *Law of Hywel Dda*, ed. and trans. Jenkins, xxi–xxiii; and Charles-Edwards, *The Welsh Laws*, 54–67.

Pleaders or advocates (*goðar*) and legal experts (*lǫmaðr*) were prominent figures in Icelandic law and society, although they never constituted a profession in anything like the same sense that Roman advocates and *iurisperiti* had done. Icelandic advocates represented their clients not only in litigation, but also in negotiations, arbitration, and deal making of all kinds. Icelandic advocates not only argued in the law courts, but were also prepared if necessary to assist clients in physical struggles against their adversaries. In return for these services, they expected to receive payment in the form of land or other gifts. Icelandic advocates had to be trained in the law and in the art of pleading, and they received schooling of both kinds from legal experts, who were themselves experienced and successful advocates.[100]

Although advocates needed to master Iceland's intricate customary law, they had no monopoly on legal knowledge, and being an advocate or legal expert was by no means a full-time occupation. The law constituted the fundamental element of Icelandic identity, and every Icelander, man or woman, was bound to be familiar with it. Mature Icelanders literally heard the law recited every year in June when the island's Lawspeaker (Lǫgsǫgumaðr) opened the Allthing, the annual assembly, which took place at the Law Rock (Lǫgberg).[101]

The Clergy as Officials of the Law

Except for Ireland, Wales, and Iceland, the closest approach to a learned legal profession during the early Middle Ages lay in the ranks of the clergy. It would be a mistake, admittedly, to draw too rigid a dividing line between lay and clerical officials during this period. Distinctions between the spheres of authority of laity and clergy were not yet as sharp or clear-cut in this period as they would later become.[102]

Churchmen were deeply involved in every aspect of the legal and institutional structures of the early Middle Ages. They functioned as what Karl Llewellyn called "officials of the law."[103] When Roman administrative structures began to crumble in the sixth century, clergymen moved in to fill the breach. When a Germanic ruler wished to produce written versions of his people's laws, he was likely to entrust the task to the clerics in his household who routinely drafted his charters, letters, and other docu-

---

100. Byock, *Medieval Iceland*, 105–7, 112, 124–25; Miller, *Bloodtaking and Peacemaking*, 226–27.
101. Miller, *Bloodtaking and Peacemaking*, 227–28; Byock, *Medieval Iceland*, 64.
102. Cox, *A Study of the Juridic Status of Laymen*, 19–30.
103. Llewellyn, *The Bramble Bush*, 3.

ments. Bishops and other clerics participated in deliberative assemblies, where they often wielded influence out of all proportion to their numbers. Clerics sat as judges, in both ecclesiastical and civil courts. Even where lay judges predominated, as they usually did in civil courts, clerical judges and advisers remained common. Clerical members of the bench, moreover, often had readier access to law books than did their lay colleagues.[104] Even so, it would be anachronistic to describe such churchmen, however learned and skillful, as professional lawyers.

The emergence of a learned legal profession had to await the development of more sophisticated legal systems and more complex procedures for dispute resolution than were common in the Germanic kingdoms. Only then would those with legal problems come to regard the services of trained lawyers as not so much a convenience as a necessity. This began to happen when teachers in twelfth century law schools commenced to expound the texts of classical Roman law systematically to their students. In the give-and-take of disputations and lectures in the law schools, medieval jurists began to puzzle out ways of adapting Roman legal doctrines and analytical tools to the very different conditions of their own society.

---

104. Lupoi, *Origins of the European Legal Order*, 435–36.

* THREE *

The Legal Revival of the Twelfth Century

Fundamental changes that began to sweep through the culture, society, and economy of Western Christendom in the closing decades of the eleventh century radically transformed the laws and legal practices that prevailed during the early Middle Ages. Within the following century-and-a-half, a new legal culture emerged in the West. Specialized schools of civil law whose students studied Justinian's codified Roman law began to appear at Bologna shortly after 1100. In Bologna, too, an innovative textbook of canon law, appearing sometime in the 1140s and commonly known as "Gratian's Decretum," soon displaced earlier canonical collections, both in the schools and in the courts. Although no pope ever formally declared it the official version of Western canon law, the Decretum attributed to Gratian nevertheless remodeled the study of the church's law into a systematic discipline that was also taught in specialized law schools.[1] Canon law gradually began to separate itself from theology during the twelfth century and soon acquired a distinct identity as an autonomous discipline. In addition, Roman and canon law commenced to cross-fertilize one another. Bishops and popes, as well as practicing canonists and teachers of canon law, discovered that numerous Roman law concepts, categories, and analytical tools could usefully be applied to canonical problems. Canonists consequently began to integrate elements of Roman law into their discipline, while men trained primarily in Roman law found that they needed to study canon law because church courts were opening up growing oppor-

---

1. Holtzmann, "Die Benutzung Gratian's"; Noonan, "Was Gratian Approved at Ferentino?"; Classen, "Das Decretum Gratiani wurde nicht in Ferentino approbiert."

tunities for employment. The amalgamation of canon law and Roman civil law produced what came to be called the *ius commune*.[2]

The Legal Revival and the Twelfth-Century Renaissance

Signal developments in the law formed a key element in a larger intellectual movement that Charles Homer Haskins (1870–1937) christened the renaissance of the twelfth century.[3] Medievalists since Haskins have generally focused attention primarily on the literary, theological, and philosophical achievements of the twelfth-century intellectual upheaval, even though the consequences of those developments were largely confined to a social and intellectual elite.[4] The legal changes introduced in the twelfth and thirteenth centuries, by contrast, had far greater and more immediate impact on the lives and actions of virtually everyone in the West. Those changes affected not only the generations who lived through them, but have continued to touch the lives of countless people down to the present day.[5]

Accounting for twelfth-century legal developments has challenged modern scholars. "Within the whole range of history there is no more momentous and puzzling problem than that connected with the fate of Roman Law after the downfall of the Roman State," declared Sir Paul Vinogradoff (1854–1925). He went on to describe the medieval revival of Roman law as "a ghost story," a tale about a legal system that died in the early Middle Ages, only to return to life at the end of the eleventh century with such vigor that law students can still profit from reading manuals written for their late Roman predecessors nearly two thousand years ago.[6]

THE LEGAL REVIVAL AND SOCIAL NEEDS

Vinogradoff and many others have seen the twelfth-century revival of interest in Roman law as a response to challenges posed by the social and

---

2. For one example of how this might work, see Pennington, "Innocent III and the Ius Commune," as well as his "Learned Law, Droit Savant, Gelehrtes Recht."

3. Haskins, *Renaissance of the Twelfth Century*. See also the reappraisal of research on this topic in *Renaissance and Renewal in the Twelfth Century*, esp. 299–338, and C. D. Ferguson, *Europe in Transition*, as well as W. K. Ferguson's reflections in *Renaissance in Historical Thought*, 329–36.

4. Thus, e.g., Knowles, *Evolution of Medieval Thought*, 71–149; Artz, *Mind of the Middle Ages*, 225–319; Strayer, *Western Europe in the Middle Ages*, 89–100, 126–40; Nicholas, *Evolution of the Medieval World*, 320–66.

5. Southern, *Medieval Humanism*, 52–53, 126, and *Scholastic Humanism* 1:237–38, 283–85, 310–18.

6. Vinogradoff, *Roman Law in Medieval Europe*, 11–13.

commercial expansion that marked the two centuries after 1050. The legal apparatus of the early Middle Ages served the needs of a predominantly rural agricultural society reasonably well. From the mid-eleventh century onward, however, population growth, and especially a dramatic rise in city populations, coupled with a revival of long-distance trade that Robert Lopez has characterized as a commercial revolution, created a need for a legal order whose mechanisms were better suited to the demands of an urban mercantile society than the legal practices then current in the West.[7] The new society and economy that began to emerge during the twelfth century required effective methods of dealing with commercial contracts, credit and banking, property transfers, insurance, corporations, municipal government, and particularly in northern Europe, the increasing centralization of royal governments. The *Corpus iuris civilis* offered a system of commercial and municipal law that could be adapted to meet those needs. Its attractiveness was enhanced, not diminished, by its antiquity and its association with Roman imperial power.[8]

The recovery of the juristic learning embodied in Justinian's Digest came as a powerful, almost intoxicating revelation to western European scholars. The Digest had never been widely known or circulated in the successor states of the Western empire, even in the sixth century. By the seventh century, what little had been known about its contents had vanished into obscurity. No pope, for example, since Gregory I (r. 590–604) had referred directly to the Digest.[9]

Recovery of the texts of the Digest began during the last quarter of the eleventh century.[10] The intricacy and ingenuity of the legal reasoning rep-

---

7. On population growth, see Génicot, "Evidence of Growth of Population"; Russell, *Late Ancient and Medieval Population*, 99–113; Herlihy, "Demography"; and Reyerson, "Urbanism." On commercial growth, see Lopez, *Commercial Revolution*; Reynolds, *Europe Emerges*, 183–207; Bautier, *Economic Development of Medieval Europe*, 101–69; Cipolla, *Before the Industrial Revolution*, 193–203; Dotson, "Trade."

8. Robinson, Fergus, and Gordon, *European Legal History*, 42–44; Caenegem, *Historical Introduction to Private Law*, 30–31; Lange, *Römisches Recht im Mittelalter*, 29–30; Ascheri, *Diritti del medioevo italiano*, 122–23. For a case study of the process of Romanizing municipal law, see Wickham, *Legge, pratiche e conflitti*, 185–278.

9. Caenegem, "Law in the Medieval World"; Conrat, *Geschichte der Quellen*, 8–9; Fuhrmann, "Papst Gregor VII. und das Kirchenrecht," 124–26.

10. The earliest portion of the Digest that became known in the West comprised its opening books, running from book 1 to book 24, title 3, law 2. Medieval jurists invariably labeled this the portion of the work the Old Digest (*Digestum vetus*). Next to come to light were the fifteen books at the end of the work, which medieval scribes

resented in the Digest exerted a powerful attraction on the minds of those familiar with legal problems. Without the Digest, the legal revival simply could not have taken off as it did in the twelfth century.[11] Medieval jurists learned from the Digest how to frame sophisticated legal arguments, how to manipulate legal categories, how to analyze problems, and how to find solutions to them. In F. W. Maitland's words,

> The Digest was the *only* book in which medieval students could obtain a knowledge of Roman Law *at its best*. The Institutes were a slight text book. The Code is made up of detached ordinances. The Novels are not merely detached ordinances, but penned in a pompous, verbose style, likely to do as much harm as good. It seems to me that but for the Digest Roman law could never have conquered the world. . . . Men would never have become enthusiastic students of the other books.[12]

At the same time, it would be unrealistic to discount the utility factor. The Roman law texts that gradually began to become available in the West from around 1100 onward undoubtedly stimulated those who taught and studied them to think about previously unexplored ways to deal with such matters as long-distance trade and the problem of assembling large capital sums to finance it, about credit instruments, mortgages, commercial contracts, and financial liability, about municipal government, sanitation, and a host of other topics that became more and more acute as cities grew and commerce flourished.

The Legal Revival and Church Reform

Some connection between the eleventh-century church reform movement and the beginnings of the legal revival seems certain, although scholars disagree both about what form that connection took and how important it was.[13] Harold Berman, at one extreme, sees the eleventh-century church re-

---

and authors knew as the New Digest (*Digestum novum*). The middle portion of the Digest, running from book 24, title 3, law 3, to book 35, title 2, law 81, was recovered last and came to be known as the *Infortiatum*. For a detailed account of the process, so far as it can presently be reconstructed, see Müller, "Recovery of Justinian's Digest."

11. Lange, *Römisches Recht in Mittelalter*, 29–30.

12. Letter to Hastings Rashdall, 5 June 1892, in *Letters of Frederic William Maitland* 2:37; Stein, *Roman Law in European History*, 44. But cf. Radding, *Origins of Medieval Jurisprudence*, 7–8, 10, 115, and 152.

13. Blumenthal's *Investiture Controversy* provides a solid introduction to the main issues and events of the reform movement, as well as a helpful bibliographical survey. See also Tellenbach's *Church in Western Europe*.

formers as the central actors. The reform movement, according to Berman, was nothing less than a "papal revolution" that radically changed the entire course of Europe's social, religious, and legal history. Berman maintains that the "papal revolution" marked the beginning of a series of fundamental political and intellectual movements that transformed the character of European law. The canon law tradition that emerged from that revolution, he argues, provided Europe for the first time with a Europe-wide body of positive law, whose basic tenets have remained central to later Western development, not only in law, but also in political institutions, social structures, and religion.[14]

While Berman assigns greater weight to the relationship between church reform and the legal revival than some scholars deem justified,[15] the two were undoubtedly connected. Although eleventh-century reformers were keenly interested in law and legal issues, neither Pope Gregory VII (r. 1073–85) nor the members of his entourage were trained lawyers. They clearly welcomed the creation of new collections of canon law, although apparently they did not directly commission any of the compilations that appeared in the late eleventh century, or for that matter in the twelfth.[16]

The leaders of the reform movement sought to free the church from the kinds of control that kings, emperors, and other civil rulers from Constantine's time onward had exerted over ecclesiastical affairs. Reformers insisted that laymen cease to appoint bishops, abbots, the rectors of parishes, and other church officials, for when they did so, reformers declared, they committed the deadly sin of simony.[17] Reformers insisted that only the clergy had

---

14. Berman, *Law and Revolution*, 85–198, 520–38 and passim. Cf. Landau, "Einfluß des kanonischen Rechts," 42–43

15. Critics have expressed serious reservations about his sweeping version of the consequences of the church reform movement and the legal revival that went with it. They have also faulted his work for errors in detail, and pointed out blemishes and inconsistencies in his arguments. Whatever its flaws, Berman's book has stimulated reexamination of the consequences of the legal revival itself, and especially of the circumstances that surrounded its inception. See especially Schieffer, "'Papal Revolution in Law'?" Reviews of the book were often critical; e.g., Peter Landau, *University of Chicago Law Review* 51 (1984) 937–43; Kenneth Pennington, *American Journal of Comparative Law* 33 (1985) 546–48; Edward M. Peters, *Harvard Law Review* 98 (1985) 686–96; M. Damaška, *Yale Law Journal* 49 (1985) 1807–24. In a balanced and generally positive assessment, however, Helmholz, "Character of the Western Legal Tradition," 41, concluded that, despite its shortcomings, Berman's book "gets the major developments right."

16. Tellenbach, *Church in Western Europe*, 314–17.

17. So called from the magician, Simon Magus, who tried to bribe St. Peter to show him how to perform miracles (Acts 8:9–24).

the right to dispose of ecclesiastical lands, revenues, and other assets, that priests and other clerics should abstain altogether from sexual activity, and that they should be subject solely to the jurisdiction of ecclesiastical courts.

Each of these claims carried legal implications, as reform leaders were acutely aware.[18] It was no coincidence that the volume of litigation in church courts increased substantially from the late eleventh century onward, owing in considerable part to disputes that resulted from the activities of reformers. Likewise, the increasingly sophisticated procedures that started to be employed in ecclesiastical courts during the second half of the twelfth century reflected the need for greater procedural regularity in order to cope with the increase in judicial business.[19] The reform movement, moreover, made clerical careers increasingly attractive for men gifted with brains, energy, and ambition. It opened up opportunities for promotion within the church, and ambitious men quickly discovered that those with specialized knowledge of the law fared distinctly better than those without it. As an anonymous versifier put it,

> Galen gives you wealth and so does Justinian's law;
> From these you gather grain, from the others only straw.[20]

It was probably no coincidence that, for example, Lanfranc (d. 1090) and Anselm (d. 1109), the powerful archbishops of Canterbury at the height of the reform movement, were both men of substantial legal learning, coupled with a strong determination to see that the kings they served observed the prescriptions of canon law.[21]

The Beginnings of the Legal Revival at Bologna

PEPO AND IRNERIUS

The first faint beginnings of systematic legal study and teaching commenced while the church reform movement was at its height. The earliest individual who can reasonably be associated with the revival of the study of Roman law, and of the Digest in particular, was a shadowy jurist known as Master

---

18. Gilchrist, "Gregory VII and Juristic Sources"; Ryan, *Saint Peter Damiani*; Riché, *Écoles et enseignement*, 260–61; Robinson, "Church and Papacy," 266–77; Tierney, *Crisis of Church and State, 1050–1300*, 24–52.

19. Brett, "Canon Law and Litigation"; Fried, "Die Römische Kurie," 173–74.

20. Kuttner, "Dat Galienus opes," 243. The translation is by Smalley, *Becket Conflict*, 19.

21. Brooke, *The English Church*, 118–19, 149–50; Duggan, "From the Conquest to the Death of John," 80–83.

Pepo.²² His identity is not easy to pin down, since Pepo was not a particularly uncommon name, at least in Tuscany and the region around Ravenna, in the late eleventh century.²³ Certainly a *legis doctor* named Pepo was mentioned in the judgment in a case in 1076, a judgment, moreover, in which a passage from Justinian's Digest is cited.²⁴ "Pepo legis doctor" also appeared in 1076 as a legal adviser to Countess Matilda of Tuscany (1046–1115) and again in 1078.²⁵ It seems likely that these documents refer to one and the same person, and the association with Matilda of Tuscany links him as well to the church reform movement and the circle of Pope Gregory VII. This presumably was the same Pepo who intervened dramatically in a case heard in Lombardy before the German king Henry IV (1056–1106), securing a verdict based on Roman law. When he wrote his account of this episode a century later, the English theologian and canonist Ralph Niger (b. between 1140 and 1146, d. before 1199), described Pepo as the standard-bearer (*baiulus*) of Justinian's Code and Institutes, although Ralph also says that Pepo was not familiar with the Digest.²⁶ We can conclude, therefore, that Pepo the jurist was a practicing advocate and judge connected with the court of Countess Matilda, and through her with the church reform movement. Two later writers claimed that Pepo attempted to teach Roman law, but without much success. The reliability of their evidence, however, is questionable.²⁷

Scholars have long identified as the prime mover in the legal revival,

22. The meaning and implications of the titles "master" (*magister*), "professor," and "doctor" in documents from the eleventh and twelfth centuries are often difficult to determine. All three implied that the person so styled was learned, and they were often used to describe men engaged in teaching of some sort, but at this period it would be hazardous to infer that the titles indicated that the bearer had advanced academic credentials. Usage changed gradually during the latter part of the twelfth century, and by around 1200 these titles were commonly used to designate persons with an advanced academic rank or degree. See Groten, "Der Magistertitel und seine Verbreitung"; Feenstra, "Legum doctor "; Renardy, *Le monde des maîtres*, 80–90.

23. Fried, *Entstehung des Juristenstandes*, 88; Fiorelli, "Clarum Bononiensium Lumen," 423–24; Cortese, *Diritto nella storia* 2:33–45.

24. Ficker, *Forschungen* 3:125–27; Ascheri, *Diritti del medioevo italiano*, 111–13.

25. Manaresi, *Placiti del Regnum Italiae*, nos. 437, 448.

26. Schmugge, "Codicis Iustiniani et Institutionum baiulus"; Kantorowicz and Smalley, "An English Theologian's View"; and Flahiff, "Ralph Niger."

27. Azo, gloss to Dig. 1.2.2.38, quoted in Savigny, *Geschichte* 4:7 note b, as well as Kantorowicz and Smalley, "An English Theologian's View," 231. Azo added that none of Pepo's writings survived. While that may be true, other writers did refer to his opinions (Losciavo, "Secundum Peponem dicitur . . . G. vero dicit"). Odofredus (d. 1265), a still later thirteenth-century witness, refers scornfully in his *Lectura* to Dig. 1.1.6 to Pepo's

not Pepo, but another man of the same generation known as Irnerius (fl. ca. 1055–1125).[28] Irnerius, we are told, began his career as a teacher of the liberal arts at Bologna in the late eleventh century. According to the commonly received version of events, Irnerius became intrigued by the language and rhetoric of the Latin legal texts that he encountered, which led him to specialize in teaching those texts. At some point he came across a partial copy of Justinian's Digest and was captivated by the sophisticated juristic reasoning that he found in its pages. This kindled his interest in Roman jurisprudence, as well as in the language in which it was clothed. Around 1088, according to the traditional story, Irnerius set himself up as a teacher of law.[29] He also produced written comments on the newly discovered texts. Many of these appeared as marginal glosses that explicated words and phrases in the texts themselves, while others took the form of systematic expositions of legal doctrines.[30]

Inspired by stories about Irnerius's discovery of hitherto unknown treasures of ancient juristic learning, the standard account continues, students flocked to Bologna to learn from him. They came at first from the city's immediate vicinity, then from other parts of the Italian peninsula, and before long from more distant regions beyond the Alps and overseas. The stars among Irnerius's pupils, it is said, were the well-known Four Doctors of Bologna: Bulgarus de Bulgarinis (d. ca. 1166), Martinus Gosia (d. ca. 1160), Hugo da Porta Ravennate (d. between 1166 and 1171), and Jacobus (d. 1178).[31] Each of these men, and perhaps some of Irnerius's other pupils,

---

teaching (Walther, "Anfänge des Rechtsstudiums," 139–44). Pepo is described more favorably in the *Historiae Seneneses* (Fiorelli, "Clarum Bononiensium Lumen," 432–34).

28. Thus, e.g., Savigny, *Geschichte* 4:13, 18–19; Sorbelli, *Storia della Università di Bologna*, 34–38; Calasso, *Medio evo del diritto*, 507–10; Berman, *Law and Revolution*, 123–24; Caenegem, *Historical Introduction to Private Law*, 51; Bellomo, *Common Legal Past*, 58–60 (but see now "Una nuova figura," 245), and numerous others, including Brundage, *Medieval Canon Law*, 44–46. He also appears in contemporary documents as Guarnerius, Wernerius, and other variants of the common German proper name Werner. It has recently been suggested, not altogether plausibly, that he was the Garnerius Teutonicus who left "quinque libros optimos glosatos" to the canons of St. Victor in Paris (Mazzanti, "Irnerio").

29. For this reason the University of Bologna celebrates 1088 as the date of its foundation, although no documentary evidence really justifies that date. On the significance of the quest for foundation dates, see Rüegg, "Themes," 4–6.

30. Dolezalek, "Gloses des manuscrits de droit."

31. Savigny, *Geschichte* 3:75–123, 471–80; 4:124–70, 481–517; Kantorowicz, *Studies*, 68–111, 241–69, and *Rechtshistorische Schriften*, 273–85; Lange, *Römisches Recht im Mittelalter*, 162–89.

then established their own schools and carried on the teaching tradition that he had founded. Law teaching, at first of Roman law, then slightly later of canon law as well, became an established industry at Bologna. The city had emerged by around 1140 as Europe's first and foremost center of legal studies.[32]

This version of the origin of the legal revival rests upon a handful of medieval sources, especially the *Lectura* of Odofredus (d. 1265) and a short passage in the *Chronicle* of Burchard of Würzburg (d. after 11 January 1231).[33] Since both Burchard and Odofredus wrote more than a century after Irnerius's death, however, it is questionable whether either of them can be reckoned a reliable witness to events at the end of the eleventh century.[34] No eleventh- or twelfth-century accounts of Irnerius's teaching career have apparently survived.

Scholars have recently begun to question the standard account of Irnerius's career and his role in the twelfth-century legal revival. Some of what earlier scholars thought they knew about the substance of Irnerius's legal teaching depended upon the ascription to him of works that it now seems he may not have written. Irnerius's authorship of the legal commentaries conventionally attributed to him has over the past half century come to seem increasingly doubtful. Hermann Kantorowicz concluded that only two brief introductions to Justinian's Code and Institutes might be Irnerius's work, and he was not entirely sure about those. More recent scholars have voiced still more skepticism about the reliability even of those attributions.[35] To complicate matters further, a collection of theological texts known as the *Liber divinarum sententiarum*, which Gratian may conceivably have used, was compiled by one "Guarnerius iurisperitissimus," who its editor has argued must be the jurist Irnerius.

Thousands of glosses that appear in manuscripts and early printed editions of Roman law texts have traditionally been identified as the work of

32. Rashdall, *Universities* 1:113–20.
33. Odofredus, *Lectura* to Cod. 1.2.14 in c. *Qui res* (= Nov. 7.5 and Nov. 120) and Cod. 2.21(22).9, at 17ra, 101ra; *Lectura* to Dig. 1.1.6, in Savigny, *Geschichte* 3:427; Burchard of Würzburg, *Chronicon*, MGH, SSRG, 15–16.
34. The Würzburg *Chronicle* dates from the late 1220s at the earliest, while Odofredus completed his *Lectura* about 1260. Skepticism about the reliability of Odofredus's testimony is not new; Kantorowicz, *Studies*, 196, described Odofredus as "a notorious prattler" and judged his evidence about Irnerius "worthless." Fried, *Entstehung des Juristenstandes*, 104, is equally severe, calling Odofredus a "glänzende Rhetoriker."
35. Kantorowicz, *Studies*, 37–41; Lange, *Römisches Recht im Mittelalter*, 161–62; Winroth, *Making of Gratian's Decretum*, 162–64.

Irnerius and other individual commentators on the basis of the abbreviated authors' names (*sigla*) attached to them. It was long believed that Irnerius was the author of all glosses that bore the *sigla* "g" or "y," but Gero Dolezalek has shown that these *sigla* also carried other meanings.[36] It is not at all clear whether or not the practice of attaching *sigla* to Roman law glosses had even begun before 1125, the latest date at which Irnerius is known to have been alive. Some, possibly most, of the glosses formerly credited to Irnerius may have been the work of later teachers.[37]

We do know with reasonable certainty that Irnerius was a legal practitioner who worked as an advocate and judge during the first quarter of the twelfth century. He may well have had apprentices who were in some sense his pupils, but no secure evidence suggests that he conducted a formally organized school. The first appearance of his name in a contemporary document occurs in arbitration award concerning a Cornacervina property dispute in 1112, in which "Guarnerius bononiensis" appeared as a *causidicus*. The following year, he again appeared as a *causidicus* in a property award at the court of Countess Matilda of Tuscany.[38] Irnerius's association with Countess Matilda might suggest that he was a supporter of the church reform movement. He is not known to have had any connection with Matilda's circle before 1112, however, and it is clear that after 1110 Matilda's ardor for church reform had cooled noticeably.[39] It is in any event hazardous to assume that lawyers necessarily subscribe to the same views as their clients.

Countess Matilda died on 24 July 1115, leaving no direct descendants. She apparently designated as her heir the German king and emperor Henry V (r. 1106–25), who was, to say the least, no friend of the reforming forces. Henry took control of Tuscany shortly after Matilda's death. Irnerius soon thereafter began to appear as a *iudex* in Henry's court, and we have records of his participation in a series of hearings from March through November 1116. No comparable documents survive from 1117, but Irnerius was still

---

36. Dolezalek, *Repertorium Codicis* 1:463–74, but cf. the counterargument of Padovani, "Il titulo De Summa Trinitate," 1093–1100.

37. Dolezalek, *Repertorium Codicis* 1:472; Winroth, *Making of Gratian's Decretum*, 167–68; Lange, *Römisches Recht im Mittelalter*, 159–62; Bellomo, "Una nuova figura," 245.

38. On Irnerius generally, see Southern, *Scholastic Humanism* 1:279–80. The documentary evidence concerning Irnerius is conveniently collected in Spagnesi, *Wernerius*. The Cornacervina arbitration award appears at 29–35, no. 1, and the Tuscan court award at 36–42, no. 2.

39. Robinson, *The Papacy*, 424–25, 449.

functioning as an imperial judge in 1118.[40] A Milanese chronicler also reports that in 1118, Irnerius, together with numerous other men learned in the law, argued in favor of the election of the anti-pope, Gregory VIII (d. 1221), to succeed Paschal II (r. 1099–1118). On this account, Irnerius was excommunicated, along with Henry V, by the Council of Reims in 1119.[41] Irnerius appears in only one further contemporary document, an arbitration agreement dated 10 December 1125.[42] Although these documents give no hint that Irnerius taught law, they do testify that contemporaries considered him a learned legal practitioner and that he was knowledgeable about Roman law, whether he taught it or not. This is scarcely surprising: legal practice and teaching would remain closely linked throughout the twelfth and thirteenth centuries. The distinction between academic lawyers, who taught in the universities but only occasionally dealt with clients, and practitioners who dealt with clients all the time would not emerge until much later.[43]

THE FOUR DOCTORS

Only in the 1220s, almost a century after Irnerius disappeared from the records, did the claim that the Four Doctors had studied law with Irnerius first appear.[44] That time gap raises questions about its reliability. Nevertheless, they had certainly studied with someone. Martinus, for example, spoke at one point about "certain law teachers, who learned the doctrine of our predecessors." His statement attests that he and his cohorts were not

---

40. Spagnesi, *Wernerius*, 43–99, nos. 3–13.

41. The passage on the legal scholars' support of Gregory VIII appears in Spagnesi, *Wernerius*, 132–33. The reported basis for their argument—that the people of Rome, rather than the cardinals, were the legitimate electors—seems slightly sophistical in view of the provisions of the papal election decree of 1059 (Gratian, D. 23 c. 1; trans. Tierney, *Crisis of Church and State*, 42–43). On their excommunication, see Landulf of St. Paul, *Historia Mediolanensis*, s.a. 1118, in MGH, SS 20:40; Holtzmann, "Zur Geschichte des Investiturstreites," 246–319; Fried, *Entstehung des Juristenstandes*, 49; Mazzanti, "Irnerio," 118–25.

42. Spagnesi, *Wernerius*, 100–102, no. 14, although Mazzanti, "Irnerio," 119 n. 9, questioned the authenticity of this document.

43. Steffen, *Studentische Autonomie*, 153. Savigny, *Geschichte* 4:19, 73, thought it unlikely, although not impossible, that Irnerius was teaching Roman law as early as the second decade of the twelfth century.

44. The claim first occurs in an anonymous addition to Otto of Morena's *Gesta Frederici I*, s.a. 1158, quoted by Savigny, *Geschichte* 4:70; see also Cortese, *Diritto nella storia* 2:70.

autodidacts and that they learned their law from more than one teacher.[45] We cannot be certain who those predecessors may have been, and the Four Doctors thus remain the earliest systematic teachers of Roman law at Bologna about whose teaching we have firm information from contemporary sources. Evidence that they taught law and sometimes served as legal consultants first began to appear during the second quarter of the twelfth century.[46] One crucial piece of this evidence concerns the papal chancellor Cardinal Haimeric (d. 1141). Bulgarus, who described the cardinal as his "dearest friend" (*karissimus amicus*), states that Haimeric had invited him to prepare a guide to Roman procedural law.[47] In response, Bulgarus sent the chancellor a short letter about the elements of procedure, a work that is variously known as *De arbitris*, *De iudiciis*, or *Excerpta legum*. Since Haimeric became chancellor in 1123 and held that office until his death in May 1141, Bulgarus must have finished this work in the first few months of 1141 at the very latest, although he could well have done so a decade or more before that. Another document shows that Bulgarus was both teaching and serving as a papal judge-delegate in July 1151.[48] His activities as a teacher are further documented by his glosses and other writings, although none of these can be dated with certainty. It is clear, however, that Gratian adapted a passage in his Decretum from one of Bulgarus's minor works, *De iuris et facti ignorantia*, which points to its composition before about 1140.[49] The request from Cardinal Haimeric certainly implies that Bulgarus had an established reputation as a leading authority on Roman law before that date, a reputation that rested at least in part upon his teaching.

Martinus Gosia, who belonged to a Bolognese noble family, seems to have been slightly younger than Bulgarus. Martinus may have written his

---

45. Martinus, *De iure dotium* §30, in Kantorowicz, *Studies*, 264: "Set quidam iuris preceptores quorundam antecessorum doctrina instructi quasi in verba magistrorum iurantes confidenter asserunt."

46. Winroth, *Making of Gratian's Decretum*, 170. The mid-twelfth century *Dissensiones dominorum* furnish concrete evidence of the character of their teaching as well as about disagreements among them; see also *CSB* 3:103–6.

47. Bulgarus, *Excerpta legum*, ed. Wahrmund, 1. See also Fowler-Magerl, *Ordo iudiciorum*, 35–40.

48. Fried, "Die Römische Kurie," 151–52; Kantorowicz, *Studies*, 68, 70–72; Lange, *Römisches Recht im Mittelalter*, 167–68; Stein, *Regulae iuris*, 132–35; Ficker, *Forschungen* 3:470.

49. Kantorowicz, *Studies*, 68–70, 73–85, 245; Lange, *Römisches Recht im Mittelalter*, 162–70. Part of the passage from *De juris* appears in the vulgate version of the Decretum and part in the earlier recensions.

treatise on the degrees of consanguinity before the appearance of Gratian's Decretum, while his treatise on dowry law may be dated slightly later, perhaps about 1150. He appeared, together with Bulgarus, Hugo, and Jacobus, as a *causidicus* in an action in 1154.[50] Martinus and Bulgarus adopted distinctly different approaches to the interpretation of the legal texts on which they commented. Bulgarus preferred a narrow approach (*ius strictum*) that adhered closely to the letter of the law, whereas Martinus chose a freer style of equitable interpretation that construed the literal text of the law in ways that would produce fair solutions to problems. Law teachers at Bologna tended to adopt Bulgarus's approach, while their counterparts in southern France were more partial to the style favored by Martinus and his followers.[51]

Jacobus (d. 1178), who was younger than Bulgarus and Martinus, is described variously as a judge, *causidicus, legislator, legum doctor,* and *vir prudentissimus* in various documents dated between 1151 and 1169.[52] In addition to glosses on numerous passages in Justinian's Digest, Code, Novels, and Institutes, Jacobus may also have been the author of the earliest medieval treatise on criminal law.[53]

The most obscure of the Four Doctors was Hugo. His name appears in several documents dated between 1151 and 1166, most of which describe him as a *causidicus*. In addition to some scattered glosses on texts in the Digest, Code, and Novels, Hugo's principal work was the brief *Summa de petitione hereditatis*, although a number of other writings have erroneously been credited to him.[54]

Contemporary sources unequivocally testify that the Four Doctors were

---

50. The passages on consanguinity led Kantorowicz, *Studies*, 91–94, to suggest that Martinus's treatise came after Gratian's work. But since the same passages appear in the collections of Anselm of Lucca and Polycarp (completed at the latest by 1113), both of which Gratian probably used, the *De computatione graduum* could have been written earlier. On the dowry law treatise, see Kantorowicz, *Studies*, 94–102; Lange, *Römisches Recht im Mittelalter*, 170–71. On the 1154 action, Savigny, *Geschichte* 4:75; *CSB* 3:104–6.

51. Lange, *Römisches Recht im Mittelalter*, 165–66, 171–74; Stein, "Vacarius and the Civil Law," 124–27; Landau, "Development of Law," 124; but cf. Cortese, *Diritto nella storia* 2:76–79.

52. Savigny, *Geschichte* 4:142; Fried, *Entstehung des Juristenstandes*, 95.

53. On the glosses, see Savigny, *Geschichte* 4:494–96; Lange, *Römisches Recht im Mittelalter*, 180–81. Kantorowicz maintained that Jacobus was the author of the criminal law treatise in, "Il 'Tractatus Criminum,'" but Gouron raised serious doubts about this attribution in "Zu den Ursprüngen des Strafrechts."

54. Kantorowicz, *Studies*, 267–69; Lange, *Römisches Recht im Mittelalter*, 187–89.

internationally known as authoritative teachers of Roman law during the second quarter of the twelfth century and that Bologna had by that time become the foremost European center for legal studies. We have, for example, the evidence of William of Tyre (b. ca. 1130, d. 1186), who traveled to the West from the Crusader States in the Levant in the mid-1140s in order to study theology at Paris and law at Bologna. His principal teachers at Bologna were Bulgarus and Hugo da Porta Ravennate, whom he described as "jurisconsults and men of the highest authority" in legal matters. Although he did not count Martinus and Jacobus among his own teachers, William added that he frequently saw them and occasionally attended their lectures. The Four Doctors, William concluded, "stood like columns and furnished the solid foundation that supported the temple of justice."[55]

A decade or so before William of Tyre's student days, Arnulf of Séez (d. 1181), later bishop of Lisieux, spent several years as a law student in Bologna, which helped prepare him for his future role in ecclesiastical and secular politics in Normandy and England.[56] Another, far better-known figure from the Anglo-Norman realm who made his way to Bologna was Archbishop Thomas Becket (1118–70), who spent a year at Bologna during the 1140s studying law. Later, during his exile from England, he sought additional tutoring in canon law from Master Lombard of Piacenza.[57]

Even more compelling testimony to Bologna's position as an international center for the teaching and study of law comes from the *Authentica "Habita."* The German emperor Frederick Barbarossa (r. 1152–90) issued this imperial decree near Bologna in 1155, while on campaign in Italy. At the request of a delegation of law teachers and students from the city, the emperor took under his protection students who, as he put it, had made themselves exiles for the sake of learning and had on this account turned themselves from rich men into paupers, exposed to manifold perils and bodily injuries. The emperor forbade anyone to molest students. Local authorities who neglected to assure the safety of a student were to be disgraced, degraded from office, and held personally liable to the student for fourfold damages. The aggrieved student could, if he wished, have the matter adju-

---

55. William of Tyre, *Chronicon* 19.12.49, at 2:880–81; see also Edbury and Rowe, *William of Tyre*, 13–15; Fried, *Entstehung des Juristenstandes*, 21.

56. Rathbone, "Roman Law in the Anglo-Norman Realm," 259.

57. William FitzStephen, *Vita S. Thomae*, in *Materials* 3:17; see also Cheney, "William FitzStephen and His Life of Archbishop Thomas"; John of Salisbury, *Letters* 2:602–8, no. 279; see also his *Vita et passio Sancti Thomae martyris* c. 5, and Herbert of Bosham, *Vita S. Thomae archiepiscopi et martyris* 7.1, in *Materials* 2:304 and 3:523–24.

dicated by his teacher or the local bishop. Barbarossa further directed that this privilege be inserted into Justinian's Code as a supplementary imperial law.[58]

Further testimony to the fame of the Four Doctors appears from their employment by Barbarossa as his legal counselors at the Diet of Roncaglia in November 1158. Rahewin (d. after 1170), in his continuation of Otto of Freising's *Gesta Frederici*, described them as "well-spoken, religious men, extremely learned in the law, teachers of the laws in the city of Bologna, and instructors of numerous pupils."[59]

The Legal Revival outside Bologna

ITALY

Although Bologna was preeminent, it was not the only place where men in the mid-twelfth century were beginning to study law seriously. Lombard jurists at Pavia and elsewhere in northern Italy, for example, during the early twelfth century increasingly larded their arguments with references to Justinian's Institutes and Code. When they began to insert occasional citations to the Digest, a far more demanding book, it seems reasonable to infer that they were no longer studying Roman legal texts simply as sources for rhetorical flourishes, but were commencing to engage in serious legal analysis.[60] Legal studies in cities such as Mantua, Pavia, Piacenza, and Ravenna, however, seem to have reflected the enterprises and interests of isolated individuals, and did not lead to the formation until much later of schools such as those of the Four Doctors at Bologna.

58. Stelzer, "Zum Scholarenprivileg Friedrich Barbarossas," 165: "Quis eorum non misereatur, cum amore scientie facti sunt exules de divitibus pauperes semetipsos exinaniunt, vitam suam omnibus periculis exponunt, et a vilissimis sepe hominibus—quod graviter ferendum est—corporales iniurias sine causa perferunt?" The privilege appears as Auth. post Cod. 4.13.5. See Nardi, "Relations with Authority," 78–79; Landau, "Development of Law," 126–27.

59. Otto of Freising and Rahewin, *Gesta Frederici seu rectius chronica* 4.6, at 520: "[H]abensque IIIIor iudices, videlicet Bulgarum, Martinum, Iacobum, Hugonem, viros disertos, religiosos et in lege doctissimos legumque in civitate Bononiensi doctores et multorum auditorum preceptores. " Likewise, an addition (written in the 1220s) to Otto Morena, *Historia Frederici I*, s.a. 1158, quoted in Savigny, *Geschichte* 4:68–69.

60. Vaccari, *Diritto longobardo*, 20–23; Lange, *Römisches Recht im Mittelalter*, 21–28; Radding, *Origins of Medieval Jurisprudence*, 171–75. On the study of law at Ravenna see Ficker, *Forschungen* 3:110–12; and Savigny, *Geschichte* 4:1–5.

France

Evidence attesting to the study and teaching of Roman and canon law in a scattering of southern French cities also began to appear in the middle years of the twelfth century. Placentinus (d. 1192), who studied with Bulgarus at Bologna, spent much of his later career teaching law at Montpellier. His *Summa Codicis* and his *Libellus de actionum varietatibus*, as well as his unfinished *Summa trium librorum*, were products of his teaching there.[61] Rogerius (d. ca. 1170), another pupil of Bulgarus, likewise taught at Montpellier before Placentinus arrived, possibly as early as 1162. It is also likely that Pillius (d. after 1213), who studied for a time with Placentinus, taught briefly at Montpellier.[62]

The study of Roman civil law predominated at Montpellier, whereas in the north of France the emphasis was chiefly on canon law. Still, because some knowledge of Roman law was essential for students of canon law, it was taught at Paris at least by the 1160s, as it was elsewhere in cathedral and monastic schools, perhaps even earlier.[63]

Outside of Paris and Montpellier, the canons of Saint-Ruf, to cite a particularly striking example, undertook the task of providing legal representation to deserving litigants as part of their religious mission.[64] By the early twelfth century, the Saint-Ruf community was engaged in training up its own lawyers to fulfill that mission. One product of their law teaching survives as the *Justiniani est in hoc opere*, a *summa* on Justinian's Institutes, which came to light in 1974 in the Pierpont Morgan Library in New York.[65]

---

61. Gouron, "Comment dater la venue de Placentin à Montpellier?" and "Placentin et la Somme 'Cum essem Mantuae,'" as well as "Autour de Placentin à Montpellier"; Lange, *Römisches Recht im Mittelalter*, 207–14; Kantorowicz, "Poetical Sermon of a Medieval Jurist."

62. Kantorowicz, *Studies*, 122–29, 142; Lange, *Römisches Recht im Mittelalter*, 192–95, 228–29.

63. Gouron, "Canon Law in Parisian Circles," and "Une école de canonistes anglais"; Kuttner, "Débuts de l'école canoniste français"; Williams, "The Cathedral School of Reims," 104–5. Evidence from glosses in a very early twelfth-century manuscript that originated at Reims shows that Justinian's Code was being taught there not long after 1100 (Dolezalek, *Repertorium Codicis* 1:148–54).

64. Unlikely as this apostolate may seem to modern sensibilities, it seems to have responded to real needs in twelfth-century France. See Poly, "Les maîtres de Saint-Ruf."

65. Gouron, "Entstehung der französischen Rechtsschule," and "Le rôle des maîtres français."

The evidence of surviving manuscripts and records of library holdings, moreover, strongly suggests that both Roman and canon law were studied, if probably not systematically taught, in other monastic communities. Even at Clairvaux—whose abbot, St. Bernard (1090–1153), was certainly no admirer of legal learning, let alone legal practitioners—the twelfth-century library contained an impressive collection of legal texts.[66]

Several important legal texts from the mid-twelfth century also originated in the French Midi. Among these, the *Exceptiones Petri* and the closely related *Tübingen Law Book* mark a transitional stage in the study of Roman law in the West, between the era when law was taught as a branch of rhetoric and the period when it became a vocational subject, taught and studied in preparation for a career spent in litigation in the courts.[67] Opinions differ concerning the date and origin of the *Exceptiones*. Most scholars now agree that the work was composed sometime around the middle of the twelfth century, and the consensus seems to be that it is more likely to have originated in the south of France than in northern Italy, as some earlier writers claimed.[68]

An even more widely influential work that unquestionably originated in the south of France during this same period is *Lo Codi*, a *summa* on the first nine books of Justinian's Code, first written (it seems) in Provençal during the third quarter of the twelfth century and later translated into Old French, Castilian, Catalan, the dialect of Dauphiné, and Latin.[69] The work was intended primarily for a lay audience whose members did not read Latin, as is evident from the fact that it was written originally in one vernacular language and subsequently found a readership in others. At the same time, the material that its author chose to include makes it plain that the book was intended for practical use, presumably by judges, advocates,

---

66. St. Bernard, *De consideratione* 1.3.4–1.4.5, 1.10.13, 1.11.14, in his *Opera* 3:397–99, 408–10; see also *Five Books on Consideration*, 29–32, 44–46; Jacqueline, *Épiscopat et papauté chez Saint Bernard de Clairvaux*, 25–39; see also his "Les études juridiques au Mont Saint-Michel." Chodorow, *Christian Political Theory*, 260–65, argues persuasively that Msgr. Jacqueline overestimated St. Bernard's own juristic knowledge and skill.

67. Conrat, *Geschichte der Quellen*, 420–90; Lange, *Römisches Recht im Mittelalter*, 387–91; Zimmermann, "Römische und kanonische Rechtskenntnis," 784–87.

68. Lange, *Römisches Recht im Mittelalter*, 388–89; Weimar, "Zur Entstehung des sogennanten Tübinger Rechtsbuchs"; Kantorowicz, "Origines françaises des *Exceptiones Petri*"; and most recently, Gouron, "Sur la patrie et la datation du 'Livre de Tubingue' et des 'Exceptiones Petri,'" and "'Petrus' démasqué," 577–88.

69. Lange, *Römisches Recht im Mittelalter*, 415–17; Gouron, "Du nouveau sur *lo Codi*," and "*Lo Codi*."

and proctors who lacked formal legal training. The popularity and wide diffusion of *Lo Codi* clearly indicates that Roman law doctrines and procedures were in current use in the courts of Provence and neighboring regions by the second half of the twelfth century. Indeed, the influence of *Lo Codi* extended even beyond western Europe, for the noble jurists who framed the *Assises* of the Crusader States in the Holy Land and Cyprus also borrowed heavily from it.[70]

England

The Roman law revival reached England, as it did other regions outside of Italy, gradually and piecemeal. Unlike the south of France, where vestiges of Roman law had persisted throughout the early Middle Ages, the few traces of Roman legal thought or practice known in England prior to the twelfth century arrived there through canon law books brought from the Continent, first by missionaries, beginning with St. Augustine of Canterbury (d. 604 or 605), and later by champions of the church reform movement. Lanfranc, archbishop of Canterbury (r. 1070–89), a native of Pavia, is often said to have studied Roman law in his youth, and even to have taught it before he entered the monastic life, although both claims seem dubious.[71] Lanfranc was, however, well-versed in canon law and after he became archbishop, as Maitland put it, "[T]he *decreta* and *canones* were ever in his mouth."[72] Indeed, Lanfranc brought with him from the Norman monastery of Bec, where he had previously been abbot, a collection of canons, largely drawn from the *Pseudo-Isidorian Decretals*. He put this collection, known as the *Collectio Lanfranci*, to use at Canterbury, whence it became widely disseminated.

The key figure in the introduction of the newly revived legal learning into the English kingdom was a Lombard jurist named Vacarius (ca. 1120–1205) who had studied law at Bologna, very likely with Martinus. He was brought to England around 1143 by Theobald, archbishop of Canterbury (r. 1139–61), who wanted his assistance in administrative matters. Late in the following decade Roger, archbishop of York (r. 1154–81), who had

---

70. Prawer, *Crusader Institutions*, 358–412, 441–56. On the Latin jurists in the Levant, see Riley-Smith, *The Feudal Nobility*, 121–44, and Edbury, *John of Ibelin*.

71. Gouron, *La science juridique française*, 10–12.

72. Pollock and Maitland, *History of English Law* 1:78. See Kéry, *Canonical Collections*, 239–43, on the dissemination of the *Collectio Lanfranci*; for an analysis of the text, see Fowler-Magerl, *Clavis canonum*.

learned about Vacarius's legal skills at firsthand while serving as archdeacon of Canterbury, persuaded Vacarius to join his own staff.[73]

Throughout his years in England, Vacarius practiced canon law and served from time to time as a papal judge-delegate. He also wrote a treatise on canonical marriage law sometime during the years between 1156 and 1170.[74] Where, when, and under what circumstances Vacarius taught has been a matter of controversy. It was long believed that he taught at Oxford and was the founder of legal studies there, but recent reexaminations of the scanty evidence on which this rests have seriously undermined that belief.[75] It seems certain, however, that Vacarius did teach Roman law somewhere in England, for when reporting that King Stephen (r. 1135–54) attempted to ban the teaching of Roman law in England, John of Salisbury (b. ca. 1115, d. 1180) specifically noted, "Silence was imposed upon our Vacarius."[76]

Vacarius's intellectual influence stemmed not so much from his classroom teaching as from the *Liber pauperum*, literally *The Poor Men's Book*, an introductory textbook of Roman law. This work comprises a series of selections from Justinian's Code and Digest, strung together with a chain of explanatory glosses, arranged in the order of the titles of the first nine books of the Code.[77] Vacarius chose the selections in the *Liber pauperum* with a view to providing an elementary introduction to the fundamentals of Ro-

---

73. Robert of Torigny, *Chronicle*, 158–59; Helmholz, *Canon Law and Ecclesiastical Jurisdiction*, 121–24; Stein, "Vacarius and the Civil Law," 169–70; Southern, "Master Vacarius."

74. Southern, "Master Vacarius," 282–85; Maitland, "Magistri Vacarii Summa de matrimonio." Vacarius also wrote two short theological treatises; see "The *Tractatus De assumpto homine* by Magister Vacarius" and Ilario da Milano, *L'eresia di Ugo Speroni*.

75. The Oxford connection was grounded on the dubious evidence of Gervase of Canterbury (d. 1210), *Actus pontificum*, in his *Historical Works* 2:384–85; see also Zulueta's introduction to his edition of the *Liber Pauperum* of Vacarius, xiii-xxi, and Rashdall, *Universities* 3:19–21. On the unreliability of the Oxford evidence, see Southern, "Master Vacarius," 273–82; Stein, "Vacarius and the Civil Law," in Zulueta and Stein, *Teaching of Roman Law*, xxii–xxvii at xxvi–xxvii; but cf. Boyle, "Beginnings of Legal Studies at Oxford," 120–22, 125–31.

76. Stein, "Vacarius and the Civil Law," 179–81, suggests that Vacarius may perhaps have taught at Northampton or Lincoln. On his silencing by Stephen, see John of Salisbury, *Policraticus* 8.22, trans. Nederman, 215. Stephen's ban on Roman law teaching presumably reflected his belief that Roman law might support the claims of his rival, Matilda, to the English throne (Southern, *Scholastic Humanism* 2:156).

77. *Liber pauperum*, prol., at 1.

man civil law for students who were preparing to study canon law. They required some basic grounding in the principles, terminology, analytical categories, and procedural system of civil law in order to make sense of many of the underlying assumptions upon which canon law rested. A deep and thorough knowledge of the finer points of the Roman legal system was not essential for their purposes, however, and Vacarius's book provided them with just what they needed. For this reason, the *Liber pauperum* became enormously popular with students, not only at Oxford, where *pauperistae* became a slightly scornful term for students with a superficial knowledge of Roman law, but elsewhere as well.[78] In addition to the *Liber pauperum*, the content of Vacarius's teaching is also known from his *Lectura*, a commentary on Justinian's Institutes that seems to have been composed from notes that one of his students took on his lectures.[79]

The Reshaping of Canon Law

CANON LAW BEFORE GRATIAN

Important new collections of canon law, many of them linked in some way to the church reform movement, appeared around turn of the twelfth century. One of those, the *Collectio Lanfranci*, as mentioned above, secured widespread acceptance throughout England.[80] The most broadly disseminated and influential collections of this period, however, were the three attributed to Ivo, bishop of Chartres (b. ca. 1040, d. 1115). Among these, the so-called *Tripartita* (Three-Part Collection) seems to have been the earliest.[81] It is closely related to another canonical collection of the late elev-

---

78. Stein, introduction to Zulueta and Stein, *Teaching of Roman Law*, xxxiv–xxxv; Boyle, "Canon Law before 1380," 533, and "Beginnings of Legal Studies at Oxford." The presence of manuscripts of the *Liber pauperum* in libraries as distant from Oxford as those at Avranches, Bruges, Trier, Prague, St. Petersburg, and Kaliningrad (formerly Königsberg), suggests that that its influence, as well as its circulation, was not limited to England.

79. The *Lectura* has been edited and translated by Zulueta and Stein in *Teaching of Roman Law*; on its authorship see Stein's introduction, xlix–li.

80. Some thirty complete and partial manuscript copies of the *Collectio Lanfranci* survive. Its circulation was largely limited to the Anglo-Norman kingdom, as is reflected by the fact that all but four of the surviving manuscripts appear in English or Norman libraries (Kéry, *Canonical Collections*, 240–41).

81. Sprandel, *Ivo von Chartres*, 52–85 passim; Kéry, *Canonical Collections*, 244–50. On the relationship between the *Tripartita* and the other collections attributed to Ivo, see Martin Brett, "Urban II and the Collections Attributed to Ivo of Chartres." Brett's pro-

enth century, the *Collectio Britannica*.[82] Ivo's *Decretum*, a huge collection of some 3,760 canons arranged in sixteen books, was by far the largest and most comprehensive of the collections associated with his name.[83] It incorporates substantial material from the earlier *Decretum* of Burchard of Worms, to which he added a large bloc of texts from the *Tripartita*, as well as other material. Because of its size and the consequent investment in time and parchment required to copy it, few complete copies of Ivo's *Decretum* probably ever existed and even fewer now survive.[84] The third collection attributed to Ivo, the *Panormia*, with slightly more than a thousand canons, mainly drawn from his *Decretum*, was a much smaller compilation. Since the *Panormia* was not only cheaper to produce, but also easier to use than the *Decretum*, it circulated much more widely. More than a hundred manuscript copies of the *Panormia* survive.[85]

The collections attributed to Ivo bear a strong family resemblance. They all originated, so far as one can tell, in northern France. Their contents testify to a commitment to the goals of the eleventh-century church reform movement, and they draw heavily upon the letters of the reforming popes of that era. They have often been held to have been compiled within a few years of each other around the mid-1090s, although this dating is questionable. All three include decretal letters of Pope Urban II (r. 1088–99). This is scarcely surprising, since Ivo and the pope were closely connected. Urban

---

visional edition of the *Tripartita* is available on the Internet, and a translation of the preface appears in Somerville and Brasington, *Prefaces to Canon Law Books*, 131–32.

82. Kéry, *Canonical Collections*, 237–38; Somerville, *Pope Urban II*, provides a detailed analysis and partial edition of the contents of the *Collectio Britannica*.

83. Kéry, *Canonical Collections*, 250–53; Landau, "Dekret des Ivo von Chartres." The readily available version of Ivo's *Decretum*, found in *PL* 161:47–1022, reproduces an edition first published by Jean Fronteau at Paris in 1647 that, as Landau demonstrates in detail, is extremely unreliable.

84. Although only a half-dozen relatively complete MSS of Ivo's *Decretum* survive, abbreviated versions and excerpts from it are widely distributed (Brett, "Creeping up on the Panormia," 207–8).

85. Kéry, *Canonical Collections*, 253–60; Landau, "Rubriken und Inskriptionen von Ivos Panormie." The title seems to be a Latin neologism compounded from the Greek παν and ὅρμια, meaning something like "a point of departure." It may perhaps have been an adaptation from the common Greek noun πανόρμος, "a seaport;" from which comes the Greek place-name Πανόρμος, Latin *Pan[h]ormus*, i.e., Palermo. The version of the *Panormia* in *PL* 161:1041–1344 reprints (with fresh errors) the faulty edition by Melchior de Vosmédian, which appeared at Louvain in 1557. A new provisional edition by Martin Brett and Bruce Brasington is available on the Internet.

had supported Ivo's election to the see of Chartres and then consecrated him as its bishop. The two men corresponded about church affairs, and Urban sometimes sought Ivo's advice on canonical questions. How far Ivo was personally involved in preparing the canonical collections attributed to him remains an open question, and the problem of dating them is still unresolved.[86]

Despite uncertainties about their author, the collections attributed to Ivo marked an important new stage in the study of canon law. One of them, the *Decretum*, was far more extensive, and another, the *Panormia*, was better organized than any of their predecessors. Ivo believed that the massive accumulation of disparate canons that he and his contemporaries had inherited from earlier generations could be fashioned into a single unified body of law. To accomplish this, he urged canonists to adopt methods such as drawing distinctions between the different senses of terms and analyzing parallel passages from different sources that students of rhetoric, theology, and Roman law had used since late antiquity.[87] The most explicit statement of Ivo's methodological insights and innovations appeared in the elaborate prologue, which appears in numerous manuscripts of both the *Decretum* and the *Panormia*, and was occasionally even included in collections of his letters. Ivo's *Prologue* outlined his vision of what needed to be done in order to refashion the study of canon law into an intellectually rigorous discipline.[88] None of the canonical collections attributed to him, however, actually managed to carry through the program that he envisioned. Ivo's vision of canon law as a discipline was successfully realized only with the appearance in the mid-twelfth century of the *Concordia discordantium canonum*.

GRATIAN AND THE
CONCORDIA DISCORDANTIUM CANONUM

The book attributed to Gratian marked the most important turning point in the maturation of medieval canon law. Powerful regional loyalties, coupled with rudimentary transportation and communications facilities,

---

86. Brett, "Urban II and the Collections Attributed to Ivo," 27–31, 46.

87. Meyer, *Distinktionstechnik in der Kanonistik*, 26–62, 129–43; Grabmann, *Geschichte der scholastischen Methode* 1:240–46; Smalley, *Study of the Bible*, 246–48; Rouse and Rouse, *Authentic Witnesses*, 212–16.

88. Brasington, "Prologue of Ivo of Chartres." A version of Ivo's prologue appeared in the *Collectio Britannica*, where it was credited to Urban II (Kuttner, "Urban II and the Doctrine of Interpretation"). A critical edition appears in Brasington, *Ways of Mercy*, 115–42; for an English translation, see Somerville and Brasington, *Prefaces to Canon Law Books*, 132–58.

meant among other things that the use of earlier canonical collections was often restricted to a single geographical area. It is accordingly problematical to speak of a general European canon law prior to the appearance of the completed version of the *Concordia discordantium canonum*, more often called the *Decretum Gratiani*, around the middle of the twelfth century.[89] The vulgate text of Gratian's Decretum became one of the most widely read books in Western history. This version of the work was copied endlessly throughout western Europe—more than 600 medieval manuscript copies still survive. It was taught as a basic text in schools of canon law everywhere from the middle of the twelfth down to the beginning of the twentieth century. The *Decretum Gratiani* touched off an intellectual transformation that helped to shape the future development of Western legal systems.

Two features distinguish the work from earlier canon law collections: its length and its analytical approach. Gratian's Decretum is enormous. The vulgate text comprises some 3,945 excerpts drawn from a wide range of authorities, including church councils, papal letters, penitentials, Roman civil law, the administrative regulations (or capitularies) of Germanic rulers, and the writings of the church fathers, especially St. Augustine and St. Jerome. The work thus furnished twelfth-century students of canon law with a comprehensive textbook even larger than the massive *Decretum* attributed to Ivo of Chartres.

Far more important, Gratian did something else that neither Ivo nor his predecessors had done. The title *Concordia discordantium canonum* (A Harmony of Dissonant Canons) uses a musical metaphor to describe the author's objective: Gratian's aim was to resolve inconsistent canons that were, so to speak, out of tune with one another and to bring them back into melodious harmony.[90] For this reason, Gratian not only assembled a huge array of texts, but also attempted to weave them into an internally coherent legal system. Gratian's Decretum, unlike its predecessors, analyzed and systematized the

---

89. Kuttner, "Research on Gratian," 4–5; Landau, "Anfänge der Verbreitung des kanonischen Rechts," 411*–429*.

90. This was not the first use of this metaphor in canonical writing, for a mid-sixth century collection attributed to Cresconius bears the title *Concordia canonum*. This was already noted in the twelfth century by Gerard Pucelle, according to the *Lucubratiunculae* of Magister Egidius, and later by Antonio Agustín (1517–86), in *De emendatione Gratiani libri duo* 1.1, at 5–6 (Kuttner and Rathbone, "Anglo-Norman Canonists," 300–301, 343). The expression is also reminiscent of the title *De consonantia canonum* (On the Consonance of the Canons) sometimes given to the prologue of Ivo of Chartres (Kuttner, *Harmony from Dissonance*).

massive body of rules that governed the structure of the Christian church and the conduct of its business. Gratian employed dialectical analysis, especially the technique of making distinctions between terms, as a method to resolve conflicts between authoritative legal texts. He refined this ancient analytical technique, whose use had been pioneered by logicians, philosophers, rhetoricians, and jurists in antiquity, in ways that enabled him to provide reasoned solutions to problems that had vexed church authorities, as well as teachers and students of canon law, for centuries. This method, moreover, could readily be applied to other bodies of law as well.[91]

The structure of the vulgate version of Gratian's Decretum is extremely peculiar. The text is divided into three parts. Part 1 comprises 101 units labeled *distinctiones*. Each distinction consists of a group of canons or chapters (*capitula*) drawn from various authorities, interspersed with comments and analyses (*dicta*) by Gratian. Each distinction treats a single theme or a group of related topics. Part 2 divides its material into thirty-six cases (*causae*). Each case begins with a brief paragraph that describes a problematical situation and then poses one or more questions (*quaestiones*) that address particular issues that this situation presents. A series of canons that relate to the issue raised by each question then follows, usually accompanied by *dicta* that analyze the discrepancies between the canons and, more often than not, propose a solution to the difficulties. Part 3, subtitled *Tractatus de consecratione*, deals with sacramental and liturgical law. This part is divided into five distinctions, each of which contains canons related to a particular topic. Unlike the first two parts of the work, part 3 includes no *dicta*. To complicate matters further, a treatise on penance (*Tractatus de penitentia*) is thrust into the middle of case 33, question 3, and this anomalous segment is subdivided into seven distinctions, on the same pattern as in part 1 of the book.

The odd structure of the finished version of the work that circulated under Gratian's name, as well as its formidable length and the convoluted reasoning that marks many passages, have long suggested that it must have been put together in stages and that some sections were probably interpolated into an earlier version or versions of the text. It seems inherently unlikely in any event that a work of this size and complexity could have been completed at one go.[92]

---

91. Winroth, *Making of Gratian's Decretum*, 194; Kuttner, "Father of the Science of Canon Law," and "Graziano: L'uomo e l'opera"; Meyer, *Distinktionstechnik*, 144–77, 264, 269–71; Berman, *Law and Revolution*, 144–61 and passim.

92. Kuttner, "Revival of Jurisprudence," 320, and "Research on Gratian," 11–15, 18–21; Vetulani, "Gratien et le droit romain," and "Encore un mot sur le droit romain."

Although the earliest manuscripts of the vulgate text do not mention his name, authorship of the *Concordia discordantium canonum* has been attributed to a teacher named Gratian since shortly after the middle of the twelfth century. Just who Gratian was and what else he may have done (other than to compile this book) remain mysterious. Despite numerous confident assertions that have been made about the details of his life and career, scarcely any reliable evidence survives about this shadowy figure.[93] Only one contemporary document is known that might, just perhaps, attest to his existence. This is a judgment rendered by a papal legate, Cardinal Goizo, in a case heard at Venice in 1143. The notary who recorded the judgment noted that the cardinal consulted three experts (*prudentes*) before rendering his decision. One of them was named Gratianus, and he could conceivably have been the mysterious Master Gratian who is said to have been the author of the *Concordia discordantium canonum*. Still, this is no more than speculation.[94] Internal evidence in the text of the Decretum, coupled with remarks of one early commentator also incline some scholars to believe that Gratian may have been a monk, while other evidence, slightly later and considerably less robust, describes him as a bishop.[95] It seems clear, however, that whoever he may have been, Gratian shared the views of the church reformers and that their principles informed the selection of canons that he chose to include in his book.[96]

Even more problematic is the role that Gratian played in the compo-

93. See, e.g., Sarti and Fattorini, *De claris archigymnasii Bononiensis professoribus* 1:330–54; Mesini, "Postille sulla biografia del 'Magister Gratianus.'" For a critical analysis of the evidence, see Noonan, "Gratian Slept Here." Winroth, *Making of Gratian's Decretum*, 5–8, summarizes Noonan's arguments.

94. *Codice diplomatico Padovano* 1:313, no. 419; *Italia pontificia* 5:60. The other two experts, Master Walfredus and Moysis, are described elsewhere as Bolognese lawyers.

95. The early commentator wrote the *Summa Parisiensis*; see C. 2 q. 7 d.p.c. 52 and C. 16 q. 1 c. 61, 115, 181. This unknown author had apparently studied at Bologna and taught canon law at Paris ca. 1170. On Gratian as monk, see Landau, "Quellen und Bedeutung des gratianischen Dekrets," 209*; Kuttner, "Research on Gratian," 6–7; Somerville, "Pope Innocent II," 109–14. But cf. Noonan, "Gratian Slept Here," 151–53 and Winroth, *Making of Gratian's Decretum*, 6. On Gratian as bishop, see Robert of Torigny, *Chronicle*, s.a. 1130, 118. Robert wrote his chronicle about 1180. The claim that Gratian was a bishop also occurs in an anonymous gloss that appears in nine manuscripts written in the third quarter of the twelfth century (Weigand, "Frühe Kanonisten und ihre Karriere," 403*–423*, 432*).

96. Stutz, "Gratian und die Eigenkirchen"; Chodorow, *Christian Political Theory*, 47–64.

sition of the Decretum that bears his name. Scholars have long suspected that the process must have been complex and that perhaps more than one compiler was involved. The awkward placement of the *Tractatus de penitentia* in particular suggests that it was added as an afterthought, while the *Tractatus de consecratione* appears to have been tacked on to the end of a more-or-less finished work.[97] Scattered through the body of the work, moreover, are more than a hundred chapters labeled *palea*, which are certainly additions to an earlier version of the text.[98]

Manuscript evidence to support these conjectures, however, seemed lacking until 1996, when Anders Winroth announced his discovery of a recension of Gratian's Decretum earlier and considerably shorter than the vulgate text in manuscripts held by libraries at Paris, Barcelona, Florence, and Admont in Austria.[99] Close analysis of sample portions of the text found in those manuscripts and comparison of that text with the standard edition of the vulgate text demonstrated that the earlier version of the Decretum was shorter, more coherent, and markedly easier to follow.

The early version of the Decretum in Winroth's four manuscripts was probably written not long after 1140, while the vulgate version was finished perhaps as much as a decade later. Other scholars hastened to examine the four manuscripts that contained the earlier recension soon after Winroth's announcement of his discovery. Their findings corroborated many of Winroth's conclusions but raised further questions.[100]

---

97. The later insertion of the *Tractatus de penitentia* was persuasively argued by Karol Wojtyła (later Pope John Paul II), "Le traité de 'Penitentia' de Gratien"; see also Rambaud-Buhot, "Le plan," in Le Bras, Lefebvre, and Rambaud, *L'âge classique*, 82–90, and Landau, "Quellen und Bedeutung des gratianischen Dekrets," 217*. On the appending of the *Tractatus de consecratione*, see Rambaud-Buhot, in *L'âge classique*, 90–99; Chodorow, *Christian Political Theory*, 12–13; Van Engen, "Observations on 'De consecratione.'"

98. Rambaud-Buhot, "Les additions," in *L'âge classique*, 100–114.

99. Winroth reported his findings at the Tenth International Congress of Medieval Canon Law. A version of his paper appeared under the title "The Two Recensions of Gratian's Decretum," supplemented by "Les deux Gratiens et le droit romain." A fuller treatment followed with the publication in 2000 of the *Making of Gratian's Decretum*.

100. Winroth, *Making of Gratian's Decretum*, 137–44. Responses included notably Weigand, "Chancen und Probleme einer baldigen kritischen Edition der ersten Redaktion des Dekrets Gratians"; Viejo-Ximénez, "La redacción original de C. 29 del Decreto de Graciano," and "'Concordia' y 'Decretum' del maestro Graciano," (but cf. again Winroth, *Making of Gratian's Decretum*, 31–32).

In 1999, Carlos Larrainzar announced that he had found another, even shorter, recension of the Decretum in manuscript 673 of the monastery of St. Gall in Switzerland. The St. Gall manuscript contains most of the cases that constitute the second part of the vulgate recension, followed by 233 miscellaneous canonistic texts, most of which appear, although in a different arrangement, in the first part of the vulgate version. The physical layout of this manuscript, with its rubricated headings and decorated initials, as well as the 214 glosses that appear in its margins, indicate that this was a finished product in its own right and may have been used as a text for teaching.[101] Larrainzar argued that the St. Gall manuscript represents the first draft of Gratian's Decretum, an argument that carries considerable weight because the cases it contains lie at the heart of the work. They are clearly the product of classroom expositions, and the situations that they present are almost certainly derived from situations that arose in the courts.[102] Winroth and Titus Lenherr, however, maintain that the St. Gall manuscript represents an abbreviation of the vulgate text rather than its original form.[103]

While the suspicion that the Decretum ascribed to Gratian took shape in stages has been confirmed, we are little wiser about the identity of the compiler. Winroth believes that at least two compilers put the *Concordia discordantium canonum* together, and this may well be true.

---

101. Larrainzar, "El borrador de la 'Concordia' de Graciano." A detailed list of its contents appears at 652–66. The manuscript itself is now available on the Web site of the Codices Electronici Sangallenses project (http://www.cesg.unifr.ch/de/index.htm). See as well his "Datos sobre la antiguidad del manuscrito Sg." See also his "Datos sobre la antiguidad del manuscrito Sg." Larrainzar also argued that the MS in the Biblioteca Nazionale Centrale in Florence that Winroth had used actually represented a separate redaction of Gratian's Decretum, intermediate between the one earlier identified by Winroth and the vulgate text (Larrainzar, "El Decreto de Graciano del códice Fd."). Winroth rejected this argument in "Le manuscrit florentin du Décret de Gratien."

102. Brett, "Canon Law and Litigation," 28. Kenneth Pennington vigorously insisted on the primacy of the cases in the composition of Gratian's work in "Gratian, Causa 19, and the Birth of Canonical Jurisprudence."

103. Winroth, "Le Décret de Gratien et le manuscrit florentin;" Lenherr, "Ist die Handschrift 673 der St. Galler Stiftsbibliothek (Sg) der Entwurf zu Gratians Dekret?" See also Paxton, "Gratian's Thirteenth Case"; Sommar, "Gratian's Causa VII." For the current state of the problem and further bibliography, see Winroth, "Recent Work on the Making of Gratian's Decretum."

Nothing in the evidence, however, demands that more than one author be involved. The principle of economy suggests that one should provisionally assume, as near contemporaries clearly did, that at least the final version of the Decretum was the product of a single writer named Gratian, although he may well have incorporated work by others into his own collection.

The St. Gall manuscript of the Decretum strongly reinforces an assumption that canonists have held since the third quarter of the twelfth century, namely, that Gratian was a teacher. The earliest *summa* on Gratian's work, written by Paucapalea probably in the second half of the 1150s, referred to its author as *magister*, the term commonly used to describe a teacher at that period, and early manuscripts of the vulgate text of the Decretum also identify its author as "Magister Gratianus."[104] As mentioned, the cases that form the central element of the St. Gall text (and the largest part of the vulgate recension) seem very much the product of classroom teaching. Positing hypothetical situations and framing questions based on them was a well-established technique for teaching law, one that had been used in the Roman law schools of antiquity and that twelfth-century teachers of Roman law continued to employ in Gratian's day.[105] The recensions of Gratian's Decretum, especially the version in the St. Gall manuscript, are emphatically academic law books designed for, and responding to, the needs of teachers rather than practitioners.[106]

One of the most persuasive indications that Gratian's Decretum was primarily intended for teaching appears at its very beginning. The first ten distinctions of part 1, which medieval teachers often labeled the treatise on laws (*Tractatus de legibus*), formed one of Gratian's most original contributions to the development of canon law as an autonomous academic enterprise. These ten distinctions have no close parallels in earlier canonical collections. They gave teachers an opportunity to provide their students at

---

104. Paucapalea, *Summa*, 3.

105. See Frier, *Rise of the Roman Jurists*, 157–71, and Liebs, "Rechtsschulen und Rechtsunterricht," 244–75, on the origins of these techniques in antiquity; and for twelfth-century examples, *Quaestiones dominorum Bononiensium* and *Le questioni civilistiche del secolo XII*, ed. Belloni. See further Kantorowicz, "Quaestiones Disputatae," and *Studies*, 81–85, 246–53; Bellomo, "Legere, repetere, disputare"; Fransen, "Questions disputées dans les facultés de droit."

106. Paxton, "Gratian's Thirteenth Case," observes that C. 13 contains Gratian's principal attempt to address the problems of practice.

the outset with an intellectual framework for their studies. They were, at best, only marginally useful for advocates in the courtroom.[107]

The arrangement of the material in all the versions of Gratian's work is fundamentally inappropriate for use by practitioners, who need to be able to locate material relating to the problems they are dealing with readily and reliably. That this problem did not escape the notice of practicing lawyers is evident from two other twelfth-century efforts to recast the Decretum in a form that responded better to the demands of practice.[108] Neither revision caught on, presumably because Gratian's version of the Decretum met classroom needs so well that law teachers preferred its vulgate form. The vulgate Decretum retained its place as a basic textbook in the schools of canon law throughout the Middle Ages, and practitioners found ways to live with it by preparing elaborate sets of cross-references and indices so that they could find what they needed.[109]

GRATIAN'S SOURCES

The nearly 4,000 chapters or canons that make up the vulgate recension of Gratian's Decretum draw upon a vast range of authorities. These include biblical texts, church councils (ecumenical, regional, and local), papal letters, dozens of patristic writers from the early centuries of the church's history (Saints Augustine, Ambrose, and Jerome feature most prominently

---

107. See Katherine Christensen's introduction to Gratian, *Treatise on Laws with the Ordinary Gloss*, xxi–xxvii.

108. Southern's suggestion in *Scholastic Humanism* 1:303–4 that Gratian was basically a legal practitioner, rather than an academic teacher, altogether ignores this fundamental problem. See also Winroth's comments in *Making of Gratian's Decretum*, 7–8. The earlier of the revised versions is the *Summa "Elegantius in iure diuino,"* sometimes called the *Summa Coloniensis*. It was completed about 1169 and may well have been the work of Bertram of Metz; see the edition by Fransen and Kuttner. The other is the *Compilatio decretorum* prepared by Cardinal Laborans (d. 1190); see Martin, "*Compilatio decretorum* des Kardinals Laborans."

109. Brett, "Canon Law and Litigation," 23–24. As more law was created in the thirteenth century and beyond, Gratian's Decretum came to be viewed as the repository of the church's older law, and its prominence in law school curricula gradually dwindled. It continued to maintain a place as the foundation upon which the new law rested until the promulgation of the *Codex iuris canonici* by Pope Benedict XV in 1917. That code was displaced in its turn by the new *Codex iuris canonici* of Pope John Paul II in 1983. Even so, much of Gratian's material remains embedded in the most recent version of the code.

among them), penitential writers, Roman law, and the laws of the Germanic kingdoms.[110] We have no reason to believe that Gratian (however many of him there may have been) consulted all, or even any, of these material sources of his collection in their original form and context. The compilers of earlier canonical collections had done that work long since, and Gratian found most of the authorities he needed readily available in a handful of collections that comprised his formal sources.[111] The great majority of the authorities that Gratian drew upon seem to have come from the *Collectio canonum* of Bishop Anselm of Lucca (d. 1086), the *Collectio canonum* of Cardinal Polycarp (d. 1113), the *Collection in Three Books* (ca. 1112), the *Decretum* of Burchard of Worms, the *Tripartita*, and Ivo's *Panormia*.[112]

The selections from Roman law sources that appear in the vulgate recension of Gratian's work pose special problems. The early redaction of the Decretum in Winroth's four manuscripts contains significantly fewer excerpts from Roman law than appear in the vulgate, and many of these were taken from the *Codex Theodosianus*, rather than from Justinian's codification. Gratian probably took these passages from earlier canonical collections. The vulgate text of the Decretum depended more heavily and more directly than earlier versions upon Justinian. The vulgate recension also used Roman law texts and concepts with greater assurance and sophistication than earlier versions had done.[113] This perhaps indicates that the Decretum began to take shape while the teaching of Roman law at Bologna was still in its early stages and that the final, or vulgate, version of Gratian's text was only completed after the study of Roman law had become well established.

---

110. The Roman law selections in the vulgate version of the Decretum have been intensively studied because they provide important clues to the history of the collection's formation. See Vetulani, "Gratien et le droit romain" and "Encore un mot sur le droit romain "; as well as Kuttner, "New Studies on the Roman Law," and "Additional Notes on the Roman Law"; Rambaud-Buhot, in *L'âge classique*, 60–66; Winroth, *Making of Gratian's Decretum*, 146–74.

111. Landau, "Neue Forschungen zu vorgratianischen Kanonessammlungen," and "Quellen und Bedeutung des gratianischen Dekrets," 211*–212*; but note also Pennington's caveats in "Gratian, Causa 19, and the Birth of Canonical Jurisprudence," 354. For the distinction between formal and material sources, see van Hove, *Prolegomena*, 48.

112. Kéry, *Canonical Collections*, 218–27, 266–71; Landau, "Burchard de Worms et Gratien." Thaner's edition of Anselm's collection is incomplete and must be supplemented by Cushing, *Papacy and Law*.

113. Winroth, *Making of Gratian's Decretum*, 148–57. See also the analysis of Gratian's procedural law by Basdevant-Gaudemet, "Les sources de droit romain," 220–27.

Gratian's Decretum and the Teaching of Canon Law

Although canon law was certainly studied and sometimes formally taught before the middle of the twelfth century in monastic and cathedral schools, as well as in schools attached to communities of canons, it was not at that point treated as an autonomous discipline, independent from theology.[114] Gratian's contemporaries tended to think of canon law in theological terms: for them it was, so to speak, applied theology.[115] It is thus scarcely surprising to find that a great many excerpts from authorities that appear in Gratian's work also appear in the *Sentences* of his contemporary, Peter Lombard (b. ca. 1095, d. 1160). Just as Gratian's book became the most successful and widely used textbook of canon law, so the Lombard's book, *Sententiae in IV libros distinctae*, became the most successful and widely used textbook of theology through the later Middle Ages.[116] The close ties between theology and canon law began to loosen shortly after the appearance of Gratian's Decretum.[117]

The Decretum that bears Gratian's name was first and foremost an amazingly successful tool for teaching, and intending clergymen continued to study it in preparation for ordination for more than seven hundred years. It provided teachers with abundant material that encompassed the whole of the legal system that the Western Church had elaborated during the first millennium of its existence. Even more important, it showed students how to analyze that mass of accumulated material in ways that resolved a good many inconsistencies that had bedeviled earlier generations of teachers.

---

114. The glosses that appear in some MSS of pre-Gratian canonical collections show that these collections were studied thoughtfully and may have been used for teaching in monastic and other schools (Brasington, "Glossing Strategies"). Delhaye, "L'organisation scolaire," provides a useful guide to the differences between the various types of schools.

115. Thus, e.g., the preface to the *Summa "Antiquitate et tempore"* declared, "Unde palam est, summam quandam totius theologiae paginae contineri in hoc libro, nec hunc librum perfecte scienti deesse posse universitatis sacrae paginae notitiam" (quoted in Schulte, *QL* 1:249; an English translation of this passage appears in Somerville and Brasington, *Prefaces to Canon Law Books*, 202–12). This *summa* (also known as Pseudo-Rufinus) dates from the 1170s (Kuttner, *Repertorium der Kanonistik*, 178–79).

116. On Peter Lombard generally, see Colish, *Peter Lombard*. A medieval fable even asserted that Gratian and Peter Lombard were born of the same mother (Stickler, *Historia iuris canonici*, 203; Boureau, "Droit et théologie," 1113).

117. Ghellinck, *Le mouvement théologique*, 203–13, 416–510.

THE DECRETIST SCHOOLS

The Bolognese School

The earliest known teacher to use Gratian's work as a textbook was Paucapalea, but details about his career are almost as scarce as those for Gratian. Paucapalea, like Gratian, was almost certainly a cleric who taught canon law at Bologna sometime between 1146 and 1165.[118] We know that Paucapalea based his teaching on the vulgate version of Gratian's book because his *Summa*, the written product of his teaching, took the form of a systematic commentary on Gratian's work and refers specifically to the vulgate text. Paucapalea was the earliest in what soon became a distinguished line of Bolognese teachers of canon law who centered their teaching on Gratian's Decretum and hence came to be called decretists.[119]

Students from regions beyond the Alps and overseas had begun arriving in Bologna to study canon law certainly by the 1160s and probably some years before that. The city by that time had established its reputation as the foremost European center for the study of Roman law and quickly became equally attractive for students of canon law as well. The decretists who taught there during the second half of the twelfth century included numerous able jurists and a handful of brilliant ones. Noteworthy among the Bolognese masters of this period were Rolandus (fl. late 1150s),[120] Rufi-

---

118. Paucapalea, *Summa* to D. 63, at 39, refers to a decretal of Pope Eugene III (r. 1145–53) dated at the end of June 1146 (JL 9658), so that his work cannot be earlier than that. He appears as a witness in a charter dated at Bologna, 13 November 1165 (*CSB* 3:120–21, no. 105). Noonan, "The True Paucapalea?" suggested that this work might not be the work of Paucapalea. Rudolf Weigand, however, strongly rejected this contention in "Paucapalea und die frühe Kanonistik." See also his "Frühe Kanonisten und ihre Karriere," 404*.

119. Paucapalea's *Summa* can only be dated approximately to sometime in the decade of the 1150s. Some twenty MSS copies survive (Kuttner, *Repertorium der Kanonistik*, 125–27; Weigand, "Paucapalea und die frühe Kanonistik"). The term *decretista* was in use around the beginning of the thirteenth century; it appears in the *Summa super Codicem* of Azo, completed between 1208 and 1210 (Savigny, *Geschichte* 3:516 n. c).

120. The decretist Rolandus named Gratian as the author of the *Decretum*—"Magister Gratianus . . . hoc opus composuit"—in the preface to his commentary on it (*Summa magistri Rolandi*, 4). Thaner's edition conflates two distinct works and a better edition is needed (Kuttner, "Did Rolandus of Bologna write a 'Stroma ex Decretorum corpore carptum'?"). Master Rolandus the canonist was long thought to be Rolandus Bandinelli, who became Pope Alexander III (r. 1159–81). That identification has now

nus (d. before 1192),[121] Stephen of Tournai (1135–1203),[122] and, greatest of them all, Huguccio (d. 1210).[123]

The French Schools

Some version of Gratian's Decretum became known among jurists in southern France, perhaps as early as the mid-1140s. The *Quoniam egestas*, an *abbreviatio*, or shortened version, of Gratian's text possibly written for students of Roman civil law who needed a brief introduction to canon law, appeared in the Midi around 1150.[124] Unlike their contemporaries in northern France and the rest of northern Europe, however, jurists in the south of France, with few exceptions, chose overwhelmingly to focus their legal studies on the texts of Justinian's *Corpus iuris civilis*.[125]

---

been shown to be mistaken (Noonan, "Who Was Rolandus?" 21–48; Weigand, "Magister Rolandus und Papst Alexander III").

121. Rufinus studied and taught canon law at Bologna from the 1150s onward. His *Summa decretorum*, written about 1164, is longer and more detailed than earlier commentaries on the Decretum. It exercised wide influence among later decretists, especially those of the French school (Benson, "Rufin," in *DDC* 7:779–84; Gouron, "Sur les sources civilistes"). Conventional accounts of Rufinus' career have recently been questioned by Deutinger, "The Decretist Rufinus"

122. Stephen of Tournai, a native of Orléans, studied Roman law at Bologna under Bulgarus and canon law under Rufinus. Stephen later returned to France, first to Orléans, where he became a canon of St. Euverte, then in 1176 to Paris, where he became abbot of Sainte-Geneviève and served as a counselor to King Philip Augustus (r. 1179–1223). In 1191 Stephen was named bishop of Tournai. His *Summa* on Gratian's *Decretum*, written while he was teaching at Bologna between 1166 and 1169, was greatly influenced by the views of Rufinus. See Kalb, *Studien zur Summa Stephans von Tournai*; Weigand, "Studien zum kanonistischen Werk Stephans von Tournai"; Landau, "Bürgschaft und Darlehen im Dekretalenrechts."

123. Huguccio taught canon law at Bologna beginning in the 1170s and completed his *Summa decretorum* in or around 1188. His work was extremely influential among later canonists, and forty-two manuscript copies of it are known to survive. From 1190 until his death in 1210, he was bishop of Ferrara (Müller, *Huguccio*). Although modern scholars have published numerous extracts from manuscripts of Huguccio's *Summa*, the work as a whole has yet to appear in print.

124. Kuttner, *Repertorium der Kanonistik*, 263–64; Gouron, "Une école ou des écoles?" and *La science juridique française*, 76–78.

125. Gouron, "Canon Law in Parisian Circles," 503; Poly, "Les légistes provençaux," 613–35. Two important exceptions were Raymond des Arènes (fl. 1160–70), who may have been the glossator known as Cardinalis, and the "Master G." who owned the

Regular teaching of the Decretum apparently commenced in the schools of Paris during the late 1160s. Decretists who taught in those schools produced several important commentaries on Gratian's work.[126] While the authors of most of the Parisian *summae* are unknown, individuals believed to have belonged to the Parisian school of decretists included (apart from Stephen of Tournai) the elder Peter of Blois, author of a set of distinctions published under the title *Speculum iuris canonici* (ca. 1180), Odo of Dover, Everard d'Ypres, Gerard Pucelle, and Sicard of Cremona (b. ca. 1155, d. 1215), author of a widely circulated *summa*.[127]

The Parisian decretist school, like other north European schools, was

---

manuscript that is now British Library, Royal 11.B.XIV (Kantorowicz, *Studies*, 13–28; Loschiavo, "Sulle tracce bolognesi del Cardinalis").

126. Fragmentary evidence suggests that canon law may have been taught at Paris as early as ca. 1165 (Gouron, "Une école des canonistes anglais"). On the subsequent history of the Parisian school of decretists, see above all Kuttner, "Débuts de l'école canoniste française," and Gouron, "Une école ou des écoles?"; also Lefebvre-Teillard, "Magister A. sur l'école de droit canonique parisienne" and "Petrus Brito legit." On the commentaries, see Kuttner, *Repertorium der Kanonistik*, 59–66, 177–80, 206–7; Stelzer, *Gelehrtes Recht in Österreich*, 44–59; Stickler, "Zum Apparat 'Animal est substantia.'"

127. On the elder Peter of Blois's *Opusculum de distinctionibus*, see Kuttner, *Repertorium der Kanonistik*, 220–22, and Lefebvre, "Pierre de Blois." The elder Peter, archdeacon of Dreux in the diocese of Chartres, is often confused with the younger Peter of Blois, the polymath archdeacon of Bath (d. 1211) and author of a widely admired letter collection (see Southern, *Scholastic Humanism* 2:178–218). On Odo of Dover, see Kuttner, *Repertorium der Kanonistik*, 172–77, and "Sur les origines du terme 'droit positif,'" 730–31. Everard d'Ypres was a Cistercian monk of the abbey of Clairvaux, author of a *Summa decretalium questionum*, which is essentially an abbreviated version of the *Summa* of Sicard of Cremona (Kuttner, *Repertorium der Kanonistik*, 187–90; Häring, "The Cistercian Everard of Ypres," 144–46, 730–31). Gerard Pucelle belonged to the circle of John of Salisbury and Thomas Becket (John of Salisbury, *Letters* 2:68–71, 210–29, 394–97, 578–79, 590–99, 684–91, nos. 158, 184–86, 226, 275, 277, 297; Herbert of Bosham, *Vita S. Thomae* 7.1.6, in *Materials* 3:525). He taught at Paris, where Walter Map and Luke of Hungary were among his pupils (Walter Map, *De nugis curialium* 2.7, at 142; Kuttner and Rathbone, "Anglo-Norman Canonists," 296–303). Gerard was also an administrator and practitioner in the courts, as well as a teacher (*The Chronicle of Battle Abbey*, 328–34; Donahue, "Gerard Pucelle as a Canon Lawyer"). One of his opinions appears in the *Summa "Omnis qui iuste iudicat"* (Kuttner, *Repertorium der Kanonistik*, 197 n. 3). For Sicard of Cremona, see Kuttner, *Repertorium der Kanonistik*, 150–53, and "Zur Biographie des Sicardus von Cremona"; Lefebvre, "Sicard de Crémone."

short-lived. Parisian decretists formed an identifiable group for roughly a generation, between about 1170 and 1210.[128] Several decretists who taught for part of their careers at Paris during that period also figured in the establishment of canon law teaching elsewhere in northern Europe, notably in the Rhineland and in the Anglo-Norman realm.

The Rhineland School

Systematic teaching of canon law began in Germany within two decades after the completion of the vulgate version of Gratian's Decretum and spread fairly rapidly thereafter. It centered principally in the Rhineland, especially at Cologne and Mainz.[129] The earliest evidence that Gratian's work was being systematically studied in Germany appears in a procedural manual known as the *Rhetorica ecclesiastica* written around 1160 or 1161. The *Rhetorica* originated as a textbook among Premonstratensian canons in the area around Hildesheim. The most sophisticated and intellectually impressive product of the Rhineland canonists, the *Summa "Elegantius in iure diuino"* (also known as the *Summa Coloniensis*), drew in part upon the *Rhetorica ecclesiastica*.[130] Although the author of the *Summa "Elegantius"* has not been securely identified, it has been plausibly suggested that he may have been Bertram (or Bertrand) of Metz who studied at Paris and taught at Cologne. He was also the author of *Sepenumero in iudiciis*, a treatise on proof.[131] Other Rhineland canonists who wrote on procedural matters included Renerius, a canon of St. Andreas in Cologne, and Eilbert of Bremen. Gerard Pucelle also taught briefly at Cologne.[132] Sicard of Cremona is another identifiable

---

128. Gouron, "Une école ou des écoles?" 232–34.

129. Scattered evidence suggests that canon law was taught at Bamberg as well, and may also have been studied in Bavaria around 1180. See Landau, "Anfänge der Verbreitung des kanonischen Rechts," 419*–422*; Fried, "Bamberger Domschule," and "Rezeption Bologneser Wissenschaft in Deutschland."

130. *Die Rhetorica ecclesiastica*, ed. Wahrmund; Fowler-Magerl, *Ordo iudiciorum*, 45–56, and *Ordines iudiciarii*, 58, 120; Landau, "Die 'Rhetorica ecclesiastica,'" 129.

131. Kuttner, "Bertram of Metz"; Fowler-Magerl, *Ordo iudiciorum*, 219–20.

132. Renerius's brief procedural treatise, *Hactenus Magister*, written sometime after 1167, has been edited by Fowler-Magerl in *Ordo iudiciorum*, 290–93; see also 87. Eilbert of Bremen dedicated the procedural *Ordo* that he wrote after 1192 to Bishop Wolfgang of Passau; *Ordo judiciarius des Eilbert von Bremen*, ed. Wahrmund; see also Fowler-Magerl, *Ordo iudiciorum*, 122; Stelzer, "Eilbert von Bremen"; Landau, "Eilbert von Bremen, Eilbert von Hildesheim und die jüngere Hildesheimer Briefsammlung." On Gerard Pucelle's brief tenure at Cologne, see Fried, "Gerard Pucelle und Köln."

canonist who taught for a time in the Rhineland—at Mainz from about 1179 to 1183. In addition, the Rhineland decretists produced several further anonymous canonistic works.[133]

The Anglo-Norman School

Study of Gratian's Decretum began slightly later in the Anglo-Norman realm. The first full-scale commentary from the Anglo-Norman decretist school was the *Summa "De multiplici iuris diuisione,"* which dates from around 1170. It relies heavily on Stephen of Tournai's *Summa*, which, as we have seen, also formed a link between the Bolognese and Parisian schools of canon law. *De multiplici iuris diuisione* was followed a few years later (certainly before 1179) by another anonymous work, the *Summa "De iure naturali."*[134] We may reasonably infer from these two treatises that canon law was being taught from Gratian's textbook, probably in England, by the early 1170s.

We certainly know that skilled canonical practitioners were available there at the same period. One of these, Master David of London (d. after 1189), had studied at Clermont and later at Paris, before becoming a law student at Bologna. He had been there nearly three years when Gilbert Foliot, bishop of London, wrote to him in or about 1168. In 1169 David represented Foliot in an appeal to the papal court and was still advising clients at the curia until about 1173.[135] When he returned to England shortly thereafter, he brought with him testimonials from Pope Alexander III and several cardinals, who praised his forensic skills.[136] Exactly when Master Da-

133. These include the *Distinctiones "Si mulier eadem hora" seu Monacenses* (ca. 1170), as well as the *summae Antiquitate et tempore* (after 1170) and *Quoniam omissis*, and the gloss apparatus *Militant siquidem patroni* (ca. 1203–10). See Kuttner, *Repertorium der Kanonistik*, 178–79, 215–16, 326; Dolezalek, "Another Fragment of the Apparatus 'Militant siquidem patroni'"; Kuttner and Rathbone, "Anglo-Norman Canonists," 298–99; Landau, "Anfänge der Verbreitung des kanonischen Rechts," 419*–420*, and "Walter von Coutances."

134. Helmholz, *Canon Law and Ecclesiastical Jurisdiction*, 128–32; Kuttner, *Repertorium der Kanonistik*, 139–41, and "Notes on Manuscripts," 533–34; Kuttner and Rathbone, "Anglo-Norman Canonists," 293; Legendre, "Miscellanea Britannica," 494; Nörr, "Die Summen 'De iure naturali' und 'De multiplici iuris divisione.'"

135. Brooke, "Register of Master David," 236–37; Foliot, *Letters and Charters*, 262 (no. 190), 274–75, 280–82 (nos. 210–11), 520–21.

136. These recommendations served him well, for King Henry II (r. 1155–89) awarded him an annual pension of 20 pounds, and Gilbert Foliot gave him an additional 10 pounds per year from the revenues of the archdeaconry of Middlesex

vid wrote the glosses that bear his name is not certain, but they probably represent his teaching at Bologna, before his return to England. There is no evidence that David of London taught canon law in England, nor, so far as we know, did William of Canterbury, who made skillful use of Gratian's Decretum and the *Summa* of Rufinus in his account (written between 1172 and 1174) of the discord between Thomas Becket and Henry II.[137] Still, David of London and William of Canterbury make it plain that the English church by the 1170s was supplied with serious experts in canon law. Further evidence of Anglo-Normal canonical scholarship continued to appear in the following decade. The *Summa "Omnis qui iuste iudicat,"* or *Summa Lipsiensis* (written 1186), gives evidence that its unknown author was familiar with recent French and Bolognese literature.[138]

By the mid-1180s, a talented group of decretists were teaching canon law in schools at Oxford. The central figure among them was John of Tynemouth (d. ca. 1221).[139] His colleagues included Simon of Sywell, who had learned his canon law at Bologna,[140] Master Honorius, who had stud-

---

(Brooke, "Register of Master David," 238–39, 245). Thirty pounds was a substantial annual income for an English cleric in the late twelfth century (Moorman, *Church Life in England*, 110–37).

137. Kuttner and Rathbone, "Anglo-Norman Canonists," 286; Weigand, *Glossen zum Dekret Gratians* 2:625–31; William of Canterbury, *Vita et passio S. Thomae*, in *Materials* 1:25–29; Duggan, "The Reception of Canon Law," 361–65, 378–82.

138. Kuttner, *Repertorium der Kanonistik*, 196–98; Kuttner and Rathbone, "Anglo-Norman Canonists," 290, 292, 294–96; Weigand, "Anglo-Normannische Kanonistik," 257–59.

139. Abbot Samson of Bury St. Edmunds entertained the group at a dinner in Oxford in the 1190s (Jocelin of Brakelond, *Chronicle*, 94–95). On John of Tynemouth, see Kuttner, *Repertorium der Kanonistik*, 22–23, 251–52; Kuttner and Rathbone, "Anglo-Norman Canonists," 317–27; Cheney, *English Bishops' Chanceries*, 11–14, 20, 129, 158, and *Hubert Walter*, 165, Smith, "The 'Officialis' of the Bishop," 214; *BRUO* 3:1923. John represented Gerald of Wales's opponent in litigation over succession to the bishopric of St. David's, which led to bad blood between the two. John later was responsible for Gerald's arrest in France; subsequently Gerald gleefully seized the opportunity to pay him back when John, in his turn, was imprisoned (Brewer, introduction to his edition of Gerald's *Opera* 1:lxxxii–lxxxiv). On the date of John's death, see Guala Bicchieri, *Letters and Charters*, 17, no. 21.

140. Kuttner and Rathbone, "Anglo-Norman Canonists," 317–21, 326–27; Cheney, *English Bishops' Chanceries*, 11, 13, 79 n. 2, 158, and *Hubert Walter*, 165–66; Smith, "The 'Officialis' of the Bishop," 213–14; *BRUO* 3:1704; Zulueta and Stein, introduction to *Teaching of Roman Law*, li.

ied at Paris,[141] Nicholas de l'Aigle (d. 1217),[142] John of Kent,[143] and Simon of Derby.[144]

One of their students, Thomas of Marlborough (d. 1236), became primarily a legal practitioner. He studied canon law at Oxford with John of Tynemouth, Simon of Sywell, and Master Honorius between 1188 and 1193 and later spent six months studying Roman law at Bologna under Azo (fl. 1190–20). After teaching briefly at Exeter and in the Oxford schools, Thomas entered the Abbey of Evesham in 1199 or 1200 and became a Benedictine monk.[145] This did not by any means spell the end of his legal career, for Thomas spent much of his monastic life in the courts rather than the cloister, litigating on behalf of Evesham. Although Thomas was by and large a successful litigator, the cost of his efforts nearly bankrupted the monastery. The monks elected him their abbot (whether out of gratitude or revenge would be difficult to say) in 1229. After another fight, he finally took office in 1230 and held it for the remainder of his life.[146]

The work of Thomas of Marlborough's teachers in the circle of John of Tynemouth is known principally from the *Quaestiones Londonenses*, a report of questions debated in the canon law schools at Oxford, and the Caius glosses, a record of the comments of the various Oxford masters on pas-

---

141. Kuttner and Rathbone, "Anglo-Norman Canonists," 296, 304–16; Cheney, *English Bishops' Chanceries*, 11, 12, 158, and *Hubert Walter*, 164–65; Smith, "The 'Officialis' of the Bishop," 215–16; Weigand, "Bemerkungen über die Schriften und Lehren des Magister Honorius," as well as "Die Anglo-Normannische Kanonistik," 259, and *Glossen zum Dekret Gratians* 2:655–57; *English Episcopal Acta, III*, 55, no. 384.

142. Kuttner and Rathbone, "Anglo-Norman Canonists," 317, 320; *BRUO* 1:560; *The Acta of the Bishops of Chichester, 1075–1207*, 196, no. 146.

143. Kuttner and Rathbone, "Anglo-Norman Canonists," 320; Goering, "The 'Summa de penitentia' of John of Kent"; *BRUO* 2:1037. Also active at the same time, although perhaps not at Oxford, was William Longchamp (d. 1197), who wrote a procedural treatise, *Practica legum et decretorum*, between about 1183 and 1189 (Fowler-Magerl, *Ordo iudiciorum*, 113–14). Longchamp seems not to have been part of John of Tynemouth's circle.

144. Little is known about Simon of Derby, save that he is mentioned in two of the *Quaestiones Londonenses* (London, BL MS Royal 9.E.VII, qq. 3 and 4 on 191rb) and appeared as a witness in a handful of charters, mainly at Lichfield (*BRUO* 1:571–72).

145. Thomas of Marlborough, *History of the Abbey of Evesham*, 232–34, §230; 310, §313; 484, §516. See also Kuttner and Rathbone, "Anglo-Norman Canonists," 316; Cheney, *Hubert Walter*, 13, 164–65; Boyle, "Beginnings of Legal Studies at Oxford," 113–14; *BRUO* 2:1223–24.

146. Knowles, *Monastic Order in England*, 335.

sages in the Decretum. The unique manuscript that contains these glosses has since migrated to Cambridge.[147]

By the 1190s, the canon law schools at Oxford were sufficiently well known that foreign students had begun to appear there, one of them from as far away as Hungary.[148] The fame of Oxford's canon law schools soon began to diminish, however, as the masters in John of Tynemouth's group departed, one after another, to take up positions in ecclesiastical administration. Simon of Sywell may have been the first to leave. He became a canon of Lincoln Cathedral, perhaps as early as 1184, although this need not mean that he was seen no more at Oxford, which lay within the boundaries of the Lincoln diocese.[149] Master Honorius held a parish in Kent from 1184 or 1185, although it is not certain that he spent much time there. After he became *officialis* of the archbishop of York in 1195, however, he ceased to teach at Oxford. Nicholas de l'Aigle departed when he was appointed dean of Chichester Cathedral around 1197, a post that he held until his death in 1217.[150] John of Tynemouth himself was the last to leave. He finally joined

---

147. The *Quaestiones Londonenses* is now in London, whence the name (British Library MS Royal 9.E.VII, at 191ra–198vb; Kuttner, *Repertorium der Kanonistik*, 251–52; Kuttner and Rathbone, "Anglo-Norman Canonists," 319–20). A few selections from them have been published (Brundage, "A Twelfth-Century Oxford Disputation," "The Crusade of Richard I," and "Treatment of Marriage in the *Quaestiones Londonenses*"). On the Caius glosses (Cambridge, Gonville and Caius College, MS 283/676), see Kuttner, *Repertorium der Kanonistik*, 22–23; Kuttner and Rathbone, "Anglo-Norman Canonists, 317–19.

148. Nicholas of Hungary received a stipend from King Richard I to support his study of canon law at Oxford. Two brothers from Frisia, Addo and Emo, were also studying law at Oxford from about 1190. They were evidently serious students (at least as Emo later recalled), who spent their nights copying the Decretum, the decretals, and the *Liber pauperum*, together with other books of civil and canon law (*Emonis et Menkonis Werumensium Chronicon*, 467, 531; Kuttner and Rathbone, "Anglo-Norman Canonists," 323–24; *BRUO* 1:14, 641).

149. From 1189 to 1193, Simon was a member of the household of St. Hugh of Avalon, bishop of Lincoln, no doubt as a legal adviser. In or about 1193 he joined the household of archbishop Hubert Walter, and then became treasurer of Lichfield Cathedral, a position that he retained for the rest of his life (*BRUO* 3:1704).

150. Honorius's career as *officialis* was brief, for he soon fell out with the archbishop, Geoffrey Plantagenet. In 1198 he was named archdeacon of Richmond, although his appointment was vigorously contested. By 1203, Honorius had left York to join Hubert Walter's household. Lengthy and expensive litigation over his archdeaconry led Honorius to borrow more money from the king than he could repay: in 1208 his property was confiscated and he was imprisoned at Gloucester. See *BRUO* 2:956–57, and on Nicholas de l'Aigle, *BRUO* 1:560.

the household of Hubert Walter in 1198, as several of his colleagues had done earlier. Unlike them, John returned to Oxford in 1214, this time not as a teacher but as archdeacon, a post that he apparently held until his death in 1221.[151]

As archdeacon of Oxford, in addition to the routine supervision of ecclesiastical affairs that this post involved, John of Tynemouth was necessarily involved with the schools in the city. The period when he was archdeacon, as it happened, marked a critical phase in the history of the Oxford schools, which were in the process of creating a corporate structure as a university. The earliest document that refers specifically to a "chancellor of the schools of Oxford" dates from 1214, the year that John of Tynemouth became archdeacon, and directs the chancellor to act jointly with the archdeacon. Academic work was just beginning to resume at Oxford that year, following the abandonment of the city by masters and students during a series of riots in 1209.[152] By 1221, when John of Tynemouth died, not only had the Oxford schools resumed teaching, but external authorities had also acknowledged that the corporate body of masters and students at Oxford constituted a university.[153] It is difficult to believe that John of Tynemouth, a learned and experienced lawyer and a former Oxford master himself, was not involved in these developments, but precisely what his role may have been cannot be determined.

Decretals and Decretal Collections in the Twelfth Century

While the *Concordia discordantium canonum* provided canonists for the first time with a comprehensive, reasoned body of material that covered the subject more adequately than any of its predecessors, the law continued to develop in the years after the vulgate text of Gratian's Decretum appeared. Indeed, the Decretum made the need for new law more obvious than it had previously been. The more decretists and their students stud-

---

151. During his service for Hubert Walter, John spent a considerable period abroad, representing the archbishop in litigation at Rome. Upon his return to England he was rewarded with a canonry and prebend at Lincoln prior to his appointment to the archdeaconry of Oxford (*BRUO* 3:1923). John's predecessor as archdeacon of Oxford was the scholar and poet, Walter Map (ca. 1140–1208). See Brooke and Mynors's introduction to Walter Map's *De nugis curialium*, xviii.

152. *Mediaeval Archives* 1:9; Hackett, "University as a Corporate Body"; Rashdall, *Universities* 3:33–34; Southern, "From Schools to University."

153. See the 1218 mandate to the masters and scholars of Oxford from the papal legate, Cardinal Guala Bicchieri, in *Mediaeval Archives* 1:16–17, as well as Guala, *Letters and Charters*, 60–61, no. 77.

ied and reflected on the texts assembled in Gratian's book, the clearer the deficiencies, limitations, and inconsistencies in existing law became. It is probably no coincidence that the pace at which new canon law was created accelerated sharply in the decades that followed the appearance of the Decretum.[154]

New lawmaking occurred primarily through rulings on individual cases in papal decretals. Popes had issued such letters since at least the late fourth century, but prior to the appearance of Gratian's Decretum they had never constituted the principal vehicle of ecclesiastical lawmaking.[155] The growth of bureaucracy at all levels of church administration in the decades following 1150 stimulated the need to create new law. The total volume of papal letters, including decretals, consequently increased rapidly during the second half of the century.[156]

Copies of papal decretals were generally dispatched only to the parties directly involved in the case that gave rise to them. Although the new law that a decretal established—new in the sense that it added to the body of law in Gratian's book—might have broad and sometimes vitally important consequences for other individuals and other situations, it was not generally circulated to the world at large. Since it was not easy to determine whether a document that looked like a decretal was an authentic papal rescript or not, this situation opened up opportunities for the unscrupulous, who were not slow to take advantage of it.[157] Toward the end of the twelfth century, Stephen of Tournai lamented in a letter to the pope:

---

154. Duggan, *Twelfth-Century Decretal Collections*, 19–21.

155. Jasper, "Beginning of the Decretal Tradition," in Jasper and Fuhrmann, *Papal Letters*, 12–13; cf. Gratian's rather broader definition of decretals, which appears at D. 19 d.a.c. 7 and D. 20 pr. The earliest known decretal is a letter of Pope Siricius (r. 384–99) dated 10 February, 385 (JK 255; Jasper, "Beginning of the Decretal Tradition," 4).

156. Duggan, *Twelfth-Century Decretal Collections*, 24–25; Winroth, *Making of Gratian's Decretum*, 145. The average annual number of papal letters that survive from the pontificate of Alexander III (1159–81), e.g., was more then twice as great as it had been a generation earlier, during the pontificates of Honorius II (1124–30) and Innocent II (1130–43). See Murray, "Pope Gregory VII and His Letters," 165–68, 202, and on the decretals of Alexander III, see especially the studies collected in *Miscellanea Rolando Bandinelli*.

157. See, e.g., the account of the difficulties that the pope and cardinals experienced in trying to determine whether papal documents introduced in litigation in 1123 were genuine or not by Hugh the Chanter, *History of the Church of York*, 192–94. See too John of Salisbury, *Historia pontificalis* c. 43, 86–87, and Thomas of Marlborough, *History of the Abbey of Evesham*, 298, §399.

Again, if a case comes up that should be settled under canon law either by your judges-delegate or by ordinary judges, there is produced from the vendors an inextricable forest of decretal letters presumably under the name of Pope Alexander [III] of blessed memory, and older holy canons are cast aside, rejected, expunged. When this plunder has been unrolled before us, those things that were wholesomely instituted in councils of holy fathers do not settle the case, nor is conciliar prescription followed, since letters prevail which perchance advocates for hire invented and forged in their shops or chambers under the name of the Roman pontiffs. A new volume composed of these is solemnly read in the schools and offered for sale in the marketplace to the applause of a horde of notaries, who rejoice that in copying suspect opuscula both their labor is lessened and their pay increased.[158]

As Stephen's complaint suggests, twelfth-century advocates, as well as judges, church administrators, and teachers of canon law, were quick to see the importance of making and collecting copies of any papal decretals, or supposed decretals, that they happened to come across, since the rulings they contained might prove useful in dealing with future situations. Individuals soon began to make little collections of decretals and to exchange them with friends and associates, who could be expected to reciprocate the favor. Private decretal collections began to circulate from the middle of the twelfth century onward, sometimes as appendices to copies of Gratian and other canonistic texts, sometimes as independent works, which teachers of canon law used as instructional tools to supplement Gratian's book.

Early decretal collections were small, haphazard assemblages of papal decisions, which modern scholars call primitive decretal collections. In the course of time, especially as collections grew larger and less manageable, collectors began to sort their decretals by topic in order to facilitate refer-

---

158. "Rursus si ventum fuerit ad judicia, que iure canonico sint tractanda, vel a vobis commissa vel ab ordinariis iudicibus cognoscenda, profertur a venditoribus inextricabilis silva decretalium epistolarum quasi sub nomine sancte recordationis Alexandri pape, et antiquiores sacri canones abiiciuntur, respuuntur, expuuntur. Hoc involuero prolato in medium, ea que in consiliis sanctorum Patrum salubriter instituta sunt, nec formam conciliis, nec finem negociis imponunt, prevalentibus epistolis quas forsitan advocati conductivi sub nomine Romanorum pontificum in apothecis sive cubiculis suis confingunt et conscribunt. Novum volumen ex eis compactum et in scolis sollempniter legitur et in foro venaliter exponitur, applaudente cetu notariorum, qui in conscribendis suspectis opusculis et laborem suum gaudent imminui et mercedem augeri" (Steven of Tournai, *Lettres*, 345, no. 274; *CUP* 1:47–48, no. 48). I have adapted this translation from the one in Thorndike, *University Records and Life*, 23–24.

ence to them. Compilers of systematic collections of this type sometimes went further. They not merely copied decretals, but also edited them and discarded the parts that seemed juridically irrelevant. When a single decretal dealt with more than one topic, as often happened, the compiler might dissect it and group each portion with other decretals, or parts of decretals, that dealt with the same or closely related subjects. Compilers of systematic collections might add subject titles or rubrics at the head of each topical group to make them easier to find. They might also try to structure these titles in some kind of logical or functional order.[159]

THE *QUINQUE COMPILATIONES ANTIQUAE*

The appearance in 1190 of the *Breviarium extravagantium* of Bernard of Pavia signaled a watershed in the history of decretal collections. Modern scholars usually refer to this collection as *Compilatio prima*, because it became the first of a series of five particularly substantial systematic decretal collections known as the *Quinque compilationes antiquae*. Teachers in the schools of canon law at Bologna and elsewhere during the next generation called these collections "the new law" and lectured on them as supplements to Gratian's Decretum.

Bernard of Pavia organized his collection in the form of a code that comprised 912 chapters arranged under 152 titles organized within five books. Each book treated a central theme, and each title dealt with a subdivision of that theme. Medieval law students memorized a mnemonic line that summarized the topical order of the books: "The judge, the judgment, clergy, marriage, and crime" (*Iudex, iudicium, clerus, connubium, crimen*). In other words, the first book dealt with courts and their organization; the second book with civil procedure in contentious matters; the third with the law governing the clergy; the fourth with marriage, legitimacy, and other topics that related primarily to the laity; and the last with canonical criminal law. This became the standard structure that later decretal collections, both official and unofficial, would follow.[160]

This phase of decretal collecting culminated in 1234 with the publica-

---

159. Fransen, *Décrétales*, 16–26; Duggan, *Twelfth-Century Decretal Collections*, 45–65. Detailed analyses of numerous individual decretal collections appear in Holtzmann, *Studies in the Collections of Twelfth-Century Decretals*, and in Duggan, *Twelfth-Century Decretal Collections*, 152–92.

160. This pattern was already noted by Master Tancred of Bologna (ca. 1185–1236) writing ca. 1216 in the introduction to his gloss apparatus on 3 Comp. (Copenhagen, Kongelige Bibliothek, Gl. Kg. Samling 196, at 1ra, and Schulte, *QL* 1:244–45). See also Fransen, *Décrétales*, 24–26; Brundage, *Medieval Canon Law*, 194–200.

tion of the *Decretales Gregorii IX*, usually referred to in the schools as the "Liber Extra" because it contained the law that was not found in Gratian's work. Four years earlier, Pope Gregory IX (r. 1227–41) had appointed Raymond of Penyafort (d. 1275), a Dominican canonist from Catalunya who had studied and taught at Bologna, as a papal chaplain and commissioned him to prepare an authoritative collection of papal decretals.[161] When Raymond and a team of assistants completed the task, the pope promulgated the collection on 5 September 1234, in a letter addressed "to all the teachers and students at Bologna." Raymond incorporated most of the contents of the *Quinque compilationes antiquae* into the new collection, together with approximately 200 additional decretals, and the pope in his letter of promulgation directed that this official collection be used in the schools and in the courts.[162]

The rapidly swelling volume of new law forced teachers of canon law to expand their teaching in order to keep up with recent developments. Although Gratian's book remained basic, teachers needed to give increasing time and attention to the ever-growing body of decretal law in order to prepare their students adequately for ecclesiastical administration and practice in the courts. Gratian's work was slowly and inexorably overshadowed in the schools because keeping up with the church's rapid legal development demanded more and more time in the curriculum. As both teachers and writers on canon law increasingly turned their attention to explicating decretal law, the time they devoted to the Decretum inevitably dwindled. By about 1210, the decretist scholarship that had flourished so vigorously during the second half of the twelfth century began to decline.[163]

Teaching Canon Law in the Late Twelfth Century

The gloss apparatuses and *summae* of the decretists contain a mine of information about the form and content of the teaching that went on in schools of canon law. Teaching consisted primarily of text-centered lectures. Lecturers analyzed the contents of each canon or chapter, one after the other, explained its meaning, showed how it related to other legal texts, and often said something about the ways in which it might apply to practical problems. Bolognese teachers revised the lectures that underlay their glosses and *summae* before making them available in edited form (*ordinationes*) to

---

161. Kuttner, "Raymond of Peñafort as Editor"; Valls-Taberner, *San Ramón de Penyafort*; Silano, "Raymond of Peñafort," *DMA* 10:266–67.

162. Gregory IX, *Rex pacificus*, in X proem.

163. Fraher, "The Becket Dispute," 361.

be copied and distributed. Things were managed differently at Paris, Orleans, and Oxford, where students took notes of their masters' oral remarks (*reportationes*) and then transcribed these in the form of glosses—this is how the Anglo-Norman Caius glosses, for example, were put down.[164]

Early in the thirteenth century, law teachers at Bologna began to compile composite collections of glosses by various authors. These compilations soon came into general use as the standard commentaries on each of the received books of civil and canon law. The commentaries were known collectively as the *Glossa ordinaria* (ordinary gloss), and teachers lectured on them as authoritative expositions of the texts.[165] Judges as well as teachers came to regard the *Glossa ordinaria* as a leading authority in its own right. "It is not safe to depart from the ordinary gloss," declared Baldus de Ubaldis (1327–1400), and Cino da Pistoia (1270–1336) described it as "the idol of the law."[166]

The *Glossa ordinaria* for Gratian's Decretum was the work of Johannes Teutonicus (b. ca. 1170, d. 1245), who completed it before 1217.[167] The Liber Extra owes its *Glossa ordinaria* to Bernard of Parma (d. 1263), and Johannes Andreae (b. ca. 1270, d. 1348) was responsible for the *Glossa ordinaria* on the Liber Sextus and the Clementine Constitutions. The astonishingly industrious professor of Roman law Accursius (b. ca. 1185, d. 1263) was responsible for the monumental *Glossa ordinaria* on the entire *Corpus iuris civilis*, which comprises more than 96,000 individual glosses and totals about 2,000,000 words.[168]

The style of lectures in the twelfth-century law schools seems to have been relatively informal, even conversational, so that students raised ques-

---

164. *Emonis et Menkonis Werumensium Chronicon*, 524; Kuttner and Rathbone, "Anglo-Norman Canonists," 324.

165. Bologna University Statutes (1317) 2.44, ed. Denifle, 314.

166. Baldus, *Consiliorum, sive responorum* 5.169, vol. 5, at 45va: "[I]n iudicando non est tutum recedere a gl. Or., dico. . . ." See also Savigny, *Geschichte* 5:295–99; Stein, "Judge and Jurist," 234–35. Cino da Pistoia, *Commentaria in Codicem* to Cod. 4.10.1, quoted in Petrus Lenauderius, *De privilegiis doctorum* 4.42.64, at 13rb. See also Engelmann, *Wiedergeburt der Rechtskultur in Italien*, 189–204, as well as Dolezalek, "Gloses des manuscrits de droit."

167. Stelling-Michaud, "Jean le Teutonique," and Kuttner, "Johannes Teutonicus." The original version of Johannes Teutonicus's *Glossa ordinaria* was revised ca. 1245 by Bartholomew of Brescia (d. ca. 1258), who added references to the Liber Extra together with some further comments of his own. This is the version that appears in early printings of the Decretum.

168. Lange, *Römisches Recht im Mittelalter*, 335–42.

tions and made comments to which lecturers responded during the course of their presentations. Lectures, in other words, involved discussions between teacher and student, as well as the teacher's presentation of material. As organized law faculties commenced to take shape in universities during the early thirteenth century, however, this spontaneous, conversational type of lecture began to give way to a more formal and rigid style, in which communication flowed only one way: the teacher held forth, while students kept silent and took notes.[169]

Twelfth-century law teaching among both civilians and canonists also involved another kind of academic exercise, the disputation, a well-established pedagogical device commonly used in teaching liberal arts and theology at least from the time of Peter Abelard (ca. 1079–1142). The earliest disputations on technical points of law date from around 1150.[170] Disputations in the law schools were essentially debates about legal issues that arose from a fact situation. In a disputation a teacher described a scenario, which could be either hypothetical or real, and then challenged students (or other teachers) to respond to the legal questions that the scenario raised. An Oxford disputation from the 1190s, for example, posed this situation:

> While the king of England was on crusade his lands were under the protection of the Roman see. Meanwhile a certain [papal] legate dispatched to all of France wished to enter Normandy but was turned back by the seneschal of Normandy, supported by the archbishop and bishops of Normandy, on account of the region's [protected] status. Notwithstanding this, the legate excommunicated the aforesaid seneschal. Afterwards, moreover, at a council held at Tours, with the Norman bishops present and not protesting, the aforesaid legate placed all of Normandy under interdict. Question: Is the interdict binding?[171]

The disputants then analyzed the complicated legal issues that this situation involved and presented arguments for and against the validity of the interdict, together with abundant citations from Roman and canon law to support each position. Nicholas de l'Aigle, who chaired this disputation, closed it by ruling that the legate lacked the power to impose an interdict on Normandy.

169. Bellomo, *Saggio sull'università*, 66–68.
170. Fransen, "Questions disputées dans les facultés de droit," 231–32. See the account of the origins of the form in Bazàn, "Questions disputées," 21–38.
171. *Quaestiones Londonenses*, no. 39, in Brundage, "The Crusade of Richard I," 451.

Disputations complemented lectures by sharpening a different set of skills. In a lecture, a teacher explicated legal texts in order to tease out their meaning, so that students could grasp their implications. In a disputation, the participants learned how to use those texts in order to fashion arguments and to meet, and if possible demolish, the arguments put forth by their opponents.

We know little about the organization and finance of canon law teaching in the twelfth century. Canonists of that period did not teach in schools supported by public revenues. In northern Europe, the schools of the canonists sometimes had a connection with a monastery, cathedral, or other ecclesiastical institution. Stephen of Tournai, for instance, probably taught at St. Euverte when he was in Orleans and at Sainte-Geneviève when he was at Paris, while Bertram of Metz apparently taught at St. Gereon in Cologne. Instruction in schools attached to an ecclesiastical institution was, at least in principle, supposed to be free of charge.[172]

Private masters who taught independently of institutions such as these, however, expected their students to pay for tuition. Students in some places made these payments individually, directly to their teachers, sometimes daily, more often at the end of the instructional year. At Bologna, it became customary for a class of students to pay an annual group fee in one lump sum. This was known as a *collecta*, since one or two students would assume responsibility for payment and would then try to collect an appropriate share from each of their classmates.[173]

We also know little about how law students financed their studies in this period. Many of them probably received at least part of their support from family resources, while some were fortunate enough to find patrons who helped to finance their education in the expectation that once they had finished their studies they would enter the patron's service. Churches had long been encouraged to assist their own clerics to further their education so that they would be better equipped to fulfill their functions.[174] The Third Lateran Council demanded that every cathedral chapter maintain a schoolmaster to instruct clerics and poor scholars. A generation later, the Fourth Lateran Council went beyond this to require metropolitan ca-

---

172. Gratian D. 37 c.12; 3 Lat. (1179) c. 18 (= X5.5.1), in *DEC* 1:220.

173. Post, "Masters' Salaries and Student-Fees," 189–93; Rashdall, *Universities* 1:208–9; Bellomo, *Saggio sull'università*, 49, 141–43; Verger, "Teachers," 151–54.

174. E.g., Gratian, D. 37 c. 12, from the Roman council of 826, c. 34, in Mansi 14:1008. See also Rufinus, *Summa* to D. 37 c. 12 v. *De quibusdam locis*, 90, followed verbatim by Johannes Faventinus, in BL, MS Royal 9.E.VII, at 22vb.

thedrals to provide a teacher of theology as well in order to instruct their students in the skills necessary for the cure of souls.[175] Since every clergyman charged with the cure of souls needed a basic knowledge of canon law, there can be little doubt that at least some elementary canon law formed part of the curriculum of these schools.[176] Nor is it likely to be a coincidence that toward the end of the twelfth century, when bishops regularly began to add trained canon lawyers to their personal staffs, the records often describe such a man as a "schoolmaster" (*magister scholarum, scholasticus*).[177]

Teachers of canon law who lacked institutional affiliation with a monastery or cathedral chapter usually lectured and held their disputations in dwellings that they owned or rented.[178] This was certainly true of the decretists who taught at Bologna. Although nearly all of them about whom we have much personal information were clerics of one sort or another,[179] they usually carried on their teaching privately, and only occasionally taught within a permanent institution. Teachers of Roman civil law at Bologna, so far as we know, were all laymen and seem to have done their teaching and legal consulting in houses that they owned or rented.

The teacher himself typically lived on the premises where he taught and might also rent rooms in his house to students from distant parts. Not surprisingly, these houses were often in the less desirable neighborhoods of the city, where rents and prices were cheap, or at least less unreasonable than they were in more fashionable quarters. Jacques de Vitry (b. between 1160 and 1170, d. 1240) recalled that during his student days at Paris in the late twelfth century,

> In one and the same house there was a school upstairs and a brothel downstairs. The teachers lectured on the upper level, while down below the harlots carried on their sordid trade. On one level the whores fought among

175. 3 Lat. (1179) c. 18 (= X 5.5.1) in *DEC* 1:220; 4 Lat. (1215) c. 11 (= X 5.5.4), in *DEC* 1:240; *Constitutiones concilii quarti Lateranensis*, ed. García y García, 59–60.

176. Thus, e.g., D. 36 c. 3, D. 38 c. 4; Southern, "The Schools of Paris," 115–18, and *Scholastic Humanism* 1:305–10; Ghellinck, *Le mouvement théologique*, 465–67; Smalley, *Study of the Bible*, 62–63, 75–77; Sayers, *Papal Judges Delegate*, 130–31.

177. Sayers, *Papal Judges Delegate*, 130; Cheney, "England and the Roman Curia," 181.

178. Bellomo, *Saggio sull'università*, 43–45.

179. Peter the Deacon, *Chronica Montis Casinensis*, 834, seems to suggest that a layman, Walfredus, a palatine judge, may have taught canon law at Bologna in the 1130s. He appears in several charters dated between 1127 and 1146, and his son, Hildebrand, was still active in Bologna in 1192. See *CSB* 12:13–22, 84–85, 89–91, 106–7 (nos. 9–18, 74, 78, 91); Sarti-Fattorini, *De claris professoribus* 1:33–35.

themselves and with their pimps, and on the other the clergy disputed and shouted down one another.[180]

Quarters such as these sufficed for routine lectures, discussions, and disputations, but popular and well-to-do teachers obviously required more spacious accommodations, as did presentations by visiting celebrities. Gerald of Wales (1146–1223), never much given to understatement, describes how his lectures on canon law at Paris in 1177 attracted such a crowd of eager listeners that the largest house in the city could scarcely contain his audience.[181]

Whatever the building, law teachers are invariably pictured as lecturing while seated on a thronelike chair (*cathedra*) placed on a dais. Directly in front of them was a desk or lectern with the book on which they were lecturing open to the section that contained the topic for that day's lecture. Students typically sat on benches facing the lecturer. A desk stood in front of each bench so that they could take notes while following the lecture in their own copies of the text (fig. 1).

Many, perhaps most, decretists combined their teaching with other activities. They advised clients as legal consultants (*iurisperiti*) or represented them as advocates in litigation. Indeed, without prior experience and reputation as a practitioner, it seems unlikely that an individual could have attracted many students, especially during the early stages of his teaching career. Twelfth-century canonists, moreover, like other clerics, typically hoped to secure appointment to a benefice, prebend, or other revenue-producing ecclesiastical position, and a reputation as a legal expert and law teacher greatly enhanced their prospects for doing this successfully. Even those who were able to acquire a steady income from a church appointment often found that the fees their students paid could furnish a modest, but doubtless welcome, supplement to the income from their ecclesiastical appointments, litigation, or consulting practice.

In this respect, the personal status of twelfth-century canonists as a group differed sharply from that of their civilian counterparts. Teachers of Roman law (especially in Italy) seem for the most part to have been laymen.

---

180. Jacques de Vitry, *Historia occidentalis* c. 7, 91: "In una autem et eadem domo scole erant superius, prostibula inferius. In parte superiori magistri legebant; in inferiori meretrices officia turpitudinis exercebant. Ex una parte meretrices inter se et cum lenonibus litigabant; ex alia parte disputantes et contentiose agentes clerici proclamabant."

181. Gerald of Wales, *De rebus a se gestis* 2.1, in his *Opera* 1:45.

Figure 1. Azo lecturing to Bolognese law students. Bolognese, first half of the fourteenth century. Österreichische Nationalbibliothek, Cod. 2256, 1r. Reproduced by permission.

We find notices of them working as advocates, legal advisers, and judges. But no contemporary source hints that any of them held ecclesiastical benefices.

Churchmen of course studied Roman civil law and some of them taught it. Repeated efforts failed to discourage monks and clerics from doing this.[182] Because a basic familiarity with Roman law was an essential foundation for the study of canon law, monks and other clerics found that they often needed civilian as well as canonistic learning to defend their monasteries in the courts.[183] As one monk of the Abbey of St. Victor at Marseilles who sought permission to study Roman law at Pavia reminded his abbot,

---

182. Council of Clermont (1130) c. 5, in Mansi 21:438–39; repeated by the Council of Reims (1131) c. 6 (Mansi 21:459), and the Council of Tours (1163) c. 8 (Mansi 21:1179). The prohibition formally became part of the general law of the church when the Second Lateran Council adopted it (2 Lat. [1139] c. 9 in *DEC* 1:198). Later councils reiterated the prohibition numerous times. Bernard of Pavia incorporated the version of the prohibition adopted by the Council of Tours into 1 Comp. 3.37.2, and from there it ultimately found its way into the Liber Extra in 1234 as X 3.50.3.

183. See, e.g., the extensive battery of citations from Roman law that Gerald of Wales assembled to prop up his defense of the liberties of St. Davids (*Opera* 1:146–49).

"Our monastery is continually attacked by lawsuits brought both by clerics and laymen in the courts, to the detriment of the property of the upright." Knowledge of Roman civil law, he maintained, was essential if he were to defend his monastery's interests.[184]

By the end of the twelfth century, canon law had become far more systematic and sophisticated than it was around 1100. From the middle of the century onward, successive versions of Gratian's Decretum furnished students and teachers with a larger and more coherent body of material to work with than their predecessors had ever known and demonstrated how to analyze it rationally. The decretists used the tools that Gratian gave them with an energy, ardor, and ambition that might well have dismayed the author of the *Concordia discordantium canonum*.

Before Gratian, canon law was a branch of theology. By the early thirteenth century, it was emerging as an independent discipline. Canonists by that point were beginning to align themselves intellectually more with Roman law than with theology. They borrowed ideas, insights, tools, and techniques from their civilian counterparts with increasing frequency and enthusiasm, yet at the same time they sought to preserve their autonomy from civil law as well as from theology. By around 1200, canon law had its own operating rules, a specialized literature, and a distinctive way of approaching problems, none of which it had possessed a century earlier.[185]

Practitioners of the two learned laws, Roman and canon, gradually commenced to become aware of their collective identity as an advantaged social group during the latter part of the twelfth century and began to attach themselves to the elite classes that ruled Western society. As they did so, less-favored members of the population predictably began to envy and resent the privileges that lawyers enjoyed.[186] At the same time, legal procedures were becoming increasingly technical and complex, which increasingly made the services of trained lawyers indispensable, a development that only heightened the antipathy of those who had to depend upon their services when they found it necessary to have resort to the law courts to secure their rights or to defend them from others.

---

184. The monk, whose name is unknown, wrote in the 1120s (Dufour, Giordanengo, and Gouron, "L'attrait des 'leges,'" 529).
185. Weigand, "Romanisierungstendenzen"; Kalb, "Überlegungen zur Entstehung der Kanonistik als Rechtswissenschaft."
186. Aubenas, "Inconscience de juristes ou pédantisme malfaisant?"

* FOUR *

Church Courts, Civil Procedure, and the Professionalization of Law

The Church, Law, and Society, ca. 1140–1230

The completion of the vulgate version of Gratian's Decretum, coupled with the newfound interest in Roman law that had begun to appear among the learned earlier in the century, produced an intellectual climate in which parties to disputes increasingly found courts that used rules based on Roman law attractive as a forum for resolution of their disagreements.[1]

A new romano-canonical procedural system began to take shape during the second half of the twelfth century. One of its aims was to assure that each party to a dispute received a reasonable chance to present its side of a case. It also made available mechanisms to recuse judges suspected of bias and to appeal to higher authorities for correction of faulty decisions.[2] The growing use of papal judges-delegate, moreover, allowed litigants to secure a final decision from the highest earthly authority for a relatively modest investment of time and money—at least as compared with the costs of litigation at the papal curia.

From the middle of the twelfth century onward, litigants inundated the church's legal system with a mounting deluge of legal actions. This growth in demand for the services of church courts apparently originated with litigants. The increased frequency with which parties brought their disputes

---

1. Fried, *Entstehung des Juristenstandes*, 144–57; Martines, *Lawyers and Statecraft*, 4; Cortese, "Legisti, canonisti e feudisti," 234–39.

2. Gratian, C. 3 q. 5 c. 15; Tancred, *Ordo iudiciarius* 2.6.6, at 148–49; Walter of Cornut, *Ordo iudiciarius* "*Scientiam,*" 34–36, §15. Regular access to appeal procedures also diminished the importance of synods as a protective device against unjust judgments in first instance (Morris, "From Synod to Consistory," 118).

to ecclesiastical tribunals presumably reflected the litigants' desire to settle their differences through legal processes, rather than a scheme by church authorities to attract more business into their courts and thus to increase their power.[3] Although popes were not indifferent to the advantages that accompanied their exercise of jurisdiction, a massive increase in the volume of litigation threatened to turn the pope, bishops, and other church authorities into full-time judges and arbitrators and to leave them with little time, energy, or capacity to provide the religious leadership and inspiration that justified their authority, power, and privileges. Faced with this situation, popes and bishops began to search for new methods to cope with the flood of lawsuits that were pouring into their courts.[4] The search began at the top.

The Judicial Business of the Papacy

Although the early bishops of Rome had managed to give personal attention to the judicial business that came before them, by the late ninth century contentious matters referred to the papacy had grown sufficiently numerous that popes occasionally sought assistance in coping with their judicial workload. Pope John VIII (872–82) was said to have met twice a month with his cardinals in order to discuss pending judicial matters with them, although the evidence for this claim is weak.[5] It is clear, however, that during the tenth century a chancellor, styled the *cancellarius sacri palatii*, presided over a growing group of chaplains, notaries, and clerks of the papal curia, housed in the Lateran Palace. Many of these men had hands-on experience in applying church law to administrative problems. Notaries in the chancellor's office had access to a good deal of practical legal lore. Other officials under the chancellor's supervision maintained the papal archives, whose registers of letters, petitions, and related documents formed an essential record of the papacy's past legal actions. Notaries and other

---

3. Brett, "Canon Law and Litigation," 32, 40; Duggan, "Papal Judges Delegate," 195.

4. There is no reason to believe that church authorities reached this conclusion as a result of an explicit calculation or that they arrived at it solely in order to serve their own self-interest. Members of the Latin Church's hierarchy in the twelfth century do not, by and large, seem to have been cynical materialists; their ranks included saints, as well as careerists.

5. JE 3366; Hirschfield, "Gerichtswesen der Stadt Rom," 449–52. Kuttner, "Cardinalis," 173 and 193 n. 74, expressed doubts about the genuineness of this document. Those doubts were reinforced by Weigand, "Unbekannte überlieferungen von Dekretalen," 607.

papal officials could find useful precedents for proposed action—or sometimes inaction—in those records. The papal establishment at the Lateran Palace in addition included seven palatine judges (formally styled *iudices de clero*), who, among other things, advised the pope on administrative affairs, including the performance of his judicial duties.[6]

THE PAPAL SYNOD

The Lateran Palace, however, did not include any judicial body that could share the burden of deciding cases. Pope Leo IX (r. 1049–54) made a beginning toward that end when he revived, reorganized, and redefined the ancient papal synod. Although his predecessors had occasionally convened gatherings of local bishops to discuss problems of doctrine and church discipline, Leo transformed the synod into a legislative and judicial body that met periodically with the pope to settle pressing issues and deal with disputes that had been referred to the pope. The pope dictated the agenda of these sessions and presided over the deliberations of the assembled prelates, who sat with him as co-judges. The reform-minded pontiffs who succeeded Leo IX continued this practice, which gradually became a regular feature of papal administration. Under Gregory VII (r. 1073–85), the papal synod became a semi-annual affair, usually held during Advent and Lent.[7]

These arrangements no doubt helped to alleviate the problems posed by the press of litigation, but the relief soon proved short-lived in the face of a continuing increase in the pope's judicial workload. The number and complexity of the matters referred to the pope for final decision continued to grow incrementally over the years, until by the end of the eleventh century judicial business was beginning to place an intolerable strain on papal time and energy.[8] In 1095, as Pope Urban II (r. 1088–99) fretted over the demands that judicial business made upon him, he experimented with a new approach to the problem. During the last five years of his pontificate, Urban began to add a few legal advisers to the household that accompanied him even when he was away from Rome, as he was during much of his pontificate.[9] The legal analyses and guidance that he received from these men allowed him to decide cases more consistently and expeditiously.

---

6. Hinschius, *System des katholischen Kirchenrechts* 1:380–83; Jordan, "Zur päpstlichen Finanzgeschichte," 88–90; Ullmann, *Growth of Papal Government*, 325–31.

7. Schmale, "Synodus," 94–98; Cowdrey, *Pope Gregory VII*, 586–92; Robinson, *The Papacy*, 122–27.

8. Brett, "Canon Law and Litigation," 32.

9. JL 5642; Becker, *Papst Urban II*. 1:99, 219–20; Robinson, *The Papacy*, 183.

THE PAPAL CONSISTORY

Urban also called upon members of the college of cardinals for assistance in coping with judicial matters. Cardinals, originally a group of priests in charge of Rome's principal churches, together with the bishops of the city's seven suburbs, had for centuries routinely attended the pope and assisted him in performing his liturgical functions. Unlike a synod, some cardinals were always available, and at least a few of them routinely accompanied the pope when he was away from Rome.[10]

Although the cardinals' functions in the early Middle Ages were primarily ceremonial rather than advisory, popes had at least occasionally sought their aid and counsel in dealing with other matters. The papal election decree of Pope Nicholas II (r. 1059–61) in 1059 for the first time gave the college of cardinals the exclusive right to elect the pope.[11] Gregory VII dispatched cardinal-legates to carry his reform message to every corner of the Christian world and to assure that it was not merely received, but implemented. Gregory's successors continued this practice. Cardinal-legates soon became one of the primary instruments of papal government.[12]

Regular meetings between the pope and the cardinals who attended him first became a fixture of papal routine during the closing years of the pontificate of Urban II.[13] These meetings, held in a chamber of the Lateran Palace called the consistory, gradually replaced papal synods as the body that popes habitually consulted before reaching major decisions, particularly on lawsuits and other delicate or controversial matters.[14]

---

10. Sydow, "Untersuchungen," 34–35, 50–53; Schmale, "Synodus," 100–102. For the complex history of the term "cardinal" when used to describe certain members of the Roman clergy see especially Kuttner, "Cardinalis."

11. Jasper, *Das Papstwahldekret von 1059* is fundamental. A text of the decree also appears in Gratian at D. 23 c. 1.

12. Cowdrey, *Pope Gregory VII*, 12–13, 592–96; Robinson, *The Papacy*, 146–78.

13. E.g., JL 5362 (text in Somerville, *Pope Urban II*, 64–67), 5505, 5519, 5788; Sydow, "Untersuchungen," 53–55; Robinson, *The Papacy*, 188.

14. Sydow, "Il 'consistorium' dopo lo schisma del 1130," 166–68; Robinson, *The Papacy*, 99–105, 139. The term "consistory" harks back to the imperial council of the later Roman empire, which served among other things as a high court of justice (Crook, *Consilium principis*, 101–103, 139–41; Jones, *Later Roman Empire* 1:333–41). The term *consistorium Lateranense* in twelfth-century Latin usually referred to the chamber where the pope and cardinals met for judicial business (Müller, "Bericht des Abtes Hariulf," 102; the same text of this account also appears with a Dutch translation in Hariulf, *Pleidooi*, 28). By the time of Innocent III (r. 1198–1216), the term was commonly used to desig-

From consultation to delegation proved a short step. As early as the pontificate of Paschal II (1099–1118), the pope occasionally named one or more assessors (often styled *causidici*, and sometimes including cardinals) to assist him in untangling difficult or complicated cases. The assessors took over much of the work that led to the resolution of a case.[15] They commonly questioned witnesses, tested the truthfulness of their testimony, and examined documents produced to support the parties' case. The assessors were then in a position to advise the pope about their findings concerning the evidence. They also deliberated on the legal issues that the case raised and reported the results of their analysis to the pope. Assessors' reports usually included recommendations concerning the most appropriate disposition of the matter. The ultimate decision on the merits of the case and the determination of how the dispute should be resolved still remained with the pope, of course, but he commonly adopted the assessors' recommendations.[16]

Since using assessors significantly reduced the time that the pope had to invest in each case, it is scarcely surprising that the practice of delegating the preliminary hearing of cases to cardinals and other curial officials grew increasingly common as the pope's caseload continued to expand, even more rapidly from the pontificate of Innocent II (r. 1130–43) onward. In the later years of Innocent's pontificate, he occasionally empowered his chancellor, Cardinal Haimeric (who held that office between 1123 and 1141),

---

nate the meetings and their participants, as well as the meeting-place (Maleczek, *Papst und Kardinalskolleg*, 301).

15. Hirschfeld, "Gerichtswesen der Stadt Rom," 513, 529–30; Ficker, *Forschungen* 3:101–103; Rossi, *Consilium sapientis iudiciale*, 69–78. Guibert of Tournai, a Franciscan preacher in the mid-thirteenth century, provided a good short description of their functions in his *Sermones ad omnes status, Ad iudices et advocatos*, 1, at 106rb: "[H]i sunt assessores quos iudices ad consilium uocant, qui debent esse intelligentes et discreti, inquirendo diligenter omnia que ad causam pertinent ut tamdiu actio uentiletur quousque ad rei ueritatem perueniatur, unde tales assessores et consiliarii debent a iudice uocari qui sunt iurisperiti et quorum consilio possit secure fulminari." Santini, "Legis doctores," 132–34, argues that the men described as *iudices* and *advocati* in the Romagna during the eleventh century were in fact judicial assessors. By the end of the twelfth century, the term "auditor" was beginning to displace "assessor" to describe these hearing officers (see, e.g., Pflugk-Harttung, *Acta* 3:385, no. 450 [1192]).

16. Thus, e.g., the decisions of Innocent II on a lawsuit between bishop Manfred of Antibes and the monastery of Lérins (1139; JL 8306) and in a dispute between the cathedral chapter and the bishop at Cremona (1139; JL 8032) in Pflugk-Harttung, *Acta* 1:158, no. 179; 2:303, no. 341. See also Maleczek, "Kardinalskollegium," 50, 68–69.

to hear and actually dispose of minor cases.[17] A decade later, we find Anastasius IV (r. 1153–54) authorizing a group of cardinals and judges, aided by "certain prudent legal experts," to deal with a complex dispute and to recommend to the pope a final determination, which he then formally confirmed.[18] This approach proved more efficient and less expensive than repeatedly summoning synods to deal with contentious matters. The parties to a dispute benefited from a process that was easier, quicker, and cheaper than the alternative, while it also saved time for increasingly overburdened popes.[19]

The frequency with which popes named men with formal legal training to the college of cardinals beginning in the second quarter of the twelfth century provides a rough index to the swelling volume and importance of judicial business in the papal consistory. Five of the cardinals whom Innocent II named to the sacred college, for example, seem to have been trained lawyers. Cardinal Haimeric, the key figure in the curia during this period, is thought to have been a canon-regular of Santa Maria di Reno in Bologna, where he, too, had presumably enjoyed the opportunity to study law.[20] Other evidence suggests that Haimeric, like so many other canons-regular who became cardinals, had more than a casual knowledge of both Roman and canon law.[21] Bulgarus, after all, addressed Haimeric as his "dearest friend, a comrade in the mysteries of the law," in the short guide to civil procedure that he wrote at Haimeric's request. Similarly, Abbot Hariulf of

17. Maleczek, "Kardinalskollegium," 59–64, 68–69; Robinson, *The Papacy*, 190–92; Müller, "Bericht des Abtes Hariulf," 101; Hariulf, *Pleidooi*, 24.

18. Pflugk-Harttung, *Acta* 3:154, no. 145 (1154; JL 9911). Gerhoch of Reichersberg, writing in 1156, although he was no admirer of lawyers, found this sort of proceeding quite acceptable (*Letter to Pope Hadrian* 45.7, at 115).

19. Pflugk-Harttung, *Acta* 1:187–88, no. 204 (Eugene III, 1146; JL 8919)), and 1:365–66, no. 425 (Celestine III, 1194; JL 17066). Synods were infrequent and expensive. In order to attend one, bishops had to put their normal duties on hold, which was practicable only occasionally. When the pope did summon a synod, moreover, he was obliged to defray travel expenses for many of the bishops who attended and to subsidize their housing and entertainment while they were at the curia.

20. Robinson, *The Papacy*, 106–7. It seems curious that among the ten lawyers who became cardinals before 1159, no less then six were also canons-regular; Robinson, *The Papacy*, 221–22. This suggests that the canons of Saint-Ruf may not have been alone in their mission.

21. This is evident, for example, in the report of his handling of a complex lawsuit between the bishops of Arezzo and Siena in 1125; Pflugk-Harttung, *Acta* 2:252–55, no. 295 (JL 7210); Kantorowicz, *Studies*, 71; Savigny, *Geschichte* 7:66–69.

Oudenburg, who sought Haimeric's advice in a lawsuit, described him as "extremely upright and learned in the ecclesiastical laws and civil institutions." All of this suggests that Haimeric may have acquired at the very least some basic legal learning, perhaps from Bulgarus, before he joined the papal curia. Whatever his level of legal expertise, Haimeric unquestionably played a central role in the juridification of the papal curia that began under Innocent II.[22]

Innocent II's successors continued the practice of choosing law-trained men as cardinals. His immediate successor, Eugene III (r. 1145–53), added five more lawyers to the sacred college, while Adrian IV (r. 1154–59) appointed two others (one of whom, Albert of Morra, became Pope Gregory VIII in 1187), and Alexander III (r. 1159–81) added another eight or nine. Since the college of cardinals in this period seldom comprised more than forty-five or fifty men at any given time, the high proportion of lawyers among them meant that as early as the 1150s they had already begun to dominate the papal curia.[23]

Once popes had begun to surround themselves with men whose minds had been formed by puzzling their way through the juristic texts assembled in the Digest and Gratian's Decretum, the character of the curia was bound to change, and so was that of the church as a whole. These developments alarmed some contemporaries and left others at least vaguely uneasy. The pope, many felt, should first and foremost be a holy man, in the familiar scriptural metaphor, a benevolent shepherd.[24] His task was to guide his flock along the stony path toward righteousness, to bring back those who strayed, and to protect the poor and unfortunate from the wicked. His life and his household ought to provide a shining example of Christian charity.

Such was the ideal. In real life, of course, shepherds commonly rely on dogs to keep their sheep in line, and the dogs, no doubt, are more popular among shepherds than among sheep. The growing numbers of lawyers in the papal curia soon began to strike twelfth-century observers as

22. Bulgarus, *Excerpta legum*, 1; Müller, "Bericht des Abtes Hariulf," 101; Hariulf, *Pleidooi*, 24. Note also the remarks of Ludwig Wahrmund in the introduction to his edition of Bulgarus's *Excerpta legum*, xix–xx. On Haimeric's character and influence, see Robinson, *The Papacy*, 48, 68–75, 215–16; Maleczek, *Papst und Kardinalskolleg*, 220–22, and "Kardinalskollegium," 62, 67–68.

23. Robinson, *The Papacy*, 106–107, 220–21, 483–84; Smalley, *Becket Conflict*, 143–44; Classen, "Zur Geschichte Papst Anastasius IV.," 38–39.

24. Ps. 23 [22 in the Vulgate]; Jer. 23:1–5, 25:34–48, 31:10; John 10:1–16.

both alarming and sinister. Critics suspected, for one thing, that introducing lawyers was a cause, not a cure, for the growth in the volume of litigation at the curia.[25]

Detractors alleged that the curia and the lawyers who worked there encouraged litigation in order to enhance their power and swell their purses. Legal business at the papal curia unquestionably contributed in a major way to the economy of the city of Rome in the twelfth and thirteenth centuries. Advocates, proctors, notaries, and curial officials profited from litigation, and as its volume increased, their numbers grew. But they were certainly not the only ones to prosper from the growth of litigation. The influx into the city of litigants, accompanied by legal advisers and servants, benefited every segment of the Roman economy. Proprietors of inns, stables, and taverns, suppliers of parchment and ink, purveyors of cloth, wax, and thread, tailors and seamstresses, grocers and cobblers, souvenir merchants, and pickpockets—all stood to gain from the upsurge in lawsuits at the papal court. Natural as it was for visitors to resent the perceived avarice of the Romans and to suspect that the lawyers were somehow responsible for the rising tide of litigation, the critics almost certainly had the relationship wrong. The rapidly increasing prominence of lawyers among the personnel of the twelfth-century curia represented a response to, rather than a cause of, the influx of litigation at the papal court that began long before they arrived in force.[26]

St. Bernard of Clairvaux (1090–1153), while no admirer of lawyers, conceded that Christians had a right to bring their disputes to the pope for final resolution and that the pope had a moral obligation to help settle disagreements within the church:

> We cannot abandon the downtrodden; we cannot refuse judgment to those who suffer injustice. If cases are not tried and litigants heard, how can judgment be passed?[27]

25. Thus, e.g., the "Apocalypsis Goliae episcopi," in *Latin Poems*, 1–20, esp. ll. 141–72; John of Salisbury, *Policraticus* 6.24, trans. Nederman, 134–36; the "Ewangelium secundum marcham argenti," in Bayless, *Parody in the Middle Ages*, 136–42, 322–23; and Yunck, *Lineage of Lady Meed*, esp. 143–59.

26. Brett, "Canon Law and Litigation," 40.

27. Bernard of Clairvaux, *De consideratione* 1.X.13, in his *Opera* 3:408; the English version is in *Five Books on Consideration*, 43. Bernard composed *De consideratione* between 1149 and 1152. See also Jacqueline, "Le pape d'après le livre II du 'De consideratione'"; Kennan, "'De consideratione' of St. Bernard"; Somerville, "Pope Innocent II," 108; as well as Brundage, "Saint Bernard and the Jurists."

Bernard was nevertheless concerned that appeals were becoming so numerous, and the burden of deciding them so time-consuming, that legal business threatened to overwhelm his former pupil, Pope Eugene III, altogether:

> I ask you, what is the point of wrangling and listening to litigants from morning to night? And would that the evil of the day were sufficient for it, but the nights are not even free![28]

St. Bernard was particularly appalled by what he saw as the growing intrusion of Roman law, and lawyers trained in Roman law, into the curia.

> When are we to build up the Church or meditate on the law? Oh yes, every day laws resound through the palace, but these are the laws of Justinian, not of the Lord. Is this just?[29] . . . [T]hese are not so much laws as wrangling and sophistry, subverting judgment. Tell me, therefore, how can you, as a bishop and shepherd of souls, allow the Law to stand silent before you while these others rattle on?[30]

Bernard was further dismayed by the flagrant ambition that he detected among the lawyers who frequented the papal court:

> Some people are so impudent that, even when their case openly abounds with the itch of ambition, they are not embarrassed to demand a hearing. They flaunt themselves before the public conscience in a trial where they provide sufficient evidence to condemn themselves. . . . The Church is filled with ambitious men. . . . If you are Christ's disciple, let your zeal be enflamed and let your authority rise up against the widespread plague of this impudence. See what the Master did; hear what he says; "Let whoever serves me follow me." He did not take time to listen, he took a whip to beat them. . . . You too have a whip.[31]

---

28. *De consideratione* 1.III.4, at 3:397; trans. in *Five Books on Consideration*, 29.

29. An untranslatable pun: "Et quidem quotidie perstrepunt in palatio leges, sed Iustiniani, non Domini. Iustene etiam istud?" My thanks to Robert Somerville, who first called my attention to Bernard's play on words here. References to the laws of Justinian began to appear in papal documents at least as early as the mid-eleventh century and the Code and Digest were being cited in litigation at the curia by 1125; e.g., *Collectio Britannica* 29 (JL 5382), in Somerville, *Pope Urban II*, 102; Pflugk-Harttung, *Acta* 2:252–55, no. 295; Conrat, *Geschichte*, 28–30; Hirschfeld, "Gerichtswesen der Stadt Rom," 509.

30. *De consideratione* 1.IV.5, at 3:399; trans. in *Five Books on Consideration*, 31–32.

31. *De consideratione* 1.X.13–1.XI.14, at 3:409–410; trans. in *Five Books on Consideration*, 45–46.

St. Bernard was not alone in abhorring what he saw as the malign influence of the legists in the Lateran Palace. Master Gerhoch (1093–1169), provost of Reichersberg, writing just a year or two later, also deplored the influence at the papal court of lawyers trained in the laws of Theodosius and Justinian and seconded Bernard's admonitions to rid the curia of their influence.[32] The pope, Gerhoch insisted, should judge according to the law of God, rather than the laws of the emperors. He added that he had no quarrel with the civil law so long as it agreed with divine law. Gerhoch was dismayed by the intricate arguments that lawyers trained in the schools of the legists introduced into the judicial process and the procedural technicalities that they invoked. The papal court, Gerhoch maintained, ought to be free of legal sophistry. What was wanted there was simple, straightforward presentation of the facts of a dispute and a resolution of it by honest judgment, according to the practices of ancient popes.[33]

PAPAL JUDGES-DELEGATE

The volume of litigation at the papal curia continued to rise sharply during the pontificate of Alexander III and continued to climb through the remainder of the twelfth century and the first half of the thirteenth.[34] The problem was compounded by a dramatic increase in first-instance cases. Despite the long-standing doctrine that the pope was empowered to judge complaints brought by anyone from any part of Christendom,[35] litigation at the papal court in earlier times had consisted primarily of appeals against decisions by lower-ranking prelates. From the pontificate of Alexander III onward, however, increasing numbers of litigants who could afford to do so chose to bring their cases directly to the papal court without first seeking a hearing in any lower court. In short order, first-instance cases at the Roman curia came to outnumber appellate cases by a large majority.[36]

---

32. Gerhoch was familiar with Bernard's *De consideratione* and referred to it explicitly in his *Letter to Pope Hadrian* 3.8, at 28. See also Morrison's analysis of Gerhoch's commentary on Ps. 64 in "The Church as Play," 114–44.

33. *Letter to Pope Hadrian* 45.1–8, at 113–15.

34. Sayers, *Papal Judges Delegate*, 2–5; Robinson, *The Papacy*, 184–85. Müller, *Päpstliche Delegationsgerichtsbarkeit* 1:32 presents a graphic representation of the growing volume of papal judicial business that originated in the duchy of Normandy between 1090 and 1216.

35. JK 664; Ivo, *Panormia* 4.9 (*PL* 161:1184); Gratian C. 9 q. 3 c. 17.

36. Thus, e.g., 1 Comp. 1.21.6 (X 1.29.5; JL 12293), 1 Comp. 1.21.16 (X 1.29.11; JL 13835). Like almost half of the other chapters in the title on judges delegate in the Liber Extra, these are both decretals of Alexander III. See also *Papal Decretals Relating to the*

It was extremely difficult, and often impossible, for the pope and cardinals to learn all the relevant facts of cases that came to them from distant lands. Accordingly, popes from the time of Paschal II onward commonly assigned the hearing of such cases to judges-delegate. These were ad hoc judges appointed from among the prelates of the region where a case arose. Their letters of appointment outlined the case as alleged by a petitioner and directed the judges-delegate to investigate the facts of the situation. On the basis of their findings of fact, the judges were then authorized to give the appropriate remedies, as specified in their letters of appointment, with full papal authority.[37]

Since it was essential that the parties have confidence in the judges, petitioners for the appointment of judges-delegate usually suggested the names of the judges that they wished to have appointed. An opponent (or in practice, his proctor) who objected to a particular individual typically suggested the name of a judge more acceptable to him. Sensible parties, or their proctors, in fact often tried to agree in advance on the names of the judges they wanted, a procedure calculated to save both of them time, trouble, and expense.[38]

A judge-delegate was not necessarily expected to have any formal training in law, although some were in fact lawyers, occasionally well-known ones—Bulgarus, for example, decided cases as a papal judge-delegate in 1151 and 1159, and popes from time to time named other law teachers or advocates to fill this function.[39] Appointees who lacked substantial legal learning might seek advice on difficult points of law from assessors,[40] while at least a few repaired the gaps in their knowledge through private study, as did Abbot Samson of Bury St. Edmunds (b. ca. 1135, d. 1211). Upon learning that the pope proposed to appoint him as a judge-delegate, "a task of which he had neither knowledge nor experience," Samson

---

Diocese of Lincoln, xviii; Sayers, *Papal Judges Delegate*, 5–8; Maitland, *Roman Canon Law*, 103–105.

37. The procedure was reminiscent of, and may well have been modeled upon, the ancient Roman formulary system. Lists of appointees appear in Sayers, *Papal Judges Delegate*, 284–301; Müller, *Päpstliche Delegationsgerichtsbarkeit* 2:1–80; and *Twelfth-Century English Archidiaconal and Vice-Archidiaconal Acta*, 197–98.

38. Herde, *Beiträge*, 217; Müller, *Päpstliche Delegationsgerichtsbarkeit* 1:194–202; Sayers, *Papal Judges Delegate*, 109–18.

39. Kantorowicz, *Studies*, 68; Sayers, *Papal Judges Delegate*, 118–20; Müller, *Päpstliche Delegationsgerichtsbarkeit*, 1:204–207; Hirschfeld, "Gerichtswesen der Stadt Rom," 460, 530–31.

40. *Chronicle of Battle Abbey*, 232–33; Müller, *Päpstliche Delegationsgerichtsbarkeit* 1:182–83.

[F]orthwith called to him two clerks skilled in the law and associated them with himself, making use of their counsel in ecclesiastical business, and studying the decrees and decretal letters, whenever he had time, so that within a short time by reading of books and practice in causes he came to be regarded as a wise judge, proceeding in court according to the form of law.[41]

Samson was no doubt exceptional in this as he was in other respects, but his example demonstrates that in the 1180s at least it was still possible for a diligent judge-delegate to acquire an adequate working knowledge of canon law through part-time study. Not all appointees, of course, were as conscientious as the abbot of Bury St. Edmunds. Judges-delegate were subject to the usual range of human peculiarities, and a few proved perversely unfit to discharge their duties. One such pair, who operated in Germany about 1150, according to John of Salisbury, cared nothing for the law, but used their appointment to line their pockets. They were, in John's words, "tormentors of men and extorters of money, who oppressed the innocent and emptied coffers." Pope Eugene III eventually revoked their mandate.[42]

As popes, beginning with Alexander III, began to receive greater numbers of first-instance cases, the use of judges-delegate increased rapidly. The tide of such cases continued to swell until the mid-thirteenth century, when the papal administration at last began to develop a system of central courts, complete with professional judges and lawyers. At about the same time, moreover, bishops, archbishops, and some lower-ranking prelates, began to develop permanent courts of their own, staffed by trained lawyers. These developments may account for what seems to have been a slow decline in the proportion of ecclesiastical cases heard by judges-delegate beginning in the closing decades of the thirteenth century.[43]

The Courts of Bishops and Lesser Prelates

Although the pope might in all sincerity style himself "everyone's ordinary judge" (*iudex ordinarius omnium*),[44] common folk were unlikely to be aware

---

41. Jocelin of Brakelond, *Chronicle*, 33–34.

42. John of Salisbury, *Historia pontificalis* 38, at 76.

43. Cheney, "Compromise of Avranches," 180–81; Sayers, *Papal Judges Delegate*, 9–25. I am indebted to Charles Donahue, Jr., for the suggestion concerning the decline of ecclesiastical cases.

44. Innocent III in X 1.6.19 (Po 949); Tancred, *Ordo iudiciarius* 1.1.1, 2.1.2, at 91, 127; cf. Gratian C. 9 q. 3 d.p.c. 9 and c. 17. Maitland first called attention to the importance of this concept in *Roman Canon Law*, 100–31.

of his claim. Even those who knew of it could seldom have been in a position to avail themselves of his services. In a world where twenty miles represented a hard day's journey and canon law decreed that no one could lawfully be required to attend a hearing situated more than a two-day journey from the diocese in which he lived, Rome seemed very far away to most people. To travel there was costly, time-consuming, and often dangerous into the bargain. Even those who lived in the Italian peninsula were likely to deem a journey to Rome intimidating, while for those who dwelt beyond the sea or north of the Alps the prospect could be positively terrifying.[45] Confessors imposed a pilgrimage to Rome as a penance only on sinners guilty of some truly vicious crime, such as murder, arson, sacrilege, incest, or violation of the seal of confession. When Innocent III (1198–1216) summoned the bishops of Christendom to Rome for the Fourth Lateran Council, he thought it necessary to impress upon them that the perils of travel and civic unrest in Rome itself were no excuse for failure to appear. "No man," he added, "will ever cross the ocean if he is always waiting for the sea to cease its turmoil."[46]

While the use of papal judges-delegate made appeals to the papacy cheaper and less daunting than they might otherwise have been, even this involved greater effort and expense than most litigants were willing or able to bear. Instead, when ordinary people, clerics or laity, needed or wanted to seek out a church authority to settle their quarrels, other tribunals lay conveniently at hand. Although the services of local church courts were not cost-free, they were apt to be considerably cheaper than the papal judicial system. One drawback in seeking redress locally lay in the fact that the result might not be final: there was always the possibility that a dissat-

---

45. The requirement that hearings could be held no more than a two-day journey from home appears in 4 Lat. (1215) c. 37 (= X 1.3.28). Pope John XXII (r. 1316–34) later reduced this to a one-day journey (Extrav. comm. 2.1.1). On the hardships of travel, see, e.g., Parks, *The English Traveler*; Verdon, *Travel in the Middle Ages*; Ohler, *The Medieval Traveler*. Abbot Samson's account of his journey ca. 1160 to Rome and Jacques de Vitry's description of his journey through northern Italy to Genoa in 1216 illustrate the kinds of dangers, both natural and human, that travelers might encounter (Jocelin of Brakelond, *Chronicle*, 48–49; Jacques de Vitry, *Lettres*, 72–77). See also Maitland, *Roman Canon Law*, 113–15; Cheney, *From Becket to Langton*, 62–63; Birch, *Pilgrimage to Rome*, 38–71; Sumption, *Pilgrimage*, 175–82.

46. *Selected Letters of Pope Innocent III*, no. 51, at 147. On pilgrimages to Rome as penance, see Bartholomew of Exeter, *Penitential* 22, in Morey, *Bartholomew of Exeter*, 191–92; Robert of Flamborough, *Liber poenitentialis* 3.163; 5.280, 315, 350, at 160, 234, 255, 273; Sumption, *Pilgrimage*, 98–100, 104–109.

isfied opponent could appeal. Litigants, therefore, needed to make a series of tactical decisions at the outset on whether to go to a local authority in the hope that the case would not be appealed, or else to bring the matter to the papal court system from the beginning. If they opted to begin in the local courts, they must also decide which level of court was most advantageous for their purposes.

Officials-Principal

Local bishops experienced many of the same difficulties in managing their legal caseload as popes did, albeit on a smaller scale. One of the most important tasks of all bishops from early on in the history of the Christian church, in addition to their liturgical and administrative functions, was to settle quarrels and disputes that arose within the communities that they both served and ruled. Up to the middle of the twelfth century, most bishops most of the time required only intermittent assistance to deal with this part of their duties. Bishops as a rule deferred serious or complicated controversies, especially those that were not urgent, until the next meeting of the diocesan synod, which was the usual and customary setting for the adjudication of ecclesiastical disputes.[47] When a case proved especially complex or sensitive, a bishop might seek guidance from the pope on handling the matter, although this of course entailed substantial delay, as well as expense.

Faced with a problem that needed a quick decision, a bishop could decide to deal with the matter himself, and much of the time that was probably his best choice. Bishops and other prelates were supposed to know some law, and conscientious performance of their official duties required them to be (or become) men of affairs.[48] When a case presented more

---

47. Twelfth-century English bishops typically held synods twice a year (Brett, *English Church under Henry I*, 155–61; Morris, "From Synod to Consistory," 116). Cheney, *English Synodalia*, 8, 26–31 describes the judicial procedure used by English episcopal synods in the twelfth and thirteenth centuries. For a few concrete examples of how this worked in action, see, e.g., *Chronicle of Battle Abbey*, 124–27, 200; *English Episcopal Acta I*, 120–21, no. 193; *English Episcopal Acta II*, 29, no. 47A; *English Episcopal Acta V*, 78–79, no. 100–101, *English Episcopal Acta 18*, 107–108, no. 138; and cf. Foreville, "Synod of the Province of Rouen."

48. Thus, e.g., Gratian D. 39 c. 1, and Rufinus, *Summa* on this passage, 93. See also, e.g., Gratian, D. 10 c. 3, d.p.c. 6, c. 7; D. 38 c. 4 (JK 371), c. 7; C. 11 q. 1 d.p.c. 30; Stephen of Tournai, *Summa* to D. 38 c. 4 v. *canones*, 58; Rufinus, *Summa* to D. 38 c. 4 v. *lic. canon. ignorare*, 91. Prelates whose canonical learning was deficient often came to regret it, as did Abbot Odo of Battle (r. 1175–1200); *Chronicle of Battle Abbey*, 324–25.

difficult problems than he was prepared to cope with, a bishop ought to consult whatever legal experts happened to be available. As canon law grew more complex and its procedural technicalities become more numerous and arcane, many bishops began to find it not so much advisable as essential to make sure that they had trained legal advisers readily available on a regular basis.[49] Prior to the third quarter of the twelfth century, men with formal training in law occasionally appeared in the households of bishops, who presumably found it useful to have a resident source of informed legal advice.[50] Up to that point, however, such arrangements were luxuries in which few bishops indulged.

Around 1175, this gradually began to change, although the pace of change varied in different regions. More and more bishops started to recruit men knowledgeable in law to serve in their administration. At first bishops usually added these recruits to their households (*familia*). They, like the bishop's other *familiares*, were in constant attendance on him, ate at his table, slept in quarters that he provided, and accompanied him on his endless peregrinations from one end of his diocese to the other. The household literally ate up the greater part of most bishops' revenues.[51] Later, during the thirteenth century, bishops' lawyers gradually detached themselves from the episcopal *familia* and ceased to follow him on his travels. Instead bishops with increasingly frequency rewarded their lawyers with prebends

49. Fournier, *Officialités*, 7–8. Eminent canonistic authorities were apt to receive a constant stream of requests for their opinions from bishops and others who needed help with difficult problems; see, e.g., Ivo of Chartres, *Epist.* 16, 26, 27, 41, 45, 57, 67, 69, in his *Correspondence*, 64–71, 106–17, 164–69, 184–89, 228–31, 298–99, 304–309.

50. One of the earliest to do so was Robert Bloet, bishop of Lincoln, 1093–1123, who employed Master Gilbert of Sempringham as a clerk and legal adviser (Cheney, *English Bishops' Chanceries*, 11, 23). John of Salisbury, whose legal learning was impressive, served in the household of Archbishop Theobald of Canterbury (r. 1139–61) and assisted the archbishop in handling much of his legal business, as his letters make clear. Thomas Becket studied law himself during his exile and also kept Lombard of Piacenza, William FitzStephen, and Philip of Calne, all trained canonists, in his household (Knowles, *Thomas Becket*, 57; Smalley, *Becket Conflict*, 121–25).

51. See Cheney, *English Bishops' Chanceries*, 4–21. Moorman, *Church Life*, 175–79, provides a graphic picture of thirteenth-century episcopal households on the move. Italian bishops, with their considerably smaller (and poorer) dioceses, made do with smaller and cheaper households. Although they were not immune from the constant travel that was common to bishops everywhere, the small size of their dioceses made life less strenuous for them and their households than it was for their counterparts north of the Alps. Brentano, *A New World*, 45, 81–106, gives some idea of what was involved in one such diocese.

in their cathedral chapters and similar revenue-producing appointments. This not only enabled them to establish independent households of their own, but also made it convenient for the bishop to delegate much of his judicial work to a legal expert who could hold court in the bishop's name at a fixed place—usually in the bishop's cathedral city, often enough in the cathedral church itself. Such an arrangement was a considerable convenience for litigants, who no longer needed to trail the bishop from one parish to another as they waited until he found an opportunity to listen to their complaints.[52]

Sources from the British Isles provide abundant evidence about these developments from the 1170s onward. Bishop Seffrid II of Chichester (r. 1180–1204), for example, whose own legal learning was not insignificant, employed Master Ralph of Ford to assist him, among other things, in dealing with legal problems. Bishop Seffrid's contemporary, Archbishop John Comyn of Dublin (r. 1182–1212), maintained in his household a resident canonist, who was the author of the procedural treatise *Quia iudiciorum quedam*. Hubert Walter, archbishop of Canterbury (r. 1193–1205) was spectacularly successful in adding distinguished lawyers to his staff. As mentioned earlier, he enticed several outstanding teachers of canon law at Oxford, including John of Tynemouth, Simon of Sywell, and Master Honorius, to desert their classrooms and join his staff. They, like lawyers in the service of other bishops, appear in the records bearing a variety of titles and duties: they might double as a schoolmaster (*magister scholarum*), or a chancery draftsman, more often as a chaplain. Some of them also functioned as legal consultants or advocates for private clients while they were in a bishop's service.[53]

As bishops and archbishops experienced an increase in judicial business not unlike the one that threatened to overwhelm the pope, they responded in much the same way that the popes had done: they, too, delegated. Starting around 1170 in the triangular region bounded on the north and west by the British Isles, on the south by Normandy, and on the east by the Rhineland, documents from one diocese after another begin to show that the skilled legal advisers who belonged to a bishop's household or formed a regular part

52. Cheney, *English Bishops' Chanceries*, 20–21; Fournier, *Officialités*, 18–20, 60–62; Burger, "*Officiales* and the *Familiae* of the Bishops of Lincoln."

53. *Acta of the Bishops of Chichester*, 13–21; Fowler-Magerl, *Ordo iudiciorum*, 105–6; Zulueta and Stein, *Teaching of Roman Law*, xli; Cheney, *English Bishops' Chanceries*, 19–20, 23, 39, and *Hubert Walter*, 164–66; Lewis, "Canonists and Law Clerks"; Ficker, *Forschungen* 3:103–106; Santini, "Legis doctores," 124–26; Merello Altea, *Scienze e professione legale*, 56.

of his administrative team were also commencing to preside as judges for all save the most sensitive cases that came to the bishop for adjudication. Contemporary documents usually describe these judges as bishops' "officials." In the technical terminology that the canonists borrowed from Roman law, the officials exercised the bishop's ordinary jurisdiction.[54]

Bishops' officials seldom show up before the thirteenth century in documents that survive from regions outside of this triangle in northwest Europe. No bishop's official appears in Polish records, for example, until 1248 at Wrocław and 1267 at Cracow, and their earliest appearances in Bohemia occurred in 1265 at Prague and 1267 at Olomütz.[55] In Italy, where dioceses were generally smaller and poorer than those north of the Alps, busy bishops usually appointed a vicar-general, who commonly combined the functions of a judge with other administrative assignments.[56] As diocesan administrators everywhere grew more numerous and more specialized, the bishop's chief judge and legal adviser was sometimes styled the official-principal, to distinguish him from the numerous other officials who served the bishop in different capacities.[57]

54. Thus, e.g., John of Salisbury, *Letters* 2:384, no. 223 (1167); Council of Westminster (1175) c. 1 and Legatine Council of York (1195) in Whitelock, Brett & Brooke 2:978, 1045; *English Episcopal Acta II*, 107, no. 130; *Acta of the Bishops of Chichester*, 185, 201, nos. 133, 152; Fournier, *Officialités*, 4–5; Vleeschouwers-Van Melkebeek, *Officialiteit van Doornik*, 11; Cheney, *English Bishops' Chanceries*, 20–21; Morris, "From Synod to Consistory," 120–21; Graham, "Administration of the Diocese of Ely," 49. Bernard of Pavia defined the term thus: "Ordinarius iudex est qui in ecclesiasticis ab Apostolico, in secularibus ab Imperatore totalem quandam habet iurisdictionem" (*Summa decretalium* 1.21.1, at 16). For Roman usage of the term *ordinarius*, see Kaser, *Römische Zivilprozessrecht*, 529–30.

55. Trusen, "Gelehrte Gerichtsbarkeit," 468–70; Vleeschouwers-Van Melkebeek, *Officialiteit van Doornik*, 40–44; Carlen, "Zum Offizialität von Sitten," 221–22; Brouette, "La plus ancienne mention," 366; Hinschius, *System des katholischen Kirchenrechts* 2:205–208; Vetulani, "Einführung der Offiziale in Polen"; Erdö, "Mittelalterliche Offizialate."

56. See Brentano, *Two Churches*, 62–66, 78–82; Trusen, "Gelehrte Gerichtsbarkeit," 470–71. P. Fournier, *Officialités*, 3–4, maintained that bishops' officials and vicars-general originally performed much the same set of tasks, but then slowly became differentiated, with officials retaining primarily judicial functions, while vicars-general relieved the bishop of numerous more purely administrative matters. E. Fournier in *Les origines du vicaire-général*, on the other hand, insisted that the functions of the two offices had been separate from their very beginning.

57. Bishops were not the only prelates who found it helpful to appoint officials to handle most or all of their judicial business. Archdeacons, archpriests, deans, subdeans, abbots, priors, even cathedral chapters by the early thirteenth century can be

As officials became more common and more important, their position became more clearly defined. A bishop could not appoint just anyone he pleased as his official: canonical rules set limits on his choice. In order to function legitimately as an ordinary judge, the official must first, not surprisingly, be Catholic and male. He must also be a cleric of good moral character and reputation, at least twenty-five years of age, of free status, and legally sane.[58] Although no formal legal prescription specified his minimal educational qualifications, the great majority of officials whose educational background can be documented had studied law.

During the first half of the thirteenth century, the nature of the jurisdiction of bishops' officials changed. At the beginning of the century, officials exercised their bishop's ordinary jurisdiction as bishop's delegates, and their decisions could be appealed to the bishop who appointed them. By midcentury, however, custom had so enhanced the position of officials that they had virtually replaced their bishops so far as the exercise of ordinary jurisdiction was concerned. For jurisdictional purposes, the official *was* the bishop. Pope Innocent IV (r. 1243–54) ruled in 1246 that a disappointed litigant could not appeal from the decision of the official to the bishop, but must instead take his complaint to a higher court, such as that of the archbishop or the pope.[59] While the bishop retained the power to dismiss

---

found commissioning officials to adjudicate disputes brought before them (Fournier, *Officialités*, 11–12). The archdeacon of Hainault had an official as early as 1180, as did an archdeacon in the diocese of Lincoln, and an archdeacon in Wiltshire around 1190, but such appointments did not become common elsewhere until the early thirteenth century. See Brouette, "La plus ancienne mention," 367–68; Cheney, *English Bishops' Chanceries*, 143–46; Fournier, *Officialités*, 10–12, 16–17; Smith, "The Officialis," 208; Kemp, introduction to *Twelfth-Century Archidiaconal and Vice-Archidiaconal Acta*, i–liv.

58. On the first requirement, Huguccio, *Summa* to C. 3 q. 7 d.p.c. 1 v. *femine*, BAV MS Vat. lat. 2280, at 134rb, quoted in Minnucci, *La capacità processuale*, 114: "*Femine*. Hec iudicare non possunt, ut xxxiii. q. v. mulerem [C. 33 q. 5 c. 17]. Sed quid de comitissa Matilda que iudicauit et de multis aliis que cotidie iudicant? Quid denique de Delbora qui legitur in ueteri testamento iudicasse, ut xv. q. iii. § econtra [C. 15 q. 3 pr. §3]; sed in ueteri testamento ex causa fuit permissum ut femine iudicarent effeminatum populum, non autem prohibentur iudicare et si aliter fiat, non est de uir. Prohibentur tamen iudicare pro se, sed non per alios si sint regine uel ducisse uel comitisse." On his character, age, status, etc., Bernard of Pavia, *Summa decretalium* 1.23.1, at 18–19; Tancred, *Ordo iudiciarius* 1.1.2, at 92–94; Fournier, *Officialités*, 18.

59. Bernard of Pavia, *Summa decretalium* 2.20, §3, at 59–60; VI 2.15.3 (Po 12061); Trusen, "Gelehrte Gerichtsbarkeit," 474–75; Fournier, *Officialités*, 13; Morris, "From Synod to Consistory," 119, 121.

an official and replace him with another, he could not overrule him. Since the official's jurisdiction was bestowed on him by a formal mandate from the bishop, those powers expired at the bishop's death. Bishops, moreover, continued to retain some jurisdictional powers in their own hands. They exercised those powers in a court of audience, which was separate from the consistory court over which the official presided.[60]

The expansion of the powers of bishops' officials exposed them to the temptations that accompany authority. Predictably not all officials resisted those temptations successfully. Peter of Blois, the younger (b. ca. 1135, d. 1211), for one, found the behavior of bishops' officials remarkably sinister. They are filled with malice, he declared. Not merely do they shear the sheep in the bishop's flock, they scrub them down and skin them to boot.[61] Writing to the official newly appointed by the bishop of Chartres, Peter warned:

> If you believe me, or rather if you believe in God, relinquish at once the office of official, the ministry of damnation, the wheel of evil, and the spirit of giddiness, which spins you into empty space. Have mercy on your soul by pleasing God, whom you cannot please unless you put that office behind you.[62]

Peter was scarcely alone in his harsh criticism of bishops' officials. Walter of Châtillon and other poets of the late twelfth and early thirteenth centuries

---

60. X 1.29.19 (Lucius III, JL 15443); cf. Dig. 17.1.26 pr. and 17.1.27.3; Trusen, "Gelehrte Gerichtsbarkeit," 474; Fournier, *Officialités*, 19–20. On courts of audience, Owen, "An Episcopal Audience Court," 140–49, and "Ecclesiastical Jurisdiction in England," 200–201; Thompson, *The English Clergy*, 54–56; Churchill, *Canterbury Administration* 1:470–83, 489–97. Writers on the Continent often used the term *audientia* to designate an appellate court, as contrasted with *auditorium*, which usually meant a court of first instance (Morris, "From Synod to Consistory," 119 n. 1).

61. Peter of Blois, *Epist.* 25 in his *Opera* 1:91: "Tota officialium intentio est, ut ... miserrimas oves quasi vice illorum [*scil*: episcoporum] tondeant, emungant, excorient."

62. Peter of Blois, *Epist.* 25, at 1:94: "Si mihi credis, imo si credis in Deum, relinque maturius officialis officium, ministerium damnationis, rotam malorum, et spiritum vertiginis, qui te ad inania circumvolvit. Miserere animae tuae placens Deo: cui placere non potest sine perditione officii." Peter's invective is doubly ironic, since both he and his correspondent—none other than John of Salisbury, who was elected to the see of Chartres in 1176 and held it until his death in 1180—were archdeacons, an office that was even more widely criticized for the same failings that he attributed to bishops' officials.

delighted in denouncing the greed and other moral shortcomings of bishops' officials and their courts.[63] The author of the *Apocalypse of Golias* was even more indignant than Peter of Blois:

> Theire frauds, theire snares, their filthinesses bold,
> Which no great margins of a book can hold.
> These are the men that all the world affright,
> Whose very face for feare makes the earth looke white.
> . . . .
> How much by inbred mischeefe they intend,
> Or by their office how they may offend,
> What pen of swiftest scribe can thoroughly write?[64]

Bishops' Consistory Courts

The judicial activities of officials-principal during the late twelfth and early thirteenth centuries did not necessarily imply the formal existence of a standing court organization. While occasional references to bishops' consistory courts appear in northern European records as early as 1179, they were not yet full-fledged institutions.[65] Bishops' consistory courts (sometimes called officialities) typically grew into permanent institutions, complete with a supporting staff to assist the official-principal, over the course of several generations following the initial appearance of the officials, who would become their presiding judges. Institutionalized officialities first appeared in England around 1240, and by 1260 they were becoming well established.[66] Similarly in the French kingdom, the elaborate bishop's court

---

63. Walter of Châtillon, "Captivata largitas," in *Moralisch-Satirische Gedichte*, 110–12; Yunck, *Lineage of Lady Meed*, 117–22.

64. An Elizabethan translation of the "Apocalypsis Goliae episcopi," ll. 221–31; the text appears in *Latin Poems*, 11–12, and the translation at 287.

65. Ralph of Diceto, *Ymagines historiarum*, s.a. 1179, in Whitelock, Brett & Brooke 2:1015. This discussion of the development of bishops' courts has benefited from preliminary drafts of three chapters, as yet unpublished, by Charles Donahue, Jr. (France and adjoining areas), Richard H. Helmholz (England), and Gero Dolezalek (Italy), forthcoming in the *History of Medieval Canon Law*, ed. Wilfried Hartmann and Kenneth Pennington. I am exceedingly grateful to the authors and editors of the series for access to this material.

66. Morris, "A Consistory Court," 151–53, and "From Synod to Consistory," 123. Fournier assumed that the official and the officiality originated simultaneously, but more recent research makes this seem highly unlikely (Smith, "'Officialis' of the Bishop," 201–20).

at Reims, for example, described in its 1267 constitutions must have been developing for at least a decade or more prior to that time.[67]

Church courts grew more numerous and more complex as their workload increased and diversified. The records of bishops' courts show that they dealt with a broad range of matters. Matrimonial litigation was one of the mainstays of most consistories, as was the punishment of fornication, adultery, concubinage, and other sexual offences. The courts also dealt with transgressors against other disciplinary rules, such as those against usury or working on Sundays and holy days. Bishops' officials, not surprisingly, dealt with transactions involving church property, disputes over benefices, the collection of tithes and other church revenues, and the probate of decedents' estates. Beyond that, defamation fell within the jurisdiction of bishops' consistories, as did breach of sworn contracts and other agreements.[68]

In addition to the official-principal, we begin during the second half of the thirteenth century to encounter additional judges, generically entitled commissary judges, appointed to act as the official's substitute during his absence, or else to perform some particular part of the official's duties that he no longer had time to deal with in person.[69] In mid-sized English dioceses, it was common to use a commissary judge, sometimes called the corrector, to handle cases that involved disciplinary or criminal charges (often labeled *ex officio* or office matters), leaving the official free to concentrate on civil litigation. In the extraordinarily large diocese of Lincoln, on the other hand, bishops assigned commissary judges to particular regions of the diocese, where they took care of a broad variety of time-consuming business, especially the probate of wills and associated matters.[70] Elsewhere a commissary judge might be commissioned to hear cases situated in out-of-the-way places that were difficult of access.[71] Commissary judges were not infrequently men of considerable distinction, such as, for example, Henry

67. *Privilegia curie Remensis*, 3–33.
68. Woodcock, *Medieval Ecclesiastical Courts*, 79–92; Donahue, introduction to *Select Cases*, ed. Adams and Donahue, 72–103; Helmholz, *Canon Law and Ecclesiastical Jurisdiction*, 355–598, 626–42.
69. John de Grandisson, *Register*, 807–808; Churchill, *Canterbury Administration* 2:188–90; Morris, "Commissary of the Bishop," 50–51.
70. Owen, "Ecclesiastical Jurisdiction in England," 201; Morris, "Commissary of the Bishop," 53–59.
71. Thus, e.g., in 1289 the archdeacon of Lichfield appointed the rector of Hawarden to hear cases in his parish for a limited time because it was cut off by flooding (*Great Register of Lichfield Cathedral*, 316).

de Staunton, an Oxford professor of canon law who subsequently became chancellor of the university and official of the Court of Arches.[72]

In addition to commissary judges, it became common for larger consistory courts to empower one or more special officers to perform the tiresome—and occasionally hazardous—task of taking the depositions of witnesses. The mid-thirteenth-century York statutes went so far as to mandate the appointment of several diligent and discreet examiners in each deanery of the diocese.[73] Examiners, who were often drawn from the ranks of the advocates or proctors of the court, took an oath to fulfill their office faithfully and were paid a salary.[74]

The Fourth Lateran Council required ecclesiastical judges to employ notaries to maintain official records of their actions, and evidence concerning notarial staffs attached to officials' courts suggests that on the Continent at least this injunction was soon implemented in practice.[75] Court seals furnish additional evidence that consistory courts were becoming institutionalized. Officials-principal from early on had authenticated documents with a personal seal, but by the 1220s consistory courts had begun to acquire their own seals, which clearly signaled that courts had acquired an institutional identity separate from that of the official or bishop.[76]

72. Donahue, introduction to *Select Cases*, ed. Adams and Donahue, 19; BRUO 3:1768. Further examples appear in Ollivant, *Court of the Official*, 53–54; Lefebvre-Teillard, *Officialités*, 37; Steins, "Ordentliche Zivilprozeß," 228.

73. Statutes of York I (ca. 1241–55) c. 35 in Powicke & Cheney 1:493.

74. Henry Burghersh, *Statuta consistorii* §2, in Wilkins, *Concilia* 2:571–72; Donahue, introduction to *Select Cases*, ed. Adams and Donahue, 19–20; Churchill, *Canterbury Administration* 1:446–50, 2:192–95, 225–26, 240–41; Steins, "Ordentliche Zivilprozeß," 257.

75. On the Fourth Lateran Council ruling, see 4 Lat. (1215) c. 38, in *Constitutiones*, 80–81, and DEC 1:252. Record keeping of church court proceedings prior to that time had been sporadic at best. The few records that do survive from the twelfth century are usually brief and laconic. Parties and church officials presumably relied on the memories of participants and witnesses as their primary record (Morris, "From Synod to Consistory," 117). Regarding the Continent, see Fournier, *Officialités*, 46–47. Similar evidence for court notaries also survives for other dioceses in France and Flanders, including Laon, Soissons, Tournai, and Liège. See Vleeschouwers-Van Melkebeek, *Officialiteit van Doornik*, 100–102; Trusen, "Gelehrte Gerichtsbarkeit," 478–79.

76. Fournier, *Officialités*, 303–5. In England, c. 28 of the legatine council of London in 1237 specified that bishops' officials must authenticate documents with a seal that bore the title of their office and that an outgoing official would pass on to his successor (Powicke & Cheney 1:257–58; Graham, "Administration of the Diocese of Ely," 50–51).

By the middle of the thirteenth century, consistory court staffs in many places had grown large and busy enough to warrant appointing a registrar to supervise notaries, scribes, and other functionaries.[77] Registrars were paid primarily out of court fees and sometimes supplemented this income from private practice as notaries public. York Minster had a "writing house" (*domus scriptorie*) where the registrar and his scribes worked and presumably kept the court records available for consultation when required. The *Privilegia curie Remensis* described the registrar as "the donkey of the court" and added that his tasks were not only difficult, but often exceedingly unpleasant. On the other hand, the position could be very lucrative.[78] In any case, the registrar was a key figure in managing the court's operations.

In addition to notaries, scribes, and clerks, a court also needed the services of strong, muscular functionaries to carry messages, serve summonses, keep order, and enforce the judge's decisions. Scattered references to these men, variously described as apparitors, summoners, or bailiffs, began to appear in canons and court records from the thirteenth century onward. To them fell the difficult, unpleasant, and occasionally dangerous work of summoning reluctant defendants to appear to answer complaints against them. Apparitors needed to be able to defend themselves, since their work could easily make them unpopular, and it was not unknown for them to be attacked, both verbally and physically, in the course of performing their duties.[79]

In addition to serving summonses, apparitors performed numerous miscellaneous tasks. They collected the fines that the court levied on losing parties and deposited them with the court's treasurer (*camerarius*). They delivered messages of all kinds, not only for the official and his court but also for the bishop. They often took inventories of decedents' estates and brought instances of irregular conduct among the faithful to the court's attention. At Reims, an apparitor appeared at the official's house every ses-

77. Fournier, *Officialités*, 28–29; Helmholz, *Canon Law and Ecclesiastical Jurisdiction*, 213–14; Trusen, "Gelehrte Gerichtsbarkeit," 476–77. Churchill, *Canterbury Administration* 2:195–98, prints nine letters of appointment for registrars of the Court of Canterbury.

78. York, Borthwick Institute D/C.AB.1, at 73vb; *Privilegia curie Remensis*, 20: "Registri autem officium odibile est ultra modum, super omnia eciam servilia opera ponderosum, et qui ipsum exercet satis habet laqueum in colo; asinus enim est curie, et talis debet esse quod paciencer sustinere valeat clamores, noisias, jurgia, minas, rixas, convictia multipliciter eidem cotidie inferenda," Woodcock, *Medieval Ecclesiastical Courts*, 76–77.

79. *John Lydford's Book*, 141, no. 250; *An Episcopal Court Book*, 63; Council of Aschaffenburg (1292) c. 16, in Mansi 24:1090.

sion day to conduct him to the court, attended him while the court was sitting, and escorted him back home again at the close of business.[80]

Chaucer's characterization of the Summoner in the *Canterbury Tales* reflects the widespread reputation for venality among such officers. Occasional notices in episcopal records of disciplinary actions against apparitors for bribery and corruption shows that their reputation was not entirely unmerited.[81]

The Courts of Archdeacons and Other Prelates

Lesser prelates also held courts, settled disputes, and exercised jurisdiction over the faithful within their more limited spheres. Although their jurisdiction usually covered only a relatively small area and a limited range of matters, they were very numerous. Since these courts applied the disciplinary rules of canon law at the grassroots level, they were more likely than the higher church tribunals to have an impact on the everyday lives of ordinary Christians.[82]

The lesser prelate that people in northern Europe were most likely to encounter was the archdeacon, sometimes called "the bishop's eye."[83] Archdeacons, appointed by and responsible to their diocesan bishops, were responsible for safeguarding the bishop's interests and supervising the morals and manners of both clergy and laity within one of the local districts into which large dioceses were commonly divided.[84] The archdea-

---

80. Thus, e.g., Legatine Council of London (1237) c. 26, Statutes of Worcester III (1240) c. 48–49, and Statutes for the London Archdeaconry (ca. 1229–41) c. 8 in Powicke & Cheney 1:256–57, 308–309, 333–34; Vleeschouwers-Van Melkebeek, *Officialiteit van Doornik*, 113–14; *Privilegia curie Remensis*, 15–16; William Wickwane, *Register*, 215, no. 518. See also Woodcock, *Medieval Ecclesiastical Courts*, 45–49, 69–70, 72–73.

81. Chaucer, *Canterbury Tales*, General Prologue, ll. 654–65; William Wickwane, *Register*, 211, 214–15, nos. 505, 518; Wunderli, "Pre-Reformation London Summoners," 210–11; Woodcock, *Medieval Ecclesiastical Courts*, 49.

82. Owen, "Ecclesiastical Jurisdiction in England," 202–204; Helmholz, *Canon Law and Ecclesiastical Jurisdiction*, 216–17; Hinschius, *System des katholischen Kirchenrechts* 2:193–205.

83. Pseudo-Clement I §12 (JK †10); *Decretales Pseudo-Isidorianae*, ed. Hinschius, 34, also in Gratian, D. 93 c. 6; Innocent III (Po 5031), in X 1.23.7 §4.

84. Gratian, D. 23 c. 22; D. 25 c. 1 §11; D. 94 d.a.c. 3 and c. 3; X 1.23.1, 7.9; Bernard of Pavia, *Summa decretalium* 1.15–20, at 16. *Twelfth-Century English Archidiaconal and Vice-Archidiaconal Acta* provides examples of some types of archidiaconal activity, although as the editor notes in the introduction (xlii), these documents present only a partial picture of their doings. At least in England, monasteries that enjoyed exemption from

con was supposed to refer the most serious infractions of canon law that he detected to the bishop's court for judgment, although not all archdeacons regularly did so. The archdeacon also had the right to prosecute lesser offenses in his own court. An archdeacon was entitled to keep the revenue from the fines he imposed in his court, and this no doubt accounts for the ruthless zeal that many archdeacons displayed in hunting down even minor infractions of ecclesiastical regulations. Consequently, archdeacons became deeply unpopular among both clergy and laity.[85] The biographer of St. Gilbert of Sempringham (b. ca. 1084, d. 1189) noted that Gilbert was reluctant to accept appointment as an archdeacon since he did not wish to have "a financial interest in the multiplication of sin."[86] Less saintly figures were apparently not often prone to such delicate feelings.

Other prelates below the rank of bishop might also hold courts. Archdeacons who held large archdeaconries sometimes named rural deans (in some places called archpriests) to supervise some portion of their bailiwick. The rural dean, whom an unkind poet described as "the archdeacon's dog," possessed within his deanery jurisdictional authority similar to that of the archdeacon.[87] The deans of chapters in cathedral and collegiate churches often enjoyed a so-called peculiar jurisdiction over the persons and properties attached to churches that were exempt from the bishop's authority. The abbots of monasteries had the right to hear and determine controversies among members of the religious communities sub-

---

the local bishop's jurisdiction sometimes appointed archdeacons who exercised jurisdiction over the clergy and laity under monastic control (Sayers, "Monastic Archdeacons," 177–203). By contrast, because dioceses in Italy, Provence, and Dauphiné were mostly very small, archdeacons there remained cathedral dignitaries and possessed neither archdeaconries nor courts (Thompson, "Diocesan Organization in the Middle Ages," 159; Brentano, *Two Churches*, 66–68).

85. Thus, e.g., John of Salisbury, *Letters* 78, 79, 107, 118, 140, at 1:123–25, 169–81, 193–94, 2:24–25; "Apocalypsis Goliae episcopi," ll. 153–56, 161–68, in *Latin Poems*, 9. Archdeacons were commonly thought to be wealthy. Indeed, according to William FitzStephen, King Henry II once complained that archdeacons made more money than he did (*Vita S. Thomae* 33, in *Materials* 3:44).

86. Quoted by Brett, *English Church under Henry I*, 208.

87. Gratian, D. 25 c. 1 §12, D. 50 c. 64; X 1.23.7 §6, 1.24.1–4, 1.25.1; Thompson, "Diocesan Organization in the Middle Ages," 167–76, 186–88. The phrase "archdeacon's dog" comes from the "Apocalypsis Goliae episcopi," ll. 193–94, ed. Wright, 10: "Decanus canis est archidiaconi, / cujus sunt canones latratus dissoni, / canens de canone discors est canoni, / datis et venditis est concors Symoni."

ject to them. Some abbots might also exercise a peculiar jurisdiction over the inhabitants of exempt parishes in which their monastery had proprietary rights.[88]

These prelates sometimes felt the need for expert legal advice and counsel, just as bishops did, especially in carrying out their judicial business. By the late twelfth century, at least in England, many archdeacons had one or more men with formal legal training in their households. Busy archdeacons, when hard pressed, might appoint their legal advisers as vice-archdeacons and empower them to hear cases and give judgments on their behalf. By the end of the century, English archdeacons and other lesser prelates were beginning to use the title official to designate the deputies who attended to their judicial business, and their French counterparts apparently followed suit somewhat later.[89] Some archdeacons employed a registrar and an apparitor or two in their courts, although not all did so. A handful had professional staffs comparable to those of a bishop's consistory court, but this was rare. The courts of most lesser prelates commonly paid only cursory attention to the procedural niceties of the *ordo iuris*. As Maitland put it, "In inferior courts you will get inferior law." Consequently, litigants in these courts seldom felt much need or incentive to use the services of professional proctors, while advocates appeared in them rarely if at all.[90]

Procedure

Advocates, *iurisperiti*, and proctors became increasingly indispensable in canonical litigation in the late twelfth century in large part because of the growth in the complexity and formalism of judicial procedure that commenced in the middle of the century. By 1200, only a foolhardy litigant would choose to initiate a lawsuit or to defend himself against an accusation before a canonical court without some help and guidance from a person who had either formal training in the learned laws or considerable

---

88. Hinschius, *System des katholischen Kirchenrechts* 2:269–77; Thompson, *English Clergy*, 57–71; Morris, "A Consistory Court"; Hyams, "Deans and Their Doings."

89. The archdeacon of Hainault had an official as early as 1180, as did an archdeacon in the diocese of Lincoln and an archdeacon in Wiltshire around 1190, but such appointments did not become common elsewhere until the early thirteenth century. See Brouette, "La plus ancienne mention," 367–68; Cheney, *English Bishops' Chanceries*, 143–46; Smith, "The Officialis," 208; Kemp, introduction to *Twelfth Century Archidiaconal and Vice-Archidiaconal Acta*, l–liv; Fournier, *Officialités*, 10–12, 16–17.

90. Maitland, *Roman Canon Law*, 43; Helmholz, *Canon Law and Ecclesiastical Jurisdiction*, 216–17; Poos, introduction to *Lower Ecclesiastical Jurisdiction*, xii-xxxv, xlv-lii.

practical experience in the courts.[91] As the author of the *Summa "Elegantius in iure diuino,"* put it around 1169:

> [I]f someone is brash enough to presume to rely on his own devices even though he is inexperienced and does not wish to have an advocate, let him do so. Everyone is free to muck up his own case.[92]

Twelfth-century teachers of canon law liked to tell their pupils that God himself had established the foundations of canonical procedure in Paradise when he summoned Adam and Eve, questioned them about eating the forbidden fruit of the tree of the knowledge of good and evil, found their testimony inconsistent, their excuses unconvincing, and in consequence banished them from Paradise (Gen. 3:9–19). This presumably reassured both teachers and students that the basic elements of their procedural system had impeccable origins, although they were surely aware that in recent times matters had become rather more complicated.[93]

Although Roman emperors and popes in late antiquity had insisted that bishops and synods should follow the rules of Roman civil procedure when they adjudicated disputes, the fading away of law schools and the decay of legal learning that began in the fifth century made it impossible to maintain the former procedural standards during the early Middle Ages. Medieval jurists found it difficult to learn much about the technical details of classical Roman procedure because the compilers of Justinian's codification had purposefully stripped most passages dealing with procedural matters out of their sources. The procedures that appeared in the classical sources were not the same as those current in sixth-century Byzantium, and Justinian's commissioners had therefore discarded them—just as present-day law firms dispose of outdated procedural manuals as a matter of course.[94]

Mention of a few basic Roman procedural principles did survive, however, and surfaced occasionally in early medieval legal writings, sometimes

---

91. Reynolds, "Medieval Law," 494. How difficult it would have been for an uninstructed layperson to find a way through the procedural maze even in the mid-twelfth century becomes obvious from the account of it by Jacobi, "Prozeß im Decretum Gratiani."

92. *Summa "Elegantius"* 6.65, at 2:133: "[S]i quis de se presumens, etiam cum imperitus sit, aduocatum habere nolit, suo ingenio relinquatur. Liberum est cuique suam causam negligere."

93. Paucapalea, *Summa, Introductio,* 1; Stephen of Tournai, *Summa, Introductio,* 2; Fowler-Magerl, *Ordo iudiciorum,* 1.

94. Cod. Theod. 16.2.23; Fowler-Magerl, *Ordo iudiciorum,* 9–10; Metzger, *Litigation in Roman Law,* 1–4.

in unexpected places. The Pseudo-Isidorian forgers, for example, demanded that judges adhere to appropriate procedure (*iudiciarius ordo*).[95] The forgers were familiar, too, with the Roman rule that placed the burden of proof on the plaintiff and insisted that judges must require anyone who accused a cleric of misconduct to prove that accusation by clear and convincing evidence.[96] Church reformers during the eleventh century actively encouraged the study and restoration of earlier canon law and enthusiastically participated in collecting the older canonical sources. Procedural law particularly interested the reformers and bulked large in their canonical collections. Systematic study of both Roman and canonistic sources in the twelfth-century law schools acquainted law students and their teachers with the few scraps of information about the workings of the late ancient procedural system to be found in Justinian's *Corpus iuris civilis*.[97]

A firsthand account by Hariulf (b. ca. 1060, d. 1143), abbot of Oudenburg in Flanders, describing his experiences in a lawsuit at the papal consistory in 1141 provides a glimpse into the informality of canonical procedure in the papal consistory around the middle of the twelfth century. When he appeared at the Lateran Palace, Hariulf tells us, Cardinal Haimeric, the papal chancellor, who also served as his legal adviser, greeted him, offered him some words of advice, then took him by the hand and led him into the consistory chamber. There the chancellor introduced Hariulf to Pope Eugene III, who was seated in the midst of his curia, the cardinals at his right hand, Roman noblemen and other laymen on his left. Hariulf made a few preliminary remarks describing the case he wished to bring and was then dismissed so that the consistory could attend to the other matters on its calendar.

Hariulf waited impatiently for nine days until the pope and cardinals

---

95. *Decretales Pseudo-Isidorianae*, Pseudo-Isidore, *Praefatio* §5, at 18.

96. Dig. 22.3.2; Cod. 2.1.4, 7.45.4; *Decretales Pseudo-Isidorianae*, Pseudo-Victor I §1.4, Pseudo-Sixtus II §7, Pseudo-Julius I §2.15, at 128, 193, 469; Fowler-Magerl, *Ordines iudiciarii*, 20–22.

97. E.g., a substantial part of *Diuersorum patrum sententie*, tit. 5–14, c. 44–110, at 44–74, deals with procedural issues. The author of this reformist collection drew these canons in large part from the Pseudo-Isidorian material. See also Gilchrist's "Canon Law Aspects of the Gregorian Reform Programme," 33–38, and his introduction to the *Collection in Seventy-Four Titles*, 25. Our principal source of information about late ancient Roman procedure is the fourth book of the *Institutes* of Gaius, which survives in a single fifth-century palimpsest that was first identified in 1816. This has been supplemented in some details by recent archeological finds (Metzger, "Roman Judges," 245; *New Outline of the Roman Civil Trial*, 1–3; and *Litigation in Roman Law*, 11, 98–99, 111–13).

were free to consider his case. When he was finally summoned to a formal hearing, it took place in the pope's private chamber, with a group of cardinals in attendance. Hariulf was invited to sit next to his counsel, Cardinal Haimeric, on the pope's footstool. To open the proceedings, Hariulf made an oral presentation in which he stated his complaint, specified the relief he sought, and the evidence upon which he relied. He then presented to the pope and cardinals the documents he had brought to support his claims. The pope and his advisers questioned Hariulf and probed his assertions and the evidence in his documents. At the end of the hearing, Hariulf was excused, while the pope and his advisers met in private session. Hariulf was called back on the following day, and Cardinal Haimeric announced that the consistory had decided that judges-delegate should be appointed to investigate the facts of the case back in Flanders.[98]

Hariulf's account thus describes a fairly simple three-stage oral procedure used at the papal consistory around the beginning of the 1140s.[99] The pope, surrounded by cardinals and other legal advisers, first heard oral argument and examined evidence in a public session. Following that, he and his advisers met privately in a closed session to discuss the evidence and the legal issues among themselves. Once they had completed their deliberations and arrived at a decision, they summoned the parties to another public session, at which the pope read out judgment.[100]

This straightforward oral proceeding was far less intricate than the multistage procedure, much of it involving written documents, that jurists at Bologna were beginning to elaborate at about the time that Hariulf's lawsuit took place. Word about these developments in procedural law probably accounts for Cardinal Haimeric's request to Bulgarus for guidance on procedural matters.[101] Bulgarus's reply to that request, the so-called *Ex-*

---

98. Müller, "Bericht des Abtes Hariulf," 104, 111; Hariulf, *Pleidooi*, 28–30, 64–66. Similarly, informal procedures had been used in an 1123 action described by Hugh the Chanter, *History of the Church of York*, 188–90. William of Tyre, *Chronica* 15.13, at 2:692–93, provides another account concerning the same sort of lawsuit in the papal consistory against the patriarch of Antioch in 1138/1139; see also John of Salisbury, *Historia pontificalis* c. 16, at 43.

99. By the end of the century Innocent III made it a practice to hold public sessions of the consistory three times a week; *Gesta Innocentii papae III* 41, in *PL* 214:lxxx; translated as the *Deeds of Pope Innocent III*, 56.

100. Müller, "Bericht des Abtes Hariulf," 111; for other examples see Herbert of Bosham, *Vita S. Thomae* 4.8, 10, in *Materials* 3:336, 340–41; John of Salisbury, *Historia pontificalis* c. 41, at 80–82.

101. Fried, "Die römische Kurie;" 162–63, 167–70.

cerpta legum (also entitled *De arbitris* or *De iudiciis* in some manuscripts), represented an early stage in the development of an elaborate new procedural system.

As popes and jurists during the following decades slowly refined an increasingly complex procedural law for church courts, they patterned many of the new rules on what they knew about late Roman civil procedure. When an educated cleric in the High Middle Ages encountered the proverbial phrase, "The church lives by Roman law" (*Ecclesia vivit lege Romana*), procedural law may well have been the first thing that came to mind.[102]

During the generations that followed Abbot Hariulf's litigation in 1141, the conduct of lawsuits in the church courts swiftly became a complex technical art.[103] Shortly after the beginning of the thirteenth century, Thomas of Marlborough's detailed account of a lawsuit between the Abbey of Evesham and the bishop of Worcester vividly demonstrates how different and how much more complex procedure at the papal consistory had become in the sixty years that separated this lawsuit from that of Abbot Hariulf.[104] By 1216, when the Bolognese canonist Tancred (ca. 1185–1236) finished the first redaction of his landmark *Ordo iudiciarius*, inexperienced litigants would have found it extremely difficult to navigate their way successfully through a legal action in canonical courts at almost any level without access to a great deal more detailed help than Hariulf apparently required.[105]

---

102. Jacobi, "Prozeß im Decretum Gratiani"; Savigny, *Geschichte* 1:141–43; Wormald, *Making of English Law*, 31, 64, 71. Fried, *Entstehung des Juristenstandes*, 62, notes that in 1119 the bishop of Arezzo desired that "ex honore clericatus et episcopi dignitatis lege ... vivere lege Romanorum; but cf. Carl Gerald Fürst, "Ecclesia vivit lege Romana?" 25–26.

103. Hugh of Poitiers's narrative account of litigation between the bishop of Autun and the abbot of Vézelay at the papal curia shows that even by 1151 the procedure had grown more involved than it was in 1141 (Hugh of Poitiers, *Chronique de l'abbaye de Vézelay* 1:397–411, and *The Vézelay Chronicle*, 134–50).

104. Thomas of Marlborough, *History of the Abbey of Evesham*, 278–314, §§280–316.

105. On Tancred's *Ordo iudiciarius*, see Nörr, "Literatur zum gemeinen Zivilprozess," 383–84, and Fowler-Magerl, *Ordo iudiciorum*, 128–30. The demands of a more complex system were already starting to be evident by about 1200, as a note from an Austrian case observed (Gouron, "Le rôle de l'avocat," 19). By 1271, when William Durand (ca. 1230–96) was finishing his *Judicial Mirror*, which became the standard manual for romano-canonical procedure during the later Middle Ages, a litigant who lacked expert legal counsel at the papal consistory or other appellate courts, such as the Court of Arches in London, would have had no realistic chance at all of success. On Durand, see Schulte, *QL* 2:144–56; Falletti, "Guillaume Durant"; Nörr, "À propos

The new procedural system was informed throughout by older sources, both civilian and canonist—essentially the Roman law in Justinian's *Corpus* and material in Gratian's Decretum. This should not be taken to imply that writers on procedure during this period simply lifted a fully developed system from these sources. Instead, they selected individual elements, which they reinterpreted and sometimes radically transformed. Many provisions of the new procedural system were enunciated in papal decretals, especially by Alexander III and Innocent III.[106] The burgeoning use of papal judges-delegate made it essential to standardize the procedures used in ecclesiastical courts in the various regions of Western Christendom, and papal directions to those judges-delegate played a significant role in achieving that goal. A significant part of the new system was the work of law teachers and the writers of procedural *ordines*. Because it was neither purely civilian nor canonist, but included elements drawn from each of the learned laws, it is conventional to describe the system as romano-canonical procedure.[107] It proved to be exceedingly durable and has been immensely influential in shaping Western procedural practices. Many of its elements remain embedded in modern procedural codes.[108]

As procedures grew more complex, the role of trained advocates grew correspondingly more vital to success in litigation. The new civil procedure was largely responsible for the emergence of professional canon lawyers in the courts of the *ius commune*, and knowledge of procedural matters became a core element in the expertise of professional canonists and civilians alike.[109]

---

du *Speculum iudiciale*," and "Der Kanonist und sein Werk," 377–80; Fasolt, *Council and Hierarchy*, 64–72.

106. On the influence of older sources in procedure, see Jacobi, "Prozeß im Decretum Gratiani," 223–25; for interpretations in papal decretals, Nörr, "Literatur zum gemeinen Zivilprozess," 383; Fowler-Magerl, *Ordines iudiciarii*, 29–35; Hirschfeld, "Gerichtswesen der Stadt Rom," 460.

107. Holtzmann and Kemp, introduction to *Papal Decretals Relating to the Diocese of Lincoln*, xviii–xix; Fowler-Magerl, *Ordines iudiciarii*, 29–33; Stein, *Roman Law in European History*, 57–59; Caenegem, *History of European Civil Procedure*, 16–17.

108. Helmholz, *Spirit of Classical Canon Law*, 88–90; Wieacker, *History of Private Law*, 137–42; Robinson, Fergus, and Gordon, *European Legal History*, 108–21, 188–91, 196–201, 225, 249, and passim; Caenegem, *History of European Civil Procedure*, 87, 110–11, and *Historical Introduction to Private Law*, 131–34; Engelmann, *History of Continental Civil Procedure*, 507–10, 653–56, 783–94, and passim.

109. Helmholz, *Canon Law and Ecclesiastical Jurisdiction*, 312.

A brief sketch of the main stages of a lawsuit will help to show why litigants by the early thirteenth century needed trained lawyers to lead them through the procedural maze.[110] The pretrial stage of civil litigation under romano-canonical procedure formally commenced when the plaintiff (*actor*) presented either an oral complaint or a formal written complaint (*libellus*) to a judge.[111] If the judge accepted the complaint, he then summoned the defendant (*reus*) to appear in court to answer it.[112] A defendant who chose to contest the case, rather than to confess guilt or settle the matter at the outset, entered a formal denial of the complaint when he appeared in court and specified in writing his objections (*exceptiones*) to any points in the plaintiff's *libellus* that he wished to challenge.[113] At this stage, too, both parties had to satisfy the court that they would be able to meet the expenses that trial of the case would involve, either by putting down a security deposit or else by producing a guarantor who would pay the costs should the litigant fail to do so.[114] The plaintiff then made a formal reply (*replicatio*), and might amend his *libellus* in response to points raised by the defendant. This in turn gave the defendant the opportunity to file a rejoin-

110. Fowler-Magerl, *Ordines iudiciarii*, 37–49 summarizes the leading features. A paragraph-long outline of the main procedural stages, probably intended for memorization by students, appears in the twelfth-century *Questiones Oxonienses* in Fowler-Magerl, *Ordo iudiciorum*, 72 n. 2. Fowler-Magerl also provides similar brief outlines of criminal procedure, summary procedure, and arbitration procedure at 49–55. See chapter 10 below for further details.

111. Tancred, *Ordo iudiciarius* 2.8–13, at 162–74. Fuller discussions with numerous examples that reflect how the *libellus* developed later in the thirteenth century appear in William of Drogheda, *Summa aurea*, 196–291, §§168–357, and William Durand, *Speculum iudiciale* 4.1 *De libellorum conceptione*, at 2:56–77. See also Steins, "Ordentliche Zivilprozeß," 248; Fowler-Magerl, *Ordo iudiciorum*, 96–100, and *Ordines iudiciarii*, 37–40.

112. Tancred, *Ordo iudiciarus* 2.3.1, at 132–35. In practice, the summons was apparently delivered to the defendant personally by the judge's summoner (*apparitor*) or other messenger. Should the summoner be unable to locate the defendant, the summons was deemed to be served if he read it out at a Sunday mass in the defendant's parish church, according to the Legatine Council of London (1247) c. 26, in Powicke & Cheney 1:256–57.

113. Tancred, *Ordo iudiciarius* 2.5.1–4, at 139–45. This topic, too, became extremely technical and gave rise to numerous specialized treatises (Fowler-Magerl, *Ordo iudiciorum*, 185–218).

114. Bencivene, *De ordine iudiciorum* 1.1, at 5–6; Tancred, *Ordo iudiciarius* 2.15.1, at 175–76.

der (*triplicatio*), to which the plaintiff could enter a counter reply (*quadruplicatio*).[115] Parties joined issue through this process, that is, they gradually defined the precise issues in dispute and undertook to furnish proof to support their claims. The process clarified the specific questions that the judge would need to decide.

The trial proper (*litis contestatio*) commenced when each party took the calumny oath, in which they solemnly swore that they were not litigating out of malice, that the evidence they would submit was genuine, and that they believed that their arguments were proper and justified in law and in fact.[116] Once this was done, the parties restated their claims. The plaintiff supplied the judge and his opponent with a set of written *positiones*. These amounted to a revision of the complaints in the *libellus*, now cast as a set of propositions that the plaintiff expected to prove. The defendant briefly replied to each of these propositions by saying whether he accepted, rejected, or doubted the plaintiff's statements.[117] The plaintiff then furnished the judge and his opponent with a list of the witnesses he wished to call, along with a set of articles (*articuli*) that stated the points that he expected each witness to prove and the questions (*interrogationes*) that he wanted witnesses to answer on those points. The defendant received a copy of these documents and in turn submitted his own list of witnesses with articles and questions.[118] The judge retained one copy of each set of documents and passed another to the opposing party.

---

115. William of Drogheda, *Summa aurea*, 276–82, §350; William Durand, *Speculum iudiciale* 4.1 *De libellorum conceptione* §7, at 2:58–60; Tancred, *Ordo iudiciarius* 2.5.5, at 146, 2.13.2, at 173.

116. Tancred, *Ordo iudiciarius* 3.1.1–2, at 196–97 and 3.2, at 201–7; Pflugk-Harttung, *Acta* 2:254, no. 295; JL 7210; John of Salisbury, *Letters* 1:122, no. 77; Brundage, "Calumny Oath and Ethical Ideals." *Litis contestatio* was another basic procedural concept that medieval canonists borrowed from Roman law. On its history see Helmholz, "The *litis contestatio*."

117. Unlike the other elements of the court case, *positiones* were never part of Roman procedure. Canonists adopted them instead from the practice of the courts of the Italian communes in the early thirteenth century. Tancred discussed *positiones* but did not devote an entire title to them, although Gratia of Arezzo (if he was indeed the author) did so when he updated Tancred's *Ordo iudiciarius*. See Tancred, *Ordo iudiciarius* 3.3.3, at 209; Gratia, *De iudiciario ordine* 2.3, at 361–67; Donahue, introduction to *Select Cases*, ed. Adams and Donahue, 44–45; Nörr, "Reihenfolgeprinzip," 160. On the authorship and date of Gratia's work, see Fowler-Magerl, *Ordines iudiciarii*, 47, 84, 107.

118. Tancred, *Ordo iudiciarius* 3.3.1–2, at 207–8. Tancred failed to mention the *articuli*, but Gratia a few years later described their use as a customary practice in some

Next came the evidence of witnesses. Taking oral testimony lay in the hands of the judge, who questioned each witnesses individually in private and under oath, with a notary present to make a record of the questions asked and the replies given to them.[119] The judge based his examination of the witnesses on the questions supplied by the parties. Although judges were free to supplement these questions with any others that might occur to them, they seldom seem to have done so.[120]

Once all the witnesses had been examined, the judge "published" their testimony by furnishing each party with a copy of the record of the witnesses' depositions. The parties now had a chance to analyze the record and to note where the evidence sustained their contentions and undermined those of the adversary.[121] It was conventional practice for the parties (or more often their legal advisers) to mark up the margins of their copies of the depositions, usually in red ink, in order to demonstrate how the testimony of each witness supported their position and to minimize or explain away any that supported the adversary's case.[122] This analysis then became the basis for oral arguments.

Parties often wished to produce documentary as well as oral evidence, and they could do so either before or after submitting oral testimony. In preparation for argument, advocates analyzed the charters, letters, and

---

places, although his own opinion was that it was preferable to spell out these points in the *libellus* (Gratia, *Summa de iudiciario ordine* 2.5, at 369; Bonaguida de Arezzo, *Summa introductoria* 3.5–6, at 274–82; William Durand, *Speculum iudiciale* 1.4 *De teste* §5, at 1:313–18). The use of *articuli* differed considerably from one region to another and provides a good example of the ways in which local practice might very from the academic norms (Nörr, "Reihenfolgeprinzip," 165–66).

119. An early *Ordo iudiciarius* that opens with the words "Iudicium est trinus personarum trium actus" (written ca. 1179 and ed. Linda Fowler-Magerl in *Ordo iudiciorum*) reports (at 299) that in some places it was customary for the advocates of both parties to be present during the examination of witnesses, although they themselves put no questions to the witnesses. This was not, however, the usual practice.

120. Tancred, *Ordo iudiciarius* 3.9.1–2, at 236–40. Depending on the circumstances, the judge might choose to delegate the questioning of any or all of the witnesses to a special examiner or commissary judge and in practice judges often did so. The written record of testimony was deemed an adequate substitute for personal questioning by the judge who would ultimately give judgment in the case.

121. Tancred, *Ordo iudiciarius* 3.10–12, at 240–48.

122. For examples of the kinds of notes and comments that might appear, see the evidence of the witnesses in *Picheford c. Nevill* (Diocese of Lincoln, 1267–72) in *Select Cases*, ed. Adams and Donahue, 311–21.

other documents that had been introduced in much the same way that they did the depositions of witnesses.[123]

When this analysis was finished, each party had a chance to present oral arguments for its version of the case and to attempt to persuade the judge that the evidence supported its position and contradicted the opponent's assertions. This was also the time for legal arguments that, each party hoped, would convince the judge that the applicable law supported its contentions.

Although judges were supposed to allow the parties to take as long as they pleased, oral argument under the developed romano-canonical procedural system tended to be brief. As a matter of forensic tactics, parties usually reserved their detailed and fully developed arguments for the written *allegationes* that they submitted to the judge following the conclusion of oral argument.[124]

When argument was completed, the parties formally petitioned the judge to decide the case. Judges commonly adjourned proceedings at this point, rather than pronouncing an immediate decision. Since the judge who would decide the case had frequently not questioned the witnesses himself, he needed time to read the record of their testimony and the parties' analyses of it. He also wanted time to deliberate on the matter and, almost invariably, to consult with colleagues and legal experts on disputed points of law.[125] When he had reached a conclusion, the judge once more notified the parties to appear in court on an appointed day, when he delivered his decision (*sententia*) to them both orally and in writing.[126]

Canon law allowed ample room—far too much of it, some think—for

---

123. Tancred, *Ordo iudiciarius* 3.13, at 248–57.

124. Tancred, *Ordo iudiciarius* 3.15, at 261–68; Gratia, *Summa de ordine iudiciario* 2.8, at 374–78; Bonaguida, *Summa introductoria* 1.3.11, 15, at 157–60; William Durand, *Speculum iudiciale* 2.2 *De disputationibus et allegationibus aduocatorum*, at 1:742–54. See also Fournier, *Officialités*, 204–5; Steins, "Ordentliche Civilprozeß," 224, 260; and Gouron, "'Utriusque partis allegationibus auditis.'" An early example of the use of written *allegationes* appears in Thomas of Marlborough's account of Evesham's lawsuit against the bishop of Worcester (*History of the Abbey of Evesham*, 310, §313).

125. Even the pope customarily consulted the *iurisperiti* resident at the curia before announcing judicial decisions; e.g. Innocent III, *Register* 1.314, ed. Hageneder and Haidacher, 1:445–46.

126. Bencivene, *De ordine iudiciorum* 3.16, at 77–80; Tancred, *Ordo iudiciarius* 4.1, at 268–76; Gratia, *De iudiciario ordine* 3.1, at 379–80; Walter of Cornut, *Ordo iudiciarius* "Scientiam," 64–66, §32; William Durand, *Speculum iudiciale* 2.3 *De sententia*, at 1:776–812.

appeals from first-instance decisions.[127] Either party could appeal not only from the final decisions (*sententia diffinitiva*) in the case, but also from interlocutory judgments, mainly on exceptions raised by one party to assertions by the other, or else on disputed procedural rulings that the judge had made during the course of the action. Since these appeals had to be decided before the case could proceed, these aptly named dilatory appeals provided tempting opportunities to delay matters, a consequence that advocates and proctors were quick to seize upon. Defendants in disciplinary proceedings, for example, or actions in which possession of a benefice or other property was disputed, were understandably tempted to enter an appeal, regardless of its merits, since it might delay final judgment for months or perhaps even years on end.[128]

This intricate and tortuous system, which involved written documents in multiple copies at every stage, contrasted sharply with earlier medieval procedures.[129] There is little evidence, however, of a vigorous struggle for dominance between the romano-canonical procedure of the academic jurists and the earlier practices of courts and judges. Instead local courts selectively integrated features of the older procedural practices into the new system as it was introduced. This mixture of a general procedural law with local variations formed a leading characteristic of late twelfth- and early thirteenth-century practice that persisted through the later Middle Ages.[130]

The main features of the new system were in widespread use by the close of the twelfth century.[131] As the system developed, even lawyers who had studied the procedural material in Gratian's Decretum and the texts of Justinian's codification increasingly found that they needed help to make their way through the procedural thicket. Legal scholars with experience in the new style of litigation responded to this growing demand by producing specialized treatises on procedure. The procedural manual that

127. Tancred, *Ordo iudiciarius* 4.5.1–14, at 291–305.
128. Cheney, *From Becket to Langton*, 63–66.
129. Civil procedure came to depend ever more heavily on written documents and records from the late thirteenth century onward (Nörr, "Reihenfolgeprinzip," 168–70).
130. Thus, e.g., Tancred, *Ordo iudiciarius* 2.3.3, 3.1.5, at 135, 198–99; Gratia, *De iudiciario ordine* 1.8.1, at 347; see also Nörr, "À propos du *Speculum iudiciale*," 63–65. The notion of a *ius proprium* as contrasted with the general law, or *ius commune*, was familiar to medieval lawyers from the classical Roman jurists, e.g., Dig. 1.1.1.4 and 1.1.9. See also Calasso, *Medio evo del diritto*, 378–80, 453–54.
131. Vleeschouwers-Van Melkebeek, *Officialiteit van Doornik*, 35–38.

Bulgarus wrote for Cardinal Haimeric was a pioneering specimen of this new genre of legal writing.[132] It was quite short—it takes up just 17 octavo pages in a modern printed edition. As procedure grew more complex, the treatises that dealt with it correspondingly ballooned. The *Ordo iudiciarius* that Tancred wrote around 1216 occupies 225 octavo pages in Bergmann's edition, while a printed version of the great *Speculum iudiciale* of William Durand (b. ca. 1230, d. 1296) with the *Additiones* of Johannes Andreae (b. ca. 1270, d. 1348) weighs in at just under 1,500 folio-size pages.[133]

Although law teachers produced these treatises, their formal teaching centered squarely on the received legal texts—the various parts of Justinian's codification among civilians, Gratian and the decretal collections among canonists. Students certainly studied the procedural manuals that their teachers wrote, but no evidence suggests that twelfth-century law teachers lectured on them. Nor would they become part of the curriculum in the law faculties of the universities that began to appear early in the thirteenth century.[134] Detailed knowledge of their contents was nevertheless indispensable for legal practitioners, and copyists soon found profitable employment in producing copies of procedural manuals. Manuscripts of several late-twelfth-century handbooks of this type survive in respectable numbers, but Tancred's *Ordo iudiciarius* was clearly the most popular of them all. Well over a hundred medieval copies of his manual still exist, which strongly suggests that by the standards of its time it became a runaway bestseller.[135]

---

132. For a brief sketch of the history of this genre of legal literature up to 1234 see Fowler-Magerl, *Ordo iudiciorum*, 9–31. The earliest known manual devoted solely to civil procedure, known from its opening words as *Imperator Iustinianus*, dealt with a distant ancestor of the developed romano-canonical system. It formed an appendix to a manuscript of Justinian's Institutes, now in Cologne. *Imperator Iustinianus* apparently originated at Pavia in the second half of the eleventh century and was almost certainly very brief, judging from the single fragment that now survives (Fowler-Magerl, *Ordo iudiciorum*, 33–35).

133. It should be noted, however, that this page count includes the *Additiones* of Johannes Andreae and Baldus, as well as an index. Even so, the increase in size provides at least a crude measure of the way the system's complexity ballooned.

134. Fowler-Magerl, *Ordines iudiciarii*, 25.

135. As Fowler-Magerl, noted, "The ordo of Tancred was found everywhere in Europe in the Middle Ages" (*Ordines iudiciarii*, 68). Dolezalek, *Verzeichnis der Handschriften zum römischen Recht*, vol. 3, pt. 1 s.v. "Tancredus," lists more than 130 MSS in libraries ranging from Cracow to Cordoba. Medieval French and German translations also survive (Fowler-Magerl, *Ordines iudiciarii*, 88, 97). By comparison, *Ulpianus de edendo* (writ-

The development and general acceptance of romano-canonical procedure beginning in the second half of the twelfth century meant among other things that parties involved in actions before the church courts increasingly needed guidance through the process. Members of the ecclesiastical hierarchy, especially those who exercised jurisdiction, from the pope on downward, likewise felt a growing need for expert help in performing their judicial duties and frequently found it necessary to delegate at least some of them to men with legal learning. Even church authorities without formal jurisdictional obligations found it expedient to secure legal advice in performing their responsibilities. Ordinary litigants in the courts needed the services of men with legal training and experience ever more urgently as procedures grew more complex. Procedural innovations more than any other single factor made the services of trained legal advisers and representatives essential.[136] As the demand for legal services grew at an accelerating pace, the law schools predictably began to supply burgeoning numbers of men trained to fill that demand.

---

ten between 1140 and 1170) survives in 15 MSS, and Otto of Pavia's *Olim* (after 1177) in 18, while 11 MSS of Johannes Bassianus's *Quicumque vult* (ca. 1185) are known, as are 13 of Walter of Cornut's *Scientiam* (before 1234). See Fowler-Magerl, *Ordo iudiciarius*, 65–75, 96–100.

136. Litewski, *Römisch-kanonische Zivilprozeß* 1:185; Smail, *Consumption of Justice*, 66.

* FIVE *

Pre-Professional Lawyers in Twelfth-Century Church Courts

The Road to Professional Status

Canon lawyers during the "long twelfth century" gradually began to act more and more like professionals. The work they did grew increasingly technical. It required familiarity with a large and complicated body of esoteric knowledge that they could master only through years of study in specialized schools. Those who controlled wealth and power came to rely upon the advice of trained lawyers in pursuing their goals. Parties to actions in the courts found the services of skilled legal advisers and advocates increasingly essential in order to assure a successful outcome. The proliferating volume and complexity of the law made it wise to employ trained lawyers to settle controversies through arbitration, as well as for negotiating agreements, public or private, securing appointments to profitable positions in either church or state government, and participating in complex transactions. Both civil and ecclesiastical authorities, moreover, found that lawyers' knowledge and analytical skills made their services desirable for the lawful conduct of public administration.

By the mid-twelfth century clever and enterprising men could already make a living, often quite a comfortable one, from the teaching and practice of civil or canon law. The occupational skills that civilians and canonists possessed opened up opportunities for advancement in the church's hierarchy. Bishops and other prelates frequently awarded benefices, prebends, and stalls in cathedral chapters to trained lawyers in order to have them at hand for ready consultation. Canonists in considerable numbers themselves became bishops, archbishops, or abbots before 1200, as thousands more would do over the centuries that followed. The college of cardinals by the end of the twelfth century routinely included significant numbers of men with legal training. Before the century's end, one canonist was even elected pope.[1]

One traditional characteristic of professional status is the belief that, unlike those who follow less prestigious trades and occupations, professionals undertake to observe special ethical rules more demanding than those that apply to nonprofessionals. This requires them to conduct themselves (at least in their occupational affairs) in ways that serve the public good, and not solely to make a living. As lawyers, and canon lawyers in particular, became more prominent and influential in Western society, they also began to face questions about the moral boundaries of their occupation. Could clerics, whose lofty behavioral standards demanded that they abstain from involvement in worldly affairs, justifiably spend their time studying law and practicing it in the courts? Considerable numbers of twelfth-century clerics certainly did so, despite the disapproval of venerable authorities. Was it morally right for advocates, legal advisers, or law teachers, whether clerics or laymen, to collect fees from their clients or students? Eminent expositors of Christian moral doctrine had held that no one should profit from selling the God-given gift of knowledge, and a few even argued that doing so amounted to usury. Were there any limits to what a lawyer could ethically do in order to promote his client's interests? If so, what were they? What obligations did an advocate owe to his clients? What were his duties to the courts in which he practiced?

As canon lawyers became more numerous and more visible in Western Christendom, both they and their detractors searched for acceptable answers to questions such as these. Critics of the jurists grew increasingly abundant and vocal as the twelfth century progressed. By the early decades of the thirteenth century, canonists and civilians alike were under verbal assault from all sides. The frequency with which they were attacked and the

1. Weigand, "Frühe Kanonisten und ihre Karriere," furnishes numerous examples of men with a legal background in the college of cardinals. Among them, Master Albert (Albertus de Mora), a cardinal since 1157, reigned as Pope Gregory VIII for two months at the end of 1187. John Noonan and Rudolf Weigand have shown, however, that Alexander III, usually considered the earliest of the great lawyer-popes, was not the same person as the canonist Rolandus of Bologna, with whom earlier scholars had confused him (Noonan, "Who Was Rolandus?" and Weigand, "Magister Rolandus und Papst Alexander III"). Pennington has argued persuasively that if Innocent III, who is conventionally described as an expert canonist, ever studied law at all, he did so only briefly. See "Legal Education of Pope Innocent III," and "Further Thoughts." A long series of lawyer-popes commenced only with the pontificate of Gregory IX (r. 1227–41), by which time canonists had by any standard become full-fledged professionals.

virulence of the criticism to which they were subjected bear eloquent, if ironic, testimony to their emergence as a class of men to be reckoned with in society.

Lawyers in Twelfth-Century Church Courts

The renewed availability of systematic training in the learned laws and a substantial growth in the volume of litigation in the church courts, combined with the elaboration of a complex and technical procedural system and the proliferation of bishop's officials and other functionaries needed to cope with the new arrangements—all of this taken together helps to account for the reappearance in courts as well as in classrooms of lawyers steeped in the esoteric lore of Roman and canon law. By 1200, trained lawyers had begun to form an essential part of church governance. This was strikingly evident at the papal curia, in whose upper ranks trained lawyers consistently outnumbered theologians. Dioceses everywhere experienced similar changes. Throughout Western Christendom, trained lawyers had also begun to rise to prominent positions in civil government and society. This was especially true in the Italian peninsula, but it was by no means a uniquely Italian phenomenon. Similar developments occurred in France, England, Germany, Spain, and the Low Countries as well.[2]

Law became a much sought-after occupation during the long twelfth century as it became increasingly obvious that legal training often led to positions of power in the church and in royal government. Aside from the fortunate few upon whom the accidents of birth bestowed entitlement to wealth and authority, trained lawyers had surer access than did other men to the power and perquisites that went with influential positions. By 1200, even members of leading elite families were beginning to realize that a legal education supplied a useful adjunct to the advantages they already enjoyed.

Between the 1140s and the 1230s, the lawyers went from strength to strength. Colin Morris aptly described their tightening grasp on the machinery of church government as a "managerial revolution." A central feature of that revolution was the concentration of power in an ecclesiastical administration increasingly dominated by men with advanced formal education.[3] This was especially true for men learned in the law—to the

---

2. Fried, *Entstehung des Juristenstandes*, 144–57; Martines, *Lawyers and Statecraft*, 4–5.

3. Morris, "From Synod to Consistory," 117. In the diocese of Liège, Renardy, *Le monde des maîtres*, 137, finds that clerics who were formally educated outside of the diocese had largely displaced other clerics in the principal offices of ecclesiastical ad-

considerable chagrin, as we shall see, of those trained in the liberal arts or theology.[4]

At the same time, approaches to dispute settlement were also changing, although this happened at varying rates in different parts of Western Christendom. Courts and judges in the early Middle Ages almost invariably sought to settle controversies through compromise between the parties. By the twelfth century, formal legal processes that terminated in a judgment according to law were becoming ever more common. Changes of this sort occurred both in church courts and in secular tribunals.[5]

PRACTITIONERS OF CANON LAW

The developments that generated a demand for the services of advocates and *iurisperiti* trained in the mysteries of Roman and canon law also encouraged the rise of subsidiary legal personnel. Experienced proctors who appeared on behalf of litigants and helped them to avoid the hazards inherent in lawsuits were in constant demand.[6] So too were expert notaries who knew how to draft in proper form the technical documents that procedural developments made increasingly essential. Scribes and clerks, who did much of the tedious work of producing the numerous copies of official documents that romano-canonical procedure required, also found ample employment.

Already by the late eleventh century, records of court proceedings, especially in Italy, showed a modest increase in the numbers of references to learned lawyers, variously described as *advocati, causidici, iurisperiti*, or less

---

ministration by the end of the twelfth century. This pattern was not unique to Liège: much the same was true elsewhere.

4. E.g., Hilduin (fl. 1179–93), sermon *Spem oris nostri*, in CUL MS Ii.1.24, at 161va: "Qui si sacris litteris operam dare mentiuntur, tumultuosis perplexitatibus causarum et decretis Gratiani potius uolunt intendere quam intelligencie sacre scripture. Isti in defecto illud manna quod pluit fastidiunt et ad ollas carnium in Egypto redeunt"; Henri d'Andeli, "La bataille des VII ars," 41–43, ll. 49–74; Kuttner, "Dat Galienus opes," 237–40; Morris, *Discovery of the Individual*, 124–25.

5. Geary, "Extra-Judicial Means." On developments in formal processes in, e.g., Languedoc, see Cheyette, "Suum cuique tribuere," and in western France, White, "'Pactum . . . legem vincit et amor judicium.'" For Tuscany, see Wickham, *Legge, pratiche e conflitti*, 62–80.

6. The proctors dealt with here are those who functioned as litigation agents (*procuratores causarum, procuratores ad agendum*), rather than the proctors who represented a principal as managers or business agents (*procuratores omnium bonorum, negotiorum gestores*, and the like).

commonly, *legis doctores*, who appeared before both civil and ecclesiastical judges to make legal arguments on behalf of parties involved in lawsuits.[7] References to *procuratores* and *notarii* or *tabelliones* multiplied even more rapidly.

Throughout western Europe, canon lawyers who furnished specialist services in the church's evolving legal system had begun by the end of the twelfth century to occupy a visible niche in society, especially in towns and cities. John of Tynemouth noted that among the five classes of "serious men" that St. Augustine had enumerated, lawyers predominated.[8] Many of these men made the furnishing of legal service their principal employment.

Advocates and Legal Counselors

The ranks of legal practitioners included two groups of unequal prestige, differentiated from one another primarily by the extent of their formal legal education. The smaller but more highly esteemed group included advocates, legal counselors (*iurisperiti*), law teachers, and judges with legal training. These elite lawyers shared a body of recondite knowledge that was intellectually demanding, as well as time-consuming and expensive to acquire. Their teachers trained them to use dialectical reasoning to analyze problems and then to apply the legal doctrines that they learned from Gratian's book and Roman law texts to specific situations. People who lacked this preparation commonly found the intricate reasoning and subtle distinctions of trained lawyers impenetrable, baffling, and exasperating.

Proctors and Notaries

Proctors and notaries were more numerous but less prestigious than advocates and *iurisperiti*. These men were the workhorses of the medieval church's legal system. Proctors did not usually qualify for their occupation through the formal study of the law in the schools. Instead they typically

---

7. The terms "doctor" and "professor" were used to describe men of learning, but did not necessarily imply any teaching function. They were applied to jurists earlier than they were to physicians, theologians, or philosophers; Weimar, "Zur Doktorwürde," 307*; Feenstra, "Legum doctor," 72–73; Santini, "Legis doctores," 126–30; Mor, "Legis doctor," 197–98. For *advocati, causidici,* and *iurisperiti*, see, e.g., Manaresi, *Placiti del Regnum Italiae*, nos. 266, 428, 433, 439, 453, 455; Ficker, *Forschungen* 3:98–101, 103–106; Merello Altea, *Scienze e professione legale*, 33–35, 40–45, as well as Gouron, "Le rôle de l'avocat," 16–17.

8. Caius glosses, at 128ra, to C. 14 q. 5 c. 15 v. *isti*: " Jo[hannes de] [T]i[nmouth] hoc intelligat de .v. grauibus hominum, puta officialibus, medicis, aduocatis, operariis, iurisperitis, iuste sibi debent suscipientibus." The Augustinian reference is to *Epist.* 153 §23, *Ad Macedonianum*.

learned from practical experience the details of how the courts and the legal system worked. Proctors customarily began their careers as court clerks or scribes. Copying legal documents and attending to the routine needs of the court not only furnished them with a living, but also gave them an opportunity to pick up, almost by osmosis, a detailed knowledge of how legal procedures worked in practice and to learn through observation about the formalities of the courtroom, as well as the peculiarities and quirks of judges and other functionaries. They prepared the records of the court's proceedings and in so doing the fine details of the judicial system's operations. They found out how to use the court calendar to channel the workload through the system and no doubt learned as well how a proctor could manipulate it to his clients' advantage. They thus acquired an intimate familiarity with the operational details of the court's practice.

Successful scribes and court clerks often secured a commission as a notary along the way to becoming proctors. While scribes were primarily copyists who reproduced documents prepared by others, notaries specialized in the actual drafting of the documents themselves, a skill that they could gain through experience as scribes as well as by formal training in the schools of the *ars dictaminis*, or some combination of the two.[9] A notary public had to be commissioned by a high-ranking public authority, often by the pope or the emperor. Documents that a public notary prepared were presumed to be reliable records that judges and public officials could safely rely upon as authentic. Proctors often entered practice from the ranks of ambitious and successful notaries.

CANON LAWYERS IN GRATIAN'S DECRETUM

Gratian's Decretum contained a scattering of canons that concern the activities of lawyers—advocates, *iurisperiti*, and proctors, as well as notaries and other legal functionaries.[10] Predictably, a greater number of passages in the vulgate version of Gratian's text dealt with lawyers than appeared in earlier versions. Nor is it surprising to find that texts from Roman law sources figured prominently among those passages.

Much of the material about lawyers and legal functionaries that Gratian included in his Decretum appears, again not surprisingly, in the sections of his text that deal with procedures for the resolution of contentious matters under ecclesiastical jurisdiction. He had almost nothing to say about

---

9. On the *ars dictaminis*, see esp. Murphy, *Rhetoric in the Middle Ages*, 194–268; for a brief survey, see also Polak, "Dictamen," *DMA* 4:173–77.

10. Notably in C. 13.

the role of lawyers in dispensing legal advice or negotiating on behalf of clients, nor does he treat these topics even in his discussions of arbitration.[11]

Advocates in Litigation

"Advocates, also called patrons," wrote Bulgarus, "are those who in court lend their aid to either of the parties. Their task is to argue cases to the extent they deem fit." The advocate's fundamental responsibility, as Bulgarus described it, was to plead his client's case by framing arguments to convince the judge that the law was on the client's side.[12] Twelfth-century law teachers regularly described advocates as fighters, champions, or soldiers who did battle on behalf of their clients.[13]

Litigation was (and is) notoriously hazardous, and the outcome of any lawsuit can seldom be predicted with total confidence. By the latter part of the twelfth century, that uncertainty was augmented by the quick pace

---

11. E.g., D. 45 c. 10; C. 2 q. 6 d.p.c. 33 and d.p.c. 36; C. 3 q. 7 c. 2 §19; C. 11 q. 1 c. 38 and 46; see also Fowler-Magerl, "Forms of Arbitration," 133–47. Unlike Justinian's codification commissioners who left information about procedure interspersed among texts dealing with substantive law, Gratian brought a substantial part of his procedural material together in C. 2–7 of the Decretum (Fowler-Magerl, *Ordines iudiciarii*, 17–19; Kantorowicz, *Studies*, 71–72).

12. Bulgarus, *Excerpta legum*, 2: "Advocati sunt, qui et patroni dicuntur, qui ingrediuntur iudicium utrique parti suum praestantes auxilium, quorum est officium, causas perorare, quousque voluerint." Cf. Tancred, *Ordo iudiciarius* 1.5.3, at 112: "Officium advocati est stare et omnia proponere, quae clientulo suo expediant." Bulgarus's understanding of the advocate's repsonsibility echoes Dig. 3.1.1.2, endlessly quoted or paraphrased by medieval canonists; e.g., Gratian, C. 3 q. 7 c. 2 §1; Bernard of Pavia, *Summa decretalium* 1.28.1, at 23; *Summa "Elegantius"* 6.68, at 2:134, among others.

13. See, e.g., Stephen of Tournai, *Summa* to D. 51 pr. v. *decertantes aut in foro*, at 76–77: "Hic dicit [de his] qui patrocinium suum in causa sanguinis praestiterunt, vel de illis dicit qui ascripti erant advocati alicuius fori, qui quasi astricti nexibus illius fori, unde salarium suum habebant, ordinari prohibentur"; Huguccio, *Summa* in CUL, Pembroke MS 72, at 157ra, to D. 51 pr., v. *decertantes*: "Decertantes, id est aduocati." Twelfth-century canonists borrowed the fighting metaphor from Roman lawgivers and jurists, who had described advocates for example as "no less useful for mankind than those who fought in battles and suffered wounds to safeguard their homeland and their families" (Cod. 2.7.14; cf. Cod. Theod. 1.29.1; 2.10.6; Nov. Val. 2.2.4; Kantorowicz, "'Praestantia doctorum,'" 395); *Glossa Palatina* to C. 23 q. 2 c. 5 v. *milicie*, Cambridge, Trinity College, MS O.10.2, at 12ra: "Nam et clerici militant, i. q. iii. Saluator [C. 1 q. 3 c. 8] et q. ult., qui in qualibet [C. 1 q. 7 c. 10], unde et stipendia habere debent, Extra de prebend., Episcopis [1 Comp. 3.5.5 (= X3.5.4); 3 Lat. (1179) c. 5, in *DEC* 1:214], etiam patroni causarum, C. de aduoc. diuer iud., aduocati [Cod. 2.7.14]."

of innovation in both procedural and substantive law. Even influential and experienced litigants required help to succeed—or sometimes to survive.[14] "The service of advocates is essential in lawsuits," Tancred declared at the beginning of the thirteenth century, and by that time this was unquestionably true in the high-level courts in which Tancred himself was active. Advocates had become so indispensable that judges were obliged to postpone hearings when a party's advocate was unable to appear.[15]

NUMBERS OF ADVOCATES

As the volume of litigation in church courts grew, the supply of men equipped to give informed legal counsel and assist parties in litigation increased to meet the demand. Their services were not available everywhere, however, since the supply of qualified advocates and *iurisperiti* was distributed very unevenly. Trained lawyers were relatively plentiful in Italian ecclesiastical courts, most notably of course at the papal curia. This was already true as early as the 1120s, when, for example, Pope Honorius II (r. 1124–30) while deciding a lawsuit between the bishops of Siena and Arezzo noted that the parties had brought their own Tuscan advocates with them to Rome. Once there, they engaged the services of Roman advocates as well, no doubt to secure the advantage of their experience with the curia and its officers.[16] The numbers of advocates practicing in Rome continued to rise though the century. By the second half of the twelfth century, formal legal opinions produced in Rome mention at least twenty individual advocates and *iurisperiti* who were practicing in the city, in addition to judges, proctors, notaries, and administrative officials with substantial legal training or experience. Since Rome at the end of the century was a city with roughly 35,000 inhabitants, lawyers and court officials formed a

---

14. Thus, e.g., *Summa Reginensis* to D. 88 c. 4 v. *in causis*, in BAV, MS Reg. lat. 1061, at 16va: "Episcopus autem debet habere aduocatum bone fame et bone opinionis." Thomas of Marlborough, a former law teacher at Oxford, thought it essential to engage four Roman advocates to present his monastery's case at the Roman curia; for his glowing account of their qualifications and their arguments in the papal consistory see *History of the Abbey of Evesham*, 282–84, §285.

15. Tancred, *Ordo iudiciarius* 1.5 pr., at 111: "Quoniam advocatorum officium necessarium est in iudiciis, ideo de advocatis subiiciamus." On postponements, see, e.g. Innocent III, *Registrum* 1.362, ed. Hageneder and Haidacher, 1:545–57; Bernard of Pavia, *Summa decretalium* 1.28.4, at 23; Nörr, *Zur Stellung des Richters*, 8.

16. *Italia pontificia* 3:154, no. 37–40; Pflugk-Harttung, *Acta* 2:252–55, no. 1295; JL 7210; Baumgärtner, "Rat bei der Rechtsprechung," 66; Hirschfeld, "Gerichtswesen der Stadt Rom," 459–60; Wickham, *Legge, pratiche e conflitti*, 261–62.

substantial presence in the city's population. By the beginning of the thirteenth century, a litigant's complaint that he had been unable to secure an advocate's services brought a smile to Innocent III's lips as he rejected the plea. "No one," said the pope, "ever suffered from a shortage of advocates at the Roman curia!"[17]

Plentiful as advocates may have been at Rome, complaints about their scarcity elsewhere were not unusual. Peter the Venerable (b. ca. 1092, d. 1156) grumbled in a letter to Pope Eugene III in 1149 that advocates, or at any rate good ones, were so scarce in Provence that he had been unable to engage a competent lawyer to act for his brother in a lawsuit at Nîmes. Unqualified spokesmen were plentiful enough, Peter added, but he needed a properly trained advocate or legal counselor (*iurisperitus*) and had been forced to search far and wide before he finally located one.[18] In England the abbot of St. Albans in 1158, unable to secure a knowledgeable legal adviser locally, finally sought out the services of an Italian lawyer named Ambrose, whom he later dispatched to Rome to defend his monastery against claims made against it by the bishop of Lincoln. Likewise Abbot Odo of Battle Abbey was at his wits' end before he finally found an advocate capable of representing him adequately in a lawsuit against the son of the justiciar of England.[19]

This situation began to change during the second half of the twelfth century, however, and by about 1200 the supply of trained lawyers was mounting rapidly. Just a few years after Abbot Odo's frantic search for an advocate, the archdeacon of Middlesex, Ralph of Diceto (d. ca. 1200), could describe in glowing terms the skill, honesty, and integrity of the numerous lawyers at the court of Canterbury.[20] Ralph's observations surely reflect the success of Archbishop Hubert Walter's endeavor to recruit the best available English canonists into his service. By around 1200, advocates and *iurisperiti* could readily be found in many French cities—certainly at Paris, Orleans, and Montpellier, for example—but they also turned up in the

17. Thomas of Marlborough, *History of the Abbey of Evesham*, 286, §285; on numbers of lawyers practicing in Rome, Baumgärtner, "Rat bei der Rechtsprechung," 79–80, 90–94.

18. Peter the Venerable, *Letters*, 1:349–50, no. 141; Poly, "Les maîtres de St.-Ruf," 189. Peter seems to have exaggerated slightly. When the hearing actually took place no less than four respected and fully qualified canonists were on hand to take part (Gouron, "Penuria advocatorum," 2–3).

19. *Gesta abbatum monasterii Sancti Albani* 1:136–37; *Chronicle of Battle Abbey*, 324–25.

20. Ralph of Diceto, *Ymagines historiarum*, quoted in Whitelock, Brett & Brooke 2:1015.

service of abbots and bishops scattered throughout the French kingdom. Germany, too, experienced a sharp growth in the availability of trained advocates and legal counselors during this period.[21]

QUALIFICATIONS OF ADVOCATES

Gratian's Decretum included a venerable list of the minimum qualifications that advocates in the ecclesiastical courts were expected to meet, and teachers in the law schools routinely commented upon them.[22] An advocate must, among other things, be free, male, and Catholic, at least seventeen years of age, of legitimate birth and sound mind, with an unblemished reputation.[23] The vulgate recension of Gratian's Decretum presented these basic requirements in a passage adapted from standard Roman law sources.[24] By the 1190s, Bernard of Pavia and other teachers quoted a little mnemonic verse that law students no doubt memorized to sum up these elementary qualifications:

> Not everyone's fit to practice the law,
> And some kinds of people won't do:
> Knaves and slaves, kids and girls,
> The blind, the deaf, and the dumb,
> Plus convicts, actors, and poofs.[25]

---

21. On France, e.g., Peter the Venerable, *Letters*, 14, 24, 197–98, nos. 8, 19, 67; Gouron, "Dilectus Henricus," "Le rôle des maîtres français," and "Un assaut en deux vagues," as well as his "Autour de Placentin à Montpellier," "Cardinal Raymond des Arènes," and "Une école ou des écoles?" On Germany, Landau, "Anfänge der Verbreitung des kanonischen Rechts," 428–29.

22. C. 3 q. 7 c. 1–2.

23. Dig. 3.1.1.3 and 3.1.1.5; cf. 22.5.3.5 and 48.2.8; *Summa "Elegantius"* 4.7, at 2:4. In regard to these requirements, however, Peter the Chanter (d. 1197), maintained in his *Summa de sacramentis* that under some circumstances a client was justified in seeking advice from an excommunicated lawyer (Haring, "Peter Cantor's View," 106). Medieval glossators, like their Roman predecessors, found it puzzling that the praetor had set the minimum age so low (*Glosse preaccursiane alle Istituzioni*, 104, nos. 212–14).

24. C. 3 q. 7 c. 2 §§2–17 is made up from a pastiche of excerpts and paraphrases taken mainly from Dig. 3.1.3, 5–6 and Cod. 2.6.8.

25. My paraphrase of Bernard of Pavia, *Summa decretalium* 1.28.2, at 23: "Non cuicunque datur ut postulet, immo negatur / Addictus poenae, servus, puer, actor arenae, / Luminibus cassus, mulier, muliebra passus." The verse was widely quoted by others, e.g., by Tancred in his *Apparatus* to 1 Comp. 1.28.1 v. *aduocati* (Cambridge, Gonville and Caius College, MS 28/17, 24), Goffredus of Trano, *Summa super titulis decretalium*, and Bernard of Parma, *Glos. ord.* to X 1.37.1.

Practicing lawyers needed to be able to recall these categories instantly, since if their opponent fell into one or another of them, that would provide grounds for entering an exception against him.

Minimum educational requirements for advocates, a characteristic component of professional status, were not yet explicitly prescribed in ecclesiastical courts. Authorities assumed that advocates should have received some formal instruction in the law, and any lawyer who could boast even an elementary familiarity with Roman law would have been aware that Justinian had prescribed five years of legal studies as the norm. Neither Gratian nor subsequent papal decretal legislation, however, spelled out just what a minimum legal education for a canonist ought to consist of. Absent any general requirements or procedures for admission to practice, judges remained free to permit anyone they deemed qualified to plead in their tribunals.[26] Uniform educational standards would in any event have been hard to enforce in the period. The papal consistory apparently attempted to make sure that its judges had an adequate knowledge of the law, but complaints were voiced elsewhere about practitioners who knew just a few odds and ends of law soliciting business from credulous clients.[27] Formal certification of competence through examination by a university law faculty would not appear until the second decade of the thirteenth century.

CLERICAL ADVOCATES

Whether and under what circumstances members of the clergy might act as advocates in the courts was a question that decretists in the late twelfth century discussed at length. Ordained clergymen, especially priests and bishops, were naturally expected to know at least something about canon law.[28] For most clerics, however, this did not imply profound legal learning,

---

26. Dig. Const. *Omnem* 2–5; Cod. 2.7.22.4 and 24.4. Azo noted that Justinian's Code called for magistrates to examine prospective advocates and for their teachers to certify that they were knowledgeable in the law (*Summa super Codicem*, 29, to Cod. 2.7).

27. By the pontificate of Eugene III, judges in the papal courts were subject to an examination by a commission of cardinals to determine "qualiter se in legum doctrina intelligant," but what this consisted of and how it was conducted is not clear (Maleczek, "Kardinalskollegium," 68). On complaints about inadequately trained lawyers, however, see Ralph Niger, *Moralia regum*, in Kantorowicz and Smalley, "An English Theologian's View," 243: "[Q]uidem vidimus picatos legibus, qui vel aliquam particulam legum audierant, ad patrocinia causarum sine delectu currere, et cuicumque litigatori quod desiderabat promittere, collaudantes et commendantes quascumque causas."

28. Rufinus, *Summa* to D. 38 c. 4 v. *ignorare*, 91–92; *Summa "Elegantius"* 2.46, at 1:63–64.

much less possession of the skills and technical knowledge that effective advocacy required by the end of the twelfth century.

Gratian cited numerous venerable authorities, beginning with Pope Innocent I (r. 401–17), who had prohibited the ordination of functionaries whose duties he deemed incompatible with holy orders. Advocates and judges in the imperial courts fell into this category, the pope reasoned, because those courts could, and often did, impose the death penalty. Officers of those courts were thus complicit in taking human life. It would be improper to admit such men to holy orders, Pope Innocent felt, since their hands, like those of soldiers or executioners, were stained with human blood, which rendered them impure. This ritual impurity was incompatible with the clerical vocation and, the pope feared, might scandalize the faithful.[29]

Twelfth-century law teachers (many of whom also worked as advocates, judicial assessors, and legal counsel themselves) quickly began to draw distinctions when they came to explain this text to their students—some of whom were almost certain to be clerics who hoped to become advocates. Surely, said Rufinus, the pope could not have intended to ban all advocates from ordination. He must have meant to prohibit the ordination only of those who had represented accusers in death penalty cases. Besides, Rufinus added, if read literally, the pope's statement would contradict a canon of the Council of Serdica (ca. 343) that appeared elsewhere in Gratian's Decretum. Later decretists commonly adopted Rufinus's distinction between advocates who prosecuted and those who defended persons accused of capital crimes, and his position became the standard interpretation of this canon.[30]

The author of the *Summa Parisiensis*, writing a few years later than Ru-

---

29. D. 51 pr. and c. 1 (JK 292). Purity teachings of this sort were both ancient and common (Douglas, *Purity and Danger*, 61–62).

30. Rufinus, *Summa* to D. 51 pr., c. 1, at 133–34, referring to the Council of Serdica c. 13, which appears in D. 61 c. 10; see also Hess, *Early Development of Canon Law*, 157–61. The *Summa* of Johannes Faventinus on this passage in London, BL, MS Add. 18,369, at 27ra, follows Rufinus verbatim. The *Distinctiones Monacenses* to D. 51 c. 1, added the suggestion of Stephen of Tournai, *Summa* to D. 51 c. 1 v. *pertinaciam*, 77, that the advocates referred to might mean champions or perhaps boxers; *Distinctiones "Si mulier eadem hora" seu Monacenses*, at 53 and Munich, Clm. 16084, at 47v–48r: "*Aliquantos*. Dicitur in foro certantes non esse promouendos; contra di. lxi. c. Osius episcopus, 'Si diues aut scolasticus de foro aut ex administratione fuerit postulatus episcopus,' etc. [D. 61 c. 10]. Respondeo hic de his qui in ciuilibus causis experiuntur, ibi de eis qui in criminalibus ubi sanguinis effunditur, uel ibi de pugilibus agitur." The *Distinctiones Monacenses*, a product of the French school of decretists, were composed in the early 1170s (Sorice, Prolegomena to her edition, xii–xvi).

finus, proposed a further qualification. Pope Innocent had forbidden the ordination of advocates, this anonymous writer suggested, in response to a local situation in fifth-century Spain, and the pope may have intended it only as a temporary measure to meet a problem unique to one region, not as a general rule. Huguccio adopted this distinction and added that some people taught that a cleric could properly defend the accused in a case punishable by bloodshed.[31]

But could clerics already ordained legitimately serve as advocates? The emperor Justin (r. 518–27), among others, had called it shameful for clerics to be experienced in forensic arguments. Conciliar legislation included in Gratian's Decretum clearly and repeatedly forbade them to practice law in the courts of civil authorities.[32] Some authorities that Gratian cited, however, allowed exceptions to this rule. A cleric was permitted to defend himself in a secular court, and he could likewise defend the church that he served if it were sued before a secular tribunal.[33] A third exception permitted a cleric, even a bishop, to appear in the courts of worldly authorities

---

31. *Summa Parisiensis* to D. 51 c. 1, at 48. Huguccio, *Summa* to D. 51 c. 1, in CUL, Pembroke MS 72, at 157ra, Lons-le Saunier, Archives départmentales du Jura, MS 16, at 71v: "*Aliquantos*. Tangit .iiii. genera curialium, scilicet aduocatorum in causa sanguinis, militum vel officialium qui seua precepta sunt executi, et alorum, scilicet ystrionum qui exercuerunt ludibria sui corporis, quorum nullus debuit promoueri. Sed quia multi tales in yspania erant ordinati et non poterant remoueri sine scandalo, tollerat quod factum est et statuit sub pena nec de cetero talia fiant"; and *Summa* to D. 51 c. 1 v. *in forensi exercitatione uersati sunt*, CUL, Pembroke MS 72, fol. 157ra, and Lons-le-Saunier, Archives départmentales, MS 16, at 71v: "Scilicet advocati causa sanguinis, et dicunt quidam pro actore contra reum. Quid ergo si quis prestitit in tali causa sanguinis patrocinium pro reo? Dicunt quod non ideo repellitur, cum etiam clericus in tali causa possit esse aduocatus, ut xxiii. q. v. Reos [C. 23 q. 5 c. 7]." My thanks to Kenneth Pennington for emendations from the Lons-le-Saunier MS here and elsewhere.

32. Cod. 1.3.40(41), similarly the *Summa "Elegantius"* 1.64, at 1:21; C. 15 q. 2 c. 1 (Council of Tarragona [516] c. 10); D. 86 c. 26 (Council of Chalcedon [451] c. 3; *DEC* 1:88–89) and C. 21 q. 3 c. 1.

33. C. 5 q. 3 c. 3, summarized by the comment of an anonymous introduction to the Decretum that begins with the words "In prima parte agitur" on this passage in London, BL, MS Arundel 490, at 8ra–rb: "Ibidem etiam ostenditur quid sit postulare, quot sint ordines eorum qui postulare prohibentur, qui uidelicet prohibentur omnino postulare. Quibusdam permittitur pro se tantum postulare, non pro aliis, quibusdam etiam pro se et pro certis personis postulare permittitur, quibusdam pro quilibet personis postulare conceditur, qui etiam a professione aduocatorum arcentur."

on behalf of a disadvantaged person (*miserabilis persona*).³⁴ The Third Lateran Council in 1179, perhaps reflecting decretist discussions of the subject, reaffirmed the traditional rule, but explicitly allowed these exceptions.³⁵

The ban on clerical advocacy in lay courts was directed chiefly toward criminal cases, where conviction of a defendant might involve death or mutilation.³⁶ The rationale for the prohibition was twofold. Execution or mutilation involved the shedding of human blood, and participation, even indirectly, in bloodshed violated the scriptural injunction against involvement by clerics in secular affairs.³⁷ Even more fundamental, as mentioned

34. D. 84 pr.; D. 87 pr., c. 1–2; C. 12 q. 3 c. 71; C. 21 q. 3 c. 1, as well as *Summa "Elegantius"* 9.46, at 3:71, Tancred, *Ordo iudiciarius* 1.5.2, at 112, and Rufinus, *Summa* to C. 21 q. 3 pr., at 385, followed verbatim by Johannes Faventinus in London, BL, MS Royal 9.E.VII, at 117va. An Anglo-Norman gloss to C. 14 q. 5 c. 10 v. *grauari*. raised a question about bishops: "Sed hoc obiicitur, nonne etiam episcopus aduocatus esse potest in causa miserabili, ubi altera pars grauatur si conuincatur? Respondeo etiam unde quidam sic grauari iniuste" (Caius glosses, at 127va). *Miserabilis persona* was a canonical term of art that designated a class of persons to whom the church courts tried to extend protection because they were deemed to be at a disadvantage before the courts, especially those of civil rulers. This class included widows, orphans, travelers (especially pilgrims), and crusaders. See Génestal, *Le privilegium fori* 1:57–61, Tierney, *Medieval Poor Law*, 14–15, as well as Brundage, "Legal Aid for the Poor."

35. 3 Lat. (1179) c. 12 in *DEC* 1:218. Local councils occasionally reenacted this canon, e.g., Council of Avignon (1209) c. 19, in Mansi 22:792; Canterbury I (ca. 1213–14) c. 10 and Salisbury I (ca. 1217–19) c. 11, in Powicke & Cheney 1:26–27, 65–66. Bernard of Pavia incorporated this canon in 1 Comp. 1.28.1, whence Raymond of Penyafort took it into the Liber Extra (X 1.37.1).

36. C. 23 q. 8 c. 30 (11 Council of Toledo [675] c. 6); Johannes Teutonicus, *Glos. ord.* to C. 23 q. 8 c. 30 v. *truncationes, aut inferendas*, and *precipiant; Apparratus "Ecce vicit leo"* to C. 15 q. 2 c. 1 v. *more secularium*, in Cambridge, Trinity College, MS O.5.17, at 77rb: "Quod non in criminali causa forensi, tamen dixit Gandulphus quod nullo modo possunt se clerici locare. Si aliquem hic inueniuntur contraria, non sunt contraria quia hic loquitur de criminalibus secularibus in quibus non possunt clerici aduocare."

37. 2 Tim. 2:4; D. 53 c. 1; D. 54 c. 3; C. 21 q. 3 c. 1–7; Johannes Teutonicus, *Glos. ord.* to C. 21 q. 3 pr. v. *quod autem; Apparatus "Ecce vicit leo"* to C. 21 q. 3 pr., in Cambridge, Trinity College MS O.5.17, at 91vb: "Item seculare negotium dicitur a seculari persona et sub hanc acceptationem consistit in tribus: in negociacione, in administracione, in aduocacione. Negocio prohibita omni clerico, ut supra lxxxviii Fornicari [D. 88 c. 10] et xiiii. q. iiii. per totum. Similiter et aduocatio in causa criminali forensi, ut extra ne cleri. vel mo. etc. Non magnopere [1 Comp. 3.37.2 (= X 3.50.3)], Clericis [1 Comp. 3.37.6 (= X 3.50.5)], et etiam in ciuili forensi, id est coram iudice seculari, nisi sit quadam dis-

earlier, it also tarnished the ritual purity required of all clerics, but particularly of priests. It was deemed abhorrent that hands stained either literally or figuratively by human blood should touch, much less consecrate, Christ's body and blood. Some decretists taught that clerical advocates were only barred from acting for the prosecution in criminal proceedings, but that they could legitimately assist defendants, even in death penalty cases.[38] In civil cases, however, clerics, like everyone else, were free to function as advocates, even in the courts of secular rulers. Indeed, Rufinus declared, they were not only permitted, but in some circumstances might be required to do so. As an Anglo-Norman gloss noted, however, these restrictions on practice in secular courts by clerical advocates were more theoretical than real. In actuality, the glossator added, they had long been abrogated by contrary custom.[39]

Church courts were another matter. Since ecclesiastical judges could not inflict punishments that involved shedding blood, clerical advocates were free to practice in canonical courts, even in criminal cases.[40] Instead

---

tinctione ei que habetur, extra de postulando c. i [1 Comp. 1.28.1 (= X 1.37.1)]. Item administratio sub iudice seculari prohibita est clericis et etiam in ciuilibus, ut infra eodem per totum, quia de ciuilibus intelliguntur capitula et in criminalia, ut infra xxiii. q. ult. His a quibus [C. 23 q. 8 c. 30]."

38. On ritual purity, e.g., D. 50 c. 36; C. 14 q. 5 c. 2; C. 23 q. 8 cc. 4, 6. On the defense exception, Caius glosses, at 35rb, to D. 51 c. 1: "Clericus in causa sanguinis aduocatus esse non potest pro accusatore, qualiter secundum omnes pro reo autem potest, ut 23 q. 4 Reos ar. [recte: C. 23 q. 5 c. 7]. Item D. de ap. l. Non tantum ar. [Dig. 49.1.6]." Despite the glossator's belief that "everyone" shared this position, however, Johannes Teutonicus held that "Prior opinio est magis tuta, ut nec pro accusatore nec pro reo possit clericus aduocare," since if the defendant should prevail, the accuser might be liable to death or mutilation for bringing a false prosecution (*Glos. ord.* to D. 51 c. 1 v. *ad sacerdotium*).

39. Rufinus, *Summa* to C. 5 q. 3 pr., at 278; Caius glosses, at 129va, to C. 15 q. 1 c. 1: "Nonne hec causa legi potest de aduocatis, et tunc omnino abrogatus est tum per contrarium consuetudinem, tum per illud in concilio Lateranensis, Clerici in [3 Lat. (1179) c. 12 in *DEC* 1:218]. Uel loquitur de iudicibus ecclesiasticis, qui non debent uendere iusticiam, ut seculares faciunt de facto." The glossator was probably citing 3 Lat. c. 12 from the *Collectio Tanner* (Oxford, Bodleian Library, MS Tanner 8, 593–712); Kuttner, *Repertorium der Kanonistik*, 294–95, and Kuttner and Rathbone, "Anglo-Norman Canonists," 340–42; Holtzmann, "Die Dekretalensammlungen, I: Die Sammlung Tanner," 107.

40. *Summa "Prima primi"* to C. 15 q. 2 in London, BL, MS Royal 11.D.II, at 328va: "Coram iudice uero ecclesiastico, tam in causa criminali quam ciuili licite postula[n]t clerici, ut infra c. 1 Excepto episcopo, qui non admittitur nisi in sua causa criminali,

the question in church courts concerned laymen: could they practice as advocates in those courts at all? And if so, under what circumstances? In principle, at least, lay advocates were barred from participation in cases where the opposing party was a cleric. They were also barred in theory from acting, even against other laymen, in cases where "spiritual" matters, such as tithes or the validity of marriage, were at issue. These theoretical prohibitions, however, were apparently not much heeded in practice: contrary custom yet again prevailed over written law.[41]

Advocacy by Monks and Canons-Regular

The study and practice of law by monks and canons- regular raised sensitive questions about religious priorities. Canon law counted only the ordained members of religious communities as clerics in the rigor of the term.[42] Monks, canons-regular, and for that matter, nuns, shared so many clerical rights and privileges, as well as restrictions on lifestyle, however, that their legal condition closely resembled that of the clergy.[43] Authorities had long held that the ascetic and contemplative character of the monastic

---

ut 3. q. 5 Quia [C. 3 q. 5 c. 15]; Rufinus, *Summa* to C. 15 q. 2 pr., at 347–48; Johannes Faventinus's *Summa* on this passage in London, BL MS Royal 9.E.VII, at 99rb, follows Rufinus verbatim.

41. Caius glosses, at 129va, to C. 15 q. 2 pr.: "Laicus autem in causa ecclesiastica criminali aduocatus esse non potest contra clericum, quia eum accusare non potest, nisi suam uel suorum iniuriam pro se; in Extra de test., de cetero [Coll. Tanner 5.4.7 (= 1 Comp. 2.13.14; X 2.20.14; JL 14091)]. Sed nec contra laicum ubi causa criminalis est mera ecclesiastica 96 Satis, ibi illicitum namque [D. 96 c. 7]. Spirituali non potest pro alio postulare, 16 q. ul. Nona [C. 16 q. 7 c. 22]; 89 Indicatum [D. 89 c. 5]. Consuetudo tamen quandoque contra. Nam in causa decimarum et matrimonii laicus pro laico postulat. Ceterum clerico contra clericum agente, non postulat laicus. Paria: Nulla est inuidia, si laicus contra laicum admittatur."

42. D. 21 c. 1; C. 16 q. 1 c. 6 and d.p.c. 40. See also Cox, *Juridic Status of Laymen*, 27–38.

43. Shared rights and privileges included, e.g., the *privilegium fori* and immunity privileges (C. 11 q. 1 c. 38; C. 16 q. 1 c. 40; C. 17 q. 4 c. 27–29). Members of religious communities who enjoyed these privileges were technically *personae ecclesiasticae*, ecclesiastical persons (C. 17 q. 4 c. 21 and *Glos. ord.* to v. *ecclesiasticis personis*). See also Cox, *Juridic Status of Laymen*, 30, as well as Koch, *Die klerikalen Standesprivilegien*, 73 and passim; Downs, *Concept of Clerical Immunity*, 18–25; Helmholz, "Si quis suadente." The most obvious restrictions on lifestyle were those pertaining to chastity and celibacy (D. 27 c. 8; C. 27 q. 1 c. 40).

life made it scandalously inappropriate for monks to involve themselves in lawsuits or to appear in court as advocates or proctors. Monastic writers sternly censured the behavior of lawyer-monks:

> They love to defend cases, not just their own but those of outsiders, and they do this all the time. They love the decrees of councils, not the secrets of the [sacred] mysteries. They meditate on decrees, not psalms, they become orators in lawsuits, use flowery rhetoric, and love to be praised because they speak on behalf of many. But a monk who talks much offends many.[44]

Several passages in Gratian's *Decretum* reiterated the ancient ban on the study and practice of law by monks and regular canons. Nevertheless, monks did successfully study and practice law, as the careers of Stephen of Tournai and Thomas of Marlborough, for example, made abundantly clear. The standard explanation of this apparent disparity between law and reality was that monks could legitimately practice law so long as their abbot approved of their doing so.[45] Although Gratian included none of their canons in his collection, recent French councils at Clermont in 1130 and at Reims in 1131, moreover, had renewed the ancient prohibitions, as had the Second Lateran Council in 1139.[46] These renewed interdictions, however, seem to have had little effect, even on the canons-regular of Saint-Ruf, who

---

44. Hugh of Fouilloy (d. 1172 or 1173), *De claustro animae* 3.17, in *PL* 176:1069: "Nec tantum suas, sed etiam alienas defendunt causas, hoc amant, hoc frequentant. Amant decreta conciliorum, non secreta mysteriorum. Decreta, non psalmos, ruminant, fiunt oratores in causis, rhetoricis utuntur coloribus, laudari appetunt, quia pro multis loquuuntur. Sed monachus multum loquens, multis displicet." The Cistercian order made numerous efforts to prevent its members from studying civil or even canon law, but these were ultimately unsuccessful See Stutz, "Die Cistercienser"; Bock, "Les Cisterciens"; also Hausherr, "Eine Warnung," 397–98.

45. Reiteration of the ban at C. 16 q. 1 c. 20 (Pope Pelagius I [555–60], JK 986) and c. 35 (Council of Tarragona [516] c. 11). Gratian expressed his own support of the principle at C. 16 q. 1 d.a.c. 20, despite the possibility that he himself may have been a monk; the strongest evidence for this comes from the *Summa Parisiensis* to C. 2 q. 7 d.p.c. 52 and C. 16 q. 1 c. 61, at 115, 181. On required approval of the abbot, e.g., Johannes Teutonicus, *Glos. ord.* to C. 16 q. 1 c. 20 v. *defensor*.

46. Council of Clermont (1130) c. 5 and Council of Reims (1131) c. 6, in Mansi 21:438–39, 459; 2 Lat. (1139) c. 9 in *DEC* 1:198–99. Later councils continued to repeat the ban, e.g., Tours (1163) c. 8 and Montpellier (1195), Paris (1212), pt. 2, c. 20, Montpellier (1214) c. 21, in Mansi 21:1179, 22:670, 831, 944.

specialized, as we saw earlier, in furnishing legal assistance to those in need of it. On the contrary, by the mid-twelfth century, Saint-Ruf was flourishing vigorously. It had grown from a single community into a prosperous congregation of canons-regular, with more than a hundred affiliated priories, churches, and chapels. Saint-Ruf also maintained a house of studies at Avignon, which became in effect a private law school for its own members.[47] The election of Nicholas Breakspear, a former abbot of Saint-Ruf, as Pope Adrian IV (1149–54) testifies that successive prohibitions of the mission in which it engaged did no irreparable harm to the standing of the congregation's members.

LEGAL ETHICS

Twelfth-century law students learned about the norms for proper behavior by advocates and legal counsel from scattered passages that they found embedded in the ancient Roman and canonical texts they studied. Since the authors of those passages had written within the context of societies much different from those in which medieval law students lived, their prescriptions concerning the ethical duties and legal obligations of lawyers inevitably required adjustment to fit the realities of life and law in twelfth- and thirteenth-century Western Europe. Law teachers attempted to fashion out of them satisfactory rules of conduct to cope with problems that perennially arise in the relationship between lawyers, their clients, and the courts. A few of the rules they proposed were peculiar to the conditions that then prevailed. Those for the most part have since been abandoned. Rules of conduct that they fashioned, however, still remain central to European and American beliefs about the way that lawyers ought to behave.

Advocates and legal advisers incurred serious moral obligations whenever they undertook to advise or represent a client, regardless of whether they received a fee. Bolognese decretists usually discussed issues in legal ethics in terms of practical arrangements, such as the advocate's obligation to be succinct and not to waste the court's time, to stick to the point in argument, to refrain from insulting one's adversary, or the timing of fee agreements and arrangements for payment. Decretists north of the Alps, by contrast, usually centered their discussions of legal ethics on broader moral issues, such as the lawyer's duty of loyalty to his client, his responsi-

---

47. Poly, "Les maîtres de Saint-Ruf," 183–85, 199–200; Classen, "Zur Geschichte Papst Anastasius IV," 38–39; Gouron, "Entstehung der französischen Rechtsschule," 156–57.

bility to avoid conflicts of interest, or his obligation to safeguard the confidential information that clients entrusted to him.[48]

OBLIGATIONS TO THE CLIENT AND THE COURT

Forceful Advocacy of Meritorious Cases

The Roman calumny oath furnished twelfth- and thirteenth-century writers with the nucleus of many of their ideas about legal ethics. Bulgarus, writing before 1141, elaborated on a portion of the oath that the advocate took at the outset of *litis contestatio* when he had to swear that he would to do his utmost for his client so long as he remained convinced that the client's case was worthy.[49]

The civilian Otto of Pavia, a former student of Placentinus, writing after 1177, quoted an additional clause from the oath that required the advocate not only to determine whether his client's case was right and just, but also stipulated that if an advocate concluded that his client's case was unfounded, based on falsehood, or otherwise defective, he must refuse to take it on. Should he later discover that a case that he had previously accepted was in fact insupportable, he must forthwith abandon it.[50]

Twelfth-century decretists adopted this position and taught that advocates and *iurisperiti* were obliged to discourage any client whose case they deemed unfounded either in fact or in law from pursuing litigation and instead to seek some alternative way of dealing with the problem.[51] As Huguccio put it:

---

48. Trancred briefly summarized the ethical teachings of Bolognese decretists in his *Ordo iudiciarius* 1.5.3, at 112; for northern decretists, Gouron, "L'enseignement du droit civil," 196.

49. Cod 3.1.14.4; see also Brundage, "Calumny Oath and Ethical Ideal"; Bulgarus, *Excerpta legum*, 3; cf. Cod. 3.1.14.4; Litweski, *Römisch-kanonische Zivilprozeß* 1:343–44; John of Salisbury, *Policraticus* 5.13, ed. Webb, at 1:340.

50. Otto of Pavia, *Summa "Olim"* §329, which appears under the name of Johannes Bassianus as a part of his so-called *Libellus de ordine iudiciorum* 2:234. A similar formulation appeared earlier in the fragmentary *Ordo iudiciarius "Etiam testimonia removentur,"* ed. Fowler-Magerl. Contemporary theologians, such as Peter the Chanter and Robert Courson, added that an advocate who argued for a case that he knew to be unjust committed a mortal sin and was obliged to make restitution if he won the case (Baldwin, *Masters, Princes, and Merchants* 2:136 n. 154).

51. *Summa "Elegantius"* 6.18, at 2:112–13; Bernard of Pavia, *Summa decretalium* 2.17.4, at 52.

One should not offer or give unjust advocacy or legal advice to anyone. If therefore I see that someone is bringing a case that lacks merit, one should not embrace his cause nor advise him to pursue it, but instead either to settle or otherwise compromise it or else to abandon it.[52]

The advocate thus had dual obligations. To the client he owed a vigorous presentation of the case, together with undertakings to be loyal and to keep his secrets confidential. To the court he owed assurance that the case he presented warranted serious consideration. An advocate or legal adviser was accordingly required to pass a preliminary judgment on the merits of every matter on which he was consulted. He acted as the gatekeeper of the court and was responsible for weeding out frivolous or malicious claims that a client brought solely or primarily in order to harass one of his enemies.[53] Conscientious lawyers made a point of giving prospective clients fair warning about what this could mean, as did Master Robert de Camera (d. 1169):

You called on me to take on and look after your case. You should know, however, that if I should glimpse any sort of injustice in your case, I will make it known and I will join with your opponent.[54]

Once he had committed himself to accept a case, the advocate was morally bound to exert himself to present it fully and forcefully, with as much art and skill as he could muster. So long as he had exerted his utmost effort

---

52. Huguccio, *Summa* to C. 11 q. 3 c. 71 v. *iustum*, in BAV, Arch. S. Petr. C. 114, at 196rb (also quoted by Baldwin, *Masters, Princes, and Merchants* 2:136 n. 153): "Nam iniustum patrocinium uel iniustum consilium non debet quis alicui prestare uel dare. Si ergo uideo quod quis iniustum fouet causam, non debet ei prestare patrocinium nec dare ei consilium ut in causa procedat, sed uel transigat uel aliter componat, uel cedat." Presumably the compromise or settlement that Huguccio envisioned would be one that avoided whatever elements in the case that rendered it unjust. Master Honorius, writing at just about the same time as Huguccio, equated giving legal assistance in an unjust case to simony in his *Summa "De iure canonico tractaturus,"* to C. 1 q. 3 c. 10, 1:333.

53. On this aspect of the advocate's duties, see Brundage, "The Lawyer as His Client's Judge."

54. Peter the Chanter, *Verbum adbreviatum*, c. 49, at 334: "Ita et magister robertus de camera solitus erat respondere omni dicenti suo: vocasti me ad causam tuam fovendam et tuendam; scias autem quod si aliquid iniusticie in causa esse perspexero, iniusticiam revelabo et parti adversarii tui adherebo." Also in Baldwin, *Masters, Princes, and Merchants* 2:136 n. 156, and see as well 1:153–54.

for his client, an advocate had no reason to be ashamed when he lost a case, as even the ablest advocate was bound now and again to do.⁵⁵

Loyalty to the Client

Once an advocate accepted a case, both law and personal honor bound him thenceforth to be faithful to his client. Fidelity to a client, as canonists learned from Gratian, meant that they were obliged to protect the client's person and property, to safeguard his secrets, and to see to it that he received what was his due without excessive difficulty or delay. Failure on any of these counts was a breach of loyalty, and disloyalty was a variety of treachery that incurred harsh penalties.⁵⁶

The advocate's most obvious duty was to present the client's claims thoroughly, accurately, and persuasively in court. An advocate needed to be cautious and alert in conducting his case, since every word he uttered in court became binding on his client, unless the client entered a timely objection.⁵⁷ In order to avoid this embarrassment, the advocate had to persuade his client to reveal every detail of the matter long before the case ever came before a judge. Almost invariably this required the client to share with his legal adviser a great deal of information that he would prefer to keep secret. The advocate had to win his client's trust and persuade him to reveal every last morsel of information that might be relevant to the case. Implicit trust on both sides was essential to the relationship between them.

The tongue, one Anglo-Norman decretist noted, is a dangerous instrument.⁵⁸ The ability to bridle his tongue and keep silent about his client's

---

55. John of Salisbury, *Policraticus* 5.13, ed. Webb, at 1:341.

56. Johannes Teutonicus, *Glos. ord.* to D. 87 c. 5 v. *non omni fide*; see also Dig. 48.19.38.8. Gratian's definition of *fidelitas* appeared in a passage that originated in a letter that Bishop Fulbert of Chartres wrote about 1020 to Duke William of Aquitaine (C. 22 q. 5. c. 18). This same passage became part of the discussion of the loyalty that a vassal owed to his lord in the *Consuetudines feudorum*, Vulgata 2.6, at 120–21 (Pennington, "Jurisprudence of the Feudal Oath of Fealty").

57. On presenting the client's claims, Tancred, *Ordo iudiciarius* 1.5.3, at 112. If an inept advocate omitted a relevant point, however, the judge might intervene to supply it. Thus, Cod. 2.10 (11).1 and Accursius, *Glos. ord.* to this passage v. *et proferre*; Tancred, *Ordo iudiciarius* 1.5.5, at 113–14. In present-day American practice, by contrast, intervention of this sort would be gross violation of judicial ethics. On being bound by words uttered in court, Cod. 2.9 (10).1, 3; Otto of Pavia, *Summa "Olim"* §§333–34, at 234; *Dissensiones dominorum*, 265–67; John of Salisbury, *Policraticus* 5.13, ed. Webb, at 2:341.

58. Caius glosses, at 94vb, to C. 5 q. 4 c. 3 v. *non referenens*: "Lingua est parua silua, qua accensa totum nemus consummatur: litis lingua parens, os terit, olle carens."

business was a necessary virtue in an advocate or legal adviser. No lawyer, however learned or brilliant, could adequately counsel a client who was unwilling to disclose his business secrets, and a host of other potentially embarrassing information as well. No client could be expected to do that unless he trusted that whatever he told his lawyer would go no further. The legal adviser's obligation to maintain confidentiality resembled a vassal's duty to protect the household secrets of his lord. Twelfth-century lawyers, who liked to compare themselves with knights, were keenly aware of the resemblance.[59]

Church authorities, like their civil counterparts, looked upon breach of confidence by an advocate or legal adviser as a most heinous crime. A treacherous lawyer who broke faith with his client deserved no more mercy than a traitor who betrayed king and country. Just as it seemed appropriate that a spy, when detected, should pay for his treason with his head, so the traitorous advocate or counselor who revealed his client's secrets to an opponent deserved to lose his livelihood.[60]

Breach of this confidentiality duty took a variety of forms. The most heinous type of betrayal was secret collusion with his client's opponent. A less perfidious lawyer might openly switch sides and join the opponent in the middle of litigation, carrying all of his original client's secrets and strategy with him. A less critical although still serious problem arose when a lawyer deserted a client who depended upon his advice, counsel, and representation in order to take on an entirely unrelated case or client.

Roman law termed the first of these *praevaricatio*, whose English common law equivalent is ambidexterity, and treated it as an extremely serious offense. The discussion of the topic in vulgate recension of Gratian's Decretum drew heavily from the Roman sources.[61] Although Roman lawyers used the term *praevaricatio* broadly to describe any sort of double-dealing, it originally described a collusive prosecution in which the accuser conspired with the accused to assure that the accusation would fail. Medieval

---

59. The comparison appears, e.g., in Accursius, *Glos ord.* to Cod. 2.7.14 v. *militant*; Azo, *Summa super Codicem*, 29, to Cod. 2.7; Johannes Teutonicus, *Glos. ord.* to C. 23 q. 1 c. 5 v. *militie*; and *Glossa Palatina* to C. 23 q. 1 c. 5 v. *milicie*, in Cambridge, Trinity College, MS O.10.2, at 12ra: "Nam et clerici militant, i. q. iii. Saluator [C. 1 q. 3 c. 8] . . . etiam patroni causarum, C. aduoc. diuer. iudi., aduocati [Cod. 2.7.14]."

60. Johannes Teutonicus, *Glos. ord.* to C. 2 q. 3 d.p.c. 8 §2 v. *prodiderit causam*, citing Dig. 49.16.6.4: "Exploratores, qui secreta nuntiauerunt hostibus, proditores sunt et capitis poenas luunt"; C. 2 q. 3 d.p.c. 8 §§2–3, taken from Dig. 3.2.4.4 and 47.15.2.

61. See Rose, "Ambidextrous Lawyer." C. 2 q. 3 d.p.c. 8 pr. §§2–8 is a pastiche of passages from Dig. 48.16.1 pr., 1, 6–7; 47.15.1–2, 5, 7; and Cod. 9.43.3.

commentators, civilian and canonist, called this public or criminal *praevaricatio*.[62] Classical jurists also used *praevaricatio* in a broader sense to describe any sort of collusion between a lawyer and his client's opponent. Medieval jurists described this as corruption of an advocate, or sometimes as private *praevaricatio*.[63]

An archetypal betrayal scenario occurred when one party bribed the adversary's advocate or legal adviser to secretly pass along documents and other confidential information that would allow the briber to anticipate and forestall the opponent's litigation strategy. Alternatively, an advocate might deliberately put forward weak arguments or hold back evidence in order to allow his putative opponent to win the case. The penalty imposed on the briber for such chicanery, when detected while the case was still in progress and proved to the judge's satisfaction, was loss of the case.[64] If the judge had already decided the matter and closed the case before the wrongdoing came to light, the losing party might appeal to vacate the verdict on the grounds that his opponent's corruption of his advocate irredeemably flawed the process, although judges might not welcome this approach. An alternative recourse for the injured party was to seek restitution of his losses through an action for fraud against the briber.[65]

A corrupt advocate became legally disreputable (*infamis*). This label entailed numerous disabilities, which among other things barred him from further practice in the courts. If the betrayal involved furnishing his adversaries with confidential written documents, the client might also charge him with forgery.[66] Legal actions against an advocate for collusion were

---

62. Dig. 47.15.1 and 48.16.1.6; Accursius, *Glos. ord.* to Cod. 7.49.1 v. *adversario*.

63. Dig. 3.2.4.4; Cod. 2.7.1 and Accursius, *Glos. ord.* to this law at v. *si patronum praeuaricatum* as well as to Cod. 2.7.1 v. *si patronum praeuaricatum*; and to Dig. vet. 4.18.1 v. *allegat*; Stephen of Tournai, *Summa* to C. 2 q. 3 d.p.c. 8 v. *praevaricator*, at 169; *Summa "Elegantius"* 5.26, at 2:63.

64. Caius glosses, at 52rb, to D. 87 c. 5 v. *non omni fide*: "Ar. contra aduocatum non ex fide allegantem, infra 2 q. 1 preuaricator [recte: C. 2 q. 3 c. 8 §2]"; Accursius, *Glos. ord.* to Cod. 7.49.1 v. *constitit*.

65. On appeals, Cod. 2.7.1 and Accursius, *Glos. ord.* thereon at v. *queritur*; Otto of Pavia, *Summa "Olim"* §332, at 234 (but cf. Dig. 4.4.18.1); on seeking restitution, Dig. 4.8.31; Accursius, *Glos. ord.* to Cod. 7.49.1 v. *amittat*.

66. Dig. 48.10.1.6. On *infamia* more generally, Gratian, C. 2 q. 3 c. 8, drawing on Dig. 3.1.1.5 and 3.2.4.4, 47.15.4, and 47.15.5; Cod. 2.7.1. See also Accursius, *Glos. ord.* to Cod. 2.7.1 v. *commissi*; Landau, *Entstehung des kanonischen Infamiebegriffs*; Migliorino, *Fama e infamia*; Peters, "Wounded Names" and *Fama*, ed. Fenster and Smail.

brought as private prosecutions by the offended party for recovery of damages, however, rather than by public authorities as disciplinary proceedings. Even so, accusing an advocate or *iurisperitus* of collusion with an opponent was a serious business, and the person who brought the action needed to be confident that he could prove his charge. Otherwise he himself might be sued for bringing a malicious action.[67]

Avoiding Conflicts of Interest: The Lawyer-Client Privilege

Medieval jurists likewise adopted the ancient rule that protected client confidences by forbidding advocates to testify in cases in which they were professionally involved. Since an advocate's testimony was by law incompetent, his client had no power to waive the immunity, even if it might serve his interest to do so.[68] Gratian's text incorporated this immunity, and decretist writers discussed it as a basic element in the law of evidence.[69]

The same principle that forestalled advocates and legal advisers from giving evidence in cases on which they were engaged likewise prohibited them from serving in other capacities that could potentially conflict with their duties to clients. An advocate could not ethically represent both parties in a lawsuit, arguing first for one, then for the other, a scenario that Johannes Teutonicus thought absurd. A *iurisperitus*, however, could legitimately advise both parties in a dispute.[70] Opinions differed on the question

67. Accursius, *Glos. ord.* to Cod. 2.7.1 v. *quod si non docueris*.

68. Dig. 22.5.25; Radin, "Privilege of Confidential Communication," 488–89 and passim.

69. Gratian mentions immunity explicitly at C. 4 q. 2 c. 3 §19 (vulgate version only), and also indirectly in the earlier recension through the Fifth Council of Carthage (401) c. 1 at C. 2 q. 6 c. 38. The Carthage canon appears in the *Decretales Pseudo-Isidorianae*, 307; cf. a different version from the *Registri ecclesiae Carthaginensis excerpta* §59, in *Concilia Africae*, 196. For decretist commentary, see, e.g., Rufinus, *Summa* to C. 2 q. 6 c. 38 v. *fuit praeses*, 255; *Summa "Elegantius"* 6.72, at 2:136; Johannes Teutonicus, *Glos. ord.* to C. 2 q. 6 c. 38 v. *vel cognitor*, who also adds that an advocate, judge, or judicial assessor could not testify on an appeal in a case in which he had previously acted in first instance.

70. Johannes Teutonicus, *Glos. ord.* to D. 45 c. 9 v. *allegavit*. On the rules for *iurisperiti*, by contrast, *Apparatus "Ecce vicit leo"* to C. 14 q. 5 c. 15 v. *utramque partem*, in Trinity College, Cambridge, MS O.5.17, at 75vb, and Sankt Florian, Stiftsbibliothek MS XI.605, at 67vb: "Aduocatus autem potest tantum ex una parte esse et partem aduersariam grauare, ar. xxiii q. ii Dixit [*fortasse* C. 24 q. 3 c. 29] dummodo habeat iustam causam, quia iniustam fouere non debet. Iuris uero peritus reuera utrique parte potest consulere, ita dicendo 'Si ita est ut tu dicis, ita debet de iure fieri.' Set tamen processum cause tantum alteri parte potest ostendere." My thanks to Kenneth Pennington for the reading from the Sankt Florian MS.

of whether a lawyer could serve as a judge or judicial assessor in a case in which he had previously furnished legal advice or acted as advocate for one of the parties. Martinus argued that it would be improper to do so and that it had in fact been prohibited by Roman law. Bulgarus and others maintained, however, that an advocate who was appointed a magistrate after he had taken a client's instructions on a matter could hand the matter over to another advocate and then sit in judgment on the case.[71]

Distribution of Counsel

By the second half of the twelfth century, canonists had begun to assert that ecclesiastical judges possessed the right, grounded on the Roman praetorian edict, to assign advocates to litigants who lacked them. In order to try a dispute fairly, they contended, judges must make sure that the parties who appeared before them competed on a level playing field. For equal access to justice, the judge must arrange that each side had equal access to qualified counsel to argue its case.[72] The earliest medieval authorization for court appointment of an advocate appears in an undated decretal of Honorius III (r. 1216–27) in which the pope appointed a cleric from his household to act as advocate for a monastery whose monks complained that no advocate was available locally to defend them.[73]

Reappearance of judicial distribution of counsel suggests that jurists had begun to think of themselves as a social group defined by their occupational rights and public responsibilities. Distribution of counsel rested upon the unstated premise that advocates and legal advisers performed their functions in the public interest. Their public functions laid a moral obligation upon them to subordinate their private interests and private profits to the good of the community. Ideas about professional ethics in the Justinianic codification simultaneously defined their occupational responsibilities and fostered a feeling of group identity.

Advocates functioned as officers of the courts in which they worked, the argument ran, and that gave judges an implicit power to order them to

---

71. For the prohibition, *Dissensiones dominorum*, 59–60, 113, relying on Cod. 1.51.14 pr. (Rossi, *Consilium sapientis*, 86–87). Cf. Cod. 2.6.6 pr. and Johannes Teutonicus, *Glos. ord.* to C. 23 q. 5 c. 8 v. *pro se*. The counterargument rested on a slightly disingenuous reading of Dig. 2.1.17.

72. Cod. 2.6.7.1; Dig. 1.16.9.5 and 3.1.1.4, cited by Tancred, *Ordo iudiciarius* 1.5.5, at 113; John of Salisbury, *Policraticus* 5.13, ed. Webb, at 1:340–41.

73. X 1.32.1 (Po 7735); see also Roumy, "Système de l'avocat commis d'office," 359–61.

make their services available to specified clients. The authority for judicial distribution of counsel that appears in the vulgate version of Gratian's Decretum consists of an excerpt from a fourth-century imperial constitution in Justinian's Code that declared:

> If two or more advocates in a court enjoy an outstanding reputation beyond that of the others, it is incumbent upon the judge to make an even distribution of counsel so that assistance for each of the parties may be evenly balanced.[74]

Lawyers were required to accept these appointments. Judges could disbar without hope of reinstatement recalcitrant advocates who refused such an assignment.[75] In addition, if a judge discovered that some wily litigant had engaged the services of many or most of the lawyers who practiced in his court so as to deprive his opponents of access to legal assistance, the judge could punish him and should presume that his case lacked merit.[76] Since the number of practicing lawyers in church courts was seldom very

---

74. C. 3 q. 7 c. 2 §12, adapted from Cod. 2.6.7.1: "Si uero in uno auditorio duo tantum uel plures pre ceteris fuerint, quorum fama sit hilarior, in iudicantis officitio sit, ut par causidicorum distributio fiat, et exequetur pro partibus auxilium singulorum." See also the *Summa "Elegantius"* 6.65, at 2:133, as well as Accursius, *Glos. ord.* to Cod. 2.6.7.3 v. *paris*.

75. C. 3 q. 7 c. 2 §13, from Cod. 2.6.7.2; Huguccio, *Summa* to C. 3 q. 7 c. 2 §13 v. *careat foro*, in BAV, Arch. S. Petr. C. 114, at 146va: "*Careat foro*, id est, officium aduocandi in foro. Uel *careat foro* ex toto, ut de cetero non liceat ei agere ibi in aliqua causa plus. Item non dicit foro quam aduocatione cui foro interdicitur [MS canc.: aduocatione] et immo imiscebit se de cetero causis forensibus quod non est de illo cui interdicitur aduocatione, ut D. De penis, Moris § id est numquam [Dig. 48.19.9.4]." Likewise in the Caius glosses on the same passage, at 90vb: "*Foro*, id est uti officio aduocationis uel secundum quosdam *orare* uel allegare. . . . uel ut ei forum interdicatur, D. de penis, l. Moris [Dig. 48.19.9.1].Cf. John of Salisbury, *Policraticus* 5.13, ed. Webb, at 1:341. For an example of such a judge's order see Aubenas, *Recueil des lettres* 1:23.

76. C. 3 q. 7 c. 2 §14, from Cod. 2.6.7.3; Huguccio, *Summa* to C. 3 q. 7 c. 2 §14 v. *experietur*, in BAV, Arch. S. Petr. C. 113, at 146va: "*Experietur*, id est punietur extraordinarie a iudice quam uoluerit aludere ut aduersarius aduocatos non possit habere." Likewise Johannes de Deo, *Breviarium* to the same passage, v. *Si quis ex litigatoribus*, in London, BL MS Royal 11.A.II, at 34va: "Dicitur quod si aliquis subtrahit copiam defensionis aduersario deludit iudicem et iure in quam fouere causam et idcirco puniri debet, Extra De testibus, Peruenit [X 4.21.4]." But see also Accursius, *Glos. ord.* to Cod. 2.6.7.3 v. *foueri*: "Presumitur enim contra eum, sed ex tali praesumptione non damnatur."

large, this could easily have been a practical tactic for well-heeled and unscrupulous litigants, as Gerald of Wales, for one, discovered.[77]

Legal Aid for the Poor

Judges in church courts also claimed the right to appoint advocates to argue without fee on behalf of poor and disadvantaged litigants (*miserabiles personae*) who might otherwise not be able to get the assistance they required to present their claims effectively. This claim was rooted not only in Roman law, but also in theological traditions about justice and charitable concern for the poor, for in Jesus's words from Matthew 26:11: "The poor you have always with you." As the presence of the poor grew distressingly obvious in twelfth-century cities, poverty came to be viewed as a more pressing social problem than it had been during the early Middle Ages.[78]

Scripture praised those who assisted the poor by shielding them against exploitation by wealthy and powerful opponents.[79] St. Augustine listed assuring justice to the poor as one of the works of mercy, and the Council of Chalcedon (451) had decreed that the clergy should provide assistance, including legal aid, for widows, orphans, and those who lacked the means to procure counsel for themselves. More recently, the Council of Compostella (1114) had reaffirmed the church's duty to furnish poor persons with legal help, "lest perchance any poor person be stifled by the majesty of justice."[80] Azo, relying on the praetorian edict, declared that judges should see to it that women, minors, the insane, and other disadvantaged persons who came before them had access to legal assistance, whether they asked for it or not. Judges need not do this for adult men in their right mind or

---

77. Gerald of Wales, *De jure et statu Menevensis ecclesiae* in his *Opera* 3: 228, The author of the *Questiones Zwettlenses* likewise treated this as a realistic possibility (Fransen, "Deux collections de questiones," 503, no. 17).

78. Roumy, "Système de l'avocat commis d'office," 365–66; Little, *Religious Poverty*, 28–29.

79. Thus, e.g., Deut. 24:14–15; Exod. 23:6; Prov. 14:21–22 and 31:9. Likewise Acts 25:16 describes the opportunity for accused persons to face their accusers and defend themselves in the law courts as a special virtue of the Roman legal system.

80. Augustine, *De civitate Dei* 9.5; Council of Chalcedon (451) c. 3, *DEC* 1:88; Gratian D. 86 c. 26; Council of Compostella (1114) c. 11, in Mansi 21:120: "Si quis potentum judicii causam tractare adversus pauperem vel definire habuerit, similem personam introducat, quae pro se causam suam definiat: ne forte cujuspiam maiestate pauperis justitia suffocetur."

for the rich, he added, since they—and their money—can readily supply themselves with advocates.[81]

Although the praetor's assurance did not appear in Gratian's Decretum, the *Summa "Elegantius in iure diuino"* (or the *Summa Coloniensis*) cited the passage, which implies that jurists in the schools before 1170 accepted it as current law.[82] A decretal of Pope Honorius III, whose eleven-year pontificate began in 1216, explicitly sanctioned its application in practice, as did councils at Toulouse in 1229 and at Bordeaux in 1234.[83] Indeed, the 1229 council at Toulouse had gone so far as to declare that even persons accused of heresy who could not afford to pay an advocate were entitled to have help from one appointed by the court.

COMPENSATION OF ADVOCATES AND LEGAL ADVISERS

Medieval jurists followed the lead of their ancient predecessors in holding legal scholarship sacred. "You should know," declared Placentinus (b. ca. 1135, d. 1192), "that legal wisdom is a most sacred thing, not to be sullied by a price tag."[84] While they subscribed in principle to the noble ideal that the availability of legal assistance should not depend solely on an individual's financial resources and that advocates should not use their skills exclusively for sordid gain, most law teachers also supported the proposition that everyone who could afford to do so ought to pay for legal services.[85]

---

81. Dig. 3.1.1.4: "Ait praetor: 'Si non habebunt aduocatum, ego dabo'"; Azo, *Summa super Codicem*, 28, to Cod. 2, *De postulando* §3. On the judge's duty to provide legal assistance see also the *Ordo iudiciarius "Iudicium est trinum personarum trium actu."*

82. *Summa "Elegantius"* 6.65, at 2:133.

83. X 1.32.1 (Po 7735); Council of Compostella (1114) c. 11 and Council of Toulouse (1229) c. 44 in Mansi, 21:120 and 23:204; synod of Archbishop Gérard de Malemort of Bordeaux (1234) c. 123 in *Statuts de 1230 à 1260*, 100.

84. Placentinus, *Sermo de legibus*, 132, ll. 150–57: "Scire debes etenim, quod civilis sapientia est res sanctissima nec pretio numerario deturpanda est, ut ff. de variis et extraordinariis cognitionibus l. 1 § est quidem [Dig. 50.13.1.5], que etiam hominem in anxietate mori non sinit nec vivere in paupertate, ut in Aut. de heredibus et Falcidia in fine coll. 1 [Nov. 1, ep.]."

85. *Summa Parisiensis* to C. 3 q. 7 c. 2 §11 v. *ad turpe compendium*, at 121; Dig. 50.13.1.5; cf. Johannes Teutonicus in *Glos. ord.* to C. 1 q. 3 c. 11 v. *retributionis*; likewise Dig. 1.16.6.3, cited by Johannes Teutonicus in *Glos. ord.* to C. 11 q. 3 c. 71 v. *iustum*; *Summa Parisiensis* to C. 14 q. 5 c. 15, ed. McLaughlin, 171. Gandulphus, together with Huguccio and Johannes Teutonicus rejected the prevalent teaching. See also Litewski, *Römisch-kanonische Zivilprozeß* 1:283–85.

"Whoever wishes to litigate," wrote Bernard of Pavia in the 1190s, "requires an advocate." The advocate, whether cleric or layman, he added, would of course expect to be paid.[86] Bernard's seemingly offhand remark reflected the realities of the church courts in the late twelfth century. Even the occasional saint among advocates was not necessarily prepared to forgo payment from those who could afford it. A few eminent jurists, notably Azo among the civilians and Vincentius Hispanus (d. 1248) among the canonists, however, rejected the common teaching that judges could require an advocate to represent a client without compensation.[87]

Moralists were fond of scolding lawyers for their greed. Legal knowledge, critics declared, was a free gift from God. If a grateful client spontaneously rewarded his legal adviser with a modest gift, that was certainly appropriate, even admirable. But jurists who expected, or worse demanded, payment for legal advice sinned grievously. Lawyers who helped only those who were willing and able to pay engaged in the reprehensible business of selling justice. They could escape eternal perdition only by repenting their evil ways and making restitution to the clients they had victimized.[88]

Strictures such as these seem by and large not to have troubled civilians, who seldom took the effort to respond to them. The legal sources that they studied, after all, not merely permitted advocates and proctors to take fees for legal services, but by establishing a cap upon the amount that they could charge implicitly approved the practice. Canonists, however, took these criticisms more to heart and strove to discover authoritative justification for what they customarily did.[89] They found welcome support for collecting compensation for their services in a distinction that Gratian had taken from one of St. Augustine's letters. Augustine had argued that judges who allowed bribes to sway their judgment were actually selling justice, as were corrupt witnesses who gave perjured testimony. But, he continued, clients paid their lawyers for advice and assistance in resolving or preventing conflicts, which was not at all the same thing as justice. Since everyone

86. Bernard of Pavia, *Summa decretalium* 1.28 pr., 3, at 22–23: "Quia ergo litigare volens indiget postulatore scil. advocato vel patrono, ideo de postulando dicamus. . . . Olim advocati salaria a fisco accipiebant, hodie vero a clientulis suis salarium exigere possunt, et tam clerici quam laici."

87. See the texts cited by Roumy, "Système de l'avocat commis d'office," 378–79. See also Rieck, *Der Heilige Ivo von Hélory*.

88. Thus, e.g., Peter of Blois, *Epist.* 26, at 1:94–96, also in *CUP* 1:32–33; Baldwin, *Masters, Princes, and Merchants* 1:193, 2:131 n. 135; Post, Giocarinis, and Kay, " 'Medieval Heritage of a Humanistic Ideal.'"

89. Cod. 3.1.13.9; Fried, "Vermögensbildung," 30–34.

agreed that advocates were not angels, they could hardly be expected to live on air alone. Like physicians and workmen, they were entitled to compensation for their labor. Or, in a well-worn biblical phrase that Pope Innocent III and a host of others regularly employed, no one should be expected to fight at his own expense on another's behalf.[90]

In practice, twelfth-century advocates, proctors, and *iurisperiti* certainly expected, and usually received, payment for their services. Their fees technically fell into the Roman law category of *honoraria*, or gratuitous rewards, in contrast to the wages (*merces*) of hired laborers.[91] *Honoraria* had in practice long since ceased to be truly gratuitous, however, and medieval lawyers were aware that provisions in late Roman law confirmed their property rights in their fees and authorized legal action to recover unpaid fees that were owed to them. Huguccio added that an advocate should settle the question of the payment of his fee at the outset, and never later than the beginning of the *litis contestatio* stage of litigation. Fee discussions after the trial proper had begun were to be avoided, since this seemed likely to give lawyers undue influence over nervous clients who were apt to become increasingly apprehensive about the outcome as the trial progressed.[92]

90. For Augustine's position, C. 11 q. 3 c. 71 and C. 14 q. 5 c. 15, as well as Johannes Teutonicus, *Glos. ord.* to v. *patrocinium*. Augustine was personally sensitive about the issue of what constituted a bribe and what did not, since he had once been accused of bribery himself (Noonan, *Bribes*, 84–87). On entitlement to compensation, Rufinus, *Summa* to C. 14 q. 5 c. 15 to v. *sed non ideo*, at 343; followed verbatim by Johannes Faventinus in London, BL, MS Add. 18369, at 90vb; 3 Comp. 2.17.6 (= X 2.26.16; Po 1778), paraphrasing 1 Cor. 9:7; cf. C. 10 q. 2 c. 4, C. 13 q. 1 c. 1 §4, C. 28 q. 1 c. 8.

91. Johannes Teutonicus, *Glos. ord.* to C. 3 q. 7 c. 2 §12 v. *ut par*; Stephen of Tournai, *Summa* to C. 3 q. 7 c. 2 §8 v. *honorarium*, at 197, followed closely by Johannes Faventinus in London, BL, MS Royal 9.E.VII, at 72vb; Accursius, *Glos. ord.* to Cod. 4.6.11 v. *datum*. On the distinction between *honoraria* and *merces*, see Zimmermann, *Law of Obligation*s, 353–59, 384–86, 415–20.

92. Cod. 2.7.4; Dig. 50.13.1.10, and 50.13.4; Accursius, *Glos. ord.* to Dig. 17.1.7 v. *si extra ordinem*; Ricardus Anglicus, *Summa de ordine iudiciario* 26, at 34; Huguccio, *Summa* to C. 3 q. 7 c. 2 §10 v. *cum eo litigatore*, BAV, Arch. S. Petr. C.114, at 146va: "Cum eo litigatore: inuito sed uolente potest. Si enim sponte uelit promittere aliquid ei ob patrocinium [MS: patrimonium] non est hoc prohibitum, infra xi. q. 4 non licet [C. 11 q. 3 c. 71]. Contra ibi enim dicitur quod licet aduocato petere salarium, sed licet ante litis contestationem, sed non postea, cum iam clientulum in proprium receperit fidem. Ab initio enim licet aduocato pacisci de salario, ut ibi dicitur, sed lite pendente [MS corr. ex: pacte] non licet pacta innouare, sicut hic dicitur." Likewise, Azo, *Summa super Codicem*, 29, to Cod. 2.6. Similar rules still prevail in the United States (2004 American Bar Association, Model Rules of Professional Conduct 1.5 (b), in *The Law Governing Law-*

Compensation of Clerical Advocates and Legal Advisers

Payment of fees to clerical advocates raised complicated issues on which a consensus emerged only gradually. The Council of Chalcedon (451), as noted earlier, strongly disapproved of clerics who became involved in judicial business of any sort, and a council at Tarragona in 516 flatly forbade clerics to accept fees for serving as advocates.[93] Disapproval of payments to clerical advocates had weakened in the intervening centuries, but twelfth-century churchmen nonetheless remained convinced that the practice was at best morally dubious. Gratian included the Chalcedon decree twice in the vulgate version of his *Decretum*,[94] as well as the Tarragona decree.

Gratian tried to resolve the dissonance between these venerable prescriptions and actual practice by assuming that the canons applied only to members of religious communities. According to this reading of the text, secular clerics who were not monks or canons-regular were exempt from the ban on taking fees for legal services. Gratian invoked custom as the authority to support this interpretation. "It is an accepted general custom approved by the church's practice," he wrote, "that clerics may undertake to act as advocates and demand gifts for their efforts and for the expenses they incurred."[95]

Early Bolognese commentators on the *Decretum* generally ignored the whole issue, although they and their students surely knew perfectly well that clerics commonly did practice as advocates and regularly got paid for doing so.[96] Rufinus, however, faced the problem squarely. Despite the can-

---

yers, 19). On the impropriety of fee discussions after beginning of the trial, Accursius, *Glos. ord.* to Cod. 2.6.6 v. *contractum ineat*.

93. Council of Chalcedon (451) c. 3, in *DEC* 1:88; Brundage, "The Monk as Lawyer." Council of Tarragona (516) c. 10, in C. 15 q. 2 c. un. Those who transgressed the ban were liable to punishment as usurers. The canon did, however, leave room for a church to accept a free-will offering from grateful clients whom one of its clergy had served.

94. D. 86 c. 26 and C. 21 q. 3 c. 1, which was an addition in the vulgate text. See also Weigand, "Versuch einer neuen, differenzierten Liste der Paleae und Dubletten im Dekret Gratians," 117, 128.

95. C. 15 q. 2 d.p.c. 1: "Hoc autem de illis intelligendum est, qui canonicam uitam professi regulariter se uicturos proposuerunt. Generali namque ecclesiae consuetudine receptum est et moribus approbatum, ut clerici more aduocatorum patrocinia inpendant, et pro inpendendis munera exigant, et pro inpensis suscipiant."

96. Paucapalea simply repeated Gratian's *dicta* on C. 15 q. 2 without comment and Rolandus paraphrased his remarks.

ons, he observed, clerics commonly act as advocates and usually receive fees for their services. Since no other authority explicitly sanctioned this, Rufinus explained that custom had nullified the prohibition in the conciliar canons. Stephen of Tournai agreed that clerics ordinarily could and did receive fees for their legal services and that the practice was tolerated at the Roman curia. He accounted for this by stressing Gratian's distinction between what was proper for professed monks and canons-regular and what was permissible for secular clergy.[97]

Not all canonists accepted these conclusions. The decretist known simply as the Cardinal (Cardinalis),[98] for one, rejected these justifications of current practice, as did the author of the *Summa Parisiensis* and the anonymous author of the *Distinctiones Monacensis*. Clerics, these writers held, had no right to demand fees for their advocacy, for that would be the grievous sin of simony. If a grateful client spontaneously offered them a gift, however, they could legitimately accept it.[99] Gandulphus, who like the Cardinal wrote between about 1160 and 1170, likewise disapproved of advocates and legal advisers who took fees. Either a case was just or it was unjust, he reasoned. If it was just, they should provide their services free of charge; if it was unjust, they should not involve themselves with it at all.[100] The author of the *Summa "Elegantius in iure diuino"* repudiated Gratian's

97. Rufinus, *Summa* to C. 15 q. 2 pr., at 348; Stephen of Tournai, *Summa* to C. 14 q. 2, at 221. Once again, Johannes Faventinus, *Summa* in London, BL, MS Add. 18369, at 92va, followed Rufinus verbatim, and the author of the *Summa "De multiplici iuris diuisione"* to C. 15 q. 2 pr. in CUL, Pembroke MS 72, at 73vb, largely followed Stephen's line of argument.

98. He has been convincingly identified as Cardinal Raymond des Arènes (d. 1177 or 1178); Losciavo, "Sulle tracce bolognesi del Cardinalis."

99. *Summa "Prima primi"* to C. 15 q. 2 in London: BL, MS Royal 11.D.II, at 328vb: "Item nullus propriis cogitur militare stipendiis [suis], ut in dec. de simonia, Cum sit sancta [Alexander III, JL 14126]. Item iustum est eum percipere emolumentum qui prestat obsequium, ut 12 q. 2 Caritatem, Ecclesiasticis [C. 12 q. 2 c. 45, 67]. Derogatum est ergo c. sequenti per contrarium consuetudinem a papa approbatam, ut forte hoc tantum significatur per sequens c. quod nullus debet aliquid accipere pro clerico ordinando uel promouendo. Gratis tantum oblatum potest recipere, ut i q. 2 Sicut episcopum [C. 12 q. 2 c. 4]. Secundum hoc male intellexit Gratianus. C[ardinalis]." *Summa Parisiensis* to C. 14 q. 5 c. 15 v. *sed non qui contra*, at 172, and *Distinctiones Monacensis*, 116.

100. Weigand, "Gandulphusglossen zum Dekret Gratians." Huguccio repeated Gandulphus's opinion in his *Summa* to C. 11 q. 3 c. 71 v. *iustum* in Munich, Bayerische Staatsbibliothek, Clm. 10247, at 159ra–rb, quoted in Fried, "Vermögensbildung," 31 n. 19. Johannes Teutonicus also quoted this passage from Huguccio in his *Glos. ord.* on this same text.

explanation even more caustically. While he acknowledged that Roman practice allowed clerical advocates to charge for their services and even to sue clients who failed to pay, this author disapproved of both customs. "It would be far more suitable," he observed tartly, to take account not of what is done at Rome, but rather what ought to be done at Rome, and to accept what the words of the canon actually say."[101]

Bishop William of Paris accepted these conclusions and sought to enforce them in his diocese. In his 1204 constitutions, William admonished his priests that they must not work as advocates save in special situations and that even then they must perform their functions without charge, although he would allow them to accept reimbursement for the expenses they incurred, provided that these were moderate.[102] Authorities even weightier than the bishop of Paris continued occasionally to condemn clerical advocates who accepted payment for their services and to demand that they cease doing so. Pope Honorius III, for example, advised the bishop of Poitiers that this sort of activity "renders the priestly title abhorrent in the hearts of the weak" and instructed him to restrain priests in his diocese from serving as paid advocates in either civil or ecclesiastical courts. It is incongruous, the pope continued, for priests entrusted with the mystery of the Lord's body and blood to delight in lawsuits and involve themselves in worldly affairs.[103]

The Third Lateran Council (1179) introduced two further considerations into the discussion. The council decreed that beneficed clerics in higher orders should not act as advocates in secular courts, save when they defended themselves or the church they served, or when they acted on behalf of a disadvantaged person.[104] Law teachers soon broadened the council's distinctions between beneficed and unbeneficed clerics and those in major and minor orders. Whereas the council had applied these distinctions only to clerics who pleaded as advocates in secular courts, decretists applied them to all clerical advocates.[105] The council had forbidden clerics

---

101. *Summa "Elegantius"* 9:47 and 9.48, at 3:72: "De eodem magis digna imitatione sententia: Perfectius est non quid Rome fiat set quid Rome fieri debeat considerare et uerba canonis uti sonant accipere."

102. Constitutions of Bishop William of Paris (1204) c. 4, in Mansi 22:767.

103. 5 Comp. 3.1.1 (X—); Po. 7780.

104. 3 Lat. (1179) c. 12, in *DEC* 1:218; 1 Comp. 1.28.un. = X 1.37.1.

105. Thus, e.g., Sicard of Cremona, writing immediately after 3 Lat., put it this way in his *Summa* to C. 15 q. 2, London, BL, MS Add. 18367, at 42va–vb: "Queritur si pro defensione possit munera exigere. Videtur quod non, ut hic.... Respondeo. Regularibus

supported by church revenues to practice as advocates, law teachers reasoned, because it would be greedy for a clerical advocate to receive fees in addition to his clerical stipend.[106] Two anonymous decretist commentators, one belonging to the Anglo-Norman and the other to the Parisian school of decretists, developed this line of thought in greater detail. The Anglo-Norman *summa* that begins with the words "Prima primi" taught that beneficed clerics, whether in major orders or not, should not receive fees as advocates in secular courts. Although clerics could practice as advocates in church courts, the author was silent on the matter of their fees for doing so.[107] The *Ecce vicit leo*, a Parisian *apparatus*, was more explicit. An unbeneficed cleric in minor orders, according to this writer, could act as a paid advocate in civil cases in secular courts under the conditions specified by the Lateran canon, and in all types of cases, civil or criminal, before

---

non licet quia non licet eis propria possidere. Secularibus autem licet, nisi scholasticis et eis qui salaria percipiunt in illis ecclesiis ubi participant, in quo casu loquitur sicut mihi uiderit hoc capitulum Obseruandum [C. 15 q. 2 c. un.], et loquitur generaliter secundum officium humanitatis." Likewise, Johannes Teutonicus, *Glos. ord.* to C. 15 q. 2 pr. v. *pro impensis.*

106. Ricardus Anglicus, *Apparatus* to 1 Comp. 1.38.1 v. *stipendiis*, in Munich, Bayerische Staatsbibliothek, Clm. 6352, at 14ra:, followed nearly verbatim by Tancred's *Apparatus* to the same passage in London, BL, MS Royal 11.C.VII, at 18rb, and Cambridge, Gonville and Caius MS 28/17, 24b: "Uidetur ergo a sensu contrario si stipendia non habeant possunt aduocare, quod plane uerius est de minoribus ordinibus. De maioribus uero secus est, quoniam si sine titulo sunt ordinati episcopus eis tenetur prouidere, ut infra de prebendis, episcopis [1 Comp. 3.5.5 = X 3.5.4]. De regularibus planum est quod ab aduocatione repelluntur, ut xvi. q. i. alia, c. Placuit communi [C. 16 q. 1 c. 6, 8]; infra ne clerici uel monachi c. ult. Non magnopere [1 Comp. 3.37.2 = X 3.50.3]. l[aurentius]." Caius glosses, at 52rb, to D. 88 c. 1 v. *clericum*: "Hic uerum est de clericis in subdiaconatus et supra; in concilium lateranensis, Clerici in subdiaconatu [c. 12], causa cupiditatis uel turpis lucri."

107. *Summa "Prima primi"* to C. 15 q. 2 in London, BL, MS Royal 11.D.II, at 328va: "In ciuili uero causa clerici in sacris ordinibus constituti uel etiam in minoribus si sustentantur de bonis ecclesie coram ciuili iudice non debent postulare.... Qui non sunt constituti in minoribus ordinibus et non habent ecclesiastica beneficia non uidentur prohiberi, ut innuit in concilio Lateranensi, Clerici [3 Lat. c. 12]. § Coram iudice uero ecclesiastico tam in causa criminali quam ciuili licite postulant clerici, ut in c. i. Excepto episcopo, qui non admittitur nisi in sua causa criminali, ut 3 q. 5 Quia [C. 3 q. 5 c. 15]." *Summa "Prima primi"* was composed between 1203 and 1209. See Kuttner and Rathbone, "Anglo-Norman Canonists," 327; Tierney, "Two Anglo-Norman Summae"; Fraher, "Alanus Anglicus."

an ecclesiastical judge.[108] Some participants in Robert Courson's legatine council at Paris in 1212 could well have been aware of the views expressed in *Ecce vicit leo* when they adopted a canon that incorporated these ideas.[109] In the opinion of leading authorities, clerical advocates appointed by a judge to represent a poor client were bound to do so without compensation. Odofredus, however, suggested to his students that there were ways to avoid such a nonpaying assignment if they really wished to do so. They might claim that the prospective client had already consulted them and that they had found that his case lacked merit. Alternatively, they might tell the judge that the person they were asked to represent was someone with whom they had close ties (*coniuncta persona*) and hence that it would be improper for them to take the case.[110]

Contingent Fees

Authorities agreed that it was reprehensible for an advocate to demand as his fee a fraction of any award that his client might receive if he won the lawsuit for which his services were engaged. Constantine I prohibited this

---

108. *Apparatus "Ecce vicit leo"* to C. 15 q. 2 pr. v. *pro expensis* in Cambridge, Trinity College MS O.5.17, at 77ra: "Hic est ii. questio, utrum scilicet clerici possunt aduocare et pro aduocatione recipere pecuniam. Notandum ergo quod nunquam coram iudice seculari possunt aduocare in causa sanguinis, nec pro precio, nec sine precio, ut xxiii. q. ult. [His; MS: Hunc] a quibus [C. 23 q. 8 c. 30]. In causa autem ciuili possunt coram seculari iudice in causis suis et miserabilium personarum et suarum ecclesiarum, ita tamen quod sine precio, nisi forte in minoribus ordinibus constituti fuerint et carent beneficiis ecclesiasticia, quia tunc se possunt locare, ut extra De postu. c. i [1 Comp. 1.28.1 (= X 1.37.1)]. Coram autem ecclesiastico iudice se possunt omnes locare ad aduocandi in quilibet causa. Excipiuntur ab hac regula sacerdotes, qui non debent locare, ar. supra xiiii. q. v Non sane [C. 14 q. 5 c. 15]. Militant namque patroni causarum, ut C. De aduocatis diuersorum iudiciorum l. Aduocati [Cod. 2.7.14], sed non tenetur quis suis stipendiis militare. Item credimus de his qui habent ecclesiastici beneficia sibi sufficiencia, quod scilicet se locare non debent." On this Parisian gloss apparatus, written between 1202 and 1210, see Kuttner and Rathbone, "Anglo-Norman Canonists," 328.

109. Legatine Council of Paris (1212), pt. 1 c. 6, in Mansi 22:820–21. In 1217, on the other hand, Honorius III ruled that canons of two collegiate churches in the diocese of Cambrai could continue to receive the regular stipends from their canonries while pleading as proctors or advocates in the Official's court (*Regesta Honorii Papae III*, no. 289, ed. Pressutti, 1:52).

110. On the obligation to accept nonpaying assignments, Hostiensis, *Lectura* to X 1.32.1 §§4–5 [Venice 1581 ed.] vol. 1, at 169ra; Roumy, "Système de l'avocat commis d'office," 382–85 cites further authorities on this point. On ways to avoid such cases, Odofredus, *Lectura* to Cod. 2.6.7 v. *restitui* §2; and again, Roumey, 376–77.

practice in 325 on the grounds that it was wicked and gravely damaging to clients and decreed that any advocate who contracted for what we now call a contingent fee should permanently forfeit his right to practice.[111]

Gratian included Constantine's ban in the vulgate recension of the Decretum, where at first it attracted little comment.[112] The *Summa Parisiensis* noted that "some people" claimed that this passage applied only to advocates paid out of public funds, as they had been in the late Roman empire. The argument had at least a veneer of plausibility, although in fact few writers adopted it. Most legal writers, civilian and canonist alike, instead accepted the ban on contingent fees as a fundamental axiom of legal ethics.[113] A few, however, explored ways around the ban. Azo, for example, argued that if an advocate bargained for only a tiny fraction (*de minima etiam parte*) of the award, he could legitimately receive this as a bonus (*palmarium*), in addition to his normal fee.[114]

Huguccio on the other hand insisted that the ban on contingent fees should be vigorously enforced and that an advocate or proctor who made an agreement with a client to take even as little as one-thousandth of a judgment as his fee should forfeit the right of audience.[115] He did note, however, that the ban on contingent fees only forbade an advocate to seek some fraction of the total award that his client would receive if successful in his lawsuit, without further specification. This language, Huguccio suggested, would not necessarily prevent an advocate from entering into an agreement whereby his client undertook that if his lawsuit were successful

---

111. Cod. 2.6.5.

112. C. 3 q. 7 c. 2 §8. Paucapalea, Rolandus, and Rufinus, for example, passed over this passage in silence, while the author of the *Summa "Elegantius"* 6.64, at 2:132, was content simply to reproduce the words of the text.

113. *Summa Parisiensis* to C. 3 q. 7 c. 2 v. *arcentur*, at 121; Tancred, *Ordo iudiciarius* 1.5.4, at 113. In contrast, e.g., Otto of Pavia, *Summa "Olim,"* 234, §§330, 335; John of Salisbury, *Policraticus* 5.13, ed. Webb, at 1:341. According to Accursius, *Glos. ord.* to Cod. 2.6.5 v. *immensa*, Martinus maintained that a contingent fee was allowable so long as it amounted to less than half of the property at issue in the case, but Hugo and Azo as well as many later authorities rejected this argument (*Dissensiones dominorum*, 267).

114. *Dissensiones dominorum*, 267–68.

115. Huguccio, *Summa* to C. 3 q. 7 c. 2 §8 v. *certe partis*, in Vatican City, BAV Arch. S. Petr. C.114, at 146rb: "*certe partis*. id est quote, scilicet medie uel tercie uel quarte uel quinte partis uel etiam minoris, non licet aduocato quotam partem rei que petur uel defenditur etiam minimam pacisci ut dicat, 'Dabis mihi pro patrocinio mediam uel terciam uel quartam partem, uel etiam millesimam istius rei,' puta hereditatis quod petis uel defendis. Idem est et in procuratore, ut D. de pactis, sumptus [Dig. 2.14.53]."

his advocate's reward would consist of some specific item of property included in the award—say, for example, a particular farm or vineyard. Such an arrangement would not violate the ban, Huguccio declared, so long as the payment did no serious harm to the client. This meant, he explained, that the value of the property specified in such an agreement must not exceed 100 gold *solidi* in value, since that was the maximum fee established by Roman law.[116] Johannes Teutonicus in his immensely authoritative ordinary gloss on the Decretum adopted Huguccio's argument almost verbatim.[117]

Fee Levels

Huguccio and other canonists taught that the amount of advocates' fees should be determined as Roman law provided by the difficulty of the case, the skill of the advocate, the customs of the court in which the action lay, and the practices current in the region in which that court sat.[118] Fees for written legal opinions (*consilia*) were also supposed to reflect the amount of labor involved. Answering a simple question offhand did not warrant any charge, according to the ordinary gloss, but preparing a formal opinion that required extensive research could justify a substantial fee. Twelfth-century jurists admonished judges to see that practitioners abided by these principles.[119] General norms are notoriously difficult to

---

116. Huguccio, *Summa*, in Vatican City, BAV, MS. Arch. S. Petr. C.113, at 146rb–va: "Res tamen aliiqua singularis de illa re uel summa que petitur bene potest pati et in pacto promitti et si plus sit quandoque medietate, ut dicat, 'Dabis mihi illam uineam uel illum predium de hac hereditate' et huiusmodi. Item non licet aduocato pacisci de immoderato salario, id est quod excedat c. aureos in causis singulis. Hoc enim salarium et non amplius aduocato de iure permittitur pro facundia aduocati et pro magnitudine iudicii et pro consuetudine fori, ut D. De uariis cognitionibus l. i. [Dig. 50.13.1.10]." On the general principle of an appropriate fee, Huguccio was adopting an argument ascribed to Johannes Bassianus (*Dissensiones dominorum*, 267–68).

117. Johannes Teutonicus, *Glos. ord.* to C. 3 q. 7 c. 2 §8 v. *partis* and §10 v. *contractum*; likewise the *Summa "Elegantius"* 6.64, at 2:132. Martinus and other civilian writers made similar arguments, although Azo dissented and maintained that this approach amounted to a fraudulent evasion of the law; Accursius, *Glos. ord.* to Cod. 2.6.5 v. *immensa*.

118. Dig. 50.13.1.10.

119. Johannes Teutonicus, *Glos. ord.* to C. 11 q. 3 c. 71 v. *iustum*; Bellomo, *Common Legal Past*, 213–14. In addition to Johannes Teutonicus, see Azo, *Summa super Codicem*, 28, to Cod. 2.6; Accursius, *Glos. ord.* to Cod. 2.6.3 v. *certum modum*; Otto of Pavia, *Summa "Olim,"* 234, §331.

translate into detailed regulations, and fee guidelines were no exception. An advocate's skill and reputation, together with local customary practices, no doubt played a role in fixing actual fee levels, but they were almost certainly neither the only nor the most important factors in the process. Advocates, legal advisers, and proctors naturally sought to try to maximize their income and to negotiate for the highest fees that their clients could be persuaded to pay. Clients' generosity tended to vary in proportion to their wealth and the interest or anxiety they felt about the outcome of their case.

Data on the fees actually paid to ecclesiastical advocates during the long twelfth century are scanty and scattered. Surviving scraps of evidence suggest that, while their remuneration varied widely, it was often not inconsiderable. Advocates at the papal curia, not unexpectedly, were especially well rewarded. Thomas of Marlborough in 1205, for instance, engaged four advocates to argue on behalf of the monastery of Evesham in its lawsuit at the papal court against the bishop of Worcester. Their daily fees ranged from 50 to 20 *solidi*, so that advocates' fees cost him a total of 150 *solidi* each day in court. This was a very substantial sum, almost twice the minimum annual wage an English vicar was supposed to receive.[120] It was so substantial, in fact, that Thomas ran out of money. When supplementary funds failed to arrive, he was forced to forgo the services of his local advocates and plead the case himself.[121]

Fees at bishops' courts tended to be considerably more modest. A generation before Thomas of Marlborough's case at Rome, Sir Richard de Anstey set down a detailed record of his expenses in a long drawn-out lawsuit against Mabel de Francheville. In the course of his litigation, Sir Richard sought rulings at the courts of the bishop of Winchester and the archbishop of Canterbury on a key element in his case, which concerned the marriage of Mabel's parents. Sir Richard recorded payments for legal advice and representation at the archbishop's court of 11 marks (£7 6s. 8d.) and a further 14 marks (£9 5s. 6d.) at the bishop's court, in addition to 10

---

120. Merandus, a Spanish advocate, commanded the highest fee at 50 *solidi* per day. Bertrandus, a knight from Pavia, and Petrus Beneventanus, then a papal chaplain (he was later commissioned to compile 3 Comp., and ultimately became a cardinal), each received 40 *solidi* daily; while Master William, a clerk of the papal chancellor, got 20 *solidi* (Thomas of Marlborough, *History of the Abbey of Evesham*, 284, §285). The Council of Oxford (1222) c. 21, in Powicke & Cheney 1:112–13, set the minimum wage of a vicar at 5 marks (Ð3 6s. 3d.).

121. Thomas of Marlborough, *History of the Abbey of Evesham*, 344–46, §358.

marks (£6 16s. 7 ½ d.) paid to one advocate and just a single mark (13s. 3d.) to another.[122]

It is impossible to translate figures such as these directly into modern currency values, but Sir Richard's accounts also record that he lost two pack animals valued at 9 *solidi* and 12 *solidi* respectively, as well as two palfreys, or riding horses, which cost him 15 *solidi* and 2 marks (£1 6s. 8d). The cost of horses and pack animals, which were used everywhere for moving people and goods overland, provide at least some rough gauge of relative values.

Authorities, both ecclesiastical and civil, attempted to impose upper limits on charges for legal services, as Roman emperors had done in late antiquity. Stephen, chancellor of the Sicilian kingdom between 1166 and 1168, published the earliest known medieval fee schedule, which limited the amounts charged for legal documents. He expressly declared that its purpose was to restrain "the enormous greed of the notaries."[123] Innocent III at the beginning of his pontificate likewise imposed a limit on what he considered the excessive fees charged by the scribes and notaries of the papal curia. Two clauses in another early-thirteenth-century document, the *Institutio cancellarie super petitionibus dandis et recipiendis*, imposed a ceiling of 20 pounds per case on the fees payable to advocates at the papal curia.[124]

The growing frequency with which we can find evidence that wealthy and prominent individuals and institutions were commencing to retain advocates and legal advisers on a long-term basis is symptomatic of an increasing dependence upon legal experts among litigants and of emerging professionalism among lawyers. A notarial manual from Reims around the beginning of the thirteenth century, for example, includes a form for a retainer agreement between a monastery and an advocate. Instances of the practice grew increasingly common in England, Italy, and Castile by the

---

122. *English Lawsuits* 2:402. Woodcock, *Medieval Church Courts*, 135–37, provides a much later example of a litigation expense statement from 1490.

123. Accursius, *Glos. ord.* to Dig. 50.13.1 v. *aureos*; Stephen quoted in Bresslau, *Handbuch der Urkundenlehre* 1:575–76.

124. *Gesta Innocentii III*, c. 41 in PL 214:lxxx; *Deeds of Pope Innocent III*, 55–56; Sayers, *Papal Government*, 17. The early clauses of the *Institutio cancellarie*, a composite document, belong to the pontificate of Innocent III. Two clauses that were added later stipulated that no litigant was to employ more than two advocates simultaneously. See Tangl, *Päpstlichen Kanzleiordnungen*, 55, §§16–17; Heckel, "Kanzleiordnung Innozenz' III.," 258–89; Sayers, *Papal Government*, 19–21.

1220s.[125] Thus, a question debated by Johannes Teutonicus not long after 1200 highlights a complication that became more common as the use of retainers became more frequent:

> A certain legal expert, having accepted payment from a certain church, promised and swore that he would render assistance to it in any of its affairs whatever. Later, however, he swore similarly to another [church] without mentioning any exceptions. It subsequently happened that both churches were involved in some lawsuits. The prelates of these churches sought assistance from him. The question is whether he was bound to aid the first one or neither [of them].[126]

Johannes counseled the *iurisperitus* caught in this dilemma to decide which client had the greater justice on his side and to give his assistance to that party. An anonymous Anglo-Norman canonist remarked tartly that anyone who put himself in this position was ill-advised.[127]

The Functions of Proctors and Advocates

Legal theory distinguished sharply between the functions of advocates and those of proctors.[128] Both could be described as lawyers and both performed essential legal services, but procedural writers insisted that they filled sepa-

---

125. *Liber practicus de consuetudine Remensi* 1.103, ed. Varin, 1:106–107; Ramsay, "Retained Legal Counsel," 96–97; Linehan, "Will of Synibaldus de Labro," 136–37.

126. Fransen, "Questions de Jean le Teutonique," 44–45, no. 7: "Quidam iurisperitus recepto salario a quadam ecclesia promisit et iurauit se prestaturum ei patrocinium in quolibet suo negotio. Postea uero similiter cuidam alteri iurauit nec posuit aliquam exceptionem. Accedit postmodum quod ambo iste ecclesie quasdam causas habebant. Prelati harum ecclesiarum petunt patrocinium ab eo. Est in questione utrum teneatur iuuare primam uel neutram. Solutio. Dicimus quod tenetur iuuare illam que iustiorem uidetur habere causam quoniam qui dat in malo consilium, uertitur in detrimentum. Si hoc est incertum, potest illud iuramentum interpretari uel quod ei melius uisum fuerit exemplo Iosue ut xxii. q. iiii. Innocens credit [C. 22 q. 4 c. 23]." Two other collections of canonistic *questiones* from the late twelfth or early thirteenth century discussed similar situations. See Fransen, "'Questiones' des canonistes (III)," 527, no. 53.

127. Caius glosses to D. 96 c. 11 v. *potestatem*, at 57vb: "Si ergo clericus in duobus episcopatibus redditum habeat, pro quo et contra quem stabitur? Respondeo, faciat secundum id 14 q. 5 Denique [C. 14 q. 5 c. 10], uel secundum alios pro reo stare debet. Male quilibet facit qui hoc modo duobus se obligauit."

128. The distinction derived from Roman law, which assigned separate roles and different standing to advocates and proctors. See Kaser, *Römische Prozessrecht*, 563 n. 56; Litewski, *Römisch-kanonische Zivilprozeß* 1:177–78; and Landau, "Erteilung des Anwaltsmandats," 413–14.

rate and distinct duties in litigation. Advocates were skilled legal experts intimately familiar with the fine points and technicalities of the law, adept at legal analysis, and persuasive argument. Proctors, by contrast, were the law's men of affairs, experienced in the practical details of the operations of courts, adroit at smoothing over difficulties, men who knew what the judges liked and (perhaps more important) what they disliked, who mastered every detail of each client's case and had all the relevant facts at their fingertips. Since the tasks that advocates and proctors performed called for different skills, they were trained differently, received different levels of compensation, and came from different socioeconomic backgrounds.

These role distinctions were not purely academic. Thomas of Marlborough tells us how Innocent III distinguished between advocates and proctors in precisely this way:

> The pope indeed forbade the advocates to speak about the facts, but only about the law when that was needed, since, he said, the proctors know the facts and the law.[129]

But a half-century earlier, Gratian and the early decretists in the middle years of the twelfth century seldom seemed as clear about the difference between the two. The vulgate version of Gratian's *Decretum* described the functions of proctors and their duties mainly in the words of a few passages selected from Justinian's *Digest* and *Code*.[130] The decretists who commented on these texts in the schools frequently spoke of proctors and advocates as if the terms were interchangeable: "The proctor indeed is called an advocate," declared the author of the *Summa Parisiensis* on one page, and a few pages later he referred to "the advocate, that is the proctor." Likewise the *Summa "Elegantius"* flatly asserted that "the proctors of cases are advocates."[131] Huguccio commented on, but did little to clarify, the terminological ambiguity:

---

129. Thomas of Marlborough, *History of the Abbey of Evesham*, 300, §303: "Prohibuerat enim [papa] ne advocati loquerentur de facto, nisi de jure tantum et cum opus esset, quia dixit procuratores nosse factum et jura." Innocent had also made the same point a little earlier in Thomas' narrative at 282, §284: "'Non loquamini,' inquid, 'amodo de illa possessione, set tantum de subiectione et exemtione monasterii, et tantum procuratores loquantur ut per eos de facto certificemur, quia uterque vestrum iurisperitus est. Et cum opus fuerit advocati respondeant nobis de iure.'"

130. C. 2 q. 6 c. 28–29, 40; C. 3 q. 7 c. 1–2; C. 3 q. 9 d.p.c. 18; C. 5 q. 3 c. 1, 3; C. 16 q. 6 d.p.c. 7.

131. *Summa Parisiensis* to C. 3 q. 7 pr., "procurator vero dicitur advocatus," and to C. 5 q. 3 c. 3, "advocatum, i. e. procuratorem," at 121, 129 (similarly, the Caius glosses

"Proctors," or otherwise "patrons," that is, advocates. Gratian's words are categorical terms, but those that follow are the words of the law, although Gratian sometimes alters them or inserts his own [words].[132]

The uncertainties of usage reflected not only the sources in the vulgate version of Gratian's *Decretum*, but also the realities of practice in many church courts in the late twelfth century, where the mingling of roles and the terms that described them could puzzle even Innocent III, as appears in his handling of a possessory action brought against Archbishop Philip of Milan in 1198. At one stage of the proceedings, Innocent described Passaguerra as the archbishop's proctor. Passaguerra, an imperial judge under emperors Henry VI (r. 1190–96) and Otto IV (r. 1198–1218), was no novice at legal swordplay. In handling Archbishop Philip's case, he employed sophisticated tactical maneuvers calculated to take advantage of the numerous procedural opportunities for evasion that the case presented. His tactics annoyed Innocent III, who complained indignantly to Archbishop Philip about Passaguerra's behavior, and in one letter directed Philip to excommunicate "your lawyer" (*causidicus tuus*).[133]

The distinction between the roles of advocates and proctors that Innocent III described in Thomas of Marlborough's case emerged clearly in the procedural manuals that began to appear from the late 1160s onward. Writers such as Johannes Bassianus (fl. ca. 1180–85)[134] and Otto of Pavia, for example, distinguished proctors from advocates much more precisely than Gratian's texts did. Proceduralists described the *procurator litis* as a litigation agent appointed by his principal or client through a formal man-

---

to C. 3 q. 7 c. 2 v. *procurator* and C. 5 q. 3 c. 3 v. *fame, publico*, at 90rb and 94va; Rufinus, *Summa* to C. 5 q. 3 c. 3 v. *advocatum*, at 278, followed verbatim by Johannes Faventinus in London, BL, MS Add. 18369, 68va); *Summa "Elegantius"* 6.63, at 2:132: "Quia procuratores causarum aduocati sunt, congruum est ut de eorum officio breuem notitiam faciamus."

132. Huguccio, *Summa* to C. 3 q. 7 c. 2 pr. v. *procuratores* in BAV MS Arch. S. Petr. C. 114, at 146ra: "*Procuratores*, uel alias patroni, id est aduocati. Hec uerba sunt Gratiani, sed deinceps sunt uerba legis, licet Gratianus quandoque ea mutat uel sua interserat."

133. Innocent III, *Register* 1.37, at 1:51–56 (Po 31), and 1.85, at 1:123–24 (Po 77).

134. Lange, *Römisches Recht im Mittelalter*, 215–26; Savigny, *Geschichte* 4:289–311, as well as his *Summa "Quicumque vult,"* at 549–55. Belloni has argued that the civilian writer Johannes Bassianus was the same person as the canonist Johannes Bazianus; see her "Baziano, cioè Giovanni Bassiano." Other scholars have not found her argument convincing; Gouron, "À la convergence des deux droits," and "Un juriste bolonais docteur."

date, which authorized him to act in place of his client during litigation. This became the standard definition of a proctor and his duties among late-twelfth-century canonists.[135]

The proctor's mandate defined what he was authorized to do on his client's behalf. The mandate could be cast in broad terms that empowered him to act in any lawsuit in which the client was involved, or it might take the form of a special mandate that limited the proctor's powers of representation to pursuing or defending a specific legal action. Likewise the mandate might be of indefinite duration, and hence valid until superseded or revoked, or it might be limited to a specified time period.[136] Mandates were almost invariably spelled out in written documents, and the proctor had to be able to prove that his mandate was genuine.[137] He had also to demonstrate that the powers it conveyed to him were sufficient to cover the case in which he appeared, that his principal was eligible to be represented by a proctor, and that he himself met the minimum qualifications to act in that capacity. Otherwise his actions would have no force or effect. These provisions allowed parties who wished to delay matters to raise exceptions against the mandate of their opponent's proctor, an opportunity of which they often took advantage.[138]

---

135. On the *procurator litis*, Otto of Pavia, *Summa "Olim,"* 231, §§253, 258; Johannes Bassianus, *Summa "Propositum,"* 218, §§46–49; gloss to Inst. 1.20.7 in *Glosse preaccursiane*, 209, no. 500. See also Landau, "Erteilung des Anwaltsmandats," 415–19. On the standardization of the definition, e.g., *Summa "Elegantius"* 6.55–56, at 2:130–31; Bernard of Pavia, *Summa decretalium* 1.29. pr., 1, 7, at 23–24; Tancred, *Ordo iudiciarius* 1.6.1, at 114.

136. Otto of Pavia, *Summa "Olim,"* 231, §255; 2 Comp. 1.18.3 (= X 1.38.3; JL 16632); Tancred, *Ordo iudiciarius* 1.6.2 and 7, at 115, 121–22.

137. Otto of Pavia, *Summa "Olim,"* 231, §258; Johannes Bassianus, *Summa "Propositum,"* 218, §49; Tancred, *Ordo iudiciarius* 1.6.1, at 114, as well as a letter of Pope Gregory the Great that Bernard of Pavia incorporated in 1 Comp. 1.29.1 (= X 1.38.1; JE 1874). For a few examples of how this was done in practice see *John Lydford's Book*, 34–35, nos. 22 and 24; *Documenten uit de praktijk*, 57–58, nos. 40, 44. Counterfeit mandates could create serious problems if, for example, an unscrupulous proctor pretended to act on behalf of some unsuspecting person and brought a spurious action, say, to deprive a cleric of his benefice. 4 Lat. (1215) c. 37 (4 Comp. 1.2.5 = X 1.3.28) described some of these problems and sought to devise remedies for them. See the text in the council's *Constitutiones*, 79–80, as well as the glosses to this canon by Johannes Teutonicus, v. *sine domini speciali mandato*, and Vincentius Hispanus, v. *nec pro ipsius presumatur processu*, at 232–33, 342–43. Note also Heckel, "Aufkommen der ständigen Prokuratoren," 311–13.

138. A proctor must be a male Catholic who had attained his majority and was not excommunicated or disreputable (*infamis*) (Gratian, C. 3 q. 7 c. 1–2; Bernard of Pavia,

The proctor represented his client in the literal sense that whatever he did or said while acting on the client's behalf carried the same legal consequences as if the client had said or done it.[139] Similarly, actions taken against the client might affect the proctor: he could, for example, be required to pay a judgment given against his client or furnish security that his client would pay. He would, of course, seek reimbursement from his client, although this might sometimes prove easier said than done.[140] Anyone could appoint a proctor to act on his or her behalf in civil cases, and persons in eminent positions, such as bishops, who were not supposed to appear in person as litigants, had to act through proctors.[141]

Practice frequently failed to reflect the sharp functional division between proctors and advocates that procedural writers made. Highly trained advocates and legal advisers were scarce, and their services were costly. They tended to cluster in cities where courts were numerous, litigation was frequent, and the stakes at issue often large. The courts of lesser prelates and some bishops were located in small cities or country towns, the property disputes they adjudicated typically involved modest sums, and their criminal cases mostly concerned petty crimes. Advocates were unlikely to flourish in such venues. In these courts, accordingly, proctors often performed the tasks that in strict law should have been reserved to advocates. This was certainly true from the second half of the thirteenth century onward, when local court records begin to survive in considerable numbers, and there is no compelling reason to think

---

Summa decretalium 1.28.4; at 24; Walter of Cornut, *Ordo iudiciarius "Scientiam"* §12, at 29–30; Tancred, *Ordo iudiciarius* 1.6.1, at 115). For a sample of the kinds of issues that might be raised against the mandate of a proctor, see Walter of Cornut, *Ordo iudiciarius "Scientiam"* §13, at 30–33. Whole treatises were sometimes devoted to this topic (Fowler-Magerl, *Ordo iudiciorum*, 185–218).

139. *Summa "Elegantius"* 6.57, at 2:131; Bernard of Pavia, *Summa decretalium* 1.29.7, at 24; Tancred, *Ordo iudiciarius* 1.6.6–7, at 120–21.

140. Dig. 3.3.43.6; *Summa "Elegantius"* 6.62, at 2:132; Tancred, *Ordo iudiciarius* 2.16.2, 4.1.5, at 179, 274–75.

141. In criminal matters, neither an accuser nor a defendant could act through a proctor: Gratian, C. 3 q. 9 c. 18, C. 5 q. 3 c. 2–3; 2 Comp. 1.18.2 (X—; JL 17615); Rufinus, *Summa* to C. 5 q. 3 pr. and c. 3, at 278. On litigants who because of their position had to employ proctors, see Cod. 2.12.25; Gratian, C. 5 q. 3 c. 3; *Summa "Elegantius"* 6.57, 59, at 2:131; Tancred, *Ordo iudiciarius* 1.6.3–4, at 116–118; Rufinus, *Summa* to C. 5 q. 3 pr., at 278, followed nearly verbatim by the *Summa "De multiplici iuris diuisione"* to C. 5 q. 3, in CUL, Pembroke MS 72, at 71va: "Si uero causa ciuilis fuerit omnes permittuntur iure communi agere per procuratorem et respondere."

that the situation was substantially different during the long twelfth century.[142]

CLERICAL PROCTORS

Clerics, according to the texts in Gratian's Decretum, could serve as proctors, but only for certain types of clients, mainly other clerics, ecclesiastical institutions, and disadvantaged persons. While this limitation ultimately rested upon the scriptural admonition that God's warriors should not be involved in secular affairs (2 Tim. 2:4), the authorities that appear in Gratian's Decretum came from the same fourth- and fifth-century conciliar canons that banned clerics from appearing as advocates in secular courts.[143]

Teachers of canon law soon began to refine the interpretation of these texts. Rolandus, writing in the 1150s, presented arguments that could be made for either side of the proposition that clerics could act as proctors in worldly affairs. He resolved the contradictions by invoking the distinction between clerics in minor orders, who could marry, and those in major orders, who could not. Those who could marry were by definition permitted to involve themselves in worldly matters, and therefore, he concluded, clerics in minor orders could act as proctors in secular affairs, but those in major orders must not. He further distinguished between regular and secular clerics. Regular clerics could not engage in any secular business whatever, although secular clerics in minor orders were free to do so.[144] But what were "worldly affairs"? The phrase had a double meaning, according to Rufinus. It could refer to worldly things or worldly per-

---

142. See particularly Helmholz, *Marriage Litigation*, 147–51, and *Canon Law and Ecclesiastical Jurisdiction*, 222–24.

143. The *locus classicus* for the ban is C. 21 q. 3 c. 1–3; Gratian's authorities include 1 Carthage (345–348) c. 6 as well as 4 Carthage (419) c. 16 (= *Breviarium Hipponense* c. 15) and the *Canones in causa Apiarii* c. 16 in *Concilia Africae*, 6, 38, 105; Chalcedon (451) c. 3, in *DEC* 1:88–89.

144. Rolandus, *Summa* to C. 21 q. 3, at 77–78. The *Summa "De multiplici iuris diuisione"* to C. 21 q. 3 pr., in CUL, Pembroke MS 72, at 75ra, also reported Rolandus's position: "Illis uero clericis quibus nubendi licentia conceditur secularium negociorum administratio secundum quodam non negatur." The author of the *Summa Parisiensis* to C. 21 q. 3 pr., at 199–200, however, concluded that no clerics, whether regular or secular, or in major or minor orders, could represent laymen in the courts. This was essentially the position that Pope Eugene III had adopted in his 1146 response to a query from Jocelin de Bohun, bishop of Salisbury; 1 Comp. 3.37.8 (= X 3.50.2); JL 8959. Opposition to clerics serving as proctors for towns, secular rulers, and other laymen was later voiced as well by 3 Lat. (1179) c. 12; *DEC* 1:218; 1 Comp. 3.37.3 (= X 3.50.4).

sons, that is, the laity. In his reading, the canons forbade clerics to serve as proctors for laymen, save when they defended widows, orphans, and minors.[145]

How effective this prohibition may have been is problematical. It seems clear enough that clerics often did serve as proctors for laymen in actions before church courts, including those at the Roman curia. Richard de Anstey, for example, sent his chaplain as a proctor to a hearing at Rome during his long-drawn-out suit against Mabel de Francheville, and similar instances were not uncommon. Whether clergymen often represented lay clients before royal and municipal tribunals is less clear.

OCCASIONAL PROCTORS

Proctors who appeared in lower-level courts were often ad hoc appointees—family members or friends who knew something about the law or had more firsthand experience with the courts and the legal system than did the person whom they represented. Occasional proctors such as these, for whom the task of acting as a proctor was not a regular occupation, might nonetheless possess considerable legal experience. Such a one was Ralph of Ford, for example, who served Bishop Seffrid II of Chichester (r. 1180–1204) intermittently as a proctor around 1203. Ralph was certainly well-versed in legal practice, which is scarcely surprising, since he had previously served as the official of the bishop of Lincoln. Ralph of Ford, however, was an exception. Occasional proctors, even those who represented their principals before papal judges-delegate, were commonly much less experienced and less skilled than he was.[146]

---

145. Rufinus, *Summa* to C. 21 q. 3 pr., at 385. Johannes Faventinus in his *Summa* in London, BL, MS Add. 18369, at 112vb, and MS Royal 9.E.VII, at 117va, conflated Rufinus's text, which he followed closely, with a paraphrase of Rolandus's distinction. The *Summa "De multiplici iuris diuisione"* to C. 21 pr., in CUL, Pembroke MS 72, at 75ra, likewise adopted, but expanded upon, the substance of Rufinus's definition: "Secularium quidem negocia duobus modis dicuntur, et rerum secularium et personarum secularium, id est laicorum, ut milicia, tutela, aduocatio fori, conductio uectigalicum, mercimonia mandatum, et similia, in huius igitur negociis secularibus personis competentibus non debent clerici, maxime regulares necnon et in sacris ordinibus constituti, procurationis officium suscipere, in quo casu subsequenta locuntur capitula, Credo, Placuit, Ciprianus [C. 21 q. 3 c. 2–4], nisi forte pro pupillorum, orphanorum, uiduarum defensione, uel nisi episcopus rerum ecclesiasticarum sollicitudinem eis precipiat habere, ut supra di. lxxxviii c. i."

146. *Acta of the Bishops of Chichester*, 18, 143. Sayers, *Papal Judges Delegate*, 223–30, lists numerous examples of less talented proctors.

PROCTORS BY OCCUPATION

The proctors who are relevant to the study of the professionalization of medieval lawyers were those who appeared frequently and regularly in the courts, who habitually represented clients to whom they bore no obvious relationship, and who made their living, or a considerable part of it, from this occupation. Many proctors who appeared at the papal court during the second half of the twelfth century fit this description, as do some of those who frequented the courts of bishops and archbishops elsewhere. Around the beginning of the thirteenth century, such men were sufficiently numerous at Rome that Pope Innocent III thought it appropriate to issue regulations concerning the conduct and lifestyle of those who practiced in his courts.[147]

Compensation of Proctors

Despite Roman classification of the mandate as a gratuitous contract, in practical reality, men who regularly spent substantial time acting as proctors in the courts for strangers wanted to be paid for their services and needed to be able to sue clients for unpaid fees. The gratuitous mandate had in fact become little more than theoretical, even in late antiquity. In due course, the medieval *ius commune* took account of this and allowed twelfth-century proctors to make a living by representing clients in the church courts.[148]

Proctors of all kinds, whether they only occasionally represented a friend or family member in court, or whether they regularly appeared on behalf of any clients who engaged them, were entitled not only to a fee for their services, but also to compensation for expenses they incurred in performing their duties.[149] Their claims were supposed to be limited to costs actually expended on the client's behalf. If, for example, said Johannes Teu-

---

147. *Constitutiones summorum pontificum II* §§12–15, in Tangl, *Päpstliche Kanzleiordnungen*, 55. See Sayers, "Canterbury Proctors," 311–15, and "Proctors Representing British Interests"; Herde, *Beiträge*, 125–30, 136–48; Linehan, "Proctors Representing Spanish Interests," and "Spanish Litigants and Their Agents"; Bataillard, *Origines de l'histoire des procureurs*, 104.

148. Dig. 17.1.1.4; Cod. 4.35.1; Zimmermann, *Law of Obligations*, 415–20. On the *ius commune*, see among others, Bellomo, *Common Legal Past*, 55–77, Pennington, "Learned Law, Droit Savant, Gelehertes Recht," and Stein, *Roman Law in European History*, 197–209.

149. This was yet another Roman law practice that canon law adopted: Dig. 17.1.12.9 and 17.1.56.4; 4 Comp. 1.16.1 (= X 1.38.6; Po 549).

tonicus, a proctor was in Rome on other business, he could charge his client only for expenses incurred by extending his stay in order to deal with the client's business. A client, moreover, was liable only for charges based on a modest level of expenditure.[150]

NOTARIES

Notaries who drafted and copied legal documents continued to appear in papal, episcopal, and royal administrative records in some regions of the West throughout the early Middle Ages. Documents prior to the middle of the twelfth century, however, often employed the term *notarius* in ways that make it difficult to be sure whether they are describing skilled draftsmen who actually composed the documents that they wrote, or a *scriba* or *scriptor*, that is, someone who copied books or documents that others created.[151]

A notary was not necessarily a lowly ink-stained scribe. Many individuals who bore the title of notary were highly educated, well-connected men of power and influence who functioned as administrative officials and advisers to their masters. There can be little doubt that notaries such as Galbert of Bruges, for example, author of a well-known account of the murder of Charles the Good, count of Flanders, in 1127, were far from being mere scriveners.[152] Papal notaries in particular had been important curial officers since very early times and continued to play significant roles in twelfth-century papal administration. Thus, for example, one of the legates who Alexander III sent in 1169 to negotiate with King Henry II and Archbishop

---

150. Johannes Teutonicus, *Apparatus* to 4 Comp. 1.16.1 v. *propter hec*, in BL, MS Royal 11.C.VII, at 217ra: "Propter hec. Et si alias fuisset iturus romam non posset petere expensas factas nisi quatenus plus [expendisset; MS: extendisset] propter longiorem moram, ut C. famul. erisc., ex parte prin. [*recte*: Dig. 10.2.39]. Distinguitur tamen quia et si egit cum mandato et succubuit non petet expensas, ut C. mandat. Etiamsi [Cod. 4.34.4]. Set si sine mandato egit et succubuit, non petat expensas, ut ff. iudi. sol., Iam tamen § In hac [Dig. 46.7.5]. Iste autem expense non excedent probabilem modum, ut ff. de damp. infec., inter quas § ult. [Dig. 39.2.39.4] et l. [sequentem; MS: sequenciam], prin. [Dig. 39.2.40 pr.] et extra iii. de eo qui mit. in pos. c. ii in fi. [3 Comp. 2.8.2 (= X 2.15.3); Po. 1194]. Jo[hannes]." My thanks to Kenneth Pennington for emendations to this passage.

151. Amelotti and Costamagna, *Alle origini del notariato*, 151–204; Ourliac, "La pratique et la loi," 108–1, Savigny, *Geschichte* 1:71–72, 478–82, and 2:236–38; Cheney, *Notaries Public in England*, 1–2, and *English Bishops' Chanceries*, 26, 31–33, 36, 38–39; Brown, "Origin and Early History of the Office of Notary," 209–17.

152. Galbert of Bruges, *Murder of Charles the Good*, c. 35, at 164.

Thomas Becket concerning the conditions for Becket's return to Canterbury was a papal notary named Gratianus. Gratianus, a nephew of Pope Eugene III, was not only well-connected, but had studied law with Bulgarus, may have been the author of glosses on Gratian's Decretum, certainly served as one of the pope's principal legal advisers, and ultimately became a cardinal.[153]

A fundamental transformation of the notary's role took place during the second half of the twelfth century, beginning in the towns of northern Italy. Although notaries prior to that time often drafted charters, contracts, testaments, and important public and private documents, the authority of those documents rested on the signatures or seals of witnesses who warranted that they were authentic. The term "notary public" (*publicus tabellio, notarius publicus, scriptor publicus*) became current in Italy from around 1140 and by the end of the century had passed into general use. The spread in the use of public notaries seems to have been tied to the increasing frequency with which bishops committed the handling of most of their routine jurisdictional business to officials-principal.[154]

The notary public, in contrast to the plain notary or scribe, was a public official in the sense that he held a commission from a high-ranking public authority, such as the emperor or the pope. The notary's commission empowered him to produce reliable documents and assured judges that they could presume that the instruments he produced were accurate and authentic so long as they bore his signed attestation and his personal identifying sign or emblem.[155] Pope Alexander III enunciated the basic elements of the presumption in favor of the reliability of notarial records in a decretal letter to Bishop Roger of Worcester, in which the pope declared:

> Genuine documents may seem to us not to have reliable authority if the witnesses who signed them have died, unless perchance they have been re-

---

153. Maleczek, *Papst und Kardinalskolleg*, 71–73. On Gratianus's legation to Thomas Becket, see William of Canterbury, *Vita sancti Thomae* 1.64, in *Materials* 1:72; John of Salisbury, *Letters*, 2:650–58, no. 289. Cheney, *Notaries Public in England*, 5, gives further examples.

154. Meyer, *Felix et inclitus notarius*, 7–107; Guyotjeannin, Pycke, and Tock, *Diplomatique médiévale*, 120–21; Gouron, "Maître Durand," 181; Wickham, *Legge, pratiche e conflitti*, 96–97, 105–6; Wolf, "Das öffentliche Notariat," 506–7.

155. Meyer, *Felix et inclitus notarius*, 557–687; Cheney, *Notaries Public in England*, 102–3, 129–30 and plates 1–6; further examples appear in Purvis, *Notarial Signs* and *El documento notarial*.

dacted by a public hand in such a way that shows that they are public [instruments], or have a seal whereby they may be proved.[156]

Procedural writers and professors of canon law elaborated on this presumption in favor of notarial records.[157] It rested, according to Bencivenne of Siena, on the oath that the law required public notaries to take.[158] It was a presumption of fact and hence subject to rebuttal,[159] but the barriers to overcoming it were very high.

> But what if the notary stands by the instrument [asked Bencivenne] and all the witnesses deny it? Reply: Sometimes the instrument is more credible than the witnesses, and sometimes the witnesses are more credible than the instrument. . . . But what if the notary said, "I don't recall that I wrote this instrument," or "I did not write this instrument"? Would the document thereby lose its authenticity? Reply: I don't believe so, because the notary might say this out of malice.[160]

The presumption in favor of the reliability of documents prepared by notaries was further reinforced by Pope Innocent III in a constitution adopted by the Fourth Lateran Council, which required that an official re-

---

156. 2 Comp. 2.15.2 (= X 2.22.2; JL 13162), 1 September [ca. 1167–69]: "Scripta vero authentica, si testes inscripti decesserint, nisi forte per manum publicam facta fuerint, ita quod appareant publica, aut authenticum sigillum habuerint, per quod possint probari, non videntur nobis alicuius firmitatis robur habere." For the date, see Kuttner, *Repertorium der Kanonistik*, 287, and Cheney, *Roger, Bishop of Worcester*, 364, appendix 2, no. 91.

157. Thus, e.g., Bernard of Pavia, *Summa decretalium* 2.15.2, at 49; Johannes Teutonicus, *Apparatus* to 4 Lat. c. 38 v. *aut duos uiros idoneos*, in *Constitutiones*, 234–35; Tancred, *Ordo iudiciarius* 3.13.2, at 248–49.

158. Bencivenne, *De ordine iudiciorum* 3 *De testibus*, 64, §8. Bergmann credited this *ordo* to Pillius and edited it under that name. This is easily understandable, since Bencivenne depended heavily on Pillius' thought—and sometimes borrowed his very words (Fowler-Magerl, *Ordo iudiciorum*, 119–22).

159. Bernard of Pavia, *Summa decretalium* 2.16.1–3, at 50–51; Tancred, *Ordo iudicarius* 3.13.5, at 253–54.

160. Bencivenne, *De ordine iudiciorum* 3 *De testibus*, 75, §14: "Sed quid, si tabellio concordet cum instrumento, et omnes testes dissentiant ab instrumento? Resp., quandoque magis esset credendum instrumento quam testibus et quandoque magis testibus quam instrumento . . . Sed quid, si tabellio dicat: 'Non ricordor, quod fecerim hoc instrumentum,' vel dicat: 'Non feci hoc instrumentum,' an propter hoc derogabitur fidei scripturae? Resp., non credo, quoniam tabellio potest hoc dicere propter malitiam."

cord of proceedings in ecclesiastical courts be set down where possible by a notary public.[161] While notaries were abundant and their services in frequent use throughout much of southern Europe, they were considerably scarcer north of the Alps, as contemporary writers noted. This was particularly true in England, where they rarely appeared, even in church courts, until the second half of the thirteenth century.[162]

At the papal curia, by contrast, enormous numbers of notaries swarmed around the Lateran Palace. Witnesses at the end of the twelfth century describe them seated around the entrance to the palace, each with his writing desk in his appointed place, surrounded by bankers and money changers, who set up their own tables in a passageway of the palace until Innocent III ordered them removed.[163] Notaries in private practice, such as these, naturally charged fees for their services based on the number of pages in each document that they prepared. Since the procedural systems in place by the beginning of the thirteenth century called for the production of substantial numbers of often lengthy documents in contentious proceedings, the costs of document production alone could pose a serious obstacle to poor litigants. For that reason, there was considerable sentiment that notarial fees should be regulated, either by judges or by higher authorities. Innocent III directed notaries who practiced at the papal palace to prepare documents for humble and disadvantaged petitioners free of charge. He also approved measures to limit legal costs, including notarial fees, elsewhere.[164]

Lawyers and Legalism

The heightened legalism of church administration in the late twelfth and early thirteenth centuries, coupled with the increasing number of lawyers

---

161. 4 Lat. (1215) c. 38, in *Constitutiones*, 80–81, as well as 4 Comp. 2.6.3 (= X 2.19.11); *DEC* 1:252. This canon did provide, however, that when a notary was not available, *duos uiros idoneos* might be employed to record proceedings. This and the other disciplinary constitutions of the council were drafted in the papal curia and the council fathers adopted them without debate. See Kuttner and García y García, "A New Eyewitness Account," 163–64.

162. Gratia, *De iudiciario ordine* 1.8.1, at 347. Notaries never gained much of a toehold in the courts of common law, although they did appear in the court of chancery. They were especially numerous among royal civil servants and in the diplomatic activities of medieval English kings (Cheney, *Notaries Public in England*, 12–25, 55–71).

163. Heckel, "Aufkommen der ständigen Prokuratoren," 295–96.

164. Gratia, *De iudiciario ordine* 2.9, at 379; Tangl, *Päpstliche Kanzleiordnungen*, 54, Const. 2 §4; Innocent III, *Register* 1.257, at 1:359–69 (Po 270); 3 Comp. 2.7.1 (= X 2.14.5; Po 1324).

in prominent positions in the church, could hardly go unnoticed, and the attention that these developments attracted was almost entirely negative. Already in 1154, for example, John of Salisbury was grumbling about canon lawyers' "vigorous use of legal subtleties" and complained that his master, Archbishop Theobald of Canterbury (r. 1138–61), was being harassed with expensive lawsuits. Even a monastic chronicler who was himself a jurist found it remarkable that churchmen—a bishop and an abbot, no less—would interrupt the sacred mysteries of the Mass to carry on their litigation. Men such as Rupert of Deutz (d. 1129) or St. Bernard of Clairvaux, brought up in the monastic tradition of meditating on sacred texts, found the dialectical approach to textual analysis that lawyers and others learned in the new twelfth-century schools at best disconcerting, and at worst downright threatening.[165]

Critics of the lawyers were not bashful about making their discontent known, sometimes in scathing prose, sometimes in stinging verse. Moralists were disturbed by the ethical implications of the utilitarian approach to problem solving that legal training instilled. They were shocked at what they viewed as the amorality of law teachers, who trained their students to frame arguments on both sides of a controversy.[166]

Detractors often identified greed as the root of lawyers' moral shortcomings. This criticism quickly became proverbial, supported as it was by the enthusiasm with which many lawyers sought material rewards for their expertise.[167] To aggravate the affront, the size of those rewards left their critics aghast—and perhaps envious as well. Moralists regarded lawyers' preoccupation with worldly matters as unsuitable for any Christian. Legal studies, they feared, were not good for the soul. "Who ever rises contrite from the study of civil or even canon law?" asked John of Salisbury, and he added that legal scholarship "never or scarcely ever inflames devotion." Teachers of theology, philosophy, and the liberal arts felt dismay and anger, strongly tinged with jealousy, that so many promising young men were

---

165. John of Salisbury, *Letters*, 1:3–4, no. 2; *Chronicle of Battle Abbey*, 156–57; Southern, *Scholastic Humanism* 2:7–24. The opposition between monastic theology and scholastic theology described by Leclercq, *Love of Learning*, 189–231, applied even more emphatically to legal studies. See also Châtillon, "L'influence de S. Bernard," 269–74.

166. Abbot Adam of Perisegne, *Epist.* 24, in *PL* 211:666–68 at 667; Peter the Chanter, *Verbum abbreviatum*, 328–35, c. 49.

167. Alain de Lille, *Summa de arte praedicatoria* c. 41, in *PL* 210:187; Master Maurice of St. Victor, *Sermo communis* 4.3, at 218; Peter the Chanter, *Verbum abbreviatum*, 328–30, c. 49, among many others. See also Post, Giocarinis, and Kay, "Medieval Heritage of a Humanistic Ideal."

prepared to desert their classrooms for those of the lawyers.[168] They were still more dismayed to discover that popes preferred to elevate lawyers, rather than theologians, philosophers, or poets, to positions of power and authority in the church.[169] Nor was the feeling that the morality of lawyers was somehow deficient limited to the ranks of highly educated intellectuals such as John of Salisbury. "Peasants and shepherds all go to heaven," said a Catalan proverb, "advocates and merchants go burn in hell."[170]

Lawyers have seldom been highly esteemed, and condemnation of them is, in Karl Llewellyn's words, "as natural as whiskers on a cat."[171] The reactions to lawyers described above were far from novel. Roman authors in antiquity, as we have seen, had voiced many of the same complaints for many of the same reasons. Those ancient sentiments disappeared underground during the early Middle Ages. As the Western empire withered during the fifth and sixth centuries and the supply of trained lawyers dried up, strictures about the behavior of lawyers vanished too. Disparagement of lawyers only resurfaced around the middle of the twelfth century, just as men trained in law began to become plentiful once again.[172]

Some twelfth-century criticism of lawyers doubtless grew out of personal animosity or disappointment,[173] but the sheer volume of the fault-finding, the uniformity of the complaints, and the variety of the authors make it unlikely that this was the principal, much less the sole, explanation. The critics expressed a distrust and dislike of lawyers that was widely held precisely because lawyers were a rising occupational group whose numbers were growing at a rapid rate. Much of this criticism expresses dismay that intellectual figures such as Ivo of Chartres or John of Salisbury, who combined impressive legal expertise and lawyerly skills with wide-ranging

168. John of Salisbury, *Letters*, 2:32–34, no. 144; Gerald of Wales, *Gemma ecclesiastica* 2.37, in his *Opera* 2:348–49.

169. E.g., Adam of Perisegne, *Epist.* 24, in *PL* 211: 667; Jean de Blois, quoted in Haskins, *Studies in Medieval Culture*, 47 n. 8

170. "Pagès i ramader tots van al cel; advocat i comerciant a l'infern a cremar," quoted by Freedman, *Origins of Peasant Servitude*, 220 n. 39.

171. Llewellyn, *The Bramble Bush*, 173–74.

172. Kuttner, "Dat Galienus opes," 237; Chiappelli, "La polemica contro i legisti," 295; Yunck, *Lineage of Lady Meed*, 139.

173. Baldwin attributes Peter the Chanter's animus against canon lawyers to the fact that in 1193 the chapter of Tournai had elected him as their bishop, only to have the election quashed and the bishopric given instead to the canonist, Stephen of Tournai ("Critics of the Legal Profession," 249, and *Masters, Princes, and Merchants* 1:9–10).

humanistic learning were being displaced by a new type of lawyer whose specialized training in the law tended to be deeper but narrower than that found among members of earlier generations.[174]

Their complaints make it clear that these critics and other members of older, established social groups saw the newcomers as a threat to their own interests, as intruders who swiftly emerged as competitors—and even worse, successful ones—for power, wealth, influence, and authority. Nor were satirical aspersions on lawyers and legal processes confined to rival groups among the elite. Popular tales in the late twelfth century also derided legalism and the minions of the legal system.[175]

That law-trained men constituted a new social order was an insight not lost upon contemporary observers, including lawyers themselves. Azo, for example, identified himself as a member of the honorable *ordo iurisperitorum*, while an Avignon document from 1194 or 1195 described the lawyers (*causidici*) as one of the privileged classes among the city's inhabitants, and even placed them ahead of the knights.[176]

Yet although they were a visible social group and were rapidly becoming a force to be reckoned with in both civil and ecclesiastical society, did trained lawyers who made the law their principal occupation constitute a profession by the close of the long twelfth century? They unquestionably spent years of formal study in order to acquire complex and esoteric skills inaccessible to most of their contemporaries. Men with this kind of training often relied upon their earnings from the practice or teaching of law for a substantial part of their livelihood. Some formal requirements for those who pleaded in court had long been in place. Canon law had incorporated basic elements of a body of ethical standards for advocates, proctors, and notaries from Roman sources, and there was general agreement that judges had the power to discipline those who blatantly defied them. A few notions of courtroom etiquette had even begun to take hold.[177]

Professionalization was a gradual process. By the close of the twelfth century, legists and canon lawyers had made substantial strides toward be-

174. A point well made by Morris, *Discovery of the Individual*, 125.
175. See, e.g., Kaeuper, "The King and the Fox."
176. Azo, *Summa super Codicem*, 1, proem.; Poly, "Les légistes provençaux," 620.
177. E.g., the convention that judges sit, but advocates and proctors stand while speaking in court, was reasonably well established; a few prescriptions governing the calendar of ecclesiastical courts were in place, and some standards for courtroom dress and decorum had begun to take shape; C. 15 q. 4 c. 1–3; Tancred, *Ordo iudiciarius* 1.5.2, 3.15.4, at 111–12, 264; 4 Lat. (1215) c. 16 (= X 3.1.15); Council of Oxford (1222) c. 33 in Powicke & Cheney 1:116.

coming a profession by the criteria described in the introduction to this book, but as of 1200 they had not yet arrived at full-fledged professional status. In 1200 a mechanism for formal certification of professional training and competence had not yet appeared. The earliest universities were just beginning to take shape at Bologna and Paris. No surviving evidence suggests that formal law faculties had yet been organized, while a system of examinations and degrees in law apparently would not begin to take shape, so far as we can tell, until the second or third decade of the thirteenth century.

Nor is there any clear evidence that a formal process for admission to practice was in use in church courts before 1200. Judges had long asserted their right to decide who they would permit to argue before them, and Roman law had prescribed some standards that advocates were supposed to meet. Admission to practice in 1200, however, apparently remained a discretionary matter to be determined at the pleasure of individual judges, and we have no evidence for any sort of formal admissions ceremony or oath of office at that time. Although ethical norms for practitioners in the courts were studied in the law schools, church authorities prior to 1200 had not yet made their observance obligatory. Disciplinary sanctions, if any, for misbehavior by advocates and other legal functionaries have failed to leave traces in the relatively few court records that survive from that period.

Around 1200, jurists in some Italian cities were starting to become sufficiently numerous and concerned to promote their common interests that they began organizing as corporate groups, usually in the form of guilds.[178] This gave them the means to act in common to address collective issues, while still preserving the capacity to compete with one another as individuals.[179]

Lawyers by the opening decades of the thirteenth century were thus on the cusp of a new professional identity. The following chapters will explore how that transition was completed during the middle decades of the century.

---

178. See, e.g., the lists of jurists in Bologna and Modena in Fried, *Entstehung des Juristenstandes*, 144–69 and 227–44.

179. Epstein, *Wage Labor and Guilds*, 102.

* SIX *

The Formation of an Educated Elite
Law Schools and Universities

Universities were indispensable for the development of the medieval legal professions. The earliest universities at Bologna and Paris probably began to take shape late in the twelfth century, although no strong evidence for their corporate existence survives from before 1200. Students and teachers at preexisting schools created these corporate bodies in part to foster more systematic teaching and learning than had previously been available. At the same time, guilds of students and teachers gave their members the ability to take collective action to advance their common interests and to defend themselves against competing interests in church and state. The university became the mother of professions in the strict sense of the term.[1]

Securing a proper legal education was a formidable task. Walter of Châtillon (b. ca. 1132, d. 1202 or 1203) compared it to scaling a lofty mountain.[2] Mastery of its language, procedures, and substantive content required a substantial investment of time and money, as well as the expenditure of a great deal of hard intellectual labor.[3] University training in law, especially when crowned by the award of prestigious academic degrees, such as doctor of laws or doctor of decrees, provided the successful student with institutional certification of his technical competence.

When a university conferred a doctorate in law, it declared that a body of acknowledged legal experts had tested the student and had determined

---

1. Ridder-Symoens, "Training and Professionalization," 149.
2. Walter of Châtillon, "In domino confido," stanza 1, in his *Moralisch-satirische Gedichte*, 39, ll. 15–18.
3. Baker, *Law's Two Bodies*, 64–67.

that he was qualified to join the ranks of public teachers of law. Lower-ranking degrees, such as the bachelor's degree or the licentiate, although less prestigious than the doctorate, nevertheless vouched that their holder had spent several years in serious study of civil and canon law and had satisfied his teachers that he had a thorough grasp of its major branches. Even students who studied law at a university for just a year or two and left without taking a degree (as most of them did) still enhanced their chances of making successful careers as advocates or legal advisers. Wealthy and well-connected elite families often deemed it advantageous to send one or more of their sons to study law at a university in order to improve their chances of beating out competitors in the contest for prestigious appointments in church or state. University law faculties put their students (at least the serious ones) through a challenging course of study calculated to provide them with the intellectual equipment needed for practicing law in the highest courts, providing sound legal advice to clients, both public and private, for serving as judges, and for administrative careers in either church or civil government.[4]

Lawyers trained and certified by a university differed from those in earlier generations. Men who studied law before the start of the thirteenth century typically heard lectures in the schools of a few private teachers who worked independently of one another. The masters and doctors who comprised the law faculties of universities, by contrast, formed a privileged corporate body. Instead of teaching as private individuals, they lectured and engaged in disputations in schools recognized as public institutions, sometimes even supported by public funds.[5] They lectured according to the dictates of a systematic curriculum. They put their students through public disputations to refine their skills and display their knowledge for all to see. They set public and private examinations to test their students' mastery of the subject and awarded a degree that attested their competence. University masters were jealous of their reputation, individually and collectively, as elite experts. They fought hard to secure recognition for the degrees they awarded and admitted new members to their ranks only grudgingly. The study of law at a university provided institutional creden-

4. Verger, "Teachers," 146–47; Schwinges, "Student Education, Student Life," 196; Aston, Duncan, and Evans, "Medieval Alumni of Cambridge," 26–27; Gramsch, *Erfurter Juristen*, 96–100; Fuchs, *Dives, pauper, nobilis*, 15, 25–38, 113; Courtenay, *Parisian Scholars*, 99–100; Soetermeer, "Proportion entre civilistes et canonistes," 287; García y García, "Enseñanza del derecho canónico," 214–22; Bellomo, *Saggio sull'università*, 57–59, 205–12, 216–22; Moraw, "Careers of Graduates."

5. Maierù, *University Training*, 40–44.

tials that carried greater distinction and greater assurance of competence than did private study with a handful of individual masters.[6]

The Origins of Universities

Teachers of the liberal arts, theology, medicine, and law began to cluster together in Paris and Bologna around the middle of the twelfth century.[7] The presence of well-known, learned, and stimulating teachers and writers—such as the Four Doctors at Bologna or Peter Abelard (ca. 1049–1142), Peter Lombard (b. ca. 1095, d. 1160), and Hugh of St. Victor (d. 1141) at Paris—gave each city a reputation as a center for advanced studies. Bologna's fame rested first and foremost on legal studies, while Paris was principally famous for the study of the liberal arts (especially logic and philosophy) and theology. By the last quarter of the twelfth century, the schools in these two cities had emerged as Europe's foremost centers of learning in their respective specialties—each had become what later generations would call a *studium generale*.[8] The cities' renown attracted aspiring philosophers, theologians, physicians, and lawyers, who formed the nucleus around which the earliest universities gradually coalesced.

During the decades just before and after 1200, teachers and students in the previously autonomous schools of individual masters at Bologna and Paris began to organize themselves as corporate bodies, variously described as *universitates*, *studia*, or *societates*. In doing so they followed a practice common among contemporary merchants and craftsmen all across Europe. The *universitates* established by the masters of the schools at Paris and students in the schools at Bologna strove, like other trade and craft guilds, to secure occupational privileges and protections for their members.[9]

6. Verger, "Professeurs des universités françaises," 175–76.

7. Rashdall, *Universities*, remains the basic general account of the process of university formation. More recent general treatments include *History of the University in Europe* (hereafter *HUE*), Cobban, *Medieval Universities*, and Pedersen, *First Universities*. For an overview of law teaching in medieval universities, Coing, "Juristische Fakultät," is fundamental.

8. Rashdall, *Universities* 1:15–19; Verger, "Patterns," in *HUE*, 35–37.

9. *Universitas* was a common legal term for a group of persons organized as a corporate entity that possessed rights and obligations distinct and separate from those of its individual members. Academic canonists in the twelfth and thirteenth centuries gradually refined the concept of a *universitas* to produce a sophisticated corporation law, from which modern corporation law ultimately derives. On the medieval development of corporate theory and terminology, see Post, "Parisian Masters as a Corporation," 29–39, Tierney, *Foundations of the Conciliar Theory*, 89–97; and

The circumstances that initially sparked the corporate organization of teaching at Paris and Bologna remain tantalizingly obscure.[10] These two institutions developed gradually over a period of time and—barring the unexpected discovery of hitherto unknown documents—it is impossible to pinpoint a precise year when they began to assume an identifiable corporate identity. But because they, like the rest of Europe's oldest universities, developed gradually, lacked identifiable founders, and did not suddenly come into being at some precisely identifiable point in time, their loyal alumni created a thicket of gaudy fables to account for their origins. Bolognese foundation myths claimed that the emperor Theodosius II (401–50) had established the university in 433 at the request of St. Ambrose (b ca. 340, d. 397), regardless of the inconvenient fact that Ambrose had died four years before Theodosius was born. Parisian students claimed Charlemagne as the founder of their university. Oxford not only hailed King Alfred (d. 890) as its founder, but as late as 1872 saw fit to commemorate the millennial anniversary of their supposed foundation date with elaborate festivities that culminated in a celebratory banquet. Cambridge, anxious not to be outdone, traced its origin to even more misty founders, including a mythical Spanish prince named Cantaber and, slightly nearer home, to King Arthur, both of conveniently early and uncertain date.[11]

By contrast to these tales, sometimes fortified by ingeniously, if unconvincingly, forged documents, more sober historians must settle for a cloud of uncertainty about the origins of Europe's first universities. Bologna and Paris were clearly the earliest such organizations, although which of them first coalesced into an institution cannot be established with any assurance.[12]

Michaud-Quantin, *Universitas*. Coing's discussion of medieval university terminology in "Juristische Fakultät," 64–66, is also helpful.

10. As Kantorowicz and Smalley put it: "Much has been written, little is known, of the origin of the University of Bologna," or for that matter of Paris ("An English Theologian's View," 231).

11. See Rüegg, "Themes," 4–8; Rashdall, *Universities* 1:142–43, 271–73, 3:5–7, 179, 276–77; Sorbelli, *Storia*, 11–14, 19–20, 31–35; Cobban, *Medieval English Universities*, 20–26; Parker, *Early History of Oxford*, 53–57, 62; Carr, *University College*, 173–74; Ingram, *Memorials of Oxford* 1: 6; Fuller, *History of the University of Cambridge*, 4–15.

12. The medical school at Salerno, occasionally described as Europe's earliest university, never developed the organizational structure that characterized other universities and is now usually considered a "proto-university" (Rüegg, "Themes," 6).

THE UNIVERSITY OF BOLOGNA

Systematic law teaching by individual masters in their own private schools was, as we saw earlier, well established at Bologna by 1155, when the emperor Frederick I issued the *Authentica "Habita,"* which formally recognized their status.[13] A few years later, on 5 October 1159, Pope Alexander III sent a letter to "the doctors of law and other masters teaching at Bologna," as well as to the bishop and canons of the city's cathedral, to inform them of his recent election to the Holy See. The salutation of Alexander's letter implies that the teachers of Bologna formed a distinct group among other civic dignitaries. The pope's letter, however, made no mention of the students they taught. It seems reasonable to infer from this that the law students of Bologna had not yet acquired a corporate identity — or at least not one that was visible to the pope.[14] Bologna certainly had schools long before 1159, but they had not yet coalesced into a *studium* or university.

By the beginning of the thirteenth century, Bologna's students formed a small but important fraction of the city's population.[15] Bolognese law students were often no longer adolescents. Many were mature men in midcareer, often already well-to-do, and some held positions of authority before they arrived. Some were laymen who aspired to become a *iudex* or *podestà* in Italian communes and wished to study law in order to equip themselves for appointments of this kind. Others were clerics, many of whom already held a benefice or prebend, who hoped that study of canon law might improve their chances for advancement to more lucrative and prestigious ecclesiastical offices. Students of this description were in a position to wield considerable power, especially when they acted as a group.[16]

---

13. For the locations of some of these schools, see Cavazza, *Le scuole*, 47–49, 55–59, and 80–116.

14. JL 10587; Somerville, "Alexander III's Pontificate," 359–60; Nörr, "Institutional Foundations," 325. Alexander's biographer, Cardinal Boso (d. 1178), described him as eloquent and learned, "a man of the Schools" (*Life of Alexander III*, 43). See also the shrewd assessment of Alexander's personality and character by Smalley, *Becket Conflict*, 138–40, although since she wrote it has become evident that he was not the author of the *Stroma Rolandi*.

15. Pini, "Discere turba volens," 66, estimates that in the second half of the twelfth century law students at Bologna numbered roughly between 2,000 and 2,200 out of a total population between about 30,000 and 50,000. For other estimates, see Steffen, *Studentische Autonomie*, 78–79; and esp. Stelling-Michaud, *Université de Bologne*, 38–39, 77.

16. Stelling-Michaud, *Université de Bologne*, 115–16, 130–69; Walther, "Anfänge des Rechtsstudiums," 157; Schwinges, "Student Education, Student Life," 198–99;

Clusters of foreign law students (in the sense that they were not natives of the city and its immediate environs) had begun to appear by the 1170s. A group of English students in 1174 set up an altar in the Church of San Salvator in honor of St. Thomas Becket, who had himself studied at Bologna not many years previously. In 1191 an association (*universitas*) of Lombard students jointly purchased a parcel of land. These two groups mark early appearances of the foreign student organizations at Bologna that later generations would call "the Nations."[17] Early in the thirteenth century, the Nations at Bologna joined forces to create two student corporations, each styled a university. Students from the Italian peninsula outside of Bologna composed the Cismontane University (*universitas cismontanorum*), while students from "beyond the mountains," that is, all other parts of Europe, made up the Ultramontane University (*universitas ultramontanorum*). Each of these organizations annually elected a rector, who served as its representative and spokesman in dealing with civic authorities and with the professoriate. Native Bolognese students and all professors, whether Bolognese by birth or not, were excluded from both student guilds.[18] It is not possible to establish a date for the creation of the two student universities, but they had certainly come into existence before 17 May 1217, when Pope Honorius III (r. 1216–27) addressed a letter to the student *universitates* at Bologna, where he himself had once been archdeacon. In his letter, the pope deplored a recent municipal statute that forbade the students to quit the city in protest against what they viewed as unacceptable treatment by the town. In a subsequent letter, the pope urged the city government to modify its policies and to remedy the grievances that the students complained of. Honorius thus threw the weight of his office behind the student universities, as his successors would continue to do.[19]

Gramsch, *Erfurter Juristen*, 271–73, 291. Although both civil and canon law were taught at Bologna from the mid-twelfth century onward, some evidence suggests that civilians outnumbered canonists among the student body (Soetermeer, "Proportion entre civilistes et canonistes," 284–85). Leclercq argues that the power of more mature, well-established students is part of a larger set of fundamental changes in the psychological relationship between students and teachers that was not limited to Bologna ("Sviluppo dell'atteggiamento critico," 401–28).

17. Coing, "Juristische Fakultät," 52; Kibre, *The Nations*, 3–14; Sorbelli, *Storia*, 150–52.

18. Rashdall, *Universities* 1:153–59, 176; Sorbelli, *Storia*, 152–58. The Cismontane and Ultramontane universities ultimately fused for practical purposes into a single student body.

19. Honorius III, *Ex relatione venerabilis*, Po 6220; *Regesta* 1:395, no. 2383. Rashdall prints the text of both letters in *Universities* 1:585 and 586–88; see also 168–71, as well

The law teachers of Bologna had apparently begun to organize a corporate body of their own even earlier than Honorius's pontificate. In 1184 or 1185, Pope Lucius III (r. 1181–85) issued regulations concerning the leasing of properties by students and teachers at Bologna and directed that they be read "yearly in the common assembly of masters and scholars." This clearly attests that some sort of organization was taking shape, since the law teachers of Bologna were regularly meeting as a group with their students at least once a year to address common problems and concerns.[20]

Local records also show that that from the late 1180s onward, Bolognese municipal authorities required law teachers to take an oath that they would not leave the city in order to teach somewhere else. By this point the city's government had clearly come to value its lawyers as important economic assets.[21] This, too, suggests that the law teachers may have been organized in some way, although the inference is no more than speculative.

By 1210, firmer evidence began to appear. Azo (fl. 1190–1220), writing at Bologna between 1208 and 1210, declared that while members of a trade or craft (*professio*) had the legal right to elect magistrates (*consules*), students had no such right, since their occupation did not qualify as a *professio*. Azo thus maintained that while the Bolognese doctors possessed the legal capacity to form a corporate body, their students did not.[22] When Pope Innocent III (1198–1216) formally published the decretal collection known as *Compilatio tertia* in 1209 (or at latest in 1210), he addressed his bull of prom-

---

as Kibre, *The Nations*, 6–8; Sorbelli, *Storia*, 162–63. Contrary to the hope that the pope had expressed initially, many students had in fact departed from Bologna (Rashdall, *Universities* 1:170–71).

20. JL 16647; the regulations were later included in the Liber Extra at X 3.18.1. Landau, "Papst Lucius III.," identifies the letter's author as Pope Lucius III, rather then Clement III as was earlier thought, and dates it between July 1184 and November 1185.

21. *Registro grosso*, nos. 1, 6–8, in *CSB* 1:3–4, 8–10. The requirement later became part of the city's 1259 statutes and was reasserted in greater detail in the 1288 statutes (*Statuti di Bologna dell'anno 1288* 8.2, 5, at 2:96–97). A fifteenth-century addition to the statutes even went so far as to prescribe the death penalty for law professors over the age of fifty who went elsewhere to teach (Rashdall, *Universities* 1:171). On the city's recognition of its lawyers' economic value, Savigny, *Geschichte* 3:220; Weimar, "Zur Doktorwürde," 320*; Walther, "Anfänge des Rechtsstudiums," 154.

22. Azo, *Lectura* to Cod. 3.13.7 v. *Qui professiones aliquas seu negotiationes exercere noscuntur*, in Savigny, *Geschichte* 3:174 n. a.; Rashdall, *Universities* 1:164–65. Accursius likewise adopted this position (*Glos. ord.* to Cod. 3.13.7). Odofredus, however, declared that at Bologna the city had bestowed this right on the students who came there to study (*Lectura* to Cod. 3.13.7, at 148rb).

ulgation to "All the masters and students resident in Bologna."[23] Since the pope addressed the masters and students collectively, it seems reasonable to infer that an organized body of teachers had emerged alongside the student groups, although once again the evidence is scarcely unequivocal.

Anecdotal evidence corroborates these hints about the existence of some sort of corporate structure among law teachers at Bologna. Boncompagno of Signa (fl. ca. 1170–1240) mentions, for example, that he presented his *Rhetorica antiqua* at Bologna on 26 March 1215 in the presence of the "guild [*universitas*] of professors of canon and civil law and a numerous multitude of other doctors and students."[24]

Around this same time, we begin to find evidence that Bolognese professors of law were awarding degrees based on the performance of their students in formal examinations. Academic degrees originated in the license to teach, as titles such as "master of arts," "licentiate in canon law," "doctor of decrees," "doctor of laws," or "doctor of both laws" suggest.[25]

Documents dated in 1221 mention an oath that students were obliged to swear to observe the statutes relating to the Bolognese law faculty.[26] Later

---

23. Innocent III, *Devotioni vestri*, in 3 Comp. proem.: "Innocentius episcopus servus servorum Dei universis magistris et scolaribus Bononiae commorantibus salutem et apostolicam benedictionem" (Po 4157); Schulte, *QL* 1:87 n. 1; Weimar, "Zur Doktorwürde," 316*–319*.

24. "[C]oram universitate professorum iuris canonici et civilis et aliorum doctorum et scolarium multitudine numerosa" (quoted in Rashdall, *Universities* 1:146 n. 1; trans. Thorndike, *University Records and Life*, 41–42, no. 22; see also Polak, "Boncompagno of Signa").

25. For "licentitate in canon law," see, e.g., *CSB* 12:207–8 (no. 181), 218–21 (no. 191), 222–24 (no. 193); *CUP* 1:76, no. 16. On "doctor of decrees," see, e.g., *CSB* 12:146–47 (no. 138), 151 (no. 142), 154–55 (no. 146), 161 (no. 151), 163 (no. 153), 223 (no. 193); Johannes de Deo, *Liber questionum*, nos. 31, 33, 34, 39, in London, BL, MS Arundel 493, at 30va–vb, 32ra. *CSB* 3:185–86, no. 169, shows that this title was used as early as 1218, likewise Padovani, "Un 'consilium sapientis,'" 75–76. For "doctor of laws," see Feenstra, "Legum doctor," 73–75; Weimar, "Zur Doktorwürde," 307*; Verger, "*Nova et vetera*," 50. "Doctor of both laws" appears in *CSB* 12:209 (no. 182), 223–24 (no. 193), 228 (no. 196); Cortese, "Legisti, canonisti e feudisti," 240–41. Finally, see also Bernard of Pavia, *Summa decretalium* 5.4.1, at 209; and Guido de Baysio, *Rosarium decretorum* to D. 37 c. 12 v. *et doctores*, CUL, MSS Peterhouse 27, at 41va, and Peterhouse 35, at 50ra: "Hic forte est differentia inter magistros et doctores, ut magistri dicantur liberalium artium, doctores qui docent ipsa elementa, arg. Extra de vi. et hone. cle., ut quisque [X 3.1.7]."

26. *Registro grosso*, in *CSB* 1:33, no. 37; Sarti-Fattorini 2:32. The term "faculty," long used to describe an intellectual discipline, by 1220 was also beginning to mean a corporate body (Geyer, "Facultas theologica," 137).

that year, or possibly early in the following one, we find the doctors of law at Bologna meeting as a group in St. Peter's Cathedral to discuss whether they ought to add a constitution of the emperor Frederick II to their lectures on Justinian's Code. Thus by 1220 or 1221 at the latest, an organized body (*collegium*) of law teachers had beyond serious doubt come into existence at Bologna alongside the two student guilds.[27]

Although law teachers now had their own corporate body, the student *universitates* initially proved the more powerful organizations. Students successfully secured regulatory control over most aspects of the *studium*, including its academic operations.[28] By the middle of the thirteenth century, as Bologna's earliest surviving statutes make plain, the student guilds dictated the academic calendar, the method of conducting lectures and disputations, and the times and conditions for the payment of professors' fees.[29] The students required their teachers to begin lectures promptly at the sounding of the cathedral bells and to end them immediately upon the next sounding of the bells. Stiff fines payable to the student guilds awaited those who failed to do so. A teacher who planned to be away from the city during the academic year had first to secure permission for his absence from his students and must then seek approval from the rectors of the student universities. In addition, he had to deposit the sum of 100 Bolognese pounds (roughly equivalent to a year's income for a law professor) as security to guarantee his return.[30] Students further consolidated their control by forcing their teachers to swear obedience to the rectors of the student universities and to the regulations that they promulgated. Bolognese

---

27. Odofredus, *Lectura* to Auth. *Cassa* post C. l.1.12, quoted in Savigny, *Geschichte* 3:521 n. b; Weimar, "Zur Doktorwürde," 317*–319*; *Registro grosso*, nos. 37, 39, in *CSB* 1:33, 35; Sorbelli, *Storia*, 178–80; Rashdall, *Universities* 1:204–5.

28. Rashdall, *Universities* 1:165–67.

29. These previously unknown statutes appear in a manuscript acquired in 1971 by the Robbins Collection at the University of California's School of Law (Boalt Hall) in Berkeley. They were published by Domenico Maffei, "Un trattato di Bonaccorso degli Elisei," 93–101. Maffei suggested that these statutes were redacted before1252, since Innocent IV approved the university's statutes on 18 December 1251 (*Les registres d'Innocent IV* 3:256, no. 6717). Boháček, "Puncta Codicis," has argued that the version of the statutes in Robbins MS 22 must have been redacted somewhat later, perhaps between ca. 1260 and 1270.

30. Bologna University Statutes (1317) 2.44, at 313; (1432) 2.48, at 323. The statutes set the annual salary of an ordinary lecturer on the *Decretum* at 150 Bolognese pounds, while an extraordinary lecturer on the same book received only 50 pounds per year (Zaccagnini, *Vita dei maestri e degli scolari*, 28–29).

teachers did manage, however, to retain control over two vital matters: conducting examinations and awarding degrees.[31]

Other universities in northern Italy, some of which originated in migrations of students and teachers from Bologna, would replicate the pattern of student-controlled university governance that started at Bologna and sometimes reproduced provisions in Bologna's statutes word-for-word.[32] One of the best-known and most enduring of these *studia* began to take shape around 1222 as a result of a migration of Bolognese students to Padua, which by the middle of the thirteenth century was commencing to rival its parent university. Earlier migrations from Bologna to Vicenza in 1204 and to Arezzo around 1215 had proved short-lived, and those foundations soon disappeared.[33]

Even universities that were not the offspring of student migrations from Bologna sometimes adopted features of Bologna's organizational model. The earliest of these was located in the south of France at Montpellier, where private medical schools had begun to flourish as early as the mid-twelfth century. Law schools soon joined the medical schools, and they, too, began to prosper, especially after the distinguished jurist Placentinus settled at Montpellier around 1163, following difficulties that had arisen between him and some colleagues at Bologna and Mantua.[34] By 1220, the medical schools of Montpellier had joined together to form a *universitas* of the magisterial or Parisian type, headed by a chancellor appointed by the bishop in consultation with three medical teachers. When Montpellier's private law schools began to unite toward the end of the 1260s, they formed a separate university, which adopted the student-dominated Bolognese model of university governance.[35]

Perugia was another university that embraced the Bolognese style of governance. The university there began operating in 1276, although it re-

31. Bologna University Statutes (1317) 2.42, at 308–10; Rashdall, *Universities* 1:148–49, 161–73; Kibre, *The Nations*, 60; Sorbelli, *Storia*, 173–75, 216–19.

32. Gargan, "Libri, librerie e biblioteche," 228.

33. Rashdall, *Universities* 2:6–21.

34. Placentinus himself provided some autobiographical information in the preface to his *Summa in tres libros*, reproduced in Savigny, *Geschichte* 4:245–46; on the date of his arrival in Montpellier see Gouron, "Comment dater la venue de Placentin à Montpellier?"

35. *Statuts et privilèges des universités françaises* 2:4–6, no. 882; Gouron, *Juristes de l'école de Montpellier* and "Deux universités pour une ville." Gouron's studies substantially modify earlier accounts, such as Rashdall, *Universities* 2:116–39.

ceived formal recognition from the papacy only in 1308.[36] Its major strength, as was true of Bologna's other offspring, lay in its law faculty.

At Bologna itself, the power of students over their professors began to diminish toward the end of the thirteenth century. Prior to that time, each teacher at Bologna contracted with his students at the beginning of the academic year for the total fee, the *collecta*, that the students in his class were prepared to pay for a course of lectures. Two students then collected the sum due from each of the others and turned it over to the professor at the end of the term. This arrangement obviously gave students substantial power over their teachers.[37] When the commune of Bologna began in 1279 to pay selected law teachers annual salaries out of municipal funds, professors came to depend less directly upon the students for their livelihood. The commune took this step reluctantly after other cities had begun to lure away some of Bologna's best-known law teachers to staff their own universities.[38] By the last quarter of the thirteenth century, nearly a dozen other cities in Italy, Spain, and southern France either had their own functioning *studia* or were trying to establish one.[39] Civil and canon law were the dominant courses of study in all of these universities, and all were ambitious to build prominent law faculties. For this purpose, local authorities were prepared offer sizable salaries and other benefits to outstanding law teachers, who they hoped would attract students and lend their prestige to the new universities.

36. Rashdall, *Universities* 2:40–43.

37. Bologna University Statutes (1432), Appendix §104, at 385–87; Post, "Masters' Salaries," 192–94; Savigny, *Geschichte* 3:254–60.

38. Rashdall, *Universities* 1:209–10; Savigny, *Geschichte* 3:240–42; Sorbelli, *Storia*, 93–94, 183–85; Denifle, *Entstehung der Universitäten*, 198; Sarti-Fattorini 1:255–56; Cobban, "Elective Salaried Lectureships," 664–65. Communal authorities had begun to discuss establishing salaried lectureships as early as the 1220s. Such appointments began to appear during that decade, first at Palencia, then at Naples, Vercelli, Padua, and Toulouse (Honorius III, *Regesta* 2:199, no. 5273; Cobban, "Elective Salaried Lectureships," 662–63, Fried, *Entstehung des Juristenstandes*, 122–23, 206, 209–10; Denifle, *Entstehung der Universitäten*, 197; Smith, *University of Toulouse*, 32–34). Other universities followed suit (Rashdall, *Universities* 2:71, 81; Mor, *Storia dell'Università di Modena*, 46–47; Zanetti, "À l'université de Pavie," 424; Beltrán de Heredia, *Cartulario de la Universidad de Salamanca* 1:604–6, no. 23; *Liber constitutionum et statutorum generalis studii Ilerdensis an. MCCC*, in Villanueva, *Viaje literario* 16: 214).

39. See the lists in Verger, "Patterns," 62–65, and Coing, "Juristische Fakultät," 46–48, 97–128.

In order to compete with these rivals, Bologna not only offered its star professors substantial salaries, but also allowed them to continue to collect fees from their students as well, although some authorities, including Cardinal Hostiensis (d. 1271), disapproved of this practice.[40] Even after Bologna's municipal government became the chief paymaster of the professoriate, students continued to have some voice in the appointment process.[41] Students lost more of their former freedom to choose their teachers once the municipal government decided that professors from outside the city would no longer be eligible for appointments at the university. Bologna consequently became a less attractive place to study than it had previously been and "foreign" enrollments declined markedly. Student control of university governance continued to shrink steadily during the fourteenth and fifteenth centuries, not only at Bologna, but also in other student universities in northern Italy that had modeled themselves on Bologna. As academic stars began to bargain successfully for guarantees of indefinite tenure and lifetime contracts, student power inexorably withered away.[42]

THE UNIVERSITY OF PARIS

At about the same time that the Bolognese *studium* was taking shape, another university with a different institutional structure was beginning to develop at Paris. While student power predominated at Bologna, at Paris the masters controlled the university from the outset and continued to govern it throughout the Middle Ages. Historians accordingly describe Paris and the other universities that imitated and adapted its constitutional structure as magisterial universities. Magisterial universities predominated throughout northern Europe, whereas in Mediterranean Europe students either played a major role in university governance, as at Bologna, or else governments had a decisive voice in shaping university policy, as was true

40. Hostiensis, *Summa* 5.9, *De magistris* § 7, at 235rb; Raymond of Penyafort, *Summa de penitentia* 1.3.2–3, cols. 306–7; Bernard of Parma, *Glos. ord.* to X 5.5.4 v. *pauperes*; Post, "Masters' Salaries," 193–95; Savigny, *Geschichte* 3:245–46; Denifle, *Entstehung der Universitäten*, 198–99.

41. Bologna University Statutes (1317) 2.40, ed. Denifle, 304–8; Cobban, "Elective Salaried Lectureships," 664–65; Rashdall, *Universities* 1:210–12; Savigny, *Geschichte* 3:242.

42. On declining student enrollment and power, see Sorbelli, *Storia*, 182–85; Denley, "Career, Springboard or Sinecure?" 97–98; Cobban, "Elective Salaried Lectureships," 686. As early as 1260, Guido de Suzzara secured a lifetime contract to teach at Modena (Torelli and Vicini, "Documenti su Guido da Suzzara," 323–27, nos. 3–4; Cobban, "Elective Salaried Lectureships," 665–68, 686).

at Naples and Salamanca.[43] Migrations of students and masters from Paris, however, accounted for relatively few of the magisterial universities: although they imitated the Parisian model, they were not by and large direct offspring of the University of Paris.[44]

Paris differed from Bologna in other important ways. The study of the liberal arts, philosophy, and theology dominated intellectual life at Paris. Innovative legal teaching and writing, primarily in canon law, had thrived at Paris for roughly two generations, during the heyday of the Parisian decretist school that began in the mid-twelfth century. The study and teaching of law at Paris gradually grew less intellectually adventurous shortly after 1200, at roughly the same time that Parisian masters and students commenced to organize themselves as a guild (*universitas magistrorum et scholarum*). After about 1210, the Parisian school of decretists, which had produced a steady stream of original expositions of Gratian's work since the late 1160s, simply died out. The Paris law faculty produced only few jurists of the first rank during the two following centuries and only began to recover its former luster toward the close of the fifteenth century.[45]

One factor in the precipitous decline of legal studies at Paris was *Super specula*, a decretal of 1219 in which Pope Honorius III prohibited the further teaching of Roman civil law at Paris.[46] The pope complained in his letter that while trained theologians were in short supply, students were flocking to the schools of law in the hope that legal qualifications would make them wealthy. Similar lamentations appeared in the canons of several twelfth-century councils; some of them had even been incorporated into the major decretal collections.[47]

Honorius III added a new twist to previous attempts to remedy this deplorable state of affairs. He not only repeated and strengthened earlier

---

43. Rashdall, *Universities* 1:17–19; Verger, "Patterns," 37–41, 59.

44. The universities of Orleans and Angers were notable exceptions that originated from migrations of Parisian students (Rashdall, *Universities* 2:139–60).

45. Ferruolo, *Origins of the University*, 269–77; Rashdall, *Universities* 1: 321–23; Le Bras, "La faculté de droit," 98–100.

46. *CUP* 1:90–93, no. 32; *Regesta* 1:277, no. 2267; 5 Comp. 5.12.3; X 5.33.28; Po 6165. Among numerous attempts to explain the policy that underlay this peculiar but important decretal, by far the most convincing is Kuttner, "Papst Honorius III."

47. Council of Clermont (1130) c. 5, in Mansi 21:438–39; Council of Reims (1131) c. 6, in Mansi 21:459; 2 Lat. (1139) c. 9, in *DEC* 1:198–99; Council of Tours (1163) c. 8, in Mansi 21:1179 and 1 Comp. 3.37.2 (= X 3.50.3); 3 Lat. (1179) c. 12, in *DEC* 1:218, 1 Comp. 1.28.1 (= X 1.37.1), and 1 Comp. 3.37.6 (= X 3.50.4); Gilles, "Clercs et l'enseignement du droit romain," 377–79.

bans on the study of civil law or medicine by monks and canons-regular, but also extended the prohibition to secular clerics and priests who held benefices that involved the cure of souls. The pope simultaneously sought to strengthen the Paris theological faculty at the expense of the law faculty by forbidding the study or teaching of Roman civil law in the city of Paris and its immediate vicinity. Honorius and his advisers presumably calculated that forcing Parisian students of canon law to go elsewhere to secure the basic knowledge of civil law that canonists required would discourage students from pursuing legal studies at Paris.[48]

Honorius's strategy partially succeeded. Paris became the only university in medieval France where jurists formed a minority both among teachers and students. At every other French university in the thirteenth-century, the schools of law were significantly larger, more prestigious, and better attended than other faculties.[49] Paris, however, became Europe's premier center for theological studies and retained its preeminence in that subject down to the end of the Middle Ages.

One consequence of *Super specula* was to transform the earlier law schools at Orleans into a university. Honorius III had in all likelihood neither foreseen nor intended this development, but in the aftermath of his decretal, Orleans rapidly grew into a flourishing center of civilian studies that drew students from far and wide. Within a short time, Orleans became for practical purposes the civil law school of the University of Paris. Hon-

---

48. Honorius claimed in *Super specula* that knowledge of civil law was hardly ever necessary for canonists: "[O]currunt raro ecclesiastice cause tales, que non possent statutis canonicis expediri" (*CUP* 1:92, no. 32). Honorius himself was a preacher and administrator rather than a canonist (on his career see Sayers, *Papal Government*, 1–12), but it is hard to believe that he did not know better—and in any event the legally trained members of his chancery must certainly have done so. This suggests that the statement may have originated elsewhere, possibly in suggestions from Paris-trained theologians among Honorius's advisers who hoped that papal discouragement of legal studies might persuade more students to study theology instead, or perhaps as a result of a petition from the Paris theological faculty itself. Papal decretals almost always responded to a request from an interested party and not uncommonly incorporated some of the language of the petition to which they replied (Pitz, *Papstreskript und Kaiserreskript*, 171–91).

49. Gouron, "Recrutement des juristes" and "Crise des universités françaises." It must nevertheless also be noted that even at Paris jurists constituted a substantial minority. Parisian petitions for papal favors at the beginning of the fifteenth century, for example, included the names of 862 canonists, or slightly more than 36 percent of the total (Verger, "Recrutement géographique," 140).

orius's successor, Pope Gregory IX (r. 1227–41), recognized this in a decretal of 1235 in which he specifically approved the teaching of Roman law at Orleans. By the latter part of the thirteenth century, Orleans had become a serious rival of Bologna.[50]

Honorius III's ban on teaching civil law at Paris was probably never fully implemented in practice.[51] References to students reading "the laws" as well as "the decretals" in Paris and adjoining towns suggest that at least some teaching of Roman law continued there after 1219. Gregory IX, in *Parens scientiarum*, addressed to the University of Paris in 1231, authorized dispensations for those who wished to study Roman law at Paris, while Honorius IV in 1285 permitted all clerics, save for bishops, abbots, and religious, to study civil law.[52] Even the clerical students at the Roman curia's own university routinely studied civil law as well as canon law and theology, provided that they had not yet been admitted to the priesthood. Innocent IV also held that any bishop could absolve clerics excommunicated for infringing the ban in *Super specula* and further maintained that monks could study civil law in their own monasteries.[53]

Students of canon law at Paris, like their counterparts at other medieval universities, continued to study Roman law despite *Super specula* because, notwithstanding Honorius III's curious claim to the contrary, canonists really did need to know some civil law.[54] Canon law and Roman law de-

50. On the rise of Orleans, see Meijers, "Université d'Orléans," 27–28; Verger, "Recrutement géographique," 162; Bertram, "Kirchenrechtliche Vorlesungen aus Orléans," 213; Genzmer, "Hugo von Trimberg," 305. Gregory's decretal appears in *CUP* 1:156–57, no. 106. At the same time, however, the pope admonished the law professors at Orleans not to permit clerics with the cure of souls to study civil law there. See also Nardi, "Relations with Authority," 89–90; Meijers, "Université d'Orléans," 28.

51. Honorius himself occasionally granted dispensations that permitted individual clerics to study civil law; see, e.g., his *Regesta* 1:156, 458, nos. 926, 2760.

52. *Parens scientiarum*, *CUP* 1:136–39, no. 79. Question 5 of the *Questiones Andegavensis*, which date from ca. 1240, indicates that dispensations for the study and teaching of Roman law at Paris were routinely approved (Fitting, "Questions de droit," 724–25). On Honorius IV's dispensations for the study of civil law, see Savigny, *Geschichte* 3:366; Stelling-Michaud, *Université de Bologne*, 127, 130; Gilles, "Clercs et enseignement du droit romain," 383–84, cites further examples.

53. Innocent IV, *Quam de diversis* in VI 5.7.2 and *Apparatus* to X 3.50.3 v. *legendas* and 3.50.10 v. *exeuntes*, at 462ra, vb ; Paravicini-Bagliani, "Fondazione dello 'Studium Curiae'"; Rashdall, *Universities* 2:28–31.

54. *CUP* 3:320–25, no. 1486; Guido de Baysio, *Rosarium* to C. 1 q. 3 c. 8, at 130ra; Griffiths, "New Men among the Lay Counselors," 258–59. The 1370 statutes of the Parisian Faculty of Decrees provided two different curricula for canon law degrees, a

pended on one another both intellectually and institutionally. "A Romanist without canon law isn't worth much," ran a medieval proverb, "and a canonist without Roman law is worth nothing at all."[55] Every practicing lawyer, regardless of whether his degree was in civil or canon law, needed at least some familiarity with canon law in order to survive, since much of the business that he handled was virtually bound to involve canonical issues, while no canonist could ignore Roman law, since the canons themselves incorporated a wealth of Roman law rules, ideas, terms, and institutions. For precisely this reason, teachers wrote and students read elementary handbooks that attempted to cram into a nutshell the essential elements of canon law for students of Roman law and Roman law for students of canon law.[56]

The University of Paris was far more tightly linked to the church than was the University of Bologna. Most twelfth-century Parisian masters and students were at least nominally clerics, and ecclesiastical oversight of teachers, students, and the university's functioning was more rigorous and pervasive than it was at Bologna.[57] Church authorities kept a wary eye on the theologians and philosophers who were the glory of Paris during the High Middle Ages. Although they were the source of the university's international fame, their teachings sometimes seemed disquietingly unconventional and occasionally flirted dangerously with heresy. Despite these qualms, the twelfth-century schools at Paris enrolled considerable numbers of Roman aristocrats, many of whom later became members of the curia. Several of them ultimately became cardinals and at least two became popes.[58] Even so, doubts about their orthodoxy hovered over the more daring Parisian masters. Suspicions going back to the days of Peter Abelard grew ever darker during the heyday of the Parisian theological faculty, although at least until 1277, the authorities seldom took vigorous action to restrain wayward opinions.[59]

---

shorter one for those who had studied civil law and a considerably longer one for those who had not (*Faculté de décret* 1:21, no. 25 §§2–4).

55. Merzbacher, "Die Parömie 'Legista sine canonibus parum valet, canonista sine legibus nihil.'"

56. Bertram and Duynstee, "Casus legum sive suffragia monachorum"; Baumgärtner, "Was muss ein Legist vom Kirchenrecht wissen?"; Dolezalek, "Wie studierte Man bei den Glossatoren?" 58–59.

57. Paré, Brunet, and Tremblay, *Renaissance du XIIe siècle*, 60–63; Baldwin, *Masters, Princes, and Merchants* 1:73–74; Verger, "Recrutement géographique," 132, 158.

58. Classen, "Curia romana e le scuole di Francia."

59. Rashdall, *Universities* 1:349–70; Asztalos, "Faculty of Theology," 410–14; Southern, *Scholastic Humanism* 2:116–32.

Substantial numbers of masters and students were living, teaching, and studying at Paris by the middle decades of the twelfth century, as John of Salisbury, Gerald of Wales, Peter Abelard, and other witnesses testify from personal experience. Indeed, by around 1150, Paris could probably boast more schools and masters than had ever previously been assembled anywhere north of the Alps.[60] Some of this teaching took place in schools attached to one of the religious institutions located in the city and its immediate environs—notably at the cathedral of Notre Dame and the monasteries of Sainte-Geneviève, St. Germain des Près, St. Denis, and St. Victor, while at the same time numerous masters also taught independently in their own private schools.

Sometime before 1180, these masters banded together in an informal association. Precisely how and under what circumstances this happened we do not know for certain, but a group of some sort surely existed by the end of the 1170s. A description by Gerald of Wales of his lectures in canon law at Paris in 1179, coupled with an account of a sermon that Stephen Langton delivered there about 1180, show that these exercises formed part of an initiation ceremony called inception, by which new members were admitted to the ranks of the masters.[61]

This twelfth-century association of masters developed a formal corporate structure early in the thirteenth century. The royal charter of 1200 by which King Philip Augustus conferred privileges on the "Parisian scholars" did not even hint that the masters' association had yet become an autonomous corporation, but by 1209 it seems to have done so.[62] The earliest certain evidence that the Paris masters were acting as a corporate body occurs in the decretal *Ex litteris vestrae* (1208 or 1209) of Pope Innocent III, who had studied theology at Paris in his youth. The pope directed his letter to the masters of Paris as a group,[63] referred to them repeatedly as a cor-

---

60. John of Salisbury, *Metalogicon* 2.10, at 70–73, and *Epist*. 136, in his *Letters* 2:2–15; Gerald of Wales, *De rebus a se gestis* 2.1–2, in his *Opera* 1:45–48; Guy de Bazoches, *Epistola ad amicum*, in *CUP* 1:55–56, no. 54; Peter Abelard, *Historia calamitatum*, in *Letters of Abelard and Heloise*, 58–65. See also Ferruolo, *Origins*, 20–24; Rashdall, *Universities* 1:274–78; Southern, *Scholastic Humanism* 1:198–204.

61. Spatz, "Evidence of Inception Ceremonies," 7–13; Rashdall, *Universities* 1:283–87; Verger, "Le chancelier," 95–96.

62. *CUP* 1:59–61, no. 1; Rashdall, *Universities* 1:294–98; Ferruolo, *Origins*, 285–87; Kibre, *Scholarly Privileges*, 85–89.

63. The salutation, which survives only in fragmentary form, addresses "Universis Doctoribus Parisiis commorantibus," or in another version, "Universis doctoribus sacrae paginae, decretorum et liberalium artium Parisiis commorantibus."

porate body (*universitas, societas, consortium*), and ruled on problems raised by members of the organization who refused to take an oath to abide by its statutes. Those statutes, which no longer survive, were drawn up by eight of the Paris masters. They dealt with such matters as the conduct of lectures, appropriate dress for masters, and attendance at the funeral services of other members.[64] Although those statutes have disappeared, the decretal's account of them leaves little doubt that at least by 1209, and probably earlier, the Parisian masters were in the process of forming a corporate body. Thirteenth-century commentators on *Ex litteris vestrae* certainly thought so.[65] This inference is reinforced by another letter of Innocent III from around the same time. In *Quia in causis*, the pope not only referred to the "Scholars of Paris" as *universitas vestra*, but also authorized them to appoint a proctor to represent them in pending litigation, which was only possible if they constituted a legal corporation.[66]

Innocent III authorized Cardinal Robert Courson (b. ca. 1160, d. 1219), formerly a theology teacher at Paris, to revise the university's earlier statutes, and this version, which Courson promulgated in 1215, is the earliest now extant. Courson's statutes not only covered the topics previously treated, but also added further provisions, notably one that required fledgling masters to swear that they had made no payment to secure a teaching license from the chancellor of the diocese.[67]

Canon law required church authorities to examine would-be masters who intended to teach publicly and to charge fees for their instruction in order to determine whether they were competent and of suitable moral character. The law also forbade authorities to require payment for granting teaching licenses and added that the license must not be denied to candidates sufficiently learned and of upright character.[68]

64. 3 Comp. 2.15.12 (= X 1.2.11; Po 3670); *CUP* 1:67–68, no. 8.

65. See Bernard of Parma, *Casus* to X 1.2.11, as well as other writers cited by Post, "Parisian Masters as a Corporation," 34–36; see also Post, *Studies*, 59–60.

66. *CUP* 1:82–83, no. 24. The decretal also appears in 4 Comp. 1.16.2 and X 1.38.7. Po 2075 dated it in 1203, although 1210 now seems a much more likely date (Post, *Studies*, 39–47).

67. *CUP* 1:78–79, no. 20; English version in Thorndyke, *University Records and Life*, 27–30, no. 15. See also Ferruolo, *Origins*, 301–9; Baldwin, *Masters, Princes, and Merchants* 1:9–25.

68. On examination of prospective masters, Gratian, D. 37 c. 12, with *Glos. ord.* to v. *ut magistri*; on licensing, 3 Lat. (1179) c. 18, in *DEC* 1:220 (= X 5.5.1), in addition to similar provisions in two decretals of Alexander III in X 5.5.2 (JL 14157) and 5.5.3 (JL 11925), together with the Legatine Council of Westminster (1138) c. 17, in Whitelock, Brett

The bishops of Paris entrusted the authority to grant teaching licenses to their chancellors. Although they could not legally demand payment, Parisian chancellors found ways to make their power felt by those who taught in schools within the diocese. Around 1210, the chancellor began to require applicants for teaching licenses to swear an oath of obedience to him. At the same time, he also commenced to harass the masters by arresting scholars for even trivial offenses against church discipline and imposing stiff fines before he would release them. The Parisian masters asked Pope Innocent III to intervene, and in 1212 he did so with a vengeance. The pope ordered the chancellor to cease and desist from these practices forthwith and threatened him with ecclesiastical censure should he persist in his noxious ways. Disputes over the limits of the chancellor's authority continued to sour relations between the university and diocesan authorities for years, but by 1220 the University of Paris, thanks to help from both king and pope, had succeeded in establishing itself as an autonomous, self-governing institution.[69]

OXFORD AND CAMBRIDGE

Individual masters were teaching at schools in the city of Oxford by the early twelfth century. When Oxford gradually began to emerge around 1185 as an important center of learning, its academic reputation initially rested on the teaching and study of canon law. The courts of the commissary judge of the bishop of Lincoln and the official of the archdeacon regularly held sessions in Oxford, and Senatus, a learned monk of Worcester, described the city around 1190 as filled with lawyers.[70] At least some of those lawyers were prepared to bring in extra income by teaching. John of Tynemouth and the circle of canon lawyers associated with him were prominent among them. They were also apparently the first teachers to attract students to Oxford from places as far distant as Frisia and Hungary. By the 1190s, Oxford was also beginning to draw attention as an interesting

---

& Brooke 2:778; Post, "Alexander III, the *licentia docendi* and the Rise of the Universities," 255–77.

69. *CUP* 1:73–74, no. 14; Ferruolo, *Origins*, 295–301, 309–15; Rashdall, *Universities* 1:306–11; Maleczek, "Papsttum und die Anfänge der Universität im Mittelalter," 90.

70. Gerald of Wales, *De rebus a se gestis* 2.16, in his *Opera* 1:72–73; Jocelin of Brakelond, *Cronica*, 94–95; Southern, "From Schools to University," 15–21, and "Master Vacarius," 270–72. On the consistory court of the bishops of Lincoln, see the *Records of the Medieval Ecclesiastical Courts* 2:180; the remark by Senatus of Worcester Cathedral priory is quoted by Boyle, "Beginnings," 110, from Oxford, Bodleian Library, MS Bodley 633, at 209–12.

place to study liberal arts and theology. More than a hundred masters are known to have been teaching at Oxford between 1190 and 1209.[71]

Scraps of evidence suggest that the Oxford masters may have commenced to organize themselves into a corporate body during the years immediately following 1200. In a letter dated 2 January 1201, Pope Innocent III described the Oxford theologian John Grim as "Master of the Schools of Oxford," which suggests the existence of some sort of organized academic group in the city.[72] The earliest substantial evidence of their corporate activity dates from 1209, when the sheriff of Oxford first jailed and then hanged two (or perhaps three) students for the murder of a townswoman. The city was convulsed by riots, and in fear and protest, the masters teaching at Oxford closed their schools and left the city. They did not return until 1214. The decisions, first to depart, and later to return, seem to have been collective actions in which nearly all the masters participated, which strongly suggests that some kind of formal organization existed, even if it was not yet styled a *universitas*.[73]

The citizens of Oxford, whose prosperity had suffered when teachers and students deserted the city, sought absolution from Cardinal Nicholas de Romanis, a papal legate who had come to England to conduct negotiations between king and pope. The legate visited Oxford in November 1213, and on the following 25 June he imposed a settlement on the citizens and the masters. Although the settlement severely penalized the townsfolk and a handful of teachers who had remained in the city, they accepted its terms in return for tacit assurances that the masters and their pupils would now return. The legate may have intended to acknowledge the corporate status of the Oxford masters' guild when he bestowed upon its head the more imposing title of chancellor, rather than master of the schools. The first unambiguous reference to the Oxford guild of masters as a *universitas* appeared a few years thereafter in a 1218 mandate by another papal legate, Cardinal Guala Bicchieri.[74]

71. *Collectanea, Second Series*, 175–76; Hackett, "University as a Corporate Body," 37.

72. Innocent III, *Insinuavit nobis dilectus*, in *The Letters of Pope Innocent III (1198–1216) concerning England and Wales*, 46, 220–21, no. 279; *BRUO* 2:826. See also Hackett, "University as a Corporate Body," 38–40.

73. Roger of Wendover, *Flores historiarum* 2:51; *Chronicle of Melrose*, s.a. 1208, 53; Matthew Paris, *Chronica majora*, s.a. 1209, at 2:525–26. Matthew of Westminster, *Flores historiarum* 2:138; *Chronicon de Lanercost*, s.a. 1208, 4; Hackett, "University as a Corporate Body," 40–43; Rashdall, *Universities* 3:33–34.

74. Southern, "From Schools to University," 26–33; Rashdall, *Universities* 3:34–35; *Mediaeval Archives* 1:2–10, nos. 2–5, 1:16–17, no. 8; *Munimenta academica* 1:1–4; Hackett, "University as a Corporate Body," 43–47 (for a list of early chancellors of the university,

One permanent consequence of the dispersion of the Oxford schools in 1209 was the emergence of a *universitas magistrorum et scholarum* at Cambridge. When the Oxford students and masters fled the city, they resettled in various places. A few migrated to Paris, although this was hazardous in view of the ongoing hostilities between the French and English kings. Those who decided to remain in England relocated mainly at Reading and Cambridge.[75] Once the citizens of Oxford had agreed to satisfy the demands of its dispersed scholars, most of that city's erstwhile teachers and students quickly returned to reestablish their schools.

A few, however, chose to remain in the schools they had established at Cambridge. Historians have found their choice puzzling. The town's location at the edge of the flat, marshy fen country was neither especially attractive nor particularly healthy. Cambridge was a reasonably thriving commercial town, to be sure, despite the flooding to which it was intermittently subject during the winter months. Not only was it prosperous, but its population was growing, as its numerous twelfth-century churches attest, while Barnwell Priory and the Priory of St. Radegund, both moderately important religious houses, lay nearby, and the great abbey of Bury St. Edmunds was not far away. Still, no evidence survives to suggest that Cambridge had ever boasted a tradition of learning or a significant concentration of schools prior to 1209.

Several of the Oxford teachers who settled at Cambridge in 1209 were probably natives of the town. One of them was a theologian, Doctor John Grim, whose family occupied a prominent position in Cambridge society. Pope Innocent III, as noted earlier, had described Grim in 1201 as "Master of the Schools of Oxford," which implies that he exercised some sort of leadership among the Oxford masters. This at least suggests that Grim may have been instrumental in persuading his colleagues that Cambridge would be an advantageous place to relocate their schools.[76]

Whatever influence Grim and other Cambridge natives may have had on the Oxford masters' initial decision to settle in Cambridge, the town's flourishing canonical courts probably helped to induce many scholars to remain in Cambridge even after Oxford had satisfied the complaints that had led to the *suspendio studiorum*. Although Cambridge, like Oxford, was not the

---

several of whom were canonists, see *Snappe's Formulary*, 318–35); Guala Bicchieri, *Letters and Charters*, 60–61, no. 77.

75. Roger of Wendover, *Flores historiarum* 2:51.

76. The others included Geoffrey Grim, John Blund, and John de Malketon (Hackett, *Original Statutes*, 46; BRUC, 67, 272, 386.

seat of a diocese, it was, also like Oxford, home to a prominent archdeacon's court, and to the busy consistory court of the bishop of Ely as well.[77]

The bishop's court was centered at Cambridge for the same practical reasons that had long dictated that Ely's diocesan synods should take place at nearby Barnwell.[78] Ely was a tiny hamlet, nestled in the shadow of the cathedral and its attached monastery, which perched atop a steep hill that rose dramatically out of the fens. Recurrent flooding frequently rendered the fenland roads round about Ely impassable, which effectively isolated the town from the outside world. Flat and low-lying as Cambridge was, it stood just far enough above the level of the fens to be flooded only occasionally. The River Cam gave the city access to commercial centers throughout eastern and southern England. Merchants regularly flocked to the city's markets and to the Stourbridge Fair at Barnwell. The see of Ely, moreover, was counted one of the three or four wealthiest dioceses in England. Able and well-connected churchmen eagerly competed even for minor offices in the diocese. Canon lawyers stood to profit from the employment opportunities afforded by litigants who flocked to Cambridge from throughout the extensive diocese.[79]

The masters who elected to remain at Cambridge soon commenced to create a formal organization. The earliest evidence of such a structure appears in the record of a 1225 lawsuit in an ecclesiastical court against the "Chancellor of Cambridge," who, like his successors over the next century and more, was no doubt appointed by the bishop of Ely.[80] The record fails

77. Brundage, "Cambridge Faculty of Canon Law"; Owen, "Records of the Bishop's Official at Ely; Aston, *Thomas Arundel*, 55–56.

78. Cheney, *English Synodalia*, 17, 20, and 21 n. 2; Owen, Ellis, and Salzman, "Religious Houses," 242.

79. On Ely's wealth, see, e.g., the records of the Norwich taxation of 1253–59 in *Liber memorandorum ecclesie de Bernewelle*, 191–99; Miller, *Abbey and Bishopric of Ely*, 80–83. On fierce competition for offices in the diocese, see, e.g., the letter of Stephen of Tournai in 1190 congratulating Richard Barre on his promotion from archdeacon of Lisieux to archdeacon of Ely. Stephen saw this move as a great step upward: "[T]ranslatus es a planeta Cyprio ad solem, ab obscuris ad lucem, a lubricis motibus ad splendoris soliditatem" (Stephen of Tournai, *Lettres*, 346–47, no. 275). On Cambridge as a center of litigation, see Brundage, "Bar of the Ely Consistory Court," 541–42. The diocese of Ely comprised virtually all of Cambridgeshire, as well as parts of Suffolk and other adjacent counties. On its establishment, see the *Liber Eliensis* 3.1–10, ed. Blake, 245–53; Miller, *Abbey and Bishopric of Ely*, 75–77, 93–95.

80. *Curia Regis Rolls* 12:129–30, 9–10 Henry III (1225/1226), no. 646; The Cambridge chancellor was mentioned again the following year in the *Liber niger* of New College,

to mention the chancellor's name, but he may have been Richard de Leycestria (also known as Richard de Wetheringsette), a canon lawyer and author of a pastoral manual, the *Qui bene presunt presbyteri*, who was also official-principal of the bishop of Ely.[81] A royal writ in 1231 referred to a *universitas* at Cambridge, as did a papal letter of 1233. The Cambridge masters had created a corporate structure with remarkable speed.[82]

UNIVERSITIES FOUNDED BY PUBLIC AUTHORITIES

The three oldest European universities—Bologna, Paris, and Oxford—were self-generated in the sense that none of them was deliberately founded by any authority outside of the university itself. Other universities—Cambridge, Orleans, Angers, Padua, and Vercelli, for example—arose as a result of migrations in times of turmoil by students and masters from an established university. All universities relied on recognition by outside authorities, such as kings, popes, and municipal governments, to legitimize and protect the rights and privileges that their members coveted, but the earliest universities emerged in consequence of spontaneous actions by students (as at Bologna) or masters (as at Paris and Oxford), without the intervention of any outside authority.

By contrast, some other universities owed their origins to deliberate foundations by kings, princes, or other public authorities and frequently continued to depend upon the founders' successors.[83] The University of Naples, established in 1224 by the emperor Frederick II (1197–1250), is an early example of this pattern of university origin and governance. A practical advantage, much esteemed not only by Frederick but also by his successors, was that the new university furnished the rulers of southern Italy and Sicily with a steady supply of legally trained functionaries to staff the administrative offices of the Sicilian kingdom.[84]

Other thirteenth-century universities founded by rulers include the University of the Roman Curia, created in 1245 by Frederick II's remorse-

---

Oxford (Roach, "The University of Cambridge," 151). See also Brundage, "Bishop Thomas Arundel."

81. *Liber memorandorum ecclesie de Bernewelle*, 184–85; *Vetus liber archidiaconi Eliensis*, 20–23; BRUC, 367, 679; Hackett, *Original Statutes*, 48–49; Cobban, *Medieval English Universities*, 57–58.

82. Gregory IX, *Registres* 1:799, no. 1389; Hackett, *Original Statutes*, 51; Cobban, *Medieval English Universities*, 58.

83. Pryds, "*Studia* as Royal Offices," 83–86.

84. Meijers, "Università di Napoli," 21–26; Pryds, "*Studia* as Royal Offices," 86–92; Abulafia, *Frederick II*, 210–11, 263–64; Stürner, *Friedrich II*. 2:47–57.

less opponent, Pope Innocent IV, who sought to provide the clerics who flocked to the papal court with opportunities for advanced study, primarily in civil and canon law and theology, but also in the Near Eastern languages that missionaries needed.[85] The University of Toulouse, established by Count Raymond VII of Toulouse under the terms of the Treaty of Paris (1229), on the other hand, had the primary purpose of training up theologians who could confound Cathar heretics and reestablish Catholic orthodoxy firmly in the Languedoc. The treaty made Count Raymond responsible for paying the salaries of fourteen professors during the first decade of the university's existence, an obligation that he regularly contrived to evade. After this rocky beginning, however, Toulouse was well on its way to becoming one of the most important universities in the south of France by the end of the thirteenth century.[86]

Universities in the Iberian peninsula were mainly royal foundations. The earliest was the short-lived University of Palencia, founded in 1208 by Alfonso VIII of Castile (1158–1214). This experiment failed to prosper, and by around 1250 the university had disappeared.[87] The University of Salamanca, which developed out of an earlier cathedral school, was formally transformed into a university in 1218 or 1219 by Alfonso IX of León (r. 1188–1230). After a shaky beginning, Alfonso el Sabio of Castile (r. 1252–84) refounded the university in 1254 and improved its endowment. The university's financial resources were further augmented in the fourteenth century by grants from tithes and other ecclesiastical revenues, to the point where it became a viable institution.[88] Several other universities with similar governmental ties were subsequently founded by Spanish and Portuguese monarchs between the end of the thirteenth and the beginning of the sixteenth centuries, among them those at Lérida (1300), Barcelona (1450), and Coimbra (1290).[89] All of them depended upon royal funding. The Iberian universities, like Naples, served royal interests by producing a steady stream of trained functionaries for the service of both monarchy

85. Rashdall, *Universities* 2:28–31, and Paravicini Bagliani, "Fondazione dello 'Studium Curiae.'"

86. *Statuts et privilèges* 1:441, no. 505; Rashdall, *Universities* 2:160–73; Smith, *University of Toulouse*, 32–81.

87. Rashdall, *Universities* 2:65–69.

88. García y García, "Universidad de Salamanca"; O'Callaghan, *The Learned King*, 131–34; Rashdall, *Universities* 2:74–90; Cárdenas, "Alfonso's Scriptorium and Chancery," 95–96.

89. Rashdall, *Universities* 2:91–96, 100–101, 108–14.

and church.⁹⁰ Although kings supported these universities out of public revenues as a matter of royal policy, they nevertheless permitted students to play a major role in the internal governance of the universities. Indeed, students retained effective power longer in the Spanish universities than they did in the universities of northern Italy.⁹¹

Universities did not begin to appear in the lands east of the Rhine until the mid-fourteenth century. When they did so, the initiative for their foundation came from public authorities, who considered them sources both of prestige and of trained functionaries. The first such university was the University of Prague, founded in 1347 by the emperor Charles IV (r. 1347–78), who was also king of Bohemia. The new university obviously filled a long-felt need, for it immediately attracted sizeable numbers of students from German-speaking lands who might otherwise have needed to travel to Paris or Bologna for their advanced education.⁹²

Soon thereafter, universities began to appear elsewhere in central and eastern Europe. In 1364 the Polish king, Casimir the Great (r. 1333–70), founded a university under student governance in the Bolognese style at Cracow. In the following year, Duke Rudolf IV of Austria (r. 1356–65) created a university on the Parisian model at Vienna, which was immediately approved by Pope Urban V (r. 1362–70).⁹³ University foundations appeared in the western regions of the German-speaking lands slightly later, at Heidelberg in 1385, at Cologne in 1388, at Würzburg in 1402, and at Louvain in 1426. Others emerged in the region east of the Weser at Erfurt in 1392 and at Leipzig in 1409.⁹⁴

Universities in Thirteenth-Century Society

Universities marked a new approach to learning that permanently transformed Western European society and intellectual life. They required costly social and political investments, to be sure. Students and teachers needed

90. Alfonso el Sabio spelled this out explicitly in his *Siete Partidas* 2.31 pr., 1, at 2:527.

91. *Siete Partidas* 2.31.6–7; Cobban, "Elective Salaried Lectureships," 686.

92. Rashdall, *Universities* 2:211–34.

93. The University of Cracow was subsequently refounded in 1397 by King Władysław Jagiełło (r. 1385–1434). Similarly, after a difficult period in the early years, the University of Vienna was refounded in 1383 by Duke Albert III (r. 1365–95). See Rashdall, *Universities* 2:234–45, 289–94.

94. Rashdall, *Universities* 2:245–60. Papal foundation charters for a university at Erfurt were granted earlier, in 1379 by Pope Clement VII and in 1389 by Pope Urban VI, but neither was put into effect until 1392. Leipzig's foundation followed the migration of a substantial number of German students from Prague in 1409.

protection, and they frequently sought financial support from public revenues. But at the same time, universities enhanced the prosperity and prestige of the cities that housed them and they became a source of civic pride. By the fourteenth century, cities that lacked a university were beginning to feel seriously disadvantaged.[95] The claim that a university brought prestige was no mere rhetorical flourish. North Italian cities in particular were willing to offer eminent professors, particularly law professors, very handsome salaries indeed to lure them away from rival universities, even if they occasionally financed those salaries in curious ways.[96]

The interaction between the universities and the societies in which they were embedded is nowhere more evident than in the teaching of law. Law professors at Bologna and other medieval universities helped to shape the development of Europe's legal systems, while at the same time university law faculties and their curricula had to adjust to changes in the law, many of which they helped to draft.[97]

University Law Faculties

Every medieval university offered degrees in canon law. Because some acquaintance with Roman law was essential for canonists, moreover, most universities provided some teaching in Roman law, although not all offered degrees in it. Nearly all universities taught the liberal arts and many could boast a medical faculty as well. Very few, however, offered organized teaching in theology: Paris, Oxford, and Cambridge were the only universities authorized to confer theology degrees before 1300.[98]

---

95. Brucker, "Renaissance Florence," 47–58.

96. In Padua, a well-paid chair of canon law was funded from the profits of the municipal brothel (Otis, *Prostitution in Medieval Society*, 182 n. 40). For less eyebrow-raising strategies, see, e.g., the records of the struggle of Modena to secure and retain the services of Guido de Suzzara, in Torelli and Vicini, "Documenti su Guido da Suzzara," 323–27, 340–41, 344–46, nos. 3–4, 14, 17, 19; or somewhat later, Perugia's efforts to persuade Baldus de Ubaldis to decline a competing offer from Florence, in *Opera di Baldo*, 325–26, nos. 10–11, as well as Pennington, "Baldus de Ubaldis," 39–40, 42. Likewise see Pennington's study of the career of Panormitanus, "Nicolaus de Tudeschis (Panormitanus)," 10–12; Denley, "Career, Springboard, or Sinecure?" 108–9; Verger, "Teachers," 153; Gilmore, "Lawyers and the Church," 64–67.

97. Cf. the remarks of Rüegg, "Themes," 9–14 and passim; also García y García, "Faculties of Law," 392–93, 404–5.

98. The papacy only began to recognize additional theological faculties in the fourteenth century, partly as a consequence of the rivalries that attended the Great Schism (Asztalos, "Faculty of Theology," 435–38).

Legal studies, as we have seen, were central to Bologna's academic reputation from the outset. By the 1170s and 1180s, people were beginning to complain that law was gaining ascendancy at Paris and Oxford as well.[99] Individual teachers of law before universities appeared had been free, at least in principle, to teach whatever they pleased, although since they depended upon student fees for their livelihood, they had a strong incentive to present material that would attract the greatest number of students. Once they organized as corporate bodies, however, law teachers came under pressure from both students and colleagues to offer systematic, and increasingly rigorous, instruction. This was especially important because university teaching careers were typically brief. Law lecturers, like their counterparts in theology, medicine, and the liberal arts, typically taught as regent masters for a few years early in their careers to fulfill degree requirements.[100] Once they had discharged their mandatory teaching obligation they commenced to seek, and often found, more permanent and better-paid positions as beneficed clerics, judges, advocates, legal counselors, or administrators in church or civil government.[101]

Since most teachers remained at the university only for a short time, systematic organization of the teaching staff and the curriculum was essential in order to maintain institutional continuity. Teachers of liberal arts, medicine, law, and theology began to organize separate faculties around

99. Thus, e.g., Daniel of Morley, *Philosophia*, in *Collectanea*, 2nd ser., 171–72; Gautier de Coinci, "Vie de Seinte Léocad," ll. 1123–46, in *Fabliaux et contes des poètes françois* 1:307–8. See also Baldwin, "Critics of the Legal Profession," 249; Clanchy, "*Moderni* in Education and Government in England," 682–84; Southern, *Scholastic Humanism* 1:8.

100. Bologna University Statutes (1432) 2.52–53, at 325–27; Bologna University Statutes of 1397 §5, and Statutes of 1460 §12, in *Statuti delle università e dei collegi dello studio bolognese*, 344 and 375; Zaccagnini, *Vita dei maestri*, 25–26; *CUP* 4:644–45, no. 1699; Boyle, "Curriculum at Oxford," 146–48; The requirement also appears in the earliest statutes of Cambridge University, 2.1–2, at 199. These statutes, which date from between 1260 and 1270, are contained in MS 401 of the Angelica Library in Rome, where they were discovered by M. B. Hackett, who edited them with an English translation (*Original Statutes*, 196–217). He also edited the next-oldest Cambridge University statutes (dated between ca. 1304 and 1307), which come from the library of Thomas Markaunt, in (*Original Statutes*, 312–31).

101. Verger, "Teachers," in *HUE*, 148–51; Courtenay, *Teaching Careers at the University of Paris*, 21–33. When universities, especially in Mediterranean Europe, began to introduce permanent, salaried professorships during the second half of the thirteenth century, this employment pattern commenced to change. Universities in northern Europe, such as Paris, Oxford, and Cambridge introduced salaried professorships only much later.

or shortly after the time that the universities themselves appeared. The specialized faculties divided the intellectual turf and established their own standards of performance and behavior in addition to those that applied throughout the university.[102]

A law faculty thus prescribed a formally structured program of studies, defined requirements for degrees, imposed standards of conduct on teachers and students, and exercised disciplinary authority over its members. For these purposes, members of the faculty developed governance structures that could organize the work of a group of previously independent teachers into a coherent program. They had to agree what a minimum course of studies should include and to define the performance standards that degree candidates must meet. The resulting regulatory systems, usually cast in statutory form, spelled out in detail such things as the numbers, types, and subjects of the lectures that a degree candidate must attend, the number of disputations that he must participate in, the minimum period of study required, and the procedures for conducting the examinations that marked the culmination of the degree course.

The masters who comprised the University of Paris created teaching faculties at about the same time that the university's corporate structure emerged. Law teachers, both canonists and civilians, almost from the beginning held occasional meetings at which they dealt with matters of common concern.[103] By 1227 the canonists had begun to move their lectures to the left bank of the Seine and eventually settled in the Clos Brunel, well away from the precincts of the cathedral of Notre Dame where they had

---

102. The meaning of the term *facultas* itself gradually changed. Twelfth-century writers normally used it to refer to an intellectual discipline. Thus, e.g. in the *Summa "Elegantius"* 15.97, at 4:136, *facultas* designates the discipline of canon law. Geyer, "Facultas theologica," 134–37, provides further examples. In the process of faculty specialization, Bologna was exceptional because the university there originally consisted solely of students of law, while the masters' *collegium* when it emerged was composed exclusively of jurists. Hence the law faculty was identical with the university itself. Toward the end of the thirteenth century, the professorial guild at Bologna separated into two *collegia*, one for teachers of canon law, the other for teachers of civil law (Rashdall, *Universities* 1:148–49, 204–5; Sorbelli, *Storia*, 178–82; Bellomo, *Saggio sull'università*, 223–24; García y García, "Faculties of Law," 399–400). Students and teachers of liberal arts and medicine at Bologna later in the thirteenth century ultimately organized their own university, separate from the university of jurists (Rashdall, *Universities* 1:233–53; Sorbelli, *Storia*, 105–28).

103. *CUP* 1:88–90, 157–58, 173–74, 226–27, nos. 31, 108, 131, 200; Verger, "Naissance de l'université de Paris," 12 n. 39.

originally been situated.[104] By the time that a law faculty emerged at Paris, however, Roman law been banished from the university and the faculty consisted entirely of canon lawyers.

The earliest reference in Parisian records to a "faculty," in the sense of a structural unit of the university, appears in 1253, and two years later Pope Alexander IV (r. 1254–61) explicitly referred to the Faculty of Decrees at Paris.[105] The earliest surviving evidence about faculty governance at Paris dates from 1264, when a document records a dispute over the election of Étienne Tempier as dean of the theological faculty, despite the fact that he was not its most senior member. The first reference to the dean of the Faculty of Decrees followed three years later, in 1267, and evidence that the faculty possessed a common seal survives from 1270 or 1271.[106]

The Paris law faculty no doubt made rules and regulations about teaching practices, examinations, and the conduct of its members from the very beginning. Some clues about what these rules must have contained survive in Gregory IX's bull *Parens scientiarum* (1231). In addition to a summary reference to a system of degree examinations in theology and canon law, the pope expressly authorized the Parisian masters to make

> constitutions or ordinances concerning the method and hour of lectures and disputations, appropriate garb, and funerals for the dead, as well as for the hours and topics on which bachelors ought to lecture, charges for lodging or the prohibition thereof, and appropriate punishment for those who offend against these constitutions or ordinances by expulsion from the group.[107]

Unfortunately, none of the constitutions or ordinances that the pope authorized survives for the period prior to the mid-fourteenth century.[108]

---

104. *CUP* 1:111, no. 55, and 2:504, no.1040; *Faculté de décret* 1:9–10, no. 11; Le Bras, "La faculté de droit," 87.

105. *CUP* 1:242–44, no. 219, 284, no. 247; Verger, "First French Universities," 9; Le Bras, "La faculté de droit," 86–87.

106. See *CUP* 1:440–41, no. 399, 468, no. 416, 503, no. 446; Gabriel, "Le doyen," 40.

107. *CUP* 1:137, no. 79: "Ceterum quia ubi non est ordo, facile repit horror, constitutiones seu ordinationes providas faciendi de modo et hora legendi et disputandi, de habitu ordinato, de mortuorum exequiis necnon de bachellariis, qui et qua hora et quid legere debeant, ac hospitiorum taxatione seu etiam interdicto, et rebelles ipsis constitutionibus vel ordinationibus per subtractionem societatis congrue castigandi, vobis concedimus facultatem."

108. For the regulations that do survive see *Faculté de décret* 1:10–11, no. 13, and 1:15–16, no. 17; *CUP* 2:503–4, no. 1040.

At Oxford as at Paris, teachers of canon and civil law apparently organized themselves at first into a single faculty about the time that the university itself was taking corporate form. Civilians and canonists shared the same quarters, often voted as a single faculty in university assemblies, and students in both faculties looked forward to careers primarily as practitioners of canon law.[109] Several thirteenth-century chancellors of Oxford were canonists, some of whom held important posts prior to becoming chancellor. As a group, however, Oxford canonists of the thirteenth and fourteenth centuries were not notable for scholarly originality.[110]

Cambridge followed a similar pattern. Canon law was taught there from the earliest times that we know anything about the university, and its first identifiable chancellor, Richard de Leycestria or Wetheringsette, was a canon lawyer. By about 1250, when its earliest surviving statutes were drawn up, the university could boast three faculties: liberal arts, theology, and canon law. Two of the three, canon law and the arts, had been there from the beginning, but theology was a relatively recent arrival and there is no evidence that the university had an organized theological faculty before about 1240. A civil law faculty appeared only later, probably in the early 1250s, shortly after the redaction of the earliest statutes. Because students of canon law needed a basic foundation in civil law, some instruction in the subject, probably at a rudimentary level, must have been available from early in the university's development.[111]

UNIVERSITY LAW TEACHING

Teaching practices in the law faculties of medieval universities resembled those in medicine, theology, and the arts. The goals were threefold: first, each faculty sought to make sure that its students thoroughly and systematically mastered the authoritative texts of the discipline. In addition, faculties insisted that their students must learn how to analyze problems and frame persuasive arguments, so that they could effectively uphold one side of an issue while refuting the others. All faculties undertook to test students at the end of the prescribed course of study to prove they had mas-

---

109. Boyle, "Beginnings," 130–31, and "Canon Law before 1380," 534–41; Barton, "The Study of Civil Law before 1380"; Dolezalek, "Wie studierte man bei den Glossatoren?" 58–59; Catto, "Citizens, Scholars and Masters," 187; Rashdall, *Universities* 3:65 n. 2.

110. Lawrence, "University in State and Church," 113; Boyle, "Curriculum at Oxford," 162.

111. Hackett, *Original Statutes*, 29–33, 131–32; Roach, in VCH, Cambs. 3:152.

tered the knowledge and the skills necessary to practice their discipline and to teach it to others.

Lectures and Repetitiones

While each law faculty in principle set its own curriculum, the basic features of law curricula followed a common pattern. Lectures were the primary mode of instruction and were delivered in Latin, the official language of university business.[112] Civil and canon law teaching, like that in other faculties, was text-centered. Candidates for degrees had to hear a minimum number of lectures on each book in the civil or canon law *corpus*.[113] These lectures followed the order of the texts and with few exceptions took up each chapter or law in sequence. The student universities at Bologna also forbade lecturers to avoid difficult passages by postponing discussion of them to the end of the lecture hour. By the early fourteenth century at the latest, teachers at Bologna were required to read and comment on the ordinary gloss as well as the text. Surviving canonistic glosses, apparatuses, *summae*, and *lecturae* reflect the content of the lectures of the individual law professors under whose names they circulated.[114]

University statutes everywhere prescribed two basic types of lectures: ordinary and extraordinary, although the distinctions between them were fluid and seem to have changed over time.[115] Ordinary lectures, at least in principle, were those that dealt in depth with the most important texts studied in each faculty and were ideally supposed to be delivered by its most prestigious senior teachers. By the latter part of the thirteenth cen-

---

112. Thus, e.g., Statutes of the College of the Treasurer at Paris in *CUP* 1:85, no. 499; Statutes of the German Nation at Orleans, in *Statuts et privilèges* 1:249, no. 340; Statutes of the Arts Faculty at Angers §118, in *Statuts et privilèges* 1:431, no. 497. English translations of these appear in Thorndike, *University Records and Life*, 78, 364–65, and 367, nos. 36, 161, 164.

113. Bellomo, *Saggio sull'università*, 60–61.

114. Bologna University Statutes (1317) 2.44–45, at 314–16. On the various genres of medieval legal writing, see Weimar, "Legistische Literatur," and García y García, "Faculties of Law," 394–97. For students' lecture notes, see esp. Dolezalek, "Wie studierte man bei den Glossatoren?" 61–66.

115. Cardinal Robert de Sorbon used this terminology in his regulations for lectures at Paris as early as 1215 (*CUP* 1:78–79, no. 20; trans. Thorndike, *University Records and Life*, 27–30, no. 15). The distinction appears in the first known Bologna statutes between 1260 and 1270 (Bologna University Statutes §5, ed. Maffei, 94). It also appears in §3 of Cambridge University's Angelica statutes, 203. On differences (or lack thereof) between ordinary and extraordinary lectures see Maierù, *University Training*, 57–58.

tury, it was customary at least in some universities for ordinary lectures to take place in the mornings, between sunrise and noon.[116]

Extraordinary, or cursory, lectures were primarily (but not exclusively) the province of the younger scholars of the faculty. These lectures dealt either with the less central texts in the legal curriculum or else provided an elementary introduction to the principal texts, which senior professors would elaborate upon in their ordinary lectures. Advanced students who had already received the bachelor's or licentiate degree usually provided the law faculty's extraordinary lectures, and attendance at a prescribed number of extraordinary lectures formed part of the degree requirements.[117]

In thirteenth-century canon law faculties, Gratian's Decretum, joined from 1234 onward by the Liber Extra, formed the core of the curriculum and the focus of ordinary lectures. Canon law curricula everywhere changed over the course of the century as faculties assigned increasing prominence to the more recent law in the Liber Extra, while the time allocated to the study of the older law in the Decretum steadily diminished.[118]

As popes and councils continued to make new law after 1234, this legislation also had to be added to the curriculum. Five short decretal collections issued by Pope Innocent IV, Pope Gregory X, and Pope Nicholas III between 1245 and 1280 became the subject of extraordinary lectures as they appeared. Those collections vanished from the curriculum toward the end of the century, following the promulgation by Pope Boniface VIII (r. 1294–1303) of the Liber Sextus (so-called because it supplemented the five books of the Liber Extra) in 1298. This required a further adjustment in the

---

116. Senior members of the faculty were for that reason often styled "ordinary professors," a usage still common in German universities. Some law faculties also offered "quasi-ordinary" lectures, i.e., a course of lectures presented by a more junior member of the faculty on the major texts that were the subject of ordinary lectures; e.g., *Statuta antiqua universitatis Oxoniensis*, 45–46, also quoted in Boyle, "Curriculum at Oxford," 136; *Munimenta academica* 2:398–99; Cambridge, *Statuta antiqua* 1:367–69, §104; Maierù, *University Training*, 45–54; Belloni, "L'insegnamento giuridico," 146–50.

117. Boyle, "Curriculum at Oxford," 136–43, 147–49. University statutes are inconsistent in their use of the terms "extraordinary" and "cursory." Each term referred both to lectures delivered by fledgling scholars and also to the elementary approach (variously described as *lectio textualis* or *expositio litteralis*) that they employed in their explanation of the texts. This contrasted with the deeper, more wide-ranging, and literally magisterial approach taken in lectures by senior ordinary professors. See the discussion in Hackett, *Original Statutes*, 133–37, as well as Maierù, *University Training*, 49.

118. Belloni, *Professori giuristi a Padova*, 65.

lecture schedule. Then in 1317, with the promulgation of the Clementine Constitutions by Pope John XXII (r. 1316–34), professors who lectured on the Liber Sextus had to adjust their schedules to add lectures on this collection as well. A further alteration in the lecture list became necessary a few years later in order to accommodate the Extravagantes of John XXII, a brief official decretal collection that appeared between 1325 and 1327.[119] Lectures sometimes included additional material from private decretal collections that circulated in the late Middle Ages.

Bolognese law students, intent on getting their money's worth for their fees, established a schedule of "points" (*puncta*) that not only specified exactly which texts and sections of texts ordinary lectures must cover, but also prescribed the order of presentation and allotted a fixed number of lecture days to each point (typically about two weeks' worth). The aim of these statutes was to assure that lecturers explained all the important texts systematically, without wandering off into irrelevancies.[120] Each professor of civil or canon law had to deposit a substantial sum of money with the rector of the student university at the beginning of the academic year to guarantee that he would observe the schedule that the students dictated. Each time he failed to do so, he forfeited a portion of his deposit. Should he exhaust the original security deposit during the course of the year, he had to put down a further deposit.[121] By the end of the thirteenth century some

---

119. Schulte, *QL* 2:29–50; Stickler, *Historia iuris canonici*, 254–68. On the rapid incorporation of the Liber Sextus into the curriculum at Bologna, see Bellomo, *Saggio sull'università*, 197, and especially Schmidt, "Rezeption des Liber Sextus," 51–64. Provisions for lectures on the Liber Sextus and the Clementine Constitutions appear, e.g., in Bologna University Statutes (1317) 2.41, 308, and Oxford, *Statuta antiqua*, 46, 132–33, also quoted by Boyle, "Curriculum at Oxford," 136–38. On John XXII's decretals, see the introduction to Jacqueline Tarrant's edition, *Extrauagantes Iohannis XXII*, 1–27.

120. Zabarella, *Tractatus de modo docendi et discendi*, 49. Study of Roman law texts, however, was selective and the *puncta* show that lectures did not by any means treat every text (Dolezalek, "Wie studierte man bei den Glossatoren?" 61). More generally, see Boháček, "Puncta Codicis," 22, and Maierù, *University Training*, 46–47. Law faculties at other universities often imitated the practice of assigning points; see, e.g., the Toulouse statutes of 1280 and the Montpellier statutes of 1339 in *Statuts et privilèges* 1:458–61, no. 535 §§15–53, and 2:51–53, no. 947 §11; Cambridge, *Statuta antiqua* 1:367–69, §104.

121. Bologna University Statutes §5, ed. Maffei, 94; cf. Bologna University Statutes (1317) 2.44 and (1432) 3.101, ed. Denifle, 313–15, 379–80. This security deposit amounted to 25 Bolognese pounds, which represented a sizable fraction of a year's professorial salary.

law faculties were beginning to assign *puncta* for extraordinary lectures as well and to impose fines for failure to meet those deadlines.[122]

During the academic year, which commonly commenced in early October and closed at the end of July,[123] faculties usually scheduled two sets of ordinary lectures daily, save on Sundays and the major feast days of the church's liturgical calendar. These holy days were "nonreading days" (*dies non legibiles*) when ordinary lectures (and sometimes extraordinary ones as well) did not take place. Major feast days were so numerous in the Western Church that the thirteenth-century statutes of the university at Bologna forbade law teachers to observe more than one holiday per week.[124] The first ordinary lectures of the day typically began immediately after sunrise, at the liturgical hour of prime.[125] The second set of ordinary lectures then commenced in midmorning, at the liturgical hour of terce, while extraordinary lectures commonly began in midafternoon, at the liturgical hour of nones, and finished before vespers, which occurred shortly before sundown. In most cities the ringing of church bells announced these times.[126]

As university law faculties became increasingly institutionalized, they

---

122. Bologna University Statutes (1317) 2.44, 315.

123. Bologna University Statutes §4, ed. Maffei, 94; Cambridge University Angelica Statutes §3, 201.

124. Bologna University Statutes §2, ed. Maffei, 93–94; cf. Bologna University Statutes (1317) 2.44, 311–12; Bellomo, *Saggio sull'università*, 187–89; Sorbelli, *Storia*, 214–15. At the University of Paris in the fourteenth century, by contrast, all faculties observed 71 full holidays each year, to which the canon law faculty added a further 39 (*CUP* 2:709–15, Appendix; trans. Thorndike, *University Records and Life*, 175–88, no. 72). The law faculty at Montpellier canceled lectures on 78 holy days, in addition to Sundays (Montpellier University Statutes (1339) c. 14, in *Statuts et privilèges* 2:44–64, no. 947, at 53; trans. Thorndike, *University Records and Life*, 188–89, no. 73).

125. At Paris, however, the first canon law lectures of the day according to the 1386 statutes commenced in the dark, before dawn, and lecturers at that time were expected to deliver their lectures without benefit of a candle. They went on until it was light enough to see a book, at which point the second lecture period began (*CUP* 3:426, no. 1528, and 3:636, no. 1700 §13). The hours of the liturgical day were computed according to the Roman system of reckoning time, which divided the period between sunrise and sunset into twelve roughly equal hours, of which the first hour (prime) began at sunrise, the third hour (terce) occurred at midmorning, the sixth hour (sext) at noon, and the ninth hour (none) in midafternoon. The actual length of the hours varied with the seasons, so that winter hours were considerably shorter than summer hours.

126. Bologna University Statutes (1317) 1.11, 2.44, 267, 313; Hackett, *Original Statutes*, 136–38, as well as Angelica Statutes §2.5, 201. This useful service was not cost-free. In Cambridge, as at many other universities, lecturers in the law faculty had to swear an

adopted a standardized template for lectures that professors were expected to follow. Hostiensis (b. between 1190 and 1200, d. 1271) described the practices current at Bologna around 1250. A teacher, he said, ought to begin by explaining the *casus*, that is, the fact situation that gave rise to a particular law or canon.[127] He should then read out the text, explicating its meaning as he went along. Following this, the lecturer should point out analogous cases, where the same rules might apply, and contrary cases, where they would not. Next he should address questions that this particular passage might raise and the solutions to them. Finally he should summarize the major themes (*notabilia*) of the text he was discussing and their application in practice. Hostiensis was aware of course that the lecture method he was describing might not work equally well for every passage in the law books.[128] What he described for his readers was the basic format of a Bolognese professorial lecture, which teachers could adapt as different situations might require.[129] Hostiensis added in a sardonic aside:

> There are indeed some who read the gloss as well as the text, which delights the feebleminded, and they correct the apparatus and in this way merely concentrate on the words. But it is clear that this is profitable neither to student nor teacher for understanding and storing [the material] in the mind. The master at his podium should not spare himself or others by stating anything less than the truth according to what he has learned and believed... because if he goes against his conscience he stokes the fires of hell and sins even more gravely than an advocate.[130]

---

oath that they would contribute to the bell-ringer's stipend (Cambridge, *Statuta antiqua* §106, at 1:369).

127. Schulte, *QL* 2:123–29; Lefebvre, "Hostiensis"; and esp. Pennington, "Henricus de Segusio," with the literature cited therein. The *casus* on the Decretum by Benencasa of Arezzo (d. 1206) and on the Liber Extra by Bernard of Parma (d. 1266) became the standard introductory expositions in most canon law faculties (Schulte, *QL* 1:170–71, 2:114–17; Kuttner and Smalley, "The Glossa Ordinaria"; Paul Ourliac, "Bernard de Parme ou de Botone").

128. Hostiensis, *Summa* 5.9 *De magistris* §6, at 235ra. This approach formed the basis for what came to be known in the later Middle Ages and the early Modern period as "the Italian method" (*mos Italicus*) of legal exposition (Kelley, *The Human Measure*, 128–47; Brugi, *Per la storia della giurisprudenza*, 50–58).

129. Bologna University Statutes (1317) 2.44, 314; Odofredus, *Comm. in Dig. vet.*, proem., quoted in Savigny, *Geschichte* 3:553 n. a; Bellomo, *Saggio sull'università*, 65–68; Dolezalek, "Wie studierte Man bei den Glossatoren?" 68–74.

130. *Summa* 5.9 *De magistris* §6, at 235ra: "Sunt enim qui glossam legunt sicut textuum, quod idiotis placet et mouentur ex eo, quia corrigunt apparatum et sic curant de

Lecturing practices current in the Bolognese law faculty set a pattern that, with some variations, became common elsewhere. The Faculty of Decrees at Paris even went so far as to prescribe the speed at which lecturers should speak and forbade professors to lecture on the Liber Extra outside of the schools in the Clos Brunel. Many universities demanded that candidates for higher degrees possess copies of all the texts that comprised the *Corpus iuris civilis* and the *Corpus iuris canonici*, together with their *Glossa ordinaria*.[131]

In addition to formal lectures, law faculties also expected students to attend review sessions called *repetitiones*. These generally took place in the late afternoon or early evening, following the conclusion of the day's scheduled lectures. The *repetitor* in charge of these exercises was often an advanced student who went through the material covered in that morning's ordinary lectures, commented on the main points, and tried to explain intricate technical issues that beginning students usually found difficult to grasp, especially at first hearing.[132] *Repetitiones* not only clarified complex matters, they also helped students to begin the process of memorizing the large chunks of material that both academic lawyers and practitioners in the courts needed to recall instantly, especially during oral argumentation.[133]

---

verbis tantum. Sed certe quo ad intelligendum mentem et retinendem neque magistro expedit neque scholari. Magister non debet parcere in cathedra sibi nec aliis quominus veritatem dicat, secundum quod didicit et credit verum esse, ut xxxvii di. Relatum [D. 37 c. 14], quia si veniret contra conscientiam ad gehennam edificat, et grauius peccaret quam etiam aduocatus, xi q. iii Precipue [C. 11 q. 3 c. 3]." This passage may have been directed at Odofredus, who boasted to prospective students, "I shall also read all the glosses, which was not done before my time (Odofredus, *Comm. in Dig. vet.*, proem., quoted by Savigny, *Geschichte* 3:541–42 n. d, trans. Thorndike in *University Records and Life*, 66–67, no. 29; see also Bellomo, *Saggio sull'università*, 211–12).

131. Statutes of the Faculty of Decrees in *CUP* 3:643–44, no. 1698 §§23, 24; Oxford, *Statuta antiqua*, 46; *Munimenta academica* 2:398; Cambridge, *Statuta antiqua* 1:364, §95; *Constitucions i altres drets de Catalunya* 2.6.4, at 1:174; Verger, "Teachers," 155; Bellomo, *Saggio sull'università*, 110.

132. Bologna University Statutes (1317) 1.11, 267; Juan Alfonso de Benavente, *Ars et doctrina studendi et docendi* 1.12, 50; *De commendatione cleri* 4, ed. and trans. Thorndike, *University Records and Life*, 218, 421; Bellomo, "Factum proponitur certum," 5, and *Saggio sull'università*, 214–16; Maierù, *University Training*, 59–62.

133. On the importance of memorization see esp. Juan Alfonso de Benavente, *Ars et doctrina* 3.51, 5.68, 5.81, 9.96, 71, 84, 91, 99; Zabarella, *Tractatus de modo docendi et discendi*, 48; Martinus de Fano, *De regimine et modo studendi*, in Frati, "L'epistola *De regimine et modo studendi*," 27, summarized in Haskins, *Studies in Medieval Culture*, 75.

Disputations

Disputations formed the second most important learning exercises in university law faculties. These formal debates (conducted in Latin, as were all university exercises) provided degree candidates in both laws with experience in framing oral arguments on legal issues and in responding to the arguments advanced by others. Law students, like students in other faculties, were obliged to participate periodically in disputations, which were chaired by one of their masters.[134] The statutes of the student universities at Bologna, for example, provided that every salaried professor must preside least once a year at a disputation. These exercises occurred twice a week between the first week of Lent and Pentecost on days when lectures were not scheduled.[135] Law teachers fulfilled this obligation in order of seniority, starting with the most recent recipient of the doctorate. Attendance at these exercises was mandatory for professors and degree candidates alike.[136] The master in charge of a disputation proposed the question for debate, which he published in advance. During the proceedings, the other masters and advanced students of the faculty argued the issues it posed, while beginning students listened and took notes on the debate. At the close, the presiding master determined the outcome of debate with a reasoned solution to the problem, supported by ample citations to the legal texts. The master who chaired a disputation was also required to supply the university's approved booksellers (*stationarii*) with a written record of his disputation within one month, so that copies could be prepared for the university's archives and for anyone else who wished to buy them (see fig. 2).[137]

Although participation in them was required, disputations were less frequent at Oxford and Cambridge than they were at Bologna. Disputations scheduled in the latter part of the morning were styled ordinary, while those in the afternoons were called extraordinary. What substantive

---

134. Maierù, University Training, 62–69; Bellomo, *Saggio sull'università*, 216–22; Bazàn et al., *Les questions disputées*, 231–37.

135. Feast days when lectures were not held were so common in the university calendar that there was little difficulty in finding at least one in any given week (Bologna University Statutes [1317] 1.44, at 311–12).

136. Bologna University Statutes (1432) 2.46–47, at 318–23.

137. Bologna University Statutes (1317) 1.19 and 2.47, at 280–81, 322–23; Thorndike, *University Records and Life*, 167, no. 66; Schwinges, "Student Education, Student Life," 232–33. See also the comments on disputations by Colluccio Salutati (1330–1406), trans. Thorndike, *University Records and Life*, 266–69, no. 102.

Figure 2. Johannes Andreae presenting a book to Pope Boniface VIII (top panel) and delivering a copy of his book in a bookstore (bottom panel). Médiathèque Municipale, Cambrai, MS 620, 1r. Reproduced by permission.

differences there may have been between the two is not clear from the statutes.[138]

Examinations

At the close of their course of study, students who sought a law degree had to pass a series of examinations. Examinations were not an altogether novel idea. Canon law had long required bishops to examine candidates for ordination to determine whether they possessed the learning, character, and morals to fulfill their duties properly.[139] Church authorities had long claimed the right to license teachers. Bishops since at least 1138 had obliged candidates for teaching licenses to pass an examination designed to assess their knowledge and ability.[140]

It was no coincidence that Bologna's archdeacon, to whom the bishop normally delegated the task of testing the fitness of candidates for ordination, also presided over degree examinations, even though he was not necessarily a member of the university.[141] Degree examinations at Bologna differed from earlier examinations. Degree examinations marked the completion of a formal educational process, and the student who passed them received an academic degree, which conferred upon him a specific status in the educational and social hierarchy. Earlier educational institutions, such as monastic, cathedral, or palace schools, did not usually attempt to certify the competence of their graduates in any systematic way and did not grant degrees.[142]

Explicit information about examinations for the degree of doctor of laws at Bologna first survives from about 1217, which indicates that by that point a *universitas doctorum* was functioning there.[143] A letter of Pope Hon-

---

138. *Statuta antiqua Oxoniensis*, 59, at 168–69; *Calendar of Patent Rolls 1374–77*, 290–93; Boyle, "Curriculum at Oxford," 152–53; Forde, "Educational Organization of the Augustinian Canons," 36 and 54–55 n. 96; Hackett, *Original Statutes*, 138–42, 201, 321.

139. Thus, e.g., D. 24 c. 2 and d.p.c. 4; Dohar, "*Sufficienter litteratus*," 308–9; Cencetti, "La laurea," 250–54.

140. D. 38 c. 1, C. 16 q. 1 d.p.c. 40; 1 Comp. 5.4.3 (= X 5.5.3; JL 11925); Legatine Council of Westminster (1138) c. 17, in Whitelock, Brett & Brooke 2:778; Nardi, "Relations with Authority," 79–80; Cencetti, "La laurea," 256–57.

141. 4 Comp. 1.11.3 (= X 1.23.9; Po 377); Paolini, "Evoluzione di una funzione ecclesiastica," 158–63; Weimar, "Zur Doktorwürde," 321*–324*; Rashdall, *Universities* 1:221–24; Cencetti, "La laurea," 262–62.

142. Hyde, "Universities and Cities," 16.

143. "Doctor" may have been used to designate an academic rank at Bologna even earlier, although the usage is not entirely clear. See Groten, "Die Magistertitel";

orius III two years later provides the earliest unambiguous evidence that the law teachers of Bologna as a body were conferring degrees and that candidates for the doctorate were required to pass an oral examination, at which the archdeacon presided.[144] Odofredus (d. 1265) corroborates this evidence when he refers in passing to an opinion that some of his predecessors (*antiqui doctores*) had expressed while conducting an examination in the cathedral church of St. Peter. The context of Odofredus's remarks suggests that this examination must have taken place around 1220.[145] Corroborative evidence appears in a story by an Orleans law professor, Guido de Cumis, about his own examinations. Guido, who was a pupil of Jacobus Balduini (d. 1235), tells us that he had the temerity to disagree with Accursius, who was one of the examiners, but that he managed to pass despite this gaffe. Jacobus relates that a less fortunate student failed an examination about the same time for disagreeing with Accursius.[146]

Students received the bachelor's degree at Bologna without undergoing an examination. Instead, advanced students (usually in their sixth or seventh year of legal studies), upon nomination by the rector and after taking a series of prescribed oaths, were appointed to incept, that is, to commence teaching by delivering an introductory lecture on one of the basic texts they had studied. Inception automatically carried with it the style and title of bachelor of civil or canon law (*juris civilis/canonici baccalareus*, abbreviated J.C.B.) After completing a year or two of lecturing, bachelors were eligible to proceed to the private examination, the first of the examinations that led to the doctorate.[147]

Feenstra, "Legum doctor"; as well as Ingrid Baumgärtner, "'De privilegiis doctorum,'" 303; Steffen, *Studentische Autonomie*, 156–59.

144. Honorius III, *Cum sepe contingat*, 28 June 1219 (Po 6094); Sarti-Fattorini 2:260, no. 17; better texts appear in Rashdall, *Universities* 1:586, and Honorius's *Regesta* 1:351–52, no. 2127. Weimar, "Zur Doktorwürde," 310*, would place the earliest doctoral examinations slightly earlier. In a further letter in favor of the university in 1224, the pope referred specifically to the degrees of doctor of decrees (*doctor decretorum*) for canonists and doctor of laws (*doctor legum*) for civilians (Po 7305; *Regesta* 2:273, no. 5120).

145. Odofredus, *Lectura super Cod.* 4.65.22, at 259ra; Weimar, "Zur Doktorwürde," 310*–313*; Baumgärtner, "De privilegiis doctorum," 303; Conte, "Un *sermo pro petendis insigniis*," 82.

146. Meijers, "Université d'Orléans," 30–35; Weimar, "Zur Doktorwürde," 312*. The student who failed abandoned his legal studies and became a Franciscan friar.

147. Bologna University Statutes (1432) 2.52–53, at 325–27; Bellomo, *Saggio sull'università*, 232–34; Rashdall, *Universities* 1:220–21. Montpellier, Oxford, and Cambridge likewise required no formal examination for admission to inception and the

Before he could take his private examination, however, the student had to secure a sworn statement from the rector of the student university that he was properly enrolled and had attended the numbers and types of lectures prescribed by statute. He next needed to persuade one of the masters of his faculty to sponsor his application to be examined. Since no master who valued his reputation would care to present a student who seemed likely to fail, masters invariably interviewed the prospective examinee to make sure that he was adequately prepared before they would agree to sponsor him. This was in effect an informal preliminary examination, sometimes called the *tentamen*. If the master judged the candidate ready, he presented him to the archdeacon (or his representative), who appointed a professorial committee to conduct his private examination.[148]

The private examination involved a daunting test of the candidate's knowledge, skill, and resourcefulness. It was by far the most intellectually challenging hurdle that a doctoral candidate faced, "A demanding and frightening test" (*rigorosum et tremendum examen*) as one statute described it.[149] On the day before the examination, the examining board, chaired by the archdeacon, assembled in the sacristy of St. Peter's Cathedral, where they picked two passages (*puncta*) from the law books on which they would examine the candidate. The next morning shortly before lectures began for the day, the candidate presented himself to his sponsor, who informed him which sections of the law the professorial committee had selected for his examination. The student had the balance of the day to prepare (perhaps with help from his sponsor) for questioning on the assigned passages. At sundown, the hour for vespers, the archdeacon summoned the candidate to enter the sacristy of the cathedral, where the examining committee was assembled behind closed doors. After the candidate had sworn the oaths prescribed by statute, the examiners, beginning with the most junior member of the board, began to question him. They challenged his answers, debated with him, and sought to determine how thoroughly he knew his subject and how well he could defend his views. Questioning proceeded

---

baccalaureate, but did require payment of fees (Hackett, *Original Statutes*, 92, 119–22). The fee for the baccalaureate in canon law at Cambridge amounted to 40 shillings (or alternatively, one-third of the annual revenues from the candidate's benefice), while the civil law degree cost only 26 shillings, 8 pence; the baccalaureate in theology was even cheaper at 20 shillings (*Statuta antiqua*, 373–74, §116).

148. Bologna University Statutes (1432) 2.54–56, at 327–31; (1397) §10 as well as the 1460 statutes §12, ed. Malagola, 343–44, 383; Bellomo, *Saggio sull'università*, 234–36.

149. Bologna University Statutes (1432) 2.57, at 332 n. 2.

in reverse order of seniority. Once the senior examiner had finished, the candidate was excused, and the committee voted by secret ballots either to pass or fail him. The presiding doctor counted the ballots, recorded the result in the secret book of the College of Doctors, and announced the outcome to the candidate.[150] Success in the private examination carried with it the title of licentiate in civil or canon law (*juris civilis/canonici licentiatus*, or J.C.L.).[151]

The student now became eligible to proceed to the public final examination (*conventus* or *principium*), which led to the doctorate. The public examination more nearly resembled a pageant than a rigorous test of the candidate's legal knowledge or skill; indeed, the most substantial test he had to pass was financial rather than intellectual. The public examination was an extremely expensive enterprise.[152] The candidate first had to make the rounds of the professors of the law faculty, paying a personal visit to each to invite them to attend his examination.[153] He must also present each professor with a gift in token of his esteem. Next, he must invite as many of his fellow students as he could afford, with gifts to each of them as well. The students who lodged with him were especially important, since they would accompany him on the appointed day in a gala procession through the streets of the town to the cathedral, whose sumptuous decoration he had to pay for.[154] Once the candidate and his escorts arrived at the cathe-

---

150. Bologna University Statutes (1432) 2.57, at 332–36; 1460 Statutes §§12–13 and 1397 Statutes §11, ed. Malagola, 343–46, 384–86; Bellomo, *Saggio sull'università*, 236–40; Rashdall, *Universities* 1:224–26. Practices at French universities were very similar (Verger, "Examen privatum, examen publicum," 33–34).

151. Verger, "Examen privatum, examen publicum," 19–26. For some purposes, the licentiate might serve as the equivalent of the doctorate (Petrus Lenauderius, *De privilegiis doctorum* 4.3.11–12, at 11rb–va).

152. Stelling-Michaud, *Université de Bologne*, 71, details some of the costs involved at Bologna. Pantin, *Canterbury College Oxford* 3:54–56, 63–67, 132–34, nos. 68, 80, 97, 160, details the actual costs for members of the college in the late fourteenth and fifteenth centuries, (from £46 17 s. 11 d. to £118 3 s. 5 ½ d.).

153. According to some authorities, a minimum of seven holders of the doctorate had to be present to approve the creation of a new doctor of laws (Petrus de Ancharano, *Lectura super Sexto Decretalium* to VI, proem. §8, at 2va; Simone da Borsano, *Lectura super Clementinas*, proem., pars prima, in Maffei, "Dottori et studenti," 237).

154. Bologna University Statutes (1432) 2.58, at 336–38, describes these ceremonies in considerable detail. See also Bellomo, *Saggio sull'università*, 243–45; Cavazza, *Le scuole*, 206–8; Rashdall, *Universities* 1:226–31; and for French universities Verger, "Examen privatum, examen publicum," 40–42.

dral, the he took a series of oaths, which bound him to honor the university's statutes. The candidate's sponsor then delivered a sermon in praise of his pupil's virtues and achievements, following which the pupil himself presented a public lecture on a legal issue.[155] Fellow students (whom the candidate presumably selected in advance) then raised objections to the points he had made in his lecture, and he responded to each of these with the most dazzling arguments of which he was capable, supported by an erudite string of citations to the supporting authorities designed to show off his command of the topic.

At the end of this ritualized disputation, the archdeacon invested the new doctor of civil or canon law (*juris civilis/canonici doctor*, or J.C.D.) with the symbols of his rank: a law book, a gold ring, and the doctoral cap (*biretta*). This final ritual attested that the new doctor was authorized to teach publicly. As Guido de Baysio (d. 1313) put it, he had received his third and final crown.[156] The ceremony in the cathedral closed with an embrace and a blessing from his professorial sponsor and the archdeacon.

A celebration then ensued, beginning with a triumphal procession with pipes and drums through the town, followed by a lavish banquet for the professors, colleagues, friends, and acquaintances who had witnessed the ceremony. The new doctor, needless to say, hosted and paid for all of this.[157] The expense involved in taking the doctorate was so enormous that impecunious students, no matter how learned, simply could not afford it. Some who received the licentiate at Bologna later took their doctorates at other universities where the costs of the public examination were more modest, despite statutes that forbade them to do so.[158] Others were able to find a wealthy patron who was willing to foot the bill. Still others left after receiving the J.C.B. or the J.C.L., and many more simply departed without any degree at all. Pope Clement V (r. 1305–14) found this state of affairs so preposterous that he tried to limit expenditures at these events by requiring degree candidates to swear publicly during the degree ceremony that they

---

155. Conte, "Un *sermo pro petendis insigniis*," 74–77, prints the text of an early example, which he dates to 1229 or 1230; for later specimens, see also Celestino Piana, *Nuove ricerche su le università di Bologna e di Parma*.

156. Guido de Baysio, *Rosarium decretorum* to D. 7 c. 12, at 52vb.

157. Bologna University Statutes (1432) 2.59, ed. Denifle, 338–42, details the mandatory fees and presents, as well as some of the other expenses involved. At Oxford and Cambridge a doctoral candidate had the option of paying a lump sum in place of hosting the banquet (Cobban, *Medieval English Universities*, 84–85).

158. Schwinges, "Student Education, Student Life," 239; Tervoort, *The* Iter italicum *and the Northern Netherlands*, 100–101, 108–10.

had spent no more than 3,000 Tournois pounds (which itself represented a small fortune) on the festivities.[159] His initiative, however well-intended, was unsuccessful, and complaints about the extravagant cost of the doctorate persisted through the later Middle Ages.

Law examinations and the ceremonies for conferring law degrees at other universities, with slight variations, closely resembled the pattern found at Bologna. Departures from Bolognese practices were generally trivial and usually reflected the circumstances of a particular university's origin and constitution.[160]

THE CANON LAW CURRICULUM

Courses of study for degrees in either canon or civil law, while not entirely uniform, closely resembled one another at different universities. Bologna furnished the original model for medieval legal education, and other universities by and large patterned their own curricula upon it, with adjustments to fit local preferences and circumstances. Oxford and Cambridge, for example, demanded two years of attendance at cursory lectures on the Bible for the bachelor of canon law degree, a requirement unknown at either Bologna or Paris.[161]

The course of study in canon law at Bologna required a *simplex canonista* to study law for at least six years in order to be eligible for the doctorate.[162] Students who had already spent five years or more in the study of civil law could qualify for the degree of doctor of both laws (*juris utriusque doctor*, or J.U.D.) by spending four additional years studying canon law. During one

---

159. Clem. 5.1.2 *Cum sit nimis absurdum*. The city of Perugia in 1400 also attempted to limit the expense of taking the doctorate at the university there by adopting a detailed schedule of maximum costs, right down to payments to the janitor who set up the benches for the public examination (2 gold florins), the bell-ringers (1 florin), and the trumpeters (2 florins); *Primum [-quartum] volumen statutorum Perusie* 1.212, vol. 1, at 71va–vb.

160. See, e.g., Gabriel, "Le doyen," 45–47; Verger, "*Examen privatum, examen publicum*," 40–42, and "Le chancelier," 92–93; Boyle, "Curriculum at Oxford," 138, 143–44, 153–57; Hackett, *Original Statutes*, 119–20, 199.

161. Cambridge, *Statuta antiqua*, 376–77, §122; Oxford, *Statuta antiqua*, 47, also quoted by Boyle, "Curriculum at Oxford," 137.

162. The University of Paris required only five years for a canon law degree (*CUP* 3:535, no. 1587). Figures of this sort, of course, do not include the years of preparatory study in the liberal arts, for as Petrus de Salinis observed in his *Lectura super Decreto*, "[Q]ui uult esse plene instructus in hac scientia debet quod vii. liberalium artium habeat aliquam nocionem" (London, BL, MS Arundel 435, at 1vb).

of those years, they attended lectures on the Decretum, then heard lectures on the Liber Extra for two years, followed by a final year of intensive study focused either on one *causa* of the Decretum or one book of the Liber Extra. Since the civil law doctorate by itself demanded at least seven or eight years of study, double qualification in both laws, although somewhat more time-consuming and expensive, was highly prestigious and desirable for those who could afford the cost and the time.[163] Johannes Bazianus (d. 1197) is the earliest jurist known to have studied and taught both laws at Bologna in the early days of the *studium* there, before the university and the system of academic degrees had fully taken shape.[164] Degrees in both laws became increasingly common during the fourteenth and fifteenth centuries, not only among those who wished to teach, but also among those who were primarily practitioners.[165]

Not all students who took degrees actually spent the number of years of study that university statutes required. University law faculties had the power to dispense individual students from statutory provisions, and they exercised that right with considerable frequency. The Cambridge University *Grace Books*, for example, show that candidates for degrees in canon law routinely received dispensations for previous experience as practitioners in the courts, for time spent studying civil law or liberal arts, and even for years spent in the cloister.[166]

Two considerations shaped the lecture schedule of the canon law faculty at Bologna and elsewhere. First, law faculties needed to provide lectures that covered all the basic texts of the discipline systematically. Second, legal texts were dense and difficult, and students needed to hear lectures on them more than once. The underlying assumption was that a beginning student (*rudis auditor et novellus*) would only be able to follow the most elementary points made in the lectures he attended. During his first year or two, the student needed to concentrate on grasping the literal meaning of the central texts of the field at a basic level. As he progressed, an advanced student (*provectus*) would gradually acquire a deeper and more

163. Bologna University Statutes (1432) 2.55, 329–30. The rules were very similar at the Universities of Florence, Padua, and Lérida (Bellomo, *Saggio sull'università*, 230–31; García y García, "Enseñanza del derecho canónico," 217–19; Davies, *Florence and Its University*, 21).

164. Savigny, *Geschichte* 5:233–34; Schulte, *QL* 1:154–56.

165. Stein, *Roman Law in European History*, 51–52; Gramsch, *Erfurter Juristen*, 465–69; Walther, "Learned Jurists," 116–17.

166. Verger, "Prosopographie et cursus universitaires," 316–18; *Grace Book Alpha*, 72, 97, 105, 141, 184; Leader, *The University to 1546*, 196, 198.

sophisticated understanding of them. During succeeding years, students focused more closely and in greater detail on the fine points of the texts they dealt with and the complexities that could arise in applying them to real problems.[167]

The earliest statutes of the University of Bologna contained detailed directions for the schedule of lectures in civil and canon law and the time allotted for individual sections of each text. In the canon law curriculum, lectures on the Decretum and the Liber Extra were scheduled in two cycles, so that students could hear two ordinary lectures each morning. During the month of October, for example, the early lecture on the Decretum at prime was supposed to deal with the first twenty-three distinctions, while the later morning lecture at terce treated *causa* 1 and the first four questions of *causa* 2. The schedule continued in the same fashion to detail a schedule that would cover the entire text during the course of one academic year. In the afternoons, the students also heard extraordinary lectures and attended review sessions. The statutes laid down similar provisions for the study of the Gregorian Decretals and the various books of Justinian's Code and Digest.[168] On days when no ordinary lectures were scheduled, students could hear extraordinary lectures. They were also expected to attend and, when they were sufficiently advanced, to participate in disputations.

Multiple lectures on each text studied meant that universities had to provide sufficient numbers of lecturers to deal with all of them. As new texts were added (which happened only in the canon law faculty), additional appointments had to be made. By the fifteenth century, consequently, the size of the teaching staff in canon law had grown substantially from what it had been in the mid-thirteenth century. Among the canonists at Bologna, for example, by the middle of the fourteenth century, four professors were responsible for morning lectures on the Liber Extra, three others were lecturing on the Liber Sextus and the Clementine Constitutions, and three gave ordinary lectures on the Decretum, while five others were assigned to give the extraordinary lectures on the Decretum in the afternoons and on certain feast days. Similar, although less ambitious, arrangements were

167. Juan Alfonso de Benavente, *Ars et doctrina studendi et docendi*, 3.50, 52–53, 55, and 7.87–88, 91–95, at 71–73, 94–98; Zabarella, *Tractatus de modo docendi et discendi*, 50–52; Bellomo, *Saggio sull'università*, 226–28.

168. Bologna University Statutes §5, ed. Maffei, 99–101 For similar provisions at Paris see *CUP* 3:535, no. 1587, and *Faculté de décret* 1:20–22, no. 25; on the Oxford course of study, see Boyle, "Curriculum at Oxford," and for Cambridge, see Brundage, "Canon Law Curriculum in Medieval Cambridge," as well as Leader, *The University to 1546*, 193–94, and Owen, *Medieval Canon Law*, 4.

in place at universities elsewhere—Padua, Florence, Toulouse, and Montpellier, for example.[169] University law faculties in the thirteenth century depended increasingly on advanced students and recently promoted doctors to do the bulk of this teaching. By the fourteenth century, especially in England, universities were even pressing students with just the J.C.B. into service to give ordinary lectures.[170]

THE PROFESSORIATE

Despite a growing demand for law teachers, few holders of the doctorate remained in teaching very long. All of them had to lecture for a few years, but only a minority made this their main, much less their sole, occupation over the long term. Doctors of law, whether they were laymen or clerics, civilians or canonists, sooner or later were apt to secure administrative or judicial appointments of some kind in the service of the church, a prince or monarch, or a municipality. They often combined one or more of these positions with private practice as advocates or *iurisperiti*. Even those who continued to teach throughout their postdoctoral careers were usually involved in practice of one sort or another from time to time in addition to their teaching duties.[171]

Since more than a few university law professors, especially in Italy, served private clients and might also hold government appointments in addition to their teaching posts, complaints about professorial absenteeism became extremely common. In addition to these sources of income, law professors commonly had at least a few students living as paying lodgers in their homes.[172] Teachers were often moneylenders as well. When expected funds failed to arrive promptly, students frequently turned to their teachers for short-term loans. Law teachers often obliged and were usually

---

169. Sorbelli, *Storia*, 84–86; Belloni, "Neue Erkenntnisse über den Rechtsunterricht," and "L'insegnamento giuridico"; Brucker, "Renaissance Florence?" 51; Gouron, "Training of Southern French Lawyers," 222–26.

170. Hackett, *Original Statutes*, 123 n. 5; Owen, *Medieval Canon Law*, 8–9; Cobban, *Medieval English Universities*, 167.

171. Verger, "Professeurs des universités françaises," 175–76, 181–84; Moraw, "Careers of Graduates," 253, 257, 261–62, 265–68; Gaudemet, "Recherches sur l'épiscopat médiéval," 144–46; Strayer, *Les gens de justice*, 21–22; Berend, "Hungarian Canon Lawyers"; Southern, "Changing Roles of Universities," 141–46; Gouron, "Le rôle de l'avocat," 18.

172. Verger, "Peut-on faire une prosopographie des professeurs?" 57; Steffen, *Studentische Autonomie*, 208–9; Petrus Lenauderius, *De privilegiis doctorum* 4.1.1, at 11ra; Bologna University Statutes (1432) 2.67, 351; Sambin, "Giuristi padovani," 368–70, 380.

ingenious enough to find ways around the canonical ban against charging interest on loans. Law professors sometimes profited handsomely from this activity.[173]

These men may have been "academic lawyers," but they were nonetheless deeply involved in affairs beyond the universities. Professorial appointments conferred a measure of prestige, which enhanced their opportunities (and their earnings) outside of the academy. Many invested heavily in real estate—gardens, vineyards, farms, city houses (both as homes and as rental properties)—as well as in bookstores, slaves, and other kinds of chattel property.[174]

While writers might insist that professors should be distinguished by their upright behavior and should not scorn those less knowledgeable than they were, in practice they all too often failed to live up to either ideal. Legal academics in the later Middle Ages had the reputation of being distinguished more often for their "insufferable arrogance and pomposity" than for their rectitude, modesty, or humility.[175]

Holders of the doctorate in law fondly fancied that the prophet Daniel must have had them in mind when he wrote, "They that are learned shall shine as the brightness of the firmament, and they that teach righteous-

173. Odofredus, *Lectura super Dig. vet.* to Dig. 1.12.1, vol. 1, at 27vb, professed to disapprove of this practice, at least when a teacher loaned money to his students so that they would frequent his lectures, but both he and his son, Albert, as well as Accursius and his son, Franciscus, and many other Bolognese professors were moneylenders on a considerable scale (Fried, "Vermögensbildung," 48–49; Sambin, "Giuristi padovani," 387).

174. Zanetti, "À l'université de Pavie," 430–31; Denley, "Career, Springboard, or Sinecure?" 112–14; Calasso, *I glossatori e la teoria della sovranità*, 85–88; Bellomo, *Saggio sull'università*, 46–48; Kibre, *Scholarly Privileges*, 30, 49–50; Fried, "Vermögensbildung," 49–51; Sambin, "Giuristi padovani," 384–86, 393–97; Soetermeer, *Utrumque ius in peciis*, 73–76, 181–88.

175. Gilmore, "Lawyers and the Church," 66–67. On the rectitude expected of professors, see Tancred, *Apparatus* to 1 Comp. 5.4.3 v. *magistri* in Cambridge, Gonville and Caius MS 28/17, at 113, and London, B.L. MS Royal 11.C.VII, at 67rb: "Huiusmodi autem magistri, studiorumque doctores primum moribus excellere debent, deinde facundia, C. De professoribus, Magistros [Cod. 10.52 (53).7]. Bene enim conuersatione debent habere testem doctrine, ut lxxiii. di. Ualentinianus [D. 63 c. 3]." On their proper bearing, see Petrus de Salinis, *Lectura* to D. 38 d.p.c. 11 in London, BL, MS Arundel 435, at 15rb: "Gratiani dictum est quod presbiteri debent ignorantem euitare, ne ergo crederet alius ipsos esse deridendos si fuerint ignorantes. Idcirco dicit magister quod licet aliud inconsonum proferant per ignorantem, non tamen propter hoc sunt a peritis scolasticis contempnendi, quia magis sunt uitanda morum uicia quam uerborum, et hoc probat per sequentem capitulum Augustini [D. 38 c. 12]."

ness to many, as stars, for all eternity" (Dan. 12:3).[176] "Doctors [of law] are gold and silver vessels, gold because of their wisdom and silver because of their eloquence," wrote Simone da Borsano (d. 1381). The very act of receiving the doctorate was equivalent to being invested with the military belt of a knight and entitled the recipient to the prerogatives that accompanied noble status. Doctors who taught law for twenty years, Simone maintained, were entitled to the rights, privileges, and social honors of a count or perhaps even a duke.[177]

Adulation of doctors of law could become very extravagant indeed. As if noble honors and knightly status were not enough, Petrus Lenauderius of Caen (b. ca. 1450, d. 1522) maintained that, even if they were married laymen, they had the power to pronounce a sentence of excommunication when acting as judges in an ecclesiastical court, since their degree bestowed a clerical "character" upon them. The great proceduralist William Durand boldly compared doctors of law to bishops in one passage and to the cherubim in another. Their tongues, he added for good measure, have the might of a flaming sword.[178]

LAW STUDENTS

University law faculties attracted swarms of students. Contemporary estimates of their numbers, such as Odofredus's claim that there were 10,000 students at Bologna in Azo's time, are often wildly improbable. In reality, slightly more than 350 law students can actually be documented at Bologna

---

176. They could find authority for this supposition in the section of Pope Honorius III's decretal *Super specula* that appeared in the title *De magistris* in the Liber Extra (X 5.5.5). The pope, however, had applied this flattering description to theologians, not lawyers (Petrus Lenauderius, *De privilegiis doctorum*, pr., 2.21.28, at 3rb, 8rb; Le Bras, "*Velut splendor firmamenti*").

177. Simone da Borsano, *Lectura Clementinarum*, proem., pt. 1, ed. Maffei, "Dottori e studenti." 238241; see also Becker, "Simone da Borsano." On doctor's knightly status, Azo, *Summa Institutionum*, proem., in *Summa super Codicem*, 346, §2; Conte, "Un sermo pro petendis insigniis," 75–76, 79–80, 82–83; Petrus Lenauderius, *De privilegiis doctorum* 2.7.8, at 7va, and 2.30.40, at 8va; Kantorowicz, "Kingship under the Impact of Scientific Jurisprudence," 92; *Statuti di Bologna* [1288] 4.91, at 1:247, 8.7, at 2:98–99; Cobban, "Elective Salaried Lectureships," 680–81; Baumgärtner, "De privilegiis doctorum," 308–16; Andreas Benellus de Barolo, *Commentarii in tres libros Codicis*, 272 to Cod. 12.15.1; Christopherus Lanfranchinus, *Utrum sit praeferendus miles, an doctor*, at. 21rb–23va, §§61–63.

178. Lenauderius, *De privilegiis doctorum* 2.15.17, at 7vb–8ra; William Durand, *Speculum iudiciale*, proem. §§8–9 and lib. 2, partic. 3 *De sententia executione* §2.12, at 1:2, 816.

in 1265. No doubt there were many more than that, but it seems extremely unlikely that there were twenty-eight times that many. Enrollment also fluctuated considerably over time. By 1269, for example, the number of known law students at Bologna had risen to well over 700, but in 1286 the figure was slightly less than 250.[179] While these data almost certainly understate the actual numbers of students, they provide a rough measure of the scale of variance in enrollment during the latter part of the thirteenth century.

Reliable enrollment figures at universities elsewhere are scarce before the fourteenth and fifteenth centuries, and even then they are scattered. When the numbers of law students can be established with reasonable precision, however, they almost always account for a sizable fraction of total university enrollments.[180] At Avignon in 1394, law students numbered 1,134 out of a total student body of 1,373, or 83 percent, an astonishingly high proportion. Toulouse in the same year counted 696 law students out of a total enrollment of 1,088 (64 percent), and at Cahors out of the 99 students enrolled in the university, 56, or well over half, were studying law. Southern French universities, however, enrolled exceptional numbers of law students. The proportion of lawyers in northern French universities was considerably smaller, although still very substantial. Thus, in 1393–94, law students accounted for 39 percent of all known university students in northern France, as against 61 percent in the universities of the Midi. Out of roughly 6,000 to 7,000 students who attended German universities in the second half of the fifteenth century, approximately 1,000 (around 14 percent) were studying law. In Spain, on the other hand, half of the 331 students enrolled at Salamanca in 1381 were studying canon law, while another 6 percent studied civil law. More than half of Oxford's medieval alumni who are known to have studied in any of the higher faculties were lawyers. The proportion of law students at Cambridge was somewhat lower and seems to have ranged between about one-third and roughly 40 percent at any given time. Theologians by comparison were less prominent in the Cambridge student body, where they accounted for about 10 to 15 percent, than they were at Oxford, where they were nearly as numerous as the lawyers.[181]

179. Odofredus, *Lectura* to Cod. 4.14.5, at 204ra; Stelling-Michaud, *Université de Bologne*, 38–39.

180. Of the English students known to have taken degrees at Padua in the late fifteenth century, exactly one-half were lawyers, with the remainder split between theology, medicine, and philosophy (Mitchell, "English Students at Padua," 117).

181. Gouron, "Recrutement des juristes," 525, 537; García y García, "Faculties of Law," 400–401; Aston, "Oxford's Medieval Alumni," 10–11; Aston, Duncan, and Evans, "Medieval Alumni of Cambridge," 58–59.

Students at the University of Bologna were often well-to-do. A good number could claim noble descent, while many others were the sons of prosperous merchants or urban professionals (judges, notaries, physicians, and the like). Relatively few came from families of artisans or small rural landowners. Among 220 Swiss students at Bologna in the second half of the thirteenth century, 10 came from families of the high nobility, 18 from lesser noble families, while 53 were sons of *milites* or *ministeriales* and 75 belonged to bourgeois families or the families of officials of one sort or another.[182] The number of Bolognese students who kept servants or chaplains indicates that many of them enjoyed a reasonably comfortable lifestyle. One calculation shows approximately one servant for every two students—some students, of course, had none, but others, such as Heinrich von Stein, a canon of the cathedral of Regensburg, employed several. A court record of 1318 shows that Heinrich's household included five *familiares*, including one described as a *scriptor*. Few students were as affluent as Heinrich, but grinding poverty seems to have been uncommon among Bolognese law students. Although any student might occasionally need to borrow money to meet a temporary cash-flow problem, crushingly impoverished students were the exception rather than the rule.[183] The description of a student as poor meant in effect that he required financial assistance, either from the university itself, a patron, or a pious foundation, such as a college. The few Bolognese students classed as poor were almost always studying canon law; they were rare among the civilians.[184]

The sons of noblemen and other powerful men appear more frequently among students at Paris and other northern French universities than in southern French universities. East of the Rhine, the socioeconomic profile of law students at Heidelberg seems to have resembled that at Paris: almost 20 percent of them were classed as nobles and more then half were

---

182. Pini, "Discere turba volens," 69–71; Stelling-Michaud, *Université de Bologne*, 116–23; Steffen, *Studentische Autonomie*, 83.

183. Pini, "Discere turba volens," 70–71; Trio, "Financing of University Students," 10; Mornet, "Pauperes scolares," 83–85. No college at Bologna, in contrast to Paris, was specifically dedicated to supporting impoverished students; likewise the names of scarcely any foreigners appear among the 217 known book scribes (a common employment for impoverished students) at Bologna in the thirteenth century. These indications further reinforce the impression that Bolognese law students tended to be reasonably well-off (Soetermeer, "roportion entre civilistes et canonistes," 276, 287).

184. Fuchs, *Dives, Pauper, Nobilis*, 60; Cobban, "John Arundel," 152–53; Paquet, "L'universitaire 'pauvre'," and "Coût des études;" Gouron, "Enseignement du droit civil," 187.

described as rich, whereas only 6 percent were reckoned poor. While the proportion of nobles was substantially lower elsewhere, students deemed well-off (*divites*) predominated at most German universities. The sons of poor families nonetheless could often manage one way or another to secure a university education, and they accounted for something on the order of 15 to 20 percent of the student population in German universities. In contrast, students of noble lineage were notably uncommon at English universities until the latter part of the fifteenth century.[185]

While most students at medieval universities were almost certainly clerics, that statement can be misleading. Students could usually claim clerical status, but that does not mean that they were necessarily "clergymen" in the sense of full-time religious professionals. "Cleric" denoted a personal status that carried with it a bundle of useful rights and privileges.[186] Prominent among them was the *privilegium fori*, known in Anglo-American law as benefit of clergy. This meant that a cleric was answerable for claims against him only in canonical courts. For clerical criminals, this was vitally important in the literal sense, because canonical judges could not impose any punishment that involved the shedding of blood.[187] A criminal cleric, no matter how heinous his crime, was in theory immune from the death penalty or mutilation, which secular courts employed as punishments for a wide range of antisocial activities. However, the vast majority of students, who were never charged with any crime, found clerical status desirable because it made them eligible to hold ecclesiastical benefices.[188] These clerical appointments could yield a steady income without necessarily re-

---

185. Courtenay, *Parisian Scholars*, 92; Gouron, "Recrutement des juristes," 543–44; Dunbabin, "Meeting the Costs of Education," 1–2; Fuchs, *Dives, Pauper, Nobilis*, 21–22; Schwinges, "Recruitment in German Universities," 46; Cobban, *Medieval English Universities*, 313–18.

186. Rashdall, *Universities* 3:393–96. Anyone who received the tonsure was entitled to clerical status and the privileges that went with it. This entailed no special religious obligations, nor did it require celibacy (X 1.14.11; VI 3.2.1).

187. Gratian, C. 23 q. 8 c. 29–30. See also Helmholz, *The Ius commune in England*, 187–239, as well as Génestal, *Le privilegium fori*, and Koch, *Die klerikalen Standesprivilegien*, 58–88. Criminal charges against students were not particularly common. Municipal court records at Bologna, for example, show 318 criminal cases brought against students between 1280 and 1350, or on average slightly less than 5 per year (Pini, "Discere turba volens," 121).

188. At least unless they married, which clerics in minor orders were free to do without loosing the other benefits of clerical status (X 3.3.2).

quiring personal performance of any religious or other duties. Clerics also claimed favorable tax treatment and exemption from most other civic obligations.

The proportion of clerics among the student population varied considerably over time and between different universities. The decretalist Nicholas de Tudeschis (1386–1445), who was commonly known as Panormitanus, maintained that most students at Paris in his day were clerics, but that at Bologna they were more often laymen. A century earlier, however, the distribution seems to have been very different. Roughly 80 percent of the documented Swiss law students at Bologna between 1265 and 1300 were clerics.[189] The difference between the two suggests a gradual decrease in the prominence of clerics among university students. In the early thirteenth century almost all university students were tonsured; by the late fifteenth century clerical students had probably become a minority at many universities.[190]

FINANCING A LEGAL EDUCATION

Costs

University courses, especially those that led to degrees in the higher faculties of medicine, theology, and law, were lengthy, and the cost of living in university towns tended to be high. A serious student who aimed at taking a law degree required not only intellectual aptitude and stamina, but also substantial financial resources, which surely accounts for the disproportionately large numbers of law students who either came from wealthy and well-placed families or enjoyed revenues from ecclesiastical benefices.

Adequate funding also reflected pride and status: too small an allowance, as an anonymous glossator noted, detracted from a student's reputation and his family's honor.[191] Students' expectations and expenditures var-

---

189. Panormitanus, *Questiones* 5.4, at 160rb; Stelling-Michaud, *Université de Bologne*, 130. Likewise at Liège in the thirteenth and fourteenth centuries the great majority of university graduates were clerics (Renardy, *Le monde des maîtres*, 188–92).

190. Schwinges, "Student Education, Student Life," 200–201.

191. Gloss to Gratian, D. 37 d.p.c. 8 v. *unde* in CUL, MS Pembroke 162, at 38v: "[E]t tunc numquid minimum honorarium pater debet scolaris prebere, sed pro modo facultatum suarum et nobilitatis et generis, ut ff. de administ. tu. Cum plures § Cum [Dig. 26.7.12.2], ut ff de uariis et extraord. cog. l. In honorariis [Dig. 50.13.1.10]; nam si modicum minus accepit uel reputabitur, ut infra iii. q. vii. c. Tria l. § Apud urbem [C. 3 q. 7 d.p.c. 1 §11]."

ied considerably, depending on their social status and the funds they had available. Odofredus calculated that a student at Paris or Bologna could manage comfortably on a budget of 100 Bolognese pounds a year.[192] Basic living expenses would require roughly between a quarter and half of that amount. Thus, for example, in 1286 two German students contracted with the rector of the Church of Saints Philip and James for a room, a fire in winter, two daily meals, and a servant to carry their books at a cost of 50 *bolognini piccoli*. To this must be added outlays for such everyday necessities as shoes, clothing, laundry, baths, candles, and travel.[193] Tuition and fees to the student's guild and university took another considerable toll on student budgets, along with the accoutrements of study—pens and ink, penknives and parchment.

Books were yet another expensive necessity for law students, who were expected to bring them—or have a servant carry them—to every lecture they attended.[194] Universities typically appointed official stationers who undertook to stock not only the basic texts required in the various faculties, but also other treatises and commentaries that students and teachers were likely to need or want, either for purchase or for rental. Records of Bolognese transactions show that between 1265 and 1350, law books cost on

---

192. Odofredus, *Lectura super Cod.* 4.28.5, at 226rb. In the mid-fifteenth century, a townsman of Lyon calculated that it cost between 30 and 50 *livres tournois* to maintain a student for a year. This works out to somewhere between two and a half and four times the wages of a daily laborer, or the capital return from an investment in a small house (Fédou, *Les hommes de loi lyonnais*, 300–301). The *livre tournois*, a substantial silver coin (it contained 4.2 grams of silver) introduced by the French king Louis IX (r. 1226–70) in 1266, was the most widely circulated currency in Europe north of the Alps in the late thirteenth century. For the fluctuation of its value against other currencies, see the tables in Spufford, *Handbook of Medieval Exchange*.

193. Zaccagnini, *La vita dei maestri*, 74–75; Schwinges, "Student Education, Student Life," 236; Bellomo, *Saggio sull'università*, 49, 225–26, 245.

194. *CUP* 2:503–4, no. 1040; Juan Alfonso de Benavente, *Ars et doctrina studendi et docendi* 2.40, at 64. Students were required to have the basic legal texts at the time they took their degrees (e.g., *CUP* 3:643–44, no. 1689; *Forma procedentium in facultate decretorum*, in *Munimenta academica* 2:398). Law teachers, practicing lawyers, and judges needed to rely on their own private law libraries, which commonly represented the largest single part of their estates at death. See Verger, "Teachers," 155; Stelling-Michaud, *Université de Bologne*, 109–14; Sambin, "Giuristi Padovani," 390–93; Whitwell, "Libraries"; Martin V, *In apostolice dignitatis* (1418) §20, in Tangl, *Päpstliche Kanzleiordnungen*, 140; Grafton, *Commerce with the Classics*, 59–60.

average roughly thirty-five Bolognese pounds apiece. By way of comparison, houses in Bologna sold for as little as thirty pounds in 1265, a judge's annual salary was ninety pounds, and the services of a notary cost the *podestà* twenty-five pounds for the year.[195]

At such prices, only wealthy students could afford ready-made copies of the eight or nine volumes that comprised the basic texts of the civil and canon law with their ordinary glosses.[196] Ordinary students either made their own copies of the texts they needed or hired scribes to make copies for them from the authorized copies that stationers happily rented to them in small sections (*peciae*), each containing a few pages. Students typically rented a single *pecia* at a time, then returned it and rented another. They could thus gradually accumulate a supply of the essential texts over the course of their years of study, together with other books they needed. The task of copying any of the basic legal texts was likely to take a year or more. Universities often regulated the terms and conditions for the rental of *peciae* in considerable detail.[197]

---

195. On university stationers, see Bologna University Statutes (1317) 1.29–32, at 291–95; Brugi, "Il catalogo dei libri degli stationarii"; Boháček, "Nuova fonte per la storia degli stazionari bolognesi," 419–27; Gargan, "Libri, librerie e biblioteche," and "Le note 'conduxit.'" On the cost of law books, see Perez Martin, "Büchergeschäfte in Bologneser Regesten," based on transactions involving 3,295 books, more than 90 percent of them law books. The cheapest recorded was a copy of the *Speculum iudiciale* of William Durand that sold for 4 pounds Bolognese, while the most expensive was a deluxe copy of Gratian's Decretum, which went for 300 pounds. Variance in prices between these extremes reflects the size of the book, the style of writing, the binding, and the number and quality of miniatures and other decorations. See also Stelling-Michaud, *Université de Bologne*, 106–9. For comparative prices, see houses: *CSB* 5:51, no. 104 (£30 bol.), 5:66, no. 138 (£46 bol.), 5:67, no. 141 (£140 bol.), 5:120–21, no. 259 (£62 bol.), 5:167–68, no. 360 (£150 bol.); judge: *CSB* 5:79–80, no. 148 (£90 bol.); notary: *CSB* 5:147–48, no. 316 (£25 bol.).

196. The texts of Justinian's *Corpus iuris civilis* were customarily bound in five volumes (Digestum vetus, Digestum novum, Infortiatum, Codex 1–9, and Volumen, which included the Institutes, Codex 10–12, and the Authenticum), while glossed copies of the *Corpus iuris canonici* might be bound as either three or four volumes.

197. Destrez, *La pecia*, is the basic study of the practice. See in addition Dolezalek, "La pecia"; Pollard, "The 'Pecia' System"; *Production du livre universitaire*; Soetermeer, *Utrumque ius in peciis*; as well as Rouse and Rouse, *Manuscripts and Their Makers* 1:85–89. On regulation of *peciae* see, e.g., Bologna University Statutes (1317) 1.36, ed. Denifle, 298–302; *CUP* 1:648–49, no. 530.

SOURCES OF STUDENT SUPPORT

Family and Patrons

Some law students came from affluent families who could readily afford the costs of a protracted university education and presumably saw the expenditure as a potentially profitable investment. One such was Cardinal Francesco Lando (d. 1326), who set aside property specifically to subsidize the legal education of his nephews.[198] The father of Jean de Roaix, a well-to-do patrician of Toulouse, likewise earmarked money in his will to support Jean while he studied law at university and to provide him with the books he would require. Unfortunately for Jean, his elder brothers who administered their father's estate failed to carry out these provisions, and on that account Jean was forced to abandon his studies after two years—or so he claimed in his lawsuit against them.[199] Humbler families than these nonetheless shared similar ambitions for the next generation of their members and somehow managed to scrape together the money to send a son to study law. This could be a hazardous gamble, as a peasant described in a poem by Rutebeuf (fl. ca. 1248–77) discovered to his sorrow.[200] Still some parents were prepared to take the risks, as did, for example, the family of the Frisian brothers Addo and Emo, who studied liberal arts, theology, and canon law at Paris, Orleans, and Oxford.

Kings, bishops, and others with power, wealth, and influence likewise calculated that by using a trifling part of their excess income to subsidize a few law students they could assure themselves of the future services of the lawyers they and their successors were bound to need. The bargain seemed especially attractive because men in positions of this sort were usually able to see to it that the students they patronized would receive an ecclesiastical benefice or some other office, which would end the need for further direct support. Towns, as well as confraternities and other charitable organiza-

---

198. The cardinal provided generously for them: their annual subsidy amounted to 80 gold ducats for clothes and living expenses, plus another 40 ducats for books (Bellomo, *Saggio sull'università*, 225–26). Similarly, Cardinal Comes of Casate (d. 1287), a former curial advocate, provided in a codicil to his will that his extensive collection of law books should go to his nephews should they wish to study law (Mather, "Codicil of Cardinal Comes").

199. Verger, "Le livre dans les universités," 407–8.

200. Rutebeuf, "Li dis de l'universitei," in his *Poèmes concernant l'Université de Paris*, 31–32. As Dunbabin notes in "Meeting the Costs of Education," 9, "Had there been no students from backgrounds as poor as this, the poet's lesson would have been lost on its readers." See also Schwinges, "Student Education, Student Life," 209–10

tions, now and again provided financial assistance to university students. Some did so sporadically, while others made this their main concern.[201]

Colleges

Patronage might also take the more costly but more enduring form of founding a college for poor students. Colleges were endowed charitable foundations that provided students with housing, meals, and often a modest annual stipend, usually on condition that the students pray for the souls of the founder and the founder's family. In addition, college founders sometimes included in their endowment the nucleus of a library, another considerable boon for members of the college, since universities were slow to develop libraries available to all students.[202] Charitable foundations of this type commenced to appear even before the universities themselves took on corporate form. The earliest example was the Collège des Dixhuit established in 1180 to provide housing for eighteen poor clerics who were studying in Paris. Other foundations soon followed at Paris. The best known was the Sorbonne, founded around 1257 by Robert de Sorbon, a chaplain of King Louis IX (1226–70).[203] The first such institution at Bologna was the Avignonese College, founded by Zoen Tencarari, bishop of Avignon, in 1267. It was soon joined by several others, the most important of which was the Spanish College, established in 1364 by Cardinal Gil Albornoz (b. between 1301 and 1303, d. 1367).[204] Colleges began to take shape

---

201. Pegues, "Royal Support of Students," and "Ecclesiastical Provisions"; Trio, "Financing of University Students," 10–12; Ridder-Symoens, "Training and Professionalization," 153, 155.

202. *Statuts et privilèges* 1:548–51, no. 593 §50, lists the books left by Arnaud de Verdale to the college that he founded at Toulouse; see also Pantin, *Canterbury College* 1:1–59; Sanderlin, *Mediaeval Statutes of the College of Autun*, 52; Highfield, "Early Colleges," 257; Powicke, *Medieval Books of Merton College*, lo–11; Cobban, *King's Hall*, 247–58. On university libraries, see Verger, "Le livre dans les universités," 414–16; Gargan, "Libri, librerie e biblioteche," 242–44; Gieysztor, "Management and Resources," 128; Aston and Faith, "University and College Endowments" 1:272–73.

203. *CUP* 1:49–50, no.50, 1:349, 372–75, 377–78, nos. 302, 325, 329; Rashdall, *Universities* 1:497–539; Schwinges, "Student Education, Student Life," 213–16; Glorieux, *Les origines du Collège de Sorbon*. The early statutes of the Sorbonne, which date from around 1274, provide numerous details about the internal governance and routines of the college's life (*CUP* 1:505–14, no. 448; trans. Thorndike, *University Records and Life*, 88–98, no. 42).

204. Sorbelli, *Storia*, 224–28; Rashdall, *Universities* 1:197–203; Denley, "Collegiate Movement in Italian Universities," 33–40; Marti, *Spanish College at Bologna*.

during the late thirteenth century at Oxford and Cambridge, where colleges continue to thrive, unlike most of their medieval counterparts on the Continent, almost all of which were suppressed at the end of the eighteenth century. Walter de Merton (d. 1277), the chancellor of King Henry III and later bishop of Rochester, founded the Oxford college that still bears his name in 1264. His foundation established the pattern not only for the further collegiate foundations that soon followed at Oxford, but also for Cambridge. When Hugh Balsham, bishop of Ely (r. 1256–86), founded Peterhouse, the earliest of the Cambridge colleges, in 1284, he directed that his college should adopt the rules laid down in the Merton statutes.[205]

Founders typically anticipated that most beneficiaries of their largess would be men studying for degrees in the higher faculties of theology, civil and canon law, or medicine. They only occasionally designated law students as their first choice for the receipt of their benefactions. Instead, they commonly favored students of theology over students of law or medicine. College founders, whether clerics or not, were after all men (or less often women) of wealth with considerable experience in the ways of the world. Their preferences no doubt reflected the not unreasonable expectation that lawyers and physicians were likely to prosper, while the worldly prospects of theologians were less bountiful.[206] They may well have calculated, too, that God might be inclined to listen more indulgently to prayers on their behalf uttered by a group of grateful theologians than to supplications from a band of lawyers.

Colleges that catered largely or even entirely to law students were a distinct minority at Oxford and Cambridge. A few universities on the Continent had similar colleges, but there too they were few and far between.[207]

205. Martin and Highfield, *History of Merton College*, 1–45; *Documents Relating to the University and Colleges of Cambridge* 2:1; Leader, *The University to 1546*, 60–66; Cobban, *Medieval English Universities*, 111–45.

206. John Bromyard, *Summa predicantium*, s.v. "Advocatus" §30, at 16va; Genzmer, "Kleriker als Berufsjuristen," 1216–17; Meynial, "Remarques sur la réaction populaire," 572–82.

207. Eighty-two percent of the students in the higher faculties at King's Hall, Cambridge, between 1337 and 1499 were studying law, while only 17 percent studied theology (Aston, Duncan, and Evans, "Medieval Alumni of Cambridge," 52–53). Trinity Hall, Cambridge (founded in 1352 by William Bateman, bishop of Norwich), was exceptional in that its founder directed that its members be restricted to students of Roman and canon law (Trinity Hall Statutes [1352], c. 1, in *Documents Relating to the University and Colleges of Cambridge* 2:417–18; Crawley, *Trinity Hall*, 2–4, 11–12). Continental colleges catering to lawyers were founded at Salamanca, Montpellier, Toulouse, Avi-

Instead, collegiate founders, especially in northern Europe, commonly placed fixed limits on the numbers of law students admitted to the institutions they created. The Sorbonne, at one extreme, excluded them altogether, and admitted only students of theology, as did the College of the Treasurer, founded in 1268 by William of Saône, Treasurer of Rouen. Others made only marginal allowance for the admission of law students, as did Walter de Merton, for example, in the statutes of his college at Oxford. Similarly at Cambridge, the statutes of Peterhouse permitted only two students to study law and one to study medicine at any given time. Other colleges were more egalitarian, such as the College of Autun in Paris, founded in 1341 by Cardinal Pierre Bertrand, whose statutes provided places for fifteen students, five in theology, five in canon law, and five in philosophy or logic.[208]

Ecclesiastical Benefices

Clerics who held parishes, canonries, or other ecclesiastical offices and benefices accounted for a considerable fraction of students in the schools of canon law at Bologna and elsewhere even before the appearance of formal university structures. Prior to the early thirteenth century, the propriety of benefice holders deserting their parishioners in order to pursue higher education seemed doubtful. Rufinus, writing around 1164, asserted that some authorities maintained that any cleric who sought permission from his bishop to leave his assigned position in order to improve his education ought to forfeit his benefice and its income. Some even claimed that to retain the income in this situation would constitute simony, although Rufinus rejected that position.[209]

Pope Honorius III's decretal *Super specula* clarified the situation in 1219:

> Let those who teach in the theological faculty receive the revenue of their prebends and benefices while they teach in the schools; students in the

---

gnon, Angers, Perugia, Pavia, Siena, and Prague (Rashdall, *Universities* 2:89–90, 134–35, 160, 172–73, 179–80, 220–21; Denley, "Collegiate Movement," 40–48; García y García, "Medieval Students of Salamanca," 102–3).

208. CUP 1:476–78 and 584–85, no. 423 and 499; Peterhouse, *Statuta antiqua* c. 24 in *Documents Relating to the University and Colleges of Cambridge* 2:21–22; Martin and Highfield, *History of Merton College*, 16, 21, 257; Sanderlin, *Mediaeval Statutes of the College of Autun*, 38.

209. Rufinus, *Summa* to D. 37 c. 12 v. *De quibusdam locis*, 90; Johannes Faventinus in his *Summa* on the same passage adopted Rufinus' argument verbatim (London, BL, MS Add. 18369, at 16va–17ra).

same may do likewise for five full years by permission of the Apostolic See, notwithstanding any contrary custom or provision, since workers in the Lord's vineyard should not be deprived of their wages.[210]

The pope thus gave beneficed clerics the opportunity to seek what we would call paid leave to study theology, funded for up to five years by the churches in which they held benefices. Implementing such a policy had become easier than it once was, since by the early thirteenth century clerics often received the income from their benefices in cash, which was readily portable, rather than in agricultural produce and food distributions.[211]

Pope Honorius clearly aimed to promote the advanced study of theology through this scholarship scheme, a goal that was evident in other provisions of his decretal. Clerics who took advantage of the opportunities that *Super specula* offered frequently chose to study canon law or the liberal arts instead of theology, as contemporary observers noticed.[212] A few applauded the pope's action. Gerald of Wales, for one, expressed the hope that these new opportunities for study would make it easier for students to acquire a firm foundation in Latin grammar and literature before they embarked on the study and teaching of law.[213]

Pope Boniface VIII (r. 1294–1303) improved earlier study leave provisions for the parochial clergy. In the decretal *Cum ex eo* (1298), Boniface authorized bishops to dispense clerics from canonical residency requirements for up to seven years for purposes of study, provided that good and sufficient curates were available to take over their pastoral duties during their absence. Pope Boniface's aim apparently was to attract young men to the clergy by offering them a subsidized education. Men who took advantage of the provisions of *Cum ex eo* were free to study in any faculty they

210. 5 Comp. 5.2.1 (= X 5.5.5; Po 6165): "Docentes vero in theologica facultate, dum in scholis docuerint, et studentes in ipsa integre per annos quinque, percipiant de licentia sedis apostolicae proventus praebendarum et beneficiorum suorum, non obstante aliqua alia consuetudine vel statuto, quum denario fraudari non debeant in vinea Domini operantes [cf. Matt. 20:1–2; Luke 10:7]."

211. Barrow, "German Cathedrals"; Stelling-Michaud, *Uuniversité de Bologne*, 89–90.

212. Stelling-Michaud, *Université de Bologne*, 125–30, and *Les juristes Suisses*; Pegues, "Ecclesiastical Provisions," 314–15. Scrupulous student clerics might even secure a papal dispensation for this purpose, as Johannes de Curtiniaco did in 1264, but most apparently did not (*CUP* 1:442, no. 401).

213. Hunt, "Preface to the 'Speculum ecclesiae,'" 195, 209.

pleased. They were bound, however, to become subdeacons (and thus to incur the obligation to observe celibacy) during their first year of study and had to be ordained to the priesthood within one year after they finished their leaves of absence. The pope's initiative appears to have been enormously successful, at least to judge by the impressive number of licenses for study leaves that appear in bishops' registers beginning in the early fourteenth century.[214]

The allure that spending five—or even better, seven—years in, say, Paris, Bologna, Oxford, Toulouse, or Salamanca must have had for clergymen in country rectories is not difficult to imagine. Neither is it surprising that some looked upon study leaves as paid vacations during which they engaged in little, if any, serious academic work.[215] Innocent IV was well aware that clerics all too readily yielded to such a temptation. In a letter to the archbishops of France, he complained about clerics on study leave, "who are present bodily in the schools, but mentally absent," unwilling to let academic work break into their night's sleep or to allow useful reading to interfere with a lazy vacation. This, he declared, was not the reason why clerical students were allowed to receive the income from their benefices, and he directed the archbishops to keep track of the academic progress of their clerics who were supposed to be studying at universities. Some bishops in fact did so and demanded reports from university authorities concerning their students' attendance at lectures and academic progress.[216]

Friars, Monks, and Canons

Secular clerics who held benefices were not the only churchmen eligible for financial assistance from ecclesiastical institutions in pursuing their studies. Monasteries, houses of canons, and the mendicant orders—mainly Franciscans and Dominicans, to a lesser extent Augustinians, Carmelites,

---

214. VI 1.6.34 (Po 24634); Boyle, "Constitution 'Cum ex eo,'" 275–76, 297–98.

215. Jacques de Vitry claimed in a sermon that canon law was so popular among Parisian students because the decretists began their lectures later in the day than did teachers in other faculties (cited from Paris, BN ms. lat 17509, at 24rb, by Ferruolo, *Origins*, 260). The 1340 statutes of the Faculty of Decrees at Paris stipulated that students must attend at least two or three lectures a week if they wished to remain on the rolls (*CUP* 2:503, no. 1040; *Faculté de décret* 1:15, no. 17; trans. Thorndike, *University Records and Life*, 193).

216. *CUP* 1:182–83, no. 145; Pegues, "Ecclesiastical Provisions," 310; Boyle, "Constitution 'Cum ex eo,'" 282; Jeanclos, "Remarques sur les conditions d'accès au canonicat," 43–44.

and the smaller orders of friars—were also sending sizable numbers of their members to study at universities by the mid-fourteenth century. The primary purpose for doing so was to equip their members for preaching and teaching.[217] Authorities for this reason usually encouraged their students to study liberal arts and theology and positively discouraged them from entering the faculty of medicine or, with particular fervor, the faculty of law. Dominicans and Franciscans tended to be less rigid about this than other orders. By the mid-fourteenth century, Benedictines and Austin canons likewise relaxed their earlier disinclination to send their members to study and sometimes even to teach canon law.[218] The Cistercians, on the other hand, strongly disapproved of their monks studying canon law. Indeed in 1188, the general chapter of the order went so far as to direct librarians in the order's monasteries not to keep copies of Gratian's Decretum on the library shelves, but to hide them away out of sight.[219]

By the middle of the thirteenth century, virtually all the principal religious orders had begun to establish houses of study or colleges for their members at the major European universities. Only a minority of students from religious orders seem to have studied canon law, and they were legally barred (save by special dispensation) from the study of civil law. At the English universities, the majority of these students in the higher faculties studied theology. Still, considerable numbers of Benedictine monks and Austin canons, and a scattering of members from other orders, studied canon law. There were practical reasons for this: monasteries and other religious communities were perennially involved in litigation and found it useful to have at least some members with legal credentials.[220]

Grants and Loans

Needy law students could with some luck qualify for so-called flying grants (*bursae volantes*) that were available to students who were not members of a college or religious order. Support for these grants came from something resembling trust funds established by donors who designated their revenues for student support. The trustees were typically either relatives of the donor or an eleemosynary institution, such as a church, a religious house,

---

217. Greatrex, "English Cathedral Priories," 396–97.
218. Hove, *Prolegomena*, 470–71.
219. Stutz, "Die Cistercienser."
220. Aston, "Oxford's Medieval Alumni," 19; Aston, Duncan, and Evans, "Medieval Alumni of Cambridge," 59–61; Brundage, "Monk as Lawyer," and "Lawyers of the Military Orders."

or the officers of a university. They were empowered to select the recipients of these grants.[221]

Students temporarily strapped for cash could, as we have see, turn to their professors, to moneylenders, or to their colleges for short-term assistance until the funds they were expecting from their families or patrons arrived. This was a costly measure, resorted to only in an emergency. Although it is difficult to be sure just how much interest was charged, since this was often disguised to evade the laws against usury, the fact that the commune of Bologna set a maximum interest rate on loans at 20 percent per annum and Florence set the maximum at 25 percent, with penalties for charges beyond that limit, suggests that the rates charged in practice were often higher than this.[222]

Employment

Students who worked their way through university were a familiar sight in medieval university towns. We find students employed as servants to professors, deans, college and university officials, and to their wealthier brethren in the student body. They showed up as cooks and porters in colleges, as street singers, beggars, and occasionally as thieves. Undergraduate students frequently paid their university bills by teaching in schools. Advanced students often taught in liberal arts faculties or the colleges to which they belonged while they worked toward a degree in one of the higher faculties. Wealthy students, in universities such as Bologna, Orleans, Toulouse, and Salamanca, in considerable numbers sometimes employed their less well-to-do brethren as tutors.[223]

Law students could sometimes find opportunities to pick up practical experience while at the same time earning money to pay for further education. Thus, for example, John Derby (d. by 1474) supported himself while studying canon law at Cambridge by working as a notary, and John Lyd-

---

221. Herman, "Canonical Conception of the Trust"; Helmholz, "Trusts in the English Ecclesiastical Courts"; Trio, "Financing of University Students," 4–10. In addition to the examples that Trio mentions, other such grants appear in the *Liber memorandorum ecclesie de Bernewelle*, 71 and 94–95; Honorius III, *Regesta* 1:122, no. 702; Sarti-Fattorini 1:146; and Bologna University Statutes 1460 §19, ed. Malagola, 348.

222. Stelling-Michaud, *Université de Bologne*, 91–98; Aston and Faith, "Endowments of the University and Colleges"; Pollard, "Mediaeval Loan Chests"; Ditsche, "Scholares pauperes," 46.

223. Dunbabin, "Meeting the Costs of Education," 14–15, 19; Schwinges, "Student Education, Student Life," 241. Johannes Andreae, to cite an illustrious example, supported himself by tutoring (Schulte, *QL* 2:207–8).

ford (d. 1407) appeared as a proctor in several cases at the chancellor's court during his student days at Oxford. Johannes de Dulmen was excused from payment of university fees at Prague in 1382 in return for his legal services to the university, as was Olavus Johannis at Rostock in 1422.[224]

Standardized curricula in universities and law faculties fostered the systematic study of received legal texts through programs of reading, lectures, review sessions, and disputations, capped by examinations that tested how well a student had absorbed the materials and techniques he had studied. These developments not only transformed legal education, but in the process also enhanced the social standing and reputation of learned lawyers. This transformation, coupled with the procedural changes that began in the later twelfth and early thirteenth centuries and the appearance of permanent ecclesiastical courts with trained judges, provided the environment within which the medieval legal profession emerged. Lawyers rapidly took on the characteristics that we have come to associate with professions during the middle decades of the thirteenth century. University law faculties played a crucial role in this development. Law faculties turned students into lawyers not only by requiring them to master the material in the law books, but also by teaching them how to think and act like lawyers, rather than philosophers, theologians, or rhetoricians. At the same time, law teachers were transforming the law itself. Legal doctrines that made their first appearance in the lecture room and were hammered out in university disputations became part of the common culture of the profession. Basic ideas about such things as, for example, the structure and functions of corporations, representative assemblies, and limits on the power of rulers that first appeared in university lectures became central elements in the reshaping of social and political institutions.[225] These doctrines owed their inception to law teachers, while the lawyers whom they taught became instrumental in applying those ideas to practical problems in both church and state. By the beginning of the last quarter of the century, professional lawyers had already become not only a highly visible component of Western Christian society, but also an immensely influential one.

224. Owen, *Medieval Canon Law*, 5–6, 34, 38; *John Lydford's Book*, 32, 35–38, nos. 13, 24, 29–39; *BRUC*, 184; *BRUO* 2:1184–85; Dunbabin, "Meeting the Costs of Education," 19; Mornet, "Pauperes scolares," 58–59.

225. On these developments see, e.g., Baker, *Law's Two Bodies*, 75; Post, *Studies in Medieval Legal Thought*; Kantorowicz, *King's Two Bodies*; and Tierney, *Foundations of the Conciliar Theory*, and *Religion, Law, and the Growth of Constitutional Thought*.

* SEVEN *

Attaining Professional Status

Advocates and proctors began to become more visible in the records of the Western Church around the middle of the thirteenth century than they previously had been. They owed their higher visibility partly to the fact that there were simply more of them than in earlier times. But in addition, church authorities beginning in the 1230s started to transform advocates and proctors who appeared regularly in the courts into a profession in the strict sense of the term.[1] The transition from quasi-professional to full-fledged professional status occurred unevenly in different regions. It began in the French kingdom, the Anglo-Norman realm, and Sicily, then spread gradually to other areas. The change generally proceeded at a brisker pace in regions where universities flourished than it did elsewhere.

From around 1250, professional canonists appear regularly in the records of church courts in many regions of western Europe. It also became increasingly common for judges in ecclesiastical tribunals to hold univer-

---

1. Occasional proctors who represented others (usually family members or close friends) in the courts sporadically on an ad hoc basis were not affected by this process, and litigants continued to appoint ad hoc proctors throughout the later Middle Ages. The distinction between an advocate and a proctor was not always clear-cut. Even draftsmen in the papal chancery sometimes used the terms loosely and wrote "advocate" when they clearly meant "proctor," or vice-versa (e.g., X 2.1.14; trans. Cheney and Semple, *Selected Letters of Pope Innocent III*, 78, no. 22; see also William Lyndwood, *Provinciale*, 74). The version of the Cambridge University statutes in the Markaunt Statutes §23 complained that advocates sometimes passed themselves off as proctors in order to evade a university statute that prohibited advocates from appearing in cases that could be disposed of in three days or less (Hackett, *Original Statutes*, 323).

sity law degrees. So too did a good many of the advocates who appeared before them. The same was true as well of greater and greater numbers of archdeacons, cathedral deans and canons, bishops, archbishops, cardinals, and popes. By the beginning of the fourteenth century, men in these posts generally held university degrees, and their degrees, more often than not, were in law. Even those without a degree had often spent at least some time studying at a university.[2]

Legal practitioners who acted on behalf of others in church courts had always needed to persuade the presiding judge to grant them permission to be heard. By the mid-thirteenth century, judges were starting to demand that applicants for the right of audience take a solemn oath that that they would observe a body of ethical rules concerning the way they conducted themselves toward their clients and the court. Failure to abide by that undertaking could result in revocation of the right of audience, which left them ineligible to practice. This marked a crucial step in the professionalization of canon lawyers. Aside from clergymen, lawyers in church courts seem to have been the first occupational group in Western Christendom to require adherence to a set of specific ethical guidelines as a condition of admission to practice. Lawyers who frequented municipal courts in Italy and royal courts in England made similar transitions to professional status later in the century. In so doing, they followed much the same path that canonists had trod around the middle of the century—so much so that it is tempting to speculate that intentional imitation may have been involved.[3]

The convergence of developments detailed in preceding chapters enabled practitioners of canon law to create a clearly defined identity as a social and occupational elite with a professional code of ethics by the mid-thirteenth century. The increase in the sheer volume of lawmaking by popes and councils during the second half of the twelfth and the opening decades of the thirteenth century certainly speeded the process by making it increasingly difficult for anyone but a trained jurist to keep abreast of current law. That in turn meant that bishops and other prelates found it necessary to delegate many of their judicial responsibilities to specialized canonical courts presided over by legally trained judges who served at the pleasure of the appointing prelate. Once appointed, they frequently continued in office for years on end. The elaboration in those courts of a

---

2. Ridder-Symoens, "Training and Professionalization," 151–52.

3. Brand, *Origins of the English Legal Profession*, 148–57; Trusen, "Advocatus"; Smail, *Consumption of Justice*, 12.

complicated canonical procedure that only those with special skills and knowledge could readily negotiate produced a growing demand for the services of systematically trained canonists. In 1231, the emperor Frederick II (1197–1250) observed that advocates had become "not so much useful as necessary" in litigation conducted under the procedural rules of the *ius commune*.[4] University law faculties had recently emerged not only to supply systematic training in the increasingly complex mysteries of the law, but also to certify that recognized experts had tested the students to whom they awarded law degrees and had found them competent.

When university-trained canonists began to carve out a specialized occupational domain for themselves as members of a new social elite, experienced practitioners began to pass on bits of sage advice, tricks of the trade, to up-and-coming juniors in the form of how-to-do-it manuals for practitioners in church courts. These handbooks dealt not only with procedure, as earlier *ordines iudiciarii* had done, but also advised advocates on such matters as appropriate dress, decorum, courtroom etiquette, litigation tactics, and other professional lore.[5] None of this had been available — at least not in writing — around 1150 when Gratian completed his famous textbook, or even by 1216, when Tancred finished his *Ordo iudiciarius*.

By the middle of the thirteenth century, trained canonists and civilians had become a visibly privileged group among the social and political elite of western Europe. The speed with which this happened reflects the attention that canonists had begun to pay to Roman law. Roman sources provided canonists with a model for a system of providing legal services that they adapted to their own situation and circumstances. Among the many ancient practices that had fallen out of use during the early Middle Ages was the process by which judges formally admitted advocates to practice in their courts. Twelfth-century writers occasionally noted that Roman courts had required advocates to take an oath of office and have their names entered on a register before they could begin to practice, but added that this no longer happened.[6] By the beginning of the 1230s, we begin to find councils and other church authorities insisting that canonical judges had not merely the power, but a duty, to control the admission and exclu-

4. *Liber Augustalis* 1.83, at 257: "Advocatorum officium, qui dubia dirimunt facta causarum, non tam utile quam necessarium reputantes."

5. William Durand remarked briefly about the history of this literature in *Speculum iudiciale*, proem. §7, while Johannes Andreae expanded on the topic in his *Additiones* to Durand's proem. v. *plurimis* and 1.4 *De aduocato*, pr., at 1:4–5, 259; see also Nörr, "Literatur zum gemeinen Zivilprozess," 391.

6. Cod. 2.7.13; cf. Dig. 3.1.6, 7, and 9; André Gouron, "Le rôle de l'avocat," 14.

sion of advocates and proctors in their courts. Conciliar canons beginning in 1231 demanded that men admitted to practice in church courts pledge that they would abide by certain basic standards of behavior in the practice of their occupation.[7] They found many of those standards described in the Roman calumny oath, and incorporated them, sometimes verbatim, into their canons.

When judges tried to define the kinds of behavior that they expected from advocates who practiced in their courts, they, too, borrowed their criteria from Roman sources. They likewise adopted the practice of maintaining a record in their court archives of those to whom they had granted the right of audience. Individual courts added further rules and statutes of their own. Judges thus commenced to establish a rudimentary disciplinary system tailored to meet problems that arose in their courts.

Qualifications for Admission

FORMAL REQUIREMENTS

A list of formal qualifications required of those who wished to plead in church courts on behalf of others appears, as mentioned above, in the vulgate version of Gratian's Decretum. Every item on Gratian's list came from Roman sources.[8]

Advocates and proctors were expected to be men of good moral character who behaved honestly and with personal integrity. They had a greater obligation than other people to conduct themselves conscientiously and with the utmost probity, lest their misdeeds bring the judicial system into disrepute. They must not charge exorbitantly for their services or bargain with their clients for a share in the proceeds of litigation. Nor should they needlessly prolong litigation.[9]

Academic commentators elaborated on these criteria, adding further explanations and qualifications to the statements that Gratian cited.[10] They occasionally expanded on his lists of disabilities, especially the provi-

---

7. Tancred, *Ordo iudiciarius* 1.5.2, at 112; William Durand, *Speculum iudiciale* 1.4 *De aduocato* 1.3 §12, at 1:261; Council of Rouen (1231) c. 45, in Mansi 23:218–19; Council of Château-Gontier (1231) c. 35, in *Conciles de la province de Tours*, 154–55.

8. Gratian C. 3 q. 7 d.p.c. 1 and c. 2 §§1–2; Dig. 3.1.1.3, 5–6, 3.1.2, and 5.1.12.2. Gratian quoted a few passages verbatim, but paraphrased many others.

9. C. 3 q. 7 c. 2 §§8–10; see also Dilcher, "Juristisches Berufsethos," 100–102.

10. Notably in the *Summa Parisiensis*, 121–22. Rolandus barely commented at all on C. 3 q. 7, while the discussions of it by Stephen of Tournai and Rufinus are very sketchy.

sions that forbade heretics, excommunicates, and non-Christians to serve as advocates or proctors in church courts, and noted that Gratian had elsewhere mentioned provisions that forbade monks, clerics in major orders, bishops, and other prelates to serve as advocates save in certain limited situations.[11] Subsequent conciliar canons and papal decretals further amplified these prohibitions.[12]

EDUCATIONAL REQUIREMENTS

Notably missing from Gratian's discussion of the qualifications of advocates and proctors was any mention of minimal educational standards. Regulations prescribing specific standards of training began to appear during the second quarter of the thirteenth century—that is, around the same time that university law faculties began to establish fixed curricula for law degrees The Council of Tours in 1236 and the Council of Langeais in 1255, for example, insisted that advocates in the court of a bishop's official must either have studied law for at least three years or show the equivalent in practical experience, since, as the council fathers observed, the ignorance of advocates and scribes caused serious problems in the conduct of litigation.[13] In England during the provincial Council of Lambeth in 1281, Archbishop Pecham (r. 1279–92) had harsh words for the half-educated lawyers who swarmed the courts, and he deplored the numerous problems that ill-prepared practitioners created for judges and litigants alike. Although St. James had advised Christians to be swift to hear but slow to speak (James 1:19) and the school of Pythagoras had required its students to listen silently for five years before they began to teach, the council declared that

---

11. Thus, e.g., *Summa "Elegantius"* 6.68 and 14.76, at 2:134, 4:92; Tancred, *Ordo iudiciarius* 1.5.2, at 111; Ricardus Anglicus, *Distinctiones* to C. 3 q. 7 d. p. c. 1, in London, BL, MS Royal 10.C.III, at 17v: "Remouetur quis a postulatione—per constitutiones—qui non fuit orthodoxe religionis, ut C. e. Nemo [Cod. 2.6.8]," and "Remouetur quis a postulatione—per constitutiones—monachi et clericis, ut C. de episcopis et c. l. repetita [Cod. 1.3.40(41)]; xvi. q. i. De presentium, sine nonnulli [C. 16 q. 2 c. 20 and 25]." Accursius noted that although advocates must be Catholics, this did not mean that they needed to be trained theologians; it was sufficient that they were baptized and in communion with Rome (*Glos. ord.* to Cod. 1.4.15 v. *mysteriis*).

12. 3 Lat. (1179) c. 12, in *DEC* 1:218, as well as 1 Comp. 1.28.1 and X 1.37.1; 4 Lat. (1215) c. 3, ed. García y García, 49, as well as 4 Comp. 5.5.2 and X 5.7.13; Innocent III, *Vergentis in senium*, in 3 Comp. 5.4.1 and X 5.7.10 (Po. 643), and *Ex parte tua*, in 3 Comp. 3.38.3 and X 1.37.2 (Po. 2712).

13. Council of Tours (1236), 159, c. 3, as well as Mansi 23:411–12; Council of Langeais (1255) c. 15, in *Conciles de la province de Tours*, 222.

[a] great many advocates nowadays do not follow this prudent discipline, but rather after having heard [lectures on] barely half of one law book they arrogate to themselves the task of pleading publicly in canonical cases. And because they know not the truth of the law, they merely turn themselves into horrible deceivers and disrupters of judicial processes.

The council accordingly required advocates to show that they had studied canon and civil law for a minimum of three years before they could be admitted to practice in church courts.[14]

Later jurists considered three years of legal study inadequate and sought to raise this minimum educational standard. Civilians in the early thirteenth century maintained that judges should not grant an advocate the right of audience unless he could show at least five years of academic preparation, as Justinian had prescribed.[15] By the end of the thirteenth century, some church authorities and canonists had come around to the same view. Archbishop Winchelsey (r. 1293–1313) in his 1295 statutes for the Court of Arches, the appeals court of the province of Canterbury, required advocates there to have studied Roman and canon law at a university for five years before admission to practice. Henry Burghersh, bishop of Lincoln (r. 1320–40), in the 1334 statutes for his consistory court went even further: he demanded six years of university study plus an additional year as a pupil observing the conduct of court cases.[16] William Lyndwood (b ca. 1375, d. 1446) in his gloss on the Lambeth canon disparaged the three-year requirement:

> I do not see [he complained] what moved the legislator to the shorter time requirement, unless perhaps he had in mind some advocate in petty and inferior courts, where important affairs are not at issue, but only minor matters. In those courts someone with just three years of practical and academic experience might be adequate to handle cases, as provided here. And Cod. 3.1.17 supports this. In the greater courts, where difficult cases are tried, more knowledgeable advocates are required, as in Cod. 2.27.24.[17]

14. Council of Lambeth (1281) c. 26, in Powicke & Cheney 2:917–18.

15. Cod. 2.7.24.4; Azo, *Summa super Codicem*, 29, to Cod. 2.7; Accursius, *Glos. ord.* to Dig. 50.13.1 v. *quoquo*; Gouron, "Le rôle de l'avocat," 17–18.

16. Statutes of Archbishop Winchelsey (9 November 1295) §8, in Logan, *Medieval Court of Arches*, 7–8; Henry Burghersh, *Statuta consistorii episcopalis Lincolniensis*, 572, §3.

17. Lyndwood, *Provinciale* 1.17. 2 v. *per triennium*, 76: "Nec video quid moveret statuentem ad limitationem minoris temporis, nisi intelligas hoc, ut scil. aliquis advocet in Curiis pedaneis et inferioribus, ubi non tractantur causae graves, sed modici ponderis;

Lyndwood specified in addition that would-be advocates should have done legal studies at a university and must prove this with either a letter from the teachers with whom they had studied or a certificate of attendance from the university chancellor.[18]

Although academic jurists generally agreed that five years spent in the formal study of law were essential before an advocate was admitted to practice, it is not clear how many judges insisted upon this. By the late fourteenth century, however, it was not unusual to find a substantial proportion of the advocates in bishops' consistories described in court records as *magistri*, which normally signified that they had spent at least some years at a university.[19]

Observers were sometimes skeptical about how adequately academic study of the law by itself prepared novice advocates for practice in the courts. All too many students, according to Martinus de Fano (fl. ca. 1255–72),

> simply take in the words but lack the necessary understanding, whence it happens that when they return from the schools, stuffed full of learning, they encounter the day-to-day progress of a case as if it were in Greek or Armenian. They enter their pleas ahead of time or frame their arguments clumsily or deal with matters in the wrong order or seek inappropriate remedies or mix up the normal judicial process or fail to enter their exceptions and citations at the appropriate time.[20]

---

in talibus namque sufficere videtur quod aliquis sit exercitatus in Causis, et habeat Practicam cum Speculativa per triennium, ut hic. Et facit ad hoc C. de judiciis, l. certi juris [Cod. 3.1.17]. In curiis tamen majoribus, et in quibus tractantur arduae causae, opus est in Advocatis major scientia, ut d. l. jubemus, cum concor." On Lyndwood, see Cheney, "William Lyndwood's *Provinciale*," and Ferme, *Canon Law in Late Medieval England*.

18. Lyndwood, *Provinciale* 1.17 De *postulando* v. *advocatus, audiverit, testimonio*, 74, 76. This again recalls Roman practice (Cod. 2.7.11.2).

19. See e.g. Renardy, *Le monde des maîtres*, 232–35; Walter de Stapeldon, *Register*, 116–19, and Brundage, "Bar of the Ely Consistory Court," 543–47. One point that William Durand listed among the objections that an advocate might bring forward to disqualify opposing counsel was that, however experienced the opponent might be in practice, he lacked the required legal education. Durand dismissed this as a weak argument: "Sed nunc admittitur eius patrocinium, licet inter aduocatos non connumeretur." Johannes Andreae noted in his *Additio* to this passage that in Venice he had even heard advocates making their arguments in the vernacular, a practice that he obviously considered shocking (William Durand, *Speculum iudiciale* 1.4 De *aduocato* 1.11, at 1:261).

20. Martinus de Fano, *Ordo iudiciarius*, prol., 1: "Quoniam plerique causam principalem iuris civilis nec non et canonici nescientes effectum eius scire non possunt et,

Nicholas de Tudeschis (1386–1445), better known as Panormitanus, writing more than a century later, voiced a similar complaint. "Nowadays," he observed, "many improperly thrust themselves into this advocacy business."[21] Bishop Burchard III of Halberstadt felt much the same, and Andrea Alciato (d. 1550) was still grumbling about the problem in the sixteenth century.[22]

Proctors seldom had as much formal training in law as advocates. Those who practiced in lower-ranking church courts sometimes began their careers as clerks or apprentices to established practitioners, while others started as court clerks or functionaries. In either case, proctors typically learned their trade primarily through practical experience and observation. A good many proctors had also qualified as notaries public and practiced in that capacity before they moved into the ranks of the proctors.[23]

Proctors in the busier and more prestigious courts, by contrast, fre-

---

cum longo insudarunt studio, sua subiiciunt corpora non utilitati alicui, sed labori, dum verba simpliciter ruminant et intellectum necessarium non adunant, unde evenit, quod a scholis pro sapientibus redeuntes ipsam causam, scilicet principalem cotidianum cursum causarum, velut Graecum vel Armenicum arbitrantes propere vel praemature preces exponunt vel inepte intentiones concipiunt vel praepostere causas agunt vel incolorate restitui petunt vel inordinate solitum ordinem iudiciorum componunt vel exceptiones et iuris pertinentia congruo tempore non allegant. " Martinus de Fano's *Ordo* was a lightly revised version of the early thirteenth-century *ordo Ad summariam notitiam*. Similar statements appear in the preface to Walter of Cornut, *Ordo iudiciarius "Scientiam,"* 1, and Aegidius de Fuscarariis, *Ordo iudiciarius*, proem., 1–2.

21. Panormitanus, *Commentaria* to X 1.37 pr. §2, at 2:178ra: "Item quaero, numquid illiteratus possit esse aduocatus? Conclude quod non, quinimo oportet quod sit iureperitus, unde debet saltem studuisse per quinquennium, et iuramento doctorum esse approbatus, ut in l. nemini, C. de aduoc. diuer. iudi. [Cod. 2.7.11]; notat. Bartolus in d. l. 1; et hoc bene nota, quia multi iniuste se ingerant huic aduocationis officio." Panormitanus's passage in fact reproduces Bartolus's statement almost word for word.

22. Burchard III von Werberge, *Judicialis processus reformacio ordinaria servanda* §30, in Hilling, "Sechs Gerichtsordnungen," 336; Alciato, *Iudiciarius processus compendium atque iuris utriusque praxis*, at 62v.

23. Helmholz, *Marriage Litigation*, 147–49; Pedersen, *Marriage Disputes*, 98–100. It was apparently the rule for proctors to practice as notaries public in the ecclesiastical courts at York in the fourteenth and fifteenth centuries and was commonly true at Ely as well (see Brundage, "Bar of the Ely Consistory Court," 548–54; York, Borthwick Institute D/C AB3, at 20r; Dasef, "Lawyers of the York Curia," 33–34; Ritchie, *Ecclesiastical Courts of York*, 53). The situation in the *bailliage* of Senlis closely resembled that at York (Guenée, *Tribunaux et gens de justice*, 205–6).

quently had at least some university training in law. Bishop Burghersh, for instance, required proctors in the Lincoln consistory to have devoted four years to university study of canon law, in addition to having practical experience in the courts before they were formally admitted. Some proctors, particularly those who appeared regularly in appellate courts, held the licentiate or doctorate, while a good many more had received the J.C.B.[24]

Proctors who worked regularly at the papal curia for a stable of clients (they are often described as standing proctors) were likely to have advanced law degrees. It is not surprising to discover that the numbers of those with academic credentials increased substantially between the middle of the thirteenth and the end of the fourteenth century. Among the half-dozen proctors affiliated with the English hospice in Rome during the closing decades of the fourteenth century, for example, three were doctors of one or both laws, and one was a bachelor of civil law. The academic qualifications of the remaining two are unknown.[25] A constitution of Pope Martin V (r. 1417–31) in 1418 required proctors who appeared before the Audientia litterarum contradictarum and other papal tribunals to possess law degrees as well as experience in the practice of the courts.[26] A brisk increase in the volume of litigation at the curia, coupled with strong demand for favors (such as benefices and dispensations) that curial proctors could procure for their clients, produced a lively market for their services by the late fourteenth century. In addition, curial proctors were well placed to secure prestigious posts in the papal administration for themselves, above and beyond the opportunities for enrichment that practice provided. Ambitious men and their families, especially those who already enjoyed some connections in curial circles, had ample incentive to invest the time, effort, and resources required to secure entrée into the proctors' branch of the profession.

24. Donahue, introduction to *Select Cases*, 23; Gramsch, *Erfurter Juristen*, 516–18; Sayers, *Papal Judges Delegate*, 223–38; Brentano, *Two Churches*, 41 n. 136.

25. Heckel, "Aufkommen der ständigen Prokuratoren," 315–21; Stelzer, "Beiträge," 113–38; Brentano, *Two Churches*, 12–49. On improving academic credentials, see, e.g., the lists in Sayers, "Proctors Representing British Interests"; Zutshi, "Proctors Acting for English Petitioners"; Linehan, "Proctors Representing Spanish Interests," and "Spanish Litigants and Their Agents"; as well as Herde, *Beiträge*, 125–48. On the proctors at the English hospice, Harvey, *The English in Rome*, 149–52; Jacob, *Essays in Later Medieval History*, 58–78.

26. Martin V, *In apostolica dignitatis specula* §33, in Tangl, *Päpstlichen Kanzleiordnungen*, 143–44.

Admissions Examinations

Prospective advocates and proctors faced the additional hurdle of passing an admissions examination. Judges, of course, had long exercised the right to question those who sought the right of audience, but by the thirteenth century admissions examinations in some jurisdictions were becoming routine. In his *Liber Augustalis* (1231), Frederick II directed his judges or justiciars to examine would-be advocates who wished to practice in the courts of his Sicilian realm. An ordinance of Alfonso III of Aragon (1286–91), adopted by the Cortes of Montso in 1289, similarly provided that advocates in his kingdom must be examined and found competent before they could take up their duties.[27] In Germany, too, church courts established examining boards. At Würzburg the examiners of applicants for admission as advocates included the provost of the cathedral, the bishop's official, and three archdeacons, while at Bamberg the vicar-general of the bishop and the dean of the cathedral tested candidates for admission to practice on their knowledge of law, procedure, and the practices of the local court. The tribunals of the papal curia adopted similar, and often more demanding, standards.[28]

Admissions Procedure

Formal admission of advocates and proctors to practice invariably centered (as modern bar admissions ceremonies still do) on the swearing of an oath. When a candidate took the oath of office, he solemnly promised that he would observe a set of ethical norms in dealing with the court and with his clients. Taking this oath officially conferred upon the candidate the right of audience that entitled him to plead before the court on behalf of clients. As an advocate or proctor, he became an officer of the court. The unstated implication was that the presiding judge had the power to impose disciplinary sanctions upon him should he violate the terms of his pledge.

THE CALUMNY OATH

Authority for the formal pledge required of advocates and proctors ultimately went back to late Roman antiquity. The admissions oath in medieval ecclesiastical courts borrowed much of its substance from the calumny

---

27. Cod. 2.7.11.1; *Liber Augustalis* 1.83, at 257; *Constitucions y altres drets de Catalunya* 2.6.1, at 1:174.

28. Trusen, "Advocatus," 1243–44; Martin V, *In apostolice dignitatis specula* §§15, 17–19, 30, and *Romani pontificis providentia* §26, in Tangl, *Päpstlichen Kanzleiordnungen*, 139–40, 155–56.

oath that was originally devised, as we have seen, to discourage vexatious lawsuits. It disappeared from the litigation records in the West sometime after the middle of the sixth century, but commenced to reappear in court records early in the eleventh century.[29] The circumstances surrounding the oath's reemergence are obscure, the documentary evidence is sparse, and the development is not easy to explain.[30] A revival of knowledge about and interest in Justinian's Institutes, in which in two passages refer to the use of the calumny oath, is attested around this period and may perhaps help to account for the oath's abrupt comeback.[31] It is clear in any event that shortly after the turn of the first millennium, courts in the north of Italy and the south of France occasionally began to require parties to litigation to take the oath *de calumnia vitanda*. By the mid-twelfth century, it was becoming a normal feature of civil procedure in these regions.[32]

By 1125, some ecclesiastical courts had also begun to require litigants to take the calumny oath. The legal advisers of Pope Honorius II (r. 1124–30), for example, debated whether bishops needed to take the oath when they were parties to a lawsuit, and scattered references to the oath appear in other papal documents from time to time during the mid-twelfth century. Honorius' successor, Innocent II (r. 1130–43), authorized an annual subsidy to Roman judges and advocates, in return for which he required the advocates to take an oath that they would not bring malicious or baseless cases to court and would not demand fees from their clients for cases that they judged worthy enough to pursue.[33] Specific references to use of the calumny oath, like many other technical features of Roman civil procedure, are absent from the vulgate version of Gratian's Decretum. This implies that its use had not yet become a regular feature of canonical procedural law by the 1140s when the final redaction of its text was finished.[34]

29. Ficker, *Forschungen* 1:56, 58, 4:64, no. 43; 67–68, no. 46; and 74–75, no. 51; Engelmann, *History of Continental Civil Procedure*, 419–21, 429, 434, 436.

30. Vaccari, *Diritto longobardo e letteratura longobardistica*, and Trifone, *Diritto romano comune e diritti particolari nell'Italia meridionale*.

31. Inst. 2.23.12 and 4.16.1; Lange, *Römisches Recht im Mittelalter*, 85–86; Stein, *Roman Law in European History*, 55–56.

32. Poly, "Les maîtres de Saint-Ruf," 202.

33. X 2.7.1 (1 Comp. 1.35[34].2; JL 7401); X 2.7.2 (1 Comp 1.35.3; JL 9654); Fried, "Römische Kurie und die Anfänge der Proceßliteratur," 168; Boso, *Vitae Romanorum pontificum*, in *Liber pontificalis*, ed. Duchesne, 2:383–84; see also Hirschfeld, "Gerichtswesen der Stadt Rom," 513–14.

34. Winroth, *Making of Gratian's Decretum*, 156–57. Gratian's treatment of procedural law was relatively brief, perhaps because he was not much interested in it, or

Around the time of the completion of the vulgate Decretum, however, John of Salisbury mentioned in his *Policraticus* (completed by 1159) that in ecclesiastical courts,

> [a]dvocates, in order to make the investigation more searching, are constrained to [seek] truth and fidelity from the beginning of the trial [*contestatio litis*] by an oath in which they swear that with all their strength and resources, omitting no effort that they can muster, they will seek to secure what is true and just for their clients, and that they will not attempt through their efforts to prolong trials.[35]

John's words in this passage are simply a lightly edited quotation from the passage in Justinian's Code that required advocates to take the calumny oath at the outset of each trial in which they appeared.[36]

The *Summa "Elegantius in iure diuino,"* written roughly a decade later than the *Policraticus*, maintained that clerics could be required to take the calumny oath only in civil cases that did not involve tithes and similar matters.[37] The author of the *Summa "Elegantius"* also mentioned in a different context that the law had formerly required advocates to swear that they would do their utmost to persuade their clients to seek only what was right and just and further that they themselves would not represent clients in frivolous cases based on bad law—again a summary of provisions in the calumny oath.[38] By about 1190, when Bernard of Pavia composed his *Summa decretalium*, use of the calumny oath had become sufficiently routine that he devoted a whole title to it, as he also did in his decretal collection, the *Breviarium extravagantium*.[39]

---

perhaps because practices in the courts were still fluid when the vulgate version of the Decretum appeared (Jacoby, "Prozeß im Decretum Gratiani," 280–81).

35. John of Salisbury, *Policracticus* 5.13, at 1:340: "Sed et ipsi patroni causarum, quo fidelior possit esse examinatio, ab ipsa contestatione litis iuramento artantur ad ueritatem et fidem, iurantes quod, cum omni uirtute sua omnique ope quod iustum et uerum existimauerint clientibus suis inferre procurabunt, nichil studii relinquentes prout cuique possibile est et quod ex industria sua non protrahent lites."

36. Cod. 3.1.14.4: "Patroni [autem] causarum . . . [sacrosanctis evangeliis tactis iuramentum praestent,] quod omni [quidem] virtute sua omnique ope quod iustum et verum existimaverint clientibus suis inferre [procurent,] nihil studii relinquentes, [quod sibi] possibile est."

37. *Summa "Elegantius"* 9.44a, at 3:71. The author based this passage on the decretal *Inherentes*, 1 Comp. 1.35.2 (= X 2.7.1; JL 7401).

38. *Summa "Elegantius"* 6.18, at 2:112–13; the ancient law referred to is Cod. 3.1.14.4.

39. *Summa decretalium* 1.34.5, at 31; 1 Comp. 1.35 (34).

Procedural writers at the beginning of the thirteenth century occasionally referred, much as John of Salisbury had done, to advocates swearing at the outset of the trial proper (*litis contestatio*) that the case they were about to present had merit and was not intended simply to harass the other party.[40] They did this, however, as spokesmen on behalf of clients in a particular case, not as a general prerequisite for the exercise of their occupation.

THE ADMISSIONS OATH

During the latter part of the twelfth century, Pisa began to require that advocates who wished to practice in the municipal courts of the city swear an oath before they received the right of audience. As early as 1162, the consuls of the city decreed that advocates (except for communal officials and clerics) who appeared in the town's courts must swear this oath in terms prescribed by the statute within the forty days next following the first of January. This admissions oath, which differed substantially from the form of the calumny oath used in Pisa at this time, required Pisan advocates to swear that they would not harm their opponents by fraudulently protracting the cases in which they appeared.[41] They also had to promise that they would limit their fees to the amounts fixed in a sliding scale that proportioned fees to the value of the property at issue. Two years later, another consular decree required advocates to add to their earlier oath a promise that they would not withdraw from cases without adequate cause and that they would accept the case of any litigant who was unable to find another advocate and was able to pay the prescribed *honorarium*.[42]

Hints that church authorities were thinking along similar lines began to crop up in the French kingdom and Normandy early in the thirteenth century. At councils in Paris (1212) and Rouen (1216), the papal legate Robert Courson demanded that advocates and proctors reject clients whose cases

---

40. Thus, e.g., Bencivenne ["Pillius"], writing shortly after 1198, *Ordo iudiciorum* 3.3.3, at 52–53. Tancred, in turn, drew upon this in his *Ordo iudiciarius* 3.2.4, at 204–5.

41. The municipal law of Pisa in the mid-twelfth century drew heavily on Roman law as Wickham shows in *Legge, pratiche e conflitti*, 196–217; on the consuls see also Storti Storchi, *Intorno ai Costituti pisani*, 115–18. The Pisan form of the calumny oath appears in the *Constitutum usus* §10; for the text, see Storti Storchi, *Intorno ai Costituti pisani*, 134 n. 492.

42. *Statuti inediti della città di Pisa* 1:7; Pisa, *Statuti* (1164), ed. Bonaini, 1:25–26. The practice of limiting fees was apparently similar in Florence, where advocates' fees are said to have averaged about 7 percent of the amount at issue in a case (Davidsohn, *Storia di Firenze* 4/2: 226; but see Martines, *Lawyers and Statecraft*, 100–101).

they deemed frivolous, unjust, or unfounded. Lawyers, he maintained, had a duty to inquire into their clients' bona fides before they agreed to advise or represent them. A canon of the Council of Melun in 1216 likewise commanded that "advocates hereafter take the calumny oath, both in cases already under way and those just beginning, or else they may not be allowed to participate in them."[43]

The oaths of admission that began to come into use in thirteenth-century ecclesiastical courts, unlike those prescribed earlier at Pisa, drew a substantial part of their content from Justinian's version of the calumny oath. When an advocate took the calumny oath that appeared in Justinian's Code, he made four promises:

1. that he would use all his strength and resources, knowledge and skill to procure what was right and just for his client;
2. that he would not accept any case that he believed was improper, desperate, or based on false allegations;
3. that if he discovered during the course of litigation that he had accepted a flawed case, he would at once withdraw from it; and
4. that he would not permit the abandoned client to seek the assistance of another advocate.[44]

Each of these undertakings would appear in the admissions oaths adopted by thirteenth-century ecclesiastical courts.

Church courts first began to require advocates and proctors to swear admissions oaths during the 1230s. The earliest clear evidence appears in the canons of two church councils held in 1231, one at Rouen in Normandy, the other at Château-Gontier, in the County of Maine.[45] Both councils adopted canons that required advocates who wished to practice in local

---

43. Council of Paris (1212), pt. 1, c. 6, and Council of Rouen (1214), c. 6, in Mansi 22:820–21, 900; also Baldwin, *Masters, Princes, and Merchants* 1:195; Council of Melun (1216) c. 1, in Mansi 22:1087: "Statuimus ut advocati jurent de calumnia de cetero, in causis tam inchoatis quam inchoandis, aut non admittantur ad eas tractandus."

44. Summarized from Cod. 3.1.14.4. A mnemonic verse that encapsulated the contents of the oath was circulating among law students by 1227 and appears in Accursius's *Glos. ord.* to Auth. coll. 9 c. 5 (= Nov. 124.1) in Cod. 2.58(59).2 v. *existimat*: "Istud iuretur, quod lis sibi iusta videtur, / Et si quaeritur, verum non inficietur;/ Nil promittetur, nec falso probatio detur, / Ut lis tardetur, dilatio nulla petetur."

45. Provincial Council of Rouen (1231) c. 48, in Mansi 23:218–19, and in Martène and Durand, *Thesaurus novus anecdotorum* 4:181–82 (see also Kay, "Mansi and Rouen," 171, and Cuillieron, "Un concile de réformation," 363); Council of Château-Gontier (1231) c. 35, in *Conciles de la province de Tours*, 154–55; also in Mansi 23:240–41.

church courts to swear that they would faithfully observe a set of obligations toward the court and toward their clients. The texts of the two oaths resemble one another and each drew elements from the calumny oath. The council fathers outlined in these oaths what they considered the essential duties of an ecclesiastical advocate. These oaths define the ethical aspirations and duties of a legal profession that was beginning to take shape in several different regions around the same time.

The Rouen canon required every advocate to promise

1. that he would perform his duties faithfully;
2. that he would not present unjust or hopeless cases;
3. that he would not steal his client's documents or cause them to be purloined;
4. that he would not knowingly or maliciously raise false or groundless exceptions against an opponent;
5. that he would not put forward perjured testimony or forged documents;
6. that he would not unduly prolong litigation;
7. that he would not conceal from the judge his opinion about the truth of matters at issue;
8. that if he came to believe that his case was defective he would consult with the proctors;
9. that he would personally prepare or have prepared the complaint (*libellus*) and the record of court proceedings (*acta*).[46]

The Château-Gontier text began with a preamble that stated explicitly that no advocate who customarily received fees could enjoy the right of audience until he took the admissions oath. The council then required the advocate to swear

---

46. "Jurabit autem unusquisque advocatus se fideliter facturum officium suum, et quod injustas causas seu desperatas contra conscientiam suam non sustinebit, nec instrumenta partis suae subtrahi vel subtrahi faciet, nec exceptionibus falsis, quod sciat, seu per malitiam excogitatis utetur, nec procurabit quod falsitates vel subreptiones, seu falsa instrumenta in causa sua producantur; et quod causam clientuli sui quantum credet quod faciat ad utilitatem ipsius clientuli, non prorogabit: et quod de eis quae in curia facta fuerint, de quibus a judicibus requisitus fuerit, veritatem secundum credulitatem suam non tacebit: quod si se crediderit causae suae insufficientem, cum procuratoribus consilium habebit; et quod libellum et acta in causis susceptis fideliter pro posse suo conficiet manu propria, vel ea, si scribere nesciverit, vel noluerit, scribi faciet."

1. that he would not knowingly present an unjust case;
2. that after taking the calumny oath or the oath to tell the truth, he would not propose dilatory or peremptory exceptions in order to harass his opponent;
3. that he would not advise his client to pursue a vexatious course of action, either before or after the publication of testimony or at any time during the proceedings;
4. that he would neither suborn witnesses to perjure themselves nor cause them to be suborned;
5. that he would not allow his client to present false witnesses;
6. that should he discover that his client had done so, he would reveal this to the court;
7. that he would not leave the court before preparing a record of the day's proceedings and having it approved by the judge;
8. that he would serve his clients faithfully and as speedily as possible;
9. that he would not burden the judge with interlocutory motions that he believed would fail;
10. that he would serve the court honestly and preserve its honor.[47]

Admissions oaths enjoyed a sudden popularity in 1231, for in September of that same year the emperor Frederick II also prescribed an admissions oath for advocates in the royal and provincial courts of his kingdom of Sicily. This oath shared numerous features with those prescribed in the canons of the French and Norman councils. Advocates in the Sicilian courts were required to swear

1. that they would assist their clients truly, faithfully, and unwaveringly;
2. that they would not coach their clients on the facts;
3. that they would not plead any point of law against good conscience;

---

47. "Item, advocati, qui de consuetudine salarium receperint, nisi jurati de cetero, nullatenus admittantur. Forma juramenti talis existat, quod non fovebunt injustas causas scienter, neque proponent dilatorias, vel peremptorias malitiose post calumnie, vel de veritate dicenda sacramentum, neque instruent partem suam ad respondendum vel proponendum malitiose, nec post publicatas attestationes, vel in quacumque parte litis, neque ante juramentum testes subornabunt vel facient subornari, neque permettent, quod pars sua falsos testes producat, et si hoc sciverint, curie revelabunt, et quod in memoriis faciendis convenient bona fide, nec recedent a curia malitiose donec sit memoriale confectum et coram judice concessum, et quod partes, quam citius poterunt, expedient bona fide, nec onorabunt judicem interlocutoriis, credentes ipsos succumbere in eidem, et quod honorem servabunt curie, nec aliquam falsitatem in curia perpetrabunt."

4. that they would not accept hopeless cases;
5. that should they chance to accept a flawed case that had at first seemed plausible but turned out to lack merit in fact or in law, they would immediately withdraw their assistance and would not permit their former client to secure another advocate;
6. that they would not raise their fees during litigation;
7. that they would not seek contingent fees.[48]

The constitution further provided that advocates must not only swear this oath when they were first admitted to practice, but must also renew it annually. In addition, Frederick II's legislation included a penalty clause: an advocate who in any case, great or small, violated the undertakings in his oath became permanently *infamis*, with all the disabilities that this entailed, and might incur a fine of one pound of pure gold, payable to the royal treasury.[49]

Six years later, a papal legate to England, Cardinal Otto da Tenengo, decreed at a legatine council in London that advocates who wished to practice in the English Courts Christian must swear an admissions oath. The conciliar canon specified just two promises that they must make, namely,

1. that they would serve their clients faithfully and defend their interests by reason and law;
2. that they would neither coach their clients nor suborn perjury by their witnesses.[50]

48. *Liber Augustalis* 1.84, at 258: "Advocatus tam in curia nostra quam coram provinciarum iustitiariis statuendos necnon et per partes singulas regno nostri ante receptum officium tactis sacrosanctis evangeliis corporalia volumus sacramenta prestare, quod partes, quarum patrocinium susceperint, cum omni fide et veritate et sine tergiversatione aliqua adiuvare curabunt, ipsas de facto non instruent, contra veram conscientiam nullatenus allegabunt, et quod causas non recipient desperatas et, si quas forte receperint partis mendaciis forsitan coloratas, que in principio sibi iuste videntur et in processu iudicii de iure vel de facto comparuerint ipsis iniuste, ipsarum patrocinium in continenti dimittent, sprete parti, prout priscis legibus est statutum, licentia convolandi ad alterius patrocinium deneganda. Iurabunt etiam, quod augmentum salarii in processu iudicii non requirent nec de parte litis ineant pactiones."

49. *Liber Augustalis* 1.84, at 259.

50. Powicke & Cheney 1:258–59: "[Q]ui advocati officium voluerit generaliter promereri, apud dyocesanum cuius origine vel domicilio iurisdictionis existitit prebeat iuramentum quod in causis quarum patronus extiterit patrocinium fidele prestabit, non ad differendam vel auferendam alterius partis iustitiam, sed ad causam clientuli legibus defendendo et rationibus intendendo. . . . Caveant autem omnes advocati ne

Cardinal Otto's canon added further details that do not appear in the earlier texts. It explicitly distinguished, for one thing, between general advocates, who practiced on a continuing basis, and occasional advocates, who did so only from time to time. Any advocate who appeared in church courts for more than three legal terms must take the admissions oath, save under special circumstances. The text also stipulated that occasional advocates who appeared in cases concerning marriage or election to ecclesiastical office must take the oath each time they appeared. The 1237 canon added that an advocate who violated the terms of his oath should be suspended from office, as well as from any benefice he might hold, until he had made satisfaction. This canon further instructed judges who were not skilled in the law that, when doubtful about an issue that might have serious adverse consequences for either party, they should seek advice from an expert—and that the parties must bear the expense this involved.[51]

These four admissions oaths from the 1230s shared numerous provisions in common with the Roman calumny oath. The common ground between the admissions oaths of the church councils and the one that Frederick II prescribed, moreover, strongly suggests that their authors sought to revive late Roman ethical standards for professional advocates. The admissions oaths imply that the authors of these texts saw advocates (and perhaps some proctors) as an identifiable occupational group and demanded that its members observe a special set of ethical rules.

The prescriptions of the councils of Rouen, Château-Gontier, and London concerning the admission of advocates apparently addressed an issue that concerned church authorities elsewhere. A half-dozen councils and synods in England between 1238 and 1268 approved similar canons, while at least four French dioceses did the same.[52]

---

per se vel alios testes subornent vel partes instruant falsum ponere vel subprimere veritatem." In addition to the description of the council by Matthew Paris in Powicke & Cheney 1:241–44, see Williamson [Owen], "Some Aspects of the Legation of Cardinal Otto in England"; Sayers, *Papal Judges Delegate*, 32–34; Paravicini Bagliani, *Cardinali di curia* 1:79, 81–82, 86.

51. Powicke & Cheney 1:258–59.

52. In England: Worcester III (1240) c. 75; Salisbury II (ca. 1238–44) c. 58; Durham II (ca. 1241–49) c. 50.6; Chichester I (ca. 1245–52) c. 66; York I (ca. 1241–55) c. 36; Legatine Council of London (Cardinal Ottobuono de Fieschi, 1268) c. 26; in Powicke & Cheney 1:314–15, 386, 435, 465, 493, and 2:773. In France: statutes of Guiard de Laon, bishop of Cambrai (1238–48) c. 187, 189, in *Statuts de l'ancienne Province de Reims*, 63–64, subsequently adopted in the *Statuta antiqua* of Tournai, c. 21.3–4, in *Conciles de la*

Rules for the admission of advocates to practice in church courts remained a matter for local ecclesiastical authorities until the third session of the Second Council of Lyons in June 1274. The notion that the council should adopt a canon concerning the ethics of advocates in the church courts may have come directly from Pope Gregory X (r. 1271–76). The pope was concerned about flaws in the church's judicial administration and apparently believed that shortcomings of advocates and proctors were in part to blame for them. The pope's answer to the problem is embodied in the constitution *Properandum*, which Bishop William Durand staunchly supported and perhaps helped to draft.[53]

Properandum opens with a lament about the law's delays, for which it blamed the crafty machinations of lawyers.[54] The constitution proposed to remedy this by reviving an ancient practice that had fallen into disuse:

> We decree that each and every advocate who practices in the church courts, either at the Apostolic See or elsewhere, shall take an oath on the holy gospels that in all the ecclesiastical cases and others for which they assume or will assume the function of advocate in those courts they will use all their strength and resources to secure for their clients what they consider right and just, sparing no effort that they can muster for that purpose. Should they discover at any point in the proceedings, moreover, that the case they had accepted in good faith is unjust, they will no longer participate in it, but will abandon it altogether, will utterly cease to deal with the matter, and will faithfully observe the behavior prescribed for these situations. Proctors are likewise bound by a similar oath. Both advocates and proctors are also obliged to repeat this oath annually in the court in which they practice. Those who have not yet sworn such an oath must take a similar oath at the commencement of each and every case in which they function as an advocate or proctor at the Holy See or before the court of any other ecclesiastical judge. Let advocates and proctors who are unwilling to swear

---

province de Tours, 349; Council of Langeais (1255) c. 15, in *Conciles de la province de Tours*, 222; *Privilegia curie Remensis* (1269), 12.

53. Lefebvre, "La constitution *Properandum*," in *1274, année charnière*, 525–27; William Durand, *Speculum iudiciale* 1.1 *De legato* 4.9, at 1:34; but see also Boyle, "Date of the Commentary of William Duranti," 40. On the council's procedure and the date of *Properandum*, see Kuttner, "Conciliar Law in the Making," 43 and 50.

54. It is surely no coincidence that the opening clause of the canon is identical with the opening clause of Justinian's constitution of 530 on reform of the law courts (Cod. 3.1.13).

as aforesaid know that so long as they refuse to do so they are barred from the performance of their functions.[55]

Properandum further set a cap on legal fees: it forbade advocates to accept payment of more than twenty and proctors more then twelve *livres tournois* for their labor on any case, including any bonus (*palmarium*) that they might receive if they were successful.

Twenty *livres tournois* was not a trivial sum. It substantially exceeded the annual income of about a third of the rural clergy in southern France at the beginning of the fourteenth century, for example, and was far more than the yearly earnings of most peasant families in the diocese of Narbonne. Should any client pay more than this, the advocate was bound to return the surplus.[56] The constitution concluded with a series of penalty clauses. Ad-

---

55. My translation of 2 Lyons (1274) c. 19 from *DEC* 1:324–25: "[S]tatuimus ut omnes et singuli advocationis officium in foro ecclesiastico sive apud sedem apostolicam sive alibi exercentes, praestent, tactis sacrosanctis evangeliis, iuramentum quod, in omnibus causis ecclesiasticis et aliis in eodem foro tractandis, quarum assumpserunt patrocinium vel assument, omni virtute sua omnique ope id quod verum et iustum existimaverint, suis clientulis inferre procurent, nihil in hoc studii, quod eis sit possibile, relinquentes, quodque in quacunque parte iudicii eis innotuerit improbam fore causam, quam in sua fide receperant, amplius non patrocinabuntur eidem, immo ab ea omnino recedent, a communione illius se penitus separantes, reliquis quae circa haec sunt in eadem sanctione statuta, inviolabiliter observandis. Procuratores insuper iuramento simili astringantur. Huiusmodi quoque iuramentum tam advocati quam procuratores in foro, in quo idem assumpserunt officium, teneantur annis singulis iterare. Qui vero ad eamdem sedem veniunt vel ad curiam cuiuslibet ecclesiastici iudicis, in qua nondum tale praestiterant iuramentum, accedunt, in aliquibus singularibus causis patrocinium vel procurationis ministerium praestituri, praestent in singulis causis eisdem, mota controversia, simile iuramentum. Advocati autem et procuratores, qui iuxta praedictam formam iurare noluerint, executionem officiorum suorum, huiusmodi noluntate durante, sibi noverint interdictam" See also Roberg, *Das Zweite Konzil von Lyon*, 314–16; Fournier, "Gloses et commentaries sur les constitutions de Grégoire X," in his *Questions d'histoire du droit canonique*, 26.

56. William Durand, *Speculum iudiciale* 1.4 *De salariis* §3.3, at 1:347–48. Panormitanus disagreed, but failed to cite the provision in *Properandum* (*Commentaria* to X 3.49.5, vol. 5, at 285va–vb). For comparative incomes and wages, see Cheyette, *Ermengard of Narbonne*, 303–5. In England, the minimum wage for perpetual vicars was 5 marks sterling (£3 6s. 8d.), or 800 pence (Powicke & Cheney 1:112–13). This was barely enough to live on, given that the basic subsistence wage in London by the reign of Edward I has been calculated at 3 pence per day, or nearly 1,100 pence per year (Epstein, *Wage Labor and Guilds*, 113). Since the *livre tournois* in the late thirteenth century generally traded for approximately 80 shillings, or 960 pence, an advocate's maximum fee for a single

vocates who violated the terms of the admissions oath, in addition to incurring the usual penalties for perjury, together with the wrath of God and the pope, might also have to repay double the fees they had received from their clients and make restitution for any damages that their clients' opponents may have suffered. Advocates guilty of contravening the oath, moreover, could be suspended from practice for three years, while guilty proctors were permanently banned from representing clients in the law courts.

The ceiling that *Properandum* set on fees, stirred up deep and troublesome distress (*summa et gravissima perturbatio*) among the curial advocates at Rome, according to William Durand's commentary on the constitutions of the Second Council of Lyons. The dismay of the advocates may well account for the curious fact that this was the only canon of the council that Boniface VIII (who had himself worked as a canon lawyer for forty years before he became pope) omitted from the Liber Sextus.[57]

Attempts to resist the provisions of *Properandum* proved futile. Shortly after the council adjourned, local authorities in many regions commenced to put them into practice. William Wickwane, the new archbishop of York (r. 1279–85), for example, ordered his official-principal to make sure that the advocates in his consistory court took the oath prescribed by the council.[58] Local councils and synods, too, soon began to apply the rules enunciated in *Properandum*, or very similar ones, to the advocates and proctors of the ecclesiastical courts in their regions. Actions of this sort appeared at Liège in 1287, then at Arras, Tournai, London (1282), and Exeter (1287). In the following years, numerous other local and regional courts did the same.[59] Pope Benedict XII (r. 1334–42) not only demanded that advocates

---

case would thus work out at almost as much as the minimum annual stipend of an English country vicar. At a more exalted social level, an annual income of 20 pounds sterling was deemed adequate for an English knight, which was about what an advocate who earned the maximum fee level could expect for handling four cases a year (Cross, "Origins of Social Gradation," 156). In terms of purchasing power, e.g., it may be noted that a pilgrim complaining about the exorbitant prices charged at Rome during the Jubilee year of 1300 was outraged that a bed for himself, together with straw and fodder for his horse, cost 1 *livre tournois* (Lefebvre, "La constitution *Properandum*," 527 and 531 n. 45).

57. Lefebvre, "La constitution *Properandum*," 525, 528; Roberg, *Das Zweite Konzil von Lyon*, 314–16; Muldoon, "Boniface VIII's Experience in the Law."

58. William Wickwane, *Register*, 208–9, no. 496.

59. Council of Liège (1287) c. 28.3, in Mansi 24:933, also in Martène and Durand, *Thesaurus novus anecdotorum* 4:877; synodal statutes of Arras (ca. 1280–90) c. 92, in *Conciles de la province de Tours*, 203; *Antiqua statuta* of Tournai c. 21.2, in *Statuts de l'ancienne*

and proctors in the courts of the papal curia swear an admissions oath similar to the one prescribed in *Properandum*, but also imposed a graduated schedule that detailed the maximum fees they were permitted to receive for various types of cases. The pope added that advocates and proctors were not entitled to collect any fees if their clients either abandoned their cases or settled out of court before litigation commenced. Advocates and proctors in that situation must refund any advance payments they had received, less any amount the papal vice chancellor might award them for preliminary work on the case.[60]

Properandum and the French and English Civil Courts

The impact of *Properandum* was not confined to church courts. Shortly after the Second Council of Lyons approved that constitution, the French king, Philip III (r. 1271–85), promulgated an ordinance dated 23 October 1274 that required advocates at the Parlement de Paris and other royal law courts to swear an oath of admission that replicated almost exactly the provisions of *Properandum*.[61]

Similarly, in England the Statute of Westminster I, adopted in 1275, addressed some of the same concerns that appear in *Properandum*. The statute enjoined advocates (called serjeants in England) who practiced in the royal courts not to perpetrate any deceit or fraud upon the court or their clients. It further provided that those who contravened this injunction were to be punished by imprisonment for a year and a day and would be barred from further advocacy in the courts. The statute did not, however, deal specifically with admission to practice, nor did it explicitly require serjeants to take an oath of admission, although the swearing of such an oath became

---

province de Reims, 348; Council at the Old Temple (1282), art. 16 and reply, in Powicke & Cheney 2:925, 927, 929; Statutes of Exeter II (1287) c. 34, in Powicke & Cheney 2:1030–31. See also, e.g., *Registre de l'officialité de Cerisy*, 285; Ruffiancius (Barcelona, 1354) c. 120, in Hillgarth and Silano, "Diocesan Synods of Barcelona (1354)," 145–46; Lincoln Consistory Statutes (1334) c. 7, in London, BL, MS Cotton Vittel. A.X, at 161v–162r; synodal statutes of Tréguier (1372) c. 3, in Martène and Durand, *Thesaurus novus anecdotorum* 4:1123; the Black Book of Ely (1377/1378) in CUL, MS. Add. 3468, at 35r–36r; *Vetus liber archidiaconi Eliensis* (ca. 1429), 165–66; *Constitutiones et statuta nove reformacionis curie officialatus Gebenn* §36, at 1:376.

60. Benedict XII, *Decens et necessarium* (27 October 1340) §§18–22, 24–25, in Tangl, *Päpstlichen Kanzleiordnungen*, 121–23.

61. *Recueil général des anciennes lois françaises* 2:652–54, no. 247. The act was renewed in 1345 (*Ordonnances des roys de France de la troisième race* 2:225–26; Delachenal, *Histoire des avocats*, 393–96; Karpik, *French Lawyers*, 21–23).

part of the admissions ceremony during the fourteenth century. By the end of the 1290s, the serjeants for all practical purposes enjoyed a monopoly on practice before the Common Bench of the central royal courts.[62]

Similar developments were afoot during the same decades in the municipal courts of London. In 1280, the city authorities demanded that lawyers who practiced in the city's courts take an oath of office that incorporated many of the same undertakings as *Properandum* and prescribed standards for their conduct toward the court and their clients.[63]

ADMISSIONS REGISTERS

As ecclesiastical judges formalized the process for admitting advocates and proctors to practice in their courts, they, like their Roman predecessors, began to keep a list (*matricula*) of those admitted. References to this practice appear occasionally in conciliar decrees, papal documents, and procedural treatises.[64] Court registrars charged with maintaining official records of proceedings and related documents likewise start to appear in the second half of the thirteenth century.[65] Keeping track of the advocates and proctors sworn and admitted to practice in the court formed part of their duties. No *matriculae* of this sort seem to have survived from the thirteenth

---

62. Statute of Westminster I (1275) c. 29, in *Statutes of the Realm* 1:34; Baker, *Order of Serjeants at Law*, 26, 88; Brand, *Origins of the English Legal Profession*, 106–10, 120–21.

63. *Liber custumarum*, tit. *De countours et attounes*, in *Munimenta Gildhallae Londoniensis*, vol. 2, pt. 1, 280–82; Brand, *Origins of the English Legal Profession*, 122.

64. Cod. Theod. 2.10.2; Cod. 2.7.11 and 2.7.29.1; Kaser, *Römische Zivilprozeßrecht*, 564. An oblique reference appears in c. 26 of the Council of London (1268), in Powicke & Cheney 2:773, and Benedict XII in *Decens et necessarium* explicitly referred to the register of advocates that the papal chancellor maintained. See also Johannes Andreae, *Additiones* to the *Speculum iudiciale* of William Durand at 1.4 *De aduocato* §1.11 v. *ver. pe.*, at 1:261; Baldus, *Comm.* to Cod. 2.7.13.1, vol. 6, at 132rb; Alexander Tartagnus, *Consilia* 6.2.3, vol. 6, at 2vb.

65. The *Privilegia curie Remensis*, 19–20, which dates from 1269, describes (in strikingly unflattering terms) the functions of the registrar of the archbishop's court; see also Fournier, *Officialités*, 28–29. In England, William Bygod is described as registrar of the court of Canterbury ca. 1288, and references to other registrars appear in documents from 1290 and following (Churchill, *Canterbury Administration* 1:452–56 and 2:241–42; *Select Cases*, ed. Adams and Donahue, 467, 469, D.10.5, 7; Finucane, "Two Notaries and Their Records," 11). Section 27 of Archbishop Winchelsey's statutes (1295) for the Court of Arches briefly described the duties of the court's registrar at that point (Logan, *Medieval Court of Arches*, 13). The operations of the registry office grew much more complex over time; see especially the lengthy description in Archbishop Sudbury's letter dated 29 August 1378 (Logan, *Medieval Court of Arches*, 58–60).

century, however, and even fourteenth-century examples are not particularly common.[66]

NUMBERS OF ADVOCATES AND PROCTORS

Observers during the second half of the thirteenth century began to remark on the numbers of trained legal practitioners whose services were available. This was a recent development. At the beginning of the century, trained lawyers were plentiful only in university towns and a handful of cities, notably Rome, where opportunities for employment abounded. At the beginning of the century, Pope Innocent III scoffed at Robert Clipston's claim that he could not find an advocate to take his case at the Roman curia, while Henry the Poet (d. before 1265) pictured the proctors of Rome assembled in a flock, "perched there like winged creatures, alighted out of heaven."[67] A quarter of a century later, Rome was no longer one of the few cities blessed—or some thought, cursed—with an abundance of lawyers. Pope Gregory IX noted in 1236 that Parma and other cities swarmed with *iurisperiti*. A few years later, the First Council of Lyons (1245) directed that ecclesiastical courts should hear cases only in cities with a plentiful supply of skilled jurists.[68] By midcentury, universities had begun to turn them out in ample numbers. In 1288, some 120 doctors of law lived in Milan, a bustling city of around 60,000 inhabitants—as compared with only 28 physicians, but roughly 1,500 notaries.[69]

Proctors and notaries in diocesan courts almost always outnumbered full-fledged advocates, usually by a substantial margin. Indeed bishops and their officials often imposed limits on the number of active advocates allowed to practice in their courts at any given time. Thus, for example, just eight advocates are known to have practiced in the official's court at Tournai between 1267 and 1301, and over the period of nearly a century the

---

66. The act book of the consistory court of the bishop of Ely, for example, records the admission of two advocates on 24 January 1377 and one on 8 April 1378, while notices of the admission of advocates and proctors in the archdeacon's court are scattered in among records of the installation of rectors of churches (e.g., CUL, EDR D/2/1, at 62v and 92r; *Vetus liber archidiaconi Eliensis*, ed. Feltoe and Minns, 163–67).

67. Heinrich der Poet, "Liber de statu Curie Romane," in *Magister Heinrich der Poet*, 71; trans. Brentano, *Two Churches*, 28–29.

68. Gregory IX, *Registres* 2:252, 496, nos. 2939, 3360; 1 Lyons c. 2, in *DEC* 1:284. Local councils subsequently echoed the Lyons decree, e.g., Trier (1277) c. 11.10 and Liège (1287) c. 28.9, in Mansi 24:202, 934.

69. Hyde, *Society and Politics*, 166–67; Cipolla, "The Professions," 41; Fossier, *Histoire sociale de l'Occident médiéval*, 257.

names of just twenty-three advocates appear on the records of the bishop's officials at Liège. In England, the Ely consistory was more generously provided with advocates than most diocesan courts. Nine of them are mentioned in the court's act book between 1373 and 1382, together with an equal number of proctors.[70] Although standard teaching in the schools, as well as practice at the papal curia and many lesser courts on the Continent, drew a sharp line between the functions of advocates and proctors, English diocesan courts often ignored academic guidelines. No advocates at all are known to have practiced regularly, for example, in the consistory courts of the dioceses of Rochester, Hereford, Coventry, and Lichfield. Proctors in those courts seem to have performed all the work of advising and presenting legal arguments on behalf of litigants, a task that was in theory the exclusive province of advocates. It is surprising to find that the same situation prevailed in the consistory and commissary courts of the diocese of Canterbury, where no advocates appear in the records, while at the same time substantial numbers of them regularly worked at the Court of Arches, the archbishop's provincial appeals court in London.[71]

The Court of Arches, like some bishops' consistories, limited the number of advocates admitted to practice at any one time, as Roman courts had done in late antiquity. Fourteen advocates were permitted to practice at the bishop's consistory court in the exceptionally large diocese of Lincoln, and Bishop Burghersh granted the official the option of admitting two more if needed.[72] The number of advocates in the courts of the archbishop of York was not supposed to exceed twelve. In reality only about six

---

70. Vleeschouwers-Van Melkebeek, *Officialiteit van Doornik*, 113; Renardy, *Le monde des maîtres*, 233–34, table 25; Brundage, "Bar of the Ely Consistory Court," 543–54, and "Cambridge Faculty of Canon Law," 42–45.

71. *Acta* of the Rochester consistory court (1347–48), in Hamo Hethe, *Registrum* 2:911–1043; Helmholz, *Marriage Litigation*, 150–51; Woodcock, *Medieval Ecclesiastical Courts*, 40–45; Churchill, *Canterbury Administration* 1:450–52; Logan, *Medieval Court of Arches*, xxii, 209–17. The advocates and proctors of the Arches apparently also worked in the consistory and commissary courts of the bishop of London and in the Court of Admiralty as well, although they were by statute forbidden to do so. See Stratford, "Statutes of the Court of Arches" (1342) §4, and Chichele, "Statute" (1423), in Logan, *Medieval Court of Arches*, 35 and 54–55; Wunderli, *London Church Courts*, 19 n. 24.

72. Sections 8 and 14 of Archbishop Winchelsey's statutes of 1295 set the limits at sixteen advocates and ten proctors and forbade proctors to appear in a case without an advocate (Logan, *Medieval Court of Arches*, 7, 9; Churchill, *Canterbury Administration* 1:451). Thirteenth-century lawyers knew about this late imperial practice from Cod. Theod. 2.10.1, as well as Cod. 2.7.24 and 26. See also Kaser, *Römische Zivilprozeßrecht*,

to eight of them were usually in active practice at any given time, although several more served as judges, vicars-general, and court registrars. Opportunities for advocates were sharply restricted in the bishop's consistory court at Exeter in the southwest of England, where only three advocates formally admitted to practice were available in 1322–23, although another ten men who aspired to be advocates were working in the court as proctors while they awaited their turns for admission. Diocesan courts on the Continent sometimes imposed similar caps on the numbers of professional advocates and proctors allowed to practice.[73] No ecclesiastical courts tried to limit the numbers of occasional or nonprofessional advocates or proctors they would allow to appear on behalf of litigants. Judges had discretion to determine whether or not to permit such persons to appear on a case-by-case basis.

Standards of Professional Conduct

Regular admissions procedures gave judges the capacity to restrict competition among advocates and proctors, which served the interests of existing practitioners by assuring them of a monopoly on a service that clients needed. At the same time, this process served the interests of courts, reinforcing judicial control over the lawyers who appeared before them.

Norms of professional conduct evolved rapidly around the middle of the thirteenth century. Much of what we know about lawyers' behavioral standards is first documented in the manuals for advocates that began to appear during this period.[74] Similar information also found its way into the longer and more detailed procedural treatises produced during the second

---

564. The number of proctors at Lincoln was also limited to sixteen (Henry Burghersh, *Statuta consistorii*, 572, §3; Morris, "A Consistory Court," 156–57).

73. Some York advocates also acted as proctors for especially important clients (Dasef, "Lawyers of the York Curia," 50–52, 56–57); on Exeter, Walter de Stapeldon, *Register*, 115–19. At Cologne in the early fourteenth century, e.g., the maximum number of advocates was fixed at ten (Gescher, "Älteste kölnische Offizialitatsstatut," 482, §3.1).

74. Notably the *Cavillationes advocatorum* (completed ca. 1235) by Bagarotus (fl. ca. 1179–1246), the slightly later *Libellus* of Ubertus de Bobbio (d. after 1245), the *Cauillationes aduocatorum* (written ca. 1246) of Johannes de Deo (b. between 1189 and 1193, d. 1267), and the *Summa super officio advocationis* (written ca. 1250) by Bonaguida de Arezzo. Each of these writers borrowed heavily from his predecessors, but Bolognese authors were more inclined to concentrate on technical matters than their counterparts north of the Alps, who tended to be more concerned about the ethics of professional conduct (Gouron, "Le rôle de l'avocat," 8, 15–16, 19).

half of the century, most notably in the *Speculum iudiciale* of William Durand.[75] Guidelines were sometimes transformed into formal practice rules during the fourteenth and fifteenth centuries. The behavioral guidelines indicate that medieval advocates were aware that they belonged to a social group defined by shared values and aspirations, in short, that a sense of professional identity was taking shape. They defined how thirteenth-century advocates wished to see themselves and, equally important, how they wished others to see them.

OBLIGATIONS TO THE COURT

A basic principle of courtroom behavior required advocates to demonstrate deference and respect for the judge. Success in advocacy depended upon the goodwill of the judge, and it was essential to avoid offending him. As Bonaguida de Arezzo (fl. ca. 1250–55) noted, "It is a hazardous matter to litigate in front of a hostile judge."[76] Advocates strove sedulously to insinuate themselves into the judge's good graces and tried to do so subtly, discreetly, and persistently: "A drip wears away the stone, not by force, but by falling continually."[77] They signaled their deference in numerous symbolic ways. The judge sat while presiding, but advocates had to stand when they addressed him. Advocates usually spoke in order of seniority. When his turn came, an advocate was required to rise, remove his cap, and bow to the judge. He had to face the judge and address him directly. He also needed to take care never to turn his back on the judge. When he finished speaking and wished to return to his seat among the other advocates, he was directed to walk backward so as to keep his face toward the judge.[78]

---

75. Durand scattered numerous remarks about professional lore, many of them borrowed from writers on courtroom practice, throughout his *Speculum iudiciale*, as Johannes Andreae pointed out in his *Additiones* to Durand's work (proem. v. *plurimis*, at 1:4).

76. Bonaguida, *Summa introductoria* 1.3.6, at 156: "[R]es periculosa est sub judice offenso litigare, ff. De receptis, Non distinguemus § cum quidam [Dig. 4.8.32.14]."

77. Hostiensis, *In quinque decretalium libri commentaria* [= *Lectura*] to X 1.32.1 §13, vol. 1, at 169rb. The quotation, "Gutta cavat lapidem non vi, sed saepe cadendo," alludes to Ovid, *Epistulae ex Ponto* 4.10.5.

78. *Summa Parisiensis* to C. 3 q. 7 c. 2 v. *orbati*, at 121; Ricardus Anglicus, *Summa de ordine iudiciario* 27, at 34; Johannes de Deo, *Cauillationes aduocatorum* 1.3, in London, BL MS Arundel 459, at 1vb: "Item si plures sunt aduocati ex una parte quam ex alia, antiquior procedat, nisi euidenti sit maior sciencia minoris, ita quod de eo nulla sit dubitatio, sicut dicit hic," and 1.4, at 2rb: "Cum aduocatus fuerit coram iudice, competenter saluti eum capite inclinato, deponito birretto, nisi est episcopus uel superior, ut si esset

Writers on professional matters regularly admonished advocates to insinuate themselves into the judge's good graces by lavishing praise on him. William Durand and other writers provided novice advocates with specimen speeches of a kind calculated to win the goodwill of even the most flinty-hearted judge. How often judges were actually put off their guard by these declamations is impossible to say, although Disraeli's claim that everyone loves flattery was surely at least as true in the thirteenth century as it was in the nineteenth.[79]

Appearances were important. An advocate needed to be careful at all times to show that he was serious, dignified, and mature. His facial expressions should tell the judge and the public that he was personable, prudent, and discreet. Sly grins or chuckling, much less outright laughter, were the mark of fools: they had no place in court.[80] The advocate's body language should reinforce this message: no wild gestures, sudden movements, or shuffling about in the courtroom. His whole demeanor, and particularly his tone of voice, should proclaim his maturity and smooth self-control.[81]

The advocate needed to dress appropriately. His gown must be neat and clean, of a quality appropriate to his dignity and function, and it should reach down to his ankles.[82] He should follow the dictates of regional cus-

---

rex uel comes, uel si esset minor in clerum ei serui consuetudinem et etiam reuerenciam sicut et prouinciales, ut ff. De officio proconsu. l. i et l. ii §1 [Dig. 1.16.1–2]." Similarly Accursius, *Glos. ord.* to Cod. 2.6.6 v. *standi*; Bonaguida, *Summa introductoria* 1.1, at 136; William Durand, *Speculum iudiciale* 1.4 *De aduocato* 5.1, at 1:269.

79. William Durand, *Speculum iudiciale* 1.4 *De aduocato* §5.4, at 1:269; Bonaguida, *Summa introductoria* 1.2, at 138–54, provides twenty-six model opening statements, while Aegidius Fuscarariis (d. 1289), *Ordo iudiciarius*, 259–69, §§190–211, gives twenty-two of them. For Disraeli's quip, see his letter to Matthew Arnold, quoted by Russell, *Collections and Recollections*, 305. Disraeli presumably drew on personal experience when he added, "and when you come to Royalty you should lay it on with a trowel."

80. Johannes de Deo, *Cauillationes aduocatorum* 1.3, in London, BL, MS Arundel 459, at 2ra: "Item aduocatus non debet coram iudice irrisum prorumpere, quia risus est in ore stultorum, ut ait Salamon [cf. Prov. 10:23]." Repeated by William Durand, *Speculum iudiciale* 1.4 *De aduocato* §5.3, at 1:269.

81. Johannes de Deo, *Cauillationes aduocatorum* 1.4, in MS Arundel 459, at 2rb–va: "Item commendet loquendo humili[ter], scilicet moderate et humano, quia allegationes bene composite aduocati trahunt iudicem in suam sententiam; furor enim et ira non tractantur sermone humile. " Similarly, Bonaguida, *Summa introductoria* 1.1, at 136–37, and William Durand, *Speculum iudiciale* 1.4 *De aduocato* §5.6, at 1:269).

82. Johannes de Deo, *Cauillationes aduocatorum* 1.3, in MS Arundel 459, at 1va: "Cum ergo aduocatus accedat coram iudice exercens officium suum habeat uestes decentes

tom in these matters, but whatever the local fashion, an advocate should dress soberly. His outer garments should be neither too short nor too long, uniform in color and not too flashy. He should avoid bright reds or greens, silken fabrics, and every sort of extreme tailoring. Advocates, as Ulpian said, were "priests of the law" and accordingly they needed to dress like priests.[83]

Advocates always had to keep their temper in check, lest they undercut the effect of their own arguments.[84] They must refrain from using offensive language or quibbling with their adversaries over minor points. They were admonished to address one another politely and respectfully. The advocate's role necessarily involved disagreeing with his adversary and parrying the opponent's arguments, but he should dispute about the law, not about personalities.[85] No advocate should impugn his opponent's honesty or disrupt proceedings by hurling insults at him, although if an opponent taunted him, it was acceptable to answer back in kind. No provocation, however, could justify drawing a sword and threatening the opposing advocate with physical violence, as did two bad-tempered advocates in the bishop's consistory at Marseilles.[86]

An advocate furthermore needed to tailor the presentation of his client's

---

ad officium pertinentes et talares, ut C. de pos. l. ult. [Cod. 2.6.8]." William Durand, *Speculum iudiciale* 1.4 *De aduocato* §2 pr., 1, at 1:264, repeats this and the remainder of the passage almost verbatim.

83. Bonaguida, *Summa introductoria* 1.1, at 137; William Durand, *Speculum iudiciale* 1.4 *De aduocato* §2.4, at 1:264–65; Johannes de Deo, *Cauillationes aduocatorum* 1.3, in MS Arundel 459, at 1va–vb: "Item cum aduocati dicuntur sacerdotes, ut ff. De iustitia et iure l. i [Dig. 1.1.1.1] et sacerdotes habeant uestes conuenientes ad officium deputatas, ut C. De san. ecc. l. Sancimus, in prin. [Cod. 1.2.21 pr.] et xliii di. Sit rector [D. 43 c. 1] et xxiii. di. preterea [D. 23 c. 12], et xvi q. i reuertimini [C. 16 q. 1 c. 65] et viii q. i Licet in fi. [C. 8 q. 1 c. 15]; ergo aduocati bonas debent habere uestes" (cf. Durand, *Speculum iudiciale* 1.4 *De aduocato* §2.2, at 1:264).

84. William Durand, *Speculum iudiciale* 1.4 *De aduocato* §4.10, at 1:268.

85. Bonaguida, *Summa introductoria* 1.3.7, at 156; Hostiensis, *Lectura* to X 2.1.6 (7) §5 and 2.1.14 pr. §1, vol. 2, at 3vb, 7ra–rb; William Durand, *Speculum iudiciale* 1.4 *De aduocato* §4.3 and 7, at 1:267.

86. Johannes de Deo, *Cauillationes aduocatorum* 1.5, in MS Arundel 459, at 3ra: "Utamini uerba temperatis contra eum: 'domine salua pace uestra,' 'salue reuerencia uestra,' 'salua honestate uestra,' uel equipollentibus uerba, ut ff. De eden. l. Argentarius in fi. [Dig. 2.13.10?]; ff. De uer. Tantum [Dig. 50.16.88?]; Ricardus Anglicus, *Summa de ordine iudiciario* 27, at 34–35; William Durand, *Speculum iudiciale* 1.4 *De aduocato* §4 pr., 1, 3, 4, at 1:267; Aubenas, *Recueil des lettres* 2:15–15.

case to suit the judge's mood and temper. Writers on professional matters regularly warned that wordy, ill-organized, and irrelevant arguments were apt to annoy the judge and might well prejudice him against the advocate and the case. A wise advocate, they advised, should keep his oral arguments and his written submissions clear, concise, and short, although he must naturally be sure not to omit any points that were vital to his case.[87]

Ecclesiastical courts at every level from the thirteenth through the fifteenth centuries and beyond produced regulations that enacted a great deal of advice of this kind in the form of practice rules, such as those that appear, for example, in the constitution *Decens et necessarium*, a body of directives that Benedict XII imposed on the papal consistory and the Audientia sacri palatii, otherwise known as the Rota, in 1340. His successors, notably Martin V (r. 1417–31), reiterated and amplified these regulations. Unofficial but authoritative manuals of Rotal procedure, such as the *Ordo judiciarius qui in Romana curia consuevit communiter observari* (ca. 1337), had appeared even earlier and may well have been the proximate source of some of these details.[88]

These rules for the papal courts reflect a regulatory process that began even earlier in the courts of lesser prelates. Archbishop Kilwardby's 1273 statutes for the Court of Arches and Archbishop Winchelsey's 1295 statutes for the same court, as well as the statutes that Bishop Burghersh imposed on the episcopal consistory at Lincoln in 1334, for example, contained comparable directives for the conduct of the advocates and proctors who frequented their courts. Similar statutes and collections of practice rules dating from the second half of the thirteenth century onward survive from numerous regions. Published samples such as the practice rules of the arch-

---

87. Johannes de Deo, *Cauillationes aduocatorum* 1.4, in MS Arundel 459, at 2rb: "Item, abstineat a superfluis, Ad l. Fal. l. v [Dig 35.2.5] ad medium, et C. De preci. impera. off. l. Instrumentorum [Cod.1.19.8], C. de ap. l. ult. [Cod. 7.62.39], ff. De auro et ar. le. l. Pediculis § Labeo [Dig. 34.2.32.6].... Tales enim loquentes ratione comprehenduntur quod habent longum nasum, ut xlix di c. 1 [D. 49 c. 1 §3] et uocantur tales garruli et etiam rustici, xliii di. § ult [D. 43 d.p.c. 5]; Bonaguida, *Summa introductoria* 1.3.17, at 160–61; Baldus, *Practica iudiciaria*, tit. *De cautelis et remediis* 18.2, at 88vb; Alexander Tartagnus, *Consilia*, no. 34, vol. 2, at 41rb.

88. Benedict XII, *Decens et necessarium* §§8, 10, 29, in Tangl, *Päpstlichen Kanzleiordnungen*, 120, 124; Martin V, *In apostolice dignitatis specula* (1418) and *Romani pontificis providentia* (1423), in Tangl, *Päpstlichen Kanzleiordnungen*, 133–45 and 146–60; Barraclough, "Ordo judiciarius." For later examples of similar rules, see also Agustín, *Praxis Rotae* and Jacob Emerix, *Tractatus seu notitia*.

bishop's court at Reims, which date from 1269, the fifteenth-century regulations from Geneva and Halberstadt, and the statutes of English church courts, suggest that these regulations reflected advice found earlier in practitioners' manuals.[89]

Many of the norms for courtroom conduct by advocates that became current among canonists in the 1230s and 1240s started to appear a generation or two later among writers on royal and customary law in France. The famous treatise on French customary law by Philippe de Beaumanoir (b. ca. 1250, d. 1296), for example, and the earliest French treatise on civil procedure, the *Stilus curiae Parliamenti* of Guillaume du Breuil (d. 1344), as well as the *scholia* of Étienne Aufréri (d. 1511) on Du Breuil's *Stilus*, all prescribe behavioral rules for advocates that closely resemble those found in the *Cauillationes* of Johannes de Deo and the *Summa introductoria* of Bonaguida de Arezzo.[90]

The conversion of the rules of conduct that appear in books of advice for lawyers into court regulations marked a fundamental change in their character. What had originally described the kinds of behavior that lawyers felt were desirable and hoped to achieve were now transformed into duties that they were required to observe under pain of punishment.[91]

The personal lives of advocates and proctors outside of their professional relationships likewise became subject to regulation. The new rules forbade them, among other things, to keep concubines, frequent taverns, engage in usury, or to work at menial occupations inappropriate to their status.[92] These prohibitions reflect the Roman view that behavior of this sort was unbecoming for an officer of the court and would reflect badly on the ecclesiastical judicial system. Advocates were ideally supposed to

---

89. Fournier, *Officialités*, 32–41; Lefebvre-Teillard, *Officialités*, 38–43; Steins, "Ordentliche Zivilprozeß," 191–206; Gescher, "Älteste kölnische Offizialatsstatut"; *Constitutiones et statuta nove reformacionis curie officialatus Gebenn* 1:377–78, §§41–44. Scattered references to other such court regulations appear in *Records of the Medieval Ecclesiastical Courts* 1:87, 103, 167–68, and passim.

90. Philippe de Beaumanoir, *Coutumes de Beauvaisis* §§175–94, at 1:89–96; Guillaume Du Breuil, *Stilus superincliti Parlamenti . . . cum scholiis Stephani Auffrerii*, at 1rb–vb.

91. On the contrast between the morality of aspiration and the morality of duty, see esp. Fuller, *Morality of Law*, 3–32.

92. Statutes of Guiard de Laon, bishop of Cambrai (r. 1238–48), c. 188 in *Statuts de l'ancienne province de Reims*, 63–64; Martin V, *Romani pontificis providentia* (1422) §28, in Tangl, *Päpstlichen Kanzleiordnungen*, 156; Steins, "Ordentliche Zivilprozeß, 203.

be models of upright behavior, although Baldus added, "I believe that few such will be found."[93]

OBLIGATIONS TO CLIENTS

Medieval advocates, like their modern counterparts, sought a comfortable balance between the duties they owed to the court, the obligations they owed to their clients, and their own professional interests. Conflicts between these three sets of duties were inescapable. Judges expected advocates and proctors to serve as gatekeepers of the court. They had to swear repeatedly that they would not take on frivolous or vexatious cases and promised the judge that they would not trouble him with actions that lacked substantial merit. They also pledged that they would inform the judge should a case they had accepted turn out to be flawed.

Yet before he could even bring a case into court, the advocate must persuade his client to trust him completely and to disclose every shred of information that might relate even remotely to the matter that brought the client to see him. Ancient tradition, reiterated by contemporary writers, warned that no advocate could advise a client or present his case with confidence until he learned all the relevant facts, including secret and confidential information that could damage the client's honor and reputation and imperil his well-being or perhaps even his life if it were publicly disclosed.

William Durand advised his readers to put this squarely to their clients at the outset:

> Let [the advocate] say: "My dear fellow, there are three persons to whom you must tell the whole truth, from whom you conceal nothing. They are your confessor, your doctor, and your lawyer. . . . For even the most experienced counselor may be led astray if he does not know the facts. . . . So tell me absolutely everything, let me have the whole business, and give it to me in writing as well. Then I will be able to give you true and reliable advice and counsel . . . , for rights arise from the facts.[94]

---

93. Baldus, *Commentaria* to Cod. 2.8.3, vol. 6, at 131va: "[N]on debent vilia ministeria exercere in vilipendium togae. Declara hanc l. per l. sancimus, infra eodem [Cod. 2.7.6]"; and *Commentaria* to Cod. 2.6.6, "[S]i quis seruaret hanc legem, reputaretur sapientissimus Aduocatus quo ad Deum et mundum, sed credo quod pauci reperiantur" (cf. Vivianus Tuscus, *Casus longi* to Cod. 2.6.6).

94. William Durand, *Speculum iudiciale* 1.4 *De aduocato* §3.1–2, at 1:265: "[D]icat illi: 'Charissime, tres sunt personae quibus est omnimoda ueritas aperienda, et nihil est illis celandum, uidelicet confessor, xxii. q. ii. c. Cum humilitatis [C. 22 q. 2 c. 9]; de poe. dist. iii. Interhaec hircum ii. [D. 3 de pen. c. 35]; medicus, ut extra de poen. et re. Omnis § sacerdos et c. seq. [X 5.38.12–13]; extra de homicidi. Tua [X 5.12.19]; xlv. dist. Disci-

A client's full disclosure of his affairs placed the advocate under an obligation not to divulge the information entrusted to him. It scarcely needs saying that not every advocate lived up to this obligation. Contemporary writers complained endlessly about the untrustworthiness of lawyers.[95] Guiot de Provins (fl. late 12th–early 13th century), declared in his "Bible": "If you find a loyal [advocate], you should hold a celebration for him." Poets were not the only ones who complained. Legal writers, too, deplored "treacherous advocates who do not defend their clients in good faith," and labeled them "untrustworthy quibblers."[96]

But what did it mean to represent a client faithfully? How far must an advocate's loyalty stretch? Where the client's interests conflicted with the advocate's obligations to the judge, the advocate was bound, at least in theory, to give preference to the judge's claims on his fidelity. If he discovered at a preliminary stage that a prospective client's case was flawed or dishonest, the advocate was supposed to dissuade him from proceeding any further. We may well wonder (although we will never know) how many advocates bluntly warned prospective clients, "You should know that if I discover any injustice in your case, I will reveal it and join the other side," as Robert Chambers reportedly did. Johannes de Deo favored a more subtle approach. He suggested that the advocate tell such a client: "I'm against suing because I don't think there's any chance of winning, and therefore I don't think you should waste the money."[97] If an advocate accepted a client

---

plina in princip. [D. 45 c. 9], iuxta illud, "Si causam ignores, quomodo cures;" et Iureperitus, de poen. dist. vi. c. i uersic. Iudiciaria [D. 6 de pen. c. 1 §3]. Quia facti ignoranita sepe peritissimos fallit, ut ff. de iuris et fac. ignoran. l. ii. [Dig. 22.6.2]. Dicas mihi igitur omnimodam ueritatem et negocii exemplum da mihi scriptum, ut congruum et uerum possim tibi dare consilium seu responsum, C. de transactio. Ut responsum [Cod. 2.4.15] et extra de sponsal. De muliere [X 4.1.6]; quia ex facto ius oritur, ff. ad legem Aquil. Si ex plagis § In cliuo [Dig. 9.2.52.2]; ff. de iureiurando, Duobus § si enim et l. finali [Dig. 12.2.28, 42]; ff. de iur. codicil. Quidam [Dig. 29.7.14]."

95. On the vast literature concerning this topic, see esp. Yunck, *Lineage of Lady Meed*, 143–59; Baldwin, "Critics of the Legal Profession"; Ourliac, "Troubadours et juristes"; and Brundage, "Vultures, Whores, and Hypocrites."

96. Guiot de Provins, "La Bible," 170, ll. 72–73; Johannes Teutonicus, *Glos. ord.* to D. 87 c. 5 v. *non omni fide*: "Et quod dicit, 'fidei,' est argumentum contra perfidos aduocatos, qui plena fide clientulos non defendunt, argu. 2 q. 3 § notandum [C. 2 q. 3 d.p.c. 7 §2]"; Lyndwood, *Provinciale* 1.17.1 v. *advocatos*, 74: "Supple infideles et cavillosos, quorum malitiis justitia deperit et litium processus innumeris subterfugiis impeditur."

97. Peter the Chanter, *Verbum adbreviatum* c. 49, 334; Baldwin, *Masters, Princes, and Merchants* 1:195 and 2:136 n. 156; Johannes de Deo, *Cauillationes aduocatorum* 1.6 in BL,

in good faith, only to discover later that the case was malicious or groundless, his duty to the court obliged him to persuade the client either to drop the matter or to settle it. Should he be unsuccessful, the advocate was duty bound to abandon the client and inform the judge of his reasons for doing so. In practical terms, this deprived the client of any possibility of persisting with his claims, since no other advocate or proctor was permitted to take up his case. The client might, in addition, be punished for bringing a frivolous action.[98]

Legal writers, preachers, confessors, and theologians agreed that an advocate or proctor who allowed his loyalty to the client to prevail over his duty to the court not only violated his professional duty, but also sinned grievously. Raymond von Wiener-Neustadt, a fourteenth-century writer, even claimed that it was equivalent to homicide, although that position seems to have found no followers.[99] An advocate who pursued a case that was manifestly malicious, frivolous, or based on manufactured evidence could potentially find himself suspended from practice, fined, and possibly even condemned to bear the costs of the unjust lawsuit.[100] It was clearly in the advocate's best interest to resign from a frivolous or groundless case, and authoritative opinion held that he was even entitled to claim his fee. The chances that his former client would willingly pay up under these cir-

---

MS Arundel 459, at 3rb: "Si tamen uiderit aduocatus factum clientuli sui inefficax, uel propter se, uel propter probationes, dicat ei, 'Nolo litigare quia spem non habeo obtinendi, et ideo sumptus facere non debetis,' ut ff. De inoff. t. l. i [Dig. 5.2.1], et dicit canon quod non debemus defendere quod ratione uinci non potest, xxiiii. q. iii. Si habes [C. 24 q. 3 c. 1] et xxvi. Deinde ponitur [D. 26 c. 3], quia quod ratione caret exstirpandum est, ut lxxxiiii. di. Corepiscopi [*recte* D. 68 c. 5]."

98. Ambrosius Catharinus Politus, *De advocati officio*, at 363ra; Council of Oxford (1222) c. 4, in Powicke & Cheney 1:107; Gregory XI, *Quamvis a felicis* (1375) §3, in Tangl, *Päpstlichen Kanzleiordnungen*, 129.

99. Raymundus von Wiener-Neustadt, *Die summa legum brevis, levis et utilis* 3.39, at 603–4. See also, e.g., Goffredus de Trano, *Summa*, 128, to X 1.37 §8; Guido de Baysio, *Rosarium Decretorum* to D. 96 c. 11 v. *beneficium*; Bonaguida, *Summa introductoria* 1.3.3 and 24, at 154–55, 165–66; Guibert of Tournai, *Sermones ad omnes status*, no. 1, at 106ra–vb; Thomas Aquinas, *Summa theologiae* 2–2 q.71 a. 3; John of Fribourg, *Summa confessorum* 2.5.171, at 77rb; *Manuale presbiterorum* a. 34, in Haren, "Interrogatories," 132.

100. E.g., Council of Oxford (1222) c. 45; Courson, *Summa "Tota celestis philosophia,"* 10.2, quoted by Baldwin, *Masters, Princes, and Merchants* 2:136 n. 154; Étienne Aufréri, *Decisiones capelle sedis archiepiscopalis Tholose*, q. 6, at 4ra; Benedict XII, *Decens et necessarium* (1340) §§29–30, in Tangl. *Päpstlichen Kanzleiordnungen*, 124.

cumstances were no doubt slim, although the advocate had the option of seeking a judicial order to compel him to do so.[101]

It is impossible to discover how regularly advocates and proctors complied with these ethical duties in their practice. Refusal to accept a case was unlikely to leave any trace in the records, especially if this happened before the matter got into court. English ecclesiastical court records do show, however, that proctors really did abandon cases that they considered groundless or without merit, and did so with considerable frequency.[102]

Conflict of interest between lawyer and client was virtually inevitable. Vigilant exercise of his duty to pass judgment on prospective clients and cases might serve the lawyer's professional interests, but it relegated the client's interests to a secondary position. The lawyer naturally wished to appear only in cases where he was likely to win. Doing so would make effective use of his time and energy and would enhance his professional reputation. The client who wished to bring his claims before a disinterested judge, however, might find himself unable to secure redress for his grievances or to defend himself against claims that others had brought against him if his interests conflicted with those of his lawyer.[103]

Once an advocate agreed to assist a client with a meritorious case, he was bound to do everything he could to advance the client's interests. Other obligations, such as scheduling conflicts, for example, could not excuse him for failure to appear when he was needed. It would be a gross breach of duty for him to desert one client in order to take on a more profitable case for someone else.[104] Should an advocate actually do so, his client could bring a claim to recover compensation for the resulting expense and inconvenience. One recourse open to a client who suffered injury as a result of desertion by an advocate was to sue him through an *actio in factum* similar to that brought against a judge who handed down a faulty verdict. Experi-

---

101. Accursius, *Glos. ord.* to Cod. 3.1.14 Auth. post c. v. *litigatori*; cf. Dig. 50.13.1.13; William Durand, *Speculum iudicale* 1.4 *De salariis* §3.22, at 1:350. Actually enforcing a judgment to compel payment might, of course, prove exceedingly difficult.

102. Helmholz, "Ethical Standards," 54–55; see also his *Marriage Litigation*, 153–54, and *Canon Law and Ecclesiastical Jurisdiction*, 226.

103. The balance shifted in favor of the client in the common law world during the eighteenth century when influential writers commenced to argue that the advocate's proper task was to represent the client's interests. Determining the propriety of those interests, they asserted, was the function of the judge and jury, not of the lawyer. See Brundage, "Lawyer as Client's Judge," 605–7.

104. Cod. Theod. 2.10.2 and Cod. 3.1.13.9.

enced lawyers were aware, however, that a client's chances of securing adequate indemnification in this way were slim.[105]

Other disciplinary mechanisms might deter advocates from abandoning inconvenient clients. An advocate who deserted a client became ipso facto *infamis*, which entailed serious disabilities, both legal and social. *Infamia* automatically resulted from public knowledge that a person had done something disgraceful and disreputable, and the community as well as the courts enforced the penalties. In Edward Peters's words, "The doctrine of infamy existed in the streets and squares of early Europe, as well as in its law books."[106]

In the courts, an adversary could disqualify an opposing advocate or proctor by entering an exception of *infamia* against him. If the judge found the exception proved, the *infamis* advocate forfeited his right of audience. Consequently, he could no longer practice his profession unless or until he had purged himself of the disgrace, which required him to make reparations to the injured client.[107] Moving an exception of *infamia* against an opponent, however, was not for the fainthearted or those unsure of their grounds, because failure to sustain the accusation with adequate proof was punishable as defamation (*calumnia*), which could result in the accuser forfeiting his own right of audience.[108]

An "ambidextrous" advocate or proctor who not only abandoned a client's case, but actually betrayed him by joining his adversary and revealing the previous client's secrets, might be penalized for fraud.[109] If he tried to

---

105. Dig. 4.4.18.1 and 50.13.6; William Durand, *Speculum iudiciale* 1.4 De aduocato §9.19, at 1:282. An *actio in factum* was one based on the praetorian edict, as contrasted with an *actio in ius*, which was grounded on provisions of the civil law (Kaser, *Römische Zivilprozeßrecht*, 238–39; Thomas, *Textbook of Roman Law*, 83–84).

106. Peters, "Wounded Names," 43–89, at 84. A whole title of the Digest (Dig. 3.2) deals with those found guilty of *infamia*; see especially Dig. 3.2.4.4, as well as Accursius, *Glos. ord.* to Cod. 2.7.1 v. *commisi*. Medieval canon law incorporated many of these doctrines, e.g., Gratian, C. 3 q. 7 c. 1 and c. 2 §2; C. 6 q. 1 c. 17–19; X 1.11.17, 2.18.1, 5.1.21, etc. See further Landau, *Entstehung des kanonischen Infamiebegriffs*; Migliorino, *Fama e infamia*; *Fama*, ed. Fenster and Smail.

107. Accursius, *Casus* to Cod. 7.49.1 v. *constitit* and *Glos. ord.* v. *amittat*.

108. Accursius, *Glos. ord.* to Cod. 2.7.1 v. *quod si non docueris* and v. *notaberis*.

109. Dig. 4.3.1 pr.–2, 4.3.33, 4.8.31. Roman lawyers and lawgivers in the classical period usually described this type of behavior as *praevaricatio* (Dig. 3.2.4.4; 47.15.1; 47.15.3.2; 47.15.5; 48.16.1.8; Cod. 2.7.1). Medieval legal writers continued this usage, e.g., Gratian C. 2 q. 3 d.p.c. 8 pr., §6. During the thirteenth century, the term *ambidexter* also began to be used to describe a lawyer who took fees with both hands, i.e., from both parties in a case, and thus as a specific type of *praevaricator* (Brundage, "Ambidextrous Advocate").

win by misrepresenting the facts or the law to the judge, he could be held criminally guilty of forgery (*falsum*), which merited severe punishment.[110] Thirteenth-century legal writers agreed that keeping a client's secrets confidential was fundamental to the lawyer-client relationship, and that betrayal by an advocate warranted the harshest sanctions.[111] Medieval pastors, preachers, and confessors agreed.[112]

Even nonlawyers were aware of many of these ethical standards.[113] Unscrupulous litigants sometimes consulted many or even all of the proctors and advocates who practiced within their jurisdiction in order to create a conflict of interest that would make it impossible for their adversary to secure the services of a lawyer. "I have often seen some people seek a legal opinion," wrote William Durand, "not in order to use it, but so that [the lawyer] would blush to furnish advice to an opponent." If he were in fact in this situation, Durand added: "I should not side with any party opposing you lest I be implicated in the crime of ambidexterity (*praevaricatio*)."[114]

Individual courts often elaborated detailed rules on these matters. Thus, for example, the constitution *Romani pontificis providentia* of Pope Martin V spelled out standards of behavior for advocates and proctors at the papal curia:

---

110. Dig. 4.8.31, 48.10.1 pr.–2, 6, and 48.19.38.8; Goffredus de Trano, *Summa super titulis decretalium*, 127–28, to X 1.37 §§6, 8; Panormitanus, *Commentaria* to X 1.29.33 §5, vol. 2, at 126vb; see also Herde, "Römisches und kanonisches Recht bei der Verfolgung des Fälschungsdelikts im Mittelalter," 338–39, as well as Robinson, *Criminal Law of Ancient Rome*, 36–39.

111. William Durand, *Speculum iudiciale* 1.4 *De aduocato* §3.10–11, at 1:266; Martin V, *Romani pontificis providentia* (1423) §25, in Tangl, *Päpstlichen Kanzleiordnungen*, 155. Alfonso el sabio was even harsher: the *Siete Partidas* 3.6.15 prescribed the death penalty for advocates guilty of *praevaricatio* (Alonso Romero and Garrigas Acosta, "El régimen jurídico de la abogacía en Castilla," 98–99).

112. E.g., Robert of Flamborough, *Liber poenitentialis*, 184–85, §207; see also Noonan, *Bribes*, 176–79.

113. E.g., John of Salisbury, *Policraticus* 5.13, ed. Webb, at 1:341; Peter of Blois, *Epist.* 26, at 1:95.

114. William Durand, *Speculum iudiciale* 1.4 *De aduocato* §3.11, at 1:266: "Saepe enim uidi ab aliquibus peti consilium, non ut acceptaretur, sed ut illi postea parti alteri consulere erubescant. Si autem fui aduocatus in causa nondum finita, in aliqua parte sui contra te non ero, alioquin crimine praeuaricationis inuoluar." The tactic of "conflicting out" potential opponent law firms remains to this day a not uncommon problem in American legal practice (Shapiro, *Tangled Loyalties*, 74–75, 184–86).

We ordain that, as is indeed right and proper, no advocate or proctor who has once given counsel or representation to one party in a case may thereafter advise or represent the opposing party in that same case or pursue or defend his cause, unless he may be required to do so by a judicial order for distribution of advocates or proctors. In that case he shall never reveal to his new client anything that he learned from the other party in the case, unless he is instructed to do so by that party. And if he contravenes the aforesaid, let him incur the sentence of excommunication and other penalties prescribed by law, and moreover he shall be deprived of his office, and shall nevertheless be held liable to the offended party.[115]

Other ecclesiastical courts adopted similar rules—or even copied this one verbatim, as the court of the bishop's official at Geneva did. Secular courts adopted analogous measures.[116]

Despite efforts to discourage such behavior and the gravity of the penalties prescribed for those who betrayed their clients' trust, ambidextrous advocates were certainly not unknown in medieval practice. Indeed, Hostiensis placed sabotage of a client's case at the head of his list of eleven common failings of advocates.[117]

The lawyer's duty to be loyal to his clients was an admirable ideal, but it was often neither simple nor self-evident to decide just who the client was. If two long-standing clients of an advocate resolved to sue one another, which one was he obliged to help? This question was debated in the law schools. An anonymous Anglo-Norman glossator at the end of the twelfth

---

115. *Romani pontificis providentia* §25, in Tangl, *Päpstlichen Kanzleiordnungen*, 155: "Statuimus autem, prout etiam iura disponunt, ut nullus advocatus vel procurator, qui semel uni parti in aliqua causa consilium vel patrocinium dederit, parti adverse in eadem causa patrocinium vel consilium prestet seu causam ipsius agat vel defendat, nisi facta advocatorum aut procuratorum distributione auctoritate iudicis compellatur. Quo casu de hiis, que ab illa prima parte in causa didicit, nunquam alteram doceat aut ex illis, nisi ab eadem parte didicerit, patrocinium prestet. Et si contra premissa fecerit, excommunicationis sententiam et alias penas iuris incurrat ac suo privetur officio ad interesse partis nichilominus condemnandus."

116. *Constitutiones et statuta nove reformacionis curie officialatus Gebenn* 1:377, §37; Beaumanoir, *Coutumes de Beauvaisis* 5.177, 179 at 1:90–91; *Constitutiones patriae Foriiulii*, rubr. 6, at 3r; *Statuta Veneta emendatissima*, Consulta 13, at 180v. English common law courts also penalized practitioners for breach of loyalty to clients (Brand, *Origins of the English Legal Profession*, 122–25, 139–40; Palmer, "Origins of the Legal Profession in England," 128–29, 132; and Rose, "Ambidextrous Lawyer").

117. Hostiensis, *Summa*, lib. 5, *De penitentiis et remissionibus* §32, at 275ra.

century declared that an advocate in this situation should remain neutral and side with neither party, although he noted that others maintained that he should appear for the defendant. "Whoever puts himself in the position of being obligated to two [warring clients]," the glossator added, " does so ill-advisedly."[118] Bernard of Parma likewise taught that an advocate should refrain from aiding either client in this situation, but he noted an exception if the advocate held an office from one of them. In that situation, the lawyer should assist the one from whom he held office. Innocent IV, on the other hand, adopted the first come, first served approach and advised an advocate torn between loyalties to two clients to lend his assistance to the one who had first engaged his services. Hostiensis adopted yet another plan. He suggested that advocates caught in this situation would do best for themselves and their clients if they tried to mediate between the parties so as to avoid litigation altogether, a solution that other legal authorities adopted as well.[119]

Hostiensis also explored the delicate situation that arose for an advocate who held a prebend in a cathedral chapter (as many did) if the chapter decided to sue the bishop (not an uncommon occurrence). Where should his loyalties lie and which party should he assist? Hostiensis advised him to act for the chapter, unless it seemed that the lawsuit might do the bishop an injustice, in which case he could go to the bishop's aid. But what if taking the bishop's side would mean that the chapter would be left with no skilled advocate? Then, according to Hostiensis, he should assist the chapter—unless the bishop gave him a direct order not to do so, since he was obliged to obey the bishop. William Durand further noted that an advocate caught between conflicting loyalties should consider his precise legal relationship with the church in which he held his benefice. Clerical advocates not uncommonly acquired benefices in dioceses in which they were legally strangers (*clerici peregrini*), while others were beneficed in the dioceses to which

---

118. See Fransen, "'Questiones' des canonistes (III)," 527, no. 53; gloss to D. 96 c. 11 v. *potestatem*, in Caius glosses, at 57vb: "Si ergo clericus in duobus episcopatibus redditum habeat, pro quo et contra quem stabitur? Respondeo, faciat secundum id 14 q. 5 Denique [C. 14 q. 5 c. 10] uel secundum alios pro reo stare debet. Male quilibet facit qui hoc modo duobus se obligauit."

119. Bernard of Parma, *Glos. ord.* to X 1.37.3 v. *contra ecclesiam*; Innocent IV, *Apparatus* to X 1.37.3 v. *praesumit*, at 165rb (see also Baldus's comments under the heading *De aduocato* in the *Additiones* to William Durand, *Speculum iudiciale*, at 1:282); Hostiensis, *Summa*, lib. 1, *De postulando* §8, at 62vb; Durand, *Speculum iudiciale* 1.4 *De aduocato* §1.18, at 1:262; Guido de Baysio, *Rosarium* to D. 96 c. 11, at 113ra–rb.

they were legally attached, or incardinated.[120] He also adopted distinctions voiced earlier by Vincentius Hispanus (d. 1248) and Hostiensis. They suggested that the proper course of action might depend upon how much the benefice was worth. If its value was negligible, it counted as a charitable gift that the donor could revoke at his pleasure. If the benefice was valuable and the advocate held it as compensation for his legal services, however, he could not be deprived of it for representing a close associate (*coniuncta persona*) who happened to be an adversary of the donor.[121]

Conflict-of-interest and confidentiality problems were likewise acute for an advocate who received a fief as a retainer for his services, another situation that was not unusual. He had a double obligation, both as a vassal and as an advocate, to serve his lord faithfully and to keep his secrets. Nevertheless, Durand asserted, a fief-holding vassal could ethically plead against his lord on behalf of a close associate on the same grounds that applied to a beneficed cleric. The fact that the advocate had promised fealty to the lord as a condition of receiving his fief did not cancel his higher obligations to himself and his kin, "since no one hates his own flesh." The fief-holder who appeared against his lord on behalf of someone outside of that close personal circle, however, would violate his oath and could lawfully be deprived of his fief.[122]

Durand advised advocates who held fiefs or benefices to be prudent. Although it might be ethically permissible under some circumstances for them to oppose their benefactors, he thought it more sensible to refrain from doing so, since, according to the rules of law, "not everything that is permissible is honorable."[123]

Loyalty and conflict of interest issues became particularly complicated for an advocate who maintained a long-standing professional relation-

120. Hostiensis, *Summa*, lib. 1, *De postulando* §8, at 63ra; William Durand, *Speculum iudiciale* 1.4 *De aduocato* §1.17, at 1:262; see further Condorelli, *Clerici peregrini*, and McBride, *Incardination and Excardination of Seculars*.

121. William Durand, *Speculum iudiciale* 1.4 *De aduocato* §1.21, at 1:262. Vincentius's gloss was quoted by Bernardus de Montemirato, also known as Abbas antiquus (d. 1296), in his *Lectura* to X 1.37.3 v. *clericus*, at 70rb. The distinctions he outlined remained current in the seventeenth century as appears from Prosper Fagani (1598–1678), *Jus canonicum* to X 1.37.3 §§18–19, vol. 2, at 577.

122. William Durand, *Speculum iudiciale* 1.4 *De aduocato* §1.30, at 1:263. On the obligations of advocates as fiefholders, see Gratian, C. 22 q. 5 c. 18, a passage from Fulbert of Chartres that also appears in the *Consuetudines feudorum*, Vulgata 2.6, at 121 (see chap. 5, n. 56 above).

123. William Durand, *Speculum iudiciale* 1.4 *De aduocato* §1.21, at 1:262.

ship with a corporate body, such as a monastery or a church. The problems arose out of the nature of corporate organizations. A corporation unites a number of individuals engaged in a common enterprise into a single entity that the law treats as if its members were one person.[124] The legal interests and personal goals of a corporation's individual members, however, are seldom identical and indeed are often incompatible with one another. The abbot of a monastery, for example, may wish to use a cash surplus to build a new church, while the monks, or most of them, may want to use the same resources to put more and better wine on the table. The monastery's advocate or proctor in this situation must decide who his client is. Do his professional obligations require him to further the interests of the abbot if those conflict with the interests of the community? But does the community have no claim upon his skill and assistance in these circumstances? Likewise, if a local church has granted a benefice to an advocate as a retainer to assure that his services will be available when needed, what must he do if another long-standing client wishes to sue that church?

These questions were not merely the hypothetical musings of law professors. Conflicts of interest of precisely these kinds frequently arose in practice, as they still do, and medieval lawyers were keenly aware that the way they dealt with them could have serious consequences for their livelihood and their reputation, both among their peers and among clients. Academic jurists when they dealt with problems such as these took their guiding principle from a provision in a third-century imperial rescript that forbade any advocate ever employed by the imperial treasury (*advocati fisci*) to appear in cases against the treasury. Gratian incorporated this provision in the second recension of his Decretum, but added that "nowadays, however, [former treasury advocates] can take private clients even against the treasury, although they declined to accept those cases while they were treasury advocates."[125]

---

124. An exception to the rule is the corporation sole, which has only a single member at any point in time, but nevertheless may continue to exist even after that individual's death; Kantorowicz, *The King's Two Bodies*, is the classic study of this peculiar institution and its consequences. Overall, however, the ethical problems that bedeviled medieval advocates and proctors in their relationships with corporate clients continue to present analogous problems to modern lawyers (Hazard, *Ethics in the Practice of Law*, 43–57).

125. C. 3 q. 7 c. 2 §15: "Item, quamuis illi, qui causam fisci egissent, prohibeantur aduersus fiscum patrocinium prestare, tamen hodie etiam aduersus fiscum patrocinium possunt exhibere priuatis, dum eam causam declinent suscipere, quam tractauerant, dum fisci aduocati fuerint [cf. Cod. 2.8(9).2]." The original proscription appears

A similar ethical quandary arose if an advocate was asked to oppose a former client, public or private, at the appellate stage of an action. Durand argued that although the law appeared to allow him to face a former client on appeal, he ought to reject such a brief.[126] Johannes Andreae (b. ca. 1270, d. 1348) offered a sterner view. Although he had seen it written that the doctors of Bologna agreed that a legal consultant could properly accept the case, he nevertheless declared:

> I would not appear for any reason against a client to whom I had given paid advice, especially if I had done so in writing. If I gave him proper advice, I should not attack it unjustly; if I was in error, I ought to safeguard my reputation.[127]

Pierre de Belleperche (d. 1308) likewise argued that an advocate should not act on appeal for the opponent of a client whom he had represented in first instance. The advocate, he pointed out, must by this point know all the secrets of his former client's case. If he opposed him on appeal, he would be suspected of betraying the confidences that he was obliged to keep. During the first stage of the case, moreover, the advocate must have sworn that he believed that his client's contentions were well-grounded in law and in fact. Now during the appeal, he would have to argue that they were not, which would contradict his earlier sworn statement. Rather than leave himself open to suspicions of betrayal and perjury, either of which would disqualify him from further practice, he must refuse to represent the earlier client's opponent on appeal.[128]

---

at Cod. 2.8(9).1–2; Dig. 3.1.10 (see also Azo, *Summa super Codicem*, 29, to Cod. 2.9; Baldus, *Commentaria* to Cod. 2.8[9].2 §§2–3, vol. 7, at 131va). See too Johannes Teutonicus, *Glos. ord.* to C. 3 q. 7 c. 2 §15, *Item quamuis illi* v. *causam*; *Summa "Elegantius"* 6.67, at 2:133; and Accursius, *Glos. ord.* to Cod. 2.8(9).1 v. *praestare*; but cf. Bartolus, *Commentarium* to Cod. 2.6.2, vol. 7, at 63r; likewise Jean Le Coq, *Questiones Johannis Galli*, 285, no. 237, similarly reported in *Arresta quedam Parisiis quam Tholose in parlamento prolata*, at 31rb.

126. William Durand, *Speculum iudiciale* 1.4 *De aduocato* §3.12–13, at 1:266.

127. Johannes Andreae, *Additio* to William Durand, *Speculum iudiciale* 1.4 *De aduocato* §3.11 v, *priusquam*, at 1:266: "Ego nulla ratione patrocinarer contra illud pro quo dedissem consilium recepto salario, et maxime in scriptis; si vero in eisdem terminis quos consului esset causa, si ei iuste consului, iustitiam impugnare non debeo; et si errassem, honori meo parcere debeo; et de accusa., Qualiter [X 5.1.17]." On the *communis opinio doctorum*, see Johannes Teutonicus, *Glos. ord.* to C. 3 q. 7 d.p.c. 1 v. *dum putaretur*; Helmholz, *Roman Canon Law in Reformation England*, 14–16, and *Spirit of Classical Canon Law*, 23–24, as well as Horn, "Legistische Literatur," 261.

128. Pierre de Belleperche, *Auree ac singularissime et quas nulla vidit etas Repetititiones* to Cod. 3.7.1, at 14r–v.

Similar issues concerning confidentiality and conflict of roles arose when an advocate also served as a judge, another not uncommon event. A fourth-century imperial constitution had forbidden anyone to function in both capacities in the same case, for as Justinian later observed, if he tried to do both, he could not be expected to fulfill either role adequately. Twelfth-century writers often interpreted this to mean that a judge could not properly rule on a case in which he had previously been an advocate for one of the parties, although some jurists questioned this reading of the law. Pope Lucius III (r. 1181–85) ruled that previous service as an advocate for one party in a lawsuit constituted sufficient grounds to recuse a judge.[129] The ethical question, however, continued to be debated. Eminent authorities held that previous knowledge of a litigant's secrets would inevitably compromise the judge's capacity to decide the case fairly, since this confidential information was likely to influence his rulings, which should rest exclusively on the evidence and arguments produced in court.[130]

Medieval courts followed the Roman law rule that barred advocates from testifying as witnesses in cases in which they appeared. This policy rested on two grounds: a belief that their testimony was likely to be colored by their relationship to the litigant, and concern about safeguarding privileged secrets.[131] A reference by Panormitanus to Antonio de Butrio's claim that testimony by an advocate against his client was highly credible,

---

129. Cod. 2.6.6 pr.; 1.51.14 (see also Dig. 2.1.17 and Gratian, C. 4. q. 4 c. 1 and 2); *Dissensiones dominorum, Vetus collectio*, 59–60, §76; Rossi, *Consilium sapientis*, 86–87; X 2.28.36 (JL 14966); Bernard of Parma, *Glos. ord.* to X 1.29.17 v. *dominus* and 2.28.36 v. *advocati*. The Jesuit writer Tomas Sanchez (1550–1610) would later maintain that if the advocate had only been consulted about a case but had not yet given his advice on it he could still serve as judge (*Opuscula sive consilia moralia* 3.1.26, at 1:410–21).

130. Accursius, *Casus* to Cod. 2.6.6 and *Glos. ord.* v. *negocio, opinionis,* and *imminutionem*; Gratian C. 2 q. 1 c. 19 and C. 3 q. 7 c. 4, as well as Johannes Teutonicus, *Apparatus* to 3 Comp. 2.12.13 v. *quin immo,* at 1:262. Bernard of Parma quoted part of this argument in his *Glos. ord.* to X 2.20.40 v. *recusatis*. It appears again in Panormitanus, *Commentaria* to X 1.31.13 §4, vol. 2, at 153va–vb. Among the procedural writers, see especially Tancred, *Ordo iudiciarius* 1.4.4, 2.6.6, at 109, 148; William Durand, *Speculum iudiciale* 1.4 *De teste* §1.67, at 1:297; as well as Nörr, *Zur Stellung des Richters*.

131. Dig. 22.5.25; Gratian C. 14 q. 2 pr., and d.p.c. 1; VI 2.10.3; Johannes Teutonicus, *Glos. ord.* to C. 2 q. 6 c. 38 v. *vel cognitor*; Bonaguida, *Summa introductoria* 3.3, at 265; *Ordo iudiciarius "Scientiam,"* 57, §29; Hostiensis, *Lectura* to X 1.36.6 §3, vol. 1, at 180ra; William Durand, *Speculum iudiciale* 1.4 *De teste* §1.74, at 1:298–99; Johannes Andreae, *Glos. ord.* to VI 2.10.3 v. *appellationis*; Rota Romana, *Decisiones novae, antiquae, et antiquiores, Decisiones novae, De appellationibus,* no. 52 [*alias* 381], 259.

however, suggests that in practice their immunity from testifying may not always have been observed. Elsewhere, Panormitanus also indicates that as an exception to the general rule, an advocate may give testimony concerning documents that he had prepared.[132]

A genuinely zealous advocate might go so far as to try to discover the secrets of his opponent's case. Bonaguida of Arezzo, drawing perhaps upon his experience at the Roman curia, declared:

> [H]e should take care, if he can, to get a look at the proofs and legal arguments of his opponent, so that once he learns what they are and the secrets of the business have been laid bare, he may know both how to attack and how to defend himself. . . . And I suggest that you do this if you can manage it with due honesty, but otherwise not.

Bonaguida apparently felt reservations about this course of action, for he hastened to add that he was, of course, merely offering helpful advice and no one was obliged to accept it, "but it is up to him to consider whether it would be proper to follow it."[133]

Bonaguida had reason to be cautious: Pope Alexander III had ruled that advocates could be punished for pilfering their opponent's papers or interfering with their witnesses, while theologians considered that efforts to ferret out an opponent's secrets were at best questionable and at worst morally reprehensible.[134] Tomás Sanchez (1550–1610), an eminent Jesuit casuist, summed up medieval debates on the matter. It was grievously sinful, Sanchez held, for an advocate to secure secret information about his opponent's case from a scribe, a printer, a member of the adversary's household, or a judge's servant. But what if the client, rather than the advocate, were to get his hands on the desired information in this way? Could the advocate in

---

132. Panormitanus, *Commentaria* to X 1.43.2 §12, vol. 2, at 216va, and to 1.36.6 §1, vol. 2, at 175va.

133. Bonaguida, *Summa introductoria* 1.3.19, at 161–62: "Sit cautus undevicesimo, ut videat, si potest, probationes et jura adversarii, ut, postquam sibi fuerint intimati et secreta negotii denundata, sciat et impugnare et se defendere: ex hoc compellatur arbiter pronuntiare, ff. de receptis 4.8. Labeo 3 [Dig. 4.8.25]. Et hoc consulo fieri, si cum honestate debita potest: alias non. Non enim, qui hortatur, mandatoris opera fungitur, ff. de his, qui notantur infamia 3.2 ob haec verba 20 [Dig. 3.2.20] et nemo ex consilio est obligatus, sed liberum est ei apud se explorare, an expediat consilium sequi, ff. mandati 17.1 mandatum 2 § tua 6 [Dig. 17.1.2.6]."

134. X 2.21.4 (JL 13980) and Bernard of Parma, *Glos. ord.* to v. *ostendit*; Goffredus de Trano, *Summa super titulis*, 219, to X 1.21 §4; Hostiensis, *Summa*, lib. 2, *De testibus cogendis* §4, at 102vb; Trusen, "Advocatus," 1240.

good conscience use the ill-gotten knowledge? Sanchez maintained that an ethical advocate should not employ it; indeed, he thought that it would be sinful even for his scribe to make a copy of it. If, however, the litigant were to discover his opponent's information by some lucky chance (*obiter informationes inuenit*), then the advocate could ethically make use of it.[135]

Although an advocate was not supposed to spy on his adversary or purloin his confidential information, he had no ethical obligation to reveal any information to the opponent. If his opponent overlooked a law or an argument that would bolster his case, no rule required the advocate to alert him to the oversight. An advocate was a warrior, and as William of Pagula (fl. ca. 1313–31) observed, a soldier in battle had every right to fight from a concealed position. For similar reasons, Bonaguida strongly advised his readers to arrange if they could possibly do so to be the closing speaker, so that opposing counsel would be unable to pick up any useful points from their remarks.[136]

An advocate, then as now, was by definition a partisan. His basic task was to do his utmost to make the best possible case for his client's position. If he could somehow induce an opponent to settle in a way that secured his client's goals without going to trial, so much the better, but that was not his primary function. He was fundamentally a fighter, not a peacemaker or an *amicus curiae*.[137] His task was to win lawsuits. The oath of office prescribed by *Properandum* explicitly demanded that he put all his strength, knowledge, and talent at his client's disposal.[138]

Wholehearted advocacy required the advocate or proctor to use every resource he could muster to secure his client's objectives. He needed to find ways to turn every issue in the case to his client's advantage. He must

---

135. Sanchez, *Consilia seu opuscula moralia* 3.1.44.5, at 1:460. See Brouillard, "Sanchez, Thomas," in *Dictionnaire de théologie catholique*, 14/1: 1075–85.

136. William of Pagula, *Summa summarum* 1.61, CUL, MS Pembroke 201, at 73va: "An aduocatus tenetur dare aduersario suo iura que pro ipso faciunt? Dic quod non, cum in corporali bello licitum est aduersarium decipere, [xx]iiii. q. iiii. c. i. et secundum glo. [C. 23 q. 2 c. 2; *glos. ord.* v. *insidiis*]"; Bonaguida, *Summa introductoria* 1.3.9, 15, at 157, 159–60, and 1.3.21, at 163. On William of Pagula, see further *BRUO* 3:1436–37 and Boyle, "The 'Summa summarum,'" 415–56.

137. Thus, e.g., Bulgarus, *Excerpta legum*, 2–3; Tancred, *Ordo iudiciarius* 1.5.3, at 112; Johannes Andreae, *Additio* to William Durand, *Speculum iudiciale* 1.4 De aduocato §1.14 v. *in fin.*, at 1:262; cf. Dig. 3.1.1.2 and Cod. 3.1.14.4, routinely quoted or paraphrased by innumerable medieval authors, e.g., Gratian at C. 3 q. 7 c. 2 §1; Bernard of Pavia, *Summa decretalium* 1.28.1, at 23; Bernard of Parma, *Glos. ord.* to X 1.37.3 v. *postulare*.

138. 2 Lyons (1274) c. 19 in DEC 1:324; also Crook, *Legal Advocacy*, 196–97.

search out hidden flaws in his adversary's case and discover ways to undermine the opponent's strong points. Although the advocate's prior training had equipped him with a reasonable command of the law, real-life situations were likely to raise problems and present opportunities that he had not previously considered. The advocate had to be ready and able to toil over his books and seek out the opinions of more learned jurists in order to find answers to new or unfamiliar legal problems. He also needed to be careful not to harm his client's cause through unwitting errors of omission, much less by deliberate failure to present his case adequately and fully.[139]

FEES AND COSTS

By the time that advocates and proctors had become full-fledged professionals, it had long since become generally accepted that clients normally had an obligation to pay for legal counsel and representation. "No one," declared Innocent III, invoking the usual proof text, "can be expected to fight for another at his own expense,"[140] nor were advocates so constituted that they could live on air. Payment for legal services not expected only when the lawyer was a cleric with an ample benefice or a judge had appointed him to assist a poor client.[141] Clients assumed that professional legal services would prove expensive. Popular beliefs, expressed in songs and sermons, parodies and proverbs, routinely castigated lawyers for their

---

139. William Durand, *Speculum iudiciale* 1.4 *De aduocato* §9.18–19, at 1:282; Baldus, *Commentaria* to Cod. 2.7.3–5, vol. 1, at 141ra–rb.

140. X 3.39.21, paraphrasing 1 Cor. 1:9:7; cf. the similar sentiment in Tacitus, *Annales* 11.7. Gratian a century earlier had noted that prohibitions against clerical advocates seeking fees for their services had been abrogated by custom in the church (*ecclesiae consuetudine receptum est et moribus approbatum*) and were no longer operative (C. 15 q. 2 d.p.c. un.).

141. Secular clerics who were adequately supported by income from benefices were not supposed to ask for compensation in return for legal assistance, although they were permitted to accept free-will gifts if grateful clients offered them spontaneously. See Bernard of Pavia, *Summa decretalium* 1.28.3, at 23; Rufinus, *Summa* to C. 15 q. 2 pr., at 348; Council of Paris (1222), pt. 1 c. 6, in Mansi 22:820–21; Synod of Bayonne (1300) c. 35, in Mansi 25:67; *Antiqua statuta* of Tournai (late thirteenth/early fourteenth century) c. 21.1, in *Statuts de l'ancienne province de Reims*, 348. Governments occasionally supported an official advocate whose function was to represent indigent clients in the courts. It was of course permissible for the appointee to accept compensation from the public purse, but not from the person on whose behalf he acted. See, e.g., Brundage, "Legal Aid for the Poor"; Roumy, "Système de l'avocat commis d'office"; as well as Planas Roselló, "Los abogados de Mallorca," 117.

rapaciousness and portrayed legal training as a royal road to riches, power, and influence. Lawyers could reasonably dream of accumulating substantial wealth, and elite practitioners sometimes realized that dream.[142]

The issues that dominated discussions of legal fees during the decades that followed 1200 centered largely on practical questions about fee arrangements. How much should lawyers charge for their services? What factors ought to determine their compensation level? What additional charges for expenses were permissible? When and under what circumstances should advocates and their clients settle on fees? When did payment become due? What recourse, if any, did a lawyer have against clients who failed to pay?

Thirteenth-century authorities agreed that advocates' fees ought to be reasonable and moderate and that they must not exceed the limits established by law.[143] Not surprisingly, lawyers, with the cooperation and sometimes the connivance of their clients, sought ways to circumvent those limits. A client might make a "loan" to his lawyer, above and beyond the legal limit on his fees—a hoary ploy that had been outlawed in antiquity. The *palmarium*, a bonus on top of the agreed-upon fee, was another well-worn dodge for evading fee limits that ancient authorities had caught onto and discouraged. Both practices still persisted, and renewed prohibitions in the thirteenth and fourteenth centuries proved no more effective than earlier ones.[144] Jason of Mayno (1435–1519), admittedly a hostile witness, accused curial advocates at Rome of paying greater attention to their own interests than to the law. He claimed that they operated on the principle that the cap on legal fees referred to the separate stages of a case and thus felt free to charge the maximum fee several times over on each case they handled.

142. Yunck, *Lineage of Lady Meed*, 143–59; Brundage, "Vultures, Whores, and Hypocrites"; Herlihy, *Medieval and Renaissance Pistoia*, 237–38; Hyde, *Padua in the Age of Dante*, 146; Martines, *Lawyers and Statecraft*, 100–106; Guenée, *Tribunaux et gens de justice*, 200–202; Fédou, *Les hommes de loi lyonnais*, 211–12; Reynolds, *Europe Emerges*, 188.

143. Gratian, C. 3 q. 7 c. 2 §11; *Summa "Elegantius"* 6.65, at 2:133; Tancred, *Ordo iudiciarius* 1.5.4, at 112–13; William of Drogheda, *Summa aurea*, 54–56, §54; Johannes Bassianus, *Libellus de ordine iudiciorum*, 234, §331; William Durand, *Speculum iudiciale* 1.4 De salariis §3.1, 3, at 1:347–48; cf. Cod. 2.6.6.5 and 12.61.2; Dig. 50.13.1.12.

144. Cod. 2.6.3 and 10.65.2.1; Dig. 50.13.1.12; Cod. Theod. 8.10.2 (= Cod. 12.61.2); William Durand, *Speculum iudiciale* 1.4 De salariis §§2.3 and 3.2, at 1:346, 347; Benedict XII, *Decens et necessarium* §27, in Tangl, *Päpstlichen Kanzleiordnungen*, 123. Durand in his commentary on *Properandum*, however, claimed that the maximum fee need not be construed to include minor gifts, such as chickens, fish, fruit, or wine (Lefebvre, "La constitution *Properandum*," 527).

Whether literally true or not, Jason's assertions are consistent with a statement of Franciscus de Vercelli (fl. ca. 1250–80), who two centuries earlier had asserted that advocates often exceeded the nominal limits on their fees, sometimes by as much as three times the legal maximum.[145]

The criteria that medieval jurists used, at least theoretically, to determine what constituted a reasonable and moderate fee came from a Roman model that that we encountered earlier. The primary criteria were the value of the stakes at issue, the difficulty of the case, the amount of work that the advocate put into it, and his skill and reputation, together with the customary level of fees in the region, particularly in the specific court where the case was heard.[146] Local markets for legal services no doubt influenced actual fee levels in many communities. At Bologna in 1268, for example, the customary fee for an advocate seems to have been about twenty-five Bolognese pounds, while a few highly esteemed advocates usually got about twice that amount.[147] To complicate matters, clients did not necessarily pay all their legal fees in cash. Mixed payments, part in cash and part in kind, were not unusual, as, for example, the fee of 100 *solidi* and twelve yards of scarlet cloth that Adam Usk (d. 1430) received for his work on one matter.[148]

Although authorities, including William Durand, often thought it nec-

145. Jason de Mayno, *Commentaria super titulo De actionibus* § *Tripli vero*, no. 52, at 199vb; Franciscus de Vercelli, quoted by Fournier, *Questions d'histoire du droit canonique*, 26. . Further on Jason de Mayno, see Savigny, *Geschichte* 6:397–418; Calasso, *Medio evo del diritto*, 583; and Gilmore, "Lawyers and the Church," 69–73.

146. Thus, e.g., Huguccio, *Summa* to C. 3 q. 7 c. 2 §8 v. *certe partis*, in BAV, Arch. S. Petr. C.114, at 146va (above, chap. 5, n. 115); Ricardus Anglicus, *Summa de ordine iudiciario*, 33–34, §26; Goffredus de Trano, *Summa super titulis*, 128, to X 1.37 §8; Raymond de Penyafort, *Summa de penitentia* 2.5.39, cols. 517–18; Accursius, *Glos. ord.* to Cod. 2.6.3 v. *certum modum* and to Dig. 50.13.1 v. *pro modo litis*; Azo, *Summa super Codicem*, 28, to Cod. 2.6; William Durand, *Speculum iudiciale* 1.4 *De salariis* §3.1, at 1:347; Visky, "Retribuzioni per il lavoro giuridica, 19; Johann Friedrich Autenrith, *De eo quod iustum est circa salaria ac honoraria advocatorum*, 28; and cf. above, chap. 1. These criteria came from Ulpian in Dig. 50.13.1.10 and remain part of the guidelines to this day; see, e.g., Rule 1.5 in the American Bar Association's Model Rules of Professional Conduct, in *The Law Governing Lawyers*, ed. Martyn, Fox, and Wendel, 19; and the International Bar Association's International Code of Ethics, Rule 17, in the Law Society's *Guide to the Professional Conduct of Solicitors*, 161.

147. Thus, e.g., *CSB* 7:116–17 (no. 221), 118 (no. 225), 178 (no. 349), 229 (no. 459); 8:32 (no. 60), 53 (no. 100), 83 (no. 160), 152 (no. 310); 10:9–10 (no. 15), 37 (no. 83).

148. Adam Usk, *Chronicle*, 96.

essary to remind advocates not to charge their clients too much, Durand also warned that selling their services too cheaply could damage their professional standing and besmirch their reputation just as much.[149] Master William Doune (d. 1361) likewise admonished advocates that selling their services at bargain rates was sinful. This, he declared, was every bit as bad as charging too much. An advocate or proctor who undercut his competitors' fees was engaging in unfair competition, which might deprive other, and perhaps better, advocates of a fair chance to earn a fee.[150]

In reality, the size of a lawyer's fee almost certainly depended at least as much on the client's resources as it did on any of the nominal criteria. Rich clients generally paid more, often much more, than poor ones for comparable services.[151] Most desirable of all from a lawyer's point of view were clients who were in a position to reward their advocates and proctors with a steady stream of revenue by granting them fiefs, administrative offices, or ecclesiastical benefices. It was likely to prove far more profitable in the long run to receive a bishopric or deanery as a fee than to get a one-time payment, whether in cash or cows.[152]

Authorities agreed that the classical Roman rule that forbade lawyers to enter into contingent fee arrangements with their clients represented sound policy and should remain in force.[153] The author of an addition to the ordinary gloss of Accursius explained that contingent fees were banned because such arrangements tended to reward advocates excessively for their labors. Permitting the practice, he added, would tempt them to support

---

149. William of Drogheda, *Summa aurea*, 90–91, §96; Bergfeld, "Das iustum pretium des Advokaten," 128–29; William Durand, *Speculum iudiciale* 1.4 *De aduocato* §1.15, at 1:262, and §9.13, at 1:281.

150. *Memoriale presbiterorum*, a. 34, ed. Haren, "Interrogatories," 132; cf. Hostiensis, *Summa*, lib. 5, *De penitentia et remissione* §32, at 275ra; William Durand, *Speculum iudiciale* 1.4 *De aduocato* §1.15, at 1:262. On William Doune, see *BRUO* 1:587–88, Thompson, "Will of Master William Doune," and Haren, "Confession, Social Ethics and Social Discipline," 109–10.

151. As Benedict XII explicitly recognized in *Decens et necessarium* (1340) §23, in Tangl, *Päpstlichen Kanzleiordnungen*, 123; see also Accursius, *Glos. ord.* to Cod. 2.6.6 v. *habeat*; Guenée, *Tribunaux et gens de justice*, 199.

152. Maitland, "English Law and the Renaissance," 184.

153. Azo, *Summa super Codicem*, 28, to Cod. 2.6; priests were also advised to ask advocates and proctors in confession whether they had made contingent fee arrangements with clients (*Memoriale presbiterorum*, §34, ed. Haren, "Interrogatories," 132; St. Antoninus, *Confessionale*, tit. *Ad aduocatos et procuratores et notarios*, unpaginated).

unworthy cases.[154] The principal dissenter on this issue among the civilians seems to have been Martinus. Unlike his peers, Martinus maintained, as we have seen, that an advocate could properly demand as his fee up to half of the property at issue in a case.[155]

Canonists by and large adopted policies similar to those of their civilian colleagues and cited many of the same authorities to support them.[156] They did concede, however, that an advocate or proctor could legitimately bargain that if they succeeded in winning a lawsuit, their client would turn over some specific item out of the award they won, such as a particular parcel of land or a designated horse, as the fee for their services. Civilians and canonists likewise agreed (although with a notable lack of enthusiasm) that variable fee arrangements, in which the amount that the advocate or proctor received depended on the outcome of the case, were permissible.[157]

Although preachers, poets, and even some academic legal writers insisted that lawyers should not work simply for the money, authors of professional handbooks were more realistic. They took it for granted that clients had an obligation to reward their lawyers with compensation appropriate to the learning, skill, and energy they brought to the task. Professional writers accordingly concerned themselves with practical arrangements concerning the negotiation and payment of legal fees.[158]

Writers of advice for legal professionals disagreed concerning the an-

154. *Additio* to Accursius's *Glos. ord.* on Cod. 2.6.5 v. *immensa*: "Et ratio quod non valeat huiusmodi pactum est quia inducit aduocatum ad delictum, nam cognoscens se habiturum partem eius quod prosequitur etiam calumniose aduocabit, siue igitur faciat pactum de quota litis, siue de certa specie seu quantitate; eadem semper est ratio, ergo, etc." On the authorship of the *additiones* to the *Glos. ord.*, see Lange, *Römisches Recht im Mittelalter*, 367–69.

155. *Dissensiones dominorum*, Hugolinus, 267, §22; Accursius, *Glos. ord.* to Cod. 2.6.5 v. *immensa* and *Glos. ord.* to Dig. 2.14.53 v. *datum*.

156. Thus, e.g., Johannes Teutonicus, *Glos. ord.* to C. 3 q. 7 c. 2 §8 v. *partis*; *Summa "Elegantius"* 6.64, at 2:132; Goffredus de Trano, *Summa super titulis*, 127, 128, to X 1.37 §§5, 8; Bernard of Parma, *Glos. ord.* to X 3.1.10 v. *more saecularium*; Hostiensis, *Summa*, lib. 1, *De postulando* §2, at 62rb; William Durand, *Speculum iudiciale* 1.4 *De aduocato* 1.15, as well as *De salariis* §§2.2 and 3.1, at 1:262, 346, 347.

157. On bargaining for a specific share in the award, *Dissensiones dominorum*, Hugolinus, 267–68, §23; Johannes Teutonicus, *Glos. ord.* to C. 3 q. 7 c. 2 §8 v. *partis*; Huguccio, *Summa* to the same passage v. *certe partis*, in chap. 5, n. 115. On variable fee arrangements, Pillius, *Casus questionum* 54, and Azo C.11, in *Questioni civilistiche*, 105, 145–47; William Durand, *Speculum iuris* 1.4 *De salariis* §3.6–7, at 1:348.

158. Peter the Chanter, *Verbum adbreviatum*, 334–35, c. 49; Gautier de Coinci, "Vie de Seinte Léocad," ll. 1107–16; Dante, *Convivio* 3.11.10, at 569; Dig. 50.13.1.5; Johannes

cient ethical principle that it was improper to set the price of services, much less to pay for them, before they were completed, despite the fact that no less an authority than Aristotle had supported it.[159] William Durand noted that opinions about the most appropriate time to negotiate fees varied. Some authorities advised advocates and proctors to settle the amount of their fees at the start, before the case went to court, while others deemed it more advantageous to strike fee agreements while the case was still in progress and before the judge pronounced his decision, and still others held it improper even to raise the matter of fees until the case was concluded.[160] Durand maintained that the custom of the court should be the deciding factor, although he also strongly advised, as others did, that it was best to settle fee arrangements right at the outset, as soon as the advocate or proctor decided to take the case: "If it seems to the advocate that his client ought to sue, let him first secure an agreement about an appropriate fee."[161]

Persuading a client to agree how much and on what terms he would pay his advocate or proctor was a delicate business, especially in the early stages of their relationship while the probable length and outcome of litigation remained uncertain. Actually securing payment, however, might well prove even more tricky. Clients who won their lawsuits were likely to pay, if not always as promptly or cheerfully as the advocate might have wished. If the client lost, the chances of collecting the agreed-upon fee promptly, or at all, diminished sharply. For this reason, Durand recommended that advocates, proctors, and legal advisers follow the practice of advocates at the Roman curia, who required payment of half their fee when they accepted the case, with the remaining half payable immediately following final arguments, and before the judge announced his decision.[162]

When a client resisted paying, the advocate's first recourse was a letter that reminded the client that their agreement had never stipulated vic-

---

Teutonicus, *Glos. ord.* to C. 11 q. 3 c. 71 v. *iustum* and to C. 1 q. 3 c. 11 v. *retributionis*; *Summa Parisiensis* to C. 3 q. 7 c. 2 v. *ad turpe compendium*, at 121.

159. Aristotle, *Nicomachaean Ethics* 9.1.6–7; Pliny, *Letters* 5.4, 9, and 13; Dig. 50.13.1.12; Bernard, *La rémunération*, 93–94, Visky, "Retribuzioni per il lavoro giuridico," 19–20.

160. William Durand, *Speculum iudiciale* 1.4 *De salariis* §3.14, at 1:349.

161. William Durand, *Speculum iudiciale* 1.4 *De aduocato* §3.8 and *De salariis* §3.5, at 1:266, 348; cf. Raymond de Penyafort, *Summa de penitentia* 2.5.39, at col. 517; Tancred, *Ordo iudiciarius* 1.5.3, at 112; William of Drogheda, *Summa aurea*, 90, §95; Innocent IV, *Apparatus* to X 1.37.1 §2, at 165ra, and London, BL, MS Royal 10.D.III, at 72va; Accursius, *Glos. ord.* to Cod. 2.6.6 v. *contractum ineat*.

162. William Durand, *Speculum iudiciale* 1.4 *De salariis* 3.14, at 1:349.

tory as a condition of payment, and to request immediate settlement of the account.[163] Should this fail to elicit an acceptable response, the advocate needed to resort to sterner measures. For this reason, William of Drogheda (d. 1245) admonished practitioners to make sure that their fee would be forthcoming in advance of the judge's decision. If a client seemed reluctant to pay, the advocate would have to ratchet up the psychological pressure. He could do this in several ways. Any practicing lawyer knew how to delay matters, and he could use obstruction as a tool to increase his client's apprehensions to the point that he became anxious enough to settle up. If these measures failed and the client still had not paid by the time that the judge handed down his decision, the advocate could refuse to turn over the written judgment and other records and documents connected with the case until he had received payment in full.[164] If the judge awarded costs to the winner of the case, as was the usual practice, the fees of advocates, proctors, and legal consultants on the winner's side normally formed part of his costs order and might be paid out of the security that parties were supposed to furnish at the time that they submitted their *libelli* to the judge. Although this effectively guaranteed that he would be paid, it might not constitute the optimum outcome from the lawyer's point of view, since judges reviewed claims for legal fees during the process of taxing costs and almost invariably reduced the claimed fees and expenses.[165]

If all else failed, the lawyer's final recourse to recover an unpaid fee was to sue his client. The juridical basis for such a suit was complicated by the tradition that the services rendered by lawyers and other practitioners of the arts appropriate to free men (*artes liberales*) were literally priceless, so that their value could not be measured in crude monetary terms. The traditional view held that it was dishonorable for a lawyer to demand a fee, although if his client spontaneously offered him a gift, he was free to accept it.[166]

Medieval civilians and canonists considered this position anomalous. Conciliar canons in the early church had decreed that simple promises, despite the fact that they lacked the formalities that jurists attached to

---

163. Examples of such letters appear in the mid-thirteenth-century procedural manual *"Curialis,"* 61–62, §206; Linehan, "Spanish Litigants and Their Agents," 500–501.

164. William of Drogheda, *Summa aurea*, 90, §95.

165. William Durand, *Speculum iudiciale* 2.1 *De satisdationibus* §§1–2, at 1:533–35, and 2.3 *De expensis* §6, at 1:907–11; Brundage, "Taxation of Costs."

166. Dig. 50.13.1.5.

contractual obligations, were morally binding and that church authorities ought to enforce them. Thirteenth-century canonists picked up on those texts, declaring that agreements, however informal, must be kept. Canon law authorized judges in ecclesiastical courts to enforce simple agreements, if necessary through excommunication. Teachers of civil law in the same period likewise began to modify their treatment of the subject to bring it more closely into line with that of contemporary canonists.[167] Azo introduced a distinction between what he called "clothed agreements" (*pacta vestita*), which were enforceable at law, in contrast to the classical "bare agreements" (*nuda pacta*) which were not. Accursius plainly considered that fee agreements between advocates and clients fell into the new class of enforceable agreements and treated them as the functional equivalent of the remuneration received by proctors and legal advisers. Procedural writers such as Tancred and William Durand certainly assumed that advocates had a legitimate cause of action against clients who failed to pay an agreed-upon fee, and by the second half of the thirteenth century this had become the standard view.[168]

Suits brought by advocates, proctors, and legal consultants to recover unpaid fees began to appear regularly in ecclesiastical court records around the middle of the thirteenth century.[169] An early example appears in a decision that Pope Gregory IX handed down in 1235 ordering the archbishop of Canterbury to compel the monks of St. Swithun's Cathedral Priory at Winchester to pay ten marks, in addition to an earlier partial payment of

---

167. Gratian C. 12. q. 2 c. 66 and X 1.35.1 and 3; Johannes Teutonicus, *Glos. ord.* to C. 12 q. 2 c. 66 v. *promiserint*; Bernard of Parma, *Glos. ord.* to X 1.35.1 v. *pacta custodiantur*; Innocent IV, *Apparatus* to X 1.35.1 v. *cohibuerit*, at 161va. Zimmermann, *Law of Obligations*, 538–45, explores these developments in detail.

168. Azo, *Summa super Codicem*, 23, to Cod. 2.3 §15; Accursius, *Glos. ord.* to Cod. 2.6.3 v. *honorarii*: "id est salarii;" likewise in his gloss to Cod. 2.6.5 v. *honorarium*; Tancred, *Ordo iudiciarius* 1.5.4, at 113; William Durand, *Speculum iudiciale* 1.4 *De salariis* §3.4, at 1:348. For later thirteenth-century commentators, see, e.g., Goffredus de Trano, *Summa super titulis*, 128, to X 1.37 §8; Bernard of Parma, *Glos. ord.* to X 1.35.1 v. *pacta custodiantur*; Hostiensis, *Summa*, lib. 1, *De postulando* §2, at 62rb.

169. Helmholz, "Ethical Standards," 47–48. The appearance in procedural manuals and practitioners' form books of sample bills of complaint and other documents needed for litigating such cases supplies further evidence of the increasing regularity with which such cases came to the courts; e.g., Master Arnulphus, *Summa minorum*, 20, §23; William Durand, *Speculum iudiciale* 4.4 *De magistris* §§2, 4–5, at 2:486; Herde, *Audientia litterarum contradictarum* 2:677–78, no. QV, 404.

eleven marks, to two advocates who claimed to have spent a year working on litigation in which the priory was involved.[170]

In addition to their professional fees, advocates and proctors were entitled to reimbursement for expenses incurred in connection with their clients' affairs. Collecting litigation costs presented fewer problems, at least in principle, than securing payments for noncontentious business. Medieval ecclesiastical courts operated under a cost-shifting policy based on constitutions of Justinian that had required the losing party to pay not only the expenses (including the fees and other sums owed to lawyers and notaries) that he had incurred on his own account, but also those incurred by his victorious opponent. Medieval canon law adopted those rules with minor modifications.[171] Immediately after the judge announced his decision in a lawsuit, the advocate or proctor for the victorious party routinely petitioned the judge for a costs order to cover his client's expenses. The judge then proceeded to tax the costs; that is, he examined the claims closely and reduced or disallowed items that he considered exorbitant or inappropriate.[172] The taxation procedure was simple and straightforward. William Durand used a dialogue to illustrate how it should work:

> The judge should say, "Friend, what did you spend on the case?" (or "for this appeal that your adversary wished on you?"). "How much for advocates, for witnesses, and the like?"
>
> And if [the party] replies that he spent more than seems probable—say, 20 pounds—if the judge deems it likely that he spent only 15 pounds, let the judge say, "I tax you 15 pounds. Now tell me under oath how much less than 15 pounds you [actually] spent."
>
> But if [the litigant] says that he spent 12 pounds, let the judge say, "And I award you 12 pounds as costs," seeking to minimize, rather than to in-

---

170. Gregory IX, *Registres*, no. 2686, at 2:120–21. This was a substantial reduction from the huge sum of 120 marks that the advocates, Master James of Kilkenny and Master Nicholas of Wilton, had originally claimed. The 21 marks they were awarded, however, is reasonably representative of the amounts that others received as annual retainers later in the century (see Ramsay, "Retained Legal Counsel," 97–99; introduction to *Select Cases*, ed. Adams and Donahue, 25 n. 1.

171. Cod. 3.1.13.6–7, further elaborated by Nov. 53.1 and 82.10; William Durand, *Speculum iudiciale* 2.3 *De expensis* §6.4, at 1:908.

172. X 2.2.17; 2.14.5; 2.17.1. Advocates had every incentive to apply for costs promptly, for if they failed to submit their petition on the day when the decision was handed down they might forfeit their claims (William Durand, *Speculum iudiciale* 2.3 *De expensis* §6.4, at 1:908).

crease the costs. And if [the litigant] says that he spent a penny less than 15 pounds, let the judge say, "And I therefore award you 15 pounds minus a penny as costs."

You see, therefore, how judicial taxation is done. You also see how the oath follows [taxation] and that costs are awarded for the sworn amount, not for less.[173]

Durand's dialogue assumes that, as he and other writers on professional matters advised, the advocates and proctors for both parties would have insisted on payment of their fees and other expenses prior to the announcement of the judge's decision.

Litigants of course had to make other outlays beyond those to advocates and proctors. Since Durand directed his dialogue at advocates, who were likely to be his principal readers, he barely alluded to these other expenses, but they were nonetheless essential costs in litigation. They inevitably included very substantial payments to notaries and scribes for preparing numerous documents, often in multiple copies, as well as any fees paid to *iurisperiti* for *consilia* and other legal advice. Travel and lodging expenses for litigants, their servants, and their witnesses, and sometimes disbursements for transportation, lodging, and meals for a traveling judge, commonly feature in litigation expense accounts. Over and above all of these, the victor in a lawsuit might also claim what we would describe as opportunity costs. Thus, for example, a tailor or carpenter who was unable to do his normal work while he was involved in litigation was entitled to include compensation for the income he might otherwise have earned. Taxed

---

173. William Durand, *Speculum iudiciale* 2.3 *De expensis* §6 pr., at 1:907–8: "Debet enim iudex dicere: Amice, quid expendisti in causa, uel ratione huius appellationis a tuo aduersario interpositae; quid expendisti in aduocatis, quid pro testibus et similibus, ut C. de iudi. Sancimus [Cod. 3.1.15]. Et si ille responderit, ultra quam sit uerisimile eum expendisse, puta dixerit XX. lib., iudex, si sibi uerisimiliter uidetur quod expendit tantum XV., iudex dicet, et ego taxo XV.; unde dic per tuum sacramentum, quantum expendisti infra XV. quod si ille dixerit, quod expendit XII. iudex dicet, et ego tibi condemno in XII. nomine expensarum, eas restringens potius quam laxans. Et si ille responderit se expendisse XV. minus uno denario, iudex dicat, et ego tibi in quindecim condemno minus uno denario, nomine expensarum. Vides igitur, quomodo praecedit iudicialis taxatio. Vides etiam, quomodo post eam sequitur iuratio, et post eam condemnatio in id, quod iuratum est, non enim fieri debet in minus, ut ff. de in lit. iur. In actionibus [Dig. 12.3.5]." Woodcock, *Medieval Ecclesiastical Courts*, 126, provides an example from actual practice of the reduction of a bill of costs by taxation.

costs, it should be stressed, were of course above and beyond any judgment for damages that the judge might also award to the victorious party.[174]

The taxation process aimed expressly at keeping down the expense of litigation in church courts. Judges were instructed that the costs they awarded must be "modest, not extravagant," and that they should include only disbursements incurred primarily or solely in order to litigate the cases they decided.[175] If a litigant traveled to Rome on other business, for instance, but also used part of his time there to press a lawsuit, his travel expenses on the way to and from Rome should not figure in his litigation costs. He could legitimately be reimbursed, however, for whatever it had cost him to remain in Rome while pursuing his lawsuit.[176]

However modest the taxed figure might turn out to be, those condemned to pay it predictably resented the fact that they had not only lost a lawsuit but in addition had to pay however much their opponent had spent to win. They sometimes sought ways to avoid a judgment for costs, often on the grounds of some technical irregularity.[177] If that failed, they were apt to delay actual payment as long as possible. The winning party was well advised to persuade the judge to insert into the costs judgment a stiff penalty clause for late payment.

DISCIPLINARY MECHANISMS

Judges bore the responsibility for enforcing the ethical commitments that advocates and proctors pledged to observe in return for the right of audience. Judges were not only in a position to detect infractions of the rules

---

174. William Durand, *Speculum iudiciale* 2.3 *De expensis* §6.1–4, at 1:908, and §6.9, at 1:909; Accursius, *Glos. ord.* to Cod. 1.3.25 Auth. in c., v. *sed hodie*. For a sample of the kinds of expenditures that appeared in one fourteenth-century case, see Harrison, *Life in a Medieval College*, 192–93. On further aspects of taxation procedure, see Brundage, "Taxation of Costs."

175. Johannes Teutonicus, *Glos. ord.* to C. 2 q. 1 c. 7 v. *expendisse*; X 2.17.1. Accursius defined "moderate" costs as 10 percent or less of the sum at issue (*Glos. ord.* to Cod. 1.3.25 Auth. in c. v. *partem*). See also William Durand, *Speculum iudiciale* 2.3 *De expensis* §6.2, at 1:908.

176. Johannes Teutonicus, *Apparatus* to 4 Comp. 1.16.1 (= X 1.16.1) v. *propter hoc*, in Munich, Bayerische Staatsbibliothek, Clm. 3879, at 275rb: "Quid si alias fuisset iturus Romam? Non possit petere expensas factas, nisi quatenus plus expendisset propter longiorem moram, ut ff. fama. her., Ex parte in prin. [Dig. 10.2.39 pr.]."

177. Jacques de Revigny discussed methods of achieving this in his *Lectura* to Cod. 3.1.13.6 and to Auth. Hodie (= Nov. 22.10) post Cod. 3.1.15, as well as his *Lectura* to Dig. 12.3.4.3, quoted in Benzemer, *What Jacques Saw*, 81.

of professional conduct, but also had the authority, indeed the duty, to punish offenders. Judges had a broad range of sanctions and could choose the penalty or combination of penalties that seemed appropriate for individual situations.

The ultimate sanction that an erring legal professional faced was loss of the right of audience, either permanently or for a limited time.[178] Even temporary suspension diminished his reputation, his social status, and his livelihood, while permanent disbarment ended his professional career. Authorities differed about how far loss of the right of audience extended. Some argued that it applied only in the court where the order was given and that the advocate or proctor disbarred in one jurisdiction could continue to practice elsewhere. Others maintained that a lawyer guilty of misdeeds serious enough to warrant loss of the right of audience was automatically *infamis* and hence ineligible to practice anywhere.[179] Suspension from practice, whether permanent or temporary, cast a shadow on a lawyer's professional reputation that was likely to cause clients to look elsewhere for legal services.[180] At the very least, loss of the right of audience, even briefly, disrupted existing client relationships and could jeopardize retainer arrangements.[181]

Judges normally canceled the right of audience only for the most heinous offenses. For smaller transgressions, they had a battery of lesser sanctions at their command. These included fines, orders for restitution of fees, orders to pay compensation for damages caused by lawyerly misconduct, and public rebukes from the bench.

Authorities agreed that defiance of a judge's order, such as refusing to

---

178. Gratian, C. 3 q. 7 c. 2 §§13–14 (Cod. 2.6.7.2–3); Ricardus Anglicus, *Distinctiones decretorum* to C. 3 1. q. 7 d.p.c. 1, in London, BL, MS Royal 10.C.III, at 17v: "Remouetur quis a postulatione per decretum iudicis—Ad tempus, tunc ibi post tempus, alias etiam infra tempus postulare potest, infra eodem Qui ex [Dig. 3.1.9, *sed recte* Dig. 3.1.7].—In perpetuum; si non appellauerit in perpetuum silebit, C. e. l. i. [Cod. 2.6.1]."

179. Lyndwood, *Provinciale* 1.17.1 v. *privatus existat*, 75, summarizes these arguments; see also William of Drogheda, *Summa aurea*, 48, §47; William Durand, *Speculum iudiciale* 1.4 *De aduocato* §1.13, at 1:261; Cino da Pistoia, *Lectura* to Cod. 2.6 §1, at 71ra–rb.

180. Rufinus, *Summa*, 268, on C. 3 q. 7 d.p.c. 2 v. *cuius vita despicitur*.

181. Prelates and monasteries commonly paid annual retainers to advocates and proctors, and sometimes to several of them. Examples abound; thus, e.g., London, BL, MS Harley 3720, at 13r–v; John Pecham, *Register* 1:30–31; *Liber practicus de consuetudine Remensis* 1.103 at 106–7; *CSB* 11:148, no. 355; Linehan, "Will of Synibaldus de Labro," 136; Sayers, *Papal Judges Delegate*, 221 n. 3; Guenée, *Tribunaux et gens de justice*, 199–200; Trexler, *Synodal Law*, 5, among numerous others.

argue on behalf of a litigant when appointed to do so, merited immediate and permanent disbarment without hope of readmission.[182] When advocates and proctors were admitted to practice they swore that they would serve their clients faithfully. Betrayal of a client's secrets or abandonment without cause so flagrantly violated the lawyer's oath of office as to make him disreputable and hence ineligible to continue to practice. In addition, he could be required to repay any fees he had received and became liable for any damages his betrayal had caused. The client might also sue to reopen a case that his advocate's behavior had caused him to lose.[183]

Advocates or proctors who were lazy, careless, or seriously negligent in the conduct of litigation were also subject to discipline, as were those who took on more cases than they could manage properly. In less serious situations, the culprit might get off with a public dressing down by the judge. Those who were more gravely at fault could be fined, and if their negligence was particularly gross a judge might temporarily suspend their right to practice. If the neglect resulted in loss of a case, the advocate or proctor could in addition be held liable to his client for damages.[184] A jurist who prepared a hasty, ill-considered *consilium* might be subject to similar penalties. If convicted of furnishing either a judge or a private client with a fraudulent *consilium*, he became *infamis* and was barred from acting as a legal adviser in the future. The same penalties also applied to the advocate or proctor who violated his oath by appearing in a case that he knew, or

---

182. C. 3 q. 7 c. 2 §13 (= Cod. 2.6.7.2). Many decretists ignored this particular text, while the few who dealt with it contented themselves with repeating or closely paraphrasing it, e.g., *Summa Parisiensis* v. *si quis*, at 121; *Summa "Elegantius"* 6.66, at 2:133; John of Caen, *Abbreviatio decreti* in London, BL, MS Cotton Claud. A.IV, at 138vb–139ra: "Item dicit quod si quis aduocatorum a iudice monitus ea excusacione que nequeat comprobari cuicumque parti patrocinium denegauerit careat foro. Sciat etiam nunquam sibi agendi copiam posse restitui." See, too, X 1.32.1; Goffredus de Trano, *Summa super titulis*, 126, to X 1.37 §1; Hostiensis, *Summa*, lib. 1, *De postulando* §2, at 62ra–rb.

183. C. 3 q. 7 c. 2 §1; William Durand, *Speculum iudiciale* 1.4 *De aduocato* §9.18, at 1:282; Benedict XII, *Decens et necessarium* §29, in Tangl, *Päpstlichen Kanzleiordnungen*, 124; Hostiensis, *Summa*, lib. 5, *De penitentiis et remissionibus* §32, at 275ra; as well as Brundage, "Ambidextrous Advocate."

184. X 1.41.2 and Bernard of Parma, *Glos. ord.* v. *restituimus*; Hostiensis, *Summa*, lib. 1, *De postulatione* §5, vol. 1, at 62va; William Durand, *Speculum iudiciale* 4.1 *De procuratoribus* §2, at 2:111; Gescher, "Das älteste kölnische Officialasstatut," §3.2, 483; Benedict XII, *Decens et necessarium* §§14–15, 29, in Tangl, *Päpstlichen Kanzleiordnungen*, 121, 124. For examples, see Helmholz, *Marriage Litigation*, 151–52.

should have known, was frivolous, malicious, or vexatious.[185] Advocates and proctors undertook not to suborn perjury by instructing their clients or witnesses about the testimony they were to give. Those who violated this rule stood to lose their case and might be excommunicated, which automatically made them *infames*.[186] Offensive conduct in court, such as failure to show appropriate respect and obedience to the judge, quarrelsome outbursts or other disruptive behavior, as well as making wordy, long-winded speeches, and introducing irrelevant arguments, could also bring down lesser disciplinary actions on the offender's head.[187]

Ominous as all of this may seem, records of actual disciplinary proceedings against advocates or proctors are not common. Notes on disciplinary actions did not fit easily into the classification systems that court registrars commonly employed. Consequently only scattered reports of such actions survive.[188] Few of the disciplinary actions that do survive, moreover, were

---

185. William Durand, *Speculum iudiciale* 2.2 *De requistione consilii* §5, at 1:763–64, and 2.3 *De poena temere litigantium* §§1–2, at 1:922; Guido de Baysio, *Rosarium* to C. 3 q. 7 c. 2 §2, in CUL, Peterhouse MS 35, at 162vb; 1440 *Constitutiones et statuta* of the court of the official of the bishop of Geneva, 377, §§37–38, and the Halberstadt court statutes of 1422 §32, in Hilling, "Sechs Gerichtsordnungen," 337; Rossi, *Consilium sapientis*, 155–59.

186. Bonaguida, *Summa introductoria* 1.3.12, at 158; William Durand, *Speculum iudiciale* 1.4 *De aduocato* §9.6 and 2.1 *De interrogationibus* §2.14, at 1:281, 546; Panormitanus, *Commentaria* to X 2.1.14 §8, vol. 3, at 46vb; Statutes of Exeter I (ca. 1225–27) c. 9, in Powicke & Cheney 1:231.

187. John Morton, *Register* 1:62, no. 202; John le Romeyn, *Register* 1:25, no. 60; Tancred, *Ordo iudiciarius* 1.5.3, at 112; Benedict XII, *Decens et necessarium* §10, and Martin V, *In apostolice dignitatis* (1418) §31, in Tangl, *Päpstlichen Kanzleiordnungen*, 120 and 143; Bonaguida, *Summa introductoria* 1.3.6–7, at 155–56, and 1.3.17, at 160–61; William Durand, *Speculum iudiciale* 1.4 *De aduocato* §1.9 and 9.6, at 1:261, 267–68; William of Pagula, *Summa summarum* 1.61 in CUL, Pembroke MS 201, at 73vb: "An aduocati et procuratores garulosi sunt puniendi? Dic quod sic et elicito uno negocio ceteri sileant quousque negocium inchohatum expediatur. Et qui contrafecerit arbitrio iudicis puniatur. In statuta curie de arcubus, c. Item iudex [Winchelsey statutes c. 12, in Logan, *Medieval Court of Arches*, 9]."

188. On disciplinary proceedings, see the general introduction by Donahue to *Records of the Medieval Ecclesiastical Courts* 1:28–29, as well as Owen, "Records of the Bishop's Official at Ely." See also the remarks of Le Bras, "*Velut splendor firmamenti*," 387–88. In addition to the disciplinary cases mentioned above and by Helmholz, "Ethical Standards," 51–53, and *Marriage Litigation*, 151–52, I have noticed other cases in Aubenas, *Recueil des lettres* 2:137–38, and Jean Le Coq, *Questiones Johannis Galli*, 444–46, no. 359.

actually initiated by judges. Unhappy litigants rather than outraged judges seem to have been the usual prime movers behind actions against lawyers.

It would be hazardous to conclude from the scarcity of recorded cases of disciplinary proceedings that advocates and proctors in the ecclesiastical courts rarely breached the rules of their profession. Complaints about "innumerable defects and abuses" in the observance of the disciplinary regulations, such as those made at the Council of Basel in 1429, as well as the regular reissue of decrees concerning court reform, may simply have been rhetorical outbursts, but they do suggest at the very least that such problems were sufficiently frequent to disturb high authorities.[189] So too does the career of Hugh Candlesby, a busy proctor in the courts of the diocese of Ely between 1374 and 1382. Despite numerous scrapes and scandals, including instances of fraud and professional malpractice, Candlesby was never the subject of a disciplinary hearing. He simply disappeared without a trace in the records shortly after playing a prominent if unsavory role in the Peasants' Revolt of 1381, for which several of his accomplices in the disturbances were hanged.[190]

The number of lawyers who practiced as advocates and proctors in church courts and provided clients with legal advice and assistance outside of the courts increased rapidly during the last half of the twelfth and the opening decades of the thirteenth century. Canon law commenced to become a true profession during the middle decades of the thirteenth century, once church authorities began to insist that advocates and proctors be formally admitted to practice. The admissions process required them to do two things. They first had to demonstrate to the satisfaction of a judge that they possessed a basic knowledge of substantive and procedural law, acquired through some combination of formal study, usually at a university, together with some practical experience, usually acquired through working in the courts where they sought to practice. Second, they had to make a solemn public promise that they would observe some basic rules of legal ethics and conduct in their relationship with the courts and with their clients.

The terms of that oath defined their identity as professional lawyers, and the process of admission certified their status as members of an identifiable social class with specific legal rights and obligations. The critical le-

---

189. Instructions to Cardinal Giuliano Caesarini concerning reform of the papal curia §§15–17, in Tangl, *Päpstlichen Kanzleiordnungen*, 364–65.

190. Brundage, "Professional Discipline."

gal element in defining that status was the right to present their arguments and opinions on behalf of clients to a judge with some assurance that their statements would be received with respectful attention. Admission also gave the practitioner the right to require clients to lay open their secrets to him concerning the matters on which they sought his assistance, no matter how sensitive, embarrassing, or incriminating that information might be should it fall into unfriendly hands. Admission to practice further accorded advocates, proctors, and legal advisers the right to compensation under appropriate circumstances and in appropriate amounts for the exercise of their skills and knowledge as authoritative and informed legal experts, either in litigation or in noncontentious matters.

At the time of admission, they also assumed obligations to treat the court and their clients honestly and with integrity. This included the duty to pass judgment on the cases that clients brought to them and to refuse to trouble the court with any case that they deemed malicious, vexatious, or frivolous. They were further obliged to deal frankly with the court. They had a duty to refrain from presenting false or perjured evidence, either written or oral, so that the judges before whom they appeared could have confidence that whatever evidence or arguments a professional lawyer laid before them could be taken seriously. Admission to practice required lawyers to pledge utmost fidelity to their clients. Their oath obliged them to advance the client's interests with all the strength and skill they possessed, to spare no pains in pursuit of the client's interests, and not to betray confidential information to which clients made them privy. Admission to practice, in short, tempered the rights that it conferred with corresponding duties of upright and honest behavior.

It would, of course, be unrealistic to assume that every advocate, proctor, or *iurisperitus* unfailingly lived up to the high ethical aspirations incorporated in their admissions oaths. The duty of maintaining discipline by demanding that canonical practitioners honor those undertakings and punishing those who failed to do so fell on the judges in ecclesiastical courts. They probably often chose to deal with the shortcomings they witnessed in informal ways that left no trace in the records. But the law also furnished aggrieved clients with remedies that they could invoke to redress the harm that faithless, lazy, or incompetent lawyers inflicted on them. Punishments for serious shortcomings could be harsh. Even if the more serious punitive measures were not always implemented in practice, the threat that they might be invoked hovered perpetually over canonical courtrooms and the lawyers who practiced in them.

* EIGHT *

Professional Canon Lawyers: Advocates and Proctors

Career Opportunities

The knowledge and skills acquired by those with legal training opened up a broad range of career opportunities in the thirteenth century. While high social standing, family connections, wealth, and sheer luck remained important, legal qualifications in conjunction with some or all of these could greatly enhance the number, variety, and desirability of career prospects.[1] A piece of doggerel written to honor Richard Barre attests that this was already true in 1190, while canonists were still on the road to becoming full-fledged professionals:

> You'll handle bishops' cases
> And the business deals of kings:
> They're saving up their money
> Just to give you lovely things.[2]

---

1. Fuchs, *Dives, Pauper, Nobilis*, 113; Thieme, "Le rôle des doctores legum," 47. The notion of a career in which an individual advances in authority and power by stages is not a recent invention, as has sometimes been asserted, e.g., by Brooks, *Pettyfoggers and Vipers*, 269. Thirteenth-century lawyers were certainly familiar with the notion that a clerical career, for example, involved ordination in fixed stages to a series of positions, each of which carried increasing prestige and authority. Some were surely aware, too, of the *cursus honorum* that had determined the stages of a political career in Roman antiquity.

2. My rendition of "Pontificum causas regumque negocia tractes, / Qui tibi divicias deliciasque parent," a distich that Stephen of Tournai recalled from their student days together at Bologna when he wrote to congratulate Barre on his promotion from archdeacon of Lisieux to archdeacon of Ely in 1190 (Stephen of Tournai, *Lettres*, 346–47, no. 275). Richard I named Barre a justiciar in 1194 and he is the only English royal justice known to have studied at Bologna (Turner, *English Judiciary*, 95–96, and "Richard Barre and Michael Belet"; Appleby, *England without Richard*, 163, 217).

A generation or two later, after trained lawyers had begun to secure a near-monopoly on the practice of their profession, a newly qualified lawyer faced prospects that might seem almost limitless.[3]

Competition for the available prizes was vigorous and grew more strenuous as the numbers of lawyers increased. By the beginning of the fourteenth century, lawyers turn up everywhere in contemporary documents. This is no doubt partly an artifact of the records, since activities that involved advocates, proctors, judges, and notaries produced enormous masses of written matter. The great majority of all surviving medieval records are in fact legal documents of one sort or another. While their prominence in the records may give an exaggerated impression of their ubiquity, professional lawyers, judges, and notaries constituted a substantial and prosperous element within most late medieval towns and cities whose population records have been studied.[4]

Large numbers of practicing lawyers sought, and many of them secured, ecclesiastical benefices that gave them a relatively steady and dependable income, above and beyond whatever they might receive from legal practice. Lawyers regularly outnumbered graduates in arts, medicine, and theology in the petitions for provisions to benefices that late medieval universities submitted to the papacy. Surveys of benefice-holders—not all of them in major orders and hence not obliged to remain celibate—suggest that lawyers enjoyed an exceptionally high rate of success in receiving these appointments. University-trained lawyers, both civilians and canonists, regularly received posts in local ecclesiastical administration, where they typically served as bishops' officials, chancellors, and archdeacons.[5] These appointments rarely paid high salaries; indeed they often paid none at all. Instead the men who held these offices received one or more benefices whose revenues in effect guaranteed their basic support, in addition to whatever fees their offices entitled them to collect and the gratuities that they were frequently offered, whether they were entitled to them or not. Since it was essential for a bishop to know something about canon law and often helpful if he were expert in its mysteries, trained lawyers enjoyed a

3. Thieme, "Le rôle des doctores legum," 46.

4. Elton, *England, 1200–1640*, 54, 102; for population analyses, see, e.g., Herlihy and Klapisch-Zuber, *Tuscans and Their Families*, 128–29, tables 4.7 and 4.8; Guenée, *Tribunaux et gens de justice*, 336 n. 259; Hyde, *Society and Politics*, 155, 167–68; Guillemain, *La cour pontificale d'Avignon*, 543–44, 550–51, 668; Cipolla, *Before the Industrial Revolution*, 83, table 2-11.

5. Moraw, "Careers of Graduates," 257; Aston, Duncan, and Evans, "Medieval Alumni of Cambridge," 73–76.

considerable edge in the competition for episcopal preferment.[6] The proportion by which lawyer-bishops outnumbered those trained in theology and the liberal arts is striking. No less than 45 percent of the medieval English bishops who had studied at Oxford, for example, had been law students, while 28 percent had studied theology and a mere 8 percent had studied only liberal arts. Much the same was true among the known episcopal alumni of Cambridge. Jurists, although not rare, seem to have been less conspicuous and theologians slightly more so among French bishops, which may well reflect the enormous prestige and influence of the theological faculty at Paris.[7]

The large volume of legal business at the papal curia exerted a magnetic pull that attracted a great many canonists to find employment there at one stage or another in their careers. Those who did so discovered that even a brief period of service at the curia could prove enormously helpful in advancing their careers, since it gave them opportunities to form contacts among influential officials, which in turn could readily lead to desirable preferment. "The speculative art may flourish elsewhere," observed Henry the Poet, "but practitioners flock to Rome, for Rome knows that honor flows from the springs of wealth."[8]

Papal courts and tribunals required the services of substantial numbers of trained lawyers, as did administrative offices, where they were commonly deemed more flexible and tactful than theologians.[9] A handful of lawyers found work as consistorial or rotal advocates, but these elite practitioners were never numerous and their ranks were tightly closed. Other tribunals offered more ample opportunities. The Audientia litterarum contradictarum in particular furnished work for throngs of proctors on

---

6. Gratian, D. 38 c. 6; *Summa "Elegantius in iure diuino"* 2.46, at 1:63–64; Petrus de Salinis, *Lectura* to D. 38 c. 6 v. *omnes* in London, BL, MS Arundel 435, at 15ra: "In isto c. statuit .vii. synodus ut . . . debet metropolitanus ordinandum episcopum interrogare cum ordinatur episcopus si sciat sacros canones legere et omnem scripturam diuinam, et si inueniatur ignorans repelleratur."

7. Aston, "Oxford's Medieval Alumni," 28; Aston, Duncan, and Evans, "Medieval Alumni of Cambridge," 70; Jean Gaudemet, "Recherches sur l'épiscopat médiéval," 144–46.

8. My paraphrase of Master Heinrich der Poet, *Liber de statu Curie Romane*, 86, ll. 521–22: "Ars alibi speculata viget, sed practica Romam / Novit et ex rerum fonte resultat honor." Gramsch, *Erfurter Juristen*, 389–424, provides numerous concrete examples.

9. Smalley, *Becket Conflict*, 144–45.

a continuing basis.[10] Bishops and archbishops, monasteries and religious orders, kings and princes were all liable to have frequent business at the Roman curia—so much indeed that they often found it useful to maintain permanent proctors there to keep an eye out for their interests. Even those who chose not to go quite that far still found it advantageous to maintain a long-term relationship with particular advocates and proctors, especially those who were their own countrymen or *confrères*, and employed them repeatedly whenever matters at the curia demanded legal advice or representation.[11]

Employment opportunities were also abundant in the households of cardinals, where numerous men who became prominent jurists—Raymond of Penyafort, Henricus de Segusio (later Cardinal Hostiensis), and Petrus de Salinis among others—spent part of their careers. Many of the cardinals themselves had advanced legal training. One sample of cardinals promoted during the late fourteenth and early fifteenth centuries, for example, included thirteen doctors of theology, but fifty-six who held a doctorate in one or both laws.[12] The theoretical question of whether a theologian or a canonist was better equipped to lead the church was sometimes debated as a teaching exercise in the schools. In actuality, the question was resolved in favor of the canonists, since popes from the thirteenth century onward were more often trained as canon lawyers than as theologians.[13]

Civil government, too, provided a flourishing market for the services of

---

10. Less than a dozen consistorial advocates normally practiced at any one time (Brandmüller, "Simon de Lellis de Teramo," 234; see also the index to Gregory IX, *Registres*, s.v. "Advocati curie" and "Auditores litterarum contradictarum"; Herde, *Audientia litterarum contradictarum* 1:26–29).

11. See, e.g., Herde, *Beiträge*, 136–48. Linehan, "Proctors Representing Spanish Interests" and "Spanish Litigants and Their Agents"; Sayers, "Canterbury Proctors" and "Proctors Representing British Interests"; or the voluminous records of the proctors representing the Teutonic Knights in *Die Berichte der Generalprokuratoren des Deutschen Ordens*, nos. 12, 13, 21, 29, 32, 37.

12. Paravicini Bagliani, *Cardinali di curia* 2:492–93; Girgensohn, "Wie wird Man Kardinal?" 150–52. The proportion of cardinals with law degrees seems to have been especially high at the curia in Avignon (Guillemain, *La cour pontificale d'Avignon*, 217).

13. Long, "Utrum jurista vel theologus plus proficiat ad regimen ecclesie." At least four popes in the thirteenth century were trained canonists (Gregory IX, Innocent IV, Clement IV, and Boniface VIII), as were five more in the fourteenth century (Clement V, John XXII, Innocent VI, Urban V, and Gregory XI), and another five in the fifteenth century (Innocent VII, John XXIII, Martin V, Calixtus III, and Alexander VI).

canonists and civilians, as well as enormous numbers of notaries. The administration of municipal governments in Italy became something much like a profession in its own right from the thirteenth century onward. The position of *podestà* regularly went to men with advanced legal training. They in turn brought with them their own teams of advisers and administrative assistants, and these almost invariably included still more lawyers. A successful *podestà* and his entourage might be almost constantly on the move, administering the affairs of one town after another on a series of short-term contracts year after year.[14] The legally trained officials who served the late medieval German kings, by contrast, were not only less mobile than Italian city administrators, but were also more likely to be clerics than laymen. Like their counterparts south of the Alps, German royal servants often had at least some legal training, frequently in canon law.[15] In France, although the Parlement de Paris dealt primarily with disputes that arose under one or another of the customary laws current in the French kingdom, the advocates and magistrates of the parlement were generally trained in the *ius commune*. Many of them, as well as numerous other French royal administrators, were clerics who held degrees in canon law. The English kings, especially Edward I (1272–1307), likewise employed considerable numbers of canonists not only as royal judges, but also in the chancery and elsewhere in the royal bureaucracy.[16]

A large fraction, perhaps even a majority, of the civil and canon lawyers who studied in university law faculties, however, apparently made private practice in local courts their principal occupation. This was the predominant pattern in southern France and was very likely true elsewhere, to judge from the numbers of men described as advocates, legal consultants, proctors, or notaries in court documents, tax rolls, and other local records. References to men so described occur mainly in documents from major cities, but references to men bearing these titles also surface occasionally

14. Waley, *Italian City Republics*, 66–73.

15. About one-third of them became bishops as well, which spared the monarch's purse, since they could in most cases live handsomely from their episcopal revenues (Moraw, "Gelehrten Juristen," 81, 91).

16. Clerical canon lawyers continued to constitute a majority of practitioners at the Parlement up to the middle of the fifteenth century, when laymen began to outnumber them (Bataillard, *Histoire des procureurs et des avoués*, 142–43, 151–52; Delachenal, *Histoire des avocats*, 24–36; Shennan, *Parlement of Paris*, 14–15, 110, 120, 136; Fitzsimmons, *Parisian Order of Barristers*, 2–4). For England, see Ramsay, "Retained Legal Counsel," 98–99; Aston, Duncan, and Evans, "Medieval Alumni of Cambridge," 81.

even in small towns and remote mountain villages.[17] Advocates who were fortunate enough to receive a benefice or office of some kind often combined these appointments with a private legal practice, while the few who managed to secure paid posts as law professors commonly also practiced law, especially as advisers to private clients and public bodies alike. Their academic positions enhanced the authority of their professional opinions (*consilia*), while the fees that judges, public officials, and litigants were willing to pay for these opinions considerably augmented their academic incomes.[18]

Advocates and *Iurisperiti*

Advocates in the church courts were by definition men learned in the law.[19] By the latter part of the thirteenth century, professional advocates were overwhelmingly alumni of university law faculties. By 1300, it was uncommon to encounter an advocate in the ecclesiastical courts who had not spent some time studying law in a university, and by the mid-fourteenth century, most, or even all, of the advocates who practiced regularly in a bishop's court were likely to have a law degree. It was not unusual by this time to find laymen as well as clerics working as advocates in church courts[20]

The social origins of advocates are seldom well documented, but soundings in the available evidence indicate that they came from a wide range of backgrounds. An important minority of the advocates whose antecedents are known belonged to well-to-do, powerful, and socially prominent families, as was common among university-trained men, especially those who had studied in the higher faculties. Most advocates, however, originated in families of the humbler sort, whose resources were no doubt often considerably reduced by the expense of legal studies at a university. Thomas de Sauteyrargues, who arrived at Nîmes in the late thirteenth century with "nihil aliud quam libros suos," may have been typical of many advocates when they first set up in practice. The plentiful economic and social re-

---

17. Juan Alfonso de Benavente, *Repetitio de aduocatis*, quoted by Alonso Rodriguez, *Juan Alfonso de Benavente*, 158; Guenée, *Tribunaux et gens de justice*, 335; Strayer, *Gens de justice*, 21; Gouron, "Les étapes de la pénétration du droit romain," 116–17.

18. Bellomo, *Common Legal Past*, 213–14.

19. Tancred, *Ordo iudiciarius* 1.5.3 at 112; William of Drogheda, *Summa aurea*, 36–37, §33; William Durand, *Speculum iudiciale* 1.4 *De aduocato* §1.32–33, at 1:263–64; Helmholz, *Canon Law and Ecclesiastical Jurisdiction*, 222.

20. Thus, e.g., Brundage, "Bar of the Ely Consistory Court," 543–47; Renardy, *Les maîtres universitaires*, nos. 10, 16, 38, 60, 87, 170, 172–73, 182–83, 189, 200, among others.

wards that could accompany a flourishing practice provided successful advocates with the opportunity to move into higher—sometimes much higher—social ranks than those from which they had sprung.[21]

Advocates evidently accumulated wealth more regularly and in greater abundance than other legal professionals, and this, coupled with their reputation for learning and political shrewdness, accounted for their ability to rise in the social hierarchy. Laymen typically invested surplus funds in land and houses, and frequently acquired substantial country estates in addition to their urban properties. Landed advocates frequently sought to attain noble status, and members of the profession who combined sufficient wealth with advantageous marriages slowly managed to filter into the ranks of the nobility. They apparently found this easier to do so in the south of France than in the north, where some fourteenth-century writers insisted that the advocate's profession was incompatible with nobility. Even there, however, attitudes toward the ennobling of advocates gradually became more flexible.[22]

Advocates functioned simultaneously as legal counselors and courtroom pleaders, two roles that were practically inseparable. An advocate had to probe the strengths and weaknesses of a potential client's case before he could make a rational decision whether or not to take it on. When he decided to accept a case, the advocate needed to advise his new client about the legal ramifications of the situation that brought them together, the remedies available to deal with the problems it presented, and the difficulties that he could foresee in fighting the action.

Advocates, moreover, routinely served as assessors or legal advisers to judges. In order to shield themselves from personal liability for errors in law, judges regularly sought advice from the advocates who practiced in their courts but were not involved in the case at hand before they announced a decision in a case. If those advocates disagreed among themselves, the judge might seek a formal opinion (*consilium*) from an outside legal expert, often a law professor, although he might also be another practicing advocate. When judges pronounced their decisions, they almost invariably took the precaution of stating that they had consulted with le-

---

21. Gouron, "Le rôle social des juristes," 59–61; Renardy, *Le monde des maîtres*, 162–63; Guenée, *Tribunaux et gens de justice*, 356–59, 368; Fédou, *Les hommes de loi lyonnais*, 153–78; Postan, *Medieval Economy and Society*, 175–76; Reynolds, *Europe Emerges*, 188, 267–68.

22. Gouron, "Le rôle social des juristes," 64–66; Guenée, *Tribunaux et gens de justice*, 200–202; Fédou, *Les hommes de loi lyonnais*, 212–30.

gal experts or judicial assessors before arriving at their judgment.[23] Indeed, judges themselves were often drawn from the ranks of professional advocates.

The advocate's central function, the one that literally defined his profession, was to plead (*postulare*) in court in order to persuade judges that the law supported the contentions of his clients, rather than the assertions that his opponents advanced. As an early procedural manual put it, "Advocates, therefore, are those who plead for others. 'To plead' means to 'set out one's own claim or that of one's friend in court before a presiding officer or to oppose the claim of another.'"[24]

Oral pleading provided the dramatic conclusion to the romano-canonical trial when, in the words of the emperor Leo I (r. 457–74), the unarmed soldiers known as advocates "with their glorious voices defended the lives, hopes, and descendants of their clients."[25] This was the advocate's opportunity to show off, to impress his clients, his colleagues, and hopefully the judge as well, not only with the sonority of his voice and his command of language, but even more important with the brilliance and cogency of his arguments, the depth of his legal knowledge, and the persuasiveness of his case.[26] Court clerks, however, rarely recorded what advocates actually said during their arguments. Indeed, they usually passed over argumentation in silence, since this was not a necessary part of the court's

---

23. William Durand, *Speculum iudiciale* 1.1 *De assessore* §§1 and 4.2, at 1:100, 101; 2.2 *De requisitione consilii*, pr., at 1:762. They announced their precautionary consultations in order to fend off any complaints that their decisions erred in law, for which they could be held personally liable. Durand, *Speculum iudiciale* 2.3 *De sententia* §6.6, at 1:786, provides a formula for this; for examples of actual specimens see the decisions in *Giles de Avenbury c. John de Aigueblanche* (1271) and *Roger de Aderne c. Thomas the Linen-Draper* (1293) in *Select Cases*, ed. Adams and Donahue, 92, 676, as well as Donahue's remarks in his introduction, 23.

24. *Ordo iudiciarius "Ulpianus de edendo"* in London, BL, MS Royal 10.B.IV, at 4r; the quotation within the quotation is from Dig. 3.1.1.2, which Gratian inserted in his Decretum at C. 3 q. 7 c. 2 §1, a passage that nearly every procedural handbook quoted. On this *ordo*, see Fowler-Magerl, *Ordines iudiciarii*, 61, and *Ordo iudiciorum*, 65–73.

25. Cod. 2.7.14: "[M]ilitant namque causarum patroni, qui gloriosae vocis confisi munimine laborantium spem vitam et posteros defendunt." Canonists often quoted this passage, e.g., *Summa "Elegantius"* 6.67, at 2:133; William of Drogheda, *Summa aurea*, 37 §33; William Durand, *Speculum iudiciale* 1.4 *De aduocato*, proem., at 1:259; Sicard of Cremona, *Summa* to C. 3 q. 7 in London, BL, MS Add. 18367, at 27vb; *Ordo iudiciarius "Ulpianus de edendo,"* in London, BL. MS Royal 10.B.IV, at 4r–v.

26. William Durand, *Speculum iudiciale* 1.4 *De aduocato* §6.3, at 1:272.

official *acta*. The written *allegationes* that advocates submitted to the judge at the close of oral argument presumably documented the line of thought they presented in oral pleading, but their forensic oratory itself was simply not recorded. Over the course of time, as written *positiones* and *allegationes* became more important, oral argument seems to have played a decreasing role in litigation.[27]

Although pleading in court was the most conspicuous, vivid, and public segment of an advocate's practice, it occupied only a small part of his professional time. Judges often demanded that every advocate who practiced in their courts be present at each court session, whether they had a case on the docket or not. Since church courts typically held formal sessions at most once or twice a week, advocates were likely to spend more time in their studies than in the courtroom.[28] The study was the place where an advocate was likely to do most of his professional work, poring over his books, meeting with clients, planning litigation strategy, trying to anticipate the arguments that opponents might raise, preparing the lines of reasoning he would adopt to counter them, drafting the numerous documents that litigation entailed, and framing his speeches for oral argument. His study was also the place where an advocate prepared the lucrative written legal opinions (*consilia*) that individual clients as well as judges and other authorities sometimes needed. Advocates occasionally seem to have practiced jointly in small partnerships or firms, since this allowed them to economize on expenses by sharing libraries, clerks, and other expenses. These arrangements, however, were probably not very common.[29]

---

27. William Durand, *Speculum iudiciale* 2.2 *De disputationibus et allegationibus aduocatorum* §§1 and 6.1, at 1:743, 751; Nörr, "Reihenfolgeprinzip," 168–69. Summaries of advocates' oral arguments occasionally survive, e.g., in the records of *Robert de Picheford c. Thomas de Nevill* (Lincoln, 1267–72) in *Select Cases*, ed. Adams and Donahue, 299–310 and 322–28, C. 18, documents 11, 13, and 15; also in narratives such as Thomas of Marlborough, *History of the Abbey of Evesham*, 302–10, §§305–13.

28. On the appearance and layout of the studies and consulting rooms of late medieval professional men, see Thornton, *Scholar in His Study*, esp. 77–88.

29. A *consilium* of Baldus deals with the problems that arose when two advocates, who were also brothers and shared their earnings, dwelling place, and other property, wished to set up separate households (Baldus, *Consilia* 3.452, vol. 3, at 132ra–rb). Joint practices may well have been more common among proctors than among advocates (Stelzer, "Beiträge," 124–37; Sayers, *Papal Government*, 34–35; Brentano, *Two Churches*, 28; and Herde, *Beiträge*, 130–31).

As we will discuss in greater detail in chapter 10, many advocates also devoted some of their professional time to working as arbiters or arbitrators to settle disputes quietly and confidentially without the formalities, quibbling, and delays of litigation.

Proctors

Professional proctors, unlike advocates, swarm through the pages of church court records from the thirteenth century onward.[30] These useful all-purpose agents show up at every level of ecclesiastical administration performing tasks of all sorts. When properly authorized to do so, medieval proctors, like their Roman counterparts, could perform almost any type of transaction on behalf of the client, sometimes called the principal, whom they literally represented, since whatever the proctor did or said on their behalf had the same force and effect as if the principal had done or said it himself.[31] Proctors *ad negotia*, for example, bought and sold property, negotiated and concluded contracts, performed homage, and sometimes served as intelligence agents for their principals. The records are filled with references as well to another kind of proctor (*procuratores ad impetrandum*) who lobbied and pulled strings to procure favors of every kind—benefices, dispensations, privileges, promotions, and pardons—that their clients wanted.[32] Proctors who served as litigation agents (variously described in the records as *procuratores ad agendum vel defendendum*, or

---

30. Professional proctors stand in contrast to occasional proctors who acted as agents from time to time, usually for a friend or family member. Occasional proctors seldom had any special legal training and performed their duties without compensation, although they were entitled to reimbursement for the expenses they incurred (Guillemain, *La cour pontificale d'Avignon*, 568–69).

31. A special type of proctor appointed to represent a corporate body, such as a monastery, a university, or a municipality, was known as a syndic. Syndics had powers that closely resembled those of ordinary proctors. Thus, X 1.39.1; Jacobus de Albegna, *Apparatus* to 5 Comp. 1.5.5 (X 1.6.47) v. *procuratoribus* and 1.22.2 (X 1.38.9) v. *sindicos et actores*, in Cordoba, Biblioteca del Cabildo MS 10, at 310v and 315v (I am indebted to Kenneth Pennington for these references); William Durand, *Speculum iudiciale* 1.3 De syndico, pr., and *Actor uniuersitatis* §3, at 1:234, 239.

32. Proctors *ad negotia*: Jean le Coq, *Questiones*, 385–88, no. 309; *Acta imperii Angliae et Franciae*, 32–33, 37, nos. 52, 59. Proctors *ad impetrandum*: William Durand, *Speculum iudiciale* 1.3 *De procuratore* §4.19, at 1:224–25; Bonaguida de Arezzo, *Summa introductoria* 5.4, at 342–45; Brentano, *Two Churches*, 26–28; Herde, *Beiträge*, 125–28; Stelzer, "Niederaltaicher Prokuratoren," 292–93; Guillemain, *La cour pontificale d'Avignon*, 521–22.

alternatively, *ad causas* or *ad litem*) specialized in helping their employers to conduct lawsuits. Contemporary sources regularly describe such a proctor as *dominus litis*, the master of a lawsuit, because he controlled the process and spoke instead of, but with the same authority as, the litigant whom he represented.[33] These proctors often hired the advocates who provided their principals with legal advice and argued points of law.[34] Proctors negotiated and paid the fees and charges necessary to get their clients' cases onto the court's docket in the first place and to keep it running in timely fashion. They smoothed the progress of their cases by distributing gifts, favors, or outright bribes to key officials. Instead of designating a special proctor just to manage their lawsuits, a client might alternatively choose to invest a proctor with full powers (*plena potestas*). An appointment of this kind authorized the proctor not only to conduct litigation, but also to attend to every other kind of business on the client's behalf.[35] Needless to say, investing a proctor with full powers was not risk-free, and clients who did so needed to have complete confidence in the proctor's moral integrity and trustworthiness.

LITIGATION PROCTORS

Men who practiced regularly as proctors in the courts are sometimes called proctors-general to distinguish them from occasional proctors who acted on behalf of friends and family members. Proctors-general, like advocates, had to be adult male Catholics in good standing. By the second half of the thirteenth century, they usually needed to pass an examination and had to swear the same sort of admissions oath that advocates took. Their names, again like those of advocates, had to be entered on

---

33. Thus, e.g., Cod. 2.12 (13).22 and 23; Dig. 3.3.31, 76; William Durand, *Speculum iudiciale* 1.3 *De procuratore* §1.28, at 1:211, etc. Forms for constituting a proctor *ad litem* occur in many notarial formularies, e.g., the *Formularium Florentinum artis notariae*, 23.

34. Thus Archbishop Winchelsey, for example, wrote on 24 July 1298 to Walter de Dounbrugge, his proctor in Rome, to inform him that he had deposited 100 marks to his credit with the Florentine bankers, Pulci and Rembertini. Winchelsey instructed his proctor to use this to seek the best advice of the better advocates at the curia on a dispute concerning church property that he was appealing to Rome (Robert Winchelsey, *Registrum* 2:539). For an insider's account by a proctor of how such transactions worked at the beginning of the thirteenth century, see Thomas of Marlborough's *History of the Abbey of Evesham* §§284–85, at 282–86.

35. William Durand, *Speculum iudiciale* 1.3 *De procuratore* §1.38 and 4.11, at 1:214, 223; Post, *Studies in Medieval Legal Thought*, 92–102.

the court's register before they actually began to practice. They were thus bound, at least in theory, to live up to the same standards of ethical conduct as advocates and subject to the same disciplinary sanctions should they fail to do so.[36]

Unlike advocates, however, proctors were not expected to be deeply versed in law. They were primarily practical legal technicians whose expertise lay in their intimate familiarity with the minute details of practice in the courts in which they worked. Advanced academic training was less vital for a proctor than for an advocate, although a substantial minority of proctors did in fact spend some time at a university. Some held law degrees, and the proportion of those who did so increased markedly between the mid-thirteenth century and the close of the fifteenth.[37] Proctors described in the records as doctors of either civil or canon law remained exceptional. When such a one does appear in the documents, he may well turn out to have been an advocate who was for some reason temporarily representing a client as his proctor or a professional proctor awaiting a vacancy in the ranks of the local advocates, as was true for example at the Exeter consistory court in 1322–23.[38] Hands-on experience with the ways that lawsuits were actually conducted and familiarity with the habits and preferences of the judges, clerks, and other court officials with whom they worked were far more important for proctors than mastery of the law's subtler points. Although elementary manuals for training proctors did exist, they usually learned their craft primarily through apprenticeship, supplemented by

---

36. Thus, e.g., Martin V, *Romani pontificis providentia* (1423) §24, in Tangl, *Päpstlichen Kanzleiordnungen*, 155; Halberstadt bishop's court regulations (1490) §4, (1497) §§6 and 27, (1499) §30, in Hilling, "Sechs Gerichtsordnung," 33, 47, 53, 71–72; *Constitutiones et statuta*, 375, §32; Brundage, "Entry to the Ecclesiastical Bar at Ely," 543–44; Bartołomeij Groici, *Porzadek sadów i spraw miejskich prawa majdeburskiego w Koronie Polskiej*, 44–45 (my thanks to Mark Munzinger, for bringing this reference to my attention, and especially for a translation of the oath). See also Helmholz, "Ethical Standards," 43–44.

37. Helmholz, "Education of English Proctors," 195–96; Donahue, introduction to *Select Cases*, ed. Adams and Donahue, 23. The 1361 statutes of the Lincoln consistory court required proctors to have studied law for four years at a university. They also needed to be in attendance at the court for an additional period to be determined by the bishop's official (*Statuta consistorii*, 572, §3).

38. Thus Paolo d'Arezzo (d. 1443) appeared as a proctor at Padua for Cosimo and Lorenzo de' Medici, for which he received the substantial sum of 100 ducats (Sambin, "Giuristi padovani," 381). For the situation at Exeter, see Walter de Stapeldon, *Register*, 115–19.

study of formulas and precedent books. A good many of them also functioned as notaries during part or all of their careers.[39]

When a litigant appointed a proctor to represent him in a legal action, the proctor became "master of the lawsuit" from the moment that the trial proper (*litis contestatio*) began.[40] Proctors were in charge of the case because both litigants and advocates needed their guidance through the mind-boggling but vital minutiae of court operations. They spoke on behalf of the litigant who appointed them even when he was present, and unless the client raised a timely objection to them, the proctor's statements were binding on him.[41]

The services that proctors provided required cozy familiarity with the personnel as well as the procedures of the courts in which they practiced, knowledge that could only be acquired by men who had been in and about the court day after day over a period of years. By the mid-thirteenth century, the services of a proctor were a necessity, not a luxury, for anyone who hoped to prevail in litigation. Even where no proctor appears for someone in the court record, the litigant probably received some advice and coaching, either from a professional proctor, a court clerk, or a notary.[42] Proctors regularly advised their principals about which advocate to choose and—especially when the client lived far away—might actually hire the

39. Helmholz, "Education of English Proctors," 201–7. A notable example of the notarial path can be found in the career of Master Johannes de Sancto Germano, a papal notary who also served as a proctor at the curia and even occasionally as a curial auditor between 1245 and 1257 (Stelzer, "Aus der päpstlichen Kanzlei"). Numerous other examples appear in Harvey, *The English in Rome*, 149–61. All the proctors at York in the fifteenth century were also notaries, as were many of those at Ely (Dasef, "Lawyers of the York Curia," 33–34; Brundage, "Bar of the Ely Consistory Court," 548–54).

40. Cod. 2.12 (13).22 (319), 23 (363); VI 1.19.1; Bernard of Pavia, *Summa decretalium* 1.29.7, at 24; Johannes Teutonicus, *Apparatus* to 3 Comp. 1.22.1 v. *litteras reuocatorias*, 143–44; Goffredus de Trano, *Summa super titulis*, 134, to X 1.38 §18; Hostiensis, *Summa aurea*, lib. 1, *De procuratoribus* §§11, 14, at 64va, 65ra; William Durand, *Speculum iudiciale* 1.3 *De procuratore* §1.28, at 1:211.

41. Bernard of Pavia, *Summa decretalium* 1.29.1, 6, at 24; Johannes Teutonicus, *Apparatus* to 3 Comp. 1.4.1 v. *idem magister*, 31–32; Goffredus de Trano, *Summa super titulis*, 128, 134 to X 1.38 pr. and §18; Bernard of Parma, *Glos. ord.* to X 1.29.32 v. *protinus, contraxit*, and to X 2.6.1 v. *procuratoris*; Hostiensis, *Summa aurea*, lib. 1, *De procuratore* §14, at 64vb–65ra; Tancred, *Ordo iudiciarius* 1.6.1, 1.7, at 114–15, 121–22; William Durand, *Speculum iudiciale* 1.3 *De procuratore* 4.6, at 1:222.

42. Helmholz, "Education of English Proctors," 192, as well as *Marriage Litigation*, 147–48, and "Canonists and Standards of Impartiality," 23–24; Hageneder, *Geistliche Gerichtsbarkeit*, 128–29.

advocate, negotiate his fee, and give him the client's instructions. Proctors bargained with court clerks to schedule hearings at times and places that would suit their employers, appeared in their place at routine hearings, and saw to it that they showed up when their actual presence was required. They also took charge of collecting all the necessary documents in their cases, had copies made and distributed to the proper recipients, arranged for summonses to be served by the court's bailiff or summoner (*apparitor*); they rounded up witnesses, and when necessary arranged for their transportation, housing, and meals; they gave gifts, and sometimes bribes, to secure the goodwill and cooperation of those in a position to expedite their principal's case, and paid the fees of advocates, notaries, scribes, messengers, and other court officials.[43]

Bishops, officials, and other authorities sought to restrain competition among the professional proctors who practiced in their courts, much as they did with advocates, by setting limits on their numbers. While it is possible that judges may have done this on their own initiative, it seems likely that proctors already established in practice encouraged them to take this step. The maximum authorized number of proctors, although generally larger than that for advocates, was seldom very large. Their numbers varied considerably, depending upon the volume of cases that a particular court normally heard. Thus, for example, just four proctors practiced in the commissary's court at Hereford in the late fifteenth century and the same number at the Rochester consistory, and even the much more important court of the archbishop of York had only seven authorized proctors early in the fifteenth century. Only two proctors practiced regularly at the Canterbury consistory court in 1374, but by 1486 that court had eight or nine of them, although the number later declined.[44] Ely was better provided for—nine proctors practiced in the bishop's consistory in the late fourteenth cen-

---

43. Fournier, *Officialités*, 39–40; Guillemain, *La cour pontificale d'Avignon*, 570–72; Steins, "Ordentliche Zivilprozeß," 251; Jacob, *Essays in Later Medieval History*, 59; Brentano, *Two Churches*, 10–56; Jacob Emerix, *Tractatus seu notitia* 1.35, at 131–32. The expense accounts of Richard Bachterhalle, proctor for the city of Bruges between 1292 and 1302, give a vivid impression of the range of gifts, tips, and other favors that a proctor might expect to lay out at the papal court (Guillemain, *La cour pontificale d'Avignon*, 68).

44. Helmholz, "Education of English Proctors," 192–93, and *Marriage Litigation*, 120. Five proctors seem to have been practicing regularly at the Rochester consistory court in the mid-fourteenth century, as appears from the fragment of the court's act book for 1347/1348 that appears in Hamo Hethe, *Registrum* 2:911–1043. On numbers at Canterbury, Woodcock *Medieval Ecclesiastical Courts*, 40–41.

tury—but that no doubt owed much to the presence of the university at Cambridge, where the court met. Exeter was anomalous in having ten proctors, the same number as the busier and far more important Court of Arches, while sixteen were authorized to practice in the diocese of Lincoln, which covered a greater territory than any other diocese in England.

Proctors were often more plentiful in ecclesiastical courts on the Continent than they were in England. The 1442 court statutes at Halberstadt fixed the maximum number of proctors there at six, but the 1490 statutes raised this to eight at the official's court, as well as eight more at the archdeacon's court.[45] Professional proctors were of course far more numerous at the papal curia, where they often practiced for years on end. Twenty-two proctors appear in tax records at Avignon between 1318 and 1323, and between 1326 and 1443 the number increased to thirty-eight. These figures naturally began to fall after the papacy returned to Rome in 1378, but even so they remained considerably larger than those found in other cities of comparable size during the same period.[46]

Proctors often found it useful or necessary to collaborate with one another and sometimes worked on a case as a team. In Italy, proctors seem occasionally to have formed partnerships or firms whose members shared expenses and perhaps even fees.[47] Proctors seem to have kept their books and files in their dwellings but probably did not usually deal with clients there. Rather, they normally met with clients and conducted their other

---

45. 1442 statutes §33, 1490 statutes §2 in Hilling, "Sechs Gerichtsordnungen," 337 and 32.

46. Guillemain, *La cour pontificale d'Avignon*, 544 n. 163 and 668. Peter of Assisi, the earliest identifiable standing proctor at the papal curia, practiced there regularly for thirty-three years (1241–74), and Waldinus de Bettona made regular appearances there for twenty-one years (1247–68); see Heckel, "Aufkommen der ständigen Prokuratoren," 319. Herde, *Beiträge*, 136–48, presents an extensive list of thirteenth-century curial proctors who represented Bavarian clients. Linehan, "Proctors Representing Spanish Interests," 75–109, gives a even longer list of those who acted on behalf of clients from the Iberian peninsula, while Sayers, "Canterbury Proctors," describes numerous proctors representing English interests.

47. On collaboration between proctors, Tancred, *Ordo iudiciarius* 1.6.2, at 115–16; Gratia, *De iudiciario ordine* 1.8.1, at 347; William Durand, *Speculum iudiciale* 1.3 *De procuratore* §3.16, at 1:219–20. On legal partnerships, Goffredus de Trano, *Summa super titulis*, 129–30 to X 1.38 §3; Bernard of Parma, *Glos. ord.* to X 1.38.14 v. *cum aliis*; Innocent IV, *Apparatus* to X 1.38.4 §§1–3, at 167ra–vb. For examples see Herde, *Beiträge*, 130–31; Brentano, *Two Churches*, 28, 32; Stelzer, "Beiträge," 124–37; Sayers, "Court of 'Audientia litterarum contradictarum' Revisited," 412.

professional dealings either in the court itself or in its immediate precincts. Proctors, as Peter Linehan put it, spent much of their professional lives "hanging around in curial corridors." They apparently spent a lot of time hanging around in taverns as well, to judge from the frequency with which the mandates appointing Canterbury proctors were executed in those establishments.[48]

Clients authorized their proctors to act in their name and on their behalf through a mandate contract. Actions undertaken by a proctor who lacked a proper mandate from his principal, or whose mandate had expired or been revoked, were invalid. Opponents, especially defendants who stood to gain by postponing judgments, often raised dilatory exceptions against the authenticity of the opposing proctor's mandate, since the judge had to hear arguments and rule on the exception before the trial could proceed.[49] To forestall this delaying tactic so far as possible, judges insisted that proctors produce a written mandate from their principal when they first appeared on his behalf and court clerks routinely made a note of this in their records. Consequently, the names of proctors, unlike those of advocates, regularly appear in court act books and similar documents.[50]

Mandates had long since ceased to be gratuitous, and proctors-general demanded and received remuneration for their labor. They also had, and used, the right to sue clients who withheld their compensation.[51] Numer-

48. See Jacob, *Essays in Later Medieval History*, 62, 73; Linehan, "Will of Synibaldus de Labro," 136; and Woodcock, *Medieval Ecclesiastical Courts*, 52.

49. On raising exceptions, see Bonaguida de Arezzo, *Summa introductoria* 3.1, at 256; cf. Thomas of Marlborough, *History of the Abbey of Evesham*, 240, §239. On judges' rulings in response, see Goffredus de Trano, *Summa super titulis*, 133, to X 1.38 §16; Bernard of Parma, *Glos. ord.* to X 1.38.4 v. *exceptio*; Innocent IV, *Apparatus* to X 1.38.4 §10, at 168vb–169ra. Manuals for practitioners and procedural treatises often treated this tactic as well: e.g., Bonaguida, *Summa introductoria* 1.3.22, 3.3, at 163–64, 261; Bencivenne, *De ordine iudiciorum* 2.2, Tancred, *Ordo iudiciarius* 2.2 and 3.1, and Gratia, *De iudiciario ordine* 1.2, at 23, 142–43, 199–200, 351; William Durand, *Speculum iudiciale* 1.3 *De procuratore* §1.29, at 1:211–12.

50. Bernard of Parma, *Glos. ord.* to X 1.38.1 v. *portitoribus, mandato*; Donahue, introduction to *Select Cases*, ed. Adams and Donahue, 24; Planas Rosselló, "Los abogados de Mallorca," 116.

51. Ricardus Anglicus, *Summa de ordine iudiciario*, 21, §18, strongly disapproved of the proctors' charging fees, but I have not encountered any other medieval authority who did so. On suing for fees, see Goffredus de Trano, *Summa super titulis*, 129, to X 1.38 §2; Bernard of Parma, *Glos. ord.* to X 1.38.2 v. *expensarum* as well as X 1.38.6 v. *propter hoc*; and X 3.1.10 v. *praeter expensas* and *gratis studeatis*; William of Drogheda, *Summa aurea*, 98–99, §103; Herde, *Audientia litterarum contradictarum* 2:288–89, 677–78, nos.

ous and time-consuming as a proctor's duties were, however, their fees were invariably smaller, often much smaller, than those of advocates. The constitution *Properandum* of the Second Council of Lyon, as noted earlier, set the advocate's maximum fee in a case at twenty *livres tournois*, while the highest permissible fee for a proctor was only twelve *livres tournois*.[52] The highest fee that *Properandum* allowed to a proctor thus amounted to three-fifths of the highest fee an advocate could charge.

Differences between the fees of advocates and proctors were often much greater than this. Benedict XII's constitution *Decens et necessarium* in 1340, which decreed that proctors in papal courts were to receive no more than half the fee awarded to advocates in the same case, may well have been closer to usual practice.[53] Disparities in actual fees, however, varied considerably. Consider, for example, the list of costs incurred in a suit (unfortunately undated) concerning tithes of fish that was first heard in the bishop's consistory court at Norwich and then appealed to the Court of Arches in London. The expense account shows that the advocate at Norwich received six marks and the proctor one mark for their work over a three-year period. The Norwich advocate, in other words, was paid six times as much as the proctor. In the appellate stage of the case at the Arches, which lasted a year, the difference was narrower: the advocate was paid twenty shillings (240 d.), while the proctors received one mark and eight pence (168 d.). The proctors' fees at the Arches in this case thus amounted to slightly more than two-thirds of the advocate's fee, which is reasonably close to the differential that the *Properandum* prescribed.[54]

K 140, QV 404. Proctors regularly sued to recover the fees and expenses due to them from deadbeat clients; the Act Book of the Ely consistory court, for example, shows many such actions between 1373 and 1382 (CUL, EDR D/2/1, at 37r, 46v, 49v, 52r, 79r–v, 87v, 91r, 97v, 113r, 116r, 131v, 161r, 162r–v). Actions of this sort were apparently far more common in the consistory court of Canterbury, which recorded as many as nineteen of them in 1499 (Woodcock, *Medieval Ecclesiastical Courts*, 87). See also Helmholz, *Marriage Litigation*, 150–51, and *Canon Law and the Law of England*, 47; and Donahue, introduction to *Select Cases*, ed. Adams and Donahue, 25 n. 1.

52. 2 Lyons (1274) c. 19 in *DEC* 1:324.

53. *Decens et necessarium* §22, in Tangl, *Päpstlichen Kanzleiordnungen*, 123.

54. Churchill, *Canterbury Administration* 2:202–5. It is tempting to speculate that the much greater disparity between the fees of advocates and proctors at Norwich, where advocates are likely to have been few, and those at London, where they were far more plentiful, may have been a function of differences in labor supply. Unfortunately, few records of the bishop's consistory at Norwich survive from the medieval period, so that it may be impossible to determine whether this conjecture is true.

As we've seen, institutional clients, such as bishops, monasteries, and cathedral chapters, as well as kings, cities, and powerful noblemen, frequently found it useful to keep one or more proctors on long-term retainers to represent their interests at the papal curia and other important law courts. In these situations, too, the retainers of standing proctors tended to be significantly smaller than those paid to advocates.[55]

Although proctors lacked the opportunities that advocates enjoyed for supplementing their income with added earnings from teaching, legal consulting, and preparing *consilia*, the fees they received from clients constituted only a fraction of their professional revenues. Indeed, laments about the "blind and profligate greed" of proctors were not uncommon.[56] Authorities attempted to address those complaints. The oath that the papal Audientia litterarum contradictarum required proctors to take, for example, was amended in the mid-thirteenth century to add a clause in which they explicitly promised that they would neither extort nor accept from their clients any more than the usual and customary fees or the amount awarded in judicial taxation of costs.[57] How much practical effect such measures may have had is questionable.

Prudent and well-heeled clients sometimes thought it worthwhile to encourage faithful service from their proctors by adding a small gratuity to their fees and expense claims, although a proctor could scarcely count on this.[58] The easiest, most reliable, and in all likelihood the commonest way for a proctor to augment his fee income was by fiddling his expense accounts.

Proctors, as we have seen, normally paid most of the expenses that litigation involved and then claimed reimbursement from their clients.[59] These

---

55. Guenée, *Tribunaux et gens de justice*, 209. See also Heckel, "Aufkommen der ständige Prokuratoren"; Stelzer, "Beiträge"; as well as Herde, *Beiträge*, 136–48; Linehan, "Proctors Representing Spanish Interests," esp. 78–109, and "Spanish Litigants and Their Agents"; Sayers, "Canterbury Proctors," "Proctors Representing British Interests," and "Court of 'Audientia litterarum contradictarum' Revisited." Authorities sometimes encouraged prelates, rectors, and other holders of benefices to keep a proctor on permanent retainer to represent them in lawsuits and other legal business (Council of Avignon [1282] c. 4, in Mansi 24:441–42).

56. Council of Noyon (1344) c. 17, in Mansi 26:11–12; Gregory XI, *Quamvis a felicis* (1375) pr. and §3, in Tangl, *Päpstlichen Kanzleiordnungen*, 128–29; Jason de Mayno, *Commentaria super titulo de actionibus* § *Triplici vero*, no. 51, at 200ra.

57. Tangl, *Päpstlichen Kanzleiordnungen*, 47.

58. Guenée, *Tribunaux et gens de justice*, 211.

59. William Durand, *Speculum iudiciale* 1.4 *De salariis* 2.6, at 1:346.

expenses taken together could be substantial. To take just one example, Don Suero Pérez, bishop of Zamora (r. 1255–85) lamented the expense of his lawsuit over possession of Vanialbo, Villa Mayor, and Morale de Toro in 1262:

> [It] cost me the greater part of what I had before I became bishop. Hence, so that I might prosecute my claim properly and effectively . . . I sold and destroyed the good inheritance that I had in Algarve and Cortilio de Lebrixa and my vineyards that I had at Seville and many other things of mine that I had before I became bishop.[60]

Proctors seldom attempted to cover all these disbursements out of their own pockets. Most probably lacked the surplus cash, and even those who could afford the expenditure were apt to consider that doing so would represent a risky and unprofitable interest-free loan to a client for an indefinite term. From the proctor's point of view, the best way to deal with the cash-flow problem was for the client to supply him with periodic advances against anticipated expenses. This secured the proctor against the possibility that the client might prove unwilling or unable to meet litigation costs, while at the same time it gave him a supply of cash in hand to meet expenses as they arose. No doubt it might also give him the comforting reassurance that the client had the means to reward him generously.

A client's promise to advance expense payments was not without risk. There could be no guarantee that promised payments would arrive on schedule, and they sometimes miscarried altogether—couriers might be robbed on the road, for example, or suffer accidents en route. This put the proctor in a difficult position that could well prove expensive. Court officers and others were liable to turn testy, even hostile, when a proctor delayed more than a short time in fulfilling commitments he had made to them. In this situation, the proctor usually had no alternative but to take out a loan in his client's name, often at usurious rates (despite ecclesiastical prohibitions), in the hope that the expected payment might arrive soon. The further away the client lived, the more precarious the situation became. Distance not only increased risks and delays in communication, but it was also likely to make securing a loan exceptionally troublesome and costly. Prospective lenders might have qualms about the client's creditworthiness and be unwilling to advance money without substantial collateral to guarantee repayment. Even if the proctor could persuade bank-

---

60. Don Suero Pérez, *Memorandum* (ca. 1271) §26, in Linehan and Lera Maíllo, *Postrimerías de un obispo Alfonsino*, 104–6. Even so, this did not deter Don Suero from undertaking other expensive lawsuits, as appears from his *Memorandum*, 106, 112, §§27 and 39.

ers or moneylenders to make a loan, the interest charges were apt to be burdensome. Deficit financing of lawsuits was nevertheless common, and proctors were almost invariably involved in negotiating these loans. Monastic communities and cathedral chapters were notoriously addicted to lawsuits, and the debts they ran up in litigation do much to explain the chronic chaos of their finances.[61]

Proctors of course needed to account to their clients for their expenditures in order to secure reimbursement. Although authorities repeatedly admonished proctors to keep expenses modest, it seems likely that they sometimes succumbed to the temptation to indulge themselves in a bit of luxury at their clients' expense and even more likely that the accounts they rendered occasionally exceed actual outlays.[62] Professional proctors often spent much of their working time on the road. They traveled back and forth to distant towns and villages, following itinerant judges, searching out prospective witnesses, or conveying documents to and fro between parties and judges. They represented their clients in proceedings at appellate courts, often enough at the papal curia. Given the kinds of work they did, successful proctors were almost by definition apt to be shrewd, worldly men, and most of them, one suspects, learned early on how to milk the accounts they rendered to their clients. It was not difficult to pad the actual outlays on a journey, especially a lengthy one, and travel expenses were likely to be difficult or impossible for a distant client to verify. In addition to claiming reimbursement for more money than he laid out, an enterprising proctor could often arrange to make a single journey serve the needs of several clients, each of whom he might then bill for the total cost of the trip.[63]

Even less is known about the origins and social backgrounds of professional proctors than those of professional advocates. Such information as

61. Moorman, *Church Life in England*, 302–5; Thompson, *English Clergy*, 173–77. Thomas of Marlborough provides a particularly detailed and vivid account of the difficulties he experienced in borrowing money to finance his monastery's lawsuit against the bishop of Worcester and the problems the monastery experienced in repaying the loan (*History of the Abbey of Evesham*, 274, 344, 372, 418, 428–32, 472–74, §§ 273, 358, 386, 437, 447–51, 505).

62. X 1.38.6 and the *Glos. ord.* of Bernard of Parma, v. *propter hoc*. Honorius III certainly had heard complaints about abuse of expense accounts by proctors (Sayers, "Centre and Locality," 117). The process of taxing costs was theoretically supposed to check the most blatant abuses, but its effectiveness in all likelihood depended on the experience and shrewdness of the judge who served as taxing master.

63. Woodcock, *Medieval Ecclesiastical Courts*, 35–36; Guenée, *Tribunaux et gens de justice*, 210–11; Verdon, *Travel in the Middle Ages*, 209, 211.

there is suggests that rank-and-file proctors frequently came from families of modest means, although men who attended university, especially those who took law degrees, may have had more privileged backgrounds. Successful and hard-working proctors could earn a respectable living. Master Thomas Nottingham, a professional proctor at the Canterbury consistory court provides an instructive example. The court's fifteenth-century fee schedule set proctors' fees at sixpence per court appearance. On that basis, Master Thomas, who made 567 recorded appearances in 1493, should have earned at the least more than fourteen pounds from fees alone that year, or about twice the usual income of an artisan, such as a carpenter, a shoemaker, or a blacksmith. Thomas was unusually busy that year, to be sure, and none of his fellow proctors at Canterbury handled anything like the volume of cases that he did. His colleagues with thriving practices may have averaged something closer to ten pounds a year. Busy proctors at York apparently made similar amounts.[64] Proctors seldom grew seriously rich from the practice of their profession, but successful ones sometimes left handsome estates. A handful of families nurtured procuratorial dynasties that produced proctors one generation after another, and members of these families could became extremely prosperous.[65]

Prestige was a different matter, and there proctors fared less well. They were commonly regarded as socially inferior to advocates. Academic jurists considered the advocate's profession as not only more dignified and more privileged than that of the proctor, but also noted that it involved less menial work. "It is an honor to be an advocate," said Accursius, "but to be a proctor is a burden."[66] Baldus was even more disdainful. The proctor's tasks, he declared, are thoroughly contemptible and a person who does contemptible work does not care much about personal dignity.[67]

---

64. Woodcock, *Medieval Ecclesiastical Courts*, 43–44, 61–62, 77; Dasef, "Lawyers of the York Curia," 75–76, estimates that very busy proctors there would have averaged about 11 pounds a year in fees.

65. Guenée, *Tribunaux et gens de justice*, 372; Dasef, "Lawyers of the York Curia, 25–26; Heckel, "Aufkommen der ständigen Prokuratoren," 320.

66. Accursius, *Glos. ord.* to Dig. 3.1.1 v. *certis personis:* "Si insistes quare diuersum est in uno quam in altero, respondeo esse aduocatum honor est, ut C. de aduo. diuer. iudicio. l. Laudabile i. respon. [Cod. 2.7.23.1 (= *vulgata* 2.8.4)]. Ideoque eis multa dantur priuilegia, ut C. de aduo. diuor. iudicio. Sancimus [Cod. 2.7.6]. Sed esse procuratorem onus est." Likewise, John of Acton, gloss to Otto c. 29 v. *advocati officium* in *Constitutiones legatinae*, 70.

67. Baldus *Commentaria* to Dig. 3.1.1.4: "[O]fficium procuratoris est vilissimum, et ubi agitur de vili officio, personae dignitas non curatur, ut C. de decur. l. X [Cod. 10.32

Professional Associations

The appearance in Mediterranean cities, particularly in northern Italy, of powerful local guilds of legal professionals encouraged the increase in the level of academic training that is evident among advocates and proctors, as well as notaries and judges, from the mid-thirteenth century onward. Lawyers' guilds, like the organizations of merchants and craftsmen that had begun to appear about 1100, were both public and private bodies. As private organizations of individuals who practiced the same craft and shared common interests, talents, and training, their members jointly engaged in social, religious, and political activities designed to improve their status both spiritually and temporally. These associations strove in addition to secure a monopoly on the practice of their particular line of work in their communities. Legal guilds, like other guilds, put political pressure on local authorities to allow their members to determine who might be permitted to practice their trade and to bar from practice anyone whom the guild did not approve. When they succeeded in such demands, they became in a sense an arm of local government.[68] Lawyers argued, just as craftsmen did, that granting them a monopoly on furnishing legal advice and assistance served the public interest. The common good of the community, lawyers asserted, demanded that ignorant and unqualified persons be excluded from key roles in the legal system. The functions that judges, advocates, proctors, and notaries performed, they claimed, were so vital to the integrity of the social fabric that only men with adequate training and preparation could carry them out properly.[69] Because their occupation was technical and complex, the argument continued, only men who had secured a systematic legal education coupled with successful experience in practice could be trusted to make sound judgments about the adequacy of aspirants to enter the legal establishment.[70]

As evidence of their commitment to the defense of the common good,

---

(31).10] et no. eo. li. X l. j de infami. [Cod. 10.59 (57).1]." Similar statements also appear in his *Commentaria* to Cod.2.7.4 and Cod. 2.12 (13) rubr.

68. Black, *Guilds and Civil Society*, 6–8; Meyer-Holz, "Die *Collegia iudicum*," 373.

69. Black, *Guilds and Civil Society*, 14–18. These claims were not without foundation and stories about ignorant notaries, for example, were rife. See, e.g. Martines, *Lawyers and Statecraft*, 30–31 and n. 42; Trexler, *Synodal Law*, 157.

70. Meyer-Holz, "Die *Collegia iudicum*," 374. Lawyers could also cite a Roman precedent for such organizations: a rescript of the Emperor Anastasius in 517 had approved the creation of a *consortio advocatorum* in Syria (Cod. 2.7.24 pr).

guilds of jurists adopted what we would now call quality control systems. The guilds sought the power to eliminate undesirable competitors by withdrawing the right to practice from those who were demonstrably illiterate, inadequately educated, or untrustworthy. At the same time, lawyers' guilds required intending practitioners to prove their professional skills by passing one or more examinations conducted by guild members. Since these examinations might be as costly as they were demanding, they not only assured that those who passed them were properly prepared to perform their functions, but also excluded from the ranks of the profession anyone who could not afford a long and costly professional preparation.[71]

Lawyers' guilds in northern Italy adopted two different organizational patterns. One approach, exemplified by the Bologna guilds, divided legal professionals into two groups, each with its own separate and distinct guild, one for judges and advocates and the other for notaries and proctors. The other pattern, represented by the practice at Florence, united practitioners in the various branches of the legal profession—advocates, judges, proctors, and notaries—into a single guild.[72]

At Bologna the guild of judges started to emerge early in the thirteenth century. Its existence can be securely documented from 1226 onward. The term "judge" (*iudex*) in this period could refer to practicing advocates as well as men who held judicial appointments, but it did not necessarily imply that everyone so described had a deep knowledge of the law acquired through systematic legal training.[73] By 1286, however, *iudex* had come to be used more restrictively, and the guild formally acknowledged this by changing its name to the Societas doctorum advocatorum et iudicum. The name change reflected a basic change in the educational requirements for admission, for after 1286 the new guild of advocates and judges demanded that applicants show that they were *doctores graduati* before they became eligible for membership. Guild membership had by that time become a prerequisite to practice in Bologna as a judge, legal consultant, or advocate.[74] Toward the end of the century, professors of Roman law formally separated from the practitioners' guild and established the College of Doctors of Civil Law. The canonists later created the College of Doctors of

71. Martines, *Lawyers and Statecraft*, 34–35; Trexler, *Synodal Law*, 158; Fasoli, "Giuristi, giudici e notai," 31–32.

72. Hyde, *Padua in the Age of Dante*, 122.

73. Fried, *Die Entstehung des Juristenstandes*, 24–44, traces the evolution of the term; see also Fasoli, Giuristi, giudici e notai," 35–36.

74. Cortese, "Legisti, canonisti e feudisti," 260–61; Fasoli, "Giuristi, giudici e notai," 36–37; Meyer-Holz, "Die *Collegia iudicum*," 378–82.

Canon Law, independent from the civilians.[75] Other cities that followed the Bolognese model of organizing advocates, judges, and law teachers into guilds separate from those of the notaries and proctors included Modena, Padua, Pavia, Reggio Emilia, Cremona, and Treviso. In Germany, the city of Würzburg likewise had by 1340 founded the Collegium patronarum causarum sive advocatorum.[76]

It is not clear just when the judges and notaries at Florence first established a guild, but like its Bolognese counterpart, the organization is securely documented from early in the thirteenth century.[77] The "judges" at Florence included all doctors of law, advocates, legal advisers, arbitrators, as well as judges in the usual sense of the term. The notaries (sometimes described as *iudices extraordinarii*) comprised everyone who held the *privilegium notariatus*, whether they received that status from the pope, the emperor, or lesser authorities. Membership in the guild was compulsory for anyone who wished to practice as an advocate or notary in the city or the surrounding countryside and suburbs (*contada*). Admission to the guild, at least by the time of its 1344 statutes, was restricted to laymen who either held the doctorate in law or had studied law at a university for five years and had passed the guild's own examination in civil and canon law. Admission was expensive: judges and advocates had to pay an entrance fee of sixteen gold florins, while notaries were charged half that sum. Members of this guild ranked along with knights near the top of the Florentine civic hierarchy.[78] Similar organizations that brought judges, advocates, and notaries together in a single guild are also found at Lucca, Siena, and Montpellier.[79]

Different patterns of professional association appeared among northern European lawyers trained in the *ius commune*. Practitioners at the Par-

---

75. On the civilian college, see Steffen, *Studentische Autonomie*, 196–98. The earliest surviving statutes of this organization date from 1397 and appear in the Bologna University Statutes, ed. Malagola, 367–402. See Malagola, *Statuti*, 325–51, for the canonists' statutes of 1460.

76. Fried, *Entstehung des Juristenstandes*, 237–44; Martines, *Lawyers and Statecraft*, 32–33; Stein, "College of Judges of Pavia"; Betto, "Collegio dei giudici e dottori di Treviso," 45–57, together with the statutes of the guild at 121–46; Alexander Tartagnus, *Consilia* 6.2, vol. 6, at 2va–vb; Trusen, "Advocatus," 1242–43.

77. Calleri, *L'arte dei giudici*, 4–11; Santini, *Studi sull'antica costituzione di Firenze*, 77–92; Martines, *Lawyers and Statecraft*, 11–12.

78. Calleri, *L'arte dei giudici*, 29–34; Santini, *Studi sull'antico costituzione*, 95; Martines, *Lawyers and Statecraft*, 29–31; Epstein, *Wage Labor and Guilds*, 140.

79. Waley, *Siena and the Sienese*, 86–89; Gouron, *La réglementation des métiers*, 97; Meyer, *Felix et inclitus notarius*, 71 n. 337.

lement de Paris, for example, developed no less than three professional organizations. Advocates, many of them canonists, belonged to the Order of Advocates (Ordre des avocats), proctors had a separate organization, the Communauté des procureurs, and both advocates and proctors also joined the Confraternity of St. Nicholas. The Order of Advocates, unlike guilds of advocates in Italy, remained an informal association without officially recognized corporate status or written rules. Yet it acted for all the world like a full-fledged corporate body, and a powerful one at that. Membership was mandatory, and no advocate whose name failed to appear on its membership roll could practice before the court. The leaders of the order enforced its unwritten guidelines for professional conduct and imposed sanctions upon those who failed to observe them, while the courts, the police, and municipal authorities treated the Order of Advocates as an autonomous entity with exclusive jurisdiction over both the personal and professional conduct of its members, including any crimes or offenses that they might commit. Advocates of the parlement worshipped together with proctors in the Chapel of St. Nicholas within the royal palace. Even after the chapel disappeared during reconstruction under Philip IV (1286–1314), they arranged for a daily mass to be said on a portable altar dedicated to St. Nicholas in the great hall of the palace. Both proctors and advocates supported and participated in these activities, which gave rise to the Confraternity of St. Nicholas. While the confraternity originally served primarily to advance the spiritual welfare of its members, it also provided a common meeting ground for other purposes. This confraternity, like others, served some of the functions of a guild insofar as it furnished mutual aid and assistance to members of both branches of the legal profession, particularly when their prerogatives and other common interests were involved. Membership in the Confraternity of St. Nicholas became mandatory for practitioners at the Parlement de Paris during the reign of Philip VI (1328–50).[80]

England produced no close counterpart to the Italian jurists' guilds. Pleaders at the common law bar and the royal chancery began to organize the societies that came to be known as the Inns of Court, the Serjeants Inn, and Inns of Chancery during the fourteenth century. These societies originated in housing arrangements that brought together students, practitioners, and judges in the royal courts and combined social and educational functions in ways that differed sharply from those that characterized the

80. Epstein, *Wage Labor and Guilds*, 51–52, 156–59; Fitzsimmons, *Parisian Order of Barristers*, 2–4; Delachenal, *Histoire des avocats*, 23–25, 35–38, 42–43. On the similarities between a confraternity and a guild, see Black, *Guilds and Civil Society*, 5–6.

legal guilds of Mediterranean Europe. Although some practitioners in the chancery and common law courts were clerics and a few had studied Roman and canon law at universities, their professional concerns centered primarily, although not as exclusively as is often assumed, on the common law peculiar to the English royal courts rather than on the *ius commune* that prevailed on the Continent.[81]

The closest English analogue to the Italian jurists' guilds emerged among the civilians and canonists who practiced in London. Advocates and proctors at the Court of Arches had formed an identifiable social and professional group at least as early as 1273, when Archbishop Kilwardby promulgated his statutes governing their admission to practice and their conduct once admitted.[82] They also shared interests with other civil and canon lawyers active in the courts of the bishop of London and the dean and chapter of St. Paul's Cathedral.

Ecclesiastical lawyers in London did not join together in a formal organization, however, until the latter part of the fifteenth century. The precipitating event that led them to form a professional association seems to have been the death in 1469 of Thomas Kent, a doctor of both civil and canon law. Dr. Kent's will left twenty-eight canon and civil law books for the use of the judges, examiners, advocates, and proctors of the Court of Arches. At some uncertain date thereafter, and under circumstances that remain obscure, a group of London ecclesiastical lawyers established a society that came to be known as Doctors' Commons. This society soon sought premises where its members could meet and where they could house the books that Dr. Kent had left to them.[83]

Doctors' Commons never functioned in quite the same way as the lawyers' guilds of the north Italian towns. Although the predecessors of its founding members had enjoyed a monopoly on practice at the Court of Arches for nearly two centuries before their society came into being, their

---

81. See Baker, *Introduction to English Legal History*, 182–85, as well as his *Legal Profession and the Common Law*, 3–23, 45–74, and *Third University of England*. Admiralty law (particularly important to island dwellers), merchant law, and some aspects of the English common law drew in part from Roman and canonical sources, while church courts, of course, flourished alongside of, and at times in competition with, civil jurisdictions. See Helmholz, *Canon Law and the Law of England*, as well as *Select Cases on Defamation*, and *The ius commune in England*; Sheehan, *The Will in Medieval England*; *Lex mercatoria and Legal Pluralism*; Ibbetson, *Common Law and Ius Commune* and *Historical Introduction to the Law of Obligations*, 1–23 and passim.

82. Logan, *Medieval Court of Arches*, 4.

83. Squibb, *Doctors' Commons*, 1–22, 56–65.

separation from the common lawyers who practiced in municipal and royal courts prevented them from securing the sort of political influence that their counterparts on the Continent enjoyed.

Professional lawyers who worked in the courts of the *ius commune* from the middle of the thirteenth century onward were primarily men who practiced as advocates or proctors in the ecclesiastical courts or law teachers and *iurisperiti* who furnished expert legal advice in those courts. Their education and experience made their services nearly indispensable for anyone who hoped to prevail in litigation before the church courts. In theory at least, advocates and proctors differed in the roles that they played in litigation, in their training and experience, in the cost of their services to their clients, in the social prestige they enjoyed, and sometimes in the professional associations to which they belonged. The lines of distinction between them were not always as sharp in practice as legal doctrine insisted they should be. The demarcation between the two groups seems to have been a good deal fuzzier in courts at the lower levels of the church's judicial system than it was in higher courts. In places where the volume of litigation was low and men with university training in canon law were correspondingly scarce, a single individual might do double duty as proctor and advocate.

While advocates and proctors constituted the core of the canonical legal profession, two other groups of men with varying degrees of legal training were essential to the conduct of their profession. Canonical courts needed judges in order to function at all, and after the middle of the thirteenth century, judges were increasingly drawn from the ranks of the advocates who practiced in those courts. Canonical courts likewise required the services of notaries, especially after 1215, when the Fourth Lateran Council obliged ecclesiastical courts to maintain reliable records of the cases that came before them.[84] The membership rolls of organizations of legal professionals, as we have seen, sometimes included judges and notaries along with advocates and proctors, and we turn now to consider how these men qualified to perform their professional duties.

---

84. 4 Lat. (1215) c. 38 (= X 2.19.11).

* NINE *

Judges and Notaries

Judges

The presiding officer of the consistory court of a bishop or lesser prelate was an ordinary judge usually styled the "official." The official was "ordinary" because he exercised the authority of the prelate who appointed him and did so permanently, or at least on a long-term basis, as distinguished from ad hoc judges, such as papal judges-delegate. Prelates by definition possessed the right of "ordinary jurisdiction," which is to say that they were the usual and customary judges of disputes or disciplinary infractions among the faithful who were subject to them.[1] At the pinnacle of the church's hierarchy, the pope claimed ordinary jurisdiction over all Christians, although in practice he normally authorized the auditors of the Roman Rota, the Audientia litterarum contradictarum, and other papal tribunals to exercise it on his behalf. Similarly, archbishops, bishops, abbots, archdeacons, deans, and other lesser prelates routinely deputized officials and commissary judges to deal with most matters that fell under their jurisdiction.

The official, together with the advocates, proctors, notaries, and other functionaries who carried out their duties under his direction, comprised the "officiality," a small professional community within the larger community where the court was located. Officials, rather than the prelates whose jurisdiction they exercised, were the key figures around whom these mini-

---

1. Tancred, *Ordo iudiciarius* 1.1.1, at 91; William Durand, *Speculum iudiciale* 1.1 *De officio ordinarii* §1.1–2, at 1:98, and §2.2, at 1:99. In Roman law, provincial governors were *ordinarii iudices*. Thus, Cod. 3.13.4, 11.74.2 (= Cod. Theod. 1.5.13); Cod. Theod. 1.5.12; Dig. 2.1.5–6; also Kaser, *Römische Zivilprozessrecht*, 529–30.

societies clustered. The judge set the tone for other members of the group. The officiality could comprise a fairly sizable group. The official-principal was often aided by one or more commissary judges, who dealt with the more routine kinds of judicial business.[2] Some courts had in addition a promoter, sometimes called procurator fiscal, who was in effect the official-principal's deputy for criminal matters. The staff generally included at least one notary public, and often several of them. The notaries drafted the court's official documents, maintained its records, and might on occasion serve as examiners of witnesses. Notaries were almost invariably assisted by scribes who made copies of the documents they produced. One notary might be designated as keeper of the court's seal, authorized to attach it to important official documents. Courts routinely employed in addition at least one or two apparitors, who served summonses, ran errands, and kept order during court sessions.[3]

A wise judge sought to foster a comfortable fellowship among the men attached to his court, yet at the same time he needed to keep himself sufficiently aloof that he did not compromise his dignity and authority. As Stephen of Tournai advised an old classmate who had become an ordinary judge:

> I would like to see you strike a happy mean between administering the court and indulging in cheerful chats with your staff after work, so that they neither weigh you down with burdensome honor nor make you careless with agreeable leisure. You were affable to fellow-students; be admirable to members of the court.[4]

THE PROFESSIONALIZATION OF JUDGES

Jurisdiction in the medieval church was vested in the pope, bishops, and other prelates. Authority to pass judgment on their subjects and to settle their disputes was inherent in these offices, and their holders required no

---

2. Commissary judges were basically auxiliaries to the official, appointed either to act for him during his absence or to deal with such time-consuming duties as the probate of testaments, the examination of witnesses, or handling routine minor offenses. See Archbishop Stratford, Statutes for the Court of Arches (1342) §44, in Logan, *Medieval Court of Arches*, 44; Churchill, *Canterbury Administration* 2:13–16, 229–30; Wunderli, *London Church Courts*, 10–15.

3. Fournier, *Officialités*, 25–28; Lefebvre-Teillard, *Officialités*, 33–38.

4. Letter 275, to Richard Barre in Stephen of Tournai, *Lettres*, 347, no. 275: "Inter curie curas et iocosas post laborem sodalium confabulationes sic te volo esse medium, ut nec ille gravi honore te deprimant, nec iste molli ocio te dissolvant. Qui scolaribus amabilis eras, curialibus admirabilis esto."

professional credentials in order to exercise it.[5] The canons stipulated numerous qualifications that bishops and other prelates ought to possess. They were supposed to be at least minimally literate in Latin, of course, so that they could fulfill their liturgical obligations, but familiarity with the details of ecclesiastical law, while helpful and convenient, was in no way a requirement for the exercise of their judicial authority.[6] When popes or bishops encountered situations where technical legal knowledge was vital, as they regularly did, they were expected to seek guidance from legal experts.

As the volume of legal business increased during the twelfth century, popes and bishops, as we saw earlier, began to delegate much of their judicial business to men with more substantial legal training than they themselves possessed. By the mid-thirteenth century, this had become standard practice at all levels of the hierarchy. This resulted in the appearance of a body of ecclesiastical judges trained in law who constituted a branch of the developing legal profession.

Similar developments occurred in royal and municipal jurisdictions during roughly the same period. The legitimacy of rule by kings and other civil authorities, like that of popes and bishops, did not depend upon their mastery of the intricacies of law and procedure. Like popes and bishops, civil rulers sought legal advice when needed, and by the latter part of the twelfth century they, too, often began to delegate much of the time-consuming and complex business of adjudicating disputes to men more expert in these matters than they were. While the judges who dealt with disputes that arose in the communes of northern Italy at the beginning of the twelfth century were still basically respectable men (*boni homines*) who generally lacked any formal juristic training, this changed gradually during the latter part of the century. The improvements in training reflected in part the increased availability of systematic legal education in the law schools at Bologna and elsewhere and in part the growing complexity of the new procedural system of the *ius commune* that secular courts were beginning to adopt. By the end of the century, Italian *iudices* were often men with substantial legal expertise.[7]

North of the Alps, as late as the mid-thirteenth century, Louis IX of France (r. 1226–70), still felt morally obliged to spend substantial time lis-

---

5. Gratian C. 9 q. 3 c. 2, C. 15 q. 7 c. 6, C. 25 q. 2 c. 3; X 1.23.7 and 2.1.2, 13; Bernard of Pavia, *Summa decretalium* 1.23 §§1 and 3, at 18–19.

6. Gratian D. 36 d.p.c. 2 and d.p.c. 15; X 1.14.15.

7. Fried, *Entstehung des Juristenstandes*, 144–71, 227–45; Wickham, *Legge, pratiche e conflitti*, 206–26.

tening to the pleas of litigants and giving judgment in their lawsuits, holding audience under an oak tree in the Forest of Vincennes or in the gardens of Paris. Other contemporary monarchs seldom matched St. Louis's zeal for judicial duties, but there were limits even to his ability to deal with litigation personally, and the earliest surviving records of the royal law court that became the Parlement de Paris date from his reign.[8] Even earlier, English kings had begun to appoint justiciars, officers of the crown who functioned as fiscal administrators, but who also exercised royal jurisdiction throughout the kingdom. Although royal justiciars settled cases in the king's name, they could seldom boast great legal expertise. During the reign of Henry III (1216–72), justiciars ceased to be appointed. In their place, the king appointed royal justices, who often had some legal learning and acquired more of it on the job.[9] As civil and ecclesiastical judges in various parts of Europe became more numerous and more expert in the law, they increasingly came to resemble legal professionals.

EDUCATION OF PROFESSIONAL JUDGES

Ecclesiastical judges became what Blackstone called "oracles of the law" during the latter part of the thirteenth century, slightly earlier than their brethren in courts of civil and common law.[10] To be the law's inspired interpreters, judges needed more than a vague, impressionistic knowledge of the rules by which they were supposed to decide the cases that came before them. As canon law grew more voluminous and technical decade by decade, the authorities who appointed ecclesiastical judges increasingly thought it desirable to choose candidates who had spent some time studying law in a university for to fill these positions.

Professionalization of ecclesiastical judges advanced gradually over the course of the thirteenth century. Around 1217, while Johannes Teutonicus was putting the finishing touches to his ordinary gloss on Gratian's Decretum, he equivocated on the question of whether ecclesiastical judges must have formal legal training or not. "It can be argued," he wrote, "that no one can be a judge, especially an ecclesiastical judge, unless he is learned in the law." He then went on in the usual scholastic fashion to consider the opposing view and cited in its support a constitution in which Justinian

---

8. Jean de Joinville, *Life of St. Louis* §§57–60, at 37–38; Shennan, *Parlement of Paris*, 13–15.

9. Baker, *Introduction to English Legal History*, 18–24, 177–78, 189–93.

10. Blackstone, *Commentaries*, introduction, 1:69, §3.1; cf. Cicero, *De oratore* 1.45.200.

had declared that soldiers who lacked a scintilla of formal legal education could nonetheless serve as military judges. Johannes concluded by adopting a compromise position: "A modest amount of learning" he concluded, "is quite enough for a judge, just as it is for a prelate."[11]

Twenty years later attitudes were changing. A reforming council at Tours in 1236, for example, decreed that officials appointed to preside over bishops' courts in that province must have studied law for at least five years or have the equivalent in practical experience through dealing with legal matters and procedure in the courts.[12] The next year in a legatine council at London, Cardinal Otto da Tenengo demanded that judges who handled marriage cases and other weighty matters have legal training, although he failed to specify how extensive that training ought to be. Other authorities began to voice similar sentiments during the decades that followed. By the 1270s, Hostiensis could maintain that the law now presumed that judges were legally trained.[13]

Records of judicial appointments suggest that prelates who appointed judges in ecclesiastical courts generally took the new educational standards seriously. As the volume of litigation in church courts grew and the need for learned judges became acute, appointing authorities sometimes found it difficult to secure enough men with adequate legal training to fill the available positions. "Formerly there were not as many judges as there are today," Jacques de Revigny (d. 1296) complained, "but nowadays any fool can be a judge."[14] Jacques probably had secular courts in mind and

---

11. *Glos. ord.* to Gratian D. 20 d.a.c. 1 v. *scientia*. See also *Glos. ord.* to D. 6 de pen. c. 1 v. *sciat*; Bernard of Parma, *Glos. ord.* to X 4.14.1 v. *potestatem*; and Gratia of Arezzo, *De iudiciorum ordine* 1.1, at 320.

12. Council of Tours (1236) c. 5, in *Conciles de la province de Tours*, 159–60. The council fathers (or whoever drafted this canon for them) no doubt had in mind Justinian's constitution *Omnem rei publicae* in Dig., proem., as well as Cod. 2.7.24.4 and perhaps Azo, *Summa super Codicem*, 29, to Cod. 2.7, or Accursius, *Glos. ord.* to Dig. 50.13.1 v. *quoquo*.

13. Legatine Council of London (1237) c. 23, in Powicke & Cheney 1:255–56; Hostiensis, *Lectura*, vol. 1, at 169rb, to X 1.32.1 §13. Twenty years earlier Hostiensis had simply said in his *Summa* (finished in 1253), at 46vb, lib. 1, *De officio et potestate iudicis delegati* §3, that a judge-delegate should not be unaware of canon law (*ius canonum non ignoret*). The Council of Buda (1279) c. 38 required at least three years of study for judges in matrimonial cases in Hungary and Poland (Mansi 24:287–88); likewise the statutes of Archbishop Winchelsey (1295) §7, ed. Logan, *Medieval Court of Arches*, 7–8, and the *Statuta consistorii episcopalis Lincolniensis*, 572, §3.

14. Jacques de Revigny, *Lectura* to Cod. 7.65.7; quoted by Bezemer, *What Jacques Saw*, 73.

he no doubt exaggerated somewhat, but trained lawyers, especially those with university degrees, were not readily available everywhere, especially in rural, sparsely populated regions. Despite scattered shortages of adequately trained manpower, however, many church courts managed to recruit trained judges with reasonable regularity. In Flanders, for example, all of the officials-principal chosen by the bishops of Tournai after 1234 had at least some university training in law, as did the great majority of the officials of the bishops of Liège and the advocates who practiced before them. Similarly at Lyons, twenty-two out of twenty-seven of the bishops' officials between 1300 and 1500 held degrees, while in England, judges in the dioceses of Canterbury, York, Rochester, Lichfield, and Ely from the fourteenth century onward almost always had law degrees. Much the same was true in at least some German dioceses by the end of the fourteenth century.[15] Even papal judges-delegate, whose main function was usually to press the parties in a dispute to settle their differences rather than to determine fine points of law, were more apt to be men with substantial legal learning after the mid-thirteenth century than had been true earlier.[16]

By the end of the century, judges appointed to the Audientia sacri palatii (later called the Rota) and other tribunals at the papal curia were usually men with substantial legal training, often with law degrees. By the beginning of the fifteenth century, the criteria for important judicial appointments had reached lofty heights. Although fifteenth-century popes did not quite demand the "labor of twenty dismal years" that Sir John Fortescue thought English judges required, they came pretty close.[17] Pope Martin V (r. 1417–31), in his constitution *In apostolice dignitatis specula*, directed that no one should be appointed as an auditor of the Rota unless he was a well-known doctor of law of unblemished reputation who had

15. For Flanders, Vleeschouwers-van Melkebeek, *Officialiteit van Doornik*, 75–89; for Liège, Renardy, *Le monde des maîtres*, 229–32; for Lyons, Fédou, *Les hommes de loi lyonnais*, 122–23, 137–39; for England, John Morton, *Register* 1:4 and 23, nos. 16–22, 84; Churchill, *Canterbury Administration* 1:436–40, 2:237–41; Logan, *Medieval Court of Arches*, 197–203; Helmholz, *Marriage Litigation*, 142–43, and "Officialités Anglo-Saxonnes," 97–101; Aston, Duncan, and Evans, "Medieval Alumni of Cambridge," 76, and Brundage, "Cambridge Faculty of Canon Law," 43–44; for Germany, Gramsch, *Erfurter Juristen*, 501–12.

16. Sayers, *Papal Judges Delegate*, 118–33; Helmholz, "Canonists and Standards of Impartiality," 27–28, 36–37; Sweeney, "Innocent III, Canon Law, and Papal Judges Delegate," 34–35; Duggan, "Papal Judges Delegate," 194–96.

17. Sayers, *Papal Government*, 34–35, and "Court of 'Audientia Litterarum Contradictarum' Revisited," 416–27; Sir John Fortescue, *De laudibus legum Anglie*, 24, cap. 8.

taught for at least three years since receiving the doctorate. The pope also commanded his vice chancellor to establish an examining board to test the depth of each candidate's legal knowledge before his appointment was finalized. Even candidates who met these lofty criteria could not be assured of an appointment. Judges of the Rota also had to be self-supporting, since their positions were still unpaid. Successful candidates accordingly had to possess either benefice-holdings or private means sufficient to produce an annual income of at least two hundred gold florins. Such a substantial income would presumably immunize judges against influence from litigants and other interested parties. The pope further demanded that auditors of the Rota possess the basic legal texts and have them at hand while dealing with cases.[18]

One consequence of growing juristic sophistication among judges in church courts was the occasional appearance of judicial decisions that not only announced the judge's conclusions, but also spelled out the reasoning that led to them and the authorities that he relied upon in reaching his decision. It was established law by the thirteenth century that formal judicial decisions must be given in writing,[19] but judgments usually consisted simply of a brief description of the parties and the points at issue, followed by the judge's verdict, without any indication of the factual or legal grounds that supported his conclusion. Thus, for example, a commissary judge in 1271 decided an appeal in a matrimonial case brought by Richard de Bosco against Johanna de Clopton in these terms:

> We, brother H[enry] de Depham, commissary of the lord official of Canterbury, appointed by the prior and chapter of Christ Church, Canterbury, during a vacancy in the see, having heard and understood the merits of the marriage case long contested before the official of the lord bishop of Salisbury between a woman, Johanna de Clopton, plaintiff, on the one hand and Richard de Bosco, defendant, on the other, upon appeal by the said Richard to the see of Canterbury from the definitive judgment of the aforesaid official [of Salisbury] in the same [case] on grounds that it was wrongly made, do determine, on the advice of the learned lawyers sitting with us

---

18. *In apostolice dignitatis specula* §§16–18, 20, in Tangl, *Päpstlichen Kanzleiordnungen*, 139–40; Hoberg, "Ältesten Informativprozesse." For a firsthand account of the difficulties judges faced because of their unpaid postion, see Adam Usk, *Chronicle*, 152–56, 176–78.

19. Cod. 7.44.2 pr. and 3; Gratian reproduced the latter of these in C. 2 q. 1 c. 8; VI 2.14.5; Tancred, *Ordo iudiciarius* 4.2.4, at 278–79; William Durand, *Speculum iudiciale* 2.3 *De sententia* §8.12, at 1:798–99.

and according to the demands of justice, that the same Richard appealed wrongly and the aforesaid official decided properly, confirming by the authority of the aforesaid Christ Church, Canterbury, the judgment given by the said official [of Salisbury].[20]

Jurists differed over whether it was appropriate for a judge to specify the reasons that led to his judgments. Johannes Teutonicus and Bernard of Parma both thought that he ought to do so on the grounds that the parties needed to know why he ruled as he did. They also agreed, however, that judges were not required to do this and, should they choose not to, their decisions nonetheless remained valid.[21] Hostiensis warned judges to be careful if they did specify the rationale behind their decisions. "It is not safe to give the reason for a decision," he warned, since "even though it may be a good one, for if it is poorly expressed the decision may not hold up." Hostiensis added, however, that in some situations a judge must state his reasons, particularly when a party appealed against his decision or the verdict departed from the *ius commune*.[22] The decree *Cum medicinalis* of the First Council of Lyons, moreover, expressly directed judges who imposed a sentence of excommunication to specify their reasons for doing so. Not only could the excommunication be revoked if the judge failed to state appropriate grounds, but the judge himself could be punished by exclusion from divine services for a month. He might also be held liable to com-

---

20. My translation of the decision in *Select Cases*, ed. Adams and Donahue, 102, C.1.2. Other examples from actual practice appear, e.g., in *Select Cases*, 137, 263–64, 679–80, C.6, C. 17, and D. 19, as well as in *Documenten uit de praktijk* and *Registres de sentences de l'officialité de Cambrai*, vol. 1. Specimen decisions also appear in Gratia, *De iudiciorum ordine* 3.1, at 380–81, and William Durand, *Speculum iudiciale* 2.3 *De sententia* §6.2–53, at 1:785–95. See too Ferme, "Judging Justly," 528.

21. Johannes Teutonicus, *Glos. ord.* to D. 21 c. 9 v. *quoniam secundis*; Bernard of Parma, *Glos. ord.* to X 2.27.16 v. *exprimantur*.

22. On the dangers of explaining decisions, Hostiensis, *Summa*, lib. 2, *De sententia* §5, at 122rb. In his *Lectura*, vol.1, at 89rb, to X 1.9.6 §8, Hostiensis explained further that if a reasoned decision were to cite inconsistent grounds it might be held invalid. He listed eighteen situations in which an explanation could be required in the *Summa*, which he finished around 1253 (lib. 2, *De sententia* §5, at 122rb–va), but by the time he completed his *Lectura*, shortly before his death in 1271, he was content to list only six reasons for a judge to specify his reasoning (*Lectura* to X 2.27.16 v. *in sententiis* §9, vol. 2, at 162vb). See also 1 Lyons (1245) c. 16 (= VI 2.15.1); William Durand, *Speculum iudiciale* 2.3 *De sententia* §5.14, at 1:783; and Gérard Fransen, "La valeur de la jurisprudence," 198.

pensate the person he had excommunicated for any expense and damages caused by his faulty judgment.[23]

When judges began to produce formal opinions, they generally concentrated on an evaluation of the credibility of the evidence that led to their conclusions and rarely explained their views on the legal issues involved.[24] In the mid-fourteenth century, however, judges of the Roman Rota began to compile and publish collections of selected rotal decisions. These *Decisiones Rotae* not only examined the facts of each case as the judges saw them, but also supplied analyses of the applicable law and the reasoning that underlay their conclusions. Rotal decisions commanded great respect among late medieval law professors and exercised considerable influence on the development of early modern procedural law.[25]

Rotal decisions differed substantially from the kinds of reasoned judicial decisions that modern high courts produce. The *Decisiones Rotae* were products of a preliminary stage in the Rota's procedure prior to the final verdict. The dean of the Rota assigned each case that came before the court to a panel of five auditors, or judges, and designated one of them as the *ponens*, or judge-reporter.[26] The *ponens* was responsible for assembling the evidence and arguments that the advocates submitted and presenting these to his colleagues, together with his own views on the matter. After they had read the dossier that the *ponens* circulated, each panel member prepared and circulated a statement of his own opinion (*consilium*) to his colleagues. The *ponens* then presented the case for discussion during a plenary session of all twelve auditors of the Rota. Following the general discussion, the four members of the panel other than the *ponens* voted on the matter. When a majority agreed on a verdict, the *ponens* prepared a *decisio* that drew upon the written opinions and the discussion in the case. He provided the

23. 1 Lyons (1245) c. 19 (= VI 5.11.1).

24. A good specimen of a decision of this sort appears in Linehan, "Case of the Impugned Chirograph," 488–95.

25. On the wide circulation of collections of rotal decisions before the appearance of printing, see Dolezalek, "Handschriftliche Verbreitung von Rechtsprechungssammlungen der Rota" and "Quaestiones motae in Rota." The Rota decided relatively few private law cases, and the influence of its jurisprudence in that area was accordingly slight. Procedural law was another matter altogether, and there the decisions of the Rota became widely influential in civil as well as ecclesiastical courts (Dolezalek and Nörr, "Rechtsprechungssammlungen der mittelalterlichen Rota," 851–53; Ferme, "Judging Justly," 534–35).

26. *Rota* means a wheel, and each such panel was (and still is) known as a "turn of the wheel" (*turnus Rotae*).

advocates of the parties with copies of the *decisio* for comment. In the light of their replies, the *ponens* then drew up the proposed judgment (*sententia*) and submitted it to the other members of the judicial panel for approval. When the auditors had approved the final version, the *sententia* became the Rota's formal verdict, while the *decisiones* presented a synthesis of the judges' analyses of the facts and the law.[27]

Apart from the *Decisiones Rotae*, reasoned decisions from other medieval church courts are scarce.[28] The only other widely circulated collection of reasoned judgments from late medieval church courts was the *Decisiones capellae Tholosanae*. This collection of judicial opinions from the ecclesiastical courts at Toulouse was put together by Jean Corsier, the official of the archbishop of Toulouse, between 1392 and 1400.[29] Other individual reasoned decisions may well lie scattered among medieval court records, although no inventory of them is available. The range of legal learning and the intricacy of the reasoning shown in the published collections of judicial opinions, however, demonstrate that canonical judges in these two important courts were highly skilled professionals.

Academic writers from the thirteenth century onward assumed (or at least hoped) that judges would know enough law to be able to spot and repair deficiencies in the legal arguments that advocates presented. Trained canon lawyers knew that judges in late antiquity had been expected to

---

27. Lefebvre, "Un texte inédit," 190–91; and Jacob Emerix, *Tractatus seu notitia* 1.21–23, at 98–110. See also Lefebvre's article "Rote romaine," 759–60; and Noonan, *Power to Dissolve*, 48–49. Reasoned decisions in the more usual sense of dispositive judgments that spell out the grounds for a verdict began to appear in Rotal jurisprudence only in the mid-sixteenth century (Fransen, "La valeur de la jurisprudence," 207–8; Stickler, *Historia iuris canonici*, 340–44). Other canonical courts were not required to state the reasons that underlay their decisions until the *Codex iuris canonici* of 1917, can. 1871 §§1–2 and can. 1873 §1.3, made this a condition of validity. The requirement was continued in force by the 1983 *Codex iuris canonici* of Pope John Paul II, can. 1609 §2, 1611 §3, and 1622 §2 (Ferme, "Judging Justly," 532–34).

28. No reasoned judicial decisions survive from the archbishop's court at Florence, for example, prior to the seventeenth century, and they did not become common until the late eighteenth century (Lombardi, *Matrimoni di antico regime*, 154, 296, 424–25).

29. The *Decisiones capelle sedis archiepiscopalis Tholose*, which went through sixteen printed editions between 1503 and 1617, consists partly of formal court decisions, intermingled with a larger number of the compiler's memoranda on individual cases. See Gazzaniga, "Droit et pratique"; also Gazzaniga and Peralba, "La bibliothèque imaginaire," which attempts to reconstruct an official's library from the references in his *decisiones*.

make good any defects they observed in the arguments put forward by the parties in their courts.³⁰ By the 1170s, references to this practice begin to crop up in glosses on Gratian's Decretum.³¹ Pope Innocent III in 1201 mentioned in his decretal *Bonae memoriae* that while hearing a case he himself had cited legal authorities favorable to each of the parties. The pope treated this as if it were routine, and by the beginning of the thirteenth century it may well have been. Certainly the common teaching in the law schools by this time held that ecclesiastical judges ought to make good shortcomings in the legal arguments that advocates or parties put before them.³²

Huguccio had earlier declared that a judge could not only make up for deficiencies in a litigant's legal argument, but could also take into account factual evidence that he was aware of and that the parties had failed to bring forward. The authority that Huguccio specifically cited in support of this position was the *Summa* of Placentinus on Justinian's Code.³³ Thirteenth-century procedural treatises agreed that a judge could legitimately take into account factual information that he was personally aware of, but only if he had acquired the information in the course of his judicial duties. Judges were in principle expected to disregard any information that had come to their notice privately, outside of court.³⁴

This view introduced a major inconsistency into the judicial process.

30. Cod. 2.10 (11).un. Even canonists such as the *pauperistae*, whose study of Roman law was less than profound, were probably aware of this title in Justinian's Code, since Vacarius had commented on it (*Liber pauperum*, 45).

31. E.g., in Sicard of Cremona, *Summa* on C. 30 q. 5 c. 11, the anonymous Anglo-Norman *summa Omnis qui iuste iudicat* and Huguccio, quoted by Nörr, *Zur Stellung des Richters*, 46 and 48.

32. X 1.5.3, written in November or December 1201 (Po 1546); also Johannes Teutonicus, *Glos. ord.* to C. 30 q. 5 c. 11 v. *remaneat*, as well as Bernard of Parma, *Glos. ord.* to X 1.5.3 v. *curavimus allegare*.

33. Huguccio, *Summa* to C. 30 q. 5 c. 11 v. *rimari*, in Nörr, *Zur Stellung des Richters*, 48. Gratian attributed the text that Huguccio was commenting upon to Pope Eleutherius (ca. 174–89), an ascription that stemmed from Pseudo-Isidore's *Capitula Angilramni* 23. It came, in fact, from a passage from a rescript of Constantine in Cod. 3.1.9 (= Cod. Theod. 2.18.1).

34. Azo, *Summa super Codicem*, 29–30, to Cod. 2.11; Tancred, *Ordo iudiciarius* 3.15.5, at 266–67; William of Drogheda, *Summa aurea*, 53–54, §53; William Durand, *Speculum iudiciale* 2.2 *De disputationibus et allegationibus aduocatorum* §6.7, and 3.1 *De notoriis criminibus* §8.12, at 1:751–52 and 2:50–51. Matters of general public knowledge (*fama* and *notorium*) differed from private knowledge, and judges could legitimately take account of them. See Fraher, "Conviction according to Conscience," as well as Peters, "Wounded Names," and Wickham, "*Fama* and the Law."

Judges were (and still are) supposed to decide cases exclusively on the basis of evidence and arguments presented in court. They had an ethical obligation to disregard anything else they may have learned about the litigants or their affairs.[35] A judge should even disregard the dictates of his own conscience if those happened to contradict the law or the evidence presented in court. A venerable principle of legal ethics that medieval jurists regularly invoked declared that "the judge decides according to what is presented [in court], not according to his own knowledge." The rationale for this was that a judge who drew upon private information about persons or events would in effect become an unsworn witness. Canon law not only insisted that the parties must know names of opposing witnesses and that testimony be given under oath, but also strictly forbade judges to serve as witnesses in cases that came before them.[36] If a judge, for example, had seen the defendant in San Gimigniano on the day when the woman who claimed to be his wife alleged that they had been married in Palermo, the judge could not reveal this in court, nor could he allow it to influence his decision. Instead, he was ethically obliged to disregard his personal knowledge and to hand down a verdict based solely on the evidence presented in court (although he could, of course, recuse himself as judge and then appear as a witness before another judge).

Judicial Ethics

As educational standards for ecclesiastical judges increased, expectations concerning the propriety of their conduct rose as well. The changes were interrelated, in part because legal writers and church authorities drew many of their ideas about proper judicial conduct from the same Roman legal texts that had furnished the authority for their insistence that judges should be trained in the law they administered.

To fulfill his obligations properly, a judge was expected not only to know

---

35. Thus, e.g., the American Bar Association's Model Code of Judicial Conduct (1990), canon 3 E.(1) (a) requires a judge to disqualify himself if he has "personal knowledge of disputed evidentiary facts concerning the proceedings" before him. See also *The Responsible Judge*, ed. Noonan and Winston, 113–14.

36. Gratian C. 2 q. 6 c. 38; Tancred, *Ordo iudiciarius* 3.6, and 3.9.1, at 226–27, 236–37; William Durand, *Speculum* 1.4 *De teste* §§1.79–80 and 4.6, at 1:300, 312. Nörr, *Zur Stellung des Richters*, treats in detail the history of the rule that judges must decide only on what is presented to them in court. The proposition that the parties bore sole responsibility for proof has in modern times come to be known as the *Verhandlungsmaxime*, or the "principle of party presentation" (Caenegem, *History of European Civil Procedure*, 14).

the law, but also to follow it—which is not necessarily the same thing. Should he fail to do so, he became personally liable for damages that his failure caused.[37] He was not supposed to permit his judgment to be swayed by personal knowledge or beliefs, as we have seen. He must not allow feelings of loyalty or dislike to influence his judgment. He must not take favors from litigants, although it was permissible to accept token offerings of consumable items, such as food, wine, or firewood, as symbols of respect, provided that their total value was trivial.[38]

In short, a just judge must deal with litigants fairly and in good faith.[39] Hostiensis summed up the principle this way:

> Note that a judge should be so impartial that he injures no one. Neither hatred nor favor, fear nor money should sway his judgment or cause him to do anything detrimental to a party. Accordingly, he should deny justice to no one, not to a slave or an excommunicate, or to anyone at all, however detestable they may be, not even to the devil himself could he be brought into court, nor should he condemn anyone unjustly, as is shown here. Let the judge keep fair play ever before his eyes.[40]

37. Cod 7.45.13; Gratian, D. 4 d.p.c. 2; X 1.2.1; Dig. 5.1.15.1 and 50.13.6; 1 Lyons (1245) c. 15 in *DEC* 1:288–89, later incorporated into VI 2.14.1.

38. On judges' personal knowledege, see *Summa Parisiensis* to C. 3 q. 7 c. 4 v. *nihil paratum*, at 122; Johannes Teutonicus, *Apparatus* to 3 Comp. 2.12.13 v. *quin immo*, at 1:262; Bernard of Parma, *Glos. ord.* to X 2.20.40 v. *recusatis*; William Durand, *Speculum iudiciale* 2.3 *De sententia* §5.1, at 1:781; Johannes Andreae, *Glos. ord.* to VI 2.14.1 v. *et contra*; and see further Nörr, *Zur Stellung des Richters*, 36–84. On discounting personal feelings in judging, see Alexander III in X 1.29.17 (JL 13932) and Bernard of Parma *Glos. ord.* thereon to v. *dominus*; Council of Paris (1213) c. 4.11, in Mansi 22:841; Durand, *Speculum iudiciale* 1.1 *De recusatione* §2.2, at 1:155. On gifts, see Deut. 16:18–19; Gratian, C. 11 q. 3 c. 71; X 3.1.10 and *Glos. ord.* v. *praeter*; X 5.34.16 together with *Glos. ord.* v. *venditionem*; VI 1.3.11 §4 with the *Glos. ord.* to v. *nisi forsan esculentum* and *consumi*; VI 2.14.1 with the *Glos. ord.* to v. *cum aeterni, et contra*, and *vel per sordes*; Council of Château-Gontier (1231) c. 34 and Council of Langeais (1255) c. 16, in *Conciles de la province de Tours*, 154, 222–23; Helmholz, "Money and Judges."

39. VI RJ 12; William Durand, *Speculum iudiciale* 1.1 *De officio omnium iudicum* §6.21, at 1:148.

40. Hostiensis, *Lectura*, vol. 2, at 141va, to X 2.25.5 §11 v. *sed equitas*: "Nota quod tanta debet esse iudicantis equitas ut neminem gravet, nec odio vel favore, timore, vel pecunia pervertat iudicium vel aliquid faciat in gravamen partis alterius . . . unde nec servo, nec excommunicato, nec etiam diabolo, si posset esse in iudicio, vel cuicumque vis quantumcunque odioso (quantum ad defensionem suam pertinet) debet iustitiam denegare, nec aliquem iniuste condemnare, ut hic patet. . . . Aequitatem igitur ante oculos iudex semper habeat."

Thirteenth- and fourteenth-century writers portrayed the just judge as a sublime, almost superhuman figure. For St. Thomas Aquinas, an upright judge was one of God's ministers, while Hostiensis considered him more meritorious than a contemplative monk. Albericus de Rosate (d. 1354) went them both one better and ranked just judges with the angels. Other writers, however, ruefully conceded that just judges, like other heroic figures, were rare. "We've seldom encountered a white raven or a black swan," said Hugo von Trimberg (ca. 1230–1313), "but even less often have I seen a righteous judge."[41]

JUDICIAL DISCIPLINE

The doctrine that judges had a moral obligation to deal fairly and impartially with litigants was already ancient before Abraham set out from Ur of the Chaldees. Mesopotamian laws held up the ideal of the righteous judge centuries before it found its way into texts of the Hebrew scriptures.[42] What was new in the treatment of judicial conduct by thirteenth-century canonists and church authorities lay principally in the ways that they reshaped ancient remedies and procedures to fit the situation of their own society.

Maintaining judicial discipline in the thirteenth century largely depended on the willingness of litigants to complain about irregular conduct by judges. While popes and councils condemned judges who were negligent or dishonest and prescribed penalties for their misconduct, church authorities had no systematic mechanism to detect and report judicial misbehavior.[43] Rather than attempting to remove unsatisfactory judges permanently from office by vigorous enforcement of criminal penalties, they relied instead on litigants and lawyers to remedy judicial improprieties on an ad hoc basis by recusing unsuitable judges. Litigants obviously had strong incentives to do this in order to avoid the injuries they were likely to suffer at the hands of a careless, corrupt, or biased judge.

The procedure was simple and straightforward. Any litigant who be-

41. Thomas Aquinas, *Summa theologiae* 2–2 q. 60 a. 2 ad 2, citing Deut. 1:16 as his authority; Hostiensis, *Summa*, pr. §8, at 2vb; Albericus de Rosate, *Commentarium in Digestum Vetum* to Dig. 1.1.1 §11, quoted by Kantorowicz, *King's Two Bodies*, 122 n. 104; my paraphrase of Hugo von Trimberg, *Der Renner* 1:348, ll. 8367–70: "Selten wir gesehen haben / Swarze swannen und wîze raben: / Noch seltseiner diuhte mich ein rihtêre, / Der gereht an allen sachen wêre."

42. E.g., Lev. 19:15; Deut. 16:18–20; Ps. 49:6; Job 36:17–19. For earlier expressions of the ideal, see Noonan, *Bribes*, 3–14.

43. E.g., Gratian C. 2 q. 1 c. 7 §3; 4 Lat. (1215) c. 38 (= X 2.19.11); X 5.7.11.

lieved that a judge was unqualified or suspected that he was biased, corrupt, or had a conflict of interest could initiate a process to replace him with a different judge. Early church authorities had borrowed the basic elements of this practice, as of so many others, from Roman civil procedure. Thirteenth-century writers refined earlier versions of the process and elaborated canonical doctrine on recusal in greater detail.[44]

Ideally, judges were supposed to discipline themselves. A judge who felt that he would find it difficult or impossible to deal impartially with a case had a moral obligation to remove himself voluntarily from the matter. Judges, unfortunately, can be as blind to their own shortcomings and ethical responsibilities as anyone else. Expecting judges to police themselves assumes a degree of self-awareness and moral probity more likely to be found among angels than among men.[45] Medieval canonists sought to make access to church courts easy and readily available. In order to persuade parties to bring their civil disputes to canonical courts rather than to settle their disagreements by other means, it was essential to convince litigants that judges in those courts would treat their claims fairly and impartially. Litigants needed assurance that, if they doubted that a specific judge could be fair, they would have easy access to a procedure to remove him from their case.[46]

All that a dissatisfied litigant needed to do, at least in principle, was to present a written exception to the judge to whom he objected stating a legally acceptable reason for removing the judge from the case. The litigant must do this at the pretrial stage of an action, before *litis contestatio* commenced. William of Drogheda advised advocates to pay close attention to

---

44. Cod. 3.5.1; 3.13.4; 3.1.16; Nov. 86.2; Pope Nicholas I in a letter to the Byzantine emperor Michael III in 865 (JK 2796) explained that previous popes and councils had adopted the procedure long ago and quoted from the description of it in Cod. 3.1.16. The relevant portion of the pope's letter appears in Gratian's Decretum as C. 3 q. 5 c. 15. The constitution *Cum speciali* of the Fourth Lateran Council elaborated on canonical recusal procedure in greater detail, and this constitution in turn was incorporated into the Liber Extra (X 2.28.61), where it became the subject for further commentary and discussion (4 Lat. c. 48 in *Constitutiones*, 88–89, with glosses by Johannes Teutonicus, at 253–56; Vincentius Hispanus, at 355–58; and Damasus, at 446–47). On the development of the process, see Fowler [Magerl], "Recusatio iudicis," as well as Helmholz, "Canonists and Standards of Impartiality," 34.

45. Noonan, preface to *The Responsible Judge*, xv. Or, more cynically, "the faintest of all human passions is the love of truth" (Housman *Selected Prose*, 43).

46. William Durand, *Speculum iudiciale* 1.1. De recusatione § 4.2, at 1:156–57; Helmholz, "Canonists and Standards of Impartiality," 33–34.

the judge's rulings during pretrial proceedings to see if the judge might have a predisposition to favor their opponent. If so, this would give them grounds to enter an exception against the judge.[47]

Suspicion alone was a sufficient basis for recusal, and simply raising the exception automatically suspended the judge's power to proceed with the case.[48] The action could proceed no further until the issue had been resolved. This was both a strength and a weakness in the procedure. It helped to assure litigants that their claims would be treated fairly. At the same time, it made it easy for an unscrupulous party to abuse the process by delaying matters on frivolous and unwarranted pretexts. Indeed, a defendant who persisted long enough could make the process so vexing and expensive that his opponent would choose to settle out of court or even abandon a perfectly good case rather than face additional cost and delay.[49]

Once a litigant had presented an exception against him, the judge was obliged to step aside while the parties to the action chose arbiters who would then determine whether the suspicion was adequately founded. The judge, however, could impose a time limit for the appointment of arbiters, as well as a deadline for the arbiters' decision.[50]

Three basic categories of complaint might disqualify a judge. First, a litigant could complain that the judge's personal status or reputation disqualified him. This eliminated judges who were excommunicants, schismatics, heretics, Jews, slaves, women, minors, adulterers, or those whom

---

47. X 2.28.61; Tancred, *Ordo iudiciarius* 2.6.1–3 and 5, at 147–48; William Durand, *Speculum iudiciale* 1.1 *De recusatione* §§3.2 and 4.1, at 1:156; Cod. 3.13.4; William of Drogheda, *Summa aurea*, 88, §89.

48. Auth. post Cod. 3.1.16 (= Nov. 86.2); X 2.2.10 and 2.28.41 §1; Tancred, *Ordo iudiciarius* 2.6.5, at 147; William Durand, *Speculum iudiciale* 1.1 *De recusatione* §2 pr., at 1:155.

49. For this reason Bernard of Parma (*Glos. ord.* to X 2.28.61 v. *De recusatoris*) took issue with the position of Johannes Teutonicus's *Apparatus* to 4 Lat. c. 48 (ed. García y García, 253–55). See also William of Drogheda, *Summa aurea*, 88–89, §91. Authorities recognized this problem and devised measures to avoid it by limiting the grounds for recusal, as did 4 Lat. (1215) c. 36 (= X 2.28.60); *Constitutiones*, 79, as well as the glosses of Johannes Teutonicus (at 230), Vincentius Hispanus (at 336–37), and Damasus (at 438). These efforts were only partially successful (Cheney, *From Becket to Langton*, 62–75; Helmholz. "Canonists and Standards of Impartiality," 24–27).

50. Tancred, *Ordo iudiciarius* 2.6.5, at 147–48. Hostiensis taught that arbiters were unnecessary if the grounds for recusal were notorious, since in that situation formal proof was not required (*Lectura*, vol. 2, at 23va and 24ra, to X 2.6.2 §1 v. *Ad nostram audientiam* and X 2.6.2 §6 v. *cum manifestum*). Justinian in 537 and again in 539 had decreed that the process must be completed within twenty days (Nov. 53.3.2 and 96.2.1).

the law deemed *infames*. Second, a judge could be recused if his appointment violated the hierarchical principle that persons could be judged only by their peers or their superiors.[51] On this principle, it was inappropriate for a person of lower status, such as a simple priest or a layman, to exercise jurisdiction over a person of higher status, such as a bishop. Disparity of rank thus furnished grounds for recusal. Complaints against judges based on either of these grounds seldom arose in practice, since popes, bishops, and other authorities were disinclined to name such persons as judges in the first place.

Most recusals were based instead on suspicion that a judge was biased, corrupt, or had interests that conflicted with those of one of the parties to an action. Defendants were almost invariably the parties who sought to recuse judges on these grounds. Plaintiffs could usually choose the court where they brought an action. They naturally did their best to select a forum and a judge that seemed likely to offer them the best chance to prevail and hence to disadvantage their opponents.

Plaintiffs who petitioned for the appointment of a papal judge-delegate had an especially good opportunity to secure judges of their choice. Popes long before the thirteenth century, as we have seen, had often delegated their judicial authority to others whenever that seemed useful and appropriate. What changed after 1200 was that the procedure for appointing judges-delegate became increasingly institutionalized and bureaucratized.[52]

Plaintiffs were often anxious to obtain a definitive verdict in their favor handed down by papal authority with no opportunity for appeal. The possibility that doing so might also enable them to secure the appointment of a judge favorable to their claims made this option even more attractive. Authorities consequently attempted to level the playing field by making it considerably easier to recuse a judge-delegate than it was to recuse an ordinary judge.[53]

Writers on canonical procedure tried to enumerate the kinds of prejudice or conflict of interest that might justify disqualifying a judge-delegate. Bernard of Pavia, writing at the end of the twelfth century, listed a half-

---

51. Gratian C. 3 q. 7 d.p.c. 1 and c. 2 §2 are the *locus classicus* for grounds of *infamia*. On the judgment by peers, Gratian C. 2 q. 7 d.p.c. 9, c. 10–15, d.p.c. 27.

52. X 1.6.19; Hostiensis, *Lectura*, vol. 2, at 16ra–rb, to X 2.2.17 §§3–5; Pennington, *Pope and Bishops*, 22–28; Sayers, *Papal Judges Delegate*, 9–14.

53. Bernard of Pavia, *Summa decretalium* 2.20.13, at 63. Hostiensis, *Summa*, lib. 1, *De recusationibus* §2, at 133rb, likewise remarks on this. See also Fowler [Magerl], "Recusatio iudicis," 746; Sayers, *Papal Judges Delegate*, 109–18.

dozen grounds. His thirteenth-century successors managed to discover a great many more. Tancred enumerated eight counts on which a judge could be recused, and while Hostiensis listed only six grounds for recusing an ordinary judge, he found thirteen of them for recusal of a judge-delegate. William of Drogheda was able to hit upon seventeen grounds for recusal, the Anglo-Norman author of the *ordo iudiciarius Scientiam* counted twenty, and William Durand came up with no less than thirty-six.[54]

The range of situations that could raise suspicions about possible judicial bias included personal association or mutuality of interest between a judge and a litigant or a litigant's advocate, such as close blood kinship, relationship through marriage, and other kinds of family connection, as well as personal friendship, or alternatively, enmity and hatred.[55] If the judge was the lord of one of the parties or had other close ties with a litigant or his legal advisers, his impartiality might justifiably be questioned. Likewise, if a judge or judicial assessor had formerly served as advocate for one of the parties, his appointment could be challenged.[56]

Suspicion that one's opponent had bribed the judge furnished obvious grounds to seek his recusal. The author of a passage in Deuteronomy cast the essential elements of the problem as a divine command:

> You shall appoint judges and officers in all your towns which the Lord your God gives you ... and they shall judge the people with righteous judgment. You shall not pervert justice; you shall not show partiality; and you shall not take a bribe, for a bribe blinds the eyes of the wise and subverts the cause of the righteous. (Deut. 16:18–19)

Yet at the same time, giving gifts and doing favors to others, while expecting to receive similar gifts and favors in return, was and still is a univer-

---

54. Bernard of Pavia, *Summa decretalium* 2.20.15, at 64; Tancred, *Ordo iudiciarius* 2.6.6, at 148–49; Hostiensis, *Summa*, lib. 1, *De recusatione iudicis delegati* §3, at 51ra–rb, and lib. 2, *De recusationibus* §2, at 133rb; William of Drogheda, *Summa aurea* §487, at 377–79; *Ordo iudiciarius "Scientiam,"* 34–36, §15; William Durand, *Speculum iudiciale* 1.1 *De iudice delegato* §7, at 1:19–22.

55. X 2.28.36; Johannes Teutonicus, *Glos. ord.* to C. 3 q. 5 c. 12 v. *ac dominationis* and C. 11 q. 3 c. 79 v. *inimicitiis*; Bernard of Parma, *Glos. ord.* to X 2.6.4 v. *nimis favens*; Hostiensis, *Lectura*, vol. 1, at 169rb, to X 1.32.1 §14.

56. X 1.29.17 and *Glos. ord.* v. *dominus*; Dig. 2.1.17; Cod. 1.51.14 pr. and 2.6.6 pr., as well as Accursius, *Glos. ord.* to Cod. 3.1.14 v. *iudices*. Among the canonists, see Tancred, *Ordo iudiciarius* 2.6.6, at 148–49; William of Drogheda, *Summa aurea*, 378, §487; William Durand, *Speculum iudiciale* 1.1 *De recusatione* §2.2, at 1:155; Fowler [Magerl], "Recusatio iudicis," 764–66.

sal human trait.[57] Gift-giving was the usual way in which medieval people showed respect and deference to one another. Authority figures of all kinds, lay and ecclesiastical, including judges, were routinely offered gifts, many of which they could not reject without affronting the donor. As ancient authority put it, "It is altogether uncivilized to accept gifts from no one."[58]

Legislators and legal writers wrestled with the problem of defining the point where polite offerings to judges crossed the line of acceptable behavior and became bribery, which church law had long censured as an attempt to perpetrate a fraud against God. Some authorities classified it as a species of simony.[59] Lawyers and judges who were trained in the law faculties certainly knew about these earlier pronouncements, since Gratian had incorporated them in his Decretum.[60] They were also aware that Innocent III had refined and extended earlier rulings on the subject in 1198 when he condemned the actions of some papal judges-delegate who had demanded that the victor in a lawsuit pay the judges a fraction of the award in the case, allegedly in order to compensate them for the fees they had paid to lawyers who advised them. Innocent considered that this outrageous subterfuge amounted to selling their judgment, which must not be allowed to stand. Ecclesiastical judges, he added, ought to be able to live quite adequately on the revenues from their benefices.[61]

Legal commentators maintained that although justice must not be sold, judges-delegate were entitled to claim compensation from the parties for modest travel expenses, "since no one is obliged to fight at his own expense."[62] William Durand specified that they could also claim compensation for casualty losses if, for example, they were robbed or one of their horses died while they were on the road to hear a case, or if the illness of one of their attendants required them to tarry away from home longer than an-

57. Noonan, *Bribes*, 3–4. Comparable behavior, such as, e.g., the exchange of food for sexual favors, seems to be common among other primates as well (Bullough, *History of Prostitution*, 4).

58. "Nam ualde inhumanum est a nemine accipere." Ulpian attributed these words to the Emperors Septimius Severus and Antoninus Pius (Dig. 1.16.6.3).

59. Council of Chalcedon (451) c. 2; Pope Gregory I, *Homeliae* 39; Isidore of Seville, *Sententiae* 3.54; Noonan, *Bribes*, 139–44.

60. Gratian C. 1. q. 1 c. 8; C. 1 q. 3 c. 10, C. 11 q. 3 c. 66 and c. 71; C. 14 q. 5 c. 15; also Helmholz, "Money and Judges," 311.

61. X 3.1.10; Po 382 (3 October 1198).

62. Raymond of Penyafort, *Summa de penitentia* 2.5.37, col. 513; Bernard of Parma, *Glos. ord.* to X 3.1.10 v. *praeter expensas* and to to X 5.34.16 v. *venditionem iustitiae*.

ticipated.[63] Judges, ordinary or delegate, could also accept token gifts (*xenia*), provided that these were offered freely and spontaneously. Raymond of Penyafort cautioned, however, that in order to avoid the appearance of corruption, it would be better to refuse even trifling gifts from litigants. More permissive writers held that judges could accept small amounts of food or drink from parties who appeared before them, since it would be impolite to refuse, provided the donors could readily afford them.[64] By the end of the century this view came to prevail. Boniface VIII ruled in *Statutum quod circa* that judges could properly accept trivial tokens of respect from litigants or their representatives, so long as these amounted to nothing more than inconsequential amounts of consumable goods. Boniface further stipulated that a judge must not accept more of these from one party than from the other.[65] Accordingly, a judge could accept gifts from litigants such as, for example, a chicken, a decanter of wine, or a bundle of firewood, which he could readily consume within a short time. But he was bound to refuse presents that were longer-lasting or more valuable—say, for example, a robe, a book, or a silver jug—since such gifts might at the very least arouse suspicion that they might influence his decision, regardless of whether in fact they did so.[66]

Complaints about corruption and other types of judicial misconduct were nonetheless constant and commonplace. Bernard of Montemirato (Abbas antiquus), for one, advised law students to pay particular attention to the canon of the Fourth Lateran Council concerning the recusal of judges because, he said, its provisions were in everyday use.[67] Critics of clerical misbehavior continued to voice suspicions about the integrity of the courts. Matheolus (fl. ca. 1290), among dozens of others, complained:

> The winner in the courts is not the one who has the law on his side, but the one who is most generous: he is protected by coins, not laws. The judge is corrupted by gifts, not by logic.[68]

63. William Durand, *Speculum iudiciale* 1.4 *De salariis* §1.1, at 1:344.
64. Raymond of Penyafort, *Summa de penitentia* 2.5.37, col. 513; Bernard of Parma, *Glos. ord.* to X 3.1.10 v. *praeter expensas*, and Hostiensis, *Lectura* to the same passage, §§1–13, at 3rb.
65. VI 1.3.11 §4. This decretal, according to Johannes Andreae, was a reworking of *Presenti*, an earlier decretal of Innocent IV that apparently no longer survives.
66. Johannes Andreae, *Glos. ord.* to VI 1.3.11 §4 v. *consumi* and *nisi forsan esculentum*.
67. Bernard of Montemirato, *Additio* to *Glos. ord.* to X 2.28.61 v. *cum speciali*: "[E]st causa multum allegabile et quotidianum."
68. My translation of the *Lamentations de Matheolus*, ll. 4575–77, at 1:283: "Non qui jus potius habet in re victor habetur / Sed qui dat melius; nummos, non jura tuetur /

It is difficult to say how well-founded such complaints may have been or how common judicial prejudice and corruption were in actual practice. Relatively few records from the medieval ecclesiastical courts now survive, and those that do remain are geographically scattered. Many of these records have not been published or even calendared, which makes it difficult to determine how often canonical courts took action against judicial corruption. Investigations of the surviving records of the English church courts have turned up only a handful of instances where judges were recused for bias, conflict of interest, or bribery. It is possible that the scarcity of judicial recusals may simply indicate that the threat to recuse was a successful litigation device. As William of Drogheda advised his professional readers, this was an effective way to induce an opponent to agree to arbitration rather than to face the prospect of the ensuing delay and expense.[69]

JUDICIAL CAREERS

Lawyers seldom began their professional lives as judges. Judicial appointments typically came in the middle or later years of a legal career. For some, a judgeship marked the summit of their professional lives. Fortunately for them, judicial positions in church courts were extremely numerous. Certainly in northern Europe, every bishop and many lesser prelates had an official-principal, and they might employ one or more commissary judges as well. In England, the number of ecclesiastical judges greatly exceeded the number of judges in the royal courts, with the result that an advocate in the church courts had a far better chance of securing a judicial post than did his counterparts among the serjeants and barristers in the king's courts.[70] The officials of bishops or archdeacons, to be sure, were not lavishly paid, but they were usually rewarded with cathedral prebends and other benefices that might yield substantial revenues, sometimes in return for little labor. Even auditors of the Rota, as we have seen, long served without any judicial stipends at all. By the time a man was ripe for such an ap-

---

Judex corruptus, data munera, non rationes." Likewise, John Bromyard, *Summa predicantium*, s.v. Iusticia §§2–3, at 179ra–5b; Philippe de Mézières, *Le songe du vieil pelerin* 3.245, 311, at 2:283, 492–94; John of Salisbury, *Letters* 2:24–26, no. 140. Helmholz, "Money and Judges," 309–10, cites further examples.

69. William of Drogheda, *Summa aurea*, 88–89, §91. For details on recorded evidence, see *Records of the Medieval Ecclesiastical Courts*; also Helmholz, *Marriage Litigation*, 146–47, and "Canonists and Standards of Impartiality," 36–37; Donahue, introduction to *Select Cases*, ed. Adams and Donahue, 42.

70. Helmholz, *Canon Law and Ecclesiastical Jurisdiction*, 224.

pointment, authorities assumed that he would have accumulated enough benefices and other appointments to support himself comfortably.[71]

Able and ambitious lawyers who had taken care to acquire good connections through service at the papal curia or in other high places frequently secured a judgeship along the road to higher honors. The circle of canonists around Thomas Arundel, the younger son of an important earl whose connections benefited his own career, offers some striking examples of the possibilities.

Two men who served as Arundel's officials while he was bishop of Ely were especially notable. On 16 November 1375, Arundel appointed as his official Richard Scrope, a younger son of Henry, first Baron Scrope. Richard Scrope had recently taken his licentiate in civil law at Cambridge and at the time of his appointment was fulfilling part of the requirements for the doctorate in both laws by lecturing in civil law.[72] Scrope no doubt owed this appointment in part to family connections with the bishop (one of his cousins had been executor of the estate of Arundel's father) as well as to his legal training and the convenient fact that he had a house in Cambridge, where the Ely consistory held its sessions.[73] Scrope served as Bishop Arundel's official until 1379. He then made a crucial career move by entering the service of Pope Urban VI (r. 1378–89). In short order, Scrope became a papal chaplain and secured another judgeship, this time as an auditor of the Rota. He returned to England in 1386, after the pope had consecrated him as bishop of Coventry and Lichfield.

Scrope's patron, Thomas Arundel, meanwhile was on the move himself. In 1388, he became archbishop of York. Then in 1396, after serving as lord chancellor of England, Arundel was translated to the archbishopric of Canterbury. Two years later, Scrope succeeded Arundel as archbishop of York. But now Scrope's good fortune deserted him. He became entangled in the political machinations that surrounded the deposition of King Richard II (r. 1377–99) and the accession of King Henry IV (r. 1399–1413). Scrope quickly became disillusioned with the new king and took up arms against him in an unsuccessful rebellion in the northern counties. When the uprising collapsed in 1405, Scrope was beheaded for treason. Ironically, this

---

71. X 3.1.10 and Hostiensis, *Lectura*, vol. 3, at 3va, v. *honeste vivere* §15.

72. CUL, EDR D/1/2, at 11v; Aston, *Thomas Arundel*, 305. Scrope received the doctorate in civil and canon law in 1379, after having served as the university's chancellor during the previous year (CUL, EDR D/2/1, at 109r; *BRUC*, 513–14).

73. He held at least one emergency court session in his house, although while he was official the consistory normally met in St. Michael's church (EDR D/2/1, at 35r [8 January 1376]).

led to an illustrious postmortem sequel to his earthly career. Many revered Scrope as a martyred archbishop, and he came to be venerated as a saint. Although the papacy never officially canonized him, his cult continued to attract devotion in the north of England up to the Reformation.[74]

Henry Bowet, Scrope's successor as archbishop of York, was another member of Arundel's team of canon lawyers. Bowet, like Scrope, held a Cambridge doctorate in civil and canon law. Bowet, too, came from prominent family, although his was neither as wealthy nor as distinguished as Scrope's. Bowet may perhaps have been somewhat rowdy as a young man—a Cambridge student with a name much like his was charged in 1371 with wandering about at night under suspicious circumstances—but if so he soon matured into a respectable member of the ecclesiastical bar. By 1374 he was practicing as an advocate at the Ely consistory court, at one point briefly in collaboration with Adam Usk, and by 1375 was lecturing in civil law at the university.[75] In 1376, when Bishop Arundel ordained him as an acolyte and subdeacon, Bowet became official of the archdeacon of Ely. He had already begun to collect a dazzling array of benefices and appointments—he was at various times dean of St. Patrick's Cathedral in Dublin, canon of Lincoln Cathedral, canon of St. Paul's Cathedral in London, archdeacon of Northampton and later of Lincoln, as well as rector of assorted parishes.[76] By 1382, he had left Ely to join the household of Henry Despenser, bishop of Norwich. He appeared at the Roman curia as a proctor for the king in 1383, was a papal chaplain by 1395, and in 1490 was appointed an auditor of the Apostolic Camera, the papacy's chief financial office. In 1396, he was back in royal service, first as constable of Bordeaux, then the following year as chief justice of Aquitaine.

Upon his return to England, Bowet, like Scrope, became embroiled in the events that surrounded the abdication of Richard II. Bowet, too, was condemned to death and forfeiture of all his property, but fortunately for him this happened *in absentia*, and Henry IV, whose cause he had backed, rescinded the sentence in December 1399. In 1401, the new king prevailed upon the pope to name Bowet bishop of Bath and Wells, and in 1402, he

---

74. Adam Usk, *Chronicle*, 66–68, 202; McNiven, "Scrope, Richard," in *Oxford Dictionary of National Biography* (online); Swanson, *Religion and Devotion in Europe*, 153, 298, and *Calendar of the Register of Richard Scrope*; Duffy, *Stripping of the Altars*, 164, 197.

75. CUL, EDR D/2/1, at 29r, 34r, 35r, 37v; Adam Usk, *Chronicle*, 134.

76. CUL, EDR D/2/1, 58v; G/1/2, at 119va–vb; *BRUC*, 83–84; Tout, "Bowet, Henry," rev. J. J. N. Palmer, in *Oxford Dictionary of National Biography* (online); Aston, *Thomas Arundel*, 306–7; Harvey, *The English in Rome*, 143–44.

served briefly as treasurer of England. In 1407, Bowet succeeded Scrope as archbishop of York, a position that he held until his death in 1423.

While Scrope and Bowet became more prominent and achieved higher office than most, the essential features of their professional lives resemble patterns replicated in the biographies of countless other canonists during and after the High Middle Ages, men whose legal training at one or more universities laid the foundation for their careers. That training made them useful to powerful patrons, who in return for the use of their legal skills saw to it that they secured benefices that furnished them with revenue and appointments to positions of power. Lawyers who achieved positions of power almost invariably spent a few years at the papal curia in one capacity or another, and many also held office or furnished legal advice to secular rulers as well. And at some point, nearly all of them had at least a little experience as a judge, sometimes as ordinary judges, sometimes as judges-delegate, and not uncommonly as both.[77] For high-flying lawyers, a judicial appointment was more often a way stage in their careers than the final climax of a successful professional life.

Notaries

The volume of manuscript evidence that survives from medieval Europe increased steadily from the late twelfth century onward. By the mid-thirteenth century, northern Italy in particular was producing enormous numbers of written records on a daily basis. Many, possibly most, of these documents were written by notaries. By the mid-thirteenth century, vast numbers of notaries were making a living by producing documents for individuals as well as for municipal and ecclesiastical institutions, and the demand for their services continued to grow through the later Middle Ages.[78]

Notaries show up in every corner of medieval Europe. They were more than glorified scribes, although at the lower end of their profession they were not much more than that.[79] The least skilled notaries simply copied routine kinds of documents out of a form book and adapted them to their clients' needs by filling in the appropriate names and dates. Even a barely

77. Gramsch, *Erfurter Juristen*, 389–401, and Moraw, "Gelehrte Juristen," supply further examples.

78. Meyer, *Felix et inclitus notarius*, 501.

79. The nomenclature is often vague and fails to distinguish clearly between public notaries and others who were simple scribes or copyists. The earliest clear references to a notary public date from the mid-twelfth century (Meyer, *Felix et inclitus notarius*, 72–86).

adequate notary also needed to be able to record the gist of the responses that witnesses gave in response to questions from a judge, but that was perhaps the most demanding task that a modestly competent notary faced. Men of this sort were technicians roughly comparable to the legal secretaries and paralegals in modern law firms.

Notaries of the middling sort were skilled craftsmen, able to prepare original documents that accurately described fairly complex transactions. They often developed a distinct professional identity with their own professional organizations, separate from those of professional advocates and proctors. Although men at this midlevel of the notarial profession needed to know some law, they had not usually been trained in a university law faculty.[80]

A more elite group of notaries consisted of men who had acquired some knowledge of law at a university. Members of this group often studied law part time, practicing as notaries in order to support themselves, or else they alternated periods of full-time study with periods of full-time practice during the course of their careers. Formal legal training enhanced the esteem accorded to notaries of this kind and could foster career advancement. Although they still described themselves as notaries, it was not uncommon for these men to qualify as proctors, advocates, or judges.[81]

At the top of the profession, some eminent jurists, diplomats, scholars, and holders of high office also functioned at times as notaries. Learned notaries were particularly numerous at the papal curia. Ambitious lawyers soon discovered that a period of service at the curia, often in the capacity of a notary, an abbreviator, or a *scriptor litterarum apostolicarum*, provided opportunities to make contacts that could greatly enhance their prospects for professional success. Many of these men had law degrees and more than a few of them had taken the doctorate.[82]

Notaries had become indispensable to the functioning of medieval ecclesiastical courts and administration virtually everywhere in Western Christendom by around 1250. Their services were also vital to the working

---

80. William Durand, *Speculum iudiciale* 2.2 *De instrumentorum editione* §8.1, at 1:663.

81. Meyer, *Felix et inclitus notarius*, 330–31; Gramsch, *Erfurter Juristen*, 506–8, 518–22. On the island of Mallorca in 1340, notaries were forbidden to practice as advocates in the same courts where they functioned as notaries, much as their colleagues had been at Cologne a few years earlier. See *Statuta curie Coloniensis* 3.7 (ca. 1306–31), in Gescher, "Älteste kölnische Officialatsstatut," 483; Planas Rosselló, "Los abogados de Mallorca," 121.

82. Herde, *Beiträge*, 8–20; Gramsch, *Erfurter Juristen*, 402–8; May, *Geistliche Gerichtsbarkeit*, 267; Sayers, *Papal Government*, 28–35.

of royal and municipal administrative and legal systems in many parts of Europe, especially in Italy, Spain, and the south of France.

Notaries, as we saw earlier, sometimes prepared documents for civil and ecclesiastical courts, public officials, and private clients in Mediterranean Europe during the early Middle Ages.[83] Notarial documents were almost unknown in northern Europe during this period, no doubt because few if any notaries had ever been employed in those regions in late antiquity and the notarial tradition had consequently never taken root there. Notaries remained extremely rare in northern France, England, Germany, Scandinavia, or central Europe before the latter part of the thirteenth century. Even when they grew more numerous, they never became as central to the functioning of government and commerce in these regions as they were south of the Alps and the Pyrenees.[84]

By the late thirteenth century, however, notaries were becoming almost as plentiful as proctors in ecclesiastical courts throughout Europe. This owed much to the constitution *Quoniam contra* of the Fourth Lateran Council, which directed judges to employ notaries wherever possible to record church court proceedings. Popes, bishops, and other church authorities also kept staffs of notaries to draft decrees, charters, and other administrative documents, to keep records of ordinations and other official activities, to prepare the constitutions and statutes of their councils and synods, and to make sure that important records were kept available for use when needed.[85]

Notaries were by this period also a pervasive presence in civil transactions. They prepared the decrees, statutes, and regulations for civil rulers and governmental bodies at every level, from emperors and kings to municipal councils and village elders. Royal and municipal courts employed no-

---

83. Amelotti, *Per una storia del notariato meridionale*.

84. Wolf, "Das öffentliche Notariat," 506; Fournier, *Officialités*, 42–48. Cardinal Otto noted in 1237 that notaries public were not to be found in England and the earliest known English notarial document is dated twenty years later (Legatine Council of London [1237] c. 27 in Powicke & Cheney 1:257; Cheney, *Notaries Public*, 12, 14, 64–65). They made their appearance even later in Poland, where the earliest such instrument to survive bears the date of 1287 (Mikucki, "Origines du notariat public en Pologne"; Bukowska Gorgoni, "Le notariat," 248–51; Lefebvre-Teillard, *Officialités*, 39).

85. 4 Lat. (1215) c. 38, ed. García y García, 80–81, also incorporated in 4 Comp. 2.6.3 and in X 2.19.11; Fournier, *Officialités*, 46–47; Lefebvre-Teillard, *Officialités*, 39–40; Cheney, *English Bishops' Chanceries*, 22–27; Churchill, *Canterbury Administration* 1:21–24; Paravicini Bagliani, *Cardinali di curia* 2:475; Guillemain, *La cour pontificale d'Avignon*, 561–62; Zutshi, "Office of Notary in the Papal Chancery."

taries to prepare and authenticate the instruments and records that litigation required, while other notaries drafted a vast array of other documents for private clients. Many of those documents concerned transactions—commercial contracts, land transfers, marriage and dowry agreements, last wills and testaments—over which litigation arose. Most of what we know about law, government, commerce, and society in the medieval Mediterranean world we see through the eyes of the notaries who crafted the documents that inform us about them.[86]

Many notaries made notarial practice their principal occupation, but since their profession regularly brought them into contact with entrepreneurs and men of wealth and power, they often stood to profit from the moneymaking opportunities in trade, finance, and other enterprises that they learned about in the course of their business.[87] For ambitious and well-connected men, the notariate might represent simply a passing early phase in a complex career path. To men such as these, the notariate might provide entrée into the service of a pope or bishop, a *podestà*, or a monarch. Their familiarity with legal instruments and the details of legal routines helped some to qualify for legal practice as proctors or advocates, sometimes in church courts, at other times in the courts of civil authorities, often enough in both. Notaries were practically indispensable for the orderly conduct of legal affairs, both in the courtroom and outside of it. They recorded the testimony of witnesses, prepared the records of court sessions and other documents connected with judicial proceedings, and maintained the archives of both ecclesiastical and secular courts. The courtroom scenes that enliven the pages of deluxe medieval legal manuscripts like the image that serves as the frontispiece to this book regularly depict squads of notaries and scribes scribbling furiously to record the proceedings.[88]

Beginning in the twelfth century, the numbers of notaries grew rapidly along with the general population increase, the revival of trade, and the burgeoning influence of the learned laws. In the process, the notariate was itself transformed. The *tabelliones* and *notarii* of late antiquity and the early Middle Ages were primarily scribes who relied on formulas de-

---

86. Wolf, "Das öffentliche Notariat," 508–9; Brentano, *Two Churches*, 294–95; Hyde, *Padua in the Age of Dante*, 154.

87. Hyde, *Padua in the Age of Dante*, 174–75.

88. *Statuta curie Coloniensis* (ca. 1306–31) 3.7, in Gescher, "Älteste kölnische Offizialatsstatut," 483; 4 Lat. (1215) c. 38, *Constitutiones*, 80–81, as well as 4 Comp. 2.6.3 and X 2.19.11; see also Tancred, *Ordo iudiciarius* 3.9.2, at 237; William Durand, *Speculum iudiciale* 1.4 *De teste* §7.2, at 1:324. On the depiction of notaries in medieval manuscripts, see L'Engle, "Trends in Bolognese Legal Illustration," 229.

rived from ancient documents to produce the instruments that their employers needed. The evidential value of the documents that these notaries composed rested either on the testimony of witnesses, who could testify that the transaction they recorded had in fact taken place, or on the seals that the participants had appended to the record to authenticate its contents.[89]

Although Western emperors had appointed notaries since at least the Carolingian period and popes were doing likewise from the middle of the eleventh century onward, documents prepared by imperial and papal notaries gained prestige during the second half of the twelfth century. Beginning with Alexander III and Frederick Barbarossa, popes and emperors began to describe the notaries they appointed as public notaries.[90] Public notaries, unlike earlier notaries, were technically public servants, taking an oath of office in which they solemnly swore that the instruments they produced would record honestly and without fraud matters that had actually transpired and that they would maintain a systematic record of the transactions that they witnessed and the documents they prepared.[91] Documents prepared by public notaries, Alexander III declared, were presumed to be trustworthy records of the transactions they described. They were public instruments, whose authority did not depend on witnesses, seals, or other authenticating devices. Instead, a formal declaration by a public notary (*manum publicam*) that he had prepared them, authenticated by his personal sign, guaranteed their reliability.[92] Notaries were obliged to keep a

---

89. Meyer, *Felix et inclitus notarius*, 8–10.

90. Meyer, *Felix et inclitus notarius*, 12–47.

91. Specimens of these oaths appear in Tangl, *Päpstliche Kanzleiordnungen*, 35–36, 46, 50; *Registre de l'officialité de Cerisy*, 285–86; *Statuti della Società dei Notai di Bologna dell'anno 1336*, 28–29, 32–35, §§26, 21. See also Meyer, *Felix et inclitus notarius*, 56–60. Although they were called public servants, notaries were paid by the individual clients for whom they prepared documents. They were paid out of public funds only if they happened to be employed by some public official or public body (William Durand, *Speculum iudicale* 2.2 *De instrumentorum editione* §2.14, at 1:635).

92. X 2.22.2 (JL 13162); Meyer, *Felix et inclitus notarius*, 148; Alexander III, letter to Bishop Roger of Worcester (between 1167 and 1169); 1 Comp. 2.15.2 (= X 2.22.2; JL 13162); Cheney, *Roger of Worcester*, 364, no. 91. Fournier, *Officialités*, 44–45, summarizes the elements of an *instrumentum in formam publicam* that guaranteed its authenticity. Such a notarized document, according to Johannes Teutonicus, had the same evidential force as the testimony of two, or perhaps even three, witnesses. It commanded more confident belief than the written declaration of a bishop or a judge (Johannes Teutonicus, *Apparatus* to 4 Lat. c. 38 v. *aut duos uiros idoneos*, in *Constitutiones*, 234, which

register, which served as a permanent record of the documents they drew up. Municipal authorities created archives to house these registers, which survive in considerable numbers and form one of the richest and most important sources for medieval economic, social, and literary history.[93]

"No one," observed Johannes Grassus (fl. mid-fifteenth century), "is born a notary."[94] Instead, public notaries had to be created. The right of the two authorities who claimed universal jurisdiction, the emperor and the pope, to create public notaries was not contested. Popes, however, proved to be more cautious in exercising this power than were emperors, who created vast numbers of notaries and readily granted the right to do so to lesser authorities as well. Papal notaries consequently commanded higher esteem and respect than those appointed by the emperor.[95] Other authorities, including kings, bishops, and cities, also asserted the right to appoint notaries without reference either to the pope or emperor.[96]

The probative value of a notarial document depended upon the authority who had appointed the notary who prepared it. Since both pope and emperor claimed universal jurisdiction, documents prepared by notaries whom they appointed were valid everywhere, but documents written by notaries appointed by lesser powers were, in theory, valid only within the confines of the appointing authority's jurisdiction.[97] By the end of the

---

Bernard of Parma substantially reproduced in his *Glos. ord.* to X 2.19.11 v. *duos uiros).* See the discussion in Pryor, *Business Contracts of Medieval Provence,* 31–39. On notarial signs, see esp. Meyer, *Felix et inclitus notarius,* 99–103, and the examples illustrated at 557–687.

93. Meyer, *Felix et inclitus notarius,* 141–75, traces in detail the history of the development of notarial registers and also provides an extensive list of surviving Italian notarial archives at 179–222. See also Soetermeer, "La proportion entre civilistes et canonistes," 274*–275*, on the Bolognese *Libri memoriali.*

94. Johannes de Grassis, *Tractatus de subtilitatibus procuratorii,* at 30ra; cf. William Durand, *Speculum iudiciale* 2.2 *De instrumentorum editione* §8.24, at 1:660.

95. Meyer, *Felix et inclitus notarius,* 12–47. Public notaries appointed by papal authority appear all over Europe. They should not be confused with the notaries of the papal chancery, who were a small group of high-ranking officers within the papal curia (Guillemain, *La cour pontificale d'Avignon,* 562–66).

96. Hostiensis, *Summa,* at 192ra, lib. 3, *Ne clerici vel monrchi* §5c; William Durand, *Speculum iudiciale* 1.3 *De procuratores* §3.1, at 1:217; Wolf, "Das öffentliche Notariat," 506–7; Petrucci, "An clerici artem notariae possint exercere," 583–84; Fournier, *Officialités,* 43–44.

97. William Durand, *Speculum iudiciale* 2.2 *De instrumentorum editione* §8.22–23, at 1:659–60.

twelfth century, notarial instruments had begun to eclipse all other kinds of legal documents in Italy, the French *pays de droit écrit*, and the kingdoms of northeastern Spain.

The training of notaries varied enormously. A notary had at least to be able to compose formal documents in Latin and to write them out in a legible hand. While he might well use a template taken from a form book to draft letters and routine documents where he needed to do little more than to supply the appropriate names, dates, and incidental information, the notary who undertook to draw up the partnership contract for a complicated commercial venture, for example, or a will that aimed at dividing a large estate among numerous heirs and assigns needed to know a considerable amount of law in order to produce a document that would satisfy the needs of his clients, especially if the matter could readily become the subject of litigation.

Notaries at the humbler end of the craft could acquire the fundamental skills through a few years of study in a grammar school, followed by an apprenticeship in the court or chancery of a bishop, prince, or municipal government. Those of middling status usually supplemented this basic training with some time spent studying the *ars notaria* in one of the specialized schools that grew up on the margins of the arts faculties in some universities, principally in Italy.[98] The most prestigious notaries had in addition studied at a university law faculty and not infrequently held law degrees. The academic qualifications of notaries at the papal curia, in particular, increased markedly during the fourteenth century, and by the century's end the ranks of notaries included scholars of great learning, such as Gilles de Bellemère (d. 1407), Lucas de Penna (d. after 1382), Coluccio Salutati (1331–1406), and Francesco Petrarca (1304–74)—although some of these luminaries actually practiced only briefly as notaries.[99]

The educational spectrum among notaries thus ranged from the marginally literate to the profoundly learned. These differences usually reflected social origins, and notaries came from a wide variety of backgrounds. Some were sons of the urban patriciate, although relatively few came from the ranks of the rural nobility. A good many notaries, not surprisingly, had fathers who were practicing notaries, while others were the sons of judges or

---

98. Horn, "Legistische Literatur der Kommentatoren," 354–55; Wolf, "Das öffentliche Notariat," 509; Zaccagnini, "Il insegnamento privato," 280–81.

99. Gilles, "Gilles Bellemère et le tribunal de la Rote"; Lefebvre, "Penna, Lucas de"; Ullmann, *Medieval Idea of Law*, 9; Cheney, *Notaries Public*, 76–78; Schwarz, *Organisation kurialer Schreiberkollegien*, 179.

physicians. A substantial number, however, came from families of humbler station: their fathers might be carpenters, bakers, stationers, or petty merchants.[100] For this latter group, qualification as a notary held possibilities for further upward movement in the social hierarchy. Notaries were men of some consequence. They were almost invariably present to record solemn events, and many dealt regularly with the wealthy and powerful in their community. People commonly addressed notaries with deference and accorded them honorific titles out of respect for their public functions. Successful notaries could accumulate substantial property.[101]

Public authorities early in the thirteenth century began to express concern about the shortcomings of poorly equipped notaries. Cryptic contracts or ambiguously worded wills, after all, could create conflicts between individuals and families, which in turn could lead to rivalry, brawls, extended feuds, or protracted and costly lawsuits. The communal government of Bologna took official notice of this in 1219 when it published a list that officially authorized 270 notaries in the city and its surrounding district (*contada*) to produce authentic public documents. About 70 of these men were employed by public officials, while the remainder were in private practice. In the following year, the commune established a municipal commission headed by a judge to examine would-be notaries on their knowledge of Latin, penmanship, and other subjects related to the notarial craft. Only those who passed this examination were eligible to take the oath of office as notaries. Once they had so sworn, the commissioners formally invested them with the title of notary public and entered their names on official record (*matricula*) of those permitted to practice as notaries within the city.[102]

It is possible, even likely, that notaries already in practice promoted this scheme in order to control competition, although unequivocal evidence to support this conjecture is lacking. If restraint of competition by limiting the number of practicing notaries was indeed one of the goals of the new policy, it failed miserably. Instead, the number of notaries at Bologna soared during the thirteenth century, as it did throughout northern Italy. By the mid-thirteenth century, the number of names on the approved list

100. Fasoli, "Giuristi, giudici e notai," 613–14; Meyer, *Felix et inclitus notarius*, 1, 359–90; Gramsch, *Erfurter Juristen*, 206–9, 315–16, 518–22; Hyde, *Padua in the Age of Dante*, 158–59; Waley, *Italian City Republics*, 29.

101. Cheney, *Notaries Public*, 69–70; Hyde, *Padua in the Age of Dante*, 157; Brentano, *Rome before Avignon*, 50; Fédou, *Les hommes de loi lyonnais*, 188–91.

102. Meyer, *Felix et inclitus notarius*, 51–60, 66–69; William Durand, *Speculum iudiciale* 2.2 *De instrumentorum editione* §8.37, at 1:662.

at Bologna had grown to 300, and by 1289 it had reached 1,089, at a time when the city had a population of roughly 50,000 to 60,000 people. Similarly, at Padua, a city roughly two-thirds the size of Bologna, the population of approximately 40,000 included 600 authorized notaries public, 91 of whom worked for the communal government. By 1280, Lucca had reached a ratio of 1 notary for every 100 inhabitants, and other north Italian cities showed comparable numbers.[103]

Notaries rarely made up such a large fraction of the population outside of northern Italy, although impressive numbers of them appear in the Spanish kingdoms and the French Midi. The further north one goes, as a general rule, the fewer notaries one encounters. In Flanders, for example, Bruges seldom had more than twenty-four notaries practicing at any given time and their numbers were substantially smaller in Ghent and Ypres. Not a single notary is known to have practiced in England until the second half of the thirteenth century.[104]

Church authorities soon established their own notarial examination boards and began to keep records of those admitted to practice, although notaries in church courts never grew as numerous as those employed by the municipal governments of the north Italian cities. Notaries in ecclesiastical courts were typically clerics in minor orders, some of whom were married.[105]

Admissions examinations for notaries could be extremely demanding. Examining boards typically included not only notaries already in practice, but often one or more judges and occasionally a law professor as well. The Bologna statutes demanded that successful candidates demonstrate a sound command of Latin vocabulary and syntax, knowledge of the various types of contracts, wills, and other documents that a notary might be

---

103. Meyer, *Felix et inclitus notarius*, 321–23, 333, 502; Bertram, "Neuerscheinungen zur Stadt und Universität Bologna," 482; Walther, "Anfänge des Rechtsstudiums," 128; Fasoli, "Giuristi, giudici e notai," 612–13; Carnielo, "Rise of an Administrative Elite," 324–25; Hyde, *Padua in the Age of Dante*, 162.

104. Bono, *História del derecho notarial español*; Figa Faura, "Los formularios notariles"; Pagarolas Sabaté, "Notaris i auxiliars de la funció notarial"; Hilaire, "Pratique notariale et justice"; Dossat, "Unité ou diversité dans la pratique notariale?"; Guillemain, *La cour pontificale d'Avignon*, 563–65; Murray, "Failure of Corporation," 157; Cheney, *Notaries Public*, 14.

105. Fournier, *Officialités*, 53–54; Battelli, "L'exame di idoneità dei notai pubblici"; Council of Tours (1236) c. 4, in *Conciles de la province de Tours*, 159 (also in Mansi 23:412); Schrader, "Bischöflichen Offiziale Hildesheims."

called upon to draw up, the standard formulas for each of them, and the ability to write legibly in different hands. Candidates often had to compose an elegant letter based on themes set by the examiners. Those who passed these examinations had to pay numerous fees, after which their names were entered on the register of the local notaries' guild or of the court in which they were authorized to practice.[106]

Only then could the new notary's investment in time, labor, and money start to pay off. The services of notaries were in daily demand and were seldom free of charge. On the contrary, complaints about the exorbitant cost of notarial services abound. Notarial fees, said Aegidius de Fuscarariis, often inflict hardship and trouble on those who had to pay them, while William Durand labeled them "inhuman," a characterization echoed in the 1393 Constitutions of Florence, which for good measure also denounced them as "unbridled extortions."[107] Ecclesiastical and civil authorities alike sought to establish limits on notarial fees. In contentious matters, judges reviewed the charges for notarial services and could reduce any that they considered excessive.[108] While this permitted judges to tailor costs to fit the circumstances of the case and means of the parties, it affected only notarial charges in lawsuits and other legal actions. Notaries in private practice, however, generally spent much of their time drawing up documents, such as wills and contracts that clients needed in the daily conduct of their affairs. Authorities, both civil and ecclesiastical, dealt with excessive notarial fees for these services by imposing maximum fee schedules that notaries within their jurisdiction were permitted to charge. These fee schedules sought to list every type of document that a notary might be asked to produce and fixed a ceiling on the charges allowed for each. Fee schedules sometimes prescribed a set sum per written page of each type of document. Thus, for example, the official of the bishop of Geneva allowed notaries in his court to charge one-and-a-half pennies per folio for copies of witnesses' testimony taken within the city, or two pennies per folio for testi-

---

106. *Statuti di Bologna* (1288) 7.1, at 2:49–51, and 7.2, at 2:51–52; *Statuti della Società dei Notai di Bologna*, 2–3, §7, and 22–23, §61; Synod of Tréguier (1372) c. 2, in Martène and Durand, *Thesaurus novus anecdotorum* 4:123; Fasoli, "Giuristi, giudici e notai," 611, 614–15; Tamba, *Società dei notai di Bologna*, 21–25; Schwarz; *Organisation kurialer Schreiberkollegien*, 7–22.

107. Aegidius Fuscarariis, *Ordo iudiciarius*, 122, c. 67; William Durand, *Speculum iudiciale* 1.4 *De salariis* §2.4, at 1:346; Trexler, *Synodal Law*, 333.

108. *Privilegia curie Remensis* (1267), 14; William Durand, *Speculum iudiciale* 1.4 *De salariis* §2.4–5, at 1:346.

mony taken outside of the city, and further specified the minimum number of lines and syllables that must appear on each page.[109] For other types of documents, such as contracts or bills of sale, they often imposed *ad valorem* schedules that fixed charges on a sliding scale according to the value of the property involved. Thus, again at Geneva, the bishop's official permitted notaries to charge six *solidi* for a record of a sale valued at up to ten florins; if the value lay between ten and twenty florins, the fee was set at nine *solidi*. This increased to twelve *solidi* for a value between twenty and thirty florins, and so forth.[110] Frequent complaints about overcharging by notaries, combined with repeated reenactments and revisions of regulations such as these, however, suggest that notaries may have regarded the maximum fees as the basic charge and then added a bonus for speedy production.[111]

The income of notaries varied considerably, depending upon their skill, reputation, and social networks, as well as the kinds of work they performed. It is seldom possible to determine how much a given notary actually earned, save for those who received fixed salaries from popes, bishops, or public authorities. Even there, considerable uncertainty remains, since these notaries may have supplemented their salaries with additional income from private commissions and perhaps from gratuities and bribes to secure speedy service as well. Elite notaries in influential positions could exercise considerable power over those who depended on their goodwill and seem likely to have done very well from their profession. Many of them often did paid work for private clients in addition to their official duties. At least in some places, however, they might be obliged to share part of this income with their superiors, as is evident from the fact that a few courts prohibited this practice. Although high-ranking and well-paid notaries doubtless constituted a tiny minority within the profession, they were nonetheless a

109. *Constitutiones et statuta* 24.57, at 1:381.

110. *Constitutiones et statuta* 28.85, at 1:384. Similar fee schedules for ecclesiastical courts appear, for example, in 4 Council of Ravenna (1317) c. 24, Provincial Council of Padua (1350), and Provincial Council of Cracow (1369), in Mansi 25: 623–27 and 26: 234, 559–60; Trexler, *Synodal Law*, 345; Tangl, *Päpstliche Kanzleiordnungen*, 60–61, 94–110. Municipal fee schedules for notaries worked along similar lines, e.g., *Statuti di Bologna* (1288) 6.48, at 2:38–41; *Statuta Ferrariae* 2.254–54, 273, at 138–41, 147–48; *Statuta ciuitatis Vrbini* 1.28, 2.37, at 25r, 575r–558r; Calleri, *L'arte dei giudici e notai*, 59–60.

111. Nigel Wireker (Longchamp), *Tractatus contra curiales*, 159–60; St. Antoninus, *Summa confessionalis*, tit. 3.4, *Ad aduocatos et procuratores et notarios*, at 57vb; Trexler, *Synodal Law*, 155; Martines, *Lawyers and Statecraft*, 23–24; Fédou, *Les hommes de loi lyonnais*, 180–82; Heckel, "Das Aufkommen der ständigen Prokuratoren," 296.

weighty and influential group.[112] The large numbers of notaries who appear in the larger cities suggest that not all of them could have made an adequate living from notarial work alone. For some, notarial practice may have been a sideline carried on in conjunction with other employment as clerks, commercial traders, apothecaries, or in various manual trades.[113] Successful notaries were often conspicuously involved in local politics and civic affairs as well, although the Marseilles notary who had his own armed war galley was certainly exceptional and quite possibly unique.[114]

Notaries who worked principally or entirely for private clients do not seem to have grown wealthy in great numbers. They often set up a shop (variously styled *apotheca*, *butica*, or *operarium*) in or near a civic center, conveniently close to its courts and municipal offices. Some notaries at Marseilles carried on their work in the street in front of their homes and invited passers-by to witness the documents they produced.[115] References to notaries who lived in small towns or villages are not uncommon. The demand for notarial services was sufficiently frequent and widespread that rural notaries may have been able make a living by combining their notarial functions with the practice of another trade or craft. Others carried on a peripatetic practice, as did Federico di Gionta, who traveled through the region around his home at Souviville near Siena and wrote documents for those who needed them in public places, most often in churches.[116] Although notaries seem typically to have been solo practitioners, busy and prosperous members of the profession, especially those in important cities, often employed clerks to copy the documents that the master drafted for his clients.

112. Brentano, *Rome before Avignon*, 50; Zutshi, "The Office of Notary in the Papal Chancery," 665–67; Fédou, *Les hommes de loi lyonnais*, 188–91; Trexler, *Synodal Law*, 160–63; *Privilegia curie Remensis*, reform decree of 1267, 14.

113. Hyde, *Padua in the Age of Dante*, 158–59; Waley, *Italian City Republics*, 29.

114. Hyde, *Society and Politics*, 167–68; Foote, "How the Past Becomes a Rumor," 795, 801; Martines, *Lawyers and Statecraft*, 49–50; Gouron, "Le rôle social des juristes," 55 n. 1.

115. Hyde, *Padua in the Age of Dante*, 170–72; Petrucci, "An clerici artem notariae possint exercere," 571; Trexler, *Synodal Law*, 156–57; Fasoli, "Giuristi, giudici e notai," 617; Waley, *Italian City Republics*, 29–30; Mundy, *Society and Government at Toulouse*, 146 and n. 11; Fournier, *Officialités*, 54–55; Smail, *Consumption of Justice*, 224–25.

116. Meyer, *Felix et inclitus notarius*, 391–499, presents a study of the notaries who practiced in the countryside round about Lucca between 1220 and 1280. On Federico di Gionta and his like, see Redon, "Quatre notaires et leurs clientèles," 91–92; also Hyde, *Society and Politics*, 82; Fasoli, "Giuristi, giudici e notai," 613.

A few notaries practiced in groups, such as the one headed by Jan Cramme at Bruges in the early fourteenth century.[117]

Judges and notaries were central to the functioning of the legal system, even though many of them were not trained lawyers. Members of both groups regularly interacted with advocates and proctors. These occupational categories were permeable in practice. It is not uncommon to find judges who were advocates, or notaries who also acted as proctors, while some notaries became judges. Although neither judges nor notaries were required to be trained as lawyers, it became increasingly common from the mid-thirteenth century onward to find judges and notaries who had either studied law at a university or spent some time as apprentices in the courts or, often enough, both of these. Judges and notaries certainly needed to know some law; at the very least they required access to knowledgeable advice about it in order to perform their functions properly.

Judges and notaries, especially in northern Italy, northeastern Spain, and the south of France frequently belonged to special guilds that were separate from the professional organizations made up of advocates and proctors. Judges and notaries shared occupational needs and interests different from those of advocates and proctors, and their professional associations sometimes reflected this.

117. Meyer, *Felix et inclitus notarius*, 362–90; Murray, "Failure of Corporation," 157–61.

* TEN *

The Practice of Canon Law

The Scope of Canonistic Legal Practice

Medieval lawyers practiced law in a variety of modes and settings. Advocates argued lawsuits on behalf of clients in courts, ecclesiastical and secular, and at home in their studies, they drafted the technical documents that were at least as vital as oral argument in determining the outcome of a case. Providing legal advice and counsel constituted another basic element in every advocate's practice. Clients needed guidance about their legal options when they engaged in complex transactions, filed a lawsuit, or entered a defense to a complaint. Judges likewise routinely sought advice from knowledgeable advocates before they handed down their decisions. Prominent advocates charged handsome fees for formal written opinions (*consilia*), both in connection with litigation and outside of it. In addition, advocates were sometimes involved in arbitration proceedings to settle disputes informally between individuals who preferred to settle their differences out of court and away from the public eye. Advocates served in still other capacities as negotiators between private parties and as diplomatic representatives of sovereign powers. They, together with judges (who often came from the ranks of advocates) and law professors, comprised the elite upper tier of the legal profession.

Professional proctors considerably outnumbered advocates in the courts of the *ius commune*. Their services as litigation agents were indispensable. In many courts, as we have seen, especially ones at the lower end of the jurisdictional hierarchy where the volume of litigation was comparatively light, proctors might perform the same services that advocates did in the higher courts. Although the academic legal training of professional proctors was generally neither as long, as arduous, nor as costly as that of advocates, they were nonetheless qualified lawyers whose practical experience litigants usually found necessary to prevail in the courts. Notaries, like proctors, were essential, not only to the functioning of the courts, but also to civil and ecclesiastical administration and for a host of commercial and personal transactions. They made up the most numerous but least prestigious branch of the profession.

Establishing Practice as an Advocate

Before a newly sworn advocate could begin to practice, he had to find clients willing to employ his services. Securing the first few clients was likely to be difficult. Fortunate novice advocates might be able to use family influence and social connections to secure clients at the outset of their careers, but most were not so lucky and had to find other means of getting started. Established practitioners admonished advocates not to solicit business from prospective clients by calling at their homes or approaching them in taverns and other public places to offer their services. Some judges even thought it necessary to forbid lawyers to station themselves at the doors of the court to seek employment from improvident litigants who had put off securing the services of an advocate until they were about to enter the courtroom. It was not, in fact, particularly unusual for judges to grant litigants a stay in proceedings to allow them to find an advocate or to instruct one whom they had just engaged.[1]

Prudent clients went about choosing an advocate more expeditiously. They were likely to seek advice from friends and relatives who had experience with lawsuits, as well as recommendations from proctors, notaries, and court clerks who knew the ways of the court and had ample opportunity to appraise the abilities of those who practiced there. Advocates who had themselves practiced as proctors or notaries early in their careers were likely to have an advantage here, since friends and acquaintances among their former colleagues might put in a good word for them, while clients whom they had served in their earlier roles might continue to employ them in their new capacity.[2] Since ecclesiastical courts seldom had more than a

1. Panormitanus, *Practica*, cap. 48.1, at 11va–vb; cf. Philippe de Beaumanoir, *Coutumes de Beauvaisis* 5.194, at 1:96; Bonaguida, *Summa introductoria* 3.1, at 251; Delachenal, *Histoire des avocats*, 58; Poos, *Lower Ecclesiastical Jurisdiction*, 150. Numerous examples of stays in proceedings appear, e.g., in *Registre des causes civiles de l'officialité épiscopale de Paris*, cols. 35, 43, 55, 116, 118, etc.

2. Johannes Andreae, *Additiones* to Durand, *Speculum iudiciale* 1.4 *De teste* §5 v. *nunc uidendum*, at 1:313. Panormitanus quoted this passage verbatim in his *Practica*, cap. 73.8–9, at 15rb–va.

Figure 3. Two Bolognese doctors of civil law kneeling before an ecclesiastical judge seated on an ornate judicial throne. Italian, ca. 1354. Österreichische Nationalbibliothek, Cod. 2048, 1r. Reproduced by permission.

handful of advocates in practice at any given moment, a client's range of choice was apt to be restricted.

Advocates who had studied at Bologna or one of the other universities of northern Italy, as well as those who had worked at the papal curia, found networks established through those experiences helpful in attracting clients and referrals. Less well-connected advocates might circulate announcements that their services were available, as two young Bolognese lawyers named Carlo and Romeo apparently did, although how effective this may have been is impossible to determine.[3]

The most persuasive advertising that a beginning advocate could hope for was the opportunity to display his abilities by pleading successfully in court before a judge (fig. 3). As Sicard of Cremona advised, "Advocates who want cases must argue in court." But, he added, "Let them take care to do no harm, because someone who is too daring and puts self-promotion ahead of reason is apt to suffer a loss of reputation."[4]

Once a judge had admitted an advocate to practice in his court and ordered his name entered on its rolls, the advocate forthwith became an

---

3. Gramsch, *Erfurter Juristen*, 110–15, 233–40, 394–424, furnishes numerous examples of successful networking. On the use of circulars to drum up business, see Thorndike, "Law Advertising."

4. Sicard of Cremona, *Summa* to C. 3 q. 7 in London, BL, MS Add. 18367, at 28ra: "Agere debent aduocati qui causa desiderant. Caueant ab iniuria, quia si quis adeo procax fuerit, ut non ratione sed propriis putet esse certandum, opinionis sue inmutationem patiantur."

officer (though not an employee) of the court. In return for his right of audience, the advocate assumed obligations toward the court. One of those duties was to attend the court's sessions regularly.[5] This also served the advocate's self-interest, since regular attendance helped to integrate him into the society of practitioners, clerks, notaries, and other officials attached to the court whose assistance might prove crucial in advancing his career. Equally important, regular court attendance provided a beginning lawyer with opportunities to break into professional practice by securing assignments as a court-appointed advocate, perhaps when a judge ordered a distribution of counsel, but more likely when the court needed an advocate to plead free of charge on behalf of a poor or disadvantaged litigant who could not otherwise secure legal services. Established practitioners were apt to be reluctant to accept these unpaid assignments and judges sometimes had to threaten anyone who refused them with disbarment.[6] For a novice advocate, however, the case of a poor client, although it might provide no immediate financial reward, offered an opportunity to show off his skills and learning. Success in a few such cases might, with good luck and hard work, secure him a reputation as an able advocate and encourage paying clients (although at first no doubt mainly those in search of bargain rates) to employ him.

Paying clients who sought to engage an advocate's services could usually expect to find him in his study when court was not in session. Although the advocate's public role was to present oral arguments in court, medieval advocates almost certainly spent a far larger part of their professional time doing other kinds of work. When they were not in court—and the public sessions of most church courts seldom occupied more than a few hours a week—advocates were apt to be busy at home among their books. An advocate typically set aside a room in his dwelling as a study or professional

---

5. Henry Burghersh, *Statuta consistorii* 2:573, §10, e.g., demanded that all advocates and proctors admitted to practice in his consistory court attend each of the court's sessions. They were required to remain until the court recessed, unless they received special permission from the presiding judge to leave earlier. Similar provisions appeared in Archbishop Winchelsey's statutes for the Court of Arches (1295) §13 and were repeated in Archbishop Stratford's statutes of (1342) §4, in Logan, *Medieval Court of Arches*, 9, 35.

6. Roumy, "Système de l'avocat commis d'office"; Accursius, *Glos. ord.* to Dig. 3.1.1.4 v. *non habebunt*; Hostiensis, *Lectura* to X 1.32.1 §§2–4 v. *non poterat*, at 1:169ra; Durand, *Speculum iudiciale* 1.4 *De aduocato* §§1.32–33, at 1:263–64; Raymond of Penyafort, *Summa de penitentia* 2.5.39, ed. Ochoa and Diez, col. 518, also quoted *in extenso* by William of Pagula, *Summa summarum* 1.61 in CUL, MS Pembroke 201, at 74ra.

chambers.[7] There he kept his law books and files of records and documents, met with clients, consulted with colleagues, and laid the groundwork for litigation. The unglamorous task of drafting the necessary documents, upon which the successful outcome of litigation largely depended, consumed a major share of his professional time and attention.[8] Although litigation involved oral motions and argument by the advocate, most of the time he spent on a lawsuit was likely to be occupied by submitting written instruments and responding to those that his opponent submitted. Many of these (at least in theory) had to be drafted by advocates rather than proctors or notaries, since advocates were assumed to have a superior knowledge of the law.[9] In addition, advocates (again, at least in theory) continually refreshed their stock of legal knowledge, during any spare time they could find between appearing in court, conferring with clients, consulting with colleagues, advising judges, arbitrating disputes, writing legal opinions, and drafting litigation documents.[10]

Although most advocates seem to have been sole practitioners, no matter how modest their professional standing, they usually employed at least one clerk. Busy and prosperous members of the profession, of course, might

7. Stephen of Tournai, *Lettres*, 345, no. 274, referred to advocates' studies as "their shops or cubicles" (*apothecis sive cubiculis suis*).

8. William of Drogheda, *Summa aurea*, 39, §36; Durand, *Speculum iudiciale* 1.4 *De aduocato* §6.3, at 1:272; Alonso Romero and Garrigas Acosta, "El régimen jurídico," 80. Modern barristers reportedly spend about four-fifths of their time drafting or advising on documents related to litigation (Du Cann, *Art of the Advocate*, 80). Medieval procedural treatises and practitioners' manuals suggest that it is at least plausible that thirteenth-century advocates may have devoted a comparable part of their professional lives to similar kinds of work. The fact that four out of the five sections (*particula*) of Bonaguida's *Summa introductoria* deal with the preparation of documents implies this.

9. Helmholz, *Canon Law and Ecclesiastical Jurisdiction*, 215; Halberstadt consistory court statutes (1442) §30, in Hilling, "Sechs Gerichtsordnungen," 336; Steins, "Ordentliche Zivilprozeß," 248. The fourteenth-century statutes of the archbishop's court at Cologne (§3.2) allowed proctors to prepare these documents, provided that they did so under the supervision of an advocate, who was required to put his signature on each page (Gescher, "Älteste kölnische Offizialatsstatut," 483). According to Innocent III, advocates were expected to concentrate on the legal merits of a case, while proctors were responsible for dealing with the factual evidence provided through the testimony of witnesses and written documents; Thomas of Marlborough, *History of the Abbey of Evesham*, 282, 300, §§284, 302; similarly the *Privilegia curie Remensis*, 13).

10. Giovanni da Nono, *Visio Egidii regis Patavii*, cited by Hyde, "Medieval Descriptions of Cities," 331; Fédou, *Hommes de loi lyonnais*, 309–10; Delachenal, *Histoire des avocats*, 58.

need to employ whole batteries of them.[11] These expectations were premised on the assumption that a beginning advocate would have sufficient resources to support himself while he built up his practice. That assumption was not always realistic, and occasional references suggest that advocates sometimes joined together to share chambers, clerks, and libraries, in order to minimize expenses. A few seem to have practiced jointly and shared income as well as expenses in small partnerships or firms.[12]

Whether he practiced individually or as part of a group, experienced professionals advised the newly admitted advocate to persuade his clients to provide him with an associate counsel. "Woe to him that is alone, for when he falleth he hath none to lift him up," declared Bonaguida, quoting scripture, and "what many wise men look for will more readily be found."[13] Whether the beginning advocate had a paid helper or not, Bonaguida encouraged him to discuss every case with trusted colleagues to get their insight into his adversary's likely moves so that he could avoid pitfalls that might not have occurred to him unaided.[14]

Long before this became an issue, however, the advocate first needed to interview his prospective client in order to discover why he wanted an advocate's assistance, what results he hoped for, and whether he had a viable case.[15] The advocate obviously needed to learn all the details of the situation before he could advise his client about the most appropriate strategies to pursue. He must not only explore what the dispute was about and what the client's objectives were, but he also had to protect his own reputation

---

11. Fédou, *Hommes de loi lyonnais*, 310–11.

12. Baldus, *Consilia* 3.452, at 3:132ra–rb, deals with a case that involved the division of property when a pair of brothers who practiced together as a *societas* of advocates decided to go their separate ways. See also the gloss attributed to Ludovicus Gomes in the *proemium* to *Regule cancellarie apostolica*: "[E]t tunc practicaui cum Cafarello maximo aduocato et dixit michi totum oppositum per rationes iuridicas, maxime quia ex quo lex incepit ligare et cetera et replicaui sibi quod rota ea die pronunciauit contrarium, et dixit michi quod rota aliquando rotat." Arrangements of this sort may have been more common among proctors than among advocates (Stelzer, "Beiträge," 127–28; Sayers, *Papal Government*, 34).

13. Bonaguida, *Summa introductoria* 1.3.5, at 155; The scriptural quotation is from Eccles. 4:10. See likewise Aegidius Fuscarariis, *Ordo iudiciarius*, 183, §110, and Durand, *Speculum iudiciale* 1.4 *De aduocato* §3.6–7, at 1:265–66.

14. Bonaguida, *Summa introductoria* 1.3.10, at 157.

15. Durand, *Speculum iudiciale* 1.4 *De aduocato* §3.1–2, at 1:265; William of Drogheda, *Summa aurea*, 66, §66; Cologne consistory court statutes (ca. 1306–31) §3.1, in Gescher, "Älteste kölnische Offizialatsstatut," 482.

by warning the client about the perils of litigation. It was essential that the client appreciate what he was getting into and what his chances of success were likely to be. It was likewise prudent to encourage the client to take realistic account of the limits of his own resources in comparison with those available to his opponent. While it would be improper to advise a client to abandon his just claims solely because of economic considerations, it was foolish as well as unethical to encourage him to undertake a lawsuit without a reasonable chance that he could prevail and that he could afford the unavoidable costs of doing so.[16]

If the client was determined to persist, the advocate then needed to question him about the evidence and to ask him to produce any documents relevant to his claims. Beyond that, the advocate had to learn the names of any witnesses who would support the client's version of events and what they were likely to say. Equally or perhaps even more important, he needed to learn as much as he could about witnesses the other party was likely to call upon and what evidence they might be expected to give. The advocate was forbidden to interview witnesses for either side lest he be suspected of influencing their testimony, but he also had to think about questions that he might ask the judge to put to them in order to bring out points that he hoped would tell in his client's favor.[17]

The advocate now had to secure every scrap of relevant information that he could induce his client to give him, for only when he had this would he be in a position to determine whether or not he should accept the case. Given the predictable inability of persons engaged in a dispute to take a detached view either of the weaknesses of their own or the strengths of their opponent's case, as well as the natural reluctance of people to reveal harmful or embarrassing information, the initial client interview was no easy task, and the advocate needed to question his client diligently in order to secure the required information. At the same time, he also had to be careful not to cross the fine line that separated giving his client legal advice from coaching him about what to say if or when he was questioned during the course of litigation.[18]

If the client was still resolved to bring a lawsuit or to defend an action

---

16. William of Drogheda, *Summa aurea*, 12–14, §8.

17. Bonaguida, *Summa introductoria* 1.3.12, at 158; Durand, *Speculum iudiciale* 2.1 *De interrogationibus* §2.14 and 2.2 *De positionibus* §9.6, at 1:546, 597.

18. Bonaguida, *Summa introductoria* 1.3.12, at 158; Aegidius de Fuscarariis, *Ordo iudiciarius*, 185, §110; Durand, *Speculum iudiciale* 1.4 *De aduocato* §9.4–6, at 1:280–81; Brundage, "The Advocate's Dilemma," 207.

brought against him, an advocate was well advised to warn him that litigation was unpredictable and that, no matter how strong the client felt his case was, it was always possible that something could go awry. Experienced practitioners insisted that an advocate must never overplay his hand by promising the client that he would prevail. He needed to make sure, Johannes de Deo cautioned, that the client understood that the outcome of his case would lie in the hands of the judge, not the advocate.[19]

Writers on professional matters regularly counseled their readers to settle on the amount of their fee and arrangements for its payment as soon as they decided to accept a case. The client, they pointed out, was apt to be most enthusiastic and optimistic about success in his lawsuit at the outset and was accordingly more likely to agree to a generous fee then than he might be later. The client's initial optimism was liable to diminish, along with his generous feelings, as the case proceeded, especially when unforeseen setbacks and delays arose. A firm agreement at the beginning, preferably in writing, sealed by a substantial first payment, ensured the advocate that even if the case went against him his labors would not go unrewarded. This approach allowed a Roman consistorial advocate to boast that he had never lost a case, although his clients sometimes did.[20]

Once he had committed himself to accept a client's case, had settled on his fee, agreed on arrangements for its payment, and received the first installment, the advocate then needed to secure written instructions from his client authorizing him to proceed. These provided him with a record that was useful in preparing for litigation and also furnished a safeguard in case the client should later become dissatisfied with his services—a real possibility, if the client seemed likely to lose his case—since so long as the advocate had followed his instructions, they would provide a defense against recriminations or lawsuits if things went wrong.[21] Finally, as William of Drogheda suggested, a canny advocate would do well not to publicize his acceptance of the case immediately and should warn his client not to tell

19. Johannes de Deo, *Cauillationes aduocatorum* 1.6, in London, BL, MS Arundel 459, at 3va. Likewise Bonaguida, *Summa introductoria* 1.3.4, at 155; Aegidius de Fuscarariis, *Ordo iudiciarius*, 183, §110; Durand, *Speculum iudiciale* 1.4 *De aduocato* §3.10, at 1:266.

20. Petrus de Monte, *Repertorium utriusque iuris*, s.v. "Advocatus." It was common practice to demand payment of a fraction of the fee (often one-half) at the outset, with the remainder due at the conclusion of oral argument, but before the judge announced his decision.

21. Bonaguida, *Summa introductoria* 1.3.2, at 154; Durand, *Speculum iudiciale* 1.4 *De aduocato* §3.3, at 1:265. The procedural manual *"Curialis,"* 25–26, §§80–81, gives two examples of instructions to an advocate.

people who his advocate was. This, said William, would allow the advocate to keep a sharp eye on the judge's demeanor at the outset of the action in order to determine whether he was prejudiced against the client and, if so, to prepare a motion to recuse.[22]

Civil Litigation

Litigation was the most public side of a medieval lawyer's practice.[23] This was the setting in which advocates displayed their legal skills most prominently, while a professional proctor's help was also indispensable if a litigant hoped to prevail. Nonlawyers almost invariably thought and wrote about legal professionals primarily in terms of litigation. So, for that matter, did most trained lawyers.

Advocates were by definition men skilled in the arts required for successful litigation.[24] Training in rhetoric coupled with practice in academic disputations taught them how to persuade others to acquiesce in their views. Years spent studying law at university equipped them to discover the legal authorities needed to support a client's case and to demolish, or at least to raise doubts about, the counter arguments put forward by their opponents. By the fourteenth century, judges in some courts were beginning to demand that advocates acquire some practical experience of the workings of the court (sometimes described as the *stylus curiae*) before they would admit them to practice. Intending advocates sometimes did this by working as scribes, notaries, or proctors before seeking admission as advocates.[25] Those who failed to do so risked getting their careers off to an awkward start of the sort we saw described by Martinus de Fano.

---

22. William of Drogheda, *Summa aurea*, 88, §89.

23. Advocates and proctors seldom appeared in criminal cases. Criminal defendants were generally not entitled to use their services, while prosecution under the inquisitorial procedural system was *ex officio* the duty of the judge—which is the reason why criminal cases are often referred to as office cases. Here I shall concentrate solely on civil litigation. For canonical criminal procedure, see Brundage, *Medieval Canon Law*, 142–53; Helmholz, *Spirit of Classical Canon Law*, 284–310; and Fraher's numerous articles, including "Tancred's 'Summula de criminalibus'"; "Theoretical Justification for the New Criminal Law"; "'Ut nullus describatur reus prius quam convincatur'"; "Preventing Crime in the High Middle Ages"; "IV Lateran's Revolution in Criminal Procedure"; and "Conviction according to Conscience."

24. Tancred, *Ordo iudiciarius* 1.5.3, at 112; Alonso Romero and Garriga Acosta, "El régimen jurídico," 62.

25. See e.g., Walter de Stapeldon, *Register*, 115–19; Gramsch, *Erfurter Juristen*, 224, 249–60.

PREPARING FOR LITIGATION

With his client's instructions in hand, the advocate's first task in preparing for a lawsuit was to plan his litigation strategy and to map out the lines of argument that he should pursue. An advocate was entitled to adequate time to prepare a case and writers on professional matters advised him not to be shy in seeing that he got it.[26] He might be able to prepare relatively simple, straightforward cases quickly by drawing upon what he had learned as a student and from observation and experience in practice. Complicated, novel, and challenging situations, on the other hand, might require substantial research, reflection, and consultation with more experienced advocates before he could settle on the arguments most likely to win the judge's favor and identify the legal authorities to support them.[27] Once he was satisfied that he understood the matter thoroughly, had anticipated his opponent's counterclaims, and knew how best to approach the case, the advocate could get down to work in earnest.

GETTING THE CASE INTO COURT

Civil litigation could commence in a variety of ways. Plaintiffs often enough simply came to court and made a direct oral complaint to the judge. In many instances, they did this before they had even consulted a lawyer about the matter. In other cases, the complainant appointed a proctor to pursue litigation on his behalf, and the proctor took care of lodging the complaint. In still other cases, plaintiffs engaged an advocate as well as a proctor before they commenced proceedings. In any case, someone, whether the plaintiff himself or his proctor, needed to set the process in motion by going to court to explain his grievance and asking the judge to take cognizance of it.[28] In real life, however, judges themselves were not necessarily involved at this initial stage of proceedings. Instead, the plaintiff or his proctor usually dealt with the registrar, or in some courts with a *receptor actorum* to whom the registrar had assigned the duty of receiving complaints and scheduling hearings. The registrar was a key member of the court's staff. Accepting cases and scheduling times for them to be heard commonly fell within his purview, in addition to his duty to maintain the records of what happened

---

26. C. 3 q. 3 c. 1–4 and d.p.c. 4; Cod. 7.14.3; Bonaguida, *Summa introductoria* 3.1, at 251–52; Durand, *Speculum iudiciale* 2.1 *De praeparatoriis iudiciorum* §§1–2, at 1:354.

27. Bonaguida, *Summa introductoria* 1.3.10, at 157.

28. Tancred, *Ordo iudiciarius* 2.2, at 131; William of Drogheda, *Summa aurea*, 14–15, §9.

in court.[29] He might in addition be the keeper of the judge's seal. The registrar was entitled to charge fees, and proctors were well advised to pay up promptly and graciously and to keep on good terms with him because the arrangements that the registrar made about times and places for hearings could significantly affect his clients' convenience, to say nothing of the costs they might have to bear.[30]

After accepting the plaintiff's complaint, the registrar or his deputy prepared a written citation or summons, which ordered the defendant to appear before the judge on a specified date to answer the complaint. The registrar then dispatched an apparitor to find the defendant and serve him with the summons in the presence of two witnesses. If the apparitor was able to locate the defendant, he read the citation aloud to him. If the defendant had learned that a summons was on the way and took care not to be found, however, the apparitor could alternatively direct the local priest to read the summons aloud in the defendant's parish church during Mass on the next Sunday or major feast day. In either event, the apparitor noted on the back of the citation when, where, and how he had served the summons. Service of the citation might also be confirmed by the local dean or archdeacon, who then furnished the judge with a written statement certifying that the summons had been properly delivered.[31]

Service of the summons obligated the defendant either to appear in person at the specified time and place or else to send a proctor to present a satisfactory reason for his failure to comply. Should he fail to respond, he might be summoned twice more.[32] If he or his personal representative still failed to appear after the third summons, the judge could declare him contumacious. This rendered the defendant *infamis*, which severely hand-

---

29. *Privilegia curie Remensis*, 20; Fournier, *Officialités*, 27–28; Pommeray, *Officialité archidiaconales*, 104–24.

30. Helmholz, *Canon Law and Ecclesiastical Jurisdiction*, 213; William of Drogheda, *Summa aurea*, 22–24, §18.

31. Tancred, *Ordo iudiciarius* 2.3, at 132–35; Bonaguida, *Summa introductoria* 3.1, at 248–49; William of Drogheda, *Summa aurea*, 14–22, §§9–17; Durand, *Speculum iudiciale* 2.1 *De citatione*, at 1:425–48; Donahue, introduction to *Select Cases*, ed. Adams and Donahue, 38–39, as well as samples of actual citations in cases B.1 (52), D.6 (406–407), and D.13 (527).

32. In actual practice, plaintiffs often sought a peremptory citation rather than the ordinary kind. This had the advantage that if the defendant failed to respond to a single peremptory citation the judge could immediately impose penalties upon him (Durand, *Speculum iudiciale* 2.1 *De citatione* §3, at 1:431–34).

icapped his ability to defend his case, and might result in a fine, excommunication, and perhaps a summary judgment in favor of the plaintiff as well.[33] A contumacious defendant who thought better of the matter and then made a belated appearance needed to apologize to the judge, promise to obey the orders of the court in future, and usually paid a stiff fine before he could proceed with his defense.[34]

With the case now in motion, the advocate had to draft the *libellus*, the legal instrument that in most cases formally set forth the plaintiff's claims and defined the issues that he wished to have adjudicated.[35] This was a crucial document and its composition required skill, learning, and ingenuity.[36] Procedural writers almost invariably dealt at length with the topic and usually furnished examples of *libelli* to deal with a variety of situations. Some even devoted whole treatises to the subject.[37] Preparing a libel required careful thought, since, as William Durand put it, "Almost the entire thrust of lawsuits depends upon the proper construction of the *libellus*." Few ad-

---

33. Tancred, *Ordo iudiciarius* 2.4.1, at 135–38; Durand, *Speculum iudiciale* 2.1 *De contumacia*, pr., §4, at 1:448, 454–57. On *infamia* and its consequences, see Migliorino, *Fama e infamia*, 152–57; Landau, *Entstehung des kanonischen Infamiebegriffs*, 54–57; and Peters, "Wounded Names," 69–71. See also Vodola, *Excommunication in the Middle Ages*, 36–43.

34. X 1.2.11 and 1.38.2; Durand, *Speculum iudiciale* 2.3 *De expensis* §3.6, at 1:901; Helmholz, *Canon Law and Ecclesiastical Jurisdiction*, 347–48; Donahue, introduction to *Select Cases*, ed. Adams and Donahue, 39–40.

35. William of Drogheda, *Summa aurea*, 196–99, §§168–69; Durand, *Speculum iudiciale* 1.4 *De aduocato* §3.4–6, at 1:265–66; Steins, "Ordentliche Zivilprozeß," 248; Cologne consistory court statutes §3.2, in Gescher, "Älteste kölnische Offizialatsstatut," 483. No *libellus* was required in most criminal cases, and it was normally not used in cases handled under summary procedure or in certain other circumstances. In some courts oral complaints were the norm, and it was not customary to use *libelli* at all (Bencivenne, *Summa de ordine iudiciorum* 1.8, at 18; Tancred, *Ordo iudiciarius* 3.5, at 198–99; Durand, *Speculum iudiciale* 4.1 *De libellorum conceptione* §9, at 2:61–67).

36. Clem. 5.11.2; Jacobus Balduinus, *Libellus instructionis advocatorum*, in Sarti, *Un giurista tra Azzone e Accursio*, 153–92; Bencivenne, *Summa de ordine iudiciorum* 1.2 and 8, at 6, 18; Tancred, *Ordo iudiciarius* 2.2 pr. and 3.1.5, at 131, 198–99; Gratia, *Summa de iudiciario ordine* 1.3.1, at 324; Durand, *Speculum iudiciale* 4.1 *De libellorum conceptione* §14.5, 4.3 *De clandestina desponsatione*, no. 2, and 4.4 *De matrimonio contra interdictum ecclesiae contracto*, no. 2, at 2:71, 445, 458.

37. See, e.g., Tancred, *Ordo iudiciarius* 2.8–13, at 162–73; William of Drogheda, *Summa aurea*, 196–292, §§168–357; Durand, *Speculum iudiciale* 4.1 *De libellorum conceptione*, at 2:56–76; Cortese, "Scienza di giudici e scienza di professori," 104–105; Fowler-Magerl, *Ordo iudiciorum*, 96–100, and *Ordines iudiciarii*, 37–40, 90, 98.

vocates prepared these instruments really well, in Durand's opinion, and he added that every advocate was virtually bound at some point to bungle the task.[38]

The libel presented the judge with a formal statement of the plaintiff's complaint, which defendants could answer with a written denial and counterclaim (*libellus reconventionis*).[39] The plaintiff's libel had to identify the parties, define the client's claims, explain the grounds on which he was bringing an action, and specify the remedy he sought. The advocate needed to do all of this succinctly, yet in a way that anticipated, and with luck and good draftsmanship might even forestall, the counterclaims that his opponent was likely to raise. Once he was satisfied that his draft of the libel covered all the contingencies he could foresee, the advocate had his clerk produce three copies, one for the court, one for his adversary, and the third for his own use in drafting positions and articles.[40]

Meanwhile, it was necessary to return to court with the *libellus* on the hearing date that the registrar set for the commencement of formal proceedings. The plaintiff's proctor, either in company with his client or by himself, usually handled the actual delivery of the libel.

COURT CALENDARS

Bishops' officials commonly held their formal court sessions in the mornings. At Reims in the mid-thirteenth century, sittings were supposed to begin at the hour of prime, shortly after daybreak, and to close before dinner, which in that period was customarily eaten around midday. This was a common, but by no means invariable, pattern in courts elsewhere. Scottish officials usually commenced their sessions later, around nine or ten o'clock in the morning, while by the mid-fifteenth century, the official of the bishop of Geneva only began to hear cases at eleven o'clock in the morning. Courts usually reserved the afternoons for other tasks, such as

38. William Durand, *Speculum iudiciale* 4.1 *De libellorum conceptione*, pr., no. 6, at 2:56. Cf. the anonymous *Notabilia decretalium Cantabrigiensis* to X 2.3.2, in CUL, MS Add. 3467, at 33r.

39. Bencivenne *Summa de ordine iudiciorum* 2.5, at 26–27; Tancred, *Ordo iudiciarius* 2.19 pr., 2–3, at 187–89; Durand, *Speculum iudiciale* 2.1 *De reconventione* §4.2, at 1:550.

40. Johannes Andreae, *Glos. ord.* to Clem. 5.11.2 v. *formare debeant*. For examples of *libelli* actually used in litigation, see *Select Cases*, ed. Adams and Donahue, A.15, C.1, C.2, C.3, C. 4, C.7, C.13, C.14, D.16, D.18, D.19, at 41–48, 97, 108, 115, 121, 138–39, 203–204, 208, 581, 629, 637; *Documenten uit de Praktijk*, nos. 10, 15, 20, 67, at 15–17, 24–25, 30–31, 88–89; and Hubaldus of Pisa, *Imbreviaturbuch*, nos. 2, 19, 31, 35, 45, 47, 51, 55, at 88, 104, 116–17, 120–21, 132, 134, 136, 144–45.

taking the depositions of witnesses.[41] They conducted judicial business in the evenings only in dire emergencies.

Court calendars differed considerably from one place to another. This reflected, at least in part, differences in the volume of litigation that they handled. The demand for their services apparently varied greatly. The canons forbade courts to hear lawsuits on Sundays or major feast days (*dies non sessionis*), of which there were a great many, and even the busiest judges conducted judicial business on those days only in exceptional circumstances.[42] Feast days and Sundays taken together meant that close to half the days of the year were unavailable for routine court hearings. Courts also enjoyed holiday periods, which often ran from late July to mid or late September, in addition to a week or more before and after Christmas and Easter.[43] Indeed, some courts seldom sat at all; the court of the dean and chapter of York in the early sixteenth century, for example, seems to have held its regular sessions only on Thursday mornings, and not every Thursday at that, although it occasionally transacted some incidental business between regular sittings, while the archbishop of Canterbury's audience court held sessions only about once every three weeks.[44] The constraints of court calendars meant that the limited time available was at a premium, with the result that proctors often had to compete fiercely to get hearings set down for times that would be convenient for their clients. This likewise helps to explain the irritation that judges and other authorities often ex-

---

41. On Reims, see Fournier, *Officialités*, 62; Pommeray, *Officialité archidiaconale*, 184–85; on mealtimes, Bologna, Spanish College Statutes §16, in Marti, *The Spanish College*, 206–12; Rashdall, *Universities* 3:402–403; Holmes, *Daily Living in the Twelfth Century*, 118–19; for Scotland and Geneva, Ollivant, *Court of the Official*, 49; *Constitutiones et statuta*, 367, §4; and on afternoon tasks, Lefebvre-Teillard, *Officialités*, 42.

42. Gratian C. 15 q. 4 c. 1–2.

43. Ollivant, *Court of the Official*, 48; *Constitutiones et statuta*, 392–93; Woodcock, *Medieval Ecclesiastical Courts*, 31–34; Morris, "A Consistory Court," 155–56; Donahue, introduction to *Select Cases*, ed. Adams and Donahue, 18, 34; Donahue, and Gordus, "Archbishop Stratford's Audience Act Book," 49; Logan, *Medieval Court of Arches*, 225–29; Cheney, *Handbook of Dates*, 110–11; Pommeray, *Officialité archidiaconale*, 185–89; Fournier, *Officialités*, 62–63; Lefebvre-Teillard, *Officialités*, 42–43. The *dies non sessionis* reflected the list of days when it was forbidden to take an oath on the Gospels, as detailed in Gratian's Decretum (C. 22 q. 5 c. 17), in addition to other feast days that were locally observed. The number of feast days observed by the courts approximated the nonlecturing days prescribed in universities.

44. Longley, introduction to *Ecclesiastical Cause Papers at York: Dean and Chapter's Court*, xi; Churchill, *Canterbury Administration* 1:493 n. 3.

pressed at litigants who failed to appear and at advocates and proctors who presented rambling and prolix motions or arguments.

The order in which cases were heard varied from one court to another. In the court of the official of the bishop of Geneva and elsewhere, the seniority of the proctors who brought cases in a given session determined the order of presentation. The most senior proctor began first, and the rest followed in order down to the most junior proctor in attendance.[45] By contrast, Pope Benedict XII ordered that in the Audientia sacri palatii the highest priority should be given to cases argued by advocates representing poor clients free of charge. Next in order came cases that involved contested elections or appointments to ecclesiastical positions. Once those had been heard, the remaining cases could come forward. Within each category, the order of seniority was to prevail, determined by the date when the advocate had been admitted to practice and his name entered in the court's admissions records.[46]

THE PHYSICAL SETTING: COURTROOMS

The consistory courts of bishops and other prelates conducted their formal business in a variety of settings. Ecclesiastical courts sometimes met in the residence of the prelate whose jurisdiction they exercised. Courts might be allotted a suite of rooms in the bishop's palace, as happened for example at Reims and Florence, while at Paris the archdeacon's court occupied the ground floor of the archdeacon's official residence within the cloister of the cathedral of Notre Dame. Some fortunate courts even managed to secure separate buildings of their own within the cathedral precincts.[47] The court's meeting place could even furnish the institution's name. The best-known example is the Audientia sacri palatii, established as a permanent institution by John XXII in his constitution *Ratio iuris* (1331). The pope gave the court its formal name in the preface to the constitution, but it subsequently came to be known as the "Roman Wheel" (Rota romana), perhaps because it met in a circular room or because the judges sat at a round table (fig. 4).[48]

---

45. *Constitutiones et statuta*, 373, §26; similarly, Durand, *Speculum iudiciale* 1.4 *De aduocato* §4.11, at 1:268.

46. Benedict XII, *Decens et necessarium* (1340) §§3–5, in Tangl, *Päpstlichen Kanzleiordnungen*, 119.

47. *Privilegia curie remensis*, 12; Pommeray, *Officialité archidiaconale*, 180–83; Lombardi, *Matrimoni di antico regime*, 144; Fournier, *Officialités*, 60–61; *Constitutiones et statuta*, 367, §4.

48. *Ratio iuris* (1331), in Tangl, *Päpstliche Kanzleiordnungen*, 84; Charles Lefebvre, "Rote romaine," 744–45.

Figure 4. The auditors of the Roman Rota, seated at a round table, open a court session with a prayer to the Holy Spirit. Italian, 1468. Archivio Segreto Vaticano, S. R. Rota, Miscellanea 7, 2v. Reproduced by permission.

Bishops' consistory courts in the twelfth and early thirteenth centuries often held sessions in public spaces: the porch or vestibule of the local cathedral was a frequent venue.[49] Since church entrances were traditionally guarded by figures of lions, such a court was occasionally styled the *curia*

49. Municipal courts likewise often chose public meeting places. Courts in the lower city of Marseille, e.g., held their sessions in stalls in the marketplace (Smail, *Consumption of Justice*, 22).

inter leones. This practice, however, produced serious inconveniences. The flow of traffic through and around the church entrance made it difficult to preserve decorum or even to hear what was being said, yet if pleaders and judges raised their voices in order to make themselves understood, this was likely to disturb worshippers and detract from the solemnity of services within the church. These and more serious disorders—including quarrels, brawls, bloodshed, murder, and other evils—sparked by court sessions led the Council of Salmur in 1253 to forbid judges to conduct their business in cathedrals or other churches.[50]

Over the course of time, many bishops moved their courts from the porch into the cathedral proper, where they sometimes took over a side chapel or walled off part of the transept or one of the side aisles as a courtroom.[51] We also find occasional references to court sessions held elsewhere in the cathedral precincts, perhaps in the house of the chancellor, official, or registrar, in the cathedral cloister, or in fair weather in some open space, such as the bishop's garden.

Some consistory courts went on circuit periodically. When this happened, judges, advocates, proctors, notaries, and members of the court staff packed up their books and records, together with supplies of parchment, pens, and ink, and moved on horseback from one town to another within the diocese. They typically stayed two or three days in each town

---

50. Fournier, *Officialités*, 60; Lefebvre-Teillard, *Officialités*, 41; Hayes, "Mundane Uses of Sacred Places," 25–27; Council of Salmur (1253) c. 6, in Mansi 23:811. Five years after the ruling by the Council of Salmur, another French council took a similar action (Council of Roffiac [1258] c. 10, in Mansi 23:988).

51. Thus, e.g, in England the Gloucester Consistory met until 1863 within a railed-in space in the south aisle of the cathedral. The judge sat under a window, while the registrar had a desk in an enclosed well (Hockaday, "Consistory Court of Gloucester," 207). At York the bishop's consistory had its own courtroom within the minster, while the court of the dean and chapter regularly met nearby in the north transept, which at least as late as the seventeenth century continued to produce complaints about the resulting disturbances to services (Purvis, "Ecclesiastical Courts of York," 22; Brown, *Courts of the York Minster Peculiar*, 6; Longley, introduction to *Ecclesiastical Cause Papers at York*, xi–xii. The bishop's consistory at Exeter likewise met in the cathedral; John de Grandisson, *Register*, 808. The archbishop's consistory at Canterbury normally met under the northwest tower of the cathedral nave, while the archbishop's appeals court in London held its sessions in the rear section of St. Mary of the Arches, otherwise known as St.-Mary-le-Bow (Logan, *Medieval Court of Arches*, xiv; Wunderli, *London Church Courts and Society*, 19).

they visited and held sessions at one of the local churches. Itinerant courts usually visited a fixed rotation of towns as they made their circuit through the diocese.[52]

A few bishops' consistory courts conducted their sittings in closed chambers from which outsiders were normally excluded. This was a practice more common on the Continent than it was in England. Thus, for example, the 1344 statutes of the consistory court of the bishops of Trier insisted that in addition to the judge and his attendants, only advocates, proctors, and notaries could be present during court sessions. Two *nuncii* were posted at the doors of the courtroom to keep all others out unless the judge specifically requested their presence.[53]

Regardless of where they were situated, the physical layout of courtrooms tended to follow similar patterns. The fifteenth-century Geneva consistory statutes describe the layout there in detail. The bishop's official presided over proceedings seated on a ceremonial chair, much like a professorial chair or a bishop's throne (*cathedra*), placed on a raised dais at one end of the courtroom. Directly in front of him was a desk where the official's notaries and clerks sat on a bench at his feet during court sessions. Documents submitted to the court were handed to the judge's clerks, who passed them on to the judge himself. All the "advocates learned in the law" eligible to practice in the court sat in order of seniority on elevated benches to the left and right of the official. When it came time for an advocate to speak, he rose from his seat and descended to the floor of the courtroom, where he stood facing the judge while stating his case, although the official might as a token of respect invite him to be seated. The proctors sat at floor level on benches facing the official and his clerk.[54]

PROFESSIONAL ETIQUETTE

Guidelines concerning courtroom behavior told advocates how they were expected to conduct themselves in court. While court records seldom mention judges enforcing these rules, then as now, they doubtless had in-

---

52. Woodcock, *Medieval Ecclesiastical Courts*, 33–36; Morris, "A Consistory Court, 155–56."

53. Steins, "Ordentliche Zivilprozeß," 222. The early-fourteenth-century statutes of the Cologne consistory (§9) contained a similar provision (Gescher, "Älteste kölnische Offizialitatsstatut," 484).

54. *Constitutiones et statuta*, 372–73 §§23–24; Helmholz, *Canon Law and Ecclesiastical Jurisdiction*, 215. See, for typical examples, the depictions of courtrooms in the frontispiece to this book and in fig. 2, chap. 6.

formal ways to penalize anyone rash enough to offend their sense of courtroom propriety.

Judges expected the advocates to appear properly dressed in a fashion befitting their social status and the dignity of the court. Their robes should be well made but sober and modest, not gaudy, neither too short nor too long, and not daringly cut.[55] William Durand concluded his discussion of courtroom attire with a piece of student doggerel:

> A smartly-clad man looks so learned
> That everyone believes what he says,
> For no one will guess that you're really a dope
> If you're turned out so smartly you might be the pope.
> If you don't dress the part, you'll get no ovations,
> No matter how learned may be your orations.[56]

The outer garments of advocates and proctors varied from one region to another, but commonly resembled the robes that university statutes prescribed for clerics, students, and professors. According to Durand, Italian advocates wore closed gowns with sleeves (*cappa manicata*), whereas north of the Alps they might come to court either in a sleeved robe or an open cloak.[57] At Lincoln, advocates in the consistory court were required to wear long gowns, presumably to distinguish them from proctors. Although university statutes often prescribed that academic dress should be black, illuminations frequently display advocates and proctors, like many academics, clad in blue or scarlet outer robes.[58]

---

55. Bonaguida, *Summa introductoria* 1.1, at 137.

56. My shameless paraphrase of "Vir bene vestitus pro vestibus esse peritus / Creditur a mille quanuis idiota sit ille. /Si careat veste, nec sit vestitus honeste, / Nullius est laudis, quamuis sciat omne, quod audit" (Durand, *Speculum iudiciale* 1.4 De aduocato §2.1, at 1:264).

57. William Durand, *Speculum iudiciale* 1.4 De aduocato §2.5, at 1:265. For more on the gowns of Italian advocates and judges, see Hargreaves-Mawdsley, *History of Legal Dress*, 5–7 and plates 1 and 2. For the academic garb of doctors of law, see Hargreaves-Mawdsley's *History of Academical Dress*, 14, 26, 37, and 49–50, together with plates 1a, 2a and b.

58. For examples of how style might confound proscriptions, see again the frontispiece to this book and fig. 2, chap. 6. On standards of dress at Lincoln, see Henry Burghersh, *Statuta consistorii*, 572, §6; Morris, "A Consistory Court," 157 n. 2; and Haren, *Sin and Society*, 201. More generally, see Bologna University Statutes (1432) 3.85, at 366; *CUP* 1:78–79, no. 20; Hackett, *Original Statutes*, 146–49, 203; *Statuta antiqua* c. 147, in

When an advocate's turn came to speak, courtroom etiquette required him to rise from his seat and walk to "the customary place" facing the judge. There he doffed his cap (*biretta*), and bowed to demonstrate his deference.[59] The advocate was admonished to show respect for the judge's authority, while demonstrating his own confidence and command of his case, through his facial expressions and tone of voice:

> Let him display his maturity and obedience especially in three ways: through his tone of voice, his expression, and his movements. Through his voice, in that he should neither raise nor lower his voice excessively, but rather keep it in the middle register.... Through his expression, in that he should display a pleasant and courteous face to the judge and the bystanders so that he may make them favorable toward him, for the advocate should appear humble and agreeable.... Through his movements, in that he should not bob his head, wave his hands about, or shuffle his feet. For he should in every way manifest his seriousness and maturity of mind.[60]

The advocate began by asking the judge's permission to speak. When he received it, writers on professional conduct urged him to begin by lavishing praise upon the judge, the more fulsome the better. William Durand advised advocates to compliment the judge's wisdom. An advocate, he suggested, might find something along these lines effective:

> Oh, Lord our God, how admirable is your wisdom! How brightly glows your eloquence, in which your servant delights! I rejoice in your words like one who has found a great treasure. Your speech is sweeter in my throat than

---

Documents Relating to Cambridge 1:387–88; Hargreaves-Mawdsley, *History of Legal Dress*, plates 2a and 2b; Rashdall, *Universities* 1:194–95, 200, 300;

59. Accursius, *Glos. ord.* to Cod. 2.6.6 v. *standi*; Bonaguida, *Summa introductoria* 1.1, at 136–37; William of Drogheda, *Summa aurea*, 39, §36; William Durand, *Speculum iudiciale* 1.4 *De aduocato* §5 pr., at 1:269. When a proctor made a statement to the court he was expected to behave in the same fashion; *Constitutiones et statuta*, 372–73, §§23–26.

60. Bonaguida, *Summa introductoria* 1.1, at 136–37: "Et circa tria praecipue se maturum morigerum et virum discretum ostendat: in voce, in vultu, et in gestu. In voce: ut vocem non plus debito deprimat vel calcet, quia medium tenendum est.... In vultu, ut vultum affabilem et jucundum judici et astantibus ostendat, ut reddat eos benevolos sibi. Nam humilem et benevolum debet se ostendere advocatus.... In gestu: ut caput, manus, vel pedes non ducat. Nam gravitatem quoad omnia, et mentis maturitatem debet ostendere." William Durand, *Speculum iudiciale* 1.4 *De aduocato* §5.6, at 1:269, reproduces this passage almost verbatim. Similar advice appears also in Étienne Aufréri, *Scholion* to Guillaume Du Breuil, *Stillus supercliti Parlamenti*, at 2ra.

honey in my mouth. Your word is a lamp for my feet and a light for my path. Your justice is like unto the mountains of God and unto the great abyss.[61]

Immoderately unctuous as this may seem to modern tastes, it reflects fashions current in thirteenth-century rhetoric. *Captatio benevolentiae*, the art of extravagant praise calculated to gain the reader's favor, formed a basic element in the teaching in schools of the *artes dictandi*, and students were trained to compose them. Durand, writing in the light of long judicial experience, was probably reflecting the sort of thing he had heard often enough when he sat as a judge in the papal curia.[62] While praising the judge, the advocate also needed to add a few words to commend his client and the client's case to the judge's good graces. In this portion of his statement, he needed to impress the judge not only with the strength of his case, but also with his client's honesty, piety, and good faith in bringing or defending the present action.[63]

Advocates were encouraged to maintain a dignified collegiality with fellow advocates and proctors who practiced in the same court. The bar of a bishop's consistory was invariably small—in England it seldom numbered more than a half-dozen advocates at most, although on the Continent it might be slightly larger—and its members unavoidably opposed one another regularly. Professional life in such a tiny closed community could quickly turn exceedingly unpleasant unless its members took care to behave with decorum and to treat their colleagues with wary respect.[64] Junior advocates were expected to defer to their seniors, while more mature advocates were cautioned to beware of their younger brethren:

61. William Durand, *Speculum iudiciale* 1.4 *De aduocato* §5.4, at 1:269: "Item humiliter audiat loquentem iudicem, et eius dicta laudibus extollat, dicens ei: 'Domine Deus noster, quam admirabilis est sapientia tua! Ignitum eloquium tuum vehementer, et seruus tuus dilexit illud. Letabor ego super eloquia tua, sicut qui inuenit spolia multa [cf. Ps. 118:103]. Quam dulcia faucibus meis eloquia tua super mel ori meo. Lucerna pedibus meis verbum tuum, et lumen semitis meis [Ps. 118:105]. Iustitia tua sicut montes Dei iusticia tua abyssus multa [Ps. 35:7]' et sic quasi cervica sub eius capite ponat, ut in eius suffultus laudibus iudex molliter conquiescat."

62. Haskins, *Studies in Mediaeval Culture*, 3, 187. Obsequiousness toward judges has by no means gone out of style; see the serious suggestions of Evans, *Advocacy in Court*, 15–17, and the parody by Herbert, *Uncommon Law*, 7–9.

63. William of Drogheda, *Summa aurea*, 40–43, §§38–39.

64. Helmholz, *Canon Law and Ecclesiastical Jurisdiction*, 214–15; Lefebvre-Teillard, *Officialités*, 38–41; Martin V, *In apostolice dignitatis* §32 (1418), in Tangl, *Die päpstlichen Kanzleiordnungen*, 143.

Let the older advocate take care to watch out for the new one, just taken out of the oven of the schools, as it were, since he has the laws and statutes at his fingertips. . . . [A]nd because he burns with desire for vain glory, he is excessively tireless about winning, whence it often happens that he may prevail over this elders, who are oftentimes lazy and negligent.[65]

Other authorities, however, advised would-be clients that they would do well to choose a senior advocate in preference to a junior one, because even if the older man was not as well informed about the recent law as his younger colleague, the cunning he had acquired from practical experience would more than make up for that deficiency.[66]

When they faced one another on opposite sides of a case, as happened routinely, advocates should refrain from speaking ill of each other. When they disagreed, as was also inevitable, they were counseled to address one another with emollient phrases, such as "With all respect," "Saving your reverence," and the like. While it was obviously inadvisable for an advocate to applaud his opponent's brilliant advocacy or his skill in demolishing one's own arguments, it was appropriate to commend the adversary's legal knowledge, ability, and experience.[67]

An advocate, especially one acting for a plaintiff, wrote Johannes de Deo, should be as prudent as a serpent while appearing to be as simple as a dove so as to encourage his opponent to underestimate him.[68] The defendant's advocate should try to show indifference and might even feign sleep while his adversary was speaking, a ruse that according to William Durand wise advocates often adopted. But with his eyes closed, he should pay close attention to his opponent's every statement and keep track of anything

---

65. William Durand, *Speculum iudiciale* 1.4 *De aduocato* §9.3, at 1:280: "Item cautus sit antiquus aduocatus, ut nouum timeat, qui leges et iura in promptu habet, tanquam nouiter ex studii fornace eductus. . . . [E]t qui tanquam inanis gloriae cupidus fervet nimia diligentia in uincendo, ex quo fit ut saepe obtineat contra antiquos, qui ut plurimum sunt desides et remisi."

66. So held Gregorio Lopez, gloss to *Siete Partidas* 3.6.2 §2, quoted by Alonso Romero and Garrigas Acosta, "El régimen juridico," 67: "Non confidas in medico novo, qui est homicida parentum, nec in advocato novello, qui est confusor litium . . . quia utiliores sunt antiqui advocati, licet minoris scientiae, propter practicam."

67. Aegidius de Fuscarariis, *Ordo iudiciarius* §110, at 185; Bonaguida, *Summa introductoria* 1.3.8, at 156; William Durand, *Speculum iudiciale* 1.4 *De aduocato* §4.1–2, at 1:267.

68. Johannes de Deo, *Cauillationes aduocatorum* 1.9, in London, BL, MS Arundel 459, at 4ra: "Item aduocatus actoris sit prudens sicut serpens: ostendat se esse simplicem sicut columbam [cf. Matt. 10:16] et tunc adversarius minis minus timebit."

that he could later throw back at him.[69] When his own time arrived, he should get up slowly and reluctantly, as if he had just awakened, so as to keep his adversary off guard as long as possible.

Although he might cultivate a distracted appearance, a shrewd practitioner should keep track of every word his opponent uttered and probe continually for weaknesses that he could exploit. [70] If the other man seemed to be irritable, for example, the crafty advocate could try to formulate a needling statement that, while superficially polite, carried disparaging undertones that could provoke a fit of anger. This had two advantages: at the least, it might distract the other man and disrupt his train of thought. With luck, it might precipitate an outburst of temper that would offend the judge and raise doubts about the soundness of the adversary's case. Procedural writers strongly advised their readers to take note of what their opponent said, so that when their turn came they could use his own words to trip him up. It would be immensely gratifying, for instance, to be able to tell the judge, "My lord, the advocate for the other party referred to such-and-such a law in his favor. Let me now show that it actually supports my case," and then demonstrate that the opposing counsel had misunderstood the law.[71]

An advocate had to be brave, even audacious. "The laws don't help the timid," he was told, and he must not be afraid to stand up to his opponent. He needed to keep in mind the Virgilian adage "Fortune favors the bold." Nor should he be concerned about the harsh rejoinders that an opponent might throw at him.[72]

Authorities sternly discouraged disruptive behavior in court. They frequently complained about uproar in the courts and commanded proctors to keep silent and remain in their seats save when they had a matter to present. Advocates and proctors must refrain from interrupting while another was speaking. They must not shout at their opponents or insult them, let

---

69. William Durand, *Speculum iudiciale* 1.4 *De aduocato* §4.6–8, at 1:267–68, and §8.3, at 1:279; Bonaguida, *Summa introductoria* 1.3.9, at 156–57; Johannes de Deo, *Cauillationes aduocatorum* 1.10, London, BL, MS Arundel 459, at 4vb.

70. Bonaguida, *Summa introductoria* 1.3.6, at 155–56; William Durand, *Speculum iudiciale* 1.4 *De aduocato* §4.9, at 1:268.

71. Bonaguida, *Summa introductoria* 1.3.9, at 156–57; Johannes de Deo, *Cauillationes aduocatorum* 1.10, in London, BL, MS Arundel 459, at 4rb; Aegidius de Fuscarariis, *Ordo iudiciarius*, 184, §110; William Durand, *Speculum iudiciale* 1.4 *De aduocato* §4.6–8, at 1:267–68.

72. William of Drogheda, *Summa aurea*, 57, §57. The Virgilian reference is to *Aeneid* 10.284.

alone call them names such as "Bandit!" or "Liar!"[73] Instead, when their case was called, they should rise and state their business quietly and without rancor. When they had finished, they should immediately resume their seats.[74] An advocate should wage his battles with reason and wit, not with insults and contumely. Those who ignored this advice could find themselves suspended from practice. Really egregious offenders could be disbarred permanently, although in practice this was rare.[75]

PRESENTING THE CLIENT'S CASE

The Libellus

When a case opened, proctors for the parties presented the written mandates that authorized them to appear on behalf of their clients. Once the judge had approved these documents, the plaintiff's advocate or proctor read aloud his client's *libellus*. He then presented two copies to the judge, who directed the registrar to affix the judge's seal to them as evidence that they had been officially received. The registrar gave one copy to the defendant and filed the other in the court's records. Once the defendant had heard the reading of the plaintiff's *libellus* and received a copy of it, he could either admit his opponent's assertions and attempt to reach a settlement then and there or else contest the plaintiff's claims. Authorities repeatedly urged judges to encourage parties to compromise their differences at this point in order to avoid litigation.[76] If the defendant wished to contest the matter, he could enter a general denial then and there. Alternatively he might seek an adjournment, generally for several

---

73. On not interrupting, Benedict XII, *Decens et necessarius* (1340) §§1, 11, and Gregory XI, *Quamvis a felicis* §4, in Tangl, *Die päpstlichen Kanzleiordnungen*, 118, 120, 129; William Durand, *Speculum iudiciale* 1.4 *De aduocato* §4.4, at 1:267. On avoiding insults, John Buckingham, bishop of Lincoln, in Lincoln Archive Office, Lincoln diocesan records, Register 12, at 389, quoted in Owen, *Medieval Canon Law*, 23–24.

74. *Constitutiones et statuta*, 372–73, §§23–26.

75. Martin V, *In apostolice dignitatis* §34, in Tangl, *Päpstlichen Kanzleiordnungen*, 144; Ricardus Anglicus, *Summa de ordine iudiciario*, 34–35, §27; Bonaguida, *Summa introductoria* 1.3.7, at 156; Aegidius de Fuscarariis, *Ordo iudiciarius*, 184 §110; William Durand, *Speculum iudiciale* 1.4 *De aduocato* §4.3, at 1:267.

76. Thus, e.g., Dig. 12.1.21; Gratian D. 90 c. 9; X 1.36.2, 7; Halberstadt consistory court statutes (1442) §31, in Hilling, "Sechs Gerichtsordnungen," 337; Guido de Baysio, *Rosarium* to D. 96 c. 11, in CUL, Peterhouse MS 27, at 89rb–va, and Peterhouse MS 35, at 107rb.

weeks, so that he could prepare a reply and counterclaim (*libellus reconventionalis*).⁷⁷

Exceptions

Once the plaintiff's claim and the defendant's denial and counterclaim, if any, had been submitted to the court, the defendant had an opportunity to put forward exceptions to the plaintiff's claims. Procedural writers distinguished three principal types of exceptions: dilatory, peremptory, and mixed. Dilatory exceptions raised objections about such matters as the jurisdiction of the court, the suitability of the judge to hear the case, the appropriateness and accuracy of statements in the opponent's *libellus*, or his capacity to bring or defend the action.⁷⁸ Dilatory exceptions, as the name implies, delayed the progress of a case, since they had to be heard and decided before the matter could proceed further. Consequently, they had to be raised during the opening stages of litigation, before the trial of issues formally commenced. Defendants often raised exceptions against the plaintiff's *libellus*, claiming, for example, that statements in it were vague, faulty, or redundant, or that they failed to disclose a legitimate cause of action. The plaintiff's advocate could deal with this by amending his *libellus* or making an oral rebuttal (*replicatio* or *reconventio*) contesting the grounds for the exception.⁷⁹

Peremptory exceptions, unlike dilatory exceptions, could be raised at any point prior to the pronouncement of the final decision, although in practice they were normally entered only after the trial proper had begun. Peremptory exceptions challenged the substance of the plaintiff's case. Such an exception might, for example, allege that the plaintiff's claims were fraudulent or that they breached a statute, or perhaps that the matter

---

77. Requests for adjournments were routinely granted; Tancred, *Ordo iudiciarius* 2.17.4, at 181; William Durand, *Speculum iudiciale* 2.1 *De dilationibus* §1.18–19, at 1:495. On the *libellus reconventionalis*, see Bencivene, *Summa de ordine iudiciorum* 2.5, at 26–27; Tancred, *Ordo iudiciarius* 2.19, at 187–89; Gratia, *De iudiciario ordine* 2.2, at 357–58; Durand, *Speculum iudiciale* 2.1 *De reconventione*, at 1:546–51.

78. Bernard of Parma, *Glos. ord.* to X 2.25.12 v. *in dilatoriis*; Bencivenne, *De ordine iudiciorum* 2.2, at 23–24; Tancred, *Ordo iudiciarius* 2.1, at 140–42; Gratia, *De iudiciario ordine* 1.9.2, at 351; William Durand, *Speculum iudiciale* 2.1 *De exceptionibus et replicationibus* §1 pr., 5–6, at 1:507, 508.

79. Dig. 44.1.2; Bencivenne, *De ordine iudiciorum* 2.4, at 25–26; Tancred, *Ordo iudiciarius* 2.5.5, at 146; Aegidius de Fuscarariis, *Ordo iudiciarius*, 119–21, §65; William Durand, *Speculum iudiciale* 2.1 *De exceptionibus et replicationibus* §5.1, at 1:531.

had already been adjudicated in an earlier lawsuit. If sustained, such a peremptory exception led to a summary judgment in favor of the defendant, which terminated the action.[80]

Mixed exceptions shared some characteristics of the other two kinds of exceptions and hence did not fit neatly under either classification. Thus, for example, an exception that the plaintiff was excommunicate and therefore lacked standing to pursue his claims belonged to the mixed category because if the plaintiff had once been excommunicated but the excommunication had since been lifted, then even if the exception were proved, it would not bar him from being heard in court. At the same time, excommunication was such a fundamental disqualification that it seemed preposterous not to allow it to be raised, even after the beginning of the trial proper. Hence this exception fell into the "mixed" category.[81]

The judge had to rule on each exception before the case could proceed further. This ruling took the form of an interlocutory decision. Since defendants regularly sought to delay matters in the hope that their adversaries might settle or even abandon their claims, it was not unusual for defense lawyers to interpose a cloud of exceptions in order to protract proceedings as long as possible. This tactic could become expensive, however, since if the judge concluded that a litigant was deliberately being obstructive and wasting the court's time, he could require the party who raised a failed exception to reimburse his opponent for the expenses incurred in contesting it.[82]

The purpose of this process was to define the questions at stake in the case (or in common law terms, to join issue) so that by the time that he had ruled on all the exceptions raised, the judge had a precise notion of the differences between the parties and the specific points on which he would ultimately need to rule. Only after this could the trial stage of an action, or *litis contestatio*, actually begin.

---

80. Dig. 44.1.3; Bencivenne, *De ordine iudiciorum* 2.2, at 23–24; Tancred, *Ordo iudiciarius* 2.5.3, at 143–45; Gratia, *De iudiciario ordine* 1.9.2, at 351; William Durand, *Speculum iudiciale* 2.1 *De exceptionibus et replicationibus* 1.1–3, at 1:507–508.

81. William Durand, *Speculum iudiciale* 2.1 *De exceptionibus et replicationibus* §1.7–8, at 1:508–509; Helmholz, *Canon Law and Ecclesiastical Jurisdiction*, 323–25.

82. Bernard of Parma, *Glos. ord.* to X 2.25.12 v. *condemnandus*; Bencivenne, *De ordine iudiciorum* 2.3, at 25; Tancred, *Ordo iudiciarius* 2.5.4, at 145; William of Drogheda, *Summa aurea*, 259–74, §348. Judicial rulings in many cases far more often related to exceptions than they did to factual allegations, as Smail notes in *Consumption of Justice*, 208–9.

Litis Contestatio

The parties themselves, rather than their advocates, formally opened the trial. The plaintiff (or his proctor, if the plaintiff was illiterate) read the amended form of his *libellus* that had emerged from the pretrial exchange of exceptions and replies to exceptions.[83] The defendant customarily responded with a brief general denial of each and all of the plaintiff's claims. At the Roman curia, for example, it was customary to declare: "I deny what was stated in the way that it was stated and I ask that what was requested not be granted." It was essential that some such exchange of claim and reply take place, because otherwise the entire proceedings could be declared void.[84]

Once the trial had commenced, the parties took the calumny oath in which they swore that they would present a bona fide case for the court to decide. The plaintiff declared that he truly believed that he had good cause to bring his action, that he was not doing so maliciously, that the evidence he presented would be sound, and that he would not seek unnecessary delays in the proceedings. The defendant then swore that he was defending the action in good faith, that he had good grounds for doing so, was not seeking to obstruct his opponent, and would employ no vexatious tactics in his defense. Both parties had to give their word, moreover, that they had not given or promised any payment to the judge, the witnesses, or anyone else involved in the case, save for their advocates and others, such as proctors and notaries, to whom payment was authorized. Should a plaintiff refuse to take the calumny oath, his case was forthwith dismissed, while a de-

---

83. Tancred, *Ordo iudiciarius* 3.1.2, at 196: "Litis contestatio fit per narrationem et responsionem partium in iudicio factam." This became the standard definition, repeated almost verbatim by, e.g., Geoffrey of Trani, *Summa super titulis* to X 2.5.1 §1, at 83va; Bernard of Parma, *Glos. ord.* to X 2.5.1 v. *responsiones*; Hostiensis, *Summa aurea*, lib. 2, *De litis contestatione* §1, at 79ra; William Durand, *Speculum iudiciale* 2.2 *De lite contestatione* §1, at 1:563.

84. Thus, Goffredus de Trano, *Summa super titulis* to X 2.5.1 §3, at 84ra–rb: "Sed si reus neget omnia in libello contenta, ut enim sic respondeat sicut in curia romana fieri consueuit: 'Nego narrata ut narrantur et dico petita fieri non debere,' puto plene fieri litis contestatio quasi ad omnia singulariter sit responsum." This formula was repeated by leading commentators, e.g., Hostiensis, *Summa aurea*, lib. 2, *De litis contestatione* §2, at 79ra; William Durand, *Speculum iudiciale* 2.2 *De lite contestatione* §2.2, at 1:563. See also Helmholz, *Canon Law and Ecclesiastical Jurisdiction*, 325–27, and "The *litis contestatio*," 80. On voiding proceedings for lack of claim and denial, see X 2.5.1 (Gregory IX).

fendant who failed to take the oath was deemed to have confessed and had summary judgment entered against him.[85]

Articles and Positions

Once both parties had taken the calumny oath, the judge (on the advice of his clerks) assigned court dates for the submission of written articles of proof (*articuli*) and positions (*positiones*). The plaintiff's articles consisted of a list of the points that he expected his witnesses and documents to prove, while the defendant's positions consisted of brief rejoinders to each of those points.[86] In practice, the plaintiff's articles usually amounted to little more than a slightly modified version of the claims contained in his *libellus*, divided this time into a series of separate paragraphs, each prefaced by the phrase "I maintain that" (*pono quod*) or "he maintains that" (*ponit quod*). The defendant's responses were usually even briefer. They usually consisted simply of a rehearsal of the articles, prefaced by a short denial or admission, such as "he believes" (*credit*) or "he does not believe" (*non credit*), "he believes otherwise" (*credit contrarium*) or "he doubts" (*dubitat*), and the like, concerning each article.[87] If a defendant admitted one or more of the plaintiff's positions, judges accepted this as a confession of that part of the plaintiff's claims and did not require that it be proved.

85. Bencivenne, *De ordine iudiciorum* 3.1–3, at 46–52; Tancred, *Ordo iudiciarius* 3.2.1–6, at 201–207; Bernard of Pavia, *Summa decretalium* 1.34.5 and 2.17.4, at 31, 52; Bernard of Parma, *Glos. ord.* to X 2.7.1 v. *calumniae iuramentum*; Steins, "Ordentliche Zivilprozeß," 221–22, 227, 249–51.

86. Bonaguida, *Summa introductoria* 3.5–6, at 274–82; Gratia, *Summa de iudiciario ordine* 2.5, at 369; William Durand, *Speculum iudiciale* 1.4 *De teste* §5, at 1:313–18. For some examples of articles used in practice, see *Select Cases*, ed. Adams and Donahue, C.11, C.12, C.14, C.17, D.8, D.11, at 162, 191–92, 209–10, 239–40, 436, 497–98. The use of *positiones* apparently developed during the early thirteenth century. Tancred, *Ordo iudiciarius* 3.3, at 209, barely mentions them, but Gratia of Arezzo, writing after 1237, devoted a lengthy treatment to the topic in *Summa de iudiciario ordine* 2.3, at 361–367. See also Durand, *Speculum iudiciale* 2.2 *De positionibus*, at 1:580–603. As Donahue noted in his introduction to *Select Cases* (ed. Adams and Donahue, 45), advocates' fees for drawing up *positiones* and *articuli* added significantly to the costs of litigation. This was offset to some degree by the fact that statements that the defendant admitted in his *positiones* did not have to be proved, which saved some time, and by the introduction in the late thirteenth century of the articulated *libellus*, which combined articles and *libellus* into a single document (Helmholz, *Canon Law and Ecclesiastical Jurisdiction*, 322–23).

87. For specimens from actual cases, see *Select Cases*, ed. Adams and Donahue, C.12, at 179–90; C.14, at 210; D.5, at 390–91; and D.8, at 434–35.

Evidence: Witnesses and Documents

Once the judge had received the articles and positions of the parties, he scheduled hearings for the parties to produce witnesses. The number of witnesses varied considerably. The testimony of at least two credible witnesses was necessary in most cases to provide canonical "full proof," unless documents or other kinds of evidence were available.[88] The judge also had the authority to limit the number of witnesses he would allow. He could in addition compel witnesses who failed to appear, or who appeared but refused to testify, to do so under pain of ecclesiastical sanctions, up to and including excommunication. The law did not allow him, however, to force a witness to answer questions that would incriminate him.[89]

The number of witnesses that litigants produced was partly a function of their financial and social resources. In addition to the charges that each party had to bear for travel, meals, lodging, and other expenses that his witnesses might incur, persuading friends and associates to give testimony represented a charge against a litigant's social capital.[90] When the testimony of witnesses who lived far away was required, judges commonly either sent one of the court's notaries or else appointed a cleric from the witnesses' vicinity to question them under oath, record their replies, and report the questions and answers in a sworn deposition. It was usually the proctor's job to locate his client's witnesses and to see that they appeared in court at the appointed time. Although proctors and advocates were not supposed to discuss witnesses' testimony with them, this rule may not always have been scrupulously observed.[91]

Each party produced its witnesses in the presence of the opposing party,

---

88. Tancred, *Ordo iudiciarius* 3.7, at 228–30; William Durand, *Speculum iudiciale* 1.4 *De teste* §11, at 1:335–36. The two witness rule as Gratian noted (C. 2 q. 4 pr.) came from biblical sources (Deut. 17:6; John 8:17; 2 Cor. 13.1; Heb. 10:28).

89. X 2.20.37, 2.21.1–3; Tancred, *Ordo iudiciarius* 3.6, at 228; Herde, "Zeugenzwang in den päpstlichen Delegationsreskripten"; Bernard of Parma, *Glos. ord.* to X 2.20.37 v. *de causis*; Helmholz, "The Privilege and the *Ius Commune*," 17–46.

90. Cod. 4.20.11; Johannes Teutonicus, *Glos. ord.* to C. 2 q. 1 c. 7 v. *expendisse*; Johannes Andreae, *Glos. ord.* to VI 1.3.11 v. *expensas*; William Durand, *Speculum iudiciale* 2.3 *De expensis* §6.21, at 1:910.

91. Tancred, *Ordo iudiciorum* 3.8.2, at 233–35; Bonaguida, *Summa introductoria* 1.3.12, at 158; Aegidius de Fuscarariis, *Ordo iudiciarius*, 185, §110; William Durand, *Speculum iudiciale* 1.4 *De aduocato* §9.4, at 1:280–81.

and as many as three hearings could be scheduled for this process.[92] The witnesses took an oath to tell the truth, the whole truth, and nothing but the truth about everything they knew in connection with the action in which they were to testify. The judge cautioned them that they must testify only to events they had seen or heard, but not about what they believed or thought or had heard from others. He likewise admonished witnesses not to discuss their testimony with anyone until the court had made the testimony of all the witnesses public.[93]

Before any witnesses could actually testify, the advocates (or the proctors, if no advocate was engaged in the case) had to provide the judge with the interrogatories (*interrogationes*), the lists of questions that they wished witnesses to answer. Although they were entitled to ask for a postponement to allow them time to produce these lists, drafting them did not usually demand undue time or effort, since they rarely amounted to much more than a restatement with minor verbal changes of the *articuli* and *positiones* that the parties had already submitted. *Interrogationes* were addressed to the judge and might be cast either in the form of a set of questions for the judge to put to the witnesses or as a series of directions to the judge concerning the topics that the advocate or proctor wished the witnesses to address.[94]

Once witnesses had been produced and sworn and the judge had received the interrogatories from the advocates or proctors he, or often another court functionary (sometimes a specialized examiner of witnesses, a commissary judge, or a notary), proceeded to question each witness. The judge or his substitute questioned each witness separately and privately in the presence of a notary, who recorded the questions and summarized the witnesses' responses.[95] The practice of examining witnesses individually and

---

92. Tancred, *Ordo iudiciarius* 3.8.2, at 235–36; Gratia, *Summa de iudiciario ordine* 2.4 and 2.6.1, at 368, 370; William Durand, *Speculum iudiciale* 1.4 *De teste* §4.1–3, at 1:.306–7.

93. Tancred, *Ordo iudiciarius* 3.9.1, at 236–37; Gratia, *Summa de ordine iudiciario* 2.6.1, at 371; William Durand, *Speculum iudiciale* 1.4 *De teste* §4.1–2, at 1:311. Exceptions to the rule that witnesses must not testify to hearsay arose in cases where consanguinity or matters concerning reputation (*fama*) were at issue.

94. Bonaguida, *Summa introductoria* 3.7–8, at 282–300; Aegidius de Fuscarariis, *Ordo iudiciarius*, 104–7, §§55–56; Tancred, *Ordo iudiciarius* 3.3, at 207–10; William Durand, *Speculum iudiciale* 1.4 *De teste* §6, at 1:319–23. See the examples from practice in *Select Cases*, ed. Adams and Donahue, C.11, C.12, C.14, C.18, at 162–64, 192–93, 211–13, 269–73; John Morton, *Register* 1:88–92, no. 258.

95. Tancred, *Ordo iudiciarius* 3.9.2, at 237–38; Gratia, *Summa de ordine iudiciorum* 2.6.1, at 371; Bernard of Pavia, *Glos. ord.* to X 2.20.52 v. *examinare sigillatim*; Hostiensis,

in secret rested upon the biblical tale of Susanna and the Elders that appears in the Vulgate version of the Book of Daniel (13:42–63).[96] The episode concerns two elderly judges who falsely accuse a beautiful young woman named Susanna of adultery. The prophet Daniel saves her from a death sentence by questioning each of the elders individually. By ferreting out incidental details in their allegations, Daniel is able to demonstrate that their stories are inconsistent, which casts doubt on their accusation and thus saves Susanna from wrongful conviction of a capital crime. Interrogatories followed Daniel's example by including questions about details incidental to the events they were mainly concerned with—where events took place, who was present, what they were wearing, what the weather was like, and so forth.

Judges in romano-canonical courts generally followed closely the lines of questioning set forth in the interrogatories they had been given. Although they were free to add further questions, in practice they seldom did so.[97] Judges or their substitutes usually had to translate the questions they asked into the vernacular in order to be understood, and witnesses of course replied in their native tongue. The notaries who kept the record of the proceedings then had to summarize the witnesses' responses in Latin, although occasionally they might include a phrase or two from a witness's statement in the vernacular. The resulting records of testimony are thus far from being verbatim transcripts of what was said. Not only were they filtered through multiple translations done on the fly, but also the notaries who redacted them usually provided only what they took to be the gist of what a witness said and seldom attempted to reproduce the actual dialogue between the questioner and the witness.[98]

Lectura to X 2.20.52 §2 v. *sigillatim*, vol. 2, at 105rb; William Durand, *Speculum iudiciale* 1.4 *De teste* §7.2–3, at 1:324–25.

96. It appears in the Septuagint as the Book of Susanna, immediately following the Book of Daniel, but modern scholars generally relegate it to the Apocrypha.

97. Bencivenne, *Summa de ordine iudiciorum* 3.11, at 70–71; Tancred, *Ordo iudiciarius* 3.9.2, at 238–40; Gratia *Summa de iudiciorum ordine* 2.6.2, at 371–72; Bernard of Parma, *Glos. ord.* to X 2.19.11 v. *interrogationes*; William Durand, *Speculum iudiciale* 1.4 *De teste* §7.3–5, at 1:324–25.

98. Numerous records of witnesses' depositions appear in Adams and Donahue, *Select Cases*; see, among others, A.1, at 2–3; A.2, at 4–7; C.6, at 129–32; C. 8, at 147–54, and D.17, at 618–25. Records of witnesses' depositions, sometimes with verbatim quotations in the vernacular, are particularly common in defamation cases; see, e.g., *Select Cases on Defamation*, 5–10, 13, 15. Samples of deposition records from the Continent may be found in *Documenten uit de Praktijk*, no. 43, at 59–62, and Hubald of Pisa, *Imbreviaturbuch*, nos. 4, at 89–93; 22, at 106–107; 42, at 127–28; 44, at 129–32; and 53, at 139–41.

After all the witnesses had been questioned and copies of their depositions prepared, the court scheduled a further hearing for the "publication" of their testimony. Both parties had to be present to certify that they did not intend to call any further witnesses and to petition jointly that the recorded testimony be made public. When the judge granted their petition, he directed his notary to read the depositions (or at least some of them) aloud, after which he furnished copies to each party and scheduled a further session to hear and adjudicate any exceptions the parties might wish to raise concerning the fitness of the witnesses to testify or the content of their evidence.[99]

As soon as they received the witnesses' evidence, the advocates or proctors for the parties began to review the record to discover how well the testimony bore out the points they wished to prove and where it contradicted or cast doubt on the assertions they had submitted to the court in articles and positions. They also needed to devise ways to minimize evidence that seemed unfavorable to their case. In this process, it was customary for advocates to mark up the record in red ink, noting which article or position each piece of evidence related to and commenting on the relevance of the testimony and the reliability (or unreliability) of the witness.[100]

When they had completed their study of the record, the parties or their representatives had the opportunity at the next hearing to raise objections that they hoped would offset the testimony of any damaging witnesses. If they could show, for example, that such a witness was a heretic, an excommunicant, a known enemy of one party or a relative or close friend of the opposing party, it might be possible to persuade the judge to exclude his testimony altogether. The process also gave litigants a welcome opportunity to air in public derogatory comments about their opponent and the witnesses who supported him without fear of being sued for defamation.[101]

---

99. Bencivenne, *Summa de ordine iudiciorum* 3.11, at 70–71; Tancred, *Ordo iudiciarius* 3.10, at 240–43; Gratia, *Summa de iudiciorum ordine* 2.6.3, at 372–73; William Durand, *Speculum iudiciale* 1.4 *De teste* §8.1–2, at 1:329.

100. This process is describd in detail in Bonaguida, *Summa introductoria* 3.9, at 300–303; Aegidius de Fuscarariis, *Ordo iudiciarius*, 111–13, §60; William Durand, *Speculum iudiciale* 1.4 *De teste* §9.1–3, at 1:331–332; and *Iste est modus prosequendi in causas*, in Logan, *Medieval Court of Arches*, 93. For an example of a set of depositions rubricated in this fashion, see *Picheford* c. *Nevill* (1267–72) in *Select Cases*, ed. Adams and Donahue, C.18, no. 12, at 311–21.

101. Bonaguida, *Summa introductoria* 3.10, at 303–306; Bencivenne, *De ordine iudiciorum* 3.11, at 71; Tancred, *Ordo iudiciarius* 3.6 and 3.11, at 222–28, 243–45; Gratia, *Summa de ordine iudiciario* 2.6.1 and 2.6.3, at 370–73; William Durand, *Speculum iudiciale* 1.4 *De*

As usual, the party who raised an exception needed to prove his contention, the opposing party had an opportunity to respond in an effort to forestall the exception, and the judge had to rule on the issues that this raised before matters could proceed. All of this offered yet further opportunities to delay conclusion of the lawsuit and put additional pressure on the adversary either to settle the dispute or perhaps to abandon it.

Although relevant documents could be introduced into evidence at several points in the proceedings, it was common to wait to produce them until after the testimony of witnesses and been published. Public instruments produced by a notary public, authenticated by a seal, or taken from official records, such as charters, privileges, contracts, court judgments and the like, not surprisingly carried greater evidential weight than informal private documents, such as account books, letters, or memoranda.[102] Documents introduced in evidence were read into the record by the judge or one of his clerks. The opposing party had the right to examine the original document and usually had a notary produce an authentic copy for his own use; for this, he naturally paid a fee.

Each party had the chance to raise exceptions against the documents produced by his opponent. Perhaps the most common exception was one that attacked the authenticity and reliability of key documents produced by the other party, on the grounds that they either were outright forgeries or bore signs of tampering. A document might be held suspect if, for example, any words had been erased, added, or crossed out, if the text was written in a variety of hands, or if it bore other signs of alteration.[103] Exceptions against documents, like other exceptions, had to be argued and the judge needed to examine the questioned instrument closely. If necessary, he might summon the notary who had produced it or the persons who had witnessed it to testify concerning its authenticity before rendering a judgment. All of this naturally delayed resolution of the case still further.[104]

---

teste §§1, 10, at 1:285–304, 332–35; *Iste est modus prosequendi in causas,* in Logan, *Medieval Court of Arches,* 93; Smail, *Consumption of Justice,* 95. Records of exceptions against witnesses appear in *Select Cases,* ed. Adams and Donahue, C.2, at 105–106; C.4, at 122–23; D.5, at 395–97; D.7, at 419–20; D.19, at 663–69.

102. X 2.22.2, 6, 9.

103. X 2.22.3, 6, 10. A party who relied on a forged document also ran the danger of being forced to pay his opponent's expenses, even if he won the case in first instance (Falkenstein, "Decretalia Remensia," 180–81 n. 80).

104. Bencivenne, *Summa de ordine iudiciorum* 3.12, at 71; Tancred, *Ordo iudiciarius* 3.13, at 248–57; Gratia, *De iudiciarum ordine,* 373–74; Bonaguida, *Summa introductoria* 1.3.14, at 159; William Durand, *Speculum iudiciale* 2.2 *De instrumentorum editione* §§5–6,

Argument

Once oral and written evidence had been submitted and exceptions against it had been adjudicated, the time had arrived for the advocates to display their ingenuity, erudition, and persuasive powers by arguing the legal issues in the case. Legal argumentation was both oral and written, but we know very little about what advocates actually said during the oral phase of it, since the court's notaries did not record it and only occasionally even mentioned that it took place. It is sometimes described in unofficial narratives, such as Thomas of Marlborough's account of the advocates' arguments in *Evesham* c. *Worcester* or Adam Usk's defense of the earl of Salisbury.[105]

Customary practice dictated that the plaintiff's advocate spoke first. After a brief introductory statement (*exordium*),[106] he proceeded to lay out his case, following the order of the articles of proof he had submitted earlier, and attempted to demonstrate how the testimony and documents he had introduced supported each of them. He fortified these statements with citations to the law relevant to each article. When he had finished, the defendant's advocate rose and, after a short *exordium* of his own, attempted to destroy his opponent's argument by systematically demonstrating that both the evidence and the law contradicted each point that his adversary had just made. Like his opponent, the defendant's advocate tried to convince the judge that both evidence and law supported his written *positiones*. Writers on litigation tactics warned advocates to keep their oral references to legal sources vague and general, so as to deprive their opponent of the opportunity to seize upon them and try to refute the interpretation that they put on the sources. If the judge felt that an advocate for either party had failed to refer to a relevant legal point or

---

1:647–52; *Iste est modus prosequendi in causas*, in Logan, *Medieval Court of Arches*, 93–94. X 5.20.5 describes nine ways to test the authenticity of suspect documents. Lively accounts of such two such cases appear in Linehan, "Case of the Impugned Chirograph," and Thomas of Marlborough, *History of the Abbey of Evesham*, 296–98 §299.

105. See *Select Cases*, ed. Adams and Donahue, C.18, at 299–310, and D.19, at 640–41; Hubaldus of Pisa, *Imbreviaturbuch*, nos. 24 and 35, at 111 and 122; Thomas of Marlborough, *History of the Abbey of Evesham*, 302–10, §§305–13; Adam Usk, *Chronicle*, 96; Helmholz, *Canon Law and Ecclesiastical Jurisdiction*, 342.

106. Bonaguida, *Summa introductoria* 1.2, at 138–54, furnishes twenty-six specimen *exordia* as models that advocates could adapt to various situations; further examples appear in William Durand, *Speculum iudiciale* 1.4 *De aduocato* §6, at 1:271–77.

had neglected to mention a significant factual matter, he had the right, indeed the obligation, to supplement the advocate's argument.[107] When the defendant's counsel had finished, the plaintiff's advocate could if he chose make a reply (*responsio*), which the defendant then had a chance to refute.

Authorities admonished judges to listen patiently to the arguments, however long-winded they might be, and not to cut them off. Instead, the judge was supposed to allow advocates to take as much time as required for the exposition of their case.[108] Writers on professional conduct, however, encouraged advocates to try to be economical in their arguments and repeatedly warned that wordy, repetitious, and lengthy declamations were likely to exasperate the judge and might prejudice him against their client. Recurring complaints about the verbosity of lawyers, however, suggest that advocates frequently ignored these admonitions.[109]

When oral argument was completed, the advocates for the parties could also submit a set of written *allegationes* for the judge's consideration.[110] Canny advocates spelled out the legal citations on which they relied more precisely in these documents than they did in oral argument. The advocate had a legal obligation to make sure that his citations were accurate and that the laws and canons he cited were genuine and cur-

107. Bonaguida, *Summa introductoria* 1.3.9, 17, 21, at 156–57, 160–61, 163; Tancred, *Ordo iudiciarius* 3.15.5, at 266–67; William Durand, *Speculum iudiciale* 1.4 *De aduocato* §9.9, at 1:281, and 2.2 *De disputationibus et allegationibus aduocatorum* §5.3, at 1:750, §6.4–8, at 1:751–52.

108. Bencivenne, *Summa de ordine iudiciorum* 3.15, at 76; Tancred, *Ordo iudiciarius* 3.15.2–4, at 261–66; Gratia, *Summa de iudiciarum ordine* 2.8, at 274–78; Aegidius de Fuscarariis, *Ordo iudiciarius*, 116–21, §§63–65; Bonaguida, *Summa introductoria* 1.3.11 and 15, at 157–60; William Durand, *Speculum iudiciale* 1.4 *De aduocato* 4.11, and 2.2 *De disputationibus et allegationibus aduocatorum* §3.1, 5–7, at 1:268, 743–44.

109. For these admonitions, see, e.g., Bonaguida, *Summa introductoria* 1.3.6, 17, at 155–56, 160–61; William Durand, *Speculum iudiciale* 1.4 *De aduocato* §5.2, at 1:269; Benedict XII, *Decens et necessarium* §10, in Tangl, *Päpstlichen Kanzleiordnungen*, 120; Pierre de Fontaines, *Le conseil*, 57–58. Complaints about lawyers' wordiness appear in John of Salisbury, *Policraticus* 5.16, ed. Webb, at 1:350–51; Jacques de Vitry, *Historia occidentalis*, 82, c. 4; Philippe de Mézières, *Le songe du vieil pelerin* 3.254, at 2:324; Gregory XI, *Quamvis a felicis*, in Tangl, *Päpstlichen Kanzleiordnungen*, 128; Kerr, "Legal Practice," 383, among many others.

110. Tancred, *Ordo iudiciarius* 3.15.5, at 267–68. Examples of these appear in *Select Cases*, ed. Adams and Donahue (C.2, at 109; C. 18, at 299–310; and D. 10, at 469–75). Linehan, "An Impugned Chirograph," 488–95, presents a Spanish example.

rent, had not been repealed or superseded by subsequent enactments, and were properly applicable to the present situation. Failure to do so could even leave him open to criminal charges for attempting to deceive the court.[111]

Judgment

Once the advocates had finished their legal arguments, the judge scheduled a final session to wrap up the hearing of the case. At that time, he asked the advocate or proctor for each party whether they wished to add anything further. After they had formally declared that they had completed presentation of their case, the judge gave a brief oral summary of the points that had been made. Both parties then joined in a petition asking the judge to give his final verdict (*sententia diffinitiva*) in the case, and he in turn appointed a day for announcing his judgment.[112]

Once the designated day arrived the judge, seated on his judicial throne, personally read his decision aloud. Judgments varied considerably in length and content.[113] Many were brief to the point of being terse: just three or four sentences that simply stated the verdict. Other decisions went into a bit more detail by summarizing the evidence that led the judge to his conclusion. Judges almost invariably stated for the record that they had observed the prescriptions of the *ordo iuris* and that they had sought the opinions of legal experts (*iurisperiti*) before reaching a decision. They hardly ever analyzed the legal issues involved, although file copies of judicial decisions in the official's court at Cambrai, for example, occasionally instructed the clerk to add a note concerning relevant legal references. In English church courts, the advocates or proctors of the parties sometimes furnished the judge with a draft of the decision they wanted him to

111. Hostiensis, *Summa aurea*, lib. 1, tit. *De postulatione* §5, at 62va; William Durand, *Speculum iudiciale* 1.4 *De aduocato* §9.10, at 1:281.

112. William Durand, *Speculum iudiciale* 2.2 *De renunciatione et conclusione*, no. 3, at 1:755; Fournier, *Officialités*, 205.

113. Bencivenne, *De ordine iudiciorum* 3.16, at 77–80; Tancred, *Ordo iudiciarius* 4.1.1–5, at 268–76; Gratia, *De iudiciario ordine* 3.1, at 379–81; *Ordo iudiciarius "Scientiam,"* 64–66, §32; William Durand, *Speculum iudiciale* 2.3 *De sententia*, at 1:776–812. For texts of actual decisions, see *Select Cases*, ed. Adams and Donahue (C.1, at 102; C.6, at 137; C.17, at 263–64; D.19, at 679–80); *Documenten uit de Praktijk* (nos. 1–5, at 7–11; 8–14, at 14–23; 16, at 25–26,;18–21, at 27–33); Hubaldus of Pisa, *Imbreviaturbuch* (nos. 3, at 88–89; 23–24, at 107–111; 31, at 115–17; 35, at 119–22; 45, at 132–33; 47, at 133–34; 51 at 136–37), as well as throughout the *Registres de sentences de l'officialité de Cambrai*.

hand down. The judge could then choose the one that corresponded most closely to his view of the case, although he could of course amend the text as he saw fit.[114]

When the defendant prevailed in a civil action, the judgment simply acquitted him of the complaint that the plaintiff had brought against him and no further steps were required to carry the decision into effect. As a matter of self-protection, however, a defendant might well wish to make sure that the news that his name had been cleared was officially made known. For this purpose, he might ask the judge to see to it that the outcome was proclaimed publicly.[115]

A decision in favor of the plaintiff, on the other hand, did not necessarily mean that the defendant would comply with it or suffer the consequences—excommunication, payment of a fine, or performance of some penitential act, for example—that the judge had decreed. Unless the judge had incorporated an enforcement order in his decision, the plaintiff needed to apply for an order for execution of judgment. These applications were not automatically granted, and defendants had the right to oppose them. Even if the judge granted the order, the defendant could still postpone its implementation by filing an appeal against it.[116]

Costs

The victorious party, whether plaintiff or defendant, now needed to secure a costs order to receive reimbursement for the expenses that he had incurred. This was vitally important not only to the litigant, but also to his lawyers, who were likely to be among its principal beneficiaries.[117]

Litigation was expensive, and a continuing flow of demands for money was apt to haunt even the most affluent and determined parties to a lawsuit. Religious communities, both male and female, were notably keen par-

114. See, e.g., *Registres de sentences de l'officialité de Cambrai* (nos. 8, at 8–9; 55, at 26; 61, at 29; 75, at 36; 76 at 37); *Iste est modus prosequendi causas*, in Logan, *Medieval Court of Arches*, 94; Helmholz, *Canon Law and Ecclesiastical Jurisdiction*, 344.

115. *Iste est modus prosequendi in causas*, in Logan, *Medieval Court of Arches*, 97, and see, e.g., the decision in the case of *Smith* c. *Dolling* in *Select Cases*, ed. Adams and Donahue (C.6, at 137).

116. Tancred, *Ordo iudiciarius* 4.4, at 285–90; William Durand, *Speculum iudiciale* 2.3 *De executione sententiae* §1.1–4, at 1:813–14, §5.4, 1:822. Examples of appeals in *Select Cases*, ed. Adams and Donahue (B.3, at 91–92, and D.7, at 425–27).

117. Alonso Romero and Garrigas Acosta, "El régimen jurídico," 86; Smail, *Consumption of Justice*, 71.

ticipants in litigation, "a monastic pastime," as Robert Brentano called it, which they sometimes pursued to the brink of bankruptcy.[118]

Romano-canonical procedure employed a cost-shifting rule designed to discourage needless litigation. The rule as stated in Justinian's Code seems at first glance simple and straightforward: the party who lost a lawsuit became responsible for paying all the direct expenses that the winner incurred in fighting the action.[119] In theory, this was supposed to deter harassment by pointless litigation. Anyone who brought a foolish lawsuit or defended a hopeless case potentially put himself in financial jeopardy, for if he lost he might be condemned to pay not only his own expenses, but those of his opponent as well. In practice, matters seldom worked out as neatly as they were supposed to. Even if the victorious party obtained a judgment for costs, it could prove difficult or impossible to collect on it, as happened, for example, to the convent of Barnwell in a suit against the rector of St. Andrew's, Histon, a far from unique case.[120] The risk was slightly mitigated by taxation of costs, which invariably reduced the total sum that the victor claimed. Even so, the financial hazard to the losing party was real and even after taxation could be very substantial.

The belief that people would be deterred from frivolous lawsuits by the prospect of financial ruin depended on three doubtful assumptions. The first was that persons involved in a lawsuit made a rational analysis of the likely consequences of losing before they began an action or decided to defend themselves against one. The second was that it was possible to foretell with reasonable certainty what the costs of conducting a case were likely to be. The third was that litigants devised their litigation strategies primarily in order to secure a favorable judgment. In many cases, at least one of these assumptions was likely to be erroneous.

While motives for litigation no doubt varied enormously, emotional turmoil rather than cool calculation frequently seems to have been a major factor in the decision to go to court rather than dealing with the problem in some other way. Plaintiffs sometimes launched lawsuits out of indignation, envy, or hatred of the defendant. Defendants not infrequently put up a prodigious fight out of fear, greed, or pure spite. None of these emotions is likely to be conducive to a level-headed appraisal of the chances of losing and the resulting consequences.[121]

---

118. Brentano, *Two Churches*, 246; Sayers, *Papal Judges Delegate*, 212; Graham, *English Ecclesiastical Studies*, 267.

119. Cod. 3.1.13.6.

120. *Liber memorandorum ecclesie de Bernewelle*, 142–44, no. 63

121. Cipolla, "The Professions," 46–47; Smail, *Consumption of Justice*, 14–16, 87–88, 131.

The expense of pursuing a lawsuit hung like the sword of Damocles over both parties throughout litigation since the cost could not be reliably determined until the matter was finally closed, and by then the cumulative expenditure could be ruinous. Determining the price tag of litigation depended on variables that no one could accurately predict in advance. No litigant could know at the outset, for example, whether either he or his opponent might at some stage decide to make an appeal, perhaps to Rome. Even if it were possible to foretell this, moreover, there was no reliable way to calculate how much the journey would cost, how long it would take, what problems might arise along the way, what living costs would amount to while there, or how long the parties or their proctors would need to spend at the curia.[122]

Parties, furthermore, did not necessarily go to court in order to secure a favorable verdict from a judge. Filing a complaint, serving the defendant with a summons, or putting up a determined defense against a complaint were not necessarily motivated by an intention to carry the case to conclusion. Actions at law could readily serve purposes that had nothing to do with securing a verdict. Litigation could be a formidable pressure tactic for both parties. The act of reading out a plaintiff's *libellus* in open court, in addition to the procedural purpose that it served, was a threat to the defendant, since it could easily embarrass him and blacken his reputation in the community. The exceptions that a defendant's advocate or proctor raised against the plaintiff's claims and against his witnesses could be used as weapons in a grudge fight and might harass him sufficiently to lead him to settle or to withdraw from the contest.[123]

The great majority of lawsuits in ecclesiastical courts never proceeded to a final judicial decision. They commonly ended either in an out-of-court settlement or were abandoned partway through the process. Church courts as a matter of policy encouraged parties to compromise on their differences, either through an informal agreement reached between themselves or by an accord mediated with the aid of an arbiter or arbitrator.[124]

---

122. Sayers, *Papal Judges Delegate*, 266–68, cites some examples of ruinous cases; for the way costs could mount in papal courts, see Müller, "Streitwert und Kosten," 138–42, 149–51.

123. Smail, *Consumption of Justice*, 23, 72, 90–95.

124. Donahue, introduction to *Select Cases*, ed. Adams and Donahue, 55–56; Helmholz, *Canon Law and Ecclesiastical Jurisdiction*, 328. Gratian C. 2 q. 6 d.p.c. 33 and d.p.c. 39; the Liber Extra devoted a whole title to the subject of arbitration (X 1.43), as did William Durand, *Speculum iudiciale* 1.1 *De arbitro et arbitratore*, at 1:102–32. See also Council of Oxford (1222) c. 32, in Powicke & Cheney 1:116. For the distinction between

Lawsuits often seem to have been less about getting a judicial decision than they were about arriving at some arrangement that both parties would find tolerable. From the viewpoint of the parties to an action, the costs of litigation represented an investment of time, money, and other resources that, while it might not necessarily yield monetary profit, had the potential to produce other kinds of satisfaction that may have seemed more important to them.

Case Record

After the victor's advocate submitted his client's statement of expenses and the judge gave his ruling on costs, advocates needed to attend to a further task. At the end of this and every other hearing in a case, the advocates or proctors for the parties had to supervise the preparation of the record of the session (*acta*) by the court's notary to make sure that it accurately reflected the proceedings. Any necessary corrections, however minor, had to be made before the notary organized the notes that he made on loose scraps of parchment during sessions into final form and made a fair copy for the record. Once he had entered the *acta* in his register, it could no longer be changed without leaving traces that could raise suspicions of tampering. Unaltered entries in the notary's official act book were presumed to be correct, and the judge was bound to stand by them. It was the advocate's responsibility to see that nothing that might benefit his client was omitted and that everything that could redound to his favor appeared in the record, for as Bonaguida reminded his readers, "It often happens that the whole matter may be altered by even the slightest change of fact."[125]

An advocate also needed to be careful not to leave the court's premises before his opponent did, in order to make sure that once formal business had ended the adversary had no chance to be alone with the judge. Otherwise there was always the possibility that the other side might seize the opportunity to sow doubts about the case in the judge's mind. For the same reason, William Durand added, an advocate should remind the judge fre-

---

arbiter and arbitrator, see Tancred, *Ordo iudiciarius* 1.3.5, at 107 n. 36, and Durand, *Speculum iudiciale* 1.1 *De arbitro et arbitratore* §1.2–3, at 1:102–103. This distinction was not always observed in practice; see Fowler-Magerl, "Forms of Arbitration," and Martone, *Arbiter—Arbitrator*.

125. Bonaguida, *Summa introductoria* 1.3.18, at 161. Similarly Gratia, *Summa de iudiciarum ordine* 1.3.4, at 325–27, while William Durand reproduced Bonaguida's words practically verbatim in *Speculum iudiciale* 1.4 *De aduocato* §9.14, at 1:281.

quently that he must base his decision on the evidence and the arguments in court, not on information that he received off the record.[126]

LENGTH OF ACTIONS

Litigants, especially plaintiffs, have grumbled about the law's delays since antiquity. Justinian declared that lawsuits threatened to exceed the human life span and seemed likely to become immortal. Thirteen hundred years later, Dickens (among others) echoed that lament, while complaints from lawyers and laymen alike continue to reverberate in courthouse corridors and legislative chambers in the twenty-first century.[127] It is scarcely surprising that among their complaints critics of medieval courts invariably listed the excessive time needed to conclude lawsuits. They routinely imputed this to the greed of lawyers, whom they repeatedly described as prolonging lawsuits in order to fatten their wallets. As John Bromyard (fl. ca. 1390), a Dominican preacher, claimed:

> The profit that advocates will make causes the delays and protracted lawsuits that they cunningly contrive in the law courts. If a lawsuit were quickly concluded it would not be very profitable. It follows from this that cases of little value will never be decided, while those worth a lot of money will drag on for a long time before a final decision is handed down. Advocates would be more truthful if they began their presentations not with "In the name of God, Amen," bur rather [with] "In the name of hard cash, Amen." In their courts everything yields to money, and coin rather than God is listened to and served.[128]

---

126. William Durand, *Speculum iudiciale* 1.4 *De aduocato* §8.5 and *De teste* §1.67, at 1:279, 297; Franciscus de Platea (d. 1460), *Opus restitutionum* §110; Johannes de Deo, *Cauillationes aduocatorum* 1.11, in London, BL, MS Arundel 459, at 5rb.

127. Juvenal, *Satires* 16.46–47; Martial, *Epigrammaton* 7.65; Cod. 3.1.13 pr.: "Properandum nobis visum est, ne lites fiant paene immortales et vitae hominum modum excedant"; Dickens, *Bleak House*, chap. 8: "And thus, through years and years, and lives and lives, everything goes on, constantly beginning over and over again, and nothing ever ends."

128. John Bromyard, *Summa predicantium*, s.v. "Advocatus" §32, at 16va–vb: "Hic etiam causa est dilationum et longorum processum qui in arte et curiis fiunt aduocatorum, scilicet lucrum quod capiunt. Si enim causa statim determinaretur non esset multum lucratiua. Et ex hoc sequitur quod qui pecunia non habent, nunquam determinabitur; qui vero in pecunia abundat, diu expectabit, quia diffinitiua [s]ententia in longum protraheretur; minus veraciter incipiunt processus suos dicentes: 'In dei nomine amen.' Veracius dicerent ut frequenter 'In nummi nomine amen.' Quia ibi pecunie obediunt omnia, et in curiis illorum potius nummus quam deus auditur et expeditur."

Bromyard voiced a common sentiment. At Avignon, Pope Benedict XII objected to the "superfluities and irrelevancies" that lawyers introduced into litigation, and at Cambridge the university sought to prevent advocates from appearing in its chancellor's court at all, on the grounds that banishing them from the process would enormously diminish the time it took to settle cases.[129]

Church authorities, too, were convinced that lawsuits lasted far too long and that blame for this rested squarely on the shoulders of advocates and proctors. The canon *Properandum* of the Second Council of Lyons in 1274, for example, harked back to Justinian's complaint about immortal lawsuits and expressed the hope that that malicious prolongation of lawsuits could be prevented by imposing appropriate constraints on those who furnished legal services. A century later, Pope Gregory XI (r. 1370–78) was still complaining that advocates continued to afflict litigants with their "pernicious subtleties and perplexities," despite all the efforts of his predecessors to eradicate this plague upon the courts.[130]

Although advocates and proctors sometimes used the available procedural tools—especially exceptions and appeals—to drag out proceedings for months or even years on end, they could do this only so long as their clients were willing to pay for their efforts. Clients, not lawyers, bore much of the responsibility for prolonging litigation, despite the fact that authorities almost invariably blamed the lawyers and repeatedly threatened to penalize them for it.[131]

Scattered evidence shows lawyers at least occasionally acting against their own economic interests by taking measures to shorten litigation. They filed motions to hear cases in summary fashion, rather than insisting on the more lengthy regular procedure, which would have been more profitable. They sought adjournments of a case in hope of compromise (*sub spe concordie*), which spared their clients the expense of submitting further documents and paying the costs of additional time in court.[132]

The duration of lawsuits in church courts varied enormously. So many

129. Benedict XII, *Decens et necessarium* (1340) §10, in Tangl, *Päpstlichen Kanzleiordnungen*, 120; Markaunt Statutes c. 22, in Hackett, *Original Statutes of Cambridge*, 322–23; and *Statuta antiqua* c. 30, in *Documents Relating to Cambridge* 1:326.

130. 2 Lyon (1274) c. 19; *Quamvis a felicis*, pr. (1 March 1375), in Tangl, *Päpstliche Kanzleiordnungen*, 128.

131. See, e.g., X 2.14.5; Hostiensis, *Lectura* to VI 2.2.1 §7, at 11rb; William Durand, *Speculum iudiciale* 1.4 *De aduocato* §9.20, at 1:282; also Guenée, *Tribunaux et gens de justice*, 238; Smail, *Consumption of Justice*, 72.

132. Helmholz, "Ethical Standards," cites examples at 48–50.

variables were involved—the complexity of the issues, the number of witnesses, the efficiency of the judge, the ingenuity of the advocates, and the stubbornness of the litigants, among others—that it would be difficult, and possibly meaningless, to determine how long an average case lasted. Although ecclesiastical courts were notoriously slow, there is reason to believe that long drawn-out proceedings were the exception rather than the rule. One study shows that out of 287 cases heard in the archdeacon's court at Paris in the early sixteenth century, 81 lasted only a single day, while 48 others were finished within a week. At Marseilles, 24 out of a sample of 50 cases were completed within a year. Of those, 10 lasted three months or less, while at the other extreme 3 continued for three years or more. In contrast, the sole surviving set of *acta* from the consistory court of the diocese of Lincoln shows that at least in 1430–31, no case was concluded in less than ten months.[133]

SUMMARY PROCEDURE

Efforts to curb the length of legal actions became increasingly urgent as the romano-canonical procedural system itself grew more elaborate, more time-consuming, more expensive, and more widely used. "Lawsuits should be curtailed rather than drawn out," declared the fathers of the Fourth Lateran Council. Church tribunals during the thirteenth century experimented with plans that abbreviated full-scale civil procedure by omitting some steps in the process.[134] Boniface VIII approved the use of simplified forms of procedure in the prosecution of heretics and cases that involved ecclesiastical elections. The decretal *Saepe contingit* of Pope Clement V (r. 1305–14) in 1306, supplemented shortly thereafter by the constitution *Dispendiosam* of the Council of Vienne (1311–12), clarified the structure of summary procedure and encouraged its use throughout the whole of the Western Church.[135]

Papal documents habitually described summary procedures as judicial processes conducted "simply and plainly, without the clamor of lawyers and judicial formalities" (*simpliciter et de plano ac sine strepitu advocatorum*

---

133. Lefebvre-Teillard, *Officialités*, 63–64; Morris, "A Consistory Court," 157–58.

134. 4 Lat. (1215) c. 37 (= X 1.3.28); Hostiensis, *Lectura* to X 1.3.28 §11, vol. 1, at 22vb; synodal statutes of Bordeaux (1234) c. 122, *Statuts synodaux* 1:98; Statutes of Salisbury II (ca. 1238–44) c. 58, Statutes of Wells (ca. 1258) c. 71, and Statutes of Exeter II (1287) c. 45, in Powicke & Cheney 1:386, 622, and 2:1042; Lefebvre, "Les origines romaines"; Williman, "Summary Justice," 437–41; Steins, "Ordentliche Zivilprozeß," 211–17; Donahue, introduction to *Select Cases*, ed. Adams and Donahue, 58–59.

135. VI 1.6.43 and 5.2.20; Clem. 5.11.2; Council of Vienne c. 6, in *DEC* 1:363 and Clem. 2.1.2.

et figura iudicii). Although these terms occurred in various combinations in Roman legal texts, neither ancient jurists nor medieval civilians prior to Bartolus (ca. 1313–58) attempted to define just what the phrase meant in actual practice.[136] Clement V parsed the meaning of this formula in *Saepe contingit*, and Johannes Andreae elaborated on the pope's description in his ordinary gloss on the constitution.[137] Summary procedure was a shortened form of ordinary civil procedure designed to limit the opportunities for delay that it afforded. Under summary procedure, the parties did not need to file a written *libellus* or response in order to initiate proceedings, nor did they need to go through the formalities of *litis contestatio*. Hearings could be scheduled on feast days, dilatory exceptions and appeals were eliminated, the number of witnesses was restricted, and legal arguments and maneuvers by advocates and proctors were curtailed.

Steps that were essential to fairness, however, could not be omitted. The defendant had to be summoned and informed of the complaint against him, although this could be done either orally or in writing. The parties had to identify the issues on which they disagreed by submitting articles and positions so that the judge could clearly understand what he needed to decide. Both parties must have the chance to submit relevant written evidence and to produce witnesses that they hoped would support their contentions. It was up to the judge to decide whether to question witnesses on his own initiative or to put questions to them that the parties had suggested. When the parties had finished submitting their proofs, the judge must decide the case on the basis of the evidence they had produced in court and in accordance with the law. When he had reached his decision, the judge must summon the parties to hear his final verdict, which he must deliver both orally and in writing, although it made no difference whether he sat or stood when he announced it. These provisions of *Saepe contingit* outlined the basic elements of what was coming to be called "due process of law." Pope Clement further allowed the parties themselves to tailor summary procedure to suit their own preferences, provided that they omitted none of these essential steps.[138]

136. See, e.g., X 3.35.8 and 5.1.26; VI 1.6.43 and 5.2.20; Clem. 2.1.2; Cod. 3.28.33 pr. and 9.22.22.2. When Bartolus took up the subject in his commentary on the imperial constitution *Ad reprimendum* of Henry VII of Luxembourg, moreover, he relied heavily on Clem. 5.11.2 (Betti, "Dottrina costruita da Bartolo").

137. Nörr, "Textrationalität zur Zweckrationalität," and "Rechtsgeschichtliche Apostillen."

138. Johannes Andreae, *Glos. ord.* to Clem. 5.11.2 v. *necessario, non contradicentibus* and v. *partibus*. The English term "due process" appears, e.g., in *Haywode* v. *Abbess of Wher-*

One aim of summary procedure was to save litigants' time and money by reducing their need for the services of professional lawyers, as the phrase *sine strepitu advocatorum* suggests.[139] Minimizing the number of technical instruments such as *libelli, interrogationes,* and *allegationes* not only diminished the costs of producing multiple copies of legal documents, but also enabled ordinary people to assume greater control—and responsibility—over the litigation process. Excluding dilatory exceptions reduced the length of lawsuits by diminishing the number of court appearances, while forgoing legal argument relieved the parties of the cost of engaging learned counsel. Litigants and their legal advisers were quick to grasp the benefits of choosing summary process. Woodcock estimated that in the diocese of Canterbury, for example, only about a third of recorded instance cases in the fifteenth century followed the full canonical procedure, while the remainder were dealt with by summary process.[140]

APPEALS

Although summary procedure could save litigants time and money in courts of first instance, appeals retained the potential to increase the duration and expense of civil litigation. Appeals ran from lower courts to courts higher in the jurisdictional hierarchy. Thus, an appeal from the decision of a bishop's consistory court, for example, could be carried to the provincial court of the appropriate archbishop or to the papal curia, but not to any lower court. Those who could afford the expense always had the right to bypass the intermediate levels of the hierarchy by appealing directly to the pope as "the ordinary judge of everyone."[141]

Classical canon law was notoriously generous in providing opportunities for dissatisfied litigants to appeal not only at the end of a trial, but also during it. Parties, especially defendants, were not shy about taking advantage of this. Modern scholars have often seen this as a serious flaw—"mon-

---

well (1384) in *Year Books of Richard II*, 13; cf. Stephen of Tournai, *Summa* to C. 2 q. 1, at 158 and *Magna Carta* c. 29 and c. 39; see also Pennington, *Prince and the Law*, 5–6, 155–57; Reid, "Canonistic Contribution"; Helmholz, "Magna Carta and the *ius commune*," 356–57, and *Fundamental Human Rights*, 12–15.

139. Johannes de Legnano, *Super Clementina "Saepe,"* 22–23; Bouchat, "Procédures juris ordine," 385–86; Lefebvre, "Les origines romaines," 157–58.

140. Woodcock, *Medieval Ecclesiastical Courts*, 59.

141. Tancred, *Ordo iudiciarius* 4.5.4, at 292–93; William Durand, *Speculum iudiciale* 2.3 *De appellationibus* §4 pr., at 1:839. The decision of a bishop's official, however, could not be appealed to the bishop who appointed the official (Durand, *De appellationibus* 4.4, at 1:839–40).

strous," Maitland called it—in the canonical legal system. Medieval authorities were not blind to the problem either, and occasionally complained about it.[142] Despite the abuse to which the process was open, the availability of appeals remained an important strength of the romano-canonical legal system, because it provided ready remedies for mistakes and wrongs that were difficult, and sometimes all but impossible, to correct in some other procedural systems.

Canon law made it extremely easy to appeal. A litigant could do so as soon as the judge finished reading out his verdict simply by making an oral statement that he intended to appeal. Cautious litigants who preferred to deliberate and perhaps to seek legal advice had up to ten days from the date when the judge announced his decision in which to submit a written notice of appeal (*libellus appellationis*) to the judge and also to inform the opponent.[143] The appellant had to apply to the judge from whose decision he was appealing for letters dimissory, known as *apostoli*, directed to the appellate judge. These documents certified that an appeal was being made, described the issues in the case, and identified the grounds for appeal. Letters dimissory could either endorse the grounds for an appeal (*apostoli reverentiales*) or dispute them (*apostoli refutatorii*). In either case, should the judge fail to issue them within thirty days of receiving notification from a party he could be fined.[144]

The law deliberately made it difficult for a judge to disallow notices of appeal save for good cause.[145] Church authorities were aware that not ev-

---

142. Maitland, *Roman Canon Law*, 103–4; likewise Pollock and Maitland, *History of English Law* 1:114–16; Cheney, *From Becket to Langton*, 51–54, 63–69; Helmholz, *Spirit of Classical Canon Law*, 101; 4 Lat. (1215) c. 37 (= X 5.33.24); Müller, "Streitwert und Kosten," 151–53. The proclivity to appeal was not limited to ecclesiastical courts. Smail estimates, e.g., that in the city courts of Marseille at least half of the fourteenth-century civil cases that ended with a decision were appealed (*Consumption of Justice*, 85).

143. Tancred, *Ordo iudiciarius* 4.5.6–7, at 294–95; William Durand, *Speculum iudiciale* 2.3 *De appellationibus* §§5 pr. and 6.9, at 1:843, 846–47.

144. Tancred, *Ordo iudiciarius* 4.5.10–11, at 297–98; William Durand, *Speculum iudiciale* 4.2 *De apostolis seu libellis dimissorium* §3.1, 13, at 2:195, 197. Actual practice varied in different regions. Gratia, e.g., noted that "Isti apostoli hodie raro dantur" (*Summa* 3.3, at 384), while Donahue notes in his introduction to *Select Cases* (at 59) that no examples of *apostoli* were to be found among the Canterbury court records and he and Norma Adams edited.

145. X 1.29.28; 2.28.11; Tancred, *Ordo iudiciarius* 4.5.14, at 302–5; Hostiensis, *Summa*, lib. 2, tit. *De appellationibus* §2, at 126ra–rb.

ery appeal was meritorious and attempted to discourage those that were malicious or merely designed to delay final disposition of the matter. They adopted the Roman law rule that gave appellate judges the power to punish frivolous appeals with a substantial fine of fifty pounds of silver, and the Fourth Lateran Council made such an appellant responsible in addition for the costs that his opponent incurred in responding to the appeal.[146]

Implementation of a decision would be suspended until the appeal had been decided. The judge whose decision was under review dispatched the records of the case to the appellate judge, who reexamined the entire matter and could, if he deemed it necessary, call for additional witnesses and further evidence. Once he had reached a conclusion, the appellate judge either affirmed, quashed, or amended the original decision.[147] If he affirmed or amended the original judgment, his verdict normally included a clause returning the matter to the lower court for enforcement. When the higher court affirmed the judgment of the court below, the decision usually included an order that directed the appellant to pay the costs that his opponent had incurred in opposing the appeal.[148]

Parties almost always needed the aid of advocates and proctors during an appeal. A client might continue to use the services of the same lawyers who originally handled the case, especially if the appeal was to a nearby tribunal. Doing so had two advantages for the client. His advocate and proctor were already familiar with the issues and the evidence and would not need to start afresh. They were presumably aware of the difficulties that the case presented and were prepared to deal with them. In addition, the client might hope that he could persuade them to handle the appeal without demanding supplementary fees. Lawyers usually agreed to handle a case for a set fee. Some authorities viewed an appeal as simply a continuation of the lawsuit for which the client had engaged his lawyers' services and concluded that the fee originally agreed upon included an appeal. This posi-

---

146. Dig. 49.1.1 pr.; Cod. 7.65.5.3; Tancred, *Ordo iudiciarius* 4.5.11, at 297–98; 4 Lat. (1215) c. 35 (= X 2.28.59).

147. Tancred, *Ordo iudiciarius* 4.5.12, at 298–99; William Durand, *Speculum iudiciale* 2.3 *De appellationibus* §§10.6, 11, at 1:857, 865–69.

148. If the appellate judge deemed that the appeal raised some legitimate issues, while others were merely dilatory or frivolous, the costs assessed against the appellant were supposed to be reduced proportionally to take account of that finding (Tancred, *Ordo iudiciarius* 4.5.12, at 299; William Durand, *Speculum iudiciale* 2.3 *De expensis* §§5.8, 5.15, and 6.11, at 1:906, 907, and 909).

tion was not surprisingly a matter of dispute among jurists. By the late thirteenth century, a consensus had emerged that advocates and proctors were entitled to additional payment for handling an appeal.[149]

Appeals to distant tribunals were likely to involve legal and logistical difficulties that would make it impractical or inadvisable to employ the same lawyers who had handled the matter in first instance. This was particularly true when a case was appealed to the papal curia, where advocates and proctors familiar with the personnel and the intricacies of practice there (*stylus curiae*) could enjoy a decisive advantage over those from far away. In these circumstances, parties commonly sent a proctor who had dealt with the case in the lower courts to the curia, where he, in turn, hired one or more advocates and proctors wise in the ways of the curia to deal with the actual presentation of the case.[150]

Thomas of Marlborough's account of his experiences at the curia while acting as proctor for the monastery of Evesham in its dispute with the bishop of Worcester illustrates how the process actually worked and some of the hazards involved. Thomas traveled to Rome in the company of his abbot to commence their appeal against earlier decisions in England. The abbot returned home after a short time, leaving Thomas to manage the conduct of the appellate case. Thomas, who had taught law at Oxford before he became a monk, took the opportunity to spend six months refreshing his legal learning at Bologna. Even so, he deemed it essential to engage the services of four high-priced but well-placed Roman advocates to argue Evesham's case. In order to pay his learned counsel and to meet other expenses, including gifts and gratuities to the pope and curial officials, Thomas had to pawn the monastery's privileges and other documents to Roman moneylenders as security for a loan of 400 silver marks. Through his own efforts and those of his advocates (aided and abetted by the mistakes of his opponents), Evesham won a partial victory in the appeal. By that point, however, Thomas had run through all his available funds and had to sneak out of Rome secretly to avoid his creditors.[151] He later esti-

---

149. William Durand, *Speculum iudiciale* 1.4 *De salariis* §3.11–13, at 1:348–49; Alexander Tartagnus, *Consilia*, no. 96, vol. 2, at 91ra–rb; Fransen, "Questions disputées de Maître S.," 334–35, no. 4.

150. Sayers, "Canterbury Proctors" and "Proctors Representing British Interests;" Linehan, "Proctors Representing Spanish Interests" and "Spanish Litigants and Their Agents;" Herde, *Beiträge*, 125–36.

151. Thomas of Marlborough, *History of the Abbey of Evesham*, 264, 278–314, 372, 376, §§260, 280–316, 386, 390. Evesham eventually recovered the documents that its creditors had taken as security when the English king confiscated the property of the Ro-

mated that the appeal cost Evesham a total of 2,000 marks, while his opponent, the bishop of Worcester spent approximately the same amount. Since each side won only a partial victory and the expenditures of each party were roughly the same, they ultimately had to swallow their losses and agree to a compromise settlement.[152]

Lawsuits and appeals, however, constituted only part of a professional lawyer's work, although they were its most dramatic and visible part. Trial work in the courtroom, as we saw, actually occupied a fraction of the time that a medieval advocate or proctor spent on litigation. Most of the labor that went into conducting a legal practice took place in the advocate's study, hidden from public view. Even when engaged in litigation, advocates and proctors spent most of their time preparing the documents that were critical to success in a legal action. Legal instruments—frequently amended during the course of a trial—defined the issues that the judge was supposed to decide. Much of the strategy of the trial itself centered on written exceptions and appeals. Judges and their surrogates questioned witnesses, although when they did so, they almost invariably asked the questions that lawyers for the parties had framed. Even the decision in a case might well be no more than an edited version of a draft prepared by an advocate or proctor for one of the parties.

Noncontentious Matters

Medieval lawyers performed much of their most valuable and rewarding work on matters other than lawsuits. Their professional education equipped them not only to fight for clients during litigation, but also to help them settle their disputes and achieve their goals without going to court at all. Litigation was usually a last resort, a confession of failure to resolve a difficulty by peaceful means. It could prove profoundly embarrassing as well as time-consuming, frustrating, and expensive.

At the same time, the threat of going to court was a powerful bargaining tool in the hands of an astute negotiator precisely because prudent lawyers and nervous clients were eager to avoid doing so. They were acutely conscious that bringing in public authorities to deal with their problems could not only prove costly and troublesome, but was also likely to deepen the hostility and aggravate the differences between the parties.

---

man moneylenders who had brought the privileges with them to England to seek repayment of the loan on which Thomas had defaulted (418, §437).

152. Thomas of Marlborough, *History of the Abbey of Evesham*, 414–16, §§433–34.

ADVICE AND COUNSEL

One of the most important functions that medieval advocates performed for their clients was to provide expert advice about the legal options available for achieving their objectives. Litigation was only one way to deal with a problem and might well be the least desirable choice. Out-of-court settlements were apt to offer quicker and cheaper solutions to many disagreements, particularly if the client was in a strong bargaining position and employed a shrewd negotiator. A lawyer who remained detached from his client's emotional involvement in a problem was likely to be better able to analyze the strengths and deficiencies of the client's circumstances and to anticipate the strategies open to an opponent.

We have little evidence about how much time advocates actually spent in providing legal advice and counsel. Medieval advocates, so far as we know, did not keep detailed records of the time they allocated to the affairs of individual clients, and it might not have occurred to them to do so. Devices for measuring time were relatively crude and seldom very accurate, even after mechanical clocks began to appear in Europe toward the end of the thirteenth century. Medieval Europeans, like their predecessors in antiquity, never had more than an approximate notion of what time it was. The concept of measuring the value of work in terms of the precise amount of time required to complete it appeared only much later.[153]

CONSILIA

Providing legal advice was likely to be the most lucrative part of a successful jurist's practice. Judges in the courts of the *ius commune* rarely handed down a final judgment without first taking counsel with legal experts (*iurisperiti*) and routinely stated in their decisions that they had done so. The experts they consulted naturally expected to be rewarded for their advice. A judge who faced a knotty legal problem, and who was aware that he could be held personally liable for deciding it incorrectly, had a strong incentive to protect himself by seeking a formal written legal opinion, known as a *consilium*, from a recognized authority.[154] This option was doubly attrac-

---

153. Carcopino, *Daily Life in Ancient Rome*, 146–50; Cipolla, *Clocks and Culture*, 37–60, 104–6; Bedini, "Clocks and Reckoning of Time."

154. William Durand, *Speculum iudiciale* 2.2 *De requisitione consilii*, no. 2, at 1:763. A sample letter from a judge requesting a *consilium* appears in no. 11, at 1:764; another can be found in *"Curialis,"* 40, no. 141. See also Rossi, *Consilium sapientis*, 43.

tive because it not only provided the judge with a defense, but in addition the parties in the case before him had to bear the expense.

In addition, private individuals and corporate bodies such as monasteries, when they were contemplating an important transaction, such as initiating a lawsuit, or pondering an out-of-court settlement, often sought a *consilium* for guidance about their options or to bolster the force of their own advocate's arguments during litigation or settlement negotiations. Well-known jurists received requests for *consilia* from other sources as well. Italian communes sought advice from counsel when they drafted municipal statutes lest judges later hold their measures unenforceable. For the same reasons, lawyers might be called in to revise, and even to draft, the canons that church councils and synods adopted. In these situations, the person or group who sought advice naturally had to bear its cost.[155]

Famous law professors and other renowned legal experts received impressive fees, sometimes equivalent to half a year's academic salary or more, for *consilia* that might take no more than a few days to prepare. Less eminent authorities naturally had to make do with less handsome rewards, but the market for legal opinions was brisk and profitable, especially in Italy.[156]

Just how much a *iurisperitus* received in return for his legal advice depended, at least in theory, on the quality of the services rendered. The traditional criteria were the same as those that applied to litigation: his *honorarium* was supposed to reflect the difficulty of the problem and its importance as measured by the amount at issue, as well as the skill of the advocate, and the charges customary in the community where he practiced.[157] Realistically, the wealth or poverty of the client was liable to be at least as

---

155. Odofredus, *Lectura* to Dig. 1.2.4, at 10rb–va; Bologna, *Statuta* (1288) 5.77, at 1:426–33; Trexler, *Synodal Law*, 8; Bartolomeo Scala, *De consilio sapientis in forensibus causis* 3.11, at 343vb–344ra; Johannes Franciscus Balbus, *Observationes nonnullarum in jure decisionum*, 3.222, at 84–85; Rossi, *Consilium sapientis*, 137; Calasso, *Medio evo del diritto* 1:591–92.

156. Modena and other Italian communes imposed two- or three-day limits on the time within which jurists must prepare legal opinions (*Libri quinque statutorum inclytae civitatis Mutinae* 2.41, at 19r; Rossi, *Consilium sapientis*, 178–80). More generally on the market for legal opinions, see Bellomo, *Common Legal Past*, 213–14; Fasoli, "Giuristi, giudici e notai," 620–21; Guenée, *Tribunaux et gens de justice*, 199; Baumgärtner, "Rat bei der Rechtsprechung," 77–78.

157. William Durand, *Speculum iudiciale* 1.4 *De salariis* §3.1, at 1:347. These criteria ultimately rest on the authority of Ulpian in Dig. 50.13.1.10.

important as any of these criteria when it came to setting fees for legal advice as well as for assistance in litigation. Since rich clients could afford to pay more than poor ones for legal services, they were usually asked to do so.

Writers on professional conduct assumed that the remuneration for legal advice should reflect the number of books and references that a skilled practitioner would need to page through in search of authorities to solve a problem.[158] Venerable authorities held that that if an advocate could advise on a matter without undertaking any significant research, he should provide his advice free of charge, particularly for poor clients, but by the late thirteenth century, some scholars questioned this view. As William Durand put it, "If he can advise without doing any work or consulting books, let it suffice to say that he is bound to help out free of charge, especially for poor persons... since it is written, 'Freely you have received, freely give' [Matt. 10:8]." Then he added, "But I would not hold him to this."[159]

Johannes Andreae bluntly objected to the practical consequences of the conventional view:

> By this reasoning it follows that I, who have labored at my studies for more than fifty years, so that nowadays I can deal with the present question with little effort, will be in a worse situation than someone of modest experience who has worked only a little while at his studies and now has to struggle in order to reply to it. For this reason I firmly maintain that in these matters account must be taken of past as well as present work.[160]

Johannes Andreae had reason to be concerned. Eminent law teachers, such as himself, and other members of the professional elite who were frequently asked to provide advice, whether oral or written, on difficult ques-

---

158. Johannes Teutonicus, *Glos. ord.* to C. 11 q. 3 c. 71 v. *iustum*; Fasoli, "Giuristi, giudici e notai," 620–21.

159. William Durand, *Speculum iudiciale* 1.3 *De salariis* §3.1, at 1:347: "Verumtamen si absque labore et reuolutione librorum consulere potest, satis potest dici quod teneatur gratis subuenire, maxime pauperibus... quia scriptum est 'Gratis accepistis, gratis date.'... Sed ego eum ad hoc non cogerem."

160. Johannes Andreae, *Additio* to William Durand, *Speculum iudiciale* 1.3 *De salariis* §3.1 v. *labor*, at 1:347: "Ergo si cum labore non teneatur gratis. Ex hac ratione sequitur quod ego qui ultra quinquaginta annos laboraui in studio, per quod cum modico nunc labore studii praesentis quaerentum expedio, ero deterioris conditionis quam qui parum laborauit in studio et modicum prouectus qui habet nunc ut respondeat laborare; quare constanter dico in his non solum praesentis, sed et praeteriti laboris rationem habendam."

tions of law were understandably anxious to protect a bountiful source of income.

Not all *consilia* were written in response to requests from judges or parties faced with problematic legal issues. During the later Middle Ages, the *consilium* also became a genre of academic legal writing similar to *questiones* and were not invariably prompted by a request from anyone. Collections of the *consilia* of widely known jurists were compiled, and some of these became important vehicles for the development of late medieval juristic doctrines.[161]

ARBITRATION AND NEGOTIATION

Arbitration and negotiation of settlements played a prominent role in legal practice. Parties had much to gain by choosing to arbitrate their differences rather than to contest them in court. Arbitration offered a way to resolve contentions privately and informally, through a process that the parties could tailor to suit their needs. It was frequently speedier and less expensive to employ a negotiator than to incur the costs of formal court proceedings. Litigation and arbitration were not antithetical to one another. Rather, they were alternative means to resolve a problem and might well go hand-in-hand. A proceeding that began as a lawsuit often ended in a negotiated settlement, while the enforcement of that settlement not infrequently depended upon the courts.[162]

Settlement of differences through arbitration agreements was no novelty. The practice in one form or another had been in use from time immemorial. Ancient Athenian law formally recognized arbitration awards in the fifth century BCE, Roman lawyers were familiar with *compromissum* agreements, and church authorities from early times, relying upon the authority of St. Paul (1 Cor. 6:1–8), encouraged members of their flocks to compromise their differences whenever possible.[163]

Arbitration during the early Middle Ages had been the preferred method

---

161. Fransen, "Questions disputées dans les facultés de droit," 239–40; Weimar, "Legistische Literatur der Glossatorenzeit," 242–43; Belloni, "Quaestiones e consilia," 19–32; Colli, "I *libri consiliorum*"; Ascheri, "Le fonte e la flessibilità del diritto comune"; Kirshner, "*Consilia* as Authority in Late Medieval Italy"; Rossi, *Consilium sapientis*, 294.

162. Müller, "Streitwort und Kosten," 156; Powell, "Arbitration and the Law," 55–56; Kuehn, *Law, Family, and Women*, 20–22.

163. E.g., Gratian D. 2 c. 5, C. 2 q. 6 d.p.c. 33, C. 3 q. 7 c. 2 §19, C. 11 q. 1 c. 39 and c. 46; Council of Oxford (1222) c. 32 in Powicke & Cheney 1:116; Lefebvre-Teillard, "L'arbitrage en droit canonique," 6–7; Dawson, *History of Lay Judges*, 13–14, 23–26; Stein, *Legal Institutions*, 17–18, 51–52; Kaser, *Römische Zivilprozessrecht*, 57–59, 107–11.

for settling disputes peacefully. Merchants and craftsmen in the towns and cities that began to transform Europe's social and economic landscape during the late eleventh and early twelfth centuries likewise preferred to settle disagreements among themselves when possible. Religious authorities encouraged laymen as well as clerics to appeal to bishops and other respected authorities to resolve their differences, in preference to engaging in war or referring the problem to secular judges. St. Bernard of Clairvaux and other prominent churchmen spent a great deal of time and energy dealing with quarrels among monasteries and churches, and they occasionally attempted to mediate commercial disputes or domestic contentions within families or between neighbors.[164]

Vigorous growth in the numbers of men trained in law beginning in the second half of the twelfth century further stimulated the interest in arbitration procedures that was evident in the writings of Placentinus and Azo. As trained jurists became more readily available, parties to disputes sometimes called them in to work out an amicable settlement of their disagreements, as an alternative to the untrained "good men" (*boni viri*)—typically mutual friends, respected clergymen, or local authority figures—to whom the task of mediation had traditionally been entrusted.[165] Quarreling parties who wished to settle but found it impossible to agree on a mutually acceptable intermediary sometimes agreed to ask a judge to appoint a lawyer or notary to resolve their differences. Judges insisted that advocates do their best to persuade clients to settle out of court before they undertook to assist them in litigation.[166]

Thirteenth-century jurists drew a distinction between arbitration conducted by an arbiter and that conducted by an arbitrator. Procedure that employed an arbiter to reach a compromise was known in classical Roman law, but proceedings conducted by an arbitrator led to a different re-

---

164. Lefebvre-Teillard, "L'arbitrage en droit canonique," 10–16; Martone, *Arbiter—Arbitrator*, 46–52, 63–64; Richard, "Bernard de Clairvaux," as well as Cheyette, "'Suum cuique tribuere,'" and White, "Pactum . . . legem vincit et amor judicium."

165. Azo, *Summa super Codicem*, 57–59, to Cod. 2.55; Martone, *Arbiter—Arbitrator*, 14–16, 27, 65–71; Powell, "Arbitration and the Law," 52–55. At Liège more than half of the recorded arbitration cases were conducted by men with legal training at a university See Bouchat, "Procédures *juris ordine*," 390; see also the samples from Florence summarized by Kuehn in *Law, Family, and Women*, 38–40 and table 1.2.

166. William Durand, *Speculum iudiciale* 1.1 De arbitro et arbitratore §1.4, at 1:103; Kuehn, *Law, Family, and Women*, 28–30, 38–39; Sbirccoli, *L'interpretazione dello statuto*, 74; Halberstadt consistory court statutes (1442) §31, in Hilling, "Sechs Gerichtsordnungen," 337.

sult known as a *compromissum sine poena*. This originated in the practices of bishops' courts in late antiquity and was then introduced into Roman law as a postclassical novelty.[167] The distinction between arbiters and arbitrators began to appear in the work of Johannes Bassianus and Huguccio during the second half of the twelfth century.[168] It still remained rather fuzzy in the first version of Tancred's *Ordo iudiciarius*, but a passage in the second recension of his *Ordo*, written at Paris around 1225, distinguished sharply between the powers of an arbitrator and those of an arbiter:

> An arbiter [Tancred declared] examines the case in judicial form, like a judge, whose decision prevails whether it is just or unjust.... And this is true unless he does a manifest or grave injustice to ether party; in which case his decision does not prevail.... The other kind of arbiter, the one who is styled an arbitrator, is different: he decides and settles the matter between the parties neither as a judge nor in judicial fashion, but rather just in the way that a good man would. His decision prevails if it is the sort that a good man would reach. If it is unjust, it ought to be corrected by the judgment of a good man.[169]

Johannes de Deo and William of Drogheda among others elaborated this distinction further, and around 1272, William Durand digested the discussions of his predecessors into what would become the classic exposition of *ius commune* doctrine on arbitration procedure.[170]

---

167. Dig. 17.2.76; Nov. 86.2; Kaser, *Römische Zivilprozessrecht*, 639–41; Zimmermann, *Law of Obligations*, 526–30.

168. Fowler-Magerl, "Forms of Arbitration," 135–36.

169. Tancred, *Ordo iudiciarius* 1.3.5, at 107 n. 36: "Notandum quod duo sunt genera arbitrorum. [cf. Dig. 17.2.76]. Est enim arbiter, qui causam examinat in iudicii forma, sicut iudex; cuius sententiae, sive aequa sit sive iniqua, standum est, ut C. 2 q. 6 A iudicibus [c. 33], u.d. Dig. e.t. 4.8 l. Diem § stari [Dig. 4.8.27.2]. Et hoc ita verum est, nisi manifeste vel enormiter alteram partem gravaret; tunc enim suae sententiae standum non esset, ut Cod. de arbitr. l. arbitrorum [Cod. 2.55(56).3]. Est alius arbiter, qui dicitur arbitrator, qui non ut iudex nec in forma iudicii, sed ut bonus vir rem decidit et componit inter partes, cuius sententiae tunc demum stabitur, si sit talis, qualis debet ferre a bono viro, unde, si iniusta sit, debet corrigi per arbitrium boni viri, ut Dig. pro socio l. Si societatem [Dig. 17.2.6]. Ad idem X 3. de iureiur. c. Veniens et c. Quintavallis [3 Comp. 22.15.1, 9 (= X 2.24.16, 23)]." The thought, as well as some phrases, in this passage are reminiscent of a fragment of a letter of the first-century jurist Proculus quoted in Dig. 17.2.76.

170. William of Drogheda, *Summa aurea*, 182–83, §153; Lefebvre-Teillard, "L'arbitrage en droit canonique," 17–22; Martone, *Arbiter—Arbitrator*, 75–84, 100; Kuehn, *Law, Family, and Women*, 24–25.

As Durand noted at the outset of his discussion, the parties to a dispute or their designated representatives selected both arbiters and arbitrators. Whichever procedure the parties chose, their goal was to arrive at a compromise solution to their disagreement that would have the effect of a judgment. An arbiter approached this task in ways that resembled those of a judge. He was bound to follow legal procedure, although he enjoyed greater flexibility than judges did and could tailor the process to suit the circumstances of a specific situation. His goal, like that of a judge, was to discover the facts of the case and to award a decision (*arbitrum*) based on those facts. An arbiter's decision was not subject to appeal in the courts because the parties agreed in advance to accept it.[171]

An arbitrator, in contrast, attempted to settle a dispute more informally than an arbiter. His goal was to achieve an equitable settlement that both parties would accept as fair. Since fair play rather than law guided his approach to the matter, an arbitrator was not obliged to follow the *ordo iuris*. His findings (known as a *laudum*), unlike those of an arbiter, could in exceptional situations be appealed to a court of law.[172]

Writers were sometimes careless in their use of the terms, and parties in search of a settlement may not have been entirely clear about the difference between an arbiter and an arbitrator—indeed they might even allow the person handling the arbitration to choose whichever procedure he preferred. Professional lawyers and notaries, however, were usually careful to specify the desired procedure and to use the terms accurately, since they were aware that the distinction made a difference in the process and could affect its outcome.[173]

They also knew that arbitration was no cure-all. Successful settlement of a dispute through arbitration depended fundamentally upon all parties acting in good faith and with a serious commitment to settling their differences fairly. Neither of these could be guaranteed. Even when the parties agreed to a settlement under one form of arbitration or the other, its enforcement could present formidable problems if one party had reservations about its terms. Since neither an arbiter nor an arbitrator had any very effective means to compel compliance with his decision, the only

---

171. Bouchat, "Procédures *juris ordine*," 382–83, 388–89. It was possible to bring an action on an *exceptio doli* against an arbiter who acted fraudulently, but this was technically not an appeal against his decision (William Durand, *Speculum iudiciale* 1.1 *De arbitro et arbitratore* §1.6, at 1:104; Fowler-Magerl, "Forms of Arbitration," 140).

172. William Durand, *Speculum iudiciale* 1.1 *De arbitro et arbitratore* §1.2–3, at 1:102–3.

173. Hubaldus of Pisa, *Imbreviaturbuch*, 102, no. 16; Fowler-Magerl, "Forms of Arbitration," 133–34, 142–47.

recourse if one party refused to accept it was to secure assistance from an outside authority, which usually meant going back to the courts. In addition, arbitration was no more immune than were formal legal proceedings to corruption, improper influence, intimidation, and delay, while failed attempts at arbitration could produce the kinds of vendettas and armed brawls that the process was supposed to prevent.[174]

Despite its shortcomings, arbitration remained a popular alternative to litigation in the later Middle Ages, not least because it provided litigants with a face-saving and cost-effective way to disengage from prolonged and expensive lawsuits. The numerous medieval arbitration agreements that survive attest to the wide and continuing popularity of the process.[175]

Arbitration provided a valuable source of professional employment for lawyers and notaries. In important and complicated disputes where convoluted issues had to be resolved, a lawyer's specialized skills might prove essential for arriving at a resolution that would hold up if it were challenged in court. *Iurisperiti* were not uncommonly called in as well when nonlawyer mediators encountered technical problems in formulating arbitration awards. If parties later contested an award, legal counsel was often engaged to prepare *consilia* concerning the lawfulness of its terms.[176]

DIPLOMACY

Some elite lawyers found occasional opportunities to use their professional expertise as diplomatic agents in the service of popes, emperors, kings, Italian city-states, and other rulers or governments who had the capacity to wage war. Diplomatic representation provided opportunities for a specialized use of many of the skills that lawyers employed when they acted on behalf of private individuals and corporations. Ambassadors negotiated and ratified agreements, conveyed messages, delivered protests, and rep-

---

174. William Durand, *Speculum iudiciale* 1.1 De arbitro et arbitratore §§4.3 and 7.40, at 1:107, 123; Kuehn, *Law, Family, and Women*, 70–71 and 147–50; Powell, "Arbitration and the Law," 56–57.

175. Kuehn, *Law, Family, and Women*, 34. The notebooks of notaries commonly contain numerous arbitration awards; thus, e.g., Hubaldus of Pisa, *Imbreviaturbuch*, nos. 8, 13, 16, 19, 40, 62, and 63, at 95–96, 99–100, 102, 103–5, 125–26, 155–58; *Acts of Gubertinus de Novate*, nos. 157, 209, 212, 260, at 155–58, 185, 187–88, 211–12; *John Lydford's Book*, nos. 97, 148, 169, 249, at 57, 77, 87–88, 134–41; among others.

176. A good example of the skills needed in arbitration cases appears in Kuehn's account of a dispute over the division of a deceased women's dowry property in *Law, Family, and Women*, 47–48; see also 28, 60–67.

resented the interests of governments much as lawyers conducted comparable transactions in the name of ordinary clients.

Early medieval rulers had of course employed intermediaries to deal with one another long before a legal profession appeared on the scene. The emergence of a growing body of men trained in the legal traditions of the *ius commune*, however, introduced lasting innovations in the conduct of European diplomacy. Prior to the thirteenth century, diplomatic agents were usually described as *nuntii*, an elastic term susceptible of a variety of meanings. A *nuntius* might simply be a messenger or courier, someone dispatched to deliver a letter or an oral message—or often both. A *nuntius*, said Azo, is like a magpie: he is merely a voice that recites the words of the person who employs him.[177] But even a simple *nuntius* might have the capacity to do more than parrot what his principal had told him to say. As his employer's representative he could, for example, help to facilitate an agreement on the terms of a contract regarding sale or purchase, provided that his principal had specifically instructed him on the conditions that he was authorized to accept.[178]

A diplomatic agent whose principal gave him a mandate that designated him as a proctor plenipotentiary, in other words, an agent vested with full power (*plena potestas*), could do a great deal more. When a ruler or public body sent a proctor armed with plenipotentiary power, the agent could, for example, negotiate a treaty, create or terminate an alliance, declare a war or conclude one. A proctor with a plenipotentiary mandate had the authority to do on his principal's behalf almost anything that his principal could do in person.[179]

Surviving records show Italian towns dispatching ambassadors with plenipotentiary powers to popes, emperors, kings, and other towns in the middle of the twelfth century. By the end of the century, popes had likewise begun to equip some of their legates with plenipotentiary powers, and other public authorities soon adopted this approach. This innova-

---

177. Azo, *Summa super Codicem*, 161, to Cod. 4.50: "Nuncius est is qui vicem gerit epistole estque velut pica et organum, et vox domini mittentis ipsum et recitat verba domini, puta misit dominus ut sciret an ille sibi venderet rem pro .x." Other common terms included *missus*, often used during the Merovingian and Carolingian periods, *orator*, the usual description for representatives of the Venetian Republic, and *legatus*, which came into increasingly frequent use, not only to designate representatives of the pope, but also those of kings and other secular rulers (William Durand, *Speculum iudiciale* 1.1 *De legato* §1.2, at 1:29–30; Queller, *Office of Ambassador*, 3–6).

178. Dig. 2.14.2 and 18.1.1.2; Gaius, *Inst.* 3.136; Zimmermann, *Law of Obligations*, 50; Zulueta, *Roman Law of Sale*, 20–21.

179. On *plena potestas*, see Post, *Studies in Medieval Legal Thought*, 91–162.

tion in diplomatic practice stemmed directly from the renewed systematic study of the *ius commune* during the twelfth-century.[180]

University-trained lawyers who had mastered the legal tools that undergirded the new diplomacy soon became indispensable diplomatic advisers to governments. Rulers preferred during the early stages of these developments to name men of exalted social rank to head their diplomatic missions, lest the rulers who received their embassies feel insulted if they were confronted with a representative who was their social inferior. This gradually changed over time. Even in the thirteenth century, eminent jurists, both canonists and civilians, occasionally led diplomatic missions, and this became increasingly common during the fourteenth century.[181] By the fifteenth century, it was routine to name distinguished jurists as ambassadors. *Jurisperiti* or doctors of law outnumbered other social or occupational groups among the ambassadors received in Florence during the second half of the century, for instance, and accounted for fully one-third of the sample that Donald Queller examined, while roughly a quarter of the diplomatic missions that Florence dispatched to other powers were headed by advocates or notaries with legal training.[182]

The papacy, whose interests stretched throughout the length and breadth of Christendom, was not surprisingly a pioneer in the development of rules governing the conduct of diplomacy and the status and privileges of diplomats. Secular powers soon began to adapt those rules to their own situation, and by the middle of the fifteenth century many basic elements of the system of diplomatic usages that remain in force to the present day were already in place.[183]

---

180. In 1195, e.g., Pope Celestine III informed the Emperor Henry VI that he was sending two legates "quorum verbis eam fidem adhiberi velut ac si de ore suo praesentialiter elata fuissent" (JL 17226). See also Post, *Studies in Medieval Legal Thought*, 104–5, 107–8; Queller, *Office of Ambassador*, 26–30; Mattingly, *Renaissance Diplomacy*, 18, 21–22.

181. Queller, *Office of Ambassador*, 68, 154–56. The role of social status in dipolomacy may account for jurists' increasingly vehement insistence that experienced doctors of law ranked socially with counts. Azo, Tancred, Hostiensis, Roffredus Beneventanus, and William Durand were among the eminent lawyers who headed diplomatic missions during the thirteenth century, and Johannes Andreae, Johannes de Legnano, and Johannes Monachus did so during the following century.

182. Queller, *Office of Ambassador*, 157; Martines, *Lawyers and Statecraft*, 311–15.

183. William Durand, *Speculum iudiciale* 1.1 De legato §§7–8, at 1:53–58, together with the *Additiones* of Baldus de Ubaldis; Mattingly, *Renaissance Diplomacy*, 20–25; Queller, *Office of Ambassador*, 175–208.

* ELEVEN *

Rewards and Hazards of the Legal Profession

Lawyers began to form a noticeable segment of medieval society around the middle of the twelfth century. By the middle of the thirteenth century, they had begun to acquire the basic characteristics of a profession in the rigorous sense of the term. By that time, both the rewards and the hazards that accompanied professional status had also become obvious. Feelings about professional lawyers and their place in society were seldom simple and never neutral. Lawyers inspired admiration as well as envy, hostility mixed with respect, resentment together with dependence on their skills. People commonly viewed the profession as simultaneously mysterious, threatening, and indispensable.

The Rewards

For the fortunate few who combined intellectual ability with diligence, influential connections, and good luck, the rewards of a legal career could be extremely attractive. The services of such men were in high demand. Consequently, they were well positioned to acquire riches, power, fame, prestige, and privilege, and not a few of them did precisely that. An anonymous poet around the beginning of the thirteenth century summed up the appeal of the profession succinctly: a legal career, he wrote, "produces a renowned name, attracts friends, gathers gold, builds character, rules the soul, and adds to honors."[1]

These rewards were unevenly distributed. Less fortunate practitioners

---

1. "Dat nomen clarum, dat amicos, implet aurum, / Informat mores, animum regit, auget honores" (Kuttner, "Dat Galienus opes," 243).

had to make do with a smaller—often much smaller—share of them than their more fortunate brethren enjoyed. Even so, anyone trained in Roman and canon law in the thirteenth or fourteenth century could reasonably anticipate a rewarding career. Legal training could not guarantee that every individual who had it would rise to a prominent position or accumulate great wealth, but success by association reflected at least some measure of glory even on those who fared less well. There is no reason to think that many qualified lawyers actually starved or even came close to it.[2]

In addition to material prizes, the legal profession's intangible rewards were far from negligible. Some students considered law a more attractive field of study than theology because it afforded them a measure of intellectual freedom. Lawyers were less hemmed in than theologians were by dogmatic boundaries that they could cross only at personal peril. This was crucial for canon law, which lay at the point where law and theology intersected. Canonists explored and developed novel ideas about such basic issues as natural rights, representation and consent, the corporate structure of ecclesiastical and civil government, the right to wage war, or limits on the authority of popes, bishops, and cardinals, or even monarchs, more freely than their colleagues in the theological faculty could entertain novel hypotheses about such matters as the Trinity, the Eucharist, free will, or apostolic poverty. As the disciplinary mechanisms to impose doctrinal conformity became more rigid during the fourteenth and fifteenth centuries, however, the attractiveness of canon law began to wane, while the popularity of Roman law continued to grow.[3]

WEALTH, POWER, AND AUTHORITY

It was a commonplace among the educated elite that law was holy and priceless.[4] At the same time, twelfth-century theologians, philosophers, poets, and jurists themselves described law and medicine as lucrative disciplines (*scientiae lucrativae*) because they opened the door to numerous career opportunities. "Study law and you'll not be needy," ran a fifteenth-century saying that young William Elphinstone scribbled in one of his textbooks while he was a law student at Louvain in the early 1430s.[5]

2. Ritchie, *Ecclesiastical Courts of York*, 62; Guenée, *Tribunaux et gens de justice*, 366; Martines, *Lawyers and Statecraft*, 101–6.
3. Meynial, "Remarques sur la réaction," 573–74.
4. Placentinus, *Sermo de legibus*, 132, §6, quoting Ulpian in Dig. 50.13.1.5.
5. "Ut non egeas lege leges." The advice certainly worked for Elphinstone, who became a prebendary of the cathedral of Glasgow. It worked even better for his son, also named William Elphinstone, a canon lawyer who became bishop of Aberdeen, Lord

Successful advocates typically enjoyed income from a variety of sources. Their professional earnings came chiefly from fees for providing legal advice and arguing on behalf of clients in litigation. The ancient tradition that they ought to furnish these services gratuitously was becoming a dead letter by the close of the twelfth century and was extinct by the end of the following century.[6] Save under special circumstances—when a judge appointed them to represent a poor person, for instance, or when they acted on behalf of a friend or family member—advocates expected clients to reward them for their labors and clients mostly did so, sometimes generously. By the late thirteenth century, authorities at the highest level took this for granted. The Second Council of Lyons, as we saw, implicitly confirmed the propriety of charging fees for legal services when it established an upper limit on the amount advocates and proctors could charge for their services. It is fair to assume that renowned advocates whose services were in great demand found ways to circumvent even the generous fee limits that the council set. It was also generally accepted by this point that advocates and proctors could take legal action to secure payment of their fees from clients who defaulted.

Qualified civilians and canonists seldom depended for their living solely on legal fees. Many also received annual retainers from regular clients, regardless of how much work, if any, they performed in a given year, while clerical lawyers frequently received income from benefices. Some elite lawyers received appointments as diplomatic agents, while others spent at least part of their careers as judges or administrative officials. A few frequently served as paid arbitrators, while many more regularly negotiated on behalf of clients in other matters. Whether they were clerics or laymen, lawyers also engaged in profitable enterprises not directly connected with the practice of law. They invested their surplus funds in rental properties, bought partnerships in commercial ventures, loaned out money, or per-

---

High Chancellor of Scotland, and founder of the University of Aberdeen (Ker, "For All That I May Clamp"; Macfarlane, "Elphinstone, William"). See also John of Garland, *Morale scolarium* 1.21, at 189; Kantorowicz and Smalley, "An English Theologian's View," 238; Alain de Lille, *Sermo de clericis ad theologiam non accedentibus*, in his *Textes inédits*, 274; Kuttner, "Dat Galienus opes," 243; Delhaye, "L'organisation scolaire," 54–56.

6. Stephen of Tournai, e.g., complained bitterly to the pope at the century's turn about the venality of unscrupulous advocates in the courts, and he was hardly the first to do so (*CUP* 1:48, no. 48; Post, Giocarinis, and Kay, "Medieval Heritage of a Humanistic Ideal."

haps more congenially (since their training made lawyers "people of the book") engaged in the book trade.[7]

Although some prominent lawyers, such as Johannes Andreae (b. ca. 1270, d. 1348) or Johannes de Legnano (b. ca. 1320 d. 1383), remained laymen throughout their careers, many, almost certainly a majority among the canonists, were clerics.[8] This did not necessarily mean that they spent any considerable amount of their time performing religious duties. They found it desirable to receive the tonsure and to be ordained to one or more of the minor orders because this conferred clerical status and made them eligible to hold ecclesiastical benefices without seriously limiting their lifestyle. Clerical canonists whose careers have left traces in the records almost always acquired at least one benefice, and many accumulated sizeable numbers of them.[9] These appointments provided at the least a reasonably dependable stipend, while some of them yielded very substantial incomes without demanding serious investment of time and effort. Indeed, a good many appointees may never have visited the benefices they held.

Clerical benefice holders were in principle subject to restrictions on their legal practice. Long-standing tradition strongly discouraged clerics from appearing in law courts as advocates or proctors, or even from studying civil law. As Bernard of Parma put it, "It is shameful for clerics to advertise themselves as lawyers."[10] The practice of law in order to gain riches, wealth, and power seemed to many authorities inappropriate for a cleric. These prohibitions were repeated often enough during the thirteenth century to suggest that the ban was often not observed. Even strict moralists came to tolerate the practice of law by clerical advocates and proctors. They conceded, however reluctantly, that in their increasingly commer-

---

7. Bellomo, *Saggio sull'università*, 124–28; Gargan, "Libri, librerie e biblioteche nell'università italiane," 234–40; Jeffries, "Profitable Fourteenth-Century Legal Practice."

8. Schulte, *QL* 2:205–29, 257–61; Stelling-Michaud, "Jean d'André" and "Jean de Legnano"; Rossi, "Contributi alla biografia del canonista Giovanni d'Andrea"; McCall, "Chaucer and John of Legnano" and "Writings of John of Legnano"; William Greenfield, *Register* 1:157, no. 357; Straub, *Geistliche Gerichtsbarkeit*, 196.

9. On the material benefits of clerical status, X 1.14.11 and 1.36.6; for examples of those who benefited, Aston, Duncan, and Evans, "Medieval Alumni of Cambridge," 75; Gramsch, *Erfurter Juristen*, 312–27, 353–59, 551, and passim.

10. Gratian D. 86 c. 26; C. 15 q. 2 c. 1; C. 21 q. 3 c. 1; Bernard of Parma, *Glos. ord.* to X 1.37.1 v. *secularibus* and 1.37.2 v. *ecclesiastici*.

cialized society, advocates, clerical or lay, could legitimately expect their clients to pay them for their work.[11]

Some restrictions still held. Bishops and other high-ranking prelates scarcely ever appeared as advocates, even in order to defend themselves. Instead they almost always appointed proctors and advocates to represent them and to argue their cases. The practice of law by monks and canons regular continued to be frowned upon, although they could legitimately engage in it if their religious superiors called upon them to defend their community's interests.[12] Benefice-holding clerics in major orders could represent clients only in civil cases in the ecclesiastical courts and were barred from practicing in secular courts. This ban, too, was commonly ignored in practice. Most of the advocates at the Parlement de Paris, for example, were clerics (including some bishops and monks) at least up to the fifteenth century, and many judges in the English royal courts under the Angevin kings were clerics.[13]

Beneficed clerics ordained to the rank of deacon and above were not supposed to receive payment for their legal work, since it was assumed that

11. The admonition in 2 Tim. 2:4 that those in God's service should not involve themselves in worldly affairs was routinely invoked as a scriptural basis for the prohibition; cf. also 2 Peter 2:20. On repeated attempts to ban clerics from legal practice, see, e.g., Council of Narbonne (1227) c. 11, Council of Champagne (1238) c. 12, and Council of Roffiac (1258) c. 6, in Mansi 23:24, 490, 986; Synodal statutes of Bordeaux (1234) cc. 66 and 67, of Sisteron (1249) c. 72, and of Nîmes c. 107, in *Statuts synodaux français* 1:74, 218, 354; Council of Angers (1269) c. 2, in *Conciles de la province de Tours*, 240–41; Statutes of Guiard de Laon of Cambrai (1238–48) c. 179, *Antiqua statuta* of Tournai (late 13th/early 14th century) c. 12.7 and 21.1, in *Statuts synodaux français* 4:61, 339, 348. On the rueful acceptance of the practice, see, e.g., Raymond of Penyafort, *Summa de paenitentia* 2.5.39, col. 517–18; Thomas Aquinas, *Summa theologiae* 2–2 q. 71 a. 4; Antoninus, *Summa confessionalis* 3.4, tit. *Ad advocatos et procuratores et notarios*, at 57va; Sanchez, *Consilia moralium* 2.3.21.4, at 1:214 .

12. Ricardus Anglicus, *Distinctiones* to C. 15 q. 2 c. 1, in London, BL MS Royal 10.C.III, at 26v–27r; Johannes Teutonicus, *Glos. ord.* to C. 5 q. 3 c. 3 v. *quia episcopus* and C. 11 q. 1 c. 29 v. *ne advocatus*; Raymond of Penyafort, *Summa de paenitentia* 2.5.39, col. 515; Tancred, *Apparatus* to 1 Comp. 3.37.2 v. *audiantur*, in London, BL, MS Royal 11.C.VII, at 52ra; Goffredus de Trano , *Summa super titulis* to X 1.37 §3,. at 61ra; Bernard of Parma, *Glos. ord.* to X 1.37.2 v. *imperante*; Hostiensis, *Lectura* to X 1.36.2 §2 v. *abbas nihilominus*, vol. 1, at 182rb; Bernard of Montemirato [Abbas antiquus], *Lectura aurea* to X 1.37.1, at 70ra; William Durand, *Speculum iudiciale* 1.4 De aduocato §1.2–3, at 1:260; Brundage, "The Monk as Lawyer."

13. Delachenal, *Histoire des avocats*, 3–4; Shennan, *Parlement of Paris*, 110; Turner, *Men Raised from the Dust*, 27, 92–104.

revenues from benefices would support them adequately. Subdeacons and clerics in minor orders could take payment for their professional services so long as the income they received from their benefices was inadequate to sustain them. Unbeneficed clerics in minor orders labored under none of these constraints.[14] It seems doubtful that these distinctions and qualifications were generally observed in the latter part of the thirteenth century.

The services of trained lawyers, clerics or laymen, were not cheap, and both ecclesiastical and civil authorities recognized that equitable distribution of legal services raised serious social and moral issues. Bonaguida of Arezzo explained why lawyers merited generous compensation:

> Since the advocate's craft is extremely useful and the law deemed it indispensable in men's lives, that same law properly decreed that those who strive to carry out that function should be honored and appropriately rewarded for their courage.[15]

An anonymous marginal gloss put the message even more succinctly: "Doctoribus bona dona danda sunt."[16]

Nonlawyers found this rationale unconvincing. Rulers in both church and state repeatedly attempted, although often with slight success, to cap legal fees. The maximum fees allowed by law were relatively generous. Run-of-the-mill practitioners seldom had cases that could justify the maximum compensation—or for that matter clients prepared to pay it.

Despite recurring complaints about the high cost of going to law, judges were kept busy and people of ordinary means—peasants, fishermen, cobblers, and blacksmiths, for example—abound in court records. Mechanisms existed to provide truly impoverished litigants with assistance from trained lawyers, and records show that they were used in practice. What the records cannot tell us is how adequately they filled the demand.

Most lawyers seem to have been reasonably well-off and eminent ones

---

14. Ricardus Anglicus, *Distinctiones*, at 26v–27r; Goffredus de Trano, *Summa super titulis* to X 1.37 §2, at 60vb–61ra; Bernard of Parma, *Glos. ord.* to X 1.37.1 v. *stipendiis* and 1.37.3 v. *pro seipso*; Innocent IV, *Apparatus* to X 1.37.1 v. *sustententur*, at 165ra; Hostiensis, *Lectura* to X 1.37.1 §§1–3 v. *coram seculari* and X 1.37.2 §1 v. *vel ecclesiastici*, vol. 1, at 182ra–vb; Bernard of Montemirato, *Lectura aurea* to X 1.37.1, at 70ra; William Durand *Speculum iudiciale* 1.4 *De aduocato* §1.4–5, at 1:260.

15. Bonaguida, *Summa introductoria*, prol., at 133: "Cum advocationis officium perquam utile vitaeque hominum lex suadeat necessarium fore, merito lex ipsa in eodem officio militantes, tanquam virtutum merentes praemia, inter alios extollendos decrevit."

16. Marginal gloss to C. 3 q. 7 c. 2 §12.

secured both fame and fortune. Even a moderately obscure canonist could prosper handsomely. William Doune, for example, despite being born out of wedlock, was able to study law at Oxford, where he became a fellow of Merton College and eventually in 1349 received the doctorate in both laws. He had begun to flourish even before that. A papal dispensation enabled him to become a cleric in 1342 despite his illegitimate birth, and in that same year he received the first of what soon became a sizeable collection of benefices. Early in his career, William joined the household of Bishop John Grandisson of Exeter as the registrar of his chancery. Grandisson's patronage enabled him to secure parishes in Devonshire and Buckinghamshire, as well as a canonry at Exeter Cathedral. William stayed on in Exeter until 1354, when he took up simultaneous appointments as archdeacon of Leicester, official-principal of the bishop of Worcester, and official-principal of the bishop of Lincoln. These appointments allowed him to become a still more active player in the benefice market, acquiring benefices that he held for a short time until he could trade them for more lucrative ones. He kept a few particularly choice appointments on a long-term basis, including a canonry at Lincoln Cathedral, which he held on to for the remainder of his life. It would be a mistake, however, to think of William Doune as simply a cynical exploiter of the opportunities that the benefice system offered. He seems in fact to have taken his clerical obligations seriously. To judge by the *Memoriale presbiterorum* that has been plausibly ascribed to him, William was an earnest and devout cleric, yet by the time of his death at Barbentane, near Avignon, in 1361, he had amassed considerable wealth, as his will makes plain. William left numerous sizeable bequests, including several for the support of poor students at Oxford, as well as a large and valuable library of legal texts.[17]

William Doune's career seems significant precisely because, apart from his probable authorship of the *Memoriale*, it was not particularly unusual. He was a pluralist, but apparently a conscientious one. Men who enjoyed careers similar to his were unexceptional. William Doune's life exemplifies a pattern that recurred countless times among moderately successful and reasonably prosperous civil and canon lawyers between roughly 1250 and 1500.

The degree of affluence that men like William Doune achieved depended on their ability to secure appointments that either entitled them to exercise power over others or else provided ready access to those who held

---

17. Thompson, "Will of Master William Doune," 260–66; *BRUO* 1:587–88; Haren, *Sin and Society*, 39–65, 190–216.

such positions. Study of the learned laws at a university, especially when combined with practical experience in courtroom and chancery, equipped these men with skills that enabled them to manipulate the gears and levers of ecclesiastical and civil administration. This in turn facilitated securing profitable positions.

The success of medieval lawyers in achieving positions of power and authority in church and state is documented by surviving legal and administrative records, as well as by narrative accounts. Even more abundant testimony to their success appeared in the reactions against it by critics who feared and resented what may be described as the juridification of the church during the High Middle Ages, that is, its domination not only by lawyers, but also by legalism in its approach to religious and spiritual matters.

Judges by the fourteenth century were likely to be university graduates trained in Roman and canon law.[18] Records from various regions of medieval Christendom bear evidence that large numbers of law-trained clerics likewise secured appointments to other positions, such as archdeacon, rural dean, and provost or dean of a cathedral chapter, that gave them disciplinary authority. Bishops and archbishops, too, were more likely to be trained in law than in theology.[19] At the very summit of ecclesiastical authority, lawyers became so numerous among cardinals and popes that participants in university disputations debated the question of whether a theologian or a canonist was better suited to head the church.[20]

Lay lawyers frequently achieved positions of power and renown as well. Although they were not eligible to receive ecclesiastical benefices, we often encounter them holding appointments as judges in both civil and ecclesias-

---

18. Stelling-Michaud, *Université de Bologne*, 203–30; Renardy, *Le monde des maîtres*, 229–32.

19. Stelling-Michaud, *Université de Bologne*, 130–69; Gaudemet, "Recherches sur l'épiscopat médiéval," 144–46; Aston, "Oxford's Medieval Alumni," 28; Aston, Duncan and Evans, "Medieval Alumni of Cambridge," 70, 73; Gramsch, *Erfurter Juristen*, 537–43; Renardy, *Le monde des maîtres*, 219–29. Similarly, among the university men from the diocese of Liège who became bishops, fourteen were jurists while twelve were theologians. Among those who became archbishops, the contrast was particularly striking: the jurists outnumbered theologians by five to one (Renardy, *Les maîtres universitaires*, 475–79, and *Le monde des maîtres*, 240–66).

20. Weigand, "Frühe Kanonisten und ihre Karriere"; Girgensohn, "Wie wird Man Kardinal?"; Robinson, *The Papacy*, 55, 220–21; Renardy, *Les maîtres universitaires*, nos. 55, 78, 119, 183, and 383, at 137–39, 197–98, 214, 237, and 319–20; Long, "Utrum jurista vel theologus plus proficiat ad regimen ecclesie."

tical courts. They not uncommonly secured other prominent positions as well, such as *podestà* in Italian city-states or as counselors to kings, princes, and municipal governments. They occasionally became ambassadors and royal chancellors.[21]

PRESTIGE, HONOR, AND PRIVILEGE

Wealth, power, and authority carried with them prestige, honor, and privilege. All professional lawyers, even those who failed to secure high positions or vast wealth, nonetheless shared in many of the privileges and at least some of the prestige of their more fortunate colleagues. When an advocate was admitted to practice in the late Roman empire, he had automatically become a member of the senatorial order and formed part of a *militia*. Medieval lawyers were aware of this and commonly equated the Roman terms with the social standing that knights (*milites*) enjoyed in their society.[22] Civilians and canonists stoutly maintained that advocates were every bit as useful and necessary members of society as knights. It therefore followed, the argument went, that they merited the same honors and privileges that knights received. Like knights, moreover, advocates and legal experts were entitled to compensation for their work, as the well-worn rhetorical question, "Who fights as a soldier at his own expense?" implied.[23]

The status of advocates and other trained lawyers as *milites* was not merely honorific: it entitled them to concrete civic privileges. Doctors, like knights, were styled "Sir" (*dominus*), "Ser," or "Messir."[24] Advocates

---

21. Thus, e.g., Fried, *Entstehung des Juristenstandes*, 130–39; Herlihy, *Medieval and Renaissance Pistoia*, 237–38; Gramsch, *Erfurter Juristen*, 441–64; Stelling-Michaud, *L'université de Bologne*, 170–78; Renardy, *Le monde des maîtres*, 305–47; Aston, Duncan, and Evans, "Medieval Alumni of Cambridge," 80–82.

22. Cod. 2.7.14; Bartolus, *Commentaria* to Cod. 2.7.14, vol. 7, at 63r; on the Roman nomenclature, see Jones, *Later Roman Empire* 1:507–8, 528–30. For medieval classifications, Azo, *Summa Institutionum*, proem., in *Summa super Codicem*, 346; Accursius, *Glos. ord.* to Dig. 27.13.1 v. *milites* and *glos. ord.* to Cod. 2.7.14 v. *aduocatos, militant*; William Durand, *Speculum iudiciale* 1.4 *De aduocato* §2.2, at 1:264; *Siete Partidas* 2.10.3 and 7.30.2.

23. 1 Cor. 9:7. The argument was a commonplace among medieval canonists, e.g., Johannes Teutonicus, *Glos. ord.* to C. 23 q. 1 c. 5 v. *militiae*; Johannes Andreae, *Glos. ord.* to VI 3.12.4 v. *castrense*; Simone da Borsano, *Lectura* to Clem., proem., ed. Maffei in "Dottori e studenti, 242; Baldus, *Commentaria* to Cod. 2.7.14 §2, vol. 6, at 132vb, among innumerable others. See also Post, Giocarinis, and Kay, "Medieval Heritage of a Humanistic Ideal."

24. Kantorowicz, "An English Theologian's View," and "Praestantia doctorum."

shared with knights the privilege of exemption from payment of taxes and other civic burdens borne by the lower orders of society; they could not be subjected to judicial torture; they were entitled to wear the insignia of knighthood; and like knights, they could be buried in scarlet robes. Their social position was also heritable, so that the children of advocates shared in these privileges.[25]

Some legal practitioners entertained still loftier social aspirations. Prosperous lawyers regularly invested part of their surplus wealth in great houses and landed estates in the hope that these plus a fortunate marriage might allow them to insinuate themselves into the ranks of the nobility. They were entitled to this status, according to Bartolus, because they were ennobled by knowledge.[26] Some went so far as to claim that noble status thus acquired was superior to nobility that was merely inherited. "He who earns nobility through his own accomplishments is more properly called 'noble' than someone who descends from a noble family, for that person is considered 'noble' only by presumption."[27]

Medieval lawyers liked to think of themselves not only as knights and noblemen, but also as a priesthood whose members performed sacred functions. The association between priests and legal expertise stretched far back into antiquity. Moses, to whom God revealed the law, was a priest, and he in turn entrusted custody of the ark of the covenant, which contained the tables of the law, to other priests (Exod. 40:12–15). Likewise, the earliest legal experts in the Roman republic, as we saw at the outset, were members of a priesthood. When a medieval law student commenced to study the Digest, he encountered right at the beginning Ulpian's declaration that

---

25. Baldus, *Commentaria* to Cod. 2.7.6 §§1–2, vol. 6, at 131vb, and 2.7.11 §6, vol. 6, at 132rb; Albertus Gandinus, *Tractatus de maleficiis*, ed. Kantorowicz, in *Albertus Gandinus und das Strafrecht* 2:173; Bologna, *Statuti* (1288) 4.91, at 1:247; Baumgärtner, "De privilegiis doctorum," 308–16; Bataillard, *Les origines*, 267; Martines, *Lawyers and Statecraft*, 29–30; Le Bras, "*Velut splendor firmamenti.*"

26. Bertin, *Les mariages dans l'ancienne société française*, 408, 416; Gouron, "Le rôle social des juristes," 64–66; Hyde, *Padua in the Age of Dante*, 146; Waley, *Siena and the Sienese*, 86–89, 209; Bartolus, *Commentaria* to Cod. 2.6.8, vol. 7, at 62v; cf. Zenzelinus de Cassanis, gloss to Extrav. Jo. XXII 3.un. v. *litteratis viris*.

27. Bartolomeo Scala, *De consilio sapientis in forensibus causis* 1.6, at 333rb–va, citing Cino da Pistoia: "[E]um, qui sua virtute nobilitatem meruit, magis dici nobilem, quam eum qui descendit nobili ex genere, qui non nisi praesumptiue nobilis existimatur, in l. Quod si nolit § Qui mancipia, De aedil. edict. [Dig. 21.1.31.21]."

[p]eople quite properly call us [jurists] priests, for we cultivate the virtue of justice and claim an understanding of what is good and fair, discriminating between equity and iniquity, distinguishing lawful from unlawful, aiming to make men good, not solely through fear of punishment, but also by the attraction of rewards, cultivating a philosophy that, if I am not mistaken, is genuine, not a sham.

Again, toward the end of the Digest, they saw that Ulpian repeated the claim that "[k]nowledge of the civil law is a most sacred matter."[28]

Lawyers' aspirations for ever greater eminence sometimes got out of hand. "The advocate's tongue," William Durand boasted, "may be described as a flaming sword" of the sort that scripture depicted in the hands of God's angels (Gen. 3:24). Doctors of law, Durand continued, belonged in the celestial hierarchy alongside the cherubim, the angels who guarded access to the true faith.[29]

The righteous jurist who medieval authors held up as a model that all members of the profession should strive to emulate was a remarkable figure. A lawyer, said Durand, "ought to be 'careful in giving advice, faithful in acting for his client, and impartial in exercising judgment,' for he will ultimately need to render an account for the gifts bestowed on him."[30] Others characterized the paradigmatic lawyer as intelligent, learned, upright, scrupulously honest, steadfast in the pursuit of justice, deferential to judges, and fair to his opponents. He was obliged both morally and legally to do everything in his power to save his client from harm, to deploy all resources at his command to advance the client's interests no matter what

---

28. Dig. 1.1.1.1 and 50.13.1.5.

29. William Durand, *Speculum iudiciale*, proem. §§8–9, at 1:2: "Ordo doctorum est, quorum lingua flammeus gladius dicitur, quia flamma charitatis ignita, iuxta illud Prophetae: 'Qui facit angelos suos spiritus et ministros suos ignem urentem [Ps. 103:4]. . . . Hi ergo Cherubim ad custodiendam uiam ligni uitae, id est ueritatem fidei orthodoxae, per quam peruenitur ad uitam" (Nörr, "Der Kanonist und sein Werk," 377–78). On canonists and angels, see also Hostiensis, *Summa*, proem. §12, at 3ra, and cf. Kuttner, *Harmony from Dissonance*, 48–49, also in his *History of Ideas and Doctrines*, no. I, 14–15.

30. William Durand, *Speculum iudiciale* 1.4 *De aduocato* §9.21, at 1:282: "Ex praemissis igitur collige quod iurisperitus debet esse 'in consilio cautus, in patrocinio fidelis, in iudicio iustus,' [Bernard of Pavia, proem. to 1 Comp., at 1] quoniam de talento sibi credito tenetur reddere rationem, ut in constitutione Gregorii X de postulatione, Properandum [2 Lyons (1274) c. 19]."

the cost to himself. He must steadfastly remain dignified, modest, cheerful, and temperate in all his dealings.[31]

It is scarcely to be expected that many human beings consistently measured up to these standards. An anonymous fourteenth-century Norman-French poet was sure, however, that the Blessed Virgin Mary would have had no trouble doing so. In *L'avocacie Notre-Dame*, he described with gusto her feats of advocacy (complete with citations to the Digest and the *Glossa ordinaria*) in a lawsuit against the devil, but her services were not readily available in any but the highest court of all. Church authorities deemed the conduct of a few mortal advocates, such as St. Ivo of Brittany (1247–1303), close enough to the mark to merit canonization, although according to one account, even Ivo was forced to plead his case at the pearly gates after St. Peter initially tried to send him away, saying, "There is no room for you lawyers in heaven."[32]

The Hazards

In contrast to the flattering self-image that professional lawyers painted of themselves, they faced pervasive distrust, suspicion, and outright hostility from many nonlawyers. Almost as soon as trained lawyers became a recognizable social group, people at every level of society and in all walks of life began to denigrate them. The more prominent and successful lawyers became, the more complaints about them grew in volume and vehemence.[33] A torrent of censure erupted from every region of medieval Europe and every literate sector of society. Theologians, merchants, preachers, popes, and poets complained that lawyers were bloodsuckers, hypocrites, sacrilegious, foul-mouthed, devious, deceitful, treacherous, proud, and arrogant. As if that were not bad enough, critics further claimed that they suborned

---

31. Bonaguida, *Summa introductoria*, prol., at 133–34; Accursius, *Glos. ord.* to Cod. 2.6.7.1 v. *meritum*; Alain de Lille, *Summa de arte praedicatoria* c. 41, at 187; John Bromyard *Summa predicantium*, s.v. "Advocatus" §3, at 14vb; "C'est li mariages des filles au diable," ed. Jubinal, 1:288; Coopland, introduction to Philippe de Mézières, *Le songe du vieil pelerin* 1:51–52.

32. Carr, *Travels through Flanders*, 86–87. On St. Ivo, see especially *Monuments originaux de l'histoire de Saint Yves*, as well as Rieck, *Der heilige Ivo von Hélory*. In addition four articles in *ZRG*, KA 90 (2004) deal with Ivo. At least two other medieval canonists, Ivo of Chartres and Raymond of Penyafort, were raised to the altars of the church, as was the common lawyer Thomas More considerably later.

33. Chiappelli, "La polemica contro i legisti," 295; Yunck, *Lineage of Lady Meed*, 139–59; Kuttner, "Dat Galienus opes," 137; Holtzmann, "Propter Sion non tacebo," 170–71.

perjury, oppressed the poor, and thrived on the misfortunes of others.[34] As one anonymous poet summed it up:

> Advocates do a lot of harm
> Whereby they put their souls at risk:
> Their poisonous tongues
> Deprive people of their birthright
> And doom many a good marriage,
> and they wreak havoc merely for a jug of wine.[35]

Practitioners of course sometimes failed to live up to the ethical standards that they had sworn to uphold, and some habitually fell far short of the mark. There is no reason to believe that, as one fourteenth-century jurist claimed, lawyers had to wait to learn chicanery until the curia settled at Avignon.[36] Much the same criticisms could be levied against any occupational group whose members professed noble ideals that were difficult to observe in practice—priests, nuns, monks, bishops, popes, physicians, theologians, philosophers, kings, and knights, to name a few—likewise fell short of their ethical aspirations from time to time. Hostility toward lawyers, however, seems especially bitter, vicious, generally shared, and longer sustained than that voiced against those others.

To be sure, people on the margins of medieval society, such as Jews, Saracens, and heretics, not only attracted comparable censures, but could also suffer savage physical, economic, and social persecution to the bargain. Lawyers, however, were hardly marginal to medieval society. Indeed,

34. Peter of Blois, *Epist.* 25, at 1:92–93; John Wycliffe, "Three Things Destroy This World," 184; Adam of Periseigne, *Epist.* 24, *PL* 211:667; Philippe de Mézières, *Le songe du vieil pelerin* 3.197, 215, 311, at 2:146, 179, 492–93; Hostiensis, to 1 Lyons (1245) c. 3 (= VI 1.3.3) §3, vol. 6, at 3vb; Antonio de Butrio, *In Sextum decretalium volumen commentaria* to VI 2.2.1 §2, at 116ra; John of Salisbury, *Policraticus* 5.16, ed. Webb, 1:252–53; Jacques de Vitry, *Die Exempla aus den Sermones feriales et communes*, 20, and *Exempla or Illustrative Stores from the Sermones Vulgares*, 15, 149–50; Guibert of Tournai, *Sermones ad status, Ad iudices et aduocatos,* no. 1, at 106ra-vb; "La danza de la muerte," quoted in Alonso Romero and Garrigas Acosta, "El régimen jurídico," 100; Gautier de Coinci, "Vie de Seinte Léocad," ll. 1117–22, at 1:307; Haren, *Sin and Society*, 13; Eustache Deschamps, *Oeuvres complètes*, no. 1454, at 8:144, also 145; John Gower, *Vox clamantis* 6.2, ll. 105–52, at 4:233–34; Jason de Mayno, *Commentaria super titulo de actionibus* to Inst. 4.6.24 §57, at 200ra

35. "C'est li mariages des filles au diable," ed. Jubinal, 284–85: "Avocat portent grant domage /Pourquoi metent lor âme en gage: / Lor langue est pleine de venin, / Par aus sont perdu héritage, / Et deffait maint bon mariage, / Et mal fait pour i. pot-de-vin."

36. Parieu, "Étude sur la *Pratique dorée*," 442.

their most grievous offence in the eyes of their critics lay precisely in their centrality. "Doctors of law betray the law," charged one of the pseudonymous poets collectively known as Golias, and even grave and learned jurists admitted that there might be some truth to the charge. Hostiensis, for example, excoriated perverse advocates whose fanciful interpretations twisted laws to suit their purposes, and Jason de Mayno (1435–1519) characterized advocates of this sort as scourges of the poor, dogs of the court, and devourers of the commonwealth.[37] As lawyers increasingly came to occupy key positions in government, commerce, the church, and universities, attacks upon them—mostly verbal, seldom physical—sharpened.

A constant refrain stigmatized advocates as professional hypocrites. They were enemies of the truth in Walter of Châtillon's opinion, while Ralph Niger (d. ca. 1205) declared that despite lawyers' professed devotion to justice, in reality they would take any case, no matter how flimsy, and do or say anything for any client, no matter how wicked, provided that the client paid their fees.[38] This theme was reiterated decade after decade, century after century. "[Lawyers] love the wicked just as much as the righteous," wrote Guiot de Provins in the late twelfth or early thirteenth century, "they don't care which side they take." Two hundred years later, Boniface Ferrier (1355–1417) was asking rhetorically: "Tell me if you've ever seen or heard of any litigant, plaintiff or defendant, who couldn't find grave and worthy advocates to champion his case, no matter how dreadful it was, right down to the final decision? They're men of great compassion: they never desert cases—unless the money dries up."[39] Jurists themselves sometimes admitted, however reluctantly, that these reproaches might occa-

---

37. "Sermo Goliae ad praelatos," ll. 1–4, in *Latin Poems*, 43; Hostiensis, *Lectura* to X 3.30.12 §1 v. *prava*, at 98vb; Jason de Mayno, *Commentaria super titulo de actionibus* to Inst. 4.6.24 §57, at 200ra: "[I]sti impii procuratores, notarii, et aduocati sunt excoriatores pauperum, quos Bartolus . . . appellat congruentissimo uocabulo canes curiarum et deuoratores ciuium."

38. Walter of Châtillon, "Propter Sion non tacebo," 22, stanza 9; Ralph Niger, *De re militari* 4.36, at 216; similarly in his *Moralia regum*, 243.

39. Guiot de Provins, *Le Bible Guiot*, at 307: "Autant aiment tort comme droit: / mais que il facent lor exploit, / ne lor chaut de quel part il pendent"; Boniface Ferrier, *Tractatus pro defensione Benedicti XIV*, c. 47, at 1468–69: "Rogo te, dic mihi si umquam vidisti vel audisti quod aliquis litigans actor vel reus non invenit etiam usque ad tres sententias definitivas advocatos solemnes et magnos, quantumcumque malam causam foveat? Videntur homines magnae compassionis, quia numquam deserunt lites, nisi deserantur a pecuniis."

sionally be justified. The great legal scholar Panormitanus, for example, acknowledged:

> I have heard from extremely able advocates that, swayed by the urgent pleas of friends, they have often accepted unjust cases knowingly and I believe that they were morally guilty, since they secured decisions for their clients through false and unjust arguments.[40]

This theme was so widely accepted that comparisons between lawyers and prostitutes, to the disadvantage of lawyers, became commonplace. A lawyer, like a prostitute, according to Abbot Adam of Periseigne (b ca. 1145, d. 1221), will serve any paying client, no matter how worthless his cause.[41] Matheolus (fl. ca. 1290) put it even more crudely:

> What can I tell you about a lawyer?
> He's a bit like a filthy whore,
> But nastier.
> If a whore just rents out her ass,
> He sells his tongue.
> That's even more degrading,
> Since the tongue is more precious
> Than the ass.[42]

The proverbial greed of lawyers provided the profession's critics with another dependable target. Lawyers, they asserted, were worldly men who valued temporal things above spiritual ones.[43] "No one ever became an advocate, save to deliver himself from poverty," Peter the Chanter grumbled. William Langland (ca. 1330–1400) agreed: "It would be easier to blow the mist off Malvern Hills than to get a word out of a lawyer until he's seen his fee." Or as Gautier de Coinci (1177–1236) put it, "Clerks go to Bologna to learn law and duplicity, and consequently they get rich and lose their

---

40. Panormitanus, *Commentaria* to X 2.7.1 §5, vol. 3, at 155vb: "Nam audiui a ualentissimis aduocatis quod saepe per importunas preces amicorum assumunt causas iniustas scienter et crederem ipsos teneri in foro animae ad interesse: quia per iniustas et falsas allegationes obtinent sententias pro eorum clientulo."

41. Adam of Periseigne, *Epist.* 24, in *PL* 211:667.

42. *Lamentations de Matheolus*, ll. 4579–84, at 1:283: "Quid de causidico possum tibi dicere? dici / Debet enim similis vel par vili meretrici, / Immo vilior est, quia, si meretrix locat anum, / Hic vendat linguam, quod plus reor est prophanum, / Cum sit enim lingua membrum preciosius anos." Cf. Peter the Chanter, *Verbum adbreviatum* c. 49, at 332; Zingerle, "Bericht über die Sterzinger Miscellaneen-Handschrift," 310; Yunck, *Lineage of Lady Meed*, 146.

43. Hilduin, *Sermo "Spem oris nostri,"* in CUL, MS Ii.1.24, at 161rb–va.

souls." Richard of Bury (1287–1345) maintained that the study of law turned men into enemies of God, and Dante (1265–1321) concurred: "Lawyers and physicians, and for that matter most religious, study not in order to acquire knowledge, but rather to secure money or high office."[44]

Critics also blamed the wiles and wordiness of lawyers for the frustrating delays and interminable length of legal proceedings. Popes joined in to demand repeatedly that they cease and desist from burdening the courts with their "pernicious subtleties and quibbling."[45] Delaying tactics were so emblematic of lawyers that a story widely used by preachers described a lawyer who had spent his life securing fraudulent delays in the hearing of his cases tried to worm a delay out of God on judgment day.[46] Walter of Châtillon likened the tumult that lawyers raised in court to the barking of dogs. John of Salisbury was already complaining as early as the mid-twelfth century that lawyers not only wasted inordinate amounts of time, but that to the bargain they were pompous, pretentious, and deceptive about their tactics and motives. They snared simple men in nets of impenetrable jargon. "Woe unto the ordinary man who knows not how to syllabificate," he added sarcastically.[47]

Hugo von Trimberg (ca. 1230–1313) was not alone in the opinion that, despite its utility in worldly matters, the study of law failed to teach men how to live virtuously. "Who ever arises contrite from the study of civil or even canon law?" John of Salisbury asked Thomas Becket. As the Dominican preacher John Bromyard (fl. ca. 1390) saw things, students emerged from law school more interested in adding weight to their purses than in seeing justice done.[48] Even worse, Bromyard maintained, they went down-

---

44. Peter the Chanter, *Verbum adbreviatum*, 329, c. 49,: "[N]ec fiebat aliquis aduocatus nisi in paupertatis sue remedium, ut officio uictum queritaret." William Langland, *Piers Plowman*, A-text, prologue, ll. 88–89: "Thow mihtest beter meten the myst · on Maluerne hulles, / Then getten a mom of heore mouth · til moneye weore schewed"; Gautier de Coinci, "Vie de Seinte Léocad," 306, ll. 1107–16; Fournier, "L'église et le droit romain," 112; Dante, *Convivio* 3.11.10, at 569: "[L]i legisti, [li] medici e quasi tutti li religiosi, che non per sapere studiano ma per acquistare moneta o dignitade. "

45. E.g., Benedict XII, *Decens et necessarium* §10; Gregory XI, *Quamvis a felicis*, pr., in Tangl, *Päpstlichen Kanzleiordnungen*, 120, 128.

46. Jacques de Vitry, *Exempla or Illustrative Stories from the Sermones vulgares*, 15, 150.

47. Eldredge, "Walter of Châtillon"; John of Salisbury, *Policraticus* 5.16, ed. Webb, at 1:350–51; Rand, "Ioannes Saresberiensis Sillabizat."

48. Hugo von Trimberg, *Der Renner* 1:353–54, 361–62, ll. 8477–80, 8677–80; John of Salisbury, *Letters* 2:32–34, no. 144; Bromyard, *Summa predicantium*, s.v. "Iusticia," at 179va, §5.

hill from there, for age and experience only made lawyers more reprehensible. The greater their success at the bar, the more they resembled monkeys. While they were young, during their years as law students, they might be winning, gracious, pleasant members of society. But as they grew older, and especially after they had been in practice for a while, they turned vicious and became cruel as lions, infernal demons—in short, lawyers. Then everyone cursed not merely them, but even the mothers who had borne them.[49] And on top of everything else, even lawyers sometimes found their colleagues unbearably dull.[50]

So what good did lawyers do? Not nearly enough, in the opinion of their critics, to offset the harm they did. Bromyard compared corrupt advocates to erratic stars that were pulled in two different directions. "The more expert in law they become, the less they obey the laws," according to Adam of Perseigne. "They're powerful quibblers," he added, "skilled in subverting judgments, justifying evildoers, and unjustly convicting the innocent."[51] One leading legal scholar pleaded in partial mitigation, however, that lawyers were not the only ones to blame for the profession's shortcomings. Clients, too, needed to shoulder some of the responsibility, for after all, "Bad cases breed worse advocates."[52]

No theological faculty apparently debated the question "Can a lawyer be saved?" although the prevailing opinions about the morals of the profes-

---

49. Bromyard, *Summa predicantium*, s.v. "Advocatus," at 15vb, §19: "Assimilantur ergo simie, que est animal in iuuentute sociale et aliqualiter placidum. Sed in senectute est animal odiosum et damnosum, res asportando, domos discoperiendo, et mordendo. Sic iuuenes scolares in iure ciuili vel in banco primo vel secundo anno de scola redeuntes sunt omnibus graciosi, sociales, curiose ornati. Ab omnibus vicinis benedicuntur, benedicitur etiam mater que ipsum portauit. Sed cum sciuerit modicum placitare et nocere uicinis suis, et esse attornatus et aduocatus et huiusmodi, accipit propinas a magnatibus . . . fiunt crudeles leones, infernales diabolici, nemini parcentes, nisi quem inuadere non audent. Et sic illi qui in iuuentute ab omnibus benedicuntur, in senectute simul cum matre que eos genuit ab omnibus maledicuntur."

50. Placentinus, *Sermo de legibus*, 130–31.

51. Bromyard, *Summa praedicantium*, s.v. "Advocatus," at 14vb, §14; Adam of Perseigne, *Epist.* 24, in *PL* 211:667: "[Q]uanto in jure peritiores existerint, tanto inveniuntur ad juris injuriam promptiores. Verborum cavillationibus potentibus sunt, et docti ad subversionem judicii, aut impium justificare pro muneribus, aut de injustitia convincere innocentem."

52. William Durand, *Speculum iudiciale* 1.4 *De aduocato* §9.11, at 1:281: "Turpes lites turpiores habent aduocatos." Cf. Seneca, *Dialogorum libri XII* 2.7.

sion suggest that this might have been a popular topic.[53] Widespread opinion held that advocates regularly injured both their opponents and their clients. Strenuously as lawyers might deny this, they stood scant chance of convincing people otherwise. A great many people certainly seem to have been convinced that, as a Catalan proverb held, lawyers inevitably wound up burning in hell.[54] The author of the "Dit des Patenostres" exhorted the faithful in their charity to pray for lawyers and other legal professionals that God might pardon their sins.[55]

Moralists early in the thirteenth century began to express concern about lawyers' spiritual health. Robert of Flamborough in his *Summa de poenitentia* (ca. 1208–15) suggested a series of pointed questions that priests ought to put to lawyers and judges who came to confess their sins. About a decade later, Raymond of Penyafort in his treatise on penance drew upon his own long experience in the law to provide confessors with more elaborate, if not flattering, guidance about the sins that judges and advocates were prone to commit.[56] Not long thereafter, Cardinal Hostiensis in his *Summa* on the Liber Extra (completed by 1253), which was directed to law students, lawyers, and law professors rather than pastors and parish priests, urged his readers to examine their consciences regularly about seven situations where they were liable to fall into sin. They were morally bound, he warned, to confess their sinful conduct in their professional life, to make amends, to do penance for past offenses, and not least, to take the necessary steps to avoid those mistakes in future. Hostiensis's list of professorial wrongdoings included many of the perennial faults of lawyers and academics: arrogance, delight in subtle but useless distinctions, saying things that they knew or ought to have known were wrong, and giving students or cli-

---

53. On the other hand, a question concerning the salvation of archdeacons, many of whom were trained lawyers, apparently was disputed among theologians (Haskins, *Renaissance of the Twelfth Century*, 51).

54. Bernard of Montemirato, *Lectura* to X 1.37.3, at 70ra; Freedman, *Origins of Peasant Servitude*, 220, n. 39. Likewise the *Bible moralisée*, London, BL, MS Harley 1527, at 47vd: "Hoc scilicet quod in hoc seculo bona sua naturalia circa terrena expenderint, siue clerici siue laici fuerint, dicent in iudicio, 'Domine, paupertatem timui et immo leges et decreta didici uel ad usuram commodaui ut opes et diuitias acquirerem.' Et ideo mittit eos in egestatem perpetuam."

55. "Le dit des Patenostres," in Jubinal, *Nouveau recueil* 2:40. A similar prayer beseeching God to have mercy on sinful jurists occurs in a poem by Peire Cardenal (b. 1180, d. ca. 1278), Ourliac, "Troubadours et juristes," 174.

56. Robert of Flamborough, *Liber poenitentialis* 4.207, at 184–85; Raymond of Penyafort, *Summa de paenitentia* 2.5.35–39, col. 511–18.

ents false, worthless, or unfounded advice.[57] Later manuals for confessors, such as the widely circulated *Summa confessorum* of the Dominican John of Fribourg (d. 1313) drew upon these writers when they addressed the moral shortcomings of members of the legal profession.[58] The *Memoriale presbiterorum*, probably reflecting William Doune's personal experiences, posed an especially long and detailed list of questions that confessors should put to members of the legal profession in order to make sure that they reported all their shortcomings. This list, directed explicitly to the faults of practitioners, included such items as giving false advice to a client, betraying a client's confidences, presenting frivolous cases, accepting contingent fees, charging too much or too little for legal services, suborning perjury, and carelessness or indolence in handling clients' cases.[59]

Critics such as Peter the Venerable regularly disparaged the literary solecisms that abounded in legal Latin and the intellectual airs of law school alumni. Gerald of Wales lamented that the study of law was stifling literature. One of his teachers at Paris, Gerald claimed, had predicted, "The days are coming, and woe unto them, in which the law will obliterate the knowledge of literature."[60] Theologians, too, bewailed the magnetism of legal studies, which attracted greedy students away from the study of divinity. Stephen Langton in his commentary on the book of Kings compared lawyers to the Philistines of the Old Testament and deplored the success of lawyers and physicians in luring students away from the study of theology and the liberal arts, as did Hugh of St. Cher, Walter of Châtillon, Nigel Wireker, and a host of others from the late twelfth century onward.[61] "Students would rather spend their time on the intricacies of cases and Gratian's decrees than to try to understand sacred scripture. They turn up their noses at the manna that rains down from heaven and turn back to the fleshpots of Egypt," thundered their con-

---

57. *Summa* 5.54 *De penitentia et remissione*, at 274vb–275ra, §§31–33.

58. John of Fribourg, *Summa confessorum* 2.6; Haren, *Sin and Society*, 72; Jacques Le Goff, "Métier et profession," 57.

59. Haren, "Interrogatories," 132–34, and *Sin and Society*, 84–110.

60. Peter the Venerable, *Letters* 1:14, no. 8; Gerald of Wales, *Gemma ecclesiastica* 2.37, at 348–49: "[M]agistrum Mainerium in auditorio scholae suae Parisiis dicentem, et damna sui temporis plangentem, audivi, vaticinium illud Sibillae vere nostris diebus esse completum, hoc scilicet: 'Venient dies, et vai illis, quibus leges obliterabunt scientiam literarum."

61. Hausherr, "Eine Warnung," 397; Flahiff, "Ralph Niger," 115–16; Ferruolo, *Origins of the Universities*, 100, 126.

temporary, the preacher Hilduin.[62] Two centuries later, Dante was still lamenting:

> The Gospels and the Fathers now are pushed aside,
> And tattered edges testify to bookish hours
> Spent cramming the Decretals!
> Pope and cardinals dote on these;
> They never turn their thoughts to Nazareth.[63]

Lawyers have never been popular. In Karl Llewellyn's words, "The healthy spirited men of many ages have lifted up their clubs to bring them down on the lawyer's skull."[64] Lawyers regularly deal with disputes that arise out of ambiguous circumstances in which no party is clearly right or entirely in the wrong. Human beings cling stubbornly to the illusion that it is possible to frame rules that will cut through all uncertainties so that, no matter how murky the problem, any reasonable person can reach a clearcut decision. Since human relations are seldom so straightforward, lawyers who frame complex arguments and introduce subtle distinctions inevitably come to be seen as tricksters who manipulate the rules to suit their client's wishes—and to maximize their own earnings. Given this common perception, it is little wonder that utopian thinkers invariably dream that a society without lawyers would be the best of all possible worlds.[65]

While medieval detractors found numerous reasons to account for their dislike of the legal profession, fear and envy surely underlay many of their criticisms. Critics feared lawyers' power and influence and the vigor with which they wielded their authority. Alarm was further increased by the mysterious ways in which lawyers operated, the jargon in which they clothed their arguments, the effortlessness with which they seemed able to pull reasons out of the air to justify their clients' bad behavior, and their ability to dredge up endless authorities to support their points. Academic

---

62. Hilduin, *Sermo "Spem oris nostri,"* in CUL, MS Ii.1.24, at 161va: "Qui si sacris litteris operam dare mentiuntur, tumultuosis perplexitatibus causarum et decretis Gratiani potius uolunt intendere quam intelligencio sacre scripture. Isti in defecto illud manna quod pluit fastidiunt et ad ollas carnium in Egypto redeunt."

63. Dante, *Paradiso* 9.133–37, in *Tutte le opere*, 276: "Per questo l'Evangelio e i dottor magni / son derelitti, e solo ai Decretali / si studia, sì che pare a' lor vivagni./ A questo intende il papa e' cardinali: / non vano i lor pensieri a Nazarette." Cf. *Paradiso* 12.83–85, at 285.

64. Llewellyn, *The Bramble Bush*, 169.

65. Pound, *The Lawyer*, xxv; Noonan, "From Social Engineering to Creative Charity," 197–98.

critics envied the success that lawyers enjoyed in attracting students to their schools, in securing prize positions in church and state, and in amassing considerable sums of money. Clients, too, often showed little appreciation for their lawyers' efforts on their behalf and frequently felt aggrieved by the lawyers on whom they depended. In any legal action, at least one party invariably loses and that party is apt to blame both his own and his opponent's lawyers for the loss. Even clients who emerged victorious from litigation routinely begrudged the legal fees they had to pay in order to secure what they regarded as their due.[66]

There is little evidence to suggest that the flood of criticism and suspicion that assailed jurists from all sides seriously diminished the profession's attractiveness to prospective recruits. Law faculties continued to draw large numbers of students through the end of the fifteenth century. Fluctuations in the scattered enrollment figures available for law faculties seem to reflect broader currents of economic, social, and political change within particular regions rather than widespread disenchantment with the profession. That said, signs of increased competition for desirable positions also hint that the supply of graduates slowly commenced to outstrip the number of available appointments, especially after the middle of the fifteenth century.[67]

In sum, professional lawyers constituted a small but powerful elite within medieval society. They earned their privileged position by devoting a considerable fraction of their lives to the difficult and expensive task of learning the law. That investment paid off by affording them the opportunity to secure rewards that were out of the reach of most of their contemporaries. But prosperity and privilege come at a cost. The resentment, envy, suspicion, fear, and loathing with which so many of their contemporaries regarded medieval lawyers were part of the price they paid for the rewards that their profession brought them.

The dissatisfaction so often voiced about the manners and morals of members of the legal profession helps to account for the increasing solidarity and exclusiveness that characterized the profession during the later Middle Ages. Professional organizations reacted by circling the wagons. They sought to protect their prerogatives by making entry into the profession ever more costly and more demanding. To this end, they raised fees for admission to practice, increased the difficulty of entrance examinations,

---

66. Mayer-Maly, *Der Jurist*, 3–4.

67. Moraw, "Careers of Graduates," 268, 275–76; Schwinges, "Admission," 188–89; Aston, "Oxford's Medieval Alumni," 30–32.

and accorded preferential status to the sons and nephews of existing members. Defensive measures of this sort formed part of the profession's response to rampant criticism of its members within the wider community in which they lived.

The caricature of the grasping, hypocritical, deceitful jurist that became a stock figure in literature and folklore from the mid-twelfth century onward testifies paradoxically to the fast-growing importance of the learned laws in late medieval society. Because highly specialized skills were essential to understand the romano-canonical legal system and to use it effectively, the judges and lawyers who made the legal system work struck those who lacked that expertise as awesome, mysterious, and sacred, yet at the same time both ominous and intimidating. Canon law in particular often impinged on the personal lives of ordinary people in ways that could be humiliating, painful, and expensive. Lawyers were intermediaries between the formal system of the *ius commune* and the individuals whose lives it impacted. As privileged players, lawyers were able to use the legal system to further their own personal interests as well as those of their clients. On that account, nonlawyers simultaneously admired, resented, and feared those who administered that system.[68]

---

68. Bouwsma, "Lawyers and Early Modern Culture," 315–16; Lewis, introduction to *Lawyers in Society*, 1–2; Galanter, *Lowering the Bar*, 15–22.

Conclusion
The Tradition of the Legal Profession

Advocates and proctors who practiced regularly in the courts of the medieval *ius commune*, the European general law, became full-fledged professionals during the second quarter of the thirteenth century. The gradual process that led to the emergence of professional lawyers began a little more than a century earlier when schools of Roman law began to reappear in western Europe, first at Bologna and shortly thereafter in the south of France. Alumni of these schools at first used the skills they acquired primarily to teach Roman law, although they occasionally provided legal advice to individuals who sought it. The principal occupation of the Four Doctors of Bologna, so far as we can tell, was teaching, but they also served on occasion as *iurisperiti* who advised individuals about the legal ramifications of transactions, remedies for grievances, or defenses against opponents.

Trained jurists began to appear regularly as pleaders in the courts around or shortly after the middle of the twelfth century. By around 1150, when the vulgate version of Gratian's Decretum had taken its final form, at least a few men trained in Roman and canon law were able to make a living by using their legal knowledge and forensic skills to argue on behalf of litigants in the courts. Employment opportunities for these lawyers were at first most plentiful in church courts. By the last quarter of the twelfth century, popes and bishops had begun to delegate their routine judicial duties to officials who had some formal training in Roman and canon law. The courts of municipalities, kings, and other secular rulers, which generally operated under local statutes or customary law, initially furnished fewer job prospects for lawyers trained in the learned laws. Those opportunities soon began to multiply, however, as these courts, too, began to adopt romano-canonical procedure.

The institutionalization of law teaching that occurred with the organization of universities around the turn of the thirteenth century marked a further step toward the professionalization of learned lawyers. University law faculties served two vital functions in the development of professional status. They furnished students with systematic instruction in Roman and canon law, as individual masters had previously done in their private schools. Beyond that, universities established formal curricula for law students and created a system of examinations to test their competence. University law faculties collectively certified that students to whom they awarded degrees had not only spent a substantial period of time studying the two laws that comprised the *ius commune*, but had also demonstrated skill in using that knowledge in public disputations and had proved in a demanding examination that they could argue points of law successfully.

Just as Europe's first universities commenced to take shape, the romano-canonical procedural system was starting to reach maturity. Because romano-canonical procedure required parties to submit formal written documents at every stage of proceedings, even litigants who appeared on their own behalf required knowledgeable advice and guidance from someone familiar with the system's forms and the practical details about submitting them to the appropriate authorities. In simple, straightforward cases before the court of a dean or an archdeacon, a notary or court clerk who could draw up the necessary documents might supply adequate assistance. In more complex cases in upper-level courts, such as bishops' consistories, litigants usually needed to employ a proctor who could not only provide legal guidance, but could also make the required court appearances for them. In matters that involved challenging legal issues, particularly if they were to be heard by an appellate court or in one of the tribunals of the papal curia, litigants almost invariably found it essential to employ the services of an advocate, in addition to a proctor, to present what they hoped would be compelling legal arguments on their behalf.

The simultaneous convergence of four developments created the conditions in which a legal profession in the strict sense emerged. First, the supply of practitioners with methodical training in the technical aspects of Roman and canon law grew at a sufficiently rapid rate to produce a critical mass of academically qualified lawyers. Second, university law faculties not only taught, but also tested and certified the ability of would-be practitioners to present sound legal arguments in the courts. Third, courts with judges who were able to evaluate the cogency of complex legal arguments were beginning to emerge. And fourth, those courts employed an intricate procedural system that few litigants could readily navigate without expert help.

Beginning in the 1230s, ecclesiastical and civil authorities began to restrict the right of audience to men who solemnly promised to observe a body of ethical norms. In the following decades, popes and bishops, councils and synods, slowly raised the hurdles that practitioners in church courts must surmount. They established educational standards for admission, prescribed regulations for the conduct of advocates and proctors both in and out of court, created fee schedules, and threatened to punish those who failed to follow these rules by revoking their right of audience. By the middle of the thirteenth century, advocates and proctors in the ecclesiastical courts were becoming full-blown professionals in ways that their predecessors a century earlier had never been. Church courts were in the vanguard of these developments, but civil authorities in many regions soon followed.

The demonization of lawyers that appeared in the mid-twelfth century gives clear and compelling evidence that men of law had by then become a visible, if not universally admired, element in medieval society. They grew more conspicuous and unpopular during subsequent decades. As their numbers swelled and their services became ever more indispensable, not only in litigation but also in facilitating other kinds of business, hostility toward lawyers mounted correspondingly. They made convenient scapegoats for discontent over changes that had begun to disrupt the traditional power structures of earlier medieval society.

Legal advisers, advocates, and proctors expected payment for their services of one sort or another, and by the latter part of the twelfth century income from legal practice was apparently sufficient to maintain some of them comfortably. Modern writers sometimes describe these lawyers as professionals simply because they could live on their earnings from using their legal skills. In this view, anyone who has sufficient expertise to make a living from the practice of a craft or trade qualifies as a professional rather than an amateur.

This usage has been common in English since the late eighteenth century. It is anachronistic, however, when applied to twelfth-century lawyers because it ignores the way in which they regarded themselves. Medieval lawyers described themselves as a *professio, ordo, militia,* or *corpus*. What they meant by those expressions had something, but not very much, to do with making a living. They and their contemporaries associated *professio* with a religious act that involved accepting a set of ethical commitments and behaving in accordance with them. Twelfth-century writers, for example, commonly described the affirmation of religious belief by reciting the Apostles' Creed as a profession of faith. They likewise described entrance into a monastery or other religious community as an act of profession, and called members of such communities professed monks or nuns. Twelfth-century legal practitioners were not professionals in any sense of the term that they would have recognized because courts did not require them to make a "profession" to observe a special set of ethical standards as a necessary condition for representing clients before a judge. On this understanding of "profession," twelfth-century lawyers may more accurately be described as proto-professionals.

These distinctions are not trivial or a mere semantic nicety. They involve two divergent concepts of what professionalism is all about. In the loose sense of the term, any occupation that requires special knowledge or skill and whose members are rewarded for the exercise of that knowledge or skill may be called a profession. The strict sense of the term adds to this the further qualification that profession necessarily involves an ethical commitment. "Profession" in this view means a skilled occupation in which practitioners agree to observe specific ethical standards in carrying out their work as a condition of entrance into practice. When they swore the admissions oath, medieval advocates and proctors accepted both a legal and a moral obligation. Once they had made that commitment, observance of the stipulated behavioral standards became mandatory and failure to do so was punishable at law.

Little evidence survives that would suggest that punishment followed infractions with great regularity. Complaints about misbehavior by legal practitioners were ubiquitous, but recorded actions to disbar advocates and proctors remained uncommon. The promise that medieval advocates and proctors made when they were admitted to practice represented an aspiration, rather than a rigidly enforced duty. Much the same could be said about professions of other kinds. Complaints about priests, monks, and nuns, for example, who breached their commitment to poverty, chastity, and obedience are also abundant, yet enforcement of those vows, too, was often haphazard. This does not mean that churchmen regarded the vows themselves or infractions of the obligations that they created as trivial or insignificant. A profession may be defined as much by the goals that its members strive for as by their success in achieving those goals.

The ethical aspirations enunciated in thirteenth-century admissions oaths remain largely unchanged to this day. Modern oaths of admission to the bar strikingly resemble their medieval counterparts, as do the assumptions about proper lawyerly conduct implicit in codes of professional responsibility. The ethical ideals to which lawyers aspire seem not to have changed greatly in the past seven centuries. Nor has anxiety about the gap between the profession's ideals and its performance greatly diminished.

Members of the legal profession, public authorities, and the community at large still deplore what they describe as the lamentable state of lawyerly ethics and the woeful decline in professional standards—at least as compared with past generations (usually only vaguely identified) when lawyers are thought to have been more upright and honorable than they are today. These stories, like the stock tales told by the profession's medieval critics, are myths. They are nonetheless important evidence, in the one case for how members of the profession believe they ought to behave, and in the other case for how outsiders view them.[1]

The evidence shows that prior to the mid-twelfth century nothing that could be described as a legal profession in the strict sense existed in medieval Europe, and that there had been no such social or vocational identity since the Roman law schools faded away toward the end of the sixth century. By the mid-thirteenth century, however, a legal profession had once more emerged in western Europe. It is likewise clear that this revived legal profession drew many of its ideas and much of its inspiration from the Roman law texts that its members studied in the law schools, but that medieval legal professionals also differed in many respects from their Roman predecessors. Many, probably most, of the profession's members in the thirteenth century were clerics, although the proportion of laymen in their ranks grew substantially, especially in Italy, during the fourteenth and fifteenth centuries.

The medieval legal professions survived on the Continent largely intact, despite some relatively superficial changes, until the late eighteenth century. They were abolished on much of the Continent during the French Revolution and its aftermath. When legal professions started to reappear early in the nineteenth century, they chose to revive many of the characteristics of their medieval forbearers. Even in England, where the common law that began to emerge during the late twelfth century diverged from the European *ius commune*, common lawyers nonetheless borrowed a considerable part of their professional ethos from the canonists and civilians.

The legal professions, together with the universities, the papacy, the corporation, and constitutional government, are institutions that must rank among the most influential and most enduring creations of the thousand years that constituted the European Middle Ages. They remain with us still. Without them, the world as we know it would be a poorer, less interesting place.

1. Bennett, *The Lawyer's Myth*, and Galanter, *Lowering the Bar*, explore the relationship between the two in greater depth.

Bibliography

Primary Sources

Abbas antiquus. See Bernard of Montemirato.

Accursius. *Glossa ordinaria*. In *Corpus iuris civilis, una cum glossis*. [1584].

Acta imperii Angliae et Franciae ab a. 1267 ad a. 1313. Ed. Fritz Kern. Tübingen: J. C. B. Mohr, 1911.

The Acta of the Bishops of Chichester, 1075–1207. Ed. H. Mayr-Hartung. Canterbury and York Society Publications, vol. 56. York: Canterbury and York Society, 1964.

Acts of Gubertinus de Novate, Notary of the Patriarch of Aquileia, 1328–1336: A Calendar with Selected Documents. Ed. Giulio Silano. Studies and Texts, vol. 102. Toronto: Pontifical Institute of Mediaeval Studies, 1990.

Adam of Periseigne. *Epistolae*. In *PL* 211:583–694.

Adam Usk. *The Chronicle of Adam Usk, 1377–1421*. Ed. and trans. Chris Given-Wilson. Oxford Medieval Texts. Oxford: Clarendon Press, 1997.

Aegidius Fuscarariis. *Ordo iudiciarius*. Ed. Ludwig Wahrmund. QGRKP, vol. 3, pt. 1. Innsbruck: Wagner, 1916.

Agustín, Antonio. *De emendatione Gratiani libri duo*. Ed. Étienne Baluze and Gerhard von Mastricht. Duisburg: Johann Friedrich Hagen, 1677.

———. *Praxis Rotae*. Ed. Charles Lefebvre. Monumenta Christiana Selecta, vol. 8. Tournai: Desclée, 1961.

Alain de Lille. *Summa de arte praedicatoria*. In *PL* 210:111–98.

———. *Textes inédits*. Ed. Marie-Thérèse d'Alverny. Études de philosophie médiévale, vol. 52. Paris: J. Vrin, 1965.

Alciato, Andrea. *Iudiciarius processus compendium atque iuris utriusque praxis*. Lyon: Apud Vincentium Portonarium, 1536.

———. *Le lettere di Andrea Alciato giureconsulto*. Ed. Gian Luigi Barni. Florence: Felice Le Monnier, 1953.

Alexander Tartagnus. *Consiliorum*. Venice: Bernardinus Stagninus, 1488.

———. *Consilia et responsa*. 9 vols. Lyon: Thomas Berthau, 1544.

Ambrose, St. *De officiis ministrorum*. In *PL* 16:25–284.
Ambrosius Catharinus Politis. *De advocati officio*. In *TUJ*, vol. 3, pt. 1, 362ra–364va.
Ammianus Marcellinus. *Rerum gestarum libri qui supersunt*. Ed. and trans. John C. Rolfe. 3 vols. Loeb Classical Library. Cambridge: Harvard University Press; London: William Heinemann, 1935–39. Repr., 1982–86.
Ancient Roman Statutes. Ed. and trans. Allan Chester Johnson, Paul Robinson Coleman-Norton, and Frank Card Bourne. Corpus of Roman Law, vol. 2. Austin: University of Texas Press, 1961.
Andreas Benellus de Barolo. *Commentarii in tres libros Codicis*. Venice: Apud Seslas, 1601. Repr., Bologna: Arnaldo Forni, 1975.
Anecdota quae processum civilem spectant. Ed. Agathon Wunderlich. Göttingen: Vandenhoeck & Ruprecht, 1841.
Anselm of Lucca. *Collectio canonum una cum collectione minore*. Ed. Friedrich Thaner. 2 vols. Innsbruck: Wagner, 1906–15. Repr., Aalen: Scientia, 1965.
Antoninus, St. *Confessionale*. Rome: Petrus de Torre, 1472.
———. *Summa confessionalis*. Lyon: M. Bonhomme, 1536.
Antonio de Butrio. *In quinque libros decretalium commentaria*. 3 vols. Lyon: Lucembourg de Gabiano & Hugues de la Portenarias, 1532.
———. *In Sextum decretalium volumen commentaria*. Venice: Apud Franciscum Zilletum, 1575.
"Apocalypsis Goliae episcopi." In *The Latin Poems Commonly Attributed to Walter Mapes*, 1–20.
Apparatus "Ecce vicit leo." In Cambridge, Trinity College, MS O.5.17.
Apuleius. *Metamorphoses*. Ed. and trans. J. Arthur Hanson. 2 vols. Loeb Classical Library. Cambridge: Harvard University Press, 1989. Repr., 1996–98.
Archives de la ville de Lectoure: Coutumes, statuts et records du XIIIe au XVIe siècle. Ed. P. Druilhet. Archives historiques de Gascogne, fasc. 9. Paris: H. Champion, 1885.
Archives législatives de la ville de Reims. Ed. Pierre Varin. 3 vols. in 4. Collection de documents inédits sur l'histoire de France. Paris: Crapelet, 1840–52.
Aristotle. *Nicomachaean Ethics*. Rev. ed. Ed. and trans. H. Rackham. Loeb Classical Library. Cambridge: Harvard University Press; London: William Heinemann, 1934. Repr., 1982.
Arnulphus. *Die Summa minorum*. Ed. Ludwig Wahrmund. QGRKP, vol. 1, pt. 2. Innsbruck: Wagner, 1905. Repr., Aalen: Scientia, 1962.
Arresta quedam Parisiis quam Tholose in parlamento prolata. Lyon: In Officinis S. Vincentii, 1525.
Aubenas, Roger. *Recueil des lettres des officialités de Marseille et d'Aix (XIVe-XVe s.): Contribution à l'histoire des officialités au moyen-âge*. 2 vols. Paris: Auguste Picard, 1937–38.
Augustine, St. *De civitate Dei*. Ed. Bernhard Dombart and Alfons Kalb. CCL, vols. 47–48. Turnhout: Brepols, 1955.
———. *Epistolae ex duobus codicibus nuper in lucem prolatae*. Ed. Johannes Divjak. CSEL, vol. 88. Vienna: Hoelder-Pichler-Tempsky, 1981.
L'avocacie Notre-Dame, ou la vierge Marie plaidant contre le diable. Ed. Alphonse Chassant. Paris: Auguste Aubry, 1885.

Azo. *Summa super Codicem, Instituta, Extraordinaria.* Pavia: Bernardinus & Ambrosius fratres de Rovellis, 1506. Repr., Turin: Bottega d'Erasmo, 1966.

Bacon, Roger. *Opera.* Ed. J. S. Brewer. Rolls Series, no. 15. London: Longman, Green, Longman, and Roberts, 1859.

Baldus de Ubaldis, Petrus. *Additiones ad Durantis Speculum.* In William Durand, *Speculum iudiciale.*

———. *Commentaria in corpore iuris civilis.* 20 vols. in 8. Venice: Apud Iuntas, 1586.

———. *Consiliorum, sive responsorum.* 6 vols. in 1. Venice: D. Nicolonius & Socios, 1580.

———. *L'opera di Baldo.* Perugia: Unione cooperativa, 1901.

———. *Practica iudiciaria.* Lyon: Jacobus Iuntas, 1534.

Barraclough, Geoffrey. "'Ordo judiciarius qui in Romana curia consuevit communiter observari' e codicibus manuscriptis dissertatione critica praemissa." *Jus pontificium* 17 (1937) 111–30, 209–17.

Bartolomeo Scala. *De consilio sapientis in forensibus causis.* In *TUJ*, vol. 3, pt. 1, 331va–355va.

Bartholomew of Exeter, *Penitential.* In Morey, *Bartholomew of Exeter,* 163–300.

Bartolus of Sassoferrato. *Opera.* 12 vols. Venice: Apud Iuntas, 1575–85.

Bede. *Ecclesiastical History of the English People.* Ed. and trans. Bertram Colgrave and R. A. B. Mynors. Oxford Medieval Texts. Oxford: Clarendon Press, 1969. Repr., 1992.

———. *Ecclesiastical History of the English People.* Ed. and trans. Judith McClure and Roger Collins. Oxford: Oxford University Press, 1994. Repr., 1999.

Beltrán de Heredia, Vicente. *Cartulario de la Universidad de Salamanca (1218–1600).* 6 vols. Salamanca: Universidad de Salamanca, 1970–72.

Bencivenne ["Pillius"]. *De ordine iudiciorum.* In *Pilii, Tancredi, Gratiae libri de iudiciorum ordine,* 3–86.

Die Berichte der Generalprokuratoren des Deutschen Ordens an der Kurie. Ed. Karl Forstreuter. 6 vols. Veröffentlichen der Niedersächsischen Archivverwaltung, nos. 12, 13, 21, 29, 32, 37. Göttingen: Vandenhoeck & Ruprecht, 1960–76.

Bernard of Clairvaux. *De consideratione ad Eugenium papam.* In his *Opera* 3:379–493.

———. *Five Books on Consideration: Advice to a Pope.* Trans. John D. Anderson and Elizabeth T. Kennan. Cistercian Fathers Series, no. 35. Kalamazoo: Cistercian Publications, 1976.

———. *Opera.* Ed. Jean Leclercq, C. H. Talbot, and H. M. Rochais. 8 vols. in 9. Rome: Editiones Cistercienses, 1957–77.

Bernard of Montemirato. *Lectura aurea domini abbatis antiqui super quinque libros decretalium.* Strasbourg: Johannes Schottus, 1511.

Bernard of Parma. *Glossa ordinaria super Decretales Gregorii IX.* In *Corpus iuris canonici.* [Venice, 1605].

Bernard of Pavia. *Summa decretalium.* Ed. E. A. T. Laspeyres. Regensburg: Josef Manz, 1860. Repr., Graz: Akademische Druck- u. Verlagsanstalt, 1956.

Bible moralisée. In London, BL, MS Harley 1527.

Bibliotheca iuridica medii aevi: Scripta anecdota glossatorum. Ed. Augusto Gaudenzi, Giovanni Battista Palmieri, Federico Patetta, Giovanni Tamasia, and Vittorio

Sciloia. 3 vols. Bologna: In aedibus Societatis Azzoguidianae, 1888–1901. 2nd ed., Bologna: Angelo Gandolfo, 1913. Repr., Turin: Bottega d'Erasmo, 1962.

Blackstone, William. *Commentaries on the Laws of England*. 4 vols. Oxford: Clarendon Press, 1765–69. Repr., Chicago: University of Chicago Press, 1979.

Blondel, David. *Pseudo-Isidorus et Turrianus vapulantes*. Geneva: Ex typographia Petri Chouët, 1628.

Bologna Statutes. See *Statuti di Bologna dell'anno 1288*.

Bologna University Statutes, ed. Maffei. See Maffei, "Un trattato di Bonaccorso degli Elisei."

Bologna University Statutes, 1317 and 1432. See Denifle, "Die Statuten der Juristen-Universität Bologna."

Bologna University Statutes, ed. Malagola. See *Statuti delle università e dei collegi dello studio bolognese*.

Bonaguida de Arezzo. *Summa introductoria super officio advocationis in foro ecclesiae*. In *Anecdota quae processum civilem spectant*, 122–345.

Boniface Ferrier. *Tractatus pro defensione Benedicti XIV*. In Martène and Durand, *Thesaurus novus anecdotorum* 2:1453–1532.

Boso. *Life of Alexander III*. Trans. G. M. Ellis. Oxford: Basil Blackwell, 1973.

———. *Vitae Romanorum pontificum*. In *Liber pontificalis*, ed. Duchesne, 353–446.

Bruns, Karl Georg. *Fontes iuris Romani antiqui*. 7th ed. Ed. Otto Gradenwitz. 2 vols. Tübingen: J. C. B. Mohr, 1909.

Bulgarus. *Excerpta legum*. Ed. Ludwig Wahrmund. QGRKP, vol. 4, pt. 1. Innsbruck: Wagner, 1925. Repr., Aalen: Scientia, 1962.

Burchard of Worms. *Decretum*. In *PL* 140:537–1058.

Burchard III von Werberge. *Judicialis processus reformacio ordinaria servanda*. Ed. Nikolaus Hilling. In "Sechsgerichtsordnungen für das Bistum Halberstadt aus dem 15. Jahrhundert," 324–41.

Burchard of Würzburg. *Chronicon*. Ed. Oswald Holder-Egger and Bernhard von Simson. MGH, SSRG. Hannover: Hahn, 1916.

The Burgundian Code. Trans. Katherine Fischer Drew. Philadelphia: University of Pennsylvania Press, 1949. Repr., 1972.

Caius glosses. Cambridge, Gonville and Caius College, MS 283/676.

Calendar of the Patent Rolls Preserved in the Public Record Office, 1374–1377. London: His Majesty's Stationery Office, 1916.

Cambridge University. Angelica Statutes. In Hackett, *The Original Statutes of Cambridge University*, 190–217.

———. *Statuta antiqua*. In *Documents Relating to the University and Colleges of Cambridge* 1:308–416.

Cassiodorus Senator, Flavius Magnus Aurelius. *Variae*. Ed. Åke Jason Fridh. CCL, vol. 96. Turnhout: Brepols, 1958.

Cassius Dio Cocceianus. *Roman History*. Ed. and trans. Earnest Cary. 9 vols. Loeb Classical Library. London: William Heinemann, 1914–27.

Chartularium studii Bononiensis: Documenti per la storia dell'Università di Bologna dalle origini fino al secolo XV. 14 vols. to date. Bologna: Commissione per la storia dell'Università di Bologna, 1909–. [*CSB*]

Chartularium Universitatis Parisiensis. Ed. Heinrich Denifle and Émile Chatelain. 4 vols. Paris: Delalain Frères, 1889–97. Repr., Brussels: Culture & Civilisation, 1964. [*CUP*]

Chaucer, Geoffrey. *The Poetical Works of Chaucer*. Ed. F. N. Robinson. Boston: Houghton-Mifflin, 1933.

Christopherus Lanfranchinus. *Utrum sit praeferendus miles an doctor*. In *TUJ* [1584], vol. 18, 21rb–23va.

The Chronicle of Battle Abbey. Ed. and trans. Eleanor Searle. Oxford Medieval Texts. Oxford: Clarendon Press, 1980.

The Chronicle of Melrose. Ed. Alan Orr Anderson and Marjorie Ogilvie Anderson. London School of Economics, Studies in Economics and Political Science, no. 100. London: Percy Lund Humphries, 1936.

Chronicon de Lanercost. Ed. John Stevenson. Bannatyne Club Publications, vol. 46. Edinburgh: Maitland Club, 1839.

Cicero, Marcus Tullius. *Brutus*. Rev. ed. Ed. and trans. G. L. Hendrickson. Loeb Classical Library. Cambridge: Harvard University Press, 1962. Repr., 1997.

———. *De legibus*. Ed. and trans. Clinton Walker Keyes. Loeb Classical Library. Cambridge: Harvard University Press; London: William Heinemann, 1928. Repr., 1988.

———. *De oratore*. Ed. and trans. E. W. Sutton and H. Rackham. 2 vols. Loeb Classical Library. Cambridge: Harvard University Press; London: William Heinemann, 1942. Repr., 1976.

———. *Pro Murena*. Rev. ed. Ed. and trans. Louis E. Lord. Loeb Classical Library. London: William Heinemann; Cambridge: Harvard University Press, 1946. Repr., 1953.

———. *The Verrine Orations*. Ed. and trans. L. H. G. Greenwood. 2 vols. Loeb Classical Library. Cambridge: Harvard University Press, 1928–35. Repr., 1988–89.

Cino da Pistoia. *Lectura super Codice*. 2 vols. Frankfurt a/M: Sigismund Feyerabendt, 1578. Repr., Rome: Il Cigno Galileo Galilei, 1998.

Codex iuris canonici auctoritate Ioannis Pauli PP. II promulgatus. Vatican City: Typis Polyglottis Vaticanis, 1983.

Codex iuris canonici Pii X pontificis maximi iussu digestus, Benedicti papae XV auctoritate promulgatus. New York: P. J. Kennedy & Sons, 1918.

Codex Theodosianus. Ed. Paul Krueger and Theodor Mommsen. 2 vols. in 3. Berlin: Weidmann, 1905. Repr., 1990.

Codice diplomatico Padovano dall'anno 1101 alla pace di Costanza (25 Giugno 1183). Ed. Andrea Gloria. Monumenti storici publicati dalla R. Deputazione Veneta di storia patria, ser. 1, Documenti, vols. 4, 6. Venice: a spese della Società, 1879–81.

Collectio Tanner. See Holtzmann, "Die Dekretalensammlungen des 12. Jahrhunderts, I: Die Sammlung Tanner."

Collectio vetus Gallica. Ed. Hubert Mordek. In *Kirchenrecht und Reform im Frankenreich*, 340–617.

The Collection in Seventy-Four Titles: A Canon Law Manual of the Gregorian Reform. Trans.

John T. Gilchrist. Mediaeval Sources in Translation, vol. 22. Toronto: Pontifical Institute of Mediaeval Studies, 1980.

Les Conciles de la province de Tours. Ed. Joseph Avril. Institut de recherche et d'histoire des textes, Sources d'histoire médiévale. Paris: Éditions du Centre National de la Recherche Scientifique, 1987.

Concilia Africae, A. 345–A. 525. Ed. Charles Munier. CCL, vol. 259. Turnhout: Brepols, 1974.

Constitutio Juliani de postulando: Eine unbekannte Konstitution Kaiser Julians. Ed. Bernhard Bischoff and Dieter Nörr. Bayerischen Akademie der Wissenschaften, Phil.-hist. Kl. Abhandlungen, n.s., Heft 58. Munich: Verlag der Bayerischen Akademie der Wissenschaften, 1963.

Constitucions i altres drets de Catalunya. 2 vols. in 1. Barcelona: Joan Pau Marti y Joseph Llopis, 1704. Repr., Barcelona: Editorial Base, 1973.

Constitutiones Concilii quarti Lateranensis una cum Commentariis glossatorum. Ed. Antonio García y García. MIC, Corpus glossatorum, vol. 2. Vatican City: BAV, 1981.

Constitutiones et statuta nove reformacionis curie officialatus Gebenn. In *Les sources du droit du Canton de Genève* 1:364–94.

Constitutiones patriae Foriiulii cum additionibus nouiter impresse. Venice: B. de Vitalibus, 1524.

Consuetudines feudorum. 2nd ed. Ed. Karl Lehmann, rev. by Karl August Eckhardt. Bibliotheca rerum historicarum, Neudrucke, vol. 1. Aalen: Scientia, 1971.

Corpus inscriptionum latinarum. 16 vols. to date. Berlin: G. Reimer, 1862–.

Corpus iuris canonici. Ed. Emil Friedberg. 2 vols. Leipzig: B. Tauchnitz, 1879. Repr., Graz: Akademische Druck- u. Verlagsanstalt, 1959.

Corpus iuris canonici una cum glossis. 4 vols. Venice: Apud Iuntas, 1605.

Corpus iuris civilis. 5 vols. Lyon: Jacobus Iuntas, 1584.

Corpus iuris civilis. Ed. Paul Krueger, Theodor Mommsen, Rudolf Schoell, and Wilhelm Kroll. 3 vols. Berlin: Weidmann, 1872–95. Repr., 1963–65.

Corpus iuris civilis: The Digest of Justinian. Text, ed. Paul Krueger and Theodor Mommsen; trans., ed. Alan Watson. 4 vols. Philadelphia: University of Pennsylvania Press, 1985.

Corpus iuris civilis: Justinian's Institutes. Trans. Peter Birks and Grant McLeod. Ithaca: Cornell University Press, 1987.

Councils and Synods with Other Documents Relating to the English Church I, A.D. 871–1204. Ed. Dorothy Whitelock, Martin Brett, and Christopher N. L. Brooke. 2 vols. Oxford: Clarendon Press, 1981. [Whitelock, Brett & Brooke]

Councils and Synods with Other Documents Relating to the English Church II, A.D. 1205–1313. Ed. Frederick M. Powicke and Christopher R. Cheney. 2 vols. Oxford: Clarendon Press, 1964. [Powicke & Cheney]

Cresconius. *Die Concordia canonum des Cresconius.* Ed. Klaus Zeichiel-Eckes. 2 vols. Freiburger Beiträge zur mittelalterlichen Geschichte, vol. 5. Frankfurt a/M: Peter Lang, 1992.

Curia regis Rolls Preserved in the Public Record Office. London: His Majesty's Stationery Office, 1922–.

Der *"Curialis."* Ed. Ludwig Wahrmund. QGRKP, vol. 1, pt. 3. Innsbruck: Wagner, 1905. Repr., Aalen: Scientia, 1962.

Dante Alighieri. *Tutte le opere.* Ed. Fredi Chiapelli. 4th ed. Milan: U. Mursia, 1965.

De commendatione cleri. Ed. and trans. Lynn Thorndike. In *University Records and Life,* 201–36, 409–33.

Decisiones capelle sedis archiepiscopalis Tholose. Ed. Jean Corsier, rev. by Étienne Aufréri. Lyon: Stephanus Gueynard, 1508.

Decrees of the Ecumenical Councils. Text, ed. Giuseppe Alberigo, J. A. Dossetti, P.-P. Joannou, C. Leonardi, and P. Prodi; trans., ed. Norman P. Tanner. 2 vols. London: Sheed & Ward; Washington, DC: Georgetown University Press, 1990. [*DEC*]

Decretales Gregorii IX. See *Corpus iuris canonici,* ed. Friedberg, 2:2–928.

The Deeds of Pope Innocent III. Trans. James M. Powell. Washington, DC: Catholic University of America Press, 2004.

Denifle, Heinrich. "Die Statuten der Juristen-Universität Bologna vom J. 1317–1347 und deren Verhältnis zu jenen Paduas, Perugias, Florenz." *Archiv für Literatur- und Kirchengeschichte des Mittelalters* 3 (1887) 196–397.

Dissensiones dominorum sive controversiae veterum iuris Romani interpretum qui glossatores vocantur. Ed. Gustav Haenel. Leipzig: Teubner, 1834. Repr., Aalen: Scientia, 1964.

Distinctiones "Si mulier eadem hora" seu Monacenses. Ed. Rosalba Sorice. MIC, Corpus glossatorum, vol. 4. Vatican City: BAV, 2002.

Diuersorum patrum sententie siue Collectio in LXXIV titulos digesta. Ed. John T. Gilchrist. MIC, Corpus collectionum, vol. 1. Vatican City: BAV, 1973.

Documenten uit de Praktijk van de Gedingbeslissende Rechtspraak van de Officialiteit van Doornik: Oorsprong en vroege ontwikkeling (1192–1300). Ed. Monique Vleeschouwers-Van Mclkebeek. Iuris scripta historica, vol. 1. Brussels: Wetenschappelijk comité voor rechtsgeschiedenis, Koninklijke Academie voor Wettenschappen, Letteren en Schone Kunsten van België, 1985.

Documents Relating to the University and Colleges of Cambridge. 3 vols. London: Longman, 1852.

Eilbert of Bremen. *Der Ordo judiciarius des Eilbert von Bremen.* Ed. Ludwig Wahrmund. QGRKP, vol. 1, pt. 5. Innsbruck: Wagner, 1906. Repr., Aalen: Scientia, 1962.

Emo of Frisia. *Emonis et Menkonis Werumensium chronicon.* Ed. Ludwig Weiland. MGH, SS 23:454–572. Hannover: Hahn, 1874.

English Episcopal Acta I, Lincoln 1067–1185. Ed. David M. Smith. London: Oxford University Press, 1980.

English Episcopal Acta II, Canterbury 1162–1190. Ed. Christopher R. Cheney and Bridgett E. A. Jones. London: Oxford University Press, 1986.

English Episcopal Acta, III, Canterbury 1193–1205. Ed. Christopher R. Cheney and Eric John. Oxford: Oxford University Press, 1986. Repr., 1991.

English Episcopal Acta V, York 1070–1154. Ed. Janet E. Burton. London: Oxford University Press, 1988.

English Episcopal Acta 18, Salisbury 1078–1217. Ed. B. R. Kemp. Oxford: Oxford University Press, 1999.

English Lawsuits from William I to Richard I. Ed. and trans. Raoul C. van Caenegem. 2 vols. Selden Society Publications, vols. 106–7. London: Selden Society, 1990–91.

An Episcopal Court Book for the Diocese of Lincoln, 1514–1520. Ed. Margaret Bowker. Lincoln Record Society Publications, vol. 61. Lincoln: Lincoln Record Society, 1967.

Étienne Aufréri. *Decisiones capelle sedis archiepiscopalis Tholose*. Lyon: Stephanus Gueynard, 1508.

Eusebius. *Life of Constantine*. Trans. Averil Cameron and Stuart G. Hall. Oxford: Clarendon Press, 1999.

Eustache Deschamps. *Oeuvres complètes*. Ed. Gaston Raynaud. 11 vols. Société des anciens textes français. Paris: Firmin Didot, 1878–1903. Repr., New York: Johnson Reprint Corporation, 1966.

"Ewangelium secundum marcham argenti." In Bayless, *Parody in the Middle Ages*, 322–23.

Extravagantes Iohannis XXII. Ed. Jacqueline Tarrant. MIC, Corpus collectionum, vol. 6. Vatican City: BAV, 1983.

Fabliaux et contes des poètes françois des XIIe, XIIIe, XIVe et XVe siècles. Ed. Étienne Barbazan, rev. by Dominique Martin Méon, 4 vols. Paris: B. Warée, 1808. Repr., Geneva: Slatkine Reprints, 1976.

La faculté de décret de l'Université de Paris au XVe siècle. Ed. M. Fournier and L. Dorez. 4 vols. Paris: Imprimerie Nationale, 1895–1942.

Fagani, Prosper. *Jus canonicum, sive commentaria absolutissima in quinque libros decretalium*. Cologne: Apud heredes Ioannis Widenfelt, 1676.

Foliot, Gilbert. *The Letters and Charters of Gilbert Foliot*. Ed. Adrian Morey and C. N. L. Brooke. Cambridge: Cambridge University Press, 1967.

Formularium Florentinum artis notariae (1220–1242). Ed. Gino Masi. Orbis Romanus, vol. 17. Milan: Vita & Pensiero, 1943.

Fortescue, John. *De laudibus legum Anglie*. Ed. and trans. S. B. Chrimes. Cambridge: Cambridge University Press, 1942. Repr., Holmes Beach, FL: Wm. W. Gaunt & Sons, 1986.

Fragmenta Vaticana. Ed. Theodor Mommsen and Paul Krueger. Berlin: Weidmann, 1890.

Franciscus de Platea. *Opus restitutionum*. Venice: Johannes de Colonia & Johann Manthen, 1474.

Gaius. *The Institutes of Gaius*. Ed. E. Seckel and B. Kuebler. Trans. William M. Gordon and Olivia F. Robinson. Ithaca: Cornell University Press, 1988.

Galbert of Bruges. *The Murder of Charles the Good*. Trans. James Bruce Ross. New York: Columbia University Press, 1959. Repr., New York: Harper & Row, 1967.

Galteri a Sancto Victorio et quorumdam aliorum sermones ineditos triginta sex. Ed. Jean Châtillon. CCM, vol. 40. Turnhout: Brepols, 1975.

Gautier de Coinci. "Vie de Seinte Léocad." In *Fabliaux et contes des poètes françois* 1:270–346.

Gellius, Aulus. *The Attic Nights of Aulus Gellius*. Rev. ed. Ed. and trans. John C. Rolfe. 3 vols. Loeb Classical Library. Cambridge: Harvard University Press, 1946–52. Repr., 1982–96.

Gerald of Wales. *De jure et statu Menevensis ecclesiae*. In his *Opera* 3:99–373.

———. *De rebus a se gestis*. In his *Opera* 1:1–122.

———. *Gemma ecclesiastica.* In his *Opera* 2:3–364.

———. *Giraldi Cambrensis Opera.* Ed. J. S. Brewer, J. F. Dimock, and G. F. Warner. 8 vols. Rolls Series, no. 21. London: Her Majesty's Stationery Office, 1861–91.

Gerhoch of Reichersberg. *Letter to Pope Hadrian about the Novelties of the Day.* Ed. Nikolaus M. Häring. Studies and Texts, vol. 24. Toronto: Pontifical Institute of Mediaeval Studies, 1974.

Gervase of Canterbury. *Historical Works.* Ed. William Stubbs. 2 vols. Rolls Series, no. 73. London: Longman, 1879–80.

Gesta Innocentii papae III. In *PL* 214:xvii–ccxviii.

Gesta abbatum monasterii Sancti Albani. Ed. Henry T. Riley. 3 vols. Rolls Series, no. 28, pt. 4. London: Longman, 1867–69.

Glossa Palatina. In Cambridge. Trinity College. MS O.10.2.

Glosse preaccursiane alle Istituzioni. Ed. Severino Caprioli. Fonti per la Storia d'Italia, no. 107. Rome: Istituto storico italiano per il medioevo, 1984.

Goffredus de Trano. *Summa perutilis et valde necessaria do. Goffredi de Trano super titulis decretalium.* Lyon: Joannes Moylin, alias de Cambray, 1519. Repr., Aalen: Scientia, 1968.

Grace Book Alpha, Containing the Proctors' Accounts and Other Records of the University of Cambridge for the Years 1454–1488. Ed. Stanley M. Leathes. Luard Memorial Series, vol. 1. Cambridge: Deighton Bell, 1897.

Gratia of Arezzo. *Summa de iudiciario ordine.* In *Pilii, Tancredi, Gratiae libri de iudiciorum ordine,* 317–485.

Gratian. *Concordia discordantium canonum.* In *Corpus iuris canonici,* ed. Friedberg, 1:1–1424.

———. *The Treatise on Laws with the Ordinary Gloss.* Trans. Augustine Thompson and James Gordley. Studies in Medieval and Early Modern Canon Law, vol. 2. Washington, DC: Catholic University of America Press, 1993.

The Great Register of Lichfield Cathedral Known as Magnum Registrum Album. Ed. H. E. Savage. William Salt Archaeological Society, 3rd ser. (1924). Kendal: Titus Wilson & Son, 1926.

Gregory IX. *Les registres de Grégoire IX.* Ed. L. Auvray. 4 vols. Bibliothèque des Écoles françaises d'Athènes et de Rome, ser. 2, vol. 9. Paris: Albert Fontemoing, 1890–1955.

Guala Bicchieri. *The Letters and Charters of Cardinal Guala Bicchieri, Papal Legate in England, 1216–1218.* Ed. Nicholas Vincent. Canterbury and York Society Publications, vol. 83. Woodbridge: Boydell Press, 1996.

Guibert of Tournai. *Sermones ad omnes status.* Lyon: J. de Vingle, 1511.

Guido de Baysio. *Rosarium decretorum.* In CUL, MS Peterhouse 27, 1ra–313vb.

———. *Rosarium decretorum.* In CUL, MS Peterhouse 35, 2ra–387ra.

———. *Rosarium decretorum.* Venice: Johannes Herblot, 1481.

Guillaume du Breuil. *Stilus superincliti Parlamenti cum scholiis Stephani Auffrerii.* Lyon: In officinis S. Vincentii, 1525.

Guiot de Provins. *Le Bible Guiot.* In *Fabliaux et contes des poètes françois* 2:307–93.

Hackett, M. B. *The Original Statutes of Cambridge University: The Text and Its History.* Cambridge: Cambridge University Press, 1970.

Hamo Hethe. *Registrum Hamonis Hethe Diocesis Roffensis, A.D. 1319–1352.* Ed. Charles Johnson. Canterbury and York Society Publications, vols. 48–49. London, Oxford: Canterbury and York Society Publications [imprint varies], 1914–48.

Hariulf. *Pleiddoi voor Oudenburg.* Ed. Ernst Müller, trans. Roel Vander Plaetse. Turnhout: Brepols, 2003.

———. "Der Bericht des Abtes Hariulf von Oudenburg über seine Prozessverhandlungen an der römische Kurie im Jahre 1141." Ed. Ernst Müller. *DA* 48 (1957) 97–115.

Magister Heinrich der Poet in Würzburg und die römische Kurie. Ed. Heinrich Grauert. Abhandlungen der Bayerischen Akademie der Wissenschaften, Philologische-Historische Klasse, vol. 27. Munich: Bayerische Akademie der Wissenschaften, 1925.

Henri d'Angeli. "La bataille des VII ars." In Paetow, *Two Medieval Satires on the University of Paris,* 37–60.

Henry Burghersh. *Statuta consistorii episcopalis Lincolniensis* (1334). In Wilkins, *Concilia* 2:571–74.

Herbert of Bosham. *Vita Sancti Thomae, archiepiscopi et martyris.* In *Materials for the History of Thomas Becket* 3:155–534.

Hilduin. *Sermones.* CUL MS Ii.1.24, 132rb–140rb, 143ra–169rb.

Hispana. *La colección canónica hispana.* Ed. Gonzalo Martínez Díez and Félix Rodríguez. 6 vols. to date. Monumenta Hispaniae Sacra, Serie Canónica. Madrid: Consejo Superior de Investigaciones Científicas, 1966–.

Homer. *Iliad.* 2nd ed. Ed. and trans. A. T. Murray, rev. by William F. Wyatt. 2 vols. Loeb Classical Library. Cambridge: Harvard University Press, 1999.

Honorius II. *Epistolae et privilegia.* In *PL* 166:1217–1320.

Honorius III. *Regesta Honorii Papae III.* Ed. Pietro Pressutti. 2 vols. Rome: Typographia Vaticana, 1888–95.

Honorius. *Summa "De iure canonico tractaturus."* Ed. Rudolf Weigand, Peter Landau, and Waltrud Kozur. MIC, Corpus glossatorum, vol. 5. Vatican City: BAV, 2004.

Horace [Quintus Horatius Flaccus]. *Satires, Epistles and Ars poetica.* Rev. ed. Ed. and trans. H. Rushton Fairclough. Loeb Classical Library. Cambridge: Harvard University Press; London: William Heinemann, 1929. Repr., 1978.

Hostiensis [Henricus de Segusio]. *In quinque decretalium libri commentaria* [= *Lectura*]. 5 vols. in 2. Venice: Apud Iuntas, 1581. Repr., Turin: Bottega d'Erasmo, 1965.

———. *Summa una cum summariis et adnotationibus Nicolae Superantii.* Lyon: Joannes de Lambray, 1537. Repr., Aalen: Scientia, 1962.

Hubald of Pisa. *Das imbreviaturbuch des erzbischöflichen Gerichtsnotars Hubaldus aus Pisa, Mai bis August 1230.* Ed. Gero Dolezalek. Forschungen zur neueren Privatrechtsgeschichte, vol. 13. Cologne: Böhlau, 1969.

Hugh of Fouilloy. *De claustro animae.* In *PL* 176:1017–1182.

Hugh of Poitiers. *Chronique de l'abbaye de Vézelay.* In *Monumenta Vizeliacensia* 1:397–411.

———. *The Vézelay Chronicle and Other Documents from MS. Auxerre 227 and Elsewhere.* Trans. John Scott and John O. Ward. Binghamton, NY: Medieval and Renaissance Texts and Studies, 1992.

Hugh the Chanter. *The History of the Church of York, 1066–1127.* Ed. and trans. Charles

Johnson, rev. by Martin Brett, C. N. L. Brooke, and M. Winterbottom. Oxford Medieval Texts. Oxford: Clarendon Press, 1990.

Hugo von Trimberg. *Der Renner*. Ed. Gustav Ehrismann and Günther Schweikle. 4 vols. Tübingen: Litterarischen Verein in Stuttgart, 1908. Repr., Berlin: Walter de Gruyter, 1970.

Huguccio. *Summa*. CUL, MS Pembroke 72; Vatican City, BAV, Arch. S. Petr. C.114.

Idung of Prüfening. *Dialogue between Two Monks*. Trans J. F. O'Sullivan in O'Sullivan and Leheay, *Cistercians and Cluniacs*, 19–141.

Index auctorum et librorum qui ab officio S. Rom. & uniuersalis inquisitionis ab omnibus & singulis in uniuersa Christiana Republica mandantur sub censuris contra legentes, vel tenentes libros prohibitos. Rome: Ex officina Saluiana, 1559. Available online as the *Index of Prohibited Books from the Roman Office of the Inquisition, 1559* (http://www.aloha.net/~mikesch/ILP-1559.htm).

Index librorum prohibitorum. Vatican City: Libreria Editrice Vaticana, 1948.

Innocent III. *The Letters of Pope Innocent III (1198–1216) concerning England and Wales*. Ed. C. R. Cheney and Mary G. Cheney. Oxford: Clarendon Press, 1967.

———. *Das Register Innocenz' III*. Ed. Othmar Hageneder and Anton Haidacher. 9 vols. to date. Publikationen der Österreichischen Kulturinstitut in Rom, 2. Abt., 1. Reihe. Graz: H. Böhlaus Nachfolger, 1964–.

———. *Selected Letters of Pope Innocent III*. Ed. and trans. C. R. Cheney and W. H. Semple. London: Thomas Nelson & Sons, 1953.

Innocent IV. *Apparatus toto orbe celebrandus super quinque libris Decretalium*. Frankfurt a/M: Sigismund Feyerabendt, 1570. Repr., Frankfurt a/M: Minerva, 1968.

———. *Les registres d'Innocent IV*. Ed. Élie Berger. 4 vols. Bibliothèque des Écoles français d'Athènes et de Rome, ser. 2, vols. 1–4. Paris: E. de Boccard, 1884–1921.

Introductio Decreti "In prima parte agitur." In London, BL, MS Arundel 490, 1ra–7ra.

Isidore of Seville. *Etymologiarum sive originum libri XX*. Ed. W. M. Lindsay. 2 vols. Oxford Classical Texts. Oxford: Clarendon Press, 1911. Repr., 1989.

———. *Sententiae*. Ed. Pierre Cazier. CCL, vol. 111. Turnhout: Brepols, 1998.

Italia pontificia, sive repertorium privilegiorum et litterarum a Romanis pontificibus ante annum MCLXXXVIII Italiae ecclesiis, monasteriis, civitatibus singulisque personis concessorum. Ed. Paul F. Kehr, Walther Holtzmann, and Dieter Girgensohn. 10 vols. Berlin: Weidmann, 1961–86.

Ivo of Chartres. *Collectio Tripartita*. Provisional edition by Martin Brett. http://wtamu.edu/bbrasington/tripapre.pdf.

———. *Correspondence*. Vol. 1, *1090–1098* [no more published]. Ed. and trans. Jean Leclercq. Les classiques de l'histoire de France au moyen âge, vol. 22. Paris: Les Belles Lettres, 1949.

———. *Decretum*. In *PL* 161:59–1036.

———. *Panormia*. In *PL* 161:1041–1344.

———. *Panormia*. Provisional edition by Martin Brett and Bruce Brasington. http://wtfaculty.wtamu.edu/bbrasington/panormia.html.

Jacob Emerix. *Tractatus seu notitia S. Rotae Romana*. Ed. Charles Lefebvre, Monumenta Christiana selecta, vol. 8. Tournai: Desclée, 1961.

Jacobus Balduinus. *Libellus instructionis advocatorum*. Ed. Nicoletta Sarti in *Un giurista tra Azzone e Accursio*.

Jacques de Vitry. *Die Exempla aus den Sermones feriales et communes*. Ed. Joseph Greven. Sammlung mittellateinischer Texte, vol. 9. Heidelberg: Carl Winter, 1914.

———. *Exempla or Illustrative Stories from the Sermones vulgares*. Ed. and trans. Thomas Frederick Crane. London: The Folklore Society, 1890.

———. *Historia occidentalis*. Ed. John Frederick Hinnebusch. Spicilegium Friburgense, vol. 17. Fribourg: University Press, 1972.

———. *Lettres de Jacques de Vitry*. Ed. R. B. C. Huygens. Leiden: Brill, 1960.

Jason de Mayno. *Commentaria super titulo de actionibus*. Lyon: A. Vincent, 1539.

Jean de Joinville. *The Life of St. Louis*. Trans. René Hague. New York: Sheed & Ward, 1955.

Jean Le Coq. *Questiones Johannis Galli*. Ed. Marguerite Boulet. Bibliothque des Écoles françaises d'Athènes et de Rome, fasc. 156. Paris: E. de Boccard, 1944 [i.e., 1945].

Jocelin of Brakelond. *The Chronicle of Jocelin of Brakelond Concerning the Acts of Samson, Abbot of the Monastery of St. Edmund*. Ed. and trans. H. E. Butler. New York: Oxford University Press, 1949.

Johannes Andreae. *Additiones Speculo*. In William Durand, *Speculum iudiciale*.

———. *Glossa ordinaria in VI*. In *Corpus iuris canonici* [Venice,1605].

Johannes Bassianus. *Libellus de ordine iudiciorum* [= *Summa "Propositum presentis operis"*]. Ed. Giovanni Tamassia and Giovanni Battista Palmieri. In *Bibliotheca iuridica medii aevi* 2:211–48.

———. *Summa "Quicumque vult."* Ed. Ludwig Wahrmund. QGRKP, vol. 4, pt. 2 Innsbruck: Wagner, 1925. Repr., Aalen: Scientia, 1962.

Johannes Cluniacensis. *Vita sancti Odonis*. In *PL* 133:43–76.

Johannes de Deo. *Breuiarium super toto corpore decretalium*. In London, BL MS Royal 11.A.II, 1ra–109rb.

———. *Cauillationes aduocatorum*. In London, BL, MS Arundel 459, 1ra–45rb.

———. *Liber questionum*. In London, BL, MS Arundel 493, 23r–48v.

Johannes de Grassis. *Tractatus de subtilitatibus procuratorii*. In *Tractatus plurimorum doctorum*, 17va–30vb.

Johannes de Legnano. *Super Clementina "Saepe."* Ed. Ludwig Wahrmund. QGRKP, vol. 4, pt. 6. Innsbruck: Wagner, 1928. Repr., Aalen: Scientia, 1962.

Johannes Faventinus. *Summa super Decretum Gratiani*. In London, BL MS Add. 18,369, 1ra–166rb, and MS Royal 9.E.VII, 1ra–160rb.

Johannes Franciscus Balbus. *Observationes nonnullarum in jure decisionum, causidicis ac juristudiosis magno usu futurae*. Lyon: Vincentius de Portonariis, 1535.

Johannes Teutonicus. *Apparatus in Compilationem tertiam*, vol. 1. Ed. Kenneth Pennington. MIC, Corpus glossatorum, vol. 3. Vatican City: BAV, 1981.

———. *Apparatus in Compilationem tertiam*. Books 3 to 5. Ed. Kenneth Pennington. http://faculty.cua.edu/pennington.

———. *Apparatus in Concilium quartum Lateranense*. Ed. Antonio García y García. In *Constitutiones Concilii quarti Lateranensis*, 173–270.

———. *Glossa ordinaria super Decretum Gratiani*. Rev. by Bartholomaeus Brixiensis. In *Corpus iuris canonici*. [Venice, 1605].

John Bromyard. *Summa predicantium omnibus diuini eloquii propagatoribus usui accommodatissima*. Nuremberg: Johann Stuchs, 1518.

John de Grandisson. *The Register of John de Grandisson, Bishop of Exeter (A.D. 1327–1369)*. Ed. F. C. Hingeston-Randolph. 3 vols. London: George Bell & Sons, 1894.

John Gower. *The Complete Works*. Ed. G. C. Macaulay. 4 vols. Oxford: Clarendon Press, 1899–1902.

John le Romeyn. *The Register of John le Romeyn, Lord Archbishop of York, 1286–1296*. Ed. William Brown. 2 vols. Surtees Society Publications, vols. 123, 128. London: Bernard Quaritch, 1913–17.

John Lydford's Book. Ed. Dorothy M. Owen. Historical Manuscripts Commission, no. JP 22. London: Her Majesty's Stationery Office, 1974.

John Morton. *The Register of John Morton, Archbishop of Canterbury, 1486–1500*. Ed. Christopher Harper-Bill. 3 vols. Canterbury and York Society Publications, vols. 75, 78, 89. York, Woodbridge: Canterbury and York Society, 1987–2000.

John of Acton [Athon]. *Constitutiones legatinae sive legitimae regionis Anglicana D. Othonis et D. Othoboni, cardinalium et sedis Romanae in Anglia legatorum*. Oxford H. Hall, impensis Richard Davis, 1676. Bound with William Lyndwood, *Provinciale*.

John of Caen. *Abbreviatio Decreti*. In London, BL, MS Cotton Claud. A.IV, 85ra–191va.

John of Fribourg. *Summa confessorum*. Lyon: Jacobus Saccon, 1518.

John of Garland. *Morale scolarium*. In Paetow, *Two Medieval Satires on the University of Paris*, 185–257.

John of Salisbury. *Historia pontificalis*. Ed. and trans. Marjorie Chibnall. Edinburgh: Thomas Nelson & Sons, 1956.

———. *The Letters of John of Salisbury*. Ed. and trans. W. J. Millor, H. E. Butler, and C. N. L. Brooke. 2 vols. Oxford Medieval Texts. Edinburgh: Thomas Nelson & Sons; Oxford: Clarendon Press, 1955–69.

———. *Metalogicon*. Ed. J. B. Hall and K. S. B. Keats-Rohan. CCM, vol. 98. Turnhout: Brepols, 1991.

———. *Policraticus sive de nugis curialium et vestigiis philosophorum libri VIII*. Ed. C. C. J. Webb. 2 vols. Oxford: University Press, 1909. Repr., Frankfurt a/M: Minerva, 1965.

———. *Policraticus I–IV*. ed. K. S. B. Keats-Rohan. CCM, vol. 118. Turnhout: Brepols, 1993.

———. *Policraticus: Of the Frivolities of Courtiers and the Footprints of Philosophers*. Ed. and trans. Cary J. Nederman. Cambridge: Cambridge University Press, 1990.

———. *The Statesman's Book of John of Salisbury, Being the Fourth, Fifth, and Sixth Books, and Selections from the Seventh and Eighth Books, of the Policraticus*. Trans. John Dickinson. Political Science Classics. New York: Alfred A. Knopf, 1927. Repr., New York: Russell & Russell, 1963.

———. *Vita et passio S. Thomae martyris*. In *Materials for the History of Thomas Becket* 2:302–22.

John Pecham. *The Register of John Pecham, Archbishop of Canterbury, 1279–1291*. Ed.

F. N. Davis and Decima Douie. 2 vols. Canterbury and York Society Publications, vols. 64–65. London: Canterbury and York Society, 1908–69.

John Stratford. "Statute of the Court of Arches (13 May 1342)." In Logan, *The Medieval Court of Arches*, 23–45.

John Wycliffe. *The English Works of John Wyclif*. Ed. F. O. Matthew. Early English Text Society Publications, vol. 74. London: Early English Text Society, 1880.

Juan Alfonso de Benavente *Ars et doctrina studendi et docendi*. Ed. Bernardo Alonso Rodríguez. Bibliotheca Salmanticensis, ser. 2, vol. 1. Salamanca: Universidad Pontificia, 1972.

Jubinal, Achille. *Nouveau recueil des contes, dits, fabliaux et autres pièces inédites des XIIIe, XIVe, et XVe siècles*. 2 vols. Paris: E. Pannier, 1839–42.

Juvenal [Decius Iunius Iuvenalis]. *Saturae*. Rev. ed. Ed. and trans. G. G. Ramsay. Loeb Classical Library. Cambridge: Harvard University Press, 1940. Repr., 1990.

Die Konstitutionen Friedrichs II. für das Königreich Sizilien. Ed. Wolfgang Stürner. MGH, Constitutiones et acta publica imperatorum et regum, vol. 2, Supplement. Hannover: Hahn, 1996.

Lactantius, Lucius Caecilius Firmianus. *De mortibus persecutorum*. Ed. and trans. J. L. Creed. Oxford Early Christian Texts. Oxford: Clarendon Press, 1984.

Landulf of St. Paul. *Historia Mediolanensis*. Ed. L. Bethmann and Philip Jaffé. MGH, SS 20:17–49. Hannover: Hahn, 1869.

The Latin Poems Commonly Attributed to Walter Mapes. Ed. Thomas Wright. Publications of the Camden Society, o.s., vol. 16. London: Camden Society, 1841.

The Law of Hywel Dda. Ed. and trans. Dafydd Jenkins. Llandysul, Dyfed: Gomer Press, 1986.

The Laws of the Alamans and Bavarians. Trans. Theodore John Rivers. Philadelphia: University of Pennsylvania Press, 1977.

Laws of the Salian and Ripuarian Franks. Trans. Theodore John Rivers. New York: AMS Press, 1986.

The Laws of the Salian Franks. Trans. Katherine Fischer Drew. Philadelphia: University of Pennsylvania Press, 1991.

Leges Burgundionum. Ed. L. R. de Salis. MGH, Leges, sect. 1, vol. 2, pt. 1. Hannover: Hahn, 1892.

Leges Langobardorum. Ed. F. Blume. MGH, Leges, sect. 1, vol. 4. Hannover: Hahn, 1868.

Leges Visigothorum. Ed. K. Zeumer. MGH, Leges, sect. 1, vol. 1. Hannover: Hahn, 1902.

Lex mercatoria and Legal Pluralism: A Late Thirteenth-Century Treatise and Its Afterlife. Ed. and trans. Mary Elizabeth Basile, Jane Fair Bestor, Daniel R. Coquillette, and Charles Donahue, Jr. Cambridge: Ames Foundation, Harvard Law School, 1998.

Liber Augustalis. See *Die Konstitutionen Friedrichs II. für das Königreich Sizilien*.

Liber constitutionum et statutorum generalis studii Ilerdensis an. MCCC. In Villanueva, *Viaje literario a las Iglesias de España* 16:307–46.

Liber divinarum sententiarum. Ed. Giuseppe Mazzanti. Testi, studi, strumenti, vol. 14. Spoleto: Centro italiano di studi sull'alto medioevo, 1999.

Liber Eliensis. Ed. E. O. Blake. Camden Society Publications, 3rd ser., vol. 92. London: Royal Historical Society, 1962.

Liber memorandorum ecclesie de Bernewelle. Ed. John Willis Clark. Cambridge: Cambridge University Press, 1907.

Liber pontificalis. 2nd ed. Ed. Louis Duchesne. 2 vols. in 3. Bibliothèque des Écoles françaises d'Athènes et de Rome, ser. 2, vol. 6. Paris: E. de Boccard, 1955–57.

Liber practicus de consuetudine Remensi. In *Archives législatives de la ville de Reims* 1:35–344.

Libri quinque statutorum inclytae civitatis Mutinae. Modena: I. de Nicolis, 1547.

Lichfield. *The Great Register of Lichfield Cathedral, Known as Magnum Registrum Album*. Ed. H. E. Savage. William Salt Archaeological Society Publications, 1924. Kendal: Titus Wilson & Son, 1926.

Livy [Titus Livius]. *Ab urbe condita*. Ed. and trans. B. O. Foster, Alfred C. Schlesinger, and Russell M. Geer. 14 vols. Loeb Classical Library. Cambridge: Harvard University Press; London: William Heinemann, 1919–67. Repr., 1987–88.

Logan, F. Donald. *The Medieval Court of Arches*. Canterbury and York Society Publications, vol. 95. Woodbridge: Canterbury and York Society, 2005.

The Lombard Laws. Trans. Katherine Fischer Drew. Philadelphia: University of Pennsylvania Press, 1973.

Longley, Katherine M. *Ecclesiastical Cause Papers at York: Dean and Chapter's Court, 1350–1843*. Borthwick Texts and Calendars, Records of the Northern Province, vol. 6. York: Borthwick Institute, 1980.

Lucretius [Titus Lucretius Carus]. *De rerum natura libri sex*. Ed. William Ellery Leonard and Stanley Barney Smith. Madison: University of Wisconsin Press, 1942. Repr., 1961.

Manaresi, C. *I Placiti del Regnum Italiae*. 3 vols. in 4. Fonti per la storia d'Italia, vols. 92, 96, 97. Rome: Istituto Italiano per il Medio Evo, 1955–60.

Mansi, Giovanni Domenico. *Sacrorum conciliorum nova et amplissima collectio*. 53 vols. in 60. Paris: H. Welter, 1901–27. [Mansi]

Martène, Edmond, and Ursmer Durand. *Thesaurus novus anecdotorum*. 5 vols. Paris: Florentius Delaulne [etc.], 1717. Repr., Farnborough: Gregg, 1968–69.

Martial [Marcus Valerius Martialis]. *Epigrammaton*. Ed. and trans. Walter C. A. Ker. 2 vols. Loeb Classical Library. Cambridge: Harvard University Press; London: William Heinemann, 1968. Repr., 1978–79.

Martinus de Fano. *Ordo iudiciarius*. Ed. Ludwig Wahrmund. QGRKP, vol. 1, pt. 7. Innsbruck: Wagner, 1906. Repr., Aalen: Scientia, 1962.

Materials for the History of Thomas Becket, Archbishop of Canterbury. Ed. James Cragie Robertson. 7 vols. Rolls Series, no. 67. London: Longman, 1875–85.

Matheolus. *Les Lamentations de Matheolus et le livre de leesce*. Ed. A.-G. Van Hamel. 2 vols. Bibliothèque de l'École des Hautes Études, fasc. 95–96. Paris: Émile Bouillon, 1892.

Matthew of Westminster. *Flores historiarum*. Ed. Henry Richards Luard. 3 vols. Rolls Series, no. 95. London: Eyre & Spottiswoode, 1890.

Matthew Paris. *Chronica Majora*. Ed. Henry Richards Luard. 7 vols. Rolls Series, no. 57. London: Longman, 1872–83.

Maurice of St. Victor. *Sermones sex*. In *Galteri a Sancto Victorio et quorumdam aliorum sermones ineditos*, 197–231.

Mediaeval Archives of the University of Oxford. Ed. H. E. Salter. 2 vols. Oxford Historical Society Publications, vols. 70, 73. Oxford: Oxford Historical Society, 1920–21.

Monumenta Vizeliacensia: Textes relatifs à l'histoire de l'abbaye de Vézelay. Ed. R. B. C. Huygens. CCM, vol. 42. Turnhout: Brepols, 1976–80.

Monuments originaux de l'histoire de Saint Yves. Ed. A. de La Bordone, J. Daniel, R. P. Perquis, and D. Templer. Saint-Brieuc: L. Prudhomme, 1887.

Muckle, J. T. "The Personal Letters between Abelard and Heloise and Abelard's Reply." *Mediaeval Studies* 17 (1955) 240–81.

Müller, Ernst. "Der Bericht des Abtes Hariulf von Oudenburg über seine Prozessverhandlungen an der römischen Kurie im Jahre 1141." *DA* 48 (1957) 97–115.

Munimenta academica, or Documents Illustrative of Academical Life and Studies at Oxford. Ed. Henry Anstey. 2 vols. Rolls Series, no. 50. London: Longman, 1868.

Munimenta Gildhallae Londoniensis. Ed. H. T. Riley. 3 vols. in 4. Rolls Series, no. 12. London: Longman, 1859–62.

Nigel Wireker [Longchamp]. *Tractatus contra curiales et officiales clericos.* Ed. A. Boutemy. Université libre de Bruxelles, Travaux de la Faculté de Philosophie et Lettres, vol. 16. Paris: Presses Universitaires de France, 1959.

Notabilia decretalium Cantabrigiensis. In CUL, MS Add. 3467.

Odofredus. *Lectura super Codice.* 2 vols. Lyon: Franciscus & Claudius Marchant Fratres, 1552. Repr., Bologna: Forni, 1968–69.

———. *Lectura super Digesto Veteri.* 2 vols. Lyon: Franciscus & Claudius Marchant Fratres, 1550–52. Repr., Bologna: Forni, 1967–68.

Ordo iudiciarius "Etiam testimonia removentur." Ed. Linda Fowler-Magerl in her *Ordo iudiciorum*, 264–73.

Ordo iudiciarius "Iudicium est trinum personarum trium actus." Ed. Linda Fowler-Magerl in her *Ordo iudiciorum*, 295–300.

Ordo iudiciarius "Scientiam." Ed. Ludwig Wahrmund. QGRKP, vol. 2, pt. 1. Innsbruck: Wagner, 1913. Repr., Aalen: Scientia, 1962.

Ordo iudiciarius "Ulpianus de edendo." London, British Library, MS Royal 10.B.IV.

Ordonnances des roys de France de la troisième race. Ed. Eusèbe de Laurière et al. 23 vols. Paris: Imprimerie royale, 1723–1849. Repr., Farnborough: Gregg, 1967–68.

Otto of Freising and Rahewin. *Gesta Frederici seu rectius chronica.* Ed. Franz-Joseph Schmale, trans. Adolf Schmidt. Berlin: Deutscher Verlag der Wissenschaften, 1965.

Otto Morena. *Historia Frederici I.* Ed. F. Güterbock. MGH, SSRG. Berlin: Weidmann, 1930.

Otto of Pavia. *Summa "Olim."* Ed. Giovanni Tamassia and Giovanni Battista Palmieri. In *Bibliotheca iuridica medii aevi* 2:229–48.

Ovid [Publius Ovidius Naso]. *Amores.* Ed. and trans. Guy Lee. London: John Murray, 1968.

———. *Epistulae ex Ponto.* 2nd ed. Ed. and trans. Arthur Leslie Wheeler, rev. by G. P. Goold. Loeb Classical Library. Cambridge: Harvard University Press, 1988. Repr., 2002.

———. *Metamorphoses.* 3rd ed. Ed. and trans. Frank Justus Miller, rev. by G. P. Goold. 2 vols. Loeb Classical Library. Cambridge: Harvard University Press. 1977. Repr., 1999.

Pactus legis Salicae. Ed. Karl August Eckhardt. MGH, Leges, sect. 1, vol. 4, pt. 1. Hannover: Hahn, 1962.

Panormitanus [Nicolas de Tudeschis]. *Commentaria*. 8 vols. Venice: [Johannes de Gara], 1571.

———. *Practica*. Venice: Johannes de Gara, 1571.

———. *Questiones et disputationes*. Lyon: Johannes de Jovelle, 1518.

Papal Decretals Relating to the Diocese of Lincoln in the Twelfth Century. Ed. Walther Holtzmann and Eric Waldram Kemp. Publications of the Lincoln Record Society, vol. 47. Lincoln: Lincoln Record Society, 1954.

Patrologiae cursus completus . . . series Latina. Ed. J.-P. Migne. 221 vols. Paris: J.-P. Migne, 1841–64. [*PL*]

Paucapalea. *Summa decretorum*. Ed. Johann Friedrich von Schulte. Giesen: E. Toth, 1890. Repr., Aalen: Scientia, 1965.

Paul the Deacon. *Storia dei Longobardi*. Ed. Georg Heinrich Waitz and Ludwig Bethmann. Trans. Luca Tenconti. Milan: Electa, 1985.

Peter Abelard. *The Letters of Abelard and Heloise*. Trans. Betty Radice. Harmondsworth: Penguin, 1974.

Peter of Blois. *Opera omnia*. Ed. J. A. Giles. 4 vols. London: Whittaker, 1847.

———. *Opusculum de distinctionibus in canonum interpretatione adhibendis, sive ut auctor voluit, "Speculum iuris canonici."* Ed. Theophilus Augustus Reimarus. Berlin: G. Reimer, 1837.

Peter the Chanter. *Verbum adbreviatum*. Ed. Monique Boutry. CCM, vol. 196. Turnhout: Brepols, 2004.

Peter the Deacon. *Chronica Montis Casinensis*. MGH, SS 7:727–844. Hannover: Hahn, 1846.

Peter Lombard. *Sententiae in IV libros distinctae*. 3rd ed. 2 vols. Grottaferrata: Editiones Collegii S. Bonaventurae ad Claras Aquas, 1971–81.

Peter the Venerable. *The Letters of Peter the Venerable*. Ed. Giles Constable. 2 vols. Cambridge: Harvard University Press, 1967.

Petrus de Ancharano. *Lectura super Sexto Decretalium*. Lyon: Johannes Moylin, alias de Cambray, 1535.

Petrus de Monte. *Repertorium utriusque iuris*. Padua: Johannes Herbot, 1480.

Petrus de Salinis. *Lectura super Decreto*. In London, BL, MS Arundel 435, 1ra–223ra.

Petrus Lenauderius. *De privilegiis doctorum*. In *TUJ* [1584], vol. 18, 3vb–21rb.

Pflugk-Harttung, Julius von. *Acta pontificum Romanorum inedita: Urkunden der Päpste, 749–1198*. 3 vols. Tübingen: Franz Fues, 1881–86. Repr., Graz: Akademische Druck- u. Verlagsanstalt, 1958.

Philippe de Beaumanoir. *Coutumes de Beauvaisis*. Ed. Amédée Salmon. 2 vols. Collection de textes pour servir à l'étude et à l'enseignement de l'histoire. Paris: A. & J. Picard, 1899–1900. Repr., 1970.

———. *Coutumes de Beauvaisis*. Trans. F. R. P. Akehurst. Philadelphia: University of Pennsylvania Press, 1992.

Philippe de Mézières. *Le songe du vieil pelerin*. Ed. G. W. Coopland. 2 vols. Cambridge: Cambridge University Press, 1969.

Pierre de Belleperche. *Auree ac singularissime et quas nulla vidit etas Repetitiones XLVIII in Justinianum Codicem commentarium.* Paris: Galliot du Pré, 1515.

Pierre de Fontaines. *Le conseil de Pierre de Fontaines, ou traité de l'ancienne jurisprudence française.* Ed. A. J. Marnier. Paris: Joubert, 1846.

Pilii, Tancredi, Gratiae libri de iudiciorum ordine. Ed. Friedrich Christian Bergmann. Göttingen: Vandenhoeck & Ruprecht, 1842. Repr., Aalen: Scientia, 1965.

Placentinus. *Sermo de legibus.* In Kantorowicz, *Rechtshistorische Schriften,* 127–35.

Pliny the Younger [Caius Plinius Caecilius Secundus]. *Letters and Panegyricus.* Ed. and trans. Betty Radice. 2 vols. Loeb Classical Library. Cambridge: Harvard University Press; London: William Heinemann, 1969. Repr., 1972–76.

Poos, Larry R. *Lower Ecclesiastical Jurisdiction in Late-Medieval England: The Courts of the Dean and Chapter of Lincoln, 1336–1349, and the Deanery of Wisbeach, 1458–1484.* Records of Social and Economic History, n.s., vol. 32. London: British Academy, 2001.

Prefaces to Canon Law Books in Latin Christianity: Selected Translations, 500–1245. Ed and trans. Robert Somerville and Bruce C. Brasington. New Haven: Yale University Press, 1998.

Primum [-quartum] volumen statutorum Perusie. 4 vols. in 1. Perugia: In aedibus H. F. Chartularii, 1523–28.

Privilegia curie Remensis archiepiscopi. In *Archives législatives de la ville de Reims* 1:3–33.

Pryor, John H. *Business Contracts of Medieval Provence: Selected Notulae from the Cartulary of Giraud Amalric of Marseilles, 1248.* Studies and Texts, no. 54. Toronto: Pontifical Institute of Mediaeval Studies, 1981.

Pseudo-Isidore. *Decretales Pseudo-Isidorianae et Capitula Angilramni.* Ed. Paul Hinschius. Leipzig: B. Tauchnitz, 1863. Repr., Aalen: Scientia, 1963.

———. *Decretales Pseudoisidorianae.* Ed. Karl Georg Schon. Text available on the Web site of Projekt Pseudosisdor (http://www.pseudoisidor.mgh.de/).

Quaestiones dominorum Bononiensium, Collectio Gratianopolitano. In *Bibliotheca iuridica medii aevi,* 211–42.

Le questioni civilistiche del secolo XII: Da Bulgaro a Pillio de Medicina e Azzone. Ed. Analisa Belloni. Ius commune, Sonderhefte, vol. 43. Frankfurt a/M: Vittorio Klostermann, 1989.

Quinque compilationes antiquae necnon collectio canonum Lipsiensis. Ed. Emil Friedberg. Leipzig: B. Tauchnitz, 1882. Repr., Graz: Akademische Druck- u. Verlagsanstalt, 1956.

Quintilian [Marcus Fabius Quintilianus]. *Institutio oratoria.* Ed. and trans. H. E. Butler. 4 vols. Loeb Classical Library. Cambridge: Harvard University Press; London: William Heinemann, 1920–22. Repr., 1979–80.

Ralph Niger. *De re militari et triplici via peregrinationis Ierosolimitane (1187/88).* Ed. Ludwig Schmugge. Beiträge zur Geschichte und Quellenkunde des Mittelalters, vol. 6. Berlin: Walter de Gruyter, 1977.

———. *Moralia regum.* Ed. Kantorowicz and Smalley in "An English Theologian's View of Roman Law," 241–44.

Raymond of Penyafort. *Summa de penitentia.* Ed. Xavier Ochoa and Aloisio Diez. Universa bibliotheca iuris, vol. 1B. Rome: Commentarium pro religiosis, 1976.

Raymundus von Wiener-Neustadt. *Die Summa legum brevis, levis et utilis des sogennanten Doctor Raymundus von Wiener Neustadt.* Ed. Alexander Gàl. Weimar: Böhlaus, 1926.

Recueil général des anciennes lois françaises depuis l'an 420 jusqu'à la révolution de 1789. Ed. François André Isambert et al. 20 vols. Paris: Belin-le-Prieur, 1821–33.

Regesta pontificum romanorum ab condita ecclesia ad annum post Christum natum MCXCVIII. 2nd ed. Ed. Philip Jaffé; . rev. by S. Loewenfeld, F. Kaltenbrunner, and P. Ewald. 2 vols. Leipzig: Veit, 1885–88. Repr., Graz: Akademische Druck- u. Verlagsanstalt, 1956. [JE, JK, JL]

Regesta pontificum romanorum inde ab a. post Christum natum MCXCVIII ad a. MCCCIV. Ed. August Potthast. 2 vols. Berlin: R. de Decker, 1874–75. [Po]

Regino of Prüm. *Libri duo de synodalibus causis et disciplinis ecclesiasticis.* Ed. F. G. A. Wasserschleben. Leipzig: Teubner, 1840. Repr., Graz: Akademische Druck- u. Verlagsanstalt, 1964.

———. *Das Sendbuch des Regino von Prüm.* Ed. and trans. Wilfried Hartmann. Ausgewählte Quellen zur deutschen Geschichte des Mittelalters, vol. 42. Darmstadt: Wissenschaftliche Buchgesellschaft, 2004.

Le registre de l'officialité de Cerisy, 1314–1457. Ed. M. G. Dupont. *Mémoires de la Société des Antiquaires de Normandie,* 3rd ser., 10 (1880) 271–456.

Registre des causes civiles de l'officialité épiscopal de Paris, 1384–1387. Ed. Joseph Petit. Collection de documents inédits sur l'histoire de France. Paris: Imprimerie Nationale, 1919.

Registres de sentences de l'officialité de Cambrai (1328–1453). Ed. Cyriel Vleeschouwers and Monique van Melkebeek. Recueil de l'ancienne jurisprudence de la Belgique, 7th ser., vol. 1. Brussels: Ministère de la Justice, 1998.

Regule cancellarie apostolica cum earum notabili et subtilissima glossa. Paris: Johan Richard, 1499.

Remains of Old Latin. Ed. and trans. E. H. Warmington. 4 vols. Loeb Classical Library. Cambridge: Harvard University Press; London: William Heinemann, 1938. Repr., 1979.

Die Rhetorica ecclesiastica. Ed. Ludwig Wahrmund. QGRKP, vol. 1, pt. 4. Innsbruck: Wagner, 1906. Repr., Aalen: Scientia, 1962.

Ricardus Anglicus. *Apparatus super compilationem primam.* In Munich, Bayerische Staatsbibliothek, Clm. 6352, 1ra–80rb.

———. *Distinctiones decretorum.* In London, BL, MS Royal 10.C.III, 4r–48v.

———. *Summa de ordine iudiciario.* Ed. Ludwig Wahrmund. QGRKP, vol. 2, pt. 3. Innsbruck: Wagner, 1915. Repr., Aalen: Scientia, 1962.

Robert of Flamborough. *Liber Poenitentialis.* Ed. J. J. Francis Firth. Studies and Texts, vol. 18. Toronto: Pontifical Institute of Mediaeval Studies, 1971.

Robert of Torigni. *Chronicle.* Ed. Richard Howlett. Rolls Series, no. 82, vol. 4. London: Longman, 1889.

Robert Winchelsey. *Registrum Roberti Winchelsey, Cantuariensis archiepiscopi, A.D. 1294–1313.* Ed. Rose Graham. 2 vols. Canterbury and York Society Publications, vols. 51–52. Oxford: University Press, 1952–56.

Roger of Wendover. *Flores historiarum.* Ed. Henry G. Hewlett. 3 vols. Rolls Series, no. 84. London: Longman, 1886–89.

Rolandus. *Summa magistri Rolandi nachmals Papstes Alexander III*. Ed. Friedrich Thaner. Innsbruck: Wagner, 1874.
Roman Statutes. Ed. M. H. Crawford. 2 vols. Bulletin of the Institute of Classical Studies, Supplement 64. London: Institute of Classical Studies, 1996.
Rota Romana. *Decisiones novae, antiquae, et antiquiores*. Turin: Apud Haeredes Nicolai Beuilaquae, 1579.
Rotondi, Giovanni. *Leges publicae populi Romani*. Milan: Società libreria editrice Milano, 1912. Repr., Hildesheim: Georg Olms, 1966.
Rufinus. *Summa decretorum*. Ed. Heinrich Singer. Paderborn: Ferdinand Schöningh, 1902. Repr., Aalen: Scientia, 1963.
Rutebeuf. *Poèmes concernant l'Université de Paris*. Ed. H. H. Lucas. Manchester: Manchester University Press; Paris: Librairie Nizet, 1952.
Sanchez, Tomás. *Opuscula sive consilia moralia*. 2 vols. in 1. Lyon: Iacobus Prost, 1635.
Select Cases from the Ecclesiastical Courts of the Province of Canterbury, c. 1200–1301. Ed. Norma Adams and Charles Donahue, Jr. Selden Society Publications, vol. 105. London: Selden Society, 1981.
Select Cases on Defamation to 1600. Ed. Richard H. Helmholz. Selden Society Publications, vol. 101. London: Selden Society, 1985.
Seneca the Younger [Lucius Annaeus Seneca]. *Apocolocyntosis divi Claudii*. Ed. and trans. W. H. C. Rouse. Loeb Classical Library. Cambridge: Harvard University Press; London: William Heinemann, 1969. Repr., 1987.
———. *Dialogorum libri XII*. Ed. L. E. Reynolds. Oxford Classical Texts. Oxford: Clarendon Press, 1977.
Sicard of Cremona. *Summa super Decretum*. In London, BL MS Add. 18367.
Las Siete Partidas del rey don Alfonso el Sabio cotejacas con varios codices antiguos per la Real Academia de la Historia. 3 vols. Madrid: En la imprenta real, 1807.
Las Siete Partidas. Ed. Robert I. Burns, trans. Samuel Parsons Scott. 5 vols. Philadelphia: University of Pennsylvania Press, 2001.
Simone da Borsano. *Lectura Clementinarum*. In Maffei. "Dottori e studenti."
Snappe's Formulary and Other Records. Ed. H. E. Salter. Oxford Historical Society Publications, vol. 80. Oxford: Oxford Historical Society, 1924.
Les sources du droit du Canton de Genève. Ed. Émile Rivoire and Victor van Berchem. 4 vols. Sammlung schweizerishchen Rechtsquellen, pt. 22. Arau: H. R. Sauerländer, 1927.
Statuta antiqua universitatis Oxoniensis. Ed. Strickland Gibson. Oxford: Clarendon Press, 1931.
Statuta ciuitatis Vrbini. Pesauro: B. Caesanus, 1559.
Statuta ecclesiae antiqua. Ed. Charles Munier. Bibliothèque de l'Institut de droit canonique de l'Université de Strasbourg, vol. 5. Paris: Presses Universitaires de France, 1960.
Statuta Ferrariae anno MCCLXXXVII. Ed. William Montorsi. Ferrara: Cassa di Risparmio, 1955.
Statuta Veneta emendatissima. Venice: B. Benalio, 1528.

Statutes of the Realm, from Original Records and Authentic Manuscripts. Ed. A. Luders et al. 11 vols. in 12. London: Record Commissioners, 1819–28.

Gli Statuti della Società dei Notai di Bologna dell'anno 1336. Ed. Nicoletta Sarti. Seminario giuridico dell'Università di Bologna, Pubblicazzione, vol. 124. Milan: A. Giuffrè, 1988.

Statuti delle università e dei collegi dello studio bolognese. Ed. Carlo Malagola. Bologna: Nicola Zanichelli, 1888. Repr., Turin: Bottega d'Erasmo, 1966.

Statuti di Bologna dell'anno 1288. Ed. Gina Fasoli and Pietro Sella. 2 vols. Studi e testi, vols. 73, 85. Vatican City: BAV, 1937–39.

Statuti inediti della città di Pisa del XII al XIV secolo. Ed. Francisco Bonaini. 3 vols. Florence: G. P. Viessu, 1854–70.

Statuts et privilèges des universités françaises depuis leur fondation jusqu'en 1789. Ed. Marcel Fournier. 4 vols. Paris: L. Larose & Forcel, 1890–94. Repr., Aalen: Scientia, 1970.

Les statuts de l'ancienne Province de Reims. Ed. Joseph Avril. Statuts synodaux français du XIIIe siècle, vol. 4. Paris: Éditions du Comité des travaux historiques et scientifiques, 1995.

Statuts synodaux français du XIIIe siècle. Ed. and trans. Odette Pontal. 5 vols. Paris: Éditions du Comité des travaux historiques et scientifiques, 1971–95.

Stephen of Tournai. *Lettres d'Étienne de Tournai.* Ed. Jules de Silve. Paris: Alphonse Picard, 1893.

———. *Die Summa über das Decretum Gratiani.* Ed. Johann Friedrich von Schulte. Giessen: Emil Roth, 1891. Repr., Aalen: Scientia, 1965.

Stoicorum veterum fragmenta. Ed. Hans Friedrich August von Arnim. 4 vols. Stuttgart: B. G. Teubner, 1905–24. Repr., 1968.

Suetonius [Caius Suetonius Tranqullus]. *De vita caesarum.* Ed. and trans. J. C. Rolfe. 2 vols. Loeb Classical Library. Cambridge: Harvard University Press; London: William Heinemann, 1913–14. Repr., 1979.

Summa "Elegantius in iure diuino" seu Coloniensis. Ed. Gérard Fransen and Stephan Kuttner. MIC, Corpus glossatorum, vol. 1, pts. 1–4. Vatican City: BAV, 1969–90.

The Summa Parisiensis on the Decretum Gratiani. Ed. Terence P. McLaughlin. Toronto: Pontifical Institute of Mediaeval Studies, 1952.

Summa "Prima primi uxor Ade." In London, British Library, MS Royal 11.D.II, 321ra–332ra.

Tacitus, Cornelius. *The Agricola and Germania of Tacitus.* Ed. Alfred J. Church and W. J. Brodribb. London: Macmillan, 1886. Repr., 1939.

———. *Annalium ab excessu divi Augusti libri.* Ed. C. D. Fisher. Oxford Classical Texts. Oxford: Clarendon Press, 1906.

Tancred. *Ordo iudiciarius.* In *Pilii, Tancredi, Gratiae libri de iudiciorum ordine,* 87–314.

Tangl, Michael. *Die päpstliche Kanzleiordnungen von 1200–1500.* Innsbruck: Wagner, 1894. Repr., Aalen: Scientia, 1959.

The Theodosian Code and Novels and the Sirmondian Constitutions. Trans. Clyde Pharr. Corpus of Roman Law, vol. 1. Princeton: Princeton University Press, 1952. Repr., Union, NJ: Lawbook Exchange, 2001.

Thomas Aquinas. *Opera omnia iussu Leonis XIII edita*. 48 vols. to date. Rome: Ex typographia polyglotta S.C. de Propaganda Fide, 1882–.

———. *Summa theologiae*. In his *Opera omnia iussu Leonis XIII edita*, vols. 5–12.

Thomas of Marlborough. *History of the Abbey of Evesham*. Ed. and trans. Jane Sayers and Leslie Watkiss. Oxford Medieval Texts. Oxford: Clarendon Press, 2003.

Thorndike, Lynn. *University Records and Life in the Middle Ages*. New York: Columbia University Press, 1944. Repr., New York: W. W. Norton, 1975.

Tractatus plurimorum doctorum. Lyon: Johannes Marion, 1519.

Tractatus universi juris. 22 vols. in 28. Venice: Franciscus Zilettus, 1584–86. [*TUJ*]

Twelfth-Century English Archidiaconal and Vice-Archidiaconal Acta. Ed. B. R. Kemp. Canterbury and York Society Publications, vol. 92. Woodbridge: Boydell Press, 2001.

Vacarius. *Liber pauperum*. Ed. Francis de Zulueta. Selden Society Publications, vol. 44. London: Quaritch, 1927.

———. "Magistri Vacarii Summa de matrimonio." Ed. Frederic William Maitland. *Law Quarterly Review* 13 (1897) 133–43, 270–87.

———. "The *Tractatus De assumpto homine* by Magister Vacarius." Ed. N. M. Häring. *Mediaeval Studies* 21 (1959) 147–75.

Valerius Maximus. *Factorum ac dictorum memorabilium libri X*. Ed. and trans. D. R. Shackleton Bailey. 2 vols. Loeb Classical Library. Cambridge: Harvard University Press, 2000.

Valla, Lorenzo. *De falso credito et ementita Constantini Donatione*. Ed. Wolfram Setz. MGH, Quellen zur Geistesgeschichte des Mittelalters, vol. 10. Weimar: H. Böhlaus Nachfolger, 1976.

Venantius Fortunatus. *Poèmes*. Ed. and trans. Marc Reydellet. 3 vols. Collection des universités de France. Paris: Les Belles Lettres, 1994–98.

Vetus liber archidiaconi Eliensis. Ed. C. L. Feltoe and Ellis H. Minns. Cambridge Antiquarian Society, Octavo Publications, no. 48. Cambridge: Cambridge Antiquarian Society, 1917.

Villanueva, Jaime. *Viaje literario a la Iglesias de España*. 22 vols. in 11. Madrid: Impressa Real, 1803–52.

Vincentius Hispanus. *Apparatus in Concilium quartum Lateranense*. Ed. Antonio García y García. In *Constitutiones Concilii quarti Lateranensis*, 271–384.

Vita Burchardi ep. Wormatiensis. MGH, SS 4:829–46. Hannover: Hahn, 1841.

Vivianus Tuschus. *Casus longi in Codicem*. In *Corpus iuris civilis*. [Lyon, 1584].

Walter de Stapeldon. *The Register of Walter de Stapeldon, Bishop of Exeter (A.D. 1307–1326)*. Ed. F. C. Hingeston-Randolph. London: George Bell & Sons; Exeter: Henry S. Eland, 1892.

Walter Map. *De nugis curialium*. Ed. and trans. M. R. James, rev. by C. N. L. Brooke and R. A. B. Mynors. Oxford Medieval Texts. Oxford: Clarendon Press, 1983. Repr., 1994.

Walter of Châtillon. *Moralisch-Satirische Gedichte Walters von Chatillon*. Ed. Karl Strecker. Heidelberg: Carl Winter, 1929.

Walter of Cornut. *Der Ordo judiciarius "Scientiam."* Ed. Ludwig Wahrmund. QGRKP, vol. 2, pt. 1. Innsbruck: Wagner, 1913. Repr., Aalen: Scientia, 1962.

Wilkins, David. *Concilia Magnae Britanniae et Hiberniae.* 4 vols. London: Sumptibus R. Gosling, F. Byles, T. Woodward, C. Davis, 1737. Repr., Brussels: Culture & Civilisation, 1964.
William Durand. *Speculum iudiciale.* 2 vols. Basel: Apud Ambrosium et Aurelium Froebenios Fratres, 1574. Repr., Aalen: Scientia, 1975.
William FitzStephen. *Vita S.Thomae, Cantuariensis archiepisopi et martyris.* In *Materials for the History of Thomas Becket* 3:1–154.
William Greenfield. *The Register of Archbishop Greenfield.* Ed. A. Hamilton Thompson. 5 vols. Surtees Society Publications, vols. 145, 149, 151–53. London: Bernard Quaritch, 1931–38.
William Langland. *Piers Plowman.* Ed. Walter W. Skeat. 2 vols. Oxford: Oxford University Press, 1886. Repr., 1954.
William Lyndwood. *Provinciale seu constitutiones Angliae.* Oxford: H. Hall for R. Davis, 1679. Bound with John of Acton, *Constitutiones legatinae.*
William of Canterbury. *Vita S. Thomae Cantuariensis archiepiscopi.* In *Materials for the History of Thomas Becket* 1:1–136.
William of Drogheda. *Die Summa aurea des Wilhelmus de Drokeda.* Ed. Ludwig Wahrmund. QGRKP, vol. 2, pt. 2. Innsbruck: Wagner, 1914. Repr., Aalen: Scientia, 1962.
William of Pagula. *Summa summarum.* CUL, MS Pembroke 201.
William of Tyre. *Chronicon.* Ed. R. B. C. Huygens. 2 vols. CCM, vols. 63–63A. Turnhout: Brepols, 1986.
William Wickwane. *The Register of William Wickwane.* Ed. William Brown. Surtees Society Publications, vol. 114. London: Bernard Quaritch, 1907.
Xenophon. *Memorabilia.* Ed. and trans. E. C. Marchant. Loeb Classical Library. Cambridge: Harvard University Press; London: William Heinemann, 1923. Repr., 1979.
Year Books of Richard II: 8–10 Richard II. Ed. L. C. Hector and Michael J. Hager. Cambridge, MA: Ames Foundation, 1987.
Zabarella, Francesco. *Tractatus de modo docendi et discendi ius canonicum.* Ed. Thomas E. Morrissey in "The Art of Teaching and Learning Law."
Zenzelinus de Cassanis. *Apparatus* to *Extravagantes Johannis XXII.* In *Corpus iuris canonici una cum glossis.* [Venice, 1605].

Secondary Works

Abulafia, David. *Frederick II, a Medieval Emperor.* New York: Oxford University Press, 1988.
Actes du colloque Terminologie de la vie intellectuelle au moyen âge. Ed. Olga Weijers. Études sur le vocabulaire intellectuel du moyen âge, vol. 1. Turnhout: Brepols, 1988.
Alonso Rodriguez, Bernardo. *Juan Alfonso de Benavente, canonista salmantino del siglo XV.* Cuadernos del Istituto Juridico Español, vol. 17. Rome and Madrid: Consejo superior de investigaciones cientificas, 1964.
Alonso Romero, Paz, and Carlos Garriga Acosta. "El régimen jurídico de la abogacia en Castilla (siglos XIII–XVIII). In *L'assistance dans la résolution des conflits,* 51–114.
Amelotti, Mario. *Per una storia del notariato meridionale.* Rome: Consiglio nazionle del notariato, 1982.

Amelotti, Mario, and Giorgio Costamagna. *Alle origini del notariato Italiano*. Studi storici sul notariato Italiano, vol. 2. Rome: Consiglio nazionale del notariato, 1975.

Anniversary Essays in Mediaeval History by Students of Charles Homer Haskins. Ed. Charles H. Taylor. Cambridge: Harvard University Press, 1919. Repr., Freeport, NY: Books for Libraries, 1967.

Appleby, John T. *England without Richard, 1189–1199*. Ithaca: Cornell University Press, 1965.

Arias Ramos, José. "Advocati y collegia advocatorum en la actividad legislativa Justinianea." In *Homenaje a D. Nicolas Perez Serrano* 1:47–61.

Arrighi, Gino. *Felino Sandei (1444–1503), canonista e umanista*. Accademia Lucchese di scienze, lettere e arti, Studi e testi, vol. 24. Lucca: Accademia Lucchese, 1987.

Artz, Frederick B. *The Mind of the Middle Ages: An Historical Survey, A.D. 200–1500*. 3rd ed. New York: Alfred A. Knopf, 1965.

Ascheri, Mario. *I diritti del medioevo italiano, secoli XI–XV*. Rome: Carocci, 2000.

———. "Le fonte e la flessibilità del diritto comune: Il paradosso del *consilium sapientis*." In *Legal Consulting in the Civil Law Tradition*, 11–53.

Aspects de l'Université de Paris. Ed. J. Calvet. Paris: Albin Michel, 1949.

Aspekte europäischer Rechtsgeschichte: Festgabe für Helmut Coing zum 70. Geburtstag. Ius Commune, Sonderhefte, vol. 17. Frankfurt a/M: Vittorio Klostermann, 1982.

Aspetti dell'insegnamento giuridico nelle Università medievali: Le "quaestiones disputatae." Reggio Calabria: Parallelo 38, 1974.

L'assistance dans la résolution des conflits. Parts 4–5. Recueils de la Société Jean Bodin pour l'histoire comparative des institutions, vols. 64–65. Brussels: De Boeck Université, 1997–98.

Aston, Margaret. *Thomas Arundel: A Study of Church Life in the Reign of Richard II*. Oxford: Clarendon Press, 1967.

Aston, T. H. "Oxford's Medieval Alumni." *Past and Present* 74 (1977) 3–40.

Aston, T. H., and Rosamond Faith. "University and College Endowments." In *HUO* 1:265–309.

Aston, T. H., G. D. Duncan, and T. A. R. Evans. "Medieval Alumni of the University of Cambridge." *Past and Present* 86 (1980) 9–96.

Asztalos, Monika. "The Faculty of Theology." In *HUE* 1:409–41.

Atti del Convegno internazionale di studi Accursiani. Ed. Guido Rossi. 3 vols. Milan: A. Giuffrè, 1968.

Atti del simposio internazionale cateriniano-bernardiniano. Ed. Domenico Maffei and Paolo Nardi. Siena: Accademia senese degli intronati, 1982.

Aubenas, Roger. "Inconscience de juristes ou pédantisme malfaisant? Un chapitre d'histoire juridico-sociale, XI–XVe siècles." *RHDF*, 4th ser., 56 (1978) 215–52.

Aufstieg und Niedergang der römischen Welt: Geschichte und Kultur Roms im Spiegel der neueren Forschung. Ed. Hildegard Temporini and Wolfgang Haase. Part 1, *Von den Anfängen Roms bis zum Ausgang der Republik*, 5 vols. Part 2, *Prinzipat*, 22 vols. to date. Berlin: Walter De Gruyter, 1972–. [*ANRW*]

Autenrith, Johann Friedrich. *De eo quod iustum est circa salaria ac honoraria advocatorum*. Wittemberg: Finceliana, 1727.

Authority and Power: Studies on Medieval Law and Government Presented to Walter Ullmann on His Seventieth Birthday. Ed. Brian Tierney and Peter Linehan. Cambridge: Cambridge University Press, 1980.

Baker, John H. *An Introduction to English Legal History.* 3rd ed. London: Butterworths, 1990.

———. *The Law's Two Bodies: Some Evidential Problems in English Legal History.* Oxford: Oxford University Press, 2002.

———. *The Legal Profession and the Common Law: Historical Essays.* London: Hambledon, 1986.

———. *The Order of Serjeants at Law.* Selden Society, suppl. ser., vol. 5. London: Selden Society, 1984.

———. *The Third University of England: The Inns of Court and the Common-Law Tradition.* Selden Society Lecture. London: Selden Society, 1990.

Baldwin, John W. "Critics of the Legal Profession: Peter the Chanter and His Circle." In *Proceedings II* (Boston), 249–59.

———. *Masters, Princes, and Merchants: The Social Views of Peter the Chanter and His Circle.* 2 vols. Princeton: Princeton University Press, 1970.

Barker, John W. *Justinian and the Later Roman Empire.* Madison: University of Wisconsin Press, 1966.

Barrow, Julia. "German Cathedrals and the Monetary Economy in the Twelfth Century." *JMH* 16 (1990) 13–38.

Bartlett, Robert. *Trial by Fire and Water: The Medieval Judicial Ordeal.* Oxford: Clarendon Press, 1986. Repr., 1988.

Bartolo da Sassoferrato: Studi e documenti per il VI centenario. 2 vols. Milan: A. Giuffrè, 1962.

Barton, J. L. "The Study of Civil Law before 1380." In *HUO* 1:519–30.

Basdevant-Gaudemet, Brigitte. "Les sources de droit romain en matière de procédure dans le Décret de Gratien." *RDC* 27 (1977) 193–242.

Bataillard, Charles. *Les origines de l'histoire des procureurs et des avoués depuis le Ve siècle jusqu'au XVe (411?–1453).* Paris: Cotillon, 1868.

Battelli, Giulio. "L'esame di idoneità dei notai pubblici apostolica auctoritate nel Duecento." In *Forschungen zur Reichs-, Papst- und Landesgeschichte* 1:255–63.

Bauman, Richard A. *Lawyers in Roman Republican Politics: A Study of the Roman Jurists in Their Political Setting, 316–82 B.C.* Münchener Beiträge zur Papyrusforschung und antiken Rechtsgeschichte, no. 72. Munich: C. H. Beck, 1983.

Baumgärtner, Ingrid. "'De privilegiis doctorum': Über Gelehrtenstand und Doktorwürde im späten Mittelalter." *Historisches Jahrbuch* 106 (1986) 298–321.

———. "Rat bei der Rechtsprechung: Die Anfänge der juristischen Gutachterpraxis zwischen römischer Kommune und päpstlicher Kurie im 12. und beginnenden 13. Jahrhundert."' In *Legal Consulting in the Civil Law Tradition,* 55–106.

———. "Was muss ein Legist vom Kirchenrecht wissen? Roffredus Beneventanus und seine *Libelli de iure canonico.*" In *Proceedings VII* (Cambridge), 223–45.

Bautier, Robert-Henri. *The Economic Development of Medieval Europe.* London: Thames & Hudson; New York: Harcourt Brace Jovanovich, 1971.

Bayless, Martha. *Parody in the Middle Ages: The Latin Tradition.* Ann Arbor: University of Michigan Press, 1996.

Bazàn, Bernardo. "Les questions disputées, principalement dans les facultés de théologie." In Bazàn et al, *Les questions disputées*, 13–149.

Bazàn, Bernardo, John W. Wippel, Gérard Fransen, and Danielle Jacquart. *Les questions disputées et les questions quodlibétiques dans les facultés de théologie, de droit et de médicine.* Typologie des sources du moyen âge occidental, fasc. 44–45. Turnhout: Brepols, 1985.

Becker, Alfons. *Papst Urban II. (1088–1099).* 2 vols. MGH, Schriften, vol. 19. Stuttgart: Anton Hiersemann, 1964–68.

Becker, Hans-Jürgen. "Simone da Borsano, ein Kanonist am Vorabend des grossenschismas." In *Rechtsgeschichte als Kulturgeschichte*, 179–95.

Bedini, Silvio A. "Clocks and Reckoning of Time." In *DMA* 3:457–64.

Beiträge zum Berufsbewusstsein des mittelalterlichen Menschen. Ed. Paul Wilpert. Miscellanea Mediaevalia, vol. 3. Berlin: Walter de Gruyter, 1964.

Bellomo, Manlio. *The Common Legal Past of Europe, 1000–1800.* Trans. Lydia G. Cochrane. Studies in Medieval and Early Modern Canon Law, vol. 4. Washington, DC: Catholic University of America Press, 1995.

———. "Factum proponitur certum sed dubium est de iure." In *Die Kunst der Disputationen*, 1–28.

———. "'Legere, repetere, disputare:' Introduzione ad una ricerca sulle 'quaestiones' civilistiche." In *Aspetti dell'insegnamento giuridico nelle Università medievali*, 13–81. Repr. in his *Medioevo edita e inedita* 1:51–97.

———. *Medioevo edita e inedita.* 3 vols. Rome: Il Cigno Galilee Galilei, 1997.

———. "Una nuova figura di intellettuale: Il giurista." In *Il secolo XI: Una svolta?* 237–56.

———. *Saggio sull'università nell'età del diritto comune.* Rome: Il Cigno Galileo Galilei, 1992.

Belloni, Annalisa. "Baziano, cioè Giovanni Bassiano, legista e canonista del secolo XII." *TRG* 57 (1989) 69–85.

———. "L'insegnamento giuridico in Italia e in Francia nei primi decenni del Cinquecento e l'emigrazione di Andrea Alciato." In *Università in Europa*, 137–58.

———. "L'insegnamento giuridico nelle università italiane." In *Luoghi e metodi*, 141–52.

———. "Neue Erkenntnisse über den Rechtsunterricht in Padua im fünfzehnten Jahrhundert." *Ius commune* 13 (1985) 1–12.

———. *Professori giuristi a Padova nel secolo XV: Profili bio-bibliografici e cattedre.* Ius commune, Sonderhefte, vol. 28. Frankfurt a/M: Vittorio Klostermann, 1986.

———. "Quaestiones e consilia: Agli inizi della prassi consigliare." In *Consilia im späten Mittelalter*, 19–32.

Bennett, Walter. *The Lawyer's Myth: Reviving Ideals in the Legal Profession.* Chicago: University of Chicago Press, 2001.

Benson, Robert L. "Rufin." In *DDC* 7:779–84.

Benzemer, Kees. *What Jacques Saw: Thirteenth Century France through the Eyes of Jacques de Revigny, Professor of Law at Orleans.* Ius Commune, Sonderhefte, vol. 99. Frankfurt: Vittorio Klostermann, 1997.

Berend, Nora. "Hungarian Canon Lawyers in Royal Service." In *Proceedings X* (Syracuse), 565–74.

Bergfeld, Christoph. "Das iustum pretium des advokaten nach Auffassung der spanischen Spätscholastik." In *Studien zur europäischen Rechtsgeschichte*, 118–30.

Berman, Harold J. *Law and Revolution: The Formation of the Western Legal Tradition*. Cambridge: Harvard University Press, 1983.

Bernard, Antoine. *La rémunération des professions libérales en droit romain classique*. Paris: Donat-Montchréstien, 1936.

Bertin, Ernest. *Les mariages dans l'ancienne société française*. Paris: Hachette, 1879. Repr., Geneva: Slatkine-Megarotis, 1975.

Bertram, Martin. "Kirchenrechtliche Vorlesungen aus Orléans (1285/7)." *Francia* 2 (1974) 213–33.

———. "Neuerscheinungen zur mittelalterlichen Geschichte von Stadt und Universität Bolognas." *QFIAB* 67 (1987) 477–88.

Bertram, Martin, and Marguerite Duynstee. "Casus legum sive suffragia monachorum: Legistische Hilfsmittel für Kanonisten im späteren Mittelalter." *TRG* 51 (1983) 317–63.

Betti, Emilio. "La dottrina costruita da Bartolo sulla constitutio 'Ad reprimendum.'" In *Bartolo da Sassoferrato* 2:37–47.

Betto, Bianca. "Il collegio dei giudici e dottori di Treviso dalle origini (secolo XIII) alla soppressione (anno 1806)." *Contributi dell'Istituto di Storia Medioevale dell'Università del Sacro Cuore* 3 (1975) 29–188.

Birch, Debra. *Pilgrimage to Rome in the Middle Ages: Continuity and Change*. Studies in the History of Medieval Religion, vol. 13. Woodbridge: Boydell Press, 1998.

Bischoff, Bernhard. *Latin Palaeography: Antiquity and the Middle Ages*. Trans. Dáibhí Ó Cróinín and David Ganz. Cambridge: Cambridge University Press, 1990.

Black, Antony. *Guilds and Civil Society in European Political Thought from the Twelfth Century to the Present*. Ithaca: Cornell University Press, 1984.

Blumenthal, Uta-Renate. *The Investiture Controversy: Church and Monarchy from the Ninth to the Twelfth Centuries*. Philadelphia: University of Pennsylvania Press, 1988.

Bock, Columban. "Les Cisterciens et l'étude du droit." *Analecta sacri ordinis Cisterciensis* 7 (1951) 3–31.

Boháček, Miroslav. "Nuova fonte per la storia degli stazionari bolognesi." *SG* 9 (1966) 407–69.

———. "Puncta Codicis v rukopisu XVII.A.10 národnίno museza v Praze." *Studie o rukopisech* 20 (1981) 3–22 [German summary at 19–22].

The Bond of Marriage. Ed. William Bassett. Notre Dame: Notre Dame University Press, 1968.

Bonner, Robert J. *Lawyers and Litigants in Ancient Athens: The Genesis of the Legal Profession*. Chicago: University of Chicago Press, 1927. Repr., New York: Benjamin Blom, 1969.

Bonner, Stanley F. *Education in Ancient Rome, from the Elder Cato to the Younger Pliny*. Berkeley and Los Angeles: University of California Press, 1977.

Bono, José. *História del derecho notarial español*. 2 vols. Madrid: Junta de Decanos de los Colegios Notariles de España, 1979–82.

Bouchat, Marc. "Procédures *juris ordine observato et juris ordine non observato* dans les arbitrages du diocèse de Liège au XIIIe siècle." *TRG* 60 (1992) 377–91.

Boureau, Alain. "Droit et théologie au XIIIe siècle." *Annales: Économies, sociétés, civilisations* 47 (1992) 1113–25.

Bouwsma, William J. "Lawyers and Early Modern Culture." *American Historical Review* 78 (1973) 303–27.

Boyle, Leonard E. "The Beginnings of Legal Studies at Oxford." *Viator* 14 (1983) 107–31.

———. "Canon Law before 1380." In *HUO* 1:531–64.

———. "The Constitution 'Cum ex eo' of Boniface VIII: Education of Parochial Clergy." *Mediaeval Studies* 24 (1962) 263–302. Repr. in his *Pastoral Care, Clerical Education and Canon Law*, no. VIII.

———. "The Curriculum of the Faculty of Canon Law at Oxford in the First Half of the Fourteenth Century." In *Oxford Studies Presented to Daniel Callus*, 135–62.

———. "The Date of the Commentary of William Duranti on the Constitutions of the Second Council of Lyons." *BMCL* 4 (1974) 39–47.

———. *Pastoral Care, Clerical Education and Canon Law, 1200–1400*. London: Variorum, 1981.

———. "The 'Summa summarum' and Some Other English Works of Canon Law." In *Proceedings II* (Boston), 415–56.

Brand, Paul A. *The Origins of the English Legal Profession*. Oxford: Basil Blackwell, 1992.

Brandmüller, Walter. "Simon de Lellis de Teramo: Ein Konsistorialadvokat auf den Konzilien von Konstanz und Basel." *Archivum historiae conciliorum* 12 (1980) 229–68.

Brasington, Bruce C. "Glossing Strategies in Two Manuscripts of Pre-Gratian Canonical Collections." In *Grundlagen des Rechts*, 155–62.

———. "The Prologue of Ivo of Chartres: A Fresh Consideration from the Manuscripts." In *Proceedings VIII* (San Diego), 3–22.

———. "Prologues to Canonical Collections as a Source for Jurisprudential Change to the Eve of the Investiture Contest." *Frühmittelalterliche Studien* 28 (1994) 226–42.

———. *Ways of Mercy: The Prologue of Ivo of Chartres, Edition and Analysis*. Vita regularis, Editionen, vol. 2. Münster: LIT Verlag, 2004.

Breatnach, Liam. "Lawyers in Early Ireland." In *Brehons, Serjeants and Attorneys: Studies in the History of the Irish Legal Profession*, 1–13.

Brehons, Serjeants and Attorneys: Studies in the History of the Irish Legal Profession. Ed. Daire Hogan and W. M. Osborough. Dublin: Irish Academic Press, 1990.

Brennan, T. Corey. *The Praetorship in the Roman Republic*. 2 vols. New York: Oxford University Press, 2000.

Brentano, Robert. *A New World in a Small Place: Church and Religion in the Diocese of Rieti, 1188–1378*. Berkeley and Los Angeles: University of California Press, 1994.

———. *Rome before Avignon: A Social History of Thirteenth-Century Rome*. New York: Basic Books, 1974. Repr., Berkeley and Los Angeles: University of California Press, 1990.

———. *Two Churches: England and Italy in the Thirteenth Century*. Princeton: Princeton University Press, 1968. Repr., Berkeley and Los Angeles: University of California Press, 1988.

Bresslau, Harry. *Handbuch der Urkundenlehre für Deutschland und Italien.* 2nd ed. 2 vols. Berlin: Walter de Gruyter, 1912–31.

Brett, Martin. "Canon Law and Litigation: The Century before Gratian." In *Medieval Ecclesiastical Studies*, 21–40.

———. "Creeping up on the Panormia." In *Grundlagen des Rechts*, 205–70.

———. *The English Church under Henry I.* Oxford Historical Monographs. London: Oxford University Press, 1975.

———. "Urban II and the Collections Attributed to Ivo of Chartres." In *Proceedings VIII* (San Diego), 27–46.

Brooke, Zachary N. *The English Church and the Papacy from the Conquest to the Reign of John.* Cambridge: Cambridge University Press, 1931.

———. "The Register of Master David of London and the Part He Played in the Becket Crisis." In *Essays in History Presented to R. L. Poole*, 227–45.

Brooks, Charles W. *Pettifoggers and Vipers of the Commonwealth: The "Lower Branch" of the Legal Profession in Early Modern England.* Cambridge Studies in Legal History. Cambridge: Cambridge University Press, 1986.

Brouette, Émile. "La plus ancienne mention d'un official d'archidiacre dans le diocèse de Liège." *Revue Belge de philologie et d'histoire* 51 (1973) 366–70.

Brouillard, R. "Sanchez, Tomas." In *Dictionnaire de théologie catholique*, vol. 14, pt. 2, cols. 1075–85.

Browe, P. "Die Abendmahlsprobe im Mittelalter." *Historisches Jahrbuch* 48 (1928) 193–207.

Brown, J. C. "The Origin and Early History of the Office of Notary." *Juridical Review* 47 (1935) 201–40, 355–410.

Brown, Peter. *Religion and Society in the Age of Saint Augustine.* New York: Harper & Row, 1972.

———. *The World of Late Antiquity, AD 150–750.* New York: Harcourt Brace Jovanovich, 1971.

Brown, Sandra. *The Medieval Courts of the York Minster Peculiar.* Borthwick Papers, no. 66. York: University of York, 1984.

Brucker, Gene. "Renaissance Florence: Who Needs a University?" In *The University and the City*, 47–58.

Bruggi, Biaggio. "Il catalogo dei libri degli stationarii negli statuti della università bolognese dei giuristi." *Studi e memorie per la storia dell'Università di Bologna* 5 (1920) 3–44.

———. *Per la storia della giurisprudenza e delle università italiane.* Turin: Unione tipografico-editrice Torinese, 1915.

Brundage, James A. "The Advocate's Dilemma: What Can You Tell the Client?" In *Medieval Church Law and the Origins of the Western Legal Tradition*, 201–10.

———. "The Ambidextrous Advocate: A Study in the History of Legal Ethics." In *"Ins Wasser geworfen und Ozeane durchquert,"* 39–56.

———. "The Bar of the Ely Consistory Court in the Fourteenth Century: Advocates, Proctors, and Others." *JEH* 43 (1992) 541–60. Repr. in his *The Profession and Practice of Medieval Canon Law*, no. XVI.

———. "Bishop Thomas Arundel and the University of Cambridge." In *Lex et Romanitas*, 139–48.

———. "The Calumny Oath and Ethical Ideals of Canonical Advocates." In *Proceedings IX* (Munich), 793–805. Repr. in his *The Profession and Practice of Medieval Canon Law*, no. IV.

———. "The Cambridge Faculty of Canon Law and the Ecclesiastical Courts of Ely." In *Medieval Cambridge*, 21–45. Repr. in his *The Profession and Practice of Medieval Canon Law*, no. X.

———. "The Canon Law Curriculum in Medieval Cambridge." In *Learning the Law*, 175–90. Repr. in his *The Profession and Practice of Medieval Canon Law*, no. IX.

———. "The Crusade of Richard I: Two Canonical Quaestiones." *Speculum* 38 (1963) 443–52. Repr. in his *The Crusades, Holy War and Canon Law*, no. III.

———. *The Crusades, Holy War and Canon Law*. Aldershot: Variorum, 1991.

———. "Entry to the Ecclesiastical Bar at Ely in the Fourteenth Century: The Oath of Admission." In *Proceedings VIII* (San Diego), 531–44.

———. "The Lawyer as His Client's Judge: The Medieval Advocate's Duty to the Court." In *Cristianità ed Europa* 1:591–607.

———. "The Lawyers of the Military Orders." In *The Military Orders*, 346–57. Repr. in his *The Profession and Practice of Medieval Canon Law*, no. XVIII.

———. "Legal Aid for the Poor and the Professionalization of Law in the Middle Ages." *Journal of Legal History* 9 (1988) 169–79. Repr. in his *The Profession and Practice of Medieval Canon Law*, no. XIV.

———. *Medieval Canon Law*. London: Longman, 1995.

———. "The Monk as Lawyer." *Jurist* 39 (1979) 423–36. Repr. in his *The Profession and Practice of Medieval Canon Law*, no. VI.

———. *The Profession and Practice of Medieval Canon Law*. Aldershot: Ashgate/Variorum, 2004.

———. "Professional Discipline in the Medieval Courts Christian: The Candlesby Case." *SG* 27 (1996) 41–48.

———. "Saint Bernard and the Jurists." In *The Second Crusade and the Cistercians*, 25–33.

———. *Sex, Law and Marriage in the Middle Ages*. Aldershot: Variorum, 1993.

———. "Taxation of Costs in Medieval Canonical Courts." In *Forschungen zur Reichs-, Papst- und Landesgeschichte* 1:265–74. Repr. in his *The Profession and Practice of Medieval Canon Law*, no. XIII.

———. "Thomas Arundel and the University of Cambridge." In *Lex et romanitas*, 139–48.

———. "The Treatment of Marriage in the Quaestiones Londonenses." *Manuscripta* 19 (1975) 86–97. Repr. in his *Sex, Law and Marriage in the Middle Ages*, no. XII.

———. "A Twelfth-Century Oxford Disputation Concerning the Privileges of the Knights Hospitallers." *Mediaeval Studies* 24 (1962) 153–60. Repr. in his *The Crusades, Holy War and Canon Law*, no. XII.

———. "Universities and the 'ius commune' in Medieval Europe." *RIDC* 11 (2000) 237–53. Repr. in his *The Profession and Practice of Medieval Canon Law*, no. VIII.

———. "Vultures, Whores, and Hypocrites: Images of Lawyers in Medieval Literature." *The Roman Law Tradition* 1 (2002) 56–103.

Brunyng, Lucas F. "Lawcourt Proceedings in the Lombard Kingdom before and after the Frankish Conquest." *JMH* 11 (1985) 193–214.

Buchner, Rudolf. *Die Rechtsquellen*. Supplement to *Deutschlands Geschichtsquellen im Mittelalter: Vorzeit und Karolinger*. Weimar: Böhlaus, 1953.

Buckland, W. W. *A Text-Book of Roman Law from Augustus to Justinian*. 3rd ed. Rev. by Peter Stein. Cambridge: Cambridge University Press, 1963. Repr., 1975.

Bukowska Gorgoni, Cristina. "Le notariat et la pénétration du droit romain en Pologne." In *Confluence des droits savants*, 243–62.

Bullough, Vern L. *The History of Prostitution*. New Hyde Park, NY: University Books, 1964.

Burger, Michael. "*Officiales* and the *Familiae* of the Bishops of Lincoln, 1258–99." *JMH* 16 (1990) 39–53.

Burrage, Michael. "The Professions in Sociology and History." In *Professions in Theory and History*, 1–28.

Byock, Jesse L. *Medieval Iceland: Society, Sagas, and Power*. Berkeley and Los Angeles: University of California Press, 1988. Repr., 1990.

Byrne, Francis J. *Irish Kings and High Kings*. London: Batsford, 1973.

Caenegem, Raoul C. van. *An Historical Introduction to Private Law*. Trans. D. E. L. Johnston. Cambridge: Cambridge University Press, 1992.

———. *History of European Civil Procedure*. Vol. 16, chap. 2, of *International Encyclopedia of Comparative Law*. Tübingen: J. C. B. Mohr, 1973.

———. "Law in the Medieval World." *TRG* 49 (1981) 13–46. Repr. in his *Legal History: A European Perspective*, 115–48.

———. *Legal History: A European Perspective*. London: Hambledon, 1991.

Calasso, Francesco. *I glossatori e la teoria della sovranità: Studio di diritto comune pubblico*. 2nd ed. Milan: A. Giuffrè, 1951.

———. *Medio evo del diritto I: Le fonti*. Milan: A. Giuffrè, 1954.

Calleri, Santi. *L'arte dei giudici di Firenze nell'età comunale e nel suo statuto del 1344*. Milan: A. Giuffrè, 1966.

The Cambridge History of Medieval Political Thought, c. 350–c. 1450. Ed. J. H. Burns. Cambridge: Cambridge University Press, 1988.

Carcopino, Jérôme. *Daily Life in Ancient Rome: The People and the City at the Height of the Empire*. 2nd ed. Ed. Henry T. Rowell; trans. E. O. Lorimer. New Haven: Yale University Press, 1968. Repr., 2003.

Cárdenas, Anthony J. "Alfonso's Scriptorium and Chancery: Role of the Prologue in Bonding the *Translatio Studii* to the *Translatio Potestatis*." In *Emperor of Culture*, 90–108.

Carlen, Louis. "Zum Offizialität von Sitten im Mittelalter." *ZRG*, KA 46 (1960) 221–38.

Carniello, R. R. "The Rise of an Administrative Elite in Medieval Bologna: Notaries and Popular Government, 1282–1292." *JMH* 28 (2002) 319–47.

Carr, William. *Travels through Flanders, Holland, Germany, Sweden, and Denmark, Con-

taining an Account of What is Most Remarkable in Those Countries. 7th ed. Amsterdam: Printed for Jacob ter Beek, 1744.

Carr, William. *University College.* College Histories, Oxford, vol. 1. London: F. E. Robinson, 1902.

Catto, J. I. "Citizens, Scholars and Masters." In *HUO* 1:151–92.

Cavazza, Francesco. *Le scuole dell'antico studio Bolognese.* Milan: Ulrico Hoepli, 1896.

Cencetti, Giorgio. "La laurea nelle università medievali." *Studi e memorie per la storia dell'Università di Bologna* 16 (1943) 249–73.

Chadwick, Henry. "New Letters of St. Augustine." *JTS*, n.s. 34 (1983) 425–52.

Charles-Edwards, T. M. *The Welsh Laws.* Cardiff: University of Wales Press, 1989.

Change in Medieval Society: Europe North of the Alps, 1050–1500. Ed. Sylvia L. Thrupp. New York: Appleton-Century-Crofts, 1964.

Charvet, L. "L'accession des clercs aux fonctions d'avocat." *Bulletin de littérature ecclésiastique* [Toulouse] 67 (1966) 287–98.

Châtillon, Jean. "L'influence de S. Bernard sur la pensée scolastique au XIIe et au XIIIe siècle." In *Saint Bernard théologien,* 268–88.

Cheney, Christopher R. "England and the Roman Curia under Innocent III." *JEH* 18 (1967) 173–86.

———. *English Bishops' Chanceries, 1100–1250.* Manchester: Manchester University Press, 1950.

———. *English Synodalia of the Thirteenth Century.* London: Oxford University Press, 1941. Repr., 1968.

———. *From Becket to Langton: English Church Government, 1170–1213.* Manchester: Manchester University Press, 1956. Repr., 1965.

———. *A Handbook of Dates for Students of British History.* 2nd ed. Rev. by Michael Jones. Cambridge: Cambridge University Press, 2000.

———. *Hubert Walter.* London: Nelson, 1967.

———. *Medieval Texts and Studies.* Oxford: Clarendon Press, 1973.

———. *Notaries Public in England in the Thirteenth and Fourteenth Centuries.* Oxford: Clarendon Press, 1972.

———. "William Lyndwood's *Provinciale.*" *Jurist* 21 (1961) 405–34. Repr. in his *Medieval Texts and Studies,* 158–84.

Cheney, Mary G. "The Compromise of Avranches of 1172 and the Spread of Canon Law in England." *English Historical Review* 56 (1941) 177–97.

———. *Roger, Bishop of Worcester, 1164–1179: An English Bishop in the Age of Becket.* Oxford: Clarendon Press, 1980.

———. "William FitzStephen and His Life of Archbishop Thomas." In *Church and Government in the Middle Ages,* 139–56.

Cheyette, Fredric L. *Ermengard of Narbonne and the World of the Troubadours.* Ithaca: Cornell University Press, 2001.

———. "Suum cuique tribuere." *French Historical Studies* 6 (1970) 287–99.

Chiappelli, Luigi. "La polemica contro i legisti dei secoli XIV, XV e XVI." *Archivio giuridico* 26 (1881) 295–322.

Chiesa, diritto e ordinamento della "Societas Christiana" nei secoli XI e XII. Miscellanea del Centro di Studi Medioevali, vol. 11. Milan: Vita & Pensiero, 1986.

Chodorow, Stanley. *Christian Political Theory and Church Politics in the Mid-Twelfth Century: The Ecclesiology of Gratian's Decretum*. Berkeley and Los Angeles: University of California Press, 1972.

Chrestomathie de l'ancien français (VIIIe–XVe siècles). 12th ed. Ed. Karl Bartsch. Leipzig: F. C. W. Vogel, 1920.

Chroust, Anton-Hermann. "The Emergence of Professional Standards and the Rise of the Legal Profession: The Graeco-Roman Period." *Boston University Law Review* 36 (1956) 587–98.

Church and Government in the Middle Ages: Essays Presented to C. R. Cheney on His 70th Birthday. Ed. C. N. L. Brooke, D. E. Luscombe, G. H. Martin, and Dorothy Owen. Cambridge: Cambridge University Press, 1976.

Churchill, Irene Josephine. *Canterbury Administration: The Administrative Machinery of the Archbishopric of Canterbury Illustrated from Original Documents*. 2 vols. London: Society for Promoting Christian Knowledge, 1933.

Cipolla, Carlo M. *Before the Industrial Revolution: European Society and Economy, 1000–1700*. 2nd ed. New York: W. W. Norton, 1980.

———. *Clocks and Culture, 1300–1700*. New York: W. W. Norton, 1978.

———. "The Professions: The Long View." *Journal of European Economic History* 2 (1973) 37–52.

Clanchy, Michael T. *From Memory to Written Record: England, 1066–1307*. 2nd ed. Oxford: Basil Blackwell, 1993.

———. "*Moderni* in Education and Government in England." *Speculum* 50 (1975) 671–88.

Clarence Smith, J. A. *Medieval Law Teachers and Writers, Civilian and Canonist*. Ottawa: University of Ottawa Press, 1975.

Classen, Peter. "La curia romana e le scuole di Francia nel secolo XII." In *Le istituzioni ecclesiastiche della "Societas Christiana,"* 432–36.

———. "Das Decretum Gratiani wurde nicht in Ferentino approbiert." *BMCL* 8 (1978) 38–40.

———. "Zur Geschichte Papst Anastasius IV." *QFIAB* 48 (1968) 36–63.

Cobban, Alan B. "Elective Salaried Lectureships in the Universities of Southern Europe in the Pre-Reformation Era." *Bulletin of the John Rylands Library of Manchester* 67 (1984/85) 662–87.

———. "John Arundel, the Tutorial System, and the Cost of Undergraduate Living in the Medieval English Universities." *Bulletin of the John Rylands University Library of Manchester* 77 (1995) 143–59.

———. *The King's Hall within the University of Cambridge in the Later Middle Ages*. Cambridge Studies in Medieval Life and Thought, ser. 3, vol. 1. Cambridge: Cambridge University Press, 1969.

———. *The Medieval English Universities: Oxford and Cambridge to c. 1500*. Aldershot: Scolar Press, 1988. Repr., Berkeley and Los Angeles: University of California Press, 1990.

——— . *The Medieval Universities: Their Development and Organization.* London: Methuen, 1975.

Cochrane, Charles Norris. *Christianity and Classical Culture: A Study of Thought and Action from Augustus to Augustine.* London: Oxford University Press, 1944.

Coing, Helmut. "Die juristische Fakultät und ihr Lehrprogramm." In Coing, *Handbuch* 1:39–128.

——— . *Handbuch der Quellen und Literatur der neueren europäischen Privatrechtsgeschichte.* Vol. 1, *Mittelalter (1100–1500): Die gelehrten Rechte und die Gesetzgebung.* Munich: C. H. Beck, 1973. [Coing, *Handbuch*]

Colish, Marcia. *Peter Lombard.* 2 vols. Leiden: E. J. Brill, 1994.

Collectanea, Second Series. Ed. Montagu Burrows. Oxford Historical Society Publications, ser. 1, vol. 16. Oxford: Oxford Historical Society, 1890.

Colli, Vincenzo. "I *libri consiliorum:* Note sulla formazione e diffusione delle raccolte di consilia dei giuristi dei secoli XIV–XV." In *Consilia im späten Mittelalter,* 225–35.

Condorelli, Orazio. *Clerici peregrini: Aspetti giuridici della mobilità clericale nei secoli XII–XIV.* I libri di Erice, vol. 12. Rome: Il Cigno Galileo Galilei, 1995.

Confluence des droits savants et des pratiques juridiques. Ed. Helmut Coing, Giulio Vismara, and André Gouron. Milan: A. Giuffrè, 1979.

Conrat, Max. *Geschichte der Quellen und Literatur des römischen Rechts im frühen Mittelalter.* Leipzig: B. Tauchnitz, 1891. Repr., Aalen: Scientia, 1963.

Consilia im späten Mittelalter: Zum historischen Aussagewert einer Quellengattung. Ed. Ingrid Baumgärtner. Studi: Schriftenreihe des Deutschen Studienzentrums in Venedig, vol. 13. Sigmaringen: Jan Thorbecke, 1995.

Conte, Emanuele. "Un *sermo pro petendis insigniis* al tempo di Azzone e Bagarotto." *Rivista di storia del diritto italiano* 60 (1987) 71–86.

Contreni, John J. "The Carolingian Renaissance: Education and Literary Culture." In *NCMH* 2:709–57.

Cortese, Ennio. *Il diritto nella storia medievale.* 2 vols. Rome: Il Cigno Galileo Galilei, 1995. Repr., 1999.

——— . "Legisti, canonisti e feudisti: La formazione di un ceto medievale." In *Università e società nelle secoli XII–XVI,* 196–281.

——— . "Scienza di giudici e scienza di professori tra XII e XIII secolo." In *Legge, giudici, giuristi,* 93–148.

Coudry, Marianne. "Sénatus-consultes et *Acta Senatus:* Rédaction, conservation et archivage des documents émanant du Sénat, de l'époque de César à celle des Sévères." In *La mémoire perdue,* ed. Demaugin, 65–102.

Courtenay, William J. *Parisian Scholars in the Early Fourteenth Century: A Social Portrait.* Cambridge Studies in Medieval Life and Thought, 4th ser., vol. 41. Cambridge: Cambridge University Press, 1999.

——— . *Teaching Careers at the University of Paris in the Thirteenth and Fourteenth Centuries.* Texts and Studies in the History of Mediaeval Education, no. 18. Notre Dame: University of Notre Dame, 1988.

Cowdrey, H. E. J. *Pope Gregory VII, 1073–1085.* Oxford: Clarendon Press, 1998.

Cox, Ronald J. *A Study of the Juridic Status of Laymen in the Writing of the Medieval Canon-*

ists. Catholic University of America, Canon Law Studies, no. 395. Washington, DC: Catholic University of America Press, 1959.

Crawley, Charles. *Trinity Hall: The History of a Cambridge College*. Cambridge: Printed for the College, 1976.

Crises et réformes dans l'église de la réforme grégorienne à la préréforme. Actes du 115e congrès national des sociétés savants, Section d'histoire médiévale et de philologie, vol. 1. Paris: Éditions du Comité des travaux historiques & scientifiques, 1991.

Cristianità ed Europa: Miscellanea di studi in onore di Luigi Prosdocimi. Ed. Cesare Alzati. 2 vols. in 3 Rome: Herder, 1994–2000.

Crook, John A. *Consilium principis: Imperial Councils and Counsellors from Augustus to Diocletian*. Cambridge: Cambridge University Press, 1955.

———. *Law and Life of Rome*. Ithaca: Cornell University Press, 1967.

———. *Legal Advocacy in the Roman World*. London: Duckworth, 1995.

Cross, Peter. "Knights, Esquires and the Origins of Social Gradation in England." *Transactions of the Royal Historical Society*, 6th ser., 5 (1995) 155–78.

Cuillieron, Monique. "Un concile de réformation: Le concile rouennais de 1231." *RHDF*, 4th ser., 61 (1983) 345–69.

Cultures of Power: Lordship, Status, and Process in Twelfth-Century Europe. Ed. Thomas N. Bisson. Philadelphia: University of Pennsylvania Press, 1995.

Cushing, Kathleen G. *Papacy and Law in the Gregorian Revolution: The Canonistic Work of Anselm of Lucca*. Oxford: Clarendon Press, 1998.

Dasef, David. "Lawyers of the York Curia, 1400–1435." B. Phil. thesis, University of York, 1976.

Davidsohn, Robert. *Storia di Firenze*. Trans. Giovanni Miccoli. 4 vols. Florence: Sansoni, 1972–73.

Davies, Jonathan. *Florence and Its University during the Early Renaissance*. Education and Society in the Middle Ages and the Renaissance, vol. 8. Leiden: E. J. Brill, 1998.

Davies, Wendy. "Local Participation and Legal Ritual in Early Medieval Law Courts." In *The Moral World of the Law*, 48–61.

Dawson, John P. *A History of Lay Judges*. Cambridge: Harvard University Press, 1960.

———. *The Oracles of the Law*. Ann Arbor: University of Michigan Law School, 1968.

Delachenal, Roland. *Histoire des avocats au Parlement de Paris, 1300–1600*. Paris: E. Plon, 1885.

Delhaye, Philippe. *Enseignement et morale au XIIe siècle*. Fribourg: Éditions universitaires; Paris: Éditions du Cerf, 1988.

———. "L'organisation scolaire au XIIe siècle." *Traditio* 5 (1947) 211–68. Repr. in his *Enseignement et morale*, 1–58.

Denifle, Heinrich. *Die Entstehung der Universitäten des Mittelalters bis 1400*. Berlin: Weidmann, 1885. Repr., Graz: Akademische Druck- u. Verlagsanstalt, 1956.

Denley, Peter. "Career, Springboard or Sinecure? University Teaching in Fifteenth-Century Italy." *Medieval Prosopography* 12 (1991) 95–114.

———. "The Collegiate Movement in Italian Universities in the Late Middle Ages." *History of Universities* 10 (1991) 29–91.

Destrez, Jean. *La pecia dans les manuscrits universitaires du XIIIe au XIVe siècle.* Paris: Jacques Vautrain, 1935.
Deutinger, Roman. "The Decretist Rufinus—a Well-Known Person?" *BMCL* 23 (1999) 10–15.
Dickens, Charles. *Bleak House.* London: Bradbury and Evans, 1853. Repr., New York: New American Library, 1964.
Dictionnaire de droit canonique. Ed. R. Naz. 7 vols. Paris: Letouzey & Ané, 1935–65. [*DDC*]
Dictionnaire de théologie catholique. Ed. A. Vacant and E. Mangenot. 15 vols. Paris: Letouzey & Ané, 1903–50.
Dictionary of the Middle Ages. Ed. Joseph R. Strayer et al. 13 vols. New York: Scribner, 1982–89. [*DMA*]
Dilcher, Gerhard. "Gesetzgebung als Rechtserneuerung: Eine Studie zum Selbstverständnis der mittelalterlichen Leges." In *Rechtsgeschichte als Kulturgeschichte*, 13–35.
———. "Der Kanonist als Gesetzgeber: Zur Rechtshistorischen Stellung des Hofrechts Bischof Burchard von Worms, 1024/25." In *Grundlagen des Rechts*, 105–29.
Dilcher, Hermann. "Juristisches Berufsethos nach dem sizilischen Gesetzbuch Friedrichs II. von Hohenstaufen." In *Studien zur europäischen Rechtsgeschichte*, 88–117.
A Distinct Voice: Medieval Studies in Honor of Leonard E. Boyle, O.P. Ed. Jacqueline Brown and William P. Stoneman. Notre Dame: University of Notre Dame Press, 1997.
Ditsche, Magnus. "'Scholares pauperes': Prospettive e condizioni di studio degli studenti poveri nelle università del medioevo." *Annali dell'Istituto storico italo-germanico in Trento* 5 (1979) 43–54.
El documento notarial en la historia. Madrid: Ministerio de educación nacional, 1963.
Dohar, William J. "*Sufficienter litteratus*: Clerical Examination and Instruction for the Cure of Souls." In *A Distinct Voice*, 305–21.
Dolezalek, Gero. "Another Fragment of the Apparatus 'Militant siquidem patroni.'" *BMCL* 5 (1975) 130–32.
———. "Die handschriftliche Verbreitung von Rechtsprechungssammlungen der Rota." *ZRG*, KA 58 (1972) 1–106.
———. "Les gloses des manuscrits de droit: Reflet des méthodes d'enseignement." In *Manuels, programmes de cours et techniques d'enseignement*, 235–55.
———. "La pecia e la preparazione dei libri giuridici nei secoli XII–XIII." In *Luoghi e metodi*, 201–17.
———. "Quaestiones motae in Rota: Richterliche Beratungsnotizen aus dem vierzehnten Jahrhundert." In *Proceedings V* (Salamanca), 99–114.
———. *Repertorium manuscriptorum veterum Codicis Iustiniani.* 2 vols. Ius Commune, Sonderhefte, vol. 24. Frankfurt a/M: Vittorio Klostermann, 1985.
———. *Verzeichnis der Handschriften zum römischen Recht bis 1600.* 4 vols. Frankfurt a/M: Max-Planck-Institut für europäische Rechtsgeschichte, 1972.
———. "Wie studierte man bei den Glossatoren?" In *Summe—Glosse—Kommentar*, 55–74.
Dolezalek, Gero, and Knut Wolfgang Nörr. "Die Rechtsprechungssammlungen der mittelalterlichen Rota." In Coing, *Handbuch* 1:849–56.

Donahue, Charles, Jr. "Gerard Pucelle as a Canon Lawyer: Life and the Battle Abbey Case." In *Grundlagen des Rechts*, 333–48.

Donahue, Charles, Jr., and Jeanne P. Gordus. "A Case from Archbishop Stratford's Audience Act Book and Some Comments on the Book and Its Value." *BMCL* 2 (1972) 45–59.

Dossat, Y. "Unité ou diversité dans la pratique notariale dans les pays de droit écrit." *Annales du Midi* 68 (1956) 175–83.

Dotson, John E. "Trade, Western European." In *DMA* 12:108–16.

Douglas, Mary. *Purity and Danger: An Analysis of the Concepts of Pollution and Taboo*. London: Routledge, 1966. Repr., 2000.

1274, année charnière: Mutations et continuités. Colloques internationaux du Centre National de la Recherche Scientifique, no. 558. Paris: Éditions du Centre national de la recherche scientifique, 1977.

Downs, John Emmanuel. *The Concept of Clerical Immunity: A Dissertation in Public Ecclesiastical Law*. Canon Law Studies, no. 126. Washington, DC: Catholic University of America Press, 1941.

El dret comú i Catalunya. Barcelona: Pagès, 1991.

Drew, Katherine Fischer. "Peace and Security in the Early Middle Ages." In *Law in Mediaeval Life and Thought*, 177–84.

Du Cann, Richard. *The Art of the Advocate*. Harmondsworth: Penguin, 1964.

Duffy, Eamon. *The Stripping of the Altars: Traditional Religion in England, c. 1400–c. 1580*. New Haven: Yale University Press, 1992.

Dufour, Jean, Gérard Giordanengo, and André Gouron. "L'attrait des 'leges': Note sur la lettre d'un moine victorin (vers 1124/1127)." *SDHI* 45 (1979) 504–29.

Duggan, Charles. "From the Conquest to the Reign of John." In *The English Church and the Papacy in the Middle Ages*, 63–115.

———. "Papal Judges Delegate and the Making of the 'New Law' in the Twelfth Century." In *Cultures of Power*, 172–99.

———. "The Reception of Canon Law in England in the Later-Twelfth Century." In *Proceedings II* (Boston), 359–90.

———. *Twelfth-Century Decretal Collections and Their Importance in English History*. University of London Historical Studies, vol. 12. London: Athlone Press, 1963.

Dumville, David N. *Councils and Synods of the Gaelic Early and Central Middle Ages*. Quiggin Pamphlets on the Sources of Mediaeval Gaelic History, no. 3. Cambridge: Department of Anglo-Saxon, Norse, and Celtic, 1997.

Dunbabin, Jean. "Meeting the Costs of University Education in Northern France, c. 1240–c. 1340." *History of Universities* 10 (1991) 1–27.

Edbury, Peter W. *John of Ibelin and the Kingdom of Jerusalem*. Woodbridge: Boydell Press, 1997.

Edbury, Peter W., and John Gordon Rowe. *William of Tyre, Historian of the Latin East*. Cambridge Studies in Medieval Life and Thought, 4th ser., vol. 8. Cambridge: Cambridge University Press, 1988. Repr., 1990.

L'église et culture en France méridionale (XIIe–XIVe siècle). Cahiers de Fanjeaux, vol. 35. Toulouse: Privat, 2000.

L'église et le droit dans le Midi (XIIIe–XIVe.). Ed. Jean-Louis Biget. Cahiers de Fanjeaux, no. 29. Toulouse: Privat, 1994.

Eldredge, Laurence. "Walter of Chatillon and the Decretum of Gratian: An Analysis of 'Propter Zion non tacebo.'" *Studies in Medieval Culture* 3 (1970) 59–69.

Éléments pour une histoire de la thèse. Ed. C. Jolly and B. Veneu. Mélanges de la Bibliothèque de la Sorbonne, vol. 12. Paris: Klincksieck, 1993.

Elton, Geoffrey R. *England: 1200–1640. The Sources of History: Studies in the Uses of Historical Evidence*, vol. 1. Ithaca: Cornell University Press, 1969.

Emden, A. B. *A Biographical Register of the University of Cambridge to 1500.* Cambridge: Cambridge University Press, 1963. [*BRUC*]

———. *A Biographical Register of the University of Oxford to 1500.* 3 vols. Oxford: Clarendon Press, 1957–59. [*BRUO*]

Emminghaus, B. "Vom Palmarium." *Archiv für practische Rechtswissenschaft*, n.s. 2 (1865) 227–52.

Emperor of Culture: Alfonso X the Learned of Castile and His Thirteenth-Century Renaissance. Ed. Robert I. Burns. Philadelphia: University of Pennsylvania Press, 1990.

Engelmann, Arthur. *A History of Continental Civil Procedure.* Trans. Robert Wyness Millar. Continental Legal History Series, vol. 7. Boston: Little, Brown, 1927. Repr., Buffalo: William S. Hein, 1999.

Engelmann, Woldemar. *Die Wiedergeburt der Rechtskultur in Italien durch die wissenschaftliche Lehre: Eine Darlegung der Entfaltung des gemeinen italienischen Rechts und seiner Justizkultur im Mittelalter.* Leipzig: K. F. Koehler, 1938.

The English Church and the Papacy in the Middle Ages. Ed. C. H. Lawrence. New York: Fordham University Press, 1965.

Epstein, Steven A. *Genoa and the Genoese, 958–1528.* Chapel Hill: University of North Carolina Press, 1996.

———. *Wage Labor and Guilds in Medieval Europe.* Chapel Hill: University of North Carolina Press, 1991.

Erdö, Peter. "Mittelalterliche Offizialate in Ungarn und in Polen." *BMCL* 23 (1999) 16–34.

Essays in History Presented to R. L. Poole. Ed. H. W. C. Davis. Oxford: Clarendon Press, 1927.

Ethics in Practice: Lawyers' Roles, Responsibilities, and Regulation. Ed. Deborah L. Rhode. Oxford: Oxford University Press, 2000.

Études d'histoire du droit canonique dédiées à Gabriel Le Bras. 2 vols. Paris: Sirey, 1965.

Études d'histoire du droit médiévale en souvenir de Josette Metman. Mémoires de la Société pour l'histoire du droit et institutions des anciens pays bouguinons, comtois et romands, fasc. 45. Dijon: Éditions universitaires de Dijon, 1988.

L'Europa e il diritto romano: Studi in memoria di Paolo Koschaker. 2 vols. Milan: A. Giuffrè, 1954.

Europäische Rechts- und Verfassungsgeschichte: Ergebnisse und Perspektiven der Forschung. Ed. Reiner Schulze. Berlin: Duncker & Humblot, 1991.

Evans, Keith. *Advocacy in Court.* 2nd ed. London: Blackstone Press, 1995.

Ex ipsis rerum documentis: Beiträge zur Mediävistik, Festschrift für Harald Zimmermann zum 65. Geburtstag. Ed. Klaus Herbers, Hans Henning Kortüm, and Carlo Servatius. Sigmaringen: Jan Thorbecke, 1991.

Expectations of the Law in the Middle Ages. Ed. A. Musson. Woodbridge: Boydell Press, 2001.

Faith, Rosamond. "The Endowments of the University and Colleges to *circa* 1348." In *HUO* 1:265–309.

Falkenstein, Ludwig. "Decretalia Remensia: Zu Datum und Inhalt einiger Dekretalen Alexanders III. für Empfänger in der Kirchenprovinz Reims." In *Miscellanea Rolando Bandinelli*, 153–216.

Falletti, L. "Guillaume Durant." In *DDC* 5:1014–75.

Fälschungen im Mittelalter: Internationaler Kongress der Monumenta Germaniae Historica, 16.–19. September 1986. 3 vols. MGH, Schriften, vol. 33. Hannover: Hahn, 1988.

Fama: The Politics of Talk and Reputation in Medieval Europe. Ed. Thelma Fenster and Daniel Lord Smail. Ithaca: Cornell University Press, 2003.

Fasoli, Gina. "Giuristi, giudici e notai nell'ordinamento comunale e nella vita cittadina." In *Atti del Convegno Internazionale di Studi Accursiani* 1:25–39.

Fasolt, Constantin. *Council and Hierarchy: The Political Thought of William Durant the Younger.* Cambridge Studies in Medieval Life and Thought, 4th ser., vol. 16. Cambridge: Cambridge University Press, 1991.

Fedele, Pio. "Francesco Petrarca e Giovanni d'Andrea." *Ephemerides iuris canonici* 30 (1974) 201–25.

Fédou, René. *Les hommes de loi lyonnais à la fin du moyen âge: Étude sur les origines de la classe de robe.* Annales de la Université de Lyon, ser. 3, vol. 37. Paris: Les Belles Lettres, 1964.

Feenstra, Robert. "'Legum doctor,' 'legum professor' et 'magister' comme termes pour designer des juristes au moyen âge." In *Actes du colloque Terminologie de la vie intellectuelle au moyen âge*, 72–77.

Ferguson, Chris D. *Europe in Transition: A Select, Annotated Bibliography of the Twelfth-Century Renaissance.* New York: Garland, 1989.

Ferguson, Wallace K. *The Renaissance in Historical Thought: Five Centuries of Interpretation.* Boston: Houghton Mifflin, 1948.

Ferme, Brian E. *Canon Law in Late Medieval England: A Study of William Lyndwood's Provinciale with Particular Reference to Testamentary Law.* Studia et textus historiae iuris canonici, vol. 8 Rome: Libreria Ateneo Salesiano, 1996.

———. *Introduzione alla storia del diritto canonico.* Vol. 1, *Il diritto antico fino al* Decretum *di Graziano.* Quaderni di Apollinaris, vol. 1. Rome: Pontificia università lateranense, 1998.

———. "Judging Justly: The Ecclesiastical Sentence in History." *Apollinaris* 65 (1992) 519–27.

Ferruolo, Stephen C. *The Origins of the University: The Schools of Paris and Their Critics, 1100–1215.* Stanford: Stanford University Press, 1985.

Festschrift für Dieter Medicus zum 70. Geburtstag. Ed. Volker Beuthien, Maximilian Fuchs, Herbert Roth, Gottfried Schiemann, and Andreas Wacke. Cologne: Carl Heymann, 1999.
Festschrift für Fritz Schulz. 2 vols. Weimar: Böhlaus, 1951.
Festschrift für Hans Thieme zu seinem 80. Geburtstag. Ed. Karl Kroeschell. Sigmaringen: Jan Thorbecke, 1986.
Festschrift für Martin Wolff: Beiträge zum Zivilrecht und internationalen Privatrecht. Ed. Ernst von Caemmerer. Tübingen: J. C. B. Mohr, 1952.
Festschrift für Max Pappenheim. Kiel: Ferdinand Hirt, 1931.
Ficker, Julius von. *Forschungen zur Reichs- und Rechtsgeschichte Italiens.* 4 vols. Innsbruck: Wagner, 1868–74. Repr., Aalen: Scientia, 1961.
Figa Faura, L. "Los formularios notariales y la formación del notario en Cataluña." *Anales de la Academia Matritense del Notariado* 22 (1978) 312–33.
Finucane, Ronald C. "Two Notaries and Their Records in England, 1282–1307." *JMH* 13 (1987) 1–14.
Fiorelli, Pietro. "Clarum Bononiensium lumen." In *Per Francesco Calasso*, 413–59.
Fitting, Hermann. "Questions de droit disputées à Angers et à Paris." *Nouvelle revue de droit français et étranger* 29 (1905) 709–36.
Fitzsimmons, Michael P. *The Parisian Order of Barristers and the French Revolution.* Harvard Historical Monographs, vol. 74. Cambridge: Harvard University Press, 1987.
Flahiff, G. B. "Ralph Niger: An Introduction to His Life and Works." *Mediaeval Studies* 2 (1940) 104–26.
Foote, David. "How the Past Becomes a Rumor: The Notarialization of Historical Consciousness in Medieval Orvieto." *Speculum* 75 (2000) 794–815.
Forbes, P. B. R. "Some Early Stages in European Law." *Juridical Review* 60 (1948) 31–47, 123–38, 225–43.
Forde, Simon. "The Educational Organization of the Augustinian Canons in England and Wales and Their University Life at Oxford, 1325–1448." *History of Universities* 13 (1994) 21–60.
Foreville, Raymonde. "The Synod of the Province of Rouen in the Eleventh and Twelfth Centuries. In *Church and Government in the Middle Ages*, 19–39.
Forschungen zur Reichs-, Papst- und Landesgeschichte: Peter Herde zum 65. Geburtstag von Freunden, Schülern und Kollegen dargebracht. Ed. Karl Borchardt and Enno Bünz. 2 vols. Stuttgart: Anton Hiersemann, 1988.
Fossier, Robert. *Histoire sociale de l'Occident médiéval.* Paris: Armand Colin, 1970.
Fouracre, Paul. "'Placita' and the Settlement of Disputes in Later Medieval Francia." In *The Settlement of Disputes in Early Medieval Europe*, 23–43.
Fournier, Édouard. *Les origines du vicaire-général: Étude d'histoire et de droit canon.* Paris: A. Picard, 1922.
———. *Questions d'histoire du droit canonique.* Paris: Sirey, 1936.
Fournier, Marcel. "L'église et le droit romain au XIIIe siècle, à propos de l'interprétation de la bulle *Super speculam* d'Honorius III, qui interdit l'enseignement du droit romain à Paris." *RHDF*, 2nd ser., 14 (1890) 80–119.
Fournier, Paul. *Les officialités au moyen âge: Étude sur l'organisation, la compétence et la*

procédure des tribunaux ecclésiastiques ordinaires en France de 1180 à 1328. Paris: E. Plon, 1880. Repr., Aalen: Scientia, 1984.

Fournier, Paul, and Gabriel Le Bras. *Histoire des collections canoniques en Occident depuis les fausses décrétales jusqu'au Décret de Gratien.* 2 vols. Paris: Sirey, 1931–32. Repr., Aalen: Scientia, 1972.

Fowler-Magerl, Linda. *Clavis canonum: Selected Canon Law Collections before 1140.* MGH, Hilfsmittel, vol. 21. Hannover: Hahn, 2005.

——. "Forms of Arbitration." In *Proceedings IV* (Toronto), 133–47.

——. *Ordines iudiciarii and libelli de ordine iudiciorum (from the Middle of the Twelfth to the End of the Fifteenth Century).* Typologie des sources du moyen âge occidental, fasc. 63. Turnhout: Brepols, 1994.

——. *Ordo iudiciorum vel ordo iudiciarius: Begriff und Literaturgattung.* Ius Commune, Sonderhefte, vol. 19. Frankfurt a/M: Vittorio Klostermann, 1984.

——. "*Recusatio iudicis* in Civilian and Canonist Thought." *SG* 15 (1972) 719–85.

Fraher, Richard M. "Alanus Anglicus and the Summa 'Induent sancti.'" *BMCL* 6 (1976) 47–54.

——. "The Becket Dispute and Two Decretist Traditions: The Bolognese Masters Revisited and Some New Anglo-Norman Texts." *JMH* 4 (1978) 347–68.

——. "Conviction according to Conscience: The Medieval Jurists' Debate Concerning Judicial Discretion and the Law of Proof." *Law and History Review* 7 (1989) 22–88.

——. "IV Lateran's Revolution in Criminal Procedure: The Birth of Inquisitio, the End of Ordeals, and Innocent III's Vision of Ecclesiastical Politics." In *Studia in honorem Eminentissimi Cardinalis Alfonsi M. Stickler,* 97–111.

——. "Preventing Crime in the High Middle Ages: The Medieval Lawyers' Search for Deterrence." In *Popes, Teachers, and Canon Law,* 212–33.

——. "Tancred's 'Summula de criminibus': A New Text and a Key to the Ordo iudiciarius." *BMCL* 9 (1979) 23–35.

——. "The Theoretical Justification for the New Criminal Law of the High Middle Ages: 'Rei publicae interest, ne crimina remaneant impunita.'" *University of Illinois Law Review* (1984) 577–95.

——. "'Ut nullus describatur reus prius quam convincatur:' Presumption of Innocence in Medieval Canon Law?" In *Proceedings VI* (Berkeley), 493–506.

Fransen, Gérard. "À propos des questions de Jean le Teutonique." *BMCL* 13 (1983) 39–47.

——. "La date du Décret de Gratien." *RHE* 51 (1956) 521–31.

——. *Les décrétales et les collections de décrétales.* Typologie des sources du moyen âge occidental, fasc. 2. Turnhout: Brepols, 1972.

——. "Deux collections de questiones." *Traditio* 21 (1965) 492–510.

——. "Manuscrits canoniques conservées en Espagne (II)." *RHE* 49 (1954) 152–56.

——. "Les 'questiones' des canonistes (III)." *Traditio* 19 (1963) 516–31.

——. "Les questions disputées dans les facultés de droit." In Bazàn et al., *Les questions disputées,* 224–77.

——. "Les questions disputées de Maître S." In *Satura Roberto Feenstra,* 331–43.

———. "La valeur de la jurisprudence en droit canonique." In *La norma en el derecho canónico* 1:197–230.

Frati, Ludovico. "L'epistola *De regimine et modo studendi* di Martino de Fano." *Studi e memorie per la storia dell'Università di Bologna* 6 (1921) 19–29.

Freedman, Paul. *The Origins of Peasant Servitude in Medieval Catalonia*. Cambridge: Cambridge University Press, 1991.

Fried, Johannes. "Die Bamberger Domschule und die Rezeption von Frühscholastik und Rechtswissenschaft in ihrem Umkreis bis zum Ende der Stauferzeit." In *Schulen und Studium*, 163–201.

———. *Die Entstehung des Juristenstandes im 12. Jahrhundert: Zur Sozialen Stellung und politische Bedeutung gelehrter Juristen in Bologna und Modena*. Forschungen zur neueren Privatrechtsgeschichte, vol. 21. Cologne: Böhlaus, 1974.

———. "Gerard Pucelle und Köln." *ZRG*, KA 68 (1982) 125–35.

———. "Die Rezeption Bolognese Wissenschaft in Deutschland während des 12. Jahrhunderts." *Viator* 21 (1990) 103–45.

———. "Die Römische Kurie und de Anfänge der Prozeßliteratur." *ZRG*, KA 59 (1973) 151–74.

———. "Vermögensbildung der bologneser Juristen im 12. und 13. Jahrhunderts." In *Università e società nei secoli XII–XVI*, 27–55.

Frier, Bruce. *A Casebook on the Roman Law of Delict*. American Philological Association, Classical Resources Series, no. 2. Atlanta, GA: Scholars Press, 1989.

———. *The Rise of the Roman Jurists: Studies in Cicero's Pro Caecina*. Princeton: Princeton University Press, 1985.

Fuchs, Christoph. *Dives, pauper, nobilis, magister, frater, clericus: Sozialgeschichtliche Untersuchungen über Heidelberger Universitätsbesucher des Spätmittelalters (1386–1450)*. Education and Society in the Middle Ages and Renaissance, vol. 5 Leiden: E. J. Brill, 1995.

Fürst, Carl Gerold. "Ecclesia vivit lege Romana?" *ZRG*, KA 61 (1975) 17–36.

Fuhrmann, Horst. *Einfluß und Verbreitung der pseudoisidorischen Fälschungen, von ihrem Auftrachtung bis in die neuere Zeit*. 3 vols. MGH, Schriften, vol. 24. Stuttgart: Hiersemann, 1972–74.

———. "Papst Gregor VII. und das Kirchenrecht: Zum Problem des Dictatus Papae." *Studi Gregoriani* 13 (1989) 123–49.

Fuller, Lon L. *The Morality of Law*. Rev. ed. New Haven: Yale University Press, 1969.

Fuller, Thomas. *The History of the University of Cambridge*. Ed. James Nichols. London: Thomas Tegg, 1840.

Gabriel, Astrik L. "Le doyen de la Faculté de Décret à l'Université médiévale de Paris." *Année canonique* 11 (1967) 39–56.

Galanter, Marc. *Lowering the Bar: Lawyer Jokes and Legal Culture*. Madison: University of Wisconsin Press, 2005.

García y García, Antonio. "La enseñanza del derecho canónico en la universidad medieval." In *Manuels, programmes de cours et techniques d'enseignement*, 201–34.

———. "The Faculties of Law." In *HUE* 1:388–408.

———. "Medieval Students of Salamanca." *History of Universities* 10 (1991) 93–105.

———. "La Universidad de Salamanca en la Edad Media." In *Università in Europa*, 17– 35.

Gargan, Luciano. "Libri, librerie e biblioteche nelle università italiane del due e trecento." In *Luoghi e metodi*, 219–46.

———. "Le note 'Conduxit': Libri di maestri e studenti nelle università Italiane de tre e quattrocento." In *Manuels, programmes de cours et techniques d'enseignement*, 385–400.

Gaudemet, Jean. *Le Bréviaire d'Alaric et les Epitome*. IRMÆ, pt. 1, sec. 2b. Milan: A. Giuffrè, 1965. Repr. in his *La formation du droit séculier et du droit de l'église*, no. I.

———. *L'église dans l'empire Romain (IVe–Ve siècles)*. 2nd ed. Histoire du droit et des institutions de l'église en Occident, vol. 3. Paris: Sirey, 1989.

———. *La formation du droit canonique médiéval*. London: Variorum, 1980.

———. *La formation du droit séculier et du droit de l'église aux VIe et VIIe siècles*. Paris: Sirey, 1957.

———. "Les ordalies au moyen âge: doctrine, législation et pratique canoniques." In *La preuve* 2:99–135. Repr. in his *La société ecclésiastique dans l'Occident médiéval*, no. XV.

———. "Recherches sur l'épiscopat médiéval en France." In *Proceedings II* (Boston), 139–54.

———. *La société ecclésiastique dans l'Occident médiéval*. London: Variorum, 1980.

———. *Les sources du droit de l'église en Occident du IIe au VIIe siècle*. Paris: Cerf, 1985.

———. "Survivances romaines dans le droit de la monarchie franque du Vème au Xème siècle." *TRG* 23 (1955) 149–206. Repr. in his *La formation du droit canonique médiéval*, no. II.

Gazzaniga, Jean-Louis. "Droit et pratique: Notes sur les décisions de la Chapelle toulousaine." In *L'église et le droit dans le Midi*, 321–27.

Gazzaniga, Jean-Louis, and Sophie Peralba. "La bibliothèque imaginaire d'un official à la fin du XIVe siècle et au début du XVe siècle." In *Livres et bibliothèques (XIIIe–XVe siècle)*, 355–68.

Geary, Patrick J. "Barbarians and Ethnicity." In *Late Antiquity*, 106–29.

———. "Extra-Judicial Means of Conflict Resolution." In *La giustizia nell'alto medioevo (secoli V–VIII)* 2:569–605.

Génestal, Robert. *Le privilegium fori en France du Décret de Gratien à la fin du XIVe siècle*. 2 vols. Bibliothèque de l'École des Hautes Études, Sciences religieuses, vols. 35, 39. Paris: Ernst Leroux, 1921–24.

Genicot, Léopold. "On the Evidence of Growth of Population in the West from the Eleventh to the Thirteenth Century." In *Change in Medieval Society*, 14–29.

Genzmer, Erich. "Hugo von Trimberg und die Juristen." In *L'Europa e il diritto romano* 1:289–336.

———. "Kleriker als Berufsjuristen im späten Mittelalter." In *Études d'histoire du droit canonique dédiées à Gabriel Le Bras* 2:1207–36.

Gescher, Franz. "Das älteste kölnische Offizialatsstatut (1306–1331)." *ZRG*, KA 14 (1925) 474–85.

Geschichte und Verfassungsgefüge: Frankfurter Festgabe für Walter Schlesinger. Ed. Klaus Zarnack. Wiesbaden: Steiner, 1973.

Geyer, Bernhard. "Facultas theologica: Eine bedeutungsgeschichtliche Untersuchung." *Zeitschrift für Kirchengeschichte* 75 (1964) 133–45.

Ghellinck, Joseph de. *Le mouvement théologique du XIIe siècle: Sa préparation lointaine avant et autour de Pierre Lombard, ses rapports avec les initiatives des canonistes.* 2nd ed. Bruges: Éditions "De Tempel," 1948.

Gieysztor, Aleksander. "Management and Resources." In *HUE* 1:108–43.

Gilchrist, John T. "Canon Law Aspects of the Eleventh-Century Gregorian Reform Programme." *JEH* 13 (1962) 21–38.

———. "Gregory VII and the Juristic Sources of His Ideology." *SG* 12 (1967) 1–37 [= *Collectanea Stephan Kuttner*, vol. 1].

Gilissen, John. *La coutume.* Typologie des sources du moyen âge occidental, fasc. 41. Turnhout: Brepols, 1982.

Gilles, Henri. "Les clercs et l'enseignement du droit romain." In *L'église et culture en France méridionale*, 375–87.

———. "Gilles de Bellemère et le tribunal de la Rote à la fin du XIVe siècle." *Mélanges d'archéologie et d'histoire publiés par l'École française de Rome* 67 (1955) 281–319.

Gilmore, Myron P. *Humanists and Jurists: Six Studies in the Renaissance.* Cambridge: Belknap Press of Harvard University Press, 1963.

———. "The Lawyers and the Church in the Italian Renaissance." *Studi senesi* 75 (1963) 8–28. Repr. in his *Humanists and Jurists*, 61–86.

Girgensohn, Dieter. "Wie wird Man Kardinal? Kuriale und ausserkuriale Karrieren an der Wende des 14. und 15. Jahrhundert." *QFIAB* 57 (1977) 138–62.

La giustizia nell'alto medioevo (secoli V–VIII). 2 vols. Settimane di studio del Centro italiano di studi sull'alto medioevo, no. 42. Spoleto: Presso la sede del Centro, 1995.

La giustizia nell'alto medioevo (secoli IX–XI). 2 vols. Settimane di studio del Centro italiano di studi sull'alto medioevo, no. 44. Spoleto: Presso la sede del Centro, 1997.

Glorieux, Palémon. *Les origines du Collège de Sorbon.* Texts and Studies in the History of Mediaeval Education, no. 8. Notre Dame: Mediaeval Institute, 1959.

Goering, Joseph. "The 'Summa de penitentia' of John of Kent." *BMCL* 18 (1988) 13–31.

Goffart, Walter. *Barbarians and Romans, A.D. 418–584: The Techniques of Accommodation.* Princeton: Princeton University Press, 1980.

———. *Rome's Fall and After.* London: Hambledon, 1989.

———. "What's Wrong with the Map of the Barbarian Invasions?" In *Minorities and Barbarians in Medieval Life and Thought*, 159–77.

González, Julián. "The Lex Irnitana: A New Copy of the Flavian Municipal Law." *Journal of Roman Studies* 76 (1986) 147–243.

Gouron, André. "À la convergence des deux droits: Jean Bassien et maître Jean." *TRG* 59 (1991) 319–32. Repr. in his *Droit et coutume en France*, no. XVII.

———. "Un assaut en deux vagues: La diffusion du droit romain dans l'Europe du XIIe siècle." In *El dret comú i Catalunya*, 47–63. Repr. in his *Droit et coutume en France*, no. XVI.

———. "Autour de Placentin à Montpellier, Maître Gui et Pierre de Cardona." *SG* 19 (1976) 339–54. Repr. in his *Science du droit*, no. VII.

———. "Canon Law in Parisian Circles before Stephan of Tournai's Summa." In *Proceedings VIII* (San Diego), 497–503. Repr. in his *Juristes et droits savants*, no. II.

———. "Le cardinal Raymond des Arènes: Cardinalis?" *RDC* 28 (1978) 180–92. Repr. in his *Science du droit*, no. XII.

———. "Lo Codi, source de la Somme au Code de Rogerius." In *Satura Roberto Feenstra*, 301–16. Repr. in his *Études sur la diffusion des doctrines juridiques*, no. XI.

———. "Comment dater la venue de Placentin à Montpellier?" *Mémoires de la Société pour l'histoire du droit et des institutions des anciens pays bourguignons, comtois et romands* 45 (1988) 187–94. Repr. in his *Droit et coutume en France*, no. IV.

———. "La crise des universités françaises à la fin du XIVe siècle." In *Atti del simposio internazionale cateriniano-bernardiniano*, 907–15. Repr. in his *Science du droit*, no. XIX.

———. "Deux universités pour une ville." In *Histoire de Montpellier*, 103–25. Repr. in his *Études sur la diffusion des doctrines juridiques*, no. VII.

———. "Dilectus Henricus, archévêque d'Aix et juriste." *Provence historique* 34 (1984) 96–101. Repr. in his *Études sur la diffusion des doctrines juridiques*, no. V.

———. *Droit et coutume en France aux XIIe et XIIIe siècles*. Aldershot: Variorum, 1993.

———. "Du nouveau sur lo Codi." *TRG* 43 (1975) 271–77. Repr. in his *Science du droit*, no. VIII.

———. "Une école de canonistes anglais à Paris: Maître Walter et ses disciples (vers 1170)." *Journal des savants* (2000) 47–72.

———. "Une école ou des écoles? Sur les canonistes français (vers 1150–vers 1210)." In *Proceedings VI* (Berkeley), 223–40. Repr. in his *Droit et coutume en France*, no. VIII.

———. "L'enseignement du droit civil au XIIe siècle: De la coutume à la règle." In *Manuels, programmes de cours et techniques d'enseignement*, 193–99. Repr. in his *Juristes et droits savants*, no. VII.

———. "Enseignement du droit: Légistes et canonistes dans le Midi de la France à la fin du XIIIe et au début du XIVe siècle." *Recueil de mémoires et travaux publié par la Société d'histoire du droit et des institutions des anciens pays de droit écrit* 5 (1966) 1–33.

———. "Die Entstehung der französischen Rechtsschule: *Summa Iustiniani est in hoc opere* und Tübinger Rechtsbuch." *ZRG, KA* 93 (1976) 138–60. Repr. in his *Science du droit*, no. IX.

———. "Les étapes de la pénétration du droit romain au XIIe siècle dans l'ancienne Septimanie." *Annales du Midi* 69 (1957) 103–20.

———. *Études sur la diffusion des doctrines juridiques médiévales*. London: Variorum, 1987.

———. "Un juriste bolonais docteur in utroque au XIIe siècle?" *Ius commune* 22 (1995) 17–33. Repr. in his *Juristes et droit savants*, no. XIX.

———. *Les juristes de l'école de Montpellier*. IRMÆ, vol. 4, pt. 3a. Milan: A. Giuffrè, 1970. Repr. in his *Études sur la diffusion des doctrines juridiques*, no. I.

———. *Juristes et droits savants: Bologne et la France médiévale*. Aldershot: Ashgate/Variorum, 2000.

———. "Maître Durand, pionnier du notariat savant." In *Mélanges offerts à André Colmer*, 181–87. Repr. in his *Juristes et droit savant*, no. XV.

———. "Penuria advocatorum." *Initium* 4 (1999) 1–11.

———. "'Petrus' démasqué." *RHDF* 82 (2004) 577–88.

———. "Placentin et la Somme 'Cum essem Mantuae.'" In *Trabajos de derecho histórico Europeo* 5:1335–52. Repr. in his *Droit et coutume en France*, no. II.

———. "Le recrutement des juristes dans les universités méridionales à la fin du XIVe siècle: Pays de canonistes et pays de civilistes?" In *Les universités à la fin du Moyen Age*, 524–48. Repr. in his *Science du droit*, no. XI.

———. *La réglementation des métiers en Languedoc au moyen âge*. Études d'histoire économique, politique et social, vol. 22. Geneva: E. Droz, 1958.

———. "Le rôle de l'avocat selon la doctrine romaniste du douzième siècle." In *L'assistance dans la résolution des conflits*, 7–19.

———. "Le rôle des maîtres français dans la renaissance juridique du XIIe siècle." *Académie des Inscriptions et Belles-Lettres: Comptes-rendus des séances de l'année 1989*, Jan.–Mar., 198–207. Repr. in his *Droit et coutume en France*, no. XV.

———. "Le rôle sociale des juristes dans les villes méridionales au moyen âge." *Annales de la Faculté des Lettres et Sciences Humaines de Nice* 9/10 (1969) 55–67. Repr. in his *Science du droit*, no. III.

———. *La science du droit dans le Midi de la France au moyen âge*. London: Variorum, 1984.

———. *La science juridique française aux XIe et XIIe siècles: Diffusion du droit de Justinien et influences canoniques jusqu'à Gratien*. IRMÆ, vol. 1, pt. 4, sect. d-e. Milan: A. Giuffrè, 1978. Repr. in his *Études sur la diffusion des doctrines juridiques*, no. II.

———. "Sur la patrie et la datation du 'Livre de Tubingue' et des 'Exceptiones Petri.'" *RIDC* 14 (2003) 15–39.

———. "Sur les sources civilistes et la datation des Sommes de Rufin et d'Étienne de Tournai." *BMCL* 16 (1986) 55–70. Repr. in his *Droit et coutume en France*, no. X.

———. "The Training of Southern French Lawyers during the Thirteenth and Fourteenth Centuries." *SG* 15 (1972) 219–27.

———. "'Utriusque partis allegationibus auditis.'" In *Justice et justiciables*, 35–45. Repr. in his *Juristes et droits savants*, no. XVI.

———. "Zu den Ursprüngen des Strafrechts: Die ersten Strafrrechtstraktate." In *Festschrift für Hans Thieme*, 43–57. Repr. in his *Études sur la diffusion des doctrines juridiques*, no. IX.

Grabmann, Martin. *Geschichte der scholastischen Methode*. 2 vols. Freiburg i/Br: Herder, 1909–11. Repr., Berlin: Akademie-Verlag, 1957.

Grafton, Anthony. *Commerce with the Classics: Ancient Books and Renaissance Readers*. Jerome Lectures, no. 20. Ann Arbor: University of Michigan Press, 1997.

Graham, Rose. "The Administration of the Diocese of Ely during the Vacancies of the See, 1288–9 and 1302–3." *Transactions of the Royal Historical Society*, 4th ser., 12 (1929) 49–74.

———. *English Ecclesiastical Studies, Being Some Essays in Research in Medieval History*. London: Society for the Promotion of Christian Knowledge, 1929.

Gramsch, Robert. *Erfurter Juristen im Spätmittelalter: Die Karrieremuster und Tätigkeitsfelder einer gelehrten Elite des 14. und 15. Jahrhunderts*. Education and Society in the Middle Ages and Renaissance, vol. 17. Leiden: Brill, 2003.

Greatrex, Joan. "The English Cathedral Priories and the Pursuit of Learning in the Later Middle Ages." *JEH* 45 (1944) 396–411.
Griffiths, Quentin. "New Men among the Lay Counselors of St. Louis' Parlement." *Mediaeval Studies* 32 (1970) 234–72.
Groici, Bartołmeij. *Porzadek sadów i spraw miejskich prawa majdeburskiego w Koronie Polkiej*. Warsaw: Wyadwnicto Prawnice, 1953.
Groten, Manfred. "Der Magistertitel und seine Verbreitung im deutschen Reich des 12. Jahrhunderts." *Historisches Jahrbuch* 113 (1993) 21–40.
Grundlagen des Rechts: Festschrift für Peter Landau zum 65. Geburtstag. Ed. Richard H. Helmholz, Paul Mikat, Jörg Müller, and Michael Stolleis. Rechts- und Staatswissenschaftliche Veröffentlichungen der Görres-Gesellschaft, neue Folge, vol. 91. Paderborn: Ferdinand Schöningh, 2000.
Gualazzini, Ugo. *L'insegnamento del diritto in Italia durante l'alto medioevo*. IRMÆ, vol. 1, pt. 5b, sect. aa. Milan: A. Giuffrè, 1974.
Guenée, Bernard. *Tribunaux et gens de justice dans le bailliage de Senlis à la fin du moyen âge (vers 1480–vers 1550)*. Strasbourg: Publications de la Faculté des Lettres, 1963.
Guide to the Professional Conduct of Solicitors. 7th ed. London: The Law Society, 1996.
Guillaume Durand, Éveque de Mende (v. 1230–1296): Canoniste, liturgiste, et homme politique. Ed. Pierre-Marie Gy. Paris: Éditions de la Centre Nationale de la Recherche Scientifique, 1992.
Guillemain, Bernard. *La cour pontificale d'Avignon, 1309–1376: Étude d'une société*. Bibliothèque des Écoles françaises d'Athènes et de Rome, vol. 201. Paris: E. de Boccard, 1966.
Guterman, Simeon L. *The Principle of the Personality of Law in the Germanic Kingdoms of Western Europe from the Fifth to the Eleventh Century*. American University Studies, ser. 9, vol. 44. New York: Peter Lang, 1990.
Guyotjeannin, Olivier, Jacques Pycke, and Benoît-Michel Tock. *Diplomatique médiévale*. L'atelier du médiéviste, vol. 2. Turnhout: Brepols, 1993.
Hackett, M. B. "The University as a Corporate Body." In *HUO* 1:47–95.
Häring, Nicholas M. "The Cistercian Everard of Ypres and His Appraisal of the Conflict between St. Bernard and Gilbert of Poitiers." *Mediaeval Studies* 17 (1955) 143–72.
———. "Peter Cantor's View of Ecclesiastical Excommunication and Its Practical Consequences." *Mediaeval Studies* 11 (1949) 100–12.
Hageneder, Othmar. *Die geistliche Gerichtsbarkeit in Ober- und Niederösterreich von den Anfängen bis zum Beginn des 15. Jahrhunderts*. Forschungen zur Geschichte Oberösterreichs, vol. 10. Linz: H. Böhlaus Nachfolger, 1967.
Handling Sin: Confession in the Middle Ages. Ed. Peter Biller and A. J. Minnis. York Studies in Medieval Theology, vol. 2. York: York Medieval Press, 1998.
Haren, Michael. "Confession, Social Ethics and Social Discipline in the *Memoriale presbiterorum*." In *Handling Sin*, 109–22.
———. "The Interrogatories for Officials, Lawyers and Secular Estates of the *Memoriale presbiterorum*." In *Handling Sin*, 123–63.
———. *Sin and Society in Fourteenth-Century England: A Study of the Memoriale Presbiterorum*. Oxford Historical Monographs. Oxford: Clarendon Press, 2000.

Hargreaves-Mawdsley, W. N. *A History of Academical Dress in Europe until the End of the Eighteenth Century*. Oxford: Clarendon Press, 1963.

———. *A History of Legal Dress in Europe until the End of the Eighteenth Century*. Oxford: Clarendon Press, 1963.

Harries, Jill. *Law and Empire in Late Antiquity*. Cambridge: Cambridge University Press, 1999.

Harrison, Frederick. *Life in a Medieval College: The Story of the Vicars-Choral of York Minster*. London: John Murray, 1952.

Hartmann, Wilfried. "Die Briefe Fulberts von Chartres als Quelle für die Praxis des bischöflichen Gerichts in Frankreich am Beginn des 11. Jahrhunderts." In *Grundlagen des Rechts*, 93–103.

———. "Probleme des geistlichen Gerichts im 10. und 11. Jahrhundert: Bischöfe und Synoden als Richter im ostfränkisch-Deutschen Reich." In *La giustizia nell'alto medioevo (secoli IX–XI)* 2:631–74.

Harvey, Margaret. *The English in Rome, 1362–1420: Portrait of an Expatriate Community*. Cambridge Studies in Medieval Life and Thought, 4th ser., vol. 45. Cambridge: Cambridge University Press, 1999.

Haskins, Charles Homer. *The Renaissance of the Twelfth Century*. Cambridge: Harvard University Press, 1927. Repr., New York: Meridian, 1958.

———. *Studies in Medieval Culture*. Oxford: Clarendon Press, 1929. Repr., New York: Frederick Ungar, 1965.

Hausherr, Reiner. "Eine Warnung vor dem Studium von zivilem und kanonischem Rechts in der Bible moralisée." *Frühmittelalterliche Studien* 3 (1975) 390–404.

Hayes, Dawn Marie. "Mundane Uses of Sacred Places in the Central and Later Middle Ages, with a Focus on Chartres Cathedral." *Comitatus* 30 (1999) 11–36.

Hazard, Geoffrey C., Jr. *Ethics in the Practice of Law*. New Haven: Yale University Press, 1978.

Henriot, Eugène. *Moeurs juridiques et judiciaires de l'ancienne Rome d'après les poètes latins*. 3 vols. Paris: Firmin Didot, 1865.

Heckel, Rudolf von. "Das Aufkommen der ständigen Prokuratoren an der päpstlichen Kurie im 13. Jahrhundert." In *Miscellanea Francesco Ehrle* 2:290–321.

———. "Studien über die Kanzleiordnung Innozenz' III." *Historisches Jahrbuch* 57 (1937) 258–89.

Helmholz, Richard H. *The Canon Law and Ecclesiastical Jurisdiction from 597 to the 1640s*. Oxford History of the Laws of England, vol. 1. Oxford: Oxford University Press, 2004.

———. *Canon Law and the Law of England*. London: Hambledon, 1987.

———. "Canonists and Standards of Impartiality for Papal Judges Delegate." *Traditio* 25 (1969) 386–404. Repr. in his *Canon Law and the Law of England*, 21–39.

———. "The Character of the Western Legal Tradition: Assessing Harold Berman's Contributions to Legal History." In *The Integrative Jurisprudence of Harold J. Berman*, 29–50.

———. *Common Law and Ius Commune*. Selden Society Lecture. London: Selden Society, 2001.

———. "The Education of English Proctors, 1400–1640." In *Learning the Law*, 191–219.

———. "Ethical Standards for Advocates and Proctors in Theory and Practice." In *Proceedings IV* (Toronto), 283–99. Repr. in his *Canon Law and the Law of England*, 41–57.

———. *Fundamental Human Rights in Medieval Law*. Maurice and Muriel Fulton Lecture Series. Chicago: University of Chicago Law School, 2001.

———. *The Ius commune in England: Four Studies*. Oxford: Oxford University Press, 2001.

———. "The *litis contestatio:* Its Survival in the Medieval *ius commune* and Beyond." In *Lex et Romanitas*, 73–89.

———. "Magna Carta and the *ius commune*." *University of Chicago Law Review* 66 (1999) 297–371.

———. *Marriage Litigation in Medieval England*. Cambridge Studies in English Legal History. Cambridge: Cambridge University Press, 1974.

———. "Money and Judges in the Law of the Medieval Church." *University of Chicago Law School Roundtable* 8 (2001) 309–23.

———. "Les officialités Anglo-Saxonnes et la culture juridique latine: Approches historiennes." *L'année canonique* 38 (1995–96) 97–105.

———. "The Privilege and the *Ius Commune:* The Middle Ages to the Seventeenth Century." In Helmholz et al., *The Privilege against Self-Incrimination*, 17–46.

———. *Roman Canon Law in Reformation England*. Cambridge Studies in English Legal History. Cambridge: Cambridge University Press, 1990.

———. "'Si quis suadente' (C. 17 q. 4 c. 29): Theory and Practice." In *Proceedings VII* (Cambridge), 425–38.

———. *The Spirit of Classical Canon Law*. Athens: University of Georgia Press, 1996.

———. "Trusts in the English Ecclesiastical Courts." In *Itinera fiduciae*, 153–72.

Helmholz, R. H., Charles M. Gray, John H. Langbein, and Eben Moglen. *The Privilege against Self-Incrimination: Its Origins and Development*. Chicago: University of Chicago Press, 1997.

Henriot, Eugène. *Moeurs juridiques et judiciaires de l'ancienne Rome*. 3 vols. Paris: Firmin Didot, 1865.

Herbert, A. P. *Uncommon Law*. London: Methuen, 1935. Repr., New York: Barnes & Noble, 1993.

Herde, Peter. *Audientia litterarum contradictarum: Untersuchungen über die päpstlichen Justizbriefe und die päpstliche Delegationsgerichtsbarkeit vom 13. bis zum Beginn des 16. Jahrhunderts*. 2 vols. Bibliothek des Deutschen Historischen Instituts in Rom, vols. 31–32. Tübingen: Max Niemeyer, 1970.

———. *Beiträge zum päpstlichen Kanzlei- und Urkundenwesen im 13. Jahrhundert*. 2nd ed. Münchener historische Studien, Abteilung Geschichtl. Hilfswissenschaften, vol. 1. Kallmünz: Michael Lassleben, 1967.

———. "Politische Verhaltensweisen der Florentiner Oligarchie, 1382–1402." In *Geschichte und Verfassungsgefüge*, 156–249.

———. "Römisches und kanonisches Recht bei der Verfolgung des Fälschungsdelikts im Mittelalter." *Traditio* 21 (1965) 291–362.

———. "Der Zeugenzwang in den päpstlichen Delegationsreskripten des Mittelalters." *Traditio* 18 (1962) 255–88.

Herlihy, David. "Demography." In *DMA* 4:136–48.

———. *Medieval and Renaissance Pistoia: The Social History of an Italian Town, 1200–1430*. New Haven: Yale University Press, 1967.

Herlihy, David, and Christiane Klapisch-Zuber. *Tuscans and Their Families: A Study of the Florentine Catasto of 1437*. New Haven: Yale University Press, 1985.

Herman, Shael. "The Canonical Conception of the Trust." In *Itinera fiduciae*, 85–109.

Hess, Hamilton. *The Early Development of Canon Law and the Council of Serdica*. Oxford: Oxford University Press, 2002.

Highfield, J. R. L. "The Early Colleges." In *HUO* 1:225–63.

Hilaire, J. "Pratique notariale et justice aux XIVème et XVème siècles: L'évolution coutumière des pays de droit écrit." In *Études d'histoire du droit médiévale en souvenir de Josette Metman*, 195–213.

Hillgarth, Jocelyn N., and Giulio Silano. "A Compilation of the Diocesan Synods of Barcelona (1354): A Critical Edition and Analysis." *Mediaeval Studies* 46 (1984) 78–157.

Hilling, Nikolaus. "Sechs Gerichtsordnungen für das Bistum Halberstadt aus dem 15. Jahrhundert." *AKKR* 122 (1947) 324–41; 125 (1951) 29–72.

Hinschius, Paul. *System des katholischen Kirchenrechts mit besonderer Rücksicht auf Deutschland. Das Kirchenrecht der Katholiken und Protestanten in Deutschland*. 6 vols. in 7. Berlin: J. Guttentag, 1869–97.

Hirschfeld, Theodor. "Das Gerichtswesen der Stadt Rom vom 8. bis 12. Jahrhundert wesentlich nach stadtrömischen Urkunden." *Archiv für Urkundenforschung* 4 (1912) 419–562.

Histoire de Montpellier. Ed. Gérard Cholvy. Toulouse: Privat, 1984.

A History of the University in Europe. General editor, Walter Rüegg. Vol. 1, *Universities in the Middle Ages*. Ed. Hilde de Ridder-Symoens. Cambridge: Cambridge University Press, 1992. [*HUE*]

The History of the University of Oxford. General editor, T. H. Aston. Vol. 1, *The Early Oxford Schools*. Ed. J. I. Catto. Oxford: Clarendon Press, 1984. [*HUO*]

Hoberg, Hermann. "Die ältesten Informativprozesse über die Qualifikation neuernannter Rotarichter (1492–1547)." In *Reformata reformanda* 1:129–41.

Hockaday, F. S. "The Consistory Court of the Diocese of Gloucester." *Transactions of the Bristol and Gloucester Archaeological Society* 46 (1924) 195–287.

Hoeflich, Michael H. "Between Gothia and Romania: The Image of the King in the Poetry of Ventantius Fortunatus." *Res publica litterarum* 5 (1982) 123–36.

Hoffmann, Hartmut, and Rudolf Pokorny. *Das Dekret des Bischofs Burchard von Worms*. MGH, Hilfsmittel, vol. 12. Munich: Monumenta Germaniae Historica, 1991.

Holmes, Urban Tigner, Jr. *Daily Living in the Twelfth Century, Based on the Observations of Alexander Neckam in London and Paris*. Madison: University of Wisconsin Press, 1952.

Holtzmann, Walther. "Die Benutuzung Gratians in der päpstlichen Kanzlei." *SG* 1 (1953) 325–49.

———. "Die Dekretalensammlungen des 12. Jahrhunderts, I: Die Sammlung Tanner." *Festschrift zur Feier des 200jährigen Bestehens der Akademie der Wissenschaften in Göttingen*, phil.-hist. Kl. (1951), 83–45.

———. "Propter Sion non tacebo: Zur Erklärung von Carmina Burana 41." *DA* 10 (1953) 170–75.

———. *Studies in the Collections of Twelfth-Century Decretals*. Ed. and trans. C. R. Cheney and Mary G. Cheney. MIC, Corpus collectionum, vol. 3. Vatican City: BAV, 1979.

———. "Zur Geschichte des Investiturstreites: Eine Bannsentenz des Konzils von Reims 1119." *Neues Archiv der Gesellschaft für ältere deutsche Geschichtskunde* 50 (1933) 246–319.

Homenaje a D. Nicolas Perez Serrano. 2 vols. Madrid: Reus, 1959.

Honoré, Tony. *Law in the Crisis of Empire, 379–455 AD: The Theodosian Dynasty and Its Quaestors*. Oxford: Clarendon Press, 1998.

———. *Tribonian*. Ithaca: Cornell University Press, 1978.

———. *Ulpian*. Oxford: Clarendon Press, 1982.

Horn, Norbert. "Die legistische Literatur der Kommentatoren und der Ausbreitung des gelehrten Rechts." In Coing, *Handbuch* 1:261–364.

Housman, A. E. *Selected Prose*. Ed. John Carter. Cambridge: Cambridge University Press, 1961.

Hove, A. van. *Prolegomena*. 2nd ed. Commentarium Lovaniense in Codicem Iuris Canonici, vol. 1, pt. 1. Malines: H. Dessain, 1945.

Hughes, Jonathan. "Arundel [Fitzalan], Thomas (1353–1414)." In *Oxford Dictionary of National Biography* (online ed.).

Humfress, Caroline. "Advocates." In *Late Antiquity*, 277–78.

———. "Defensor Ecclesiae." In *Late Antiquity*, 405–6.

———. "Law Schools." In *Late Antiquity*, 540–41.

———. "A New Legal Cosmos: Late Roman Lawyers and the Early Medieval Church." In *The Medieval World*, 557–75.

Hunt, R. W. "The Preface to the 'Speculum ecclesiae' of Giraldus Cambrensis." *Viator* 8 (1977) 187–213.

Hyams, Paul R. "Deans and Their Doings: The Norwich Inquiry of 1286." In *Proceedings VI* (Berkeley), 619–46.

———. "Trial by Ordeal: The Key to Proof in Early Common Law." In *On the Laws and Customs of England*, 90–126.

Hyde, J. K. "Medieval Descriptions of Cities." *Bulletin of the John Rylands Library* 48 (1966) 308–40.

———. *Padua in the Age of Dante*. New York: Barnes & Noble, 1966.

———. *Society and Politics in Medieval Italy: The Evolution of the Civil Life, 1000–1340*. New York: St. Martin's Press, 1973.

———. "Universities and Cities in Medieval Italy." In *The University and the City*, 13–21.

Ibbetson, David. *Common Law and Ius Commune*. Selden Society Lecture. London: Selden Society, 2001.

———. *A Historical Introduction to the Law of Obligations*. Oxford: Oxford University Press, 1999.

Ilario da Milano, P. *L'eresia di Ugo Speroni nella confutazione del maestro Vacario*. Studi e testi, vol. 115. Vatican City: BAV, 1945.

Ingram, James. *Memorials of Oxford.* 3 vols. Oxford: J. H. Parker, 1834–37.
"Ins Wasser geworfen und Ozeane durchquert": Festschrift für Knut Wolfgang Nörr. Ed. Mario Ascheri, Friedrich Ebel, Martin Heckel, Antonio Padoa-Schioppa, Wolfgang Pöggeler, Filippo Ranieri, and Wilhelm Rütten. Cologne: Böhlau, 2003.
The Integrative Jurisprudence of Harold J. Berman. Ed. Howard O. Hunter. Boulder: Westview Press, 1996.
Le istituzioni ecclesiastiche della "Societas Christiana" dei secoli XI–XII: Papato, cardinalato ed episcopato. Università Cattolica del Sacro Cuore, Miscellanea del Centro di studi medioevali, vol. 7. Milan: Vita & Pensiero, 1974.
Itinera fiduciae: Trust and Treuhand in Historical Perspective. Ed. Richard Helmholz and Reinhard Zimmermann. Comparative Studies in Continental and Anglo-American Legal History, vol. 19. Berlin: Duncker & Humblot, 1998.
Jacob, E. F. *Essays in Later Medieval History.* Manchester: Manchester University Press, 1968.
Jacobi, Erwin. "Der Prozeß im Decretum Gratiani und bei den ältesten Dekretisten." *ZRG, KA* 3 (1913) 223–343.
Jacqueline, Bernard. *Épiscopat et papauté chez Saint Bernard de Clairvaux.* Saint-Lô: Éditions Henri Jacqueline, 1975.
———. "Les études juridiques au Mont Saint-Michel dès origines au XVIe siècle." In *Millénaire monastique du Mont Saint-Michel* 2:257–73.
———. "Le pape d'après le livre II du 'De consideratione ad Eugenium papam' de Saint Bernard de Clairvaux." *SG* 14 (1967) 219–39 [= *Collectanea Stephan Kuttner*, vol. 4].
Jasper, Detlev. *Das Papstwahldekret von 1059: Überlieferung und Textgestalt.* Beiträge zur Geschichte und Quellenkunde des Mittelalters, vol. 12. Sigmaringen: Jan Thorbecke, 1986.
Jasper, Detlev, and Horst Fuhrmann. *Papal Letters in the Early Middle Ages.* History of Medieval Canon Law, vol. 2. Washington, DC: Catholic University of America Press, 2001.
Jeanclos, Yves. "Remarques sur les conditions d'accès au canonicat à Troyes à la fin du XIVe siècle." *RHDF*, 4th ser., 57 (1979) 21–50.
Jeffries, P. J. "Profitable Fourteenth-Century Legal Practice and Landed Investment: The Case of Judge Stonor, c. 1281–1354." *Southern History* 15 (1993) 18–35.
Jones, A. H. M. *The Later Roman Empire, 284–602: A Social, Economic and Administrative Survey.* 2 vols. Oxford: Basil Blackwell, 1964. Repr., Baltimore: Johns Hopkins University Press, 1986.
Jordan, Karl. "Zur päpstlichen Finanzgeschichte im 11. und. 12. Jahrhundert." *QFIAB* 25 (1933/1934) 61–104.
Juristische Buchproduktion im Mittelalter. Ed. Vincenzo Colli. Frankfurt a/M: Vittorio Klostermann, 2002.
Justice et justiciables: Mélanges Henri Vidal. Montpellier: Société d'histoire du droit et des institutions des anciens pays de droit écrit, 1994.
Kaeuper, Richard W. "The King and the Fox: Reaction to the Role of Kingship in Tales of Raynard the Fox." In *Expectations of the Law in the Middle Ages*, 9–21.
Kalb, Herbert. *Studien zur Summa Stephans von Tournai: Ein Beitrag zur kanonistischen*

Wissenschaftsgeschichte des späten 12. Jahrhunderts. Forschungen zur Rechts- und Kulturgeschichte, vol. 12. Innsbruck: Wagner, 1983.

———. "Überlegungen zur Entstehung der Kanonistik als Rechtswissenschaft—einige Aspekte." *Österreichisches Archiv für Kirchenrecht* 41 (1992) 1–28.

Kantorowicz, Ernst H. *The King's Two Bodies: A Study in Mediaeval Political Theology.* Princeton: Princeton University Press, 1957.

———. "Kingship under the Impact of Scientific Jurisprudence." In *Twelfth-Century Europe and the Foundations of Modern Society*, 89–111.

Kantorowicz, Hermann. *Albertus Gandinus und das Strafrecht der Scholastik.* 2 vols. Berlin: J. Guttentag, W. de Gruyter, 1907–26. Repr., Frankfurt a/M: Keip, 1978–81.

———. "An English Theologian's View of Roman Law: Pepo, Irnerius, Ralph Niger." *Medieval and Renaissance Studies* 1 (1941 [recte 1943]) 237–51. Repr. in his *Rechtshistorische Schriften*, 231–44.

———. "Les origines françaises des Exceptiones Petri." *RHDF*, 4th ser., 16 (1937) 588–640. Repr. in his *Rechtshistorische Schriften*, 197–230.

———. "The Poetical Sermon of a Medieval Jurist: Placentinus and his 'Sermo de legibus.'" *Journal of the Warburg Institute* 2 (1938) 22–41. Repr. in his *Rechtshistorische Schriften*, 111–35.

———. "Praestantia doctorum." In *Festschrift für Max Pappenheim*, 55–73. Repr. in his *Rechtshistorische Schriften*, 377–96.

———. "The Quaestiones Disputatae of the Glossators." *TRG* 16 (1939) 1–67. Repr. in his *Rechtshistorische Schriften*, 137–85.

———. "Il 'Tractatus criminum.'" In *Per il cinquantenario della Rivista Penale*, 262–76. Rome: Temi, 1925. Repr. in his *Rechtshistorische Schriften*, 273–85.

———. *Rechtshistorische Schriften.* Ed. Helmut Coing and Gerhard Immel. Freiburger Rechts- und Staatswissenschaftliche Abhandlungen, vol. 30. Karlsruhe: C. F. Müller, 1970.

———. *Studies in the Glossators of the Roman Law: Newly Discovered Writings of the Twelfth Century.* Cambridge: Cambridge University Press, 1938.

———. *Über die Entstehung der Digestenvulgata: Ergänzungen zu Mommsen.* Weimar: H. Böhlaus, 1910.

Kantorowicz, Hermann, and Beryl Smalley. "An English Theologian's View of Roman Law: Pepo Irnerius, Ralph Niger." *Medieval and Renaissance Studies* 1 (1941) 237–51. Repr. in Kantorowicz, *Rechtshistorische Schriften*, 231–44.

Karpik, Lucien. *French Lawyers: A Study in Collective Action, 1274–1994.* Trans. Nora Scott. Oxford: Clarendon Press, 1999.

Kaser, Max. *Das römische Zivilprozessrecht.* 2nd ed. Rev. by Karl Hackl. Handbuch der Altertumswissenschaft, sect, 10, pt. 3, vol. 3. Munich: C. H. Beck, 1996.

Kay, Richard. *Councils and Clerical Culture in the Medieval West.* Aldershot: Variorum, 1997.

———. "Mansi and Rouen: A Critique of the Conciliar Collections." *Catholic Historical Review* 52 (1966) 155–85. Repr. in his *Councils and Clerical Culture in the Medieval West*, no. IV.

Kelley, Donald R. *The Human Measure: Social Thought in the Western Legal Tradition.* Cambridge: Harvard University Press, 1990.

Kelly, Fergus. *A Guide to Early Irish Law.* Early Irish Law Studies, vol. 3. Dublin: Dublin Institute for Advanced Studies, 1988.

Kelly, J. M. *Roman Litigation.* Oxford: Clarendon Press, 1966.

Kennan, Elizabeth T. "The 'De consideratione' of St. Bernard of Clairvaux and the Papacy in the Mid-Twelfth Century: A Review of Scholarship." *Traditio* 23 (1967) 73–115.

Ker, Neil R. "'For All That I May Clamp': Louvain Students and Lecture Rooms in the Fifteenth Century." *Medium ævum* 39 (1970) 32–33.

Kerr, A. B. "Legal Practice in Fifteenth Century France." *Virginia Law Review* 24 (1938) 381–87.

Kéry, Lotte. *Canonical Collections of the Early Middle Ages (ca. 400–1140): A Bibliographical Guide to the Manuscripts and Literature.* History of Medieval Canon Law, vol. 1. Washington, DC: Catholic University of America Press, 1999.

Kibre, Pearl. *The Nations in the Mediaeval Universities.* Cambridge: Mediaeval Academy of America, 1948.

———. *Scholarly Privileges in the Middle Ages: The Rights, Privileges, and Immunities of Scholars and Universities at Bologna, Padua, Paris, and Oxford.* Mediaeval Academy of America Publications, no. 72. Cambridge: Mediaeval Academy of America, 1962.

King, P. D. *Law and Society in the Visigothic Kingdom.* Cambridge Studies in Medieval Life and Thought, 3rd ser., vol. 5. Cambridge: Cambridge University Press, 1972.

Kirshner, Julius. "*Consilia* as Authority in Late Medieval Italy: The Case of Florence." In *Legal Consulting in the Civil Law Tradition*, 107–40.

Knowledge and the Future of Man. Ed. Walter J. Ong. New York: Holt, Rinehart & Winston, 1978.

Knowles, David. *The Evolution of Medieval Thought.* Baltimore: Helicon Press, 1962.

———. *The Monastic Order in England: A History of Its Development from the Times of St. Dunstan to the Fourth Lateran Council.* Cambridge: Cambridge University Press, 1940.

———. *Thomas Becket.* London: Adam & Charles Black, 1970.

Koch, Walter. *Die klerikalen Standesprivilegien nach Kirchen- und Staatsrecht unter besonderer Berücksichtigung der Verhältnisse in der Schweiz.* Fribourg: Kanisiuswerk, 1949.

Kodrębski, Jan. "Der Rechtsunterricht am Ausgang der Republik und zu Beginn des Principats." In *ANRW*, pt. 2, 15:177–96.

Koschaker, Paul. *Europa und das römische Recht.* Munich: Biederstein, 1947.

Kronman, Anthony T. "The Law as a Profession." In *Ethics in Practice*, 29–41.

Kuehn, Thomas. *Law, Family, and Women: Toward a Legal Anthropology of Renaissance Italy.* Chicago: University of Chicago Press, 1991.

Kultgen, John. *Ethics and Professionalism.* Philadelphia: University of Pennsylvania Press, 1988.

Kunkel, Wolfgang. *Die römischen Juristen: Herkunft und soziale Stellung.* 2nd ed. Cologne: Böhlau, 1967. Repr., 2001.

Die Kunst der Disputationen: Probleme der Rechtsauslegung und Rechtsanwendung im 13. und

14. Jahrhundert. Ed. Manlio Bellomo. Schriften des Historischen Kollegs, Kolloquien, no. 38. Munich: R. Oldenbourg, 1997.

Kuttner, Stephan G. "Additional Notes on the Roman Law in Gratian." *Seminar* 12 (1954) 68–74. Repr. in his *Gratian and the Schools of Law*, no. V.

———. "Annual Report." *Traditio* 13 (1957) 463–66.

———. "Bertram of Metz." *Traditio* 13 (1957) 501–5.

———. "Cardinalis: The History of a Canonical Concept." *Traditio* 3 (1945) 129–214. Repr. in his *History of Ideas and Doctrines of Canon Law*, no. IX.

———. "Conciliar Law in the Making: The Lyonese Constitutions (1274) of Gregory X in a Manuscript of Washington." In *Lateranum*, n.s. 15 (1939) 39–81 [= *Miscellanea Pio Paschini*, vol. 2]. Repr. in his *Medieval Councils, Decretals, and Collections of Canon Law*, no. XII.

———. "Dat Galienus opes et sanctio Justiniana." In *Linguistic and Literary Studies in Honor of Helmut A. Hatzfeld*, 237–46. Repr. in his *History of Ideas and Doctrines of Canon Law*, no. X.

———. "Les débuts de l'école canoniste français." *SDHI* 4 (1938) 193–204. Repr. in his *Gratian and the Schools of Law*, no. VI.

———. "The Father of the Science of Canon Law." *Jurist* 1 (1941) 2–19.

———. *Gratian and the Schools of Law, 1140–1234*. London: Variorum, 1983.

———. "Graziano: L'uomo e l'opera." *SG* 1 (1953) 17–29. Repr. in his *Gratian and the Schools of Law*, no. II.

———. *Harmony from Dissonance: An Interpretation of Medieval Canon Law*. Latrobe, PA: Archabbey Press, 1960. Repr. in his *History of Ideas and Doctrines of Canon Law*, no. I.

———. *The History of Ideas and Doctrines of Canon Law in the Middle Ages*. 2nd ed. Aldershot: Variorum, 1992.

———. "Johannes Teutonicus." In *Neue Deutsche Biographie* 10:571–73.

———. "Die Konstitutionen des ersten allgemeinen Konzils von Lyon." *SDHI* 6 (1930) 70–131. Repr. in his *Medieval Councils, Decretals, and Collections of Canon Law*, no. XI.

———. *Medieval Councils, Decretals, and Collections of Canon Law: Selected Essays*. 2nd ed. Aldershot: Variorum, 1992.

———. "New Studies on the Roman Law in Gratian's Decretum." *Seminar* 11 (1953) 12–50. Repr. in his *Gratian and the Schools of Law*, no. IV.

———. "Notes on Manuscripts." *Traditio* 17 (1961) 533–34.

———. "Papst Honorius III. und das Studium des Zivilrechts." In *Festschrift für Martin Wolff*, 79–101. Repr. in his *Gratian and the Schools of Law*, no. X.

———. "Raymond of Peñafort as Editor: The 'Decretales' and Constitutiones of Gregory IX." *BMCL* 12 (1982) 65–80. Repr. in his *Studies in the History of Medieval Canon Law*, no. XII.

———. *Repertorium der Kanonistik (1140–1234)*. Studi e testi, vol. 71. Vatican City: BAV, 1937.

———. "Research on Gratian: Acta and Agenda." In *Proceedings VII* (Cambridge), 3–26. Repr. in his *Studies in the History of Medieval Canon Law*, no. V.

———. "The Revival of Jurisprudence." In *Renaissance and Renewal in the Twelfth Century*, 299–323. Repr. in his *Studies in the History of Medieval Canon Law*, no. II.

———. "Some Gratian Manuscripts with Early Glosses." *Traditio* 19 (1963) 532–36.
———. *Studies in the History of Medieval Canon Law*. Aldershot: Variorum, 1990.
———. "Sur les origines du terme 'droit positif.'" *RHDF* 4th ser., 15 (1936) 730–31.
———. "Urban II and the Doctrine of Interpretation: A Turning Point." *SG* 15 (1972) 55–85. Repr. in his *History of Ideas and Doctrines of Canon Law*, no. IV.
———. "Zur Biographie des Sicardus von Cremona." *ZRG, KA* 25 (1936) 476–91.
Kuttner, Stephan G., and Antonio García y García. "A New Eyewitness Account of the Fourth Lateran Council," *Traditio* 20 (1964) 115–78. Repr. in Kuttner's *Medieval Councils, Decretals, and Collections of Canon Law*, no. IX
Kuttner, Stephan G., and Beryl Smalley. "The Glossa Ordinaria to the Gregorian Decretals." *English Historical Review* 60 (1945) 97–105. Repr. in Kuttner's *Studies in the History of Medieval Canon Law*, no. XIII.
Kuttner, Stephan G., and Eleanor Rathbone. "Anglo-Norman Canonists of the Twelfth Century: An Introductory Study." *Traditio* 7 (1949/1951) 279–358. Repr. in Kuttner's *Gratian and the Schools of Law*, no. VIII.
Landau, Peter. "Die Anfänge der Verbreitung des klassischen kanonischen Rechts in Deutschland im 12. Jahrhundert und im ersten Drittel des 13. Jahrhunderts." In *Chiesa, diritto e ordinamento*, 272–90. Repr. in his *Kanones und Dekretalen*, 411*–429*.
———. "Bürgschaft und Darlehen im Dekretalenrechts des 12. Jahrhunderts, zugleich zur Biographie des Peter von Blois und des Stephan von Tournai." In *Festschrift für Dieter Medicus*, 297–316.
———. "Burchard de Worms et Gratien: À propos des sources immédiates de Gratien." *RDC* 48 (1998) 233–45.
———. "Das Dekret des Ivo von Chartres: Die handschriftliche Überlieferung im Vergleich zum Text in den Editionen des 16. und 17. Jahrhunderts." *ZRG, KA* 70 (1984) 1–44.
———. "The Development of Law." In *NCMH*, vol. 4, pt. 1, 113–47.
———. "Eilbert von Bremen, Eilbert von Hildesheim und die jüngere Hildesheimer Briefsammlung." In *Forschungen zur Reichs-, Papst- und Landesgeschichte* 1:231–37.
———. "Der Einfluß des kanonischen Rechts auf die europäische Rechtskultur." In *Europäische Rechts- und Verfassungsgeschichte*, 49–57.
———. *Die Entstehung des kanonischen Infamiebegriffs von Gratian bis zur Glossa Ordinaria*. Forschungen zur kirchlichen Rechtsgeschichte und zum Kirchenrecht, vol. 5. Cologne: Böhlau, 1966.
———. "Die Erteilung des Anwaltsmandats in der Geschichte des kanonischen Rechts—Zugleich zu Bernardus Papiensis und Otto Papiensis." In *Wege zur Globalisierung des Rechts*, 413–25.
———. "Gefälschtes Recht in den Rechtsamlungen bis Gratian." In *Fälschungen im Mittelalter* 2:11–49. Repr. in his *Kanones und Dekretalen*, 3*–41*.
———. *Kanones und Dekretalen: Beiträge zur Geschichte der Quellen des kanonischen Rechts*. Goldbach: Keip. 1997.
———. "Neue Forschungen zu vorgratianischen Kanonessammlungen und den Quellen des gratianischen Dekrets." *Ius Commune* 11 (1984) 1–29. Repr. in his *Kanones und Dekretalen*, 177*–205*.

———. "Papst Lucius III. und das Mietrecht in Bologna." In *Proceedings IV* (Toronto), 511–22.

———. "Quellen und Bedeutung des Gratianischen Dekrets." *SDHI* 52 (1986) 218–25. Repr. in his *Kanones und Dekretalen*, 207*–224*.

———. "Die 'Rhetorica ecclesiastica'—Deutschlands erstes juristisches Lehrbuch im Mittelalter." In *Summe—Glosse—Kommentar*, 125–39.

———. "Die Rubriken und Inskriptionen von Ivos Panormie." *BMCL* 12 (1982) 31–49. Repr. in his *Kanones und Dekretalen*, 97*–115*.

———. "Walter von Coutances und die Anfänge der anglo-normannischen Rechtswissenschaft." In *"Panta rei"* 3:183–204.

Lange, Hermann. *Römisches Recht im Mittelalter*. Vol. 1, *Die Glossatoren*. Munich: C. H. Beck, 1997.

Lapidge, Michael. "The School of Theodore and Hadrian." *Anglo-Saxon England* 15 (1986) 45–72.

Larrainzar, Carlos. "El borrador de la 'Concordia' de Graciano: Sankt Gallen, Stiftsbibliothek MS 673 (Sg)." *Ius ecclesiae* 11 (1999) 593–666.

———. "Datos sobre la antiguidad del manuscritto Sg: Su redacción de C. 27 q. 2." In *"Panta rei"* 3:205–37.

———. "El Decreto de Graciano del codice Fd (=Firenze, Biblioteca Nazionale Centrale 'Conventi Soppressi' A.I.402): In memoriam Rudolf Weigand." *Ius ecclesiae* 10 (1998) 421–89.

Late Antiquity: A Guide to the Postclassical World. Ed. G. W. Bowersock, Peter Brown, and Oleg Grabar. Cambridge: Belknap Press of Harvard University Press, 1999.

Law, Church, and Society: Essays in Honor of Stephan Kuttner. Ed. Kenneth Pennington and Robert Somerville. Philadelphia: University of Pennsylvania Press, 1977.

Law in Mediaeval Life and Thought. Ed. Edward B. King and Susan J. Ridyard. Sewanee Mediaeval Studies, no. 5. Sewanee: The Press of the University of the South, 1990.

Lawrence, C. H. "The University in State and Church." In *HUO* 1:97–150.

Lawyers in Society. Ed. Richard L. Abel and Philip S. C. Lewis. 3 vols. Berkeley and Los Angeles: University of California Press, 1988–89.

Lea, Henry Charles. *Studies in Church History*. Philadelphia: Henry C. Lea's Son & Co., 1883.

Leader, Damian Riehl. *The University to 1546. A History of the University of Cambridge*, vol. 1. Cambridge: Cambridge University Press, 1988.

Learning Institutionalized: Teaching in the Medieval University. Ed. John Van Engen. Notre Dame Conferences in Medieval Studies, no. 9. Notre Dame: University of Notre Dame Press, 2000.

Learning the Law: Teaching and the Transmission of Law in England, 1150–1900. Ed. Jonathan A. Bush and Alain Wijffels. London: Hambledon Press, 1999.

Le Bras, Gabriel. "La faculté de droit au moyen âge." In *Aspects de l'Université de Paris*, 83–100.

———. *"Velut splendor firmamenti*: Le docteur dans le droit de l'église médiévale." In *Mélanges offerts à Étienne Gilson*, 373–88.

Le Bras, Gabriel, Charles Lefebvre, and Jacqueline Rambaud. *L'âge classique, 1140–1378:*

Sources et théorie du droit. Histoire du droit et des institutions de l'église en Occident, vol. 7. Paris: Sirey, 1965.

Le Goff, Jacques. "Métier et profession d'après les manuels de confesseurs au moyen âge." In *Beiträge zum Berufsbewusstsein des mittlalterlichen Menschen,* 44–60.

Leclercq, Jean. *The Love of Learning and the Desire for God: A Study of Monastic Culture.* Trans. Catherine Misrahi. New York: Fordham University Press, 1961. Repr., New York: New American Library, 1962.

———. "Lo sviluppo dell'atteggiamento critico degli allievi verso i maestri dal X al XIII secolo." In *Università e società,* 401–28.

Lefebvre, Charles. "La constitution *Properandum* et les avocats de la curie à la fin du XIIIe siècle." In *1274, année charnière,* 525–31.

———. "Hostiensis." In *DDC* 5:1211–27.

———. "Les origines romaines de la procédure sommaire aux XIIe et XIIIe siècles." *Ephemerides iuris canonici* 12 (1956) 149–97.

———. "Pena, Lucas de." In *DDC* 6:1343–46.

———. "Pierre de Blois." In *DDC* 6:1472.

———. "Rote romaine." In *DDC* 7:742–72.

———. "Sicard de Cremone." In *DDC* 7:1008–11.

———. "Un texte inédit sur la procédure rotale au XIVe siècle." *RDC* 10 (1960) 174–91.

Lefebvre-Teillard, Anne. "L'arbitrage en droit canonique." *Revue de l'arbitrage,* no. 1 (2006) 5–34.

———. "Magister A. sur l'école de droit canonique parisienne au début du XIIIe siècle." In *"Panta rei"* 3:239–57.

———. *Les officialités à la veille du concile de Trente.* Bibliothèque d'histoire du droit et droit romain, vol. 19. Paris: R. Pichon & R. Durand-Auzias, 1973.

———. "Petrus Brito legit . . . Sur quelques aspects de l'enseignement du droit canonique à Paris au début du XIIIe siècle." *RHDF* 79 (2001) 153–77.

Legal Consulting in the Civil Law Tradition. Ed. Mario Ascheri, Ingrid Baumgärtner, and Julius Kirschner. Berkeley: The Robbins Collection, 1999.

Legal Records and the Historian. Ed. J. H. Baker. Royal Historical Society, Studies in History, no. 7. London: Royal Historical Society, 1978.

Legendre, Pierre "Miscellanea Britannica." *Traditio* 15 (1959) 491–97.

Legge, giudici, giuristi: Atti del convegno tenuto a Cagliari. Università di Cagliari, Pubblicazioni della Facoltà di Giurisprudenza, ser. 1, vol. 26. Milan: A. Giuffrè, 1982.

L'Engle, Susan. "Trends in Bolognese Legal Illustration: The Early Trecento." In *Juristische Buchproduktion,* 219–44.

L'Engle, Susan, and Robert Gibbs. *Illuminating the Law: Legal Manuscripts in Cambridge Collections.* Turnhout: Harvey Miller, 2001.

Lenherr, Titus. "Ist die Handschrift 673 der St. Galler Stiftsbibliothek (Sg) der Entwurf zu Gratians Dekret? Versuch einer Antwort aus Beobachtungen an D. 31 und D. 32." http://home.vr-wed.de/titus_lenherr/Sg.Entw.pdf.

Lewis, Andrew D. E. "The Autonomy of Roman Law." In *The Moral World of the Law,* 37–47.

Lewis, Charles E. "Canonists and Law Clerks in the Household of Archbishop Hubert Walter." In *Seven Studies in Medieval English History*, 57–64.
Lex et Romanitas: Essays for Alan Watson. Ed. Michael Hoeflich. Berkeley: The Robbins Collection, 2000.
Lexikon des Mittelalters. 10 vols. Munich: Artemis, 1977–99.
Liebs, Detlef. "Rechtsschulen und Rechtsunterricht im Prinzipat." In *ANRW*, pt. 2, 15:197–286.
Linehan, Peter A. "The Case of the Impugned Chirograph and the Juristic Culture of Early Thirteenth-Century Zamora." In *Manoscritti, editoria e biblioteche* 1:461–513.
———. *Past and Present in Medieval Spain*. Aldershot: Variorum, 1992.
———. "Proctors Representing Spanish Interests at the Papal Court, 1216–1303." *Archivum historiae pontificiae* 17 (1979) 69–123. Repr. in his *Past and Present in Medieval Spain*, no. VII.
———. "Spanish Litigants and Their Agents at the Thirteenth-Century Papal Curia." In *Proceedings V* (Salamanca), 487–501. Repr. in his *Past and Present in Medieval Spain*, no. VIII.
———. "The Will of Synibaldus de Labro." *RIDC* 7 (1966) 135–47.
Linehan, Peter A., and José Carlos de Lera Maíllo. *Las postrimerías de un obispo Alfonsino: Don Suero Pérez, el de Zamora*. Zamora: Semuret, 2003.
Linguistic and Literary Studies in Honor of Helmut A. Hatzfeld. Ed. A. S. Crisafulli. Washington, DC: Catholic University of America Press, 1964.
Litewski, Wiesław. *Der römisch-kanonische Zivilprozeß nach den älteren ordines iudiciarii*. 2 vols. Kraków: Wydawnictwo Uniwersytetu Jagiellońskiego, 1999.
Little, Lester K. *Religious Poverty and the Profit Economy in Medieval Europe*. Ithaca: Cornell University Press, 1978.
Livres et bibliothèques (XIIIe–XVe siècle). Cahiers de Fanjeaux, no. 31. Toulouse: Privat, 1996.
Llewellyn, Karl N. *The Bramble Bush: On Our Law and Its Study*. Oceana Publications, 1960. Repr., 1996.
Llewellyn, Peter. *Rome in the Dark Ages*. London: Constable, 1971. Repr., 1996.
Lombardi, Daniela. *Matrimonio di antico regime*. Annali dell'Istiuto storico italo-germanico in Trento, Monografie, no. 34. Bologna: Il Mulino, 2001.
Long, R. James. "'Utrum jurista vel theologus plus proficiat ad regimen ecclesie': A Quaestio Disputata of Francis Caraccioli." *Mediaeval Studies* 30 (1968) 134–62.
Lonza, Nella. "Un inedito 'Tractatus de dignitate et priuilegio doctoratus' di Pietro d'Arezzo." In *"Panta rei"* 3:367–76.
Lopez, Robert S. *The Commercial Revolution of the Middle Ages, 950–1350*. Cambridge: Cambridge University Press, 1976. Repr., 1985.
Loschiavo, Luca. "'Secundum Peponem dicitur . . . G. vero dicit.' In magine ad una nota etimologica da Pepo ed Ugolino." *RIDC* 6 (1995) 233–49.
———. "Sulle tracce bolognesi del Cardinalis decretista (e legista) del secolo XII." In *Manoscritti, editoria e biblioteche* 2:515–32.
Luoghi e metodi di insegnamento nell'Italia medioevale (secoli XII–XIV). Ed. Luciano Gar-

gan and Oronzo Limone. Università degli studi di Lecce, Dipartimento di scienze storiche e sociale, Saggi e ricerche, ser. 2, vol. 3. Galatina: Congedo, 1989.

Lupoi, Maurizio. *The Origins of the European Legal Order*. Trans. Adrian Belton. Cambridge: Cambridge University Press, 2000.

Luscombe, David. "John of Salisbury in Recent Scholarship." In *The World of John of Salisbury*, 21–37.

McBride, J. T. *Incardination and Excardination of Seculars*. Canon Law Studies, vol. 145. Washington, DC: Catholic University of America Press, 1941.

McCall, John P. "Chaucer and John of Legnano." *Speculum* 40 (1965) 484–89.

———. "The Writings of John of Legnano with a List of Manuscripts." *Traditio* 23 (1967) 415–37.

Macfarlane, Leslie J. "Elphinstone, William (1431–1514)." In *Oxford Dictionary of National Biography* (online edition).

McKitterick, Rosamond. *The Carolingians and the Written Word*. Cambridge: Cambridge University Press, 1989.

———. "Some Carolingian Law-Books and Their Function." In *Authority and Power*, 13–27.

McNiven, Peter. "Scrope, Richard (c. 1350–1405)." In *Oxford Dictionary of National Biography* (online ed.).

Maassen, Friedrich. *Geschichte der Quellen und der Literatur des kanonischen Rechts im Abendlande*. Graz: Leuschner & Lubensky, 1870. Repr., Graz: Akademische Druck- u. Verlagsanstalt, 1956.

Maffei, Domenico. *La donazione di Costantino nei giuristi medievali*. Milan: A. Giuffrè, 1964.

———. "Dottori e studenti nel pensiero di Simone da Borsano." *SG* 15 (1972) 229–50.

———. "Un trattato di Bonaccorso degli Elisei e i più antichi statuti dello Studio di Bologna nel manoscritto 22 della Robbins Collection." *BMCL* 5 (1975) 73–101.

Maierù, Alfonso. *University Training in Medieval Europe*. Ed. and trans. D. N. Pryds. Education and Society in the Middle Ages and Renaissance, vol. 3. Leiden: E. J. Brill, 1994.

Maitland, Frederic William. "English Law and the Renaissance." In *Select Essays in Anglo-American Legal History* 1:168–207.

———. *The Letters of Frederic William Maitland*. Vol. 2. Ed. P. N. R. Zutshi. Selden Society, suppl. ser., vol. 11. London: Selden Society, 1995.

———. *Roman Canon Law in the Church of England: Six Essays*. London: Methuen, 1898.

Maleczek, Werner. "Das Kardinalskollegium unter Innocenz II. und Anaklet II." *Archivum Historiae Pontificiae* 19 (1981) 27–78.

———. *Papst und Kardinalskolleg von 1191 bis 1216: Die Kardinäle unter Coelestin III. und Innocenz III*. Österreichischen Kulturinstitut in Rom, Publikationen des Historischen Instituts, ser. 1, vol. 6. Vienna: Österreichischen Akademie der Wissenschaften, 1984.

———. "Das Papsttum und die Anfänge der Universität im Mittelalter." *Römische historische Mitteilungen* 27 (1985) 85–143.

Manoscritti, editoria e biblioteche dall medioevo all'età contemporanea: Studi offerti a Do-

menico Maffei per il suo ottantesimo compleanno. Ed. Mario Ascheri, Gaetano Colli, and Paola Maffei. 3 vols. Rome: Roma nel Rinascimento, 2006.

Manuels, programmes de cours et techniques d'enseignement dans les universités médiévales. Ed. Jacqueline Hamesse. Louvain-la-Neuve: Institut d'études médiévales, 1994.

Marti, Berthe. *The Spanish College at Bologna in the Fourteenth Century:* Philadelphia: University of Pennsylvania Press, 1966.

Martin, G. H., and J. R. L. Highfield. *A History of Merton College.* Oxford: Oxford University Press, 1997.

The Law Governing Lawyers: National Rules, Standards, Statutes, and State Lawyer Codes. Ed. Susan R. Martyn, Lawrence J. Fox, and W. Bradley Wendel. New York: Aspen, 2005.

Mantovani, Dario. *Le formule del processo privato romano.* Padua: CEDAM, 1999.

Martin, Norbert. "Die Compilatio decretorum des Cardinals Laborans." In *Proceedings VI* (Berkeley), 125–37.

Martines, Lauro. *Lawyers and Statecraft in Renaissance Florence.* Princeton: Princeton University Press, 1968.

Martone, Luciano. *Arbiter — Arbitrator: Forme di giustizia privata nell'età del diritto comune.* Storia e diritto, vol. 13. Naples: Jovene, 1984.

Massol, Henri. "Des honoraires des avocats en droit français et en droit romain." *Recueil de l'Académie de législation de Toulouse* 27 (1878/1879) 37–85.

The Materials, Sources, and Methods of Ecclesiastical History. Ed. Derek Baker. Studies in Church History, vol. 11. Oxford: Basil Blackwell, 1975.

Mather, Richard. "The Codicil of Cardinal Comes of Casate and the Libraries of Thirteenth-Century Cardinals." *Traditio* 20 (1964) 319–50.

Mathisen, Ralph W. "*Peregrini, Barbari,* and *Cives Romani*: Concepts of Citizenship and the Legal Identity of Barbarians in the Later Roman Empire." *American Historical Review* 111 (2006) 1011–40.

Matthews, John F. *Laying Down the Law: A Study of the Theodosian Code.* New Haven: Yale University Press, 2000.

Mattingly, Garrett. *Renaissance Diplomacy.* Boston: Houghton Mifflin, 1955. Repr., Baltimore: Penguin Books, 1964.

May, Georg. *Die geistliche Gerichtsbarkeit des Erzbischofs von Mainz im Thüringen des späten Mittelalters.* Erfurter theologische Studien, vol. 2. Leipzig: St. Benno Verlag, 1956.

Mayer-Maly, Theo. *Der Jurist.* Tätigkeitsbericht der Österreichischen Akademie der Wissenschaften, Sonderdruck 1988/1989, no. 1. Vienna: Verlag der Österreichischen Akademie der Wissenschaften, 1988.

Mazzanti, Giuseppe. "Irnerio: Contributo a una biografia." *RIDC* 11 (2000) 117–82.

Mecke, Bernhard. "Die Entwicklung des 'Procurator ad litem.'" *SDHI* 28 (1962) 101–61.

Medieval Cambridge: Essays on the Pre-Reformation University. Ed. Patrick Zutshi. The History of the University of Cambridge, Texts and Studies, vol. 1. Woodbridge: Boydell Press, 1993.

Medieval Church Law and the Origins of the Western Legal Tradition: A Tribute to Kenneth Pennington. Ed. Wolfgang P. Müller and Mary E. Sommar. Washington, DC: Catholic University of America Press, 2006.

Medieval Ecclesiastical Studies in Honour of Dorothy M. Owen. Ed. M. J. Franklin and Christopher Harper-Bill. Studies in the History of Medieval Religion, vol. 7. Woodbridge: Boydell Press, 1995.

Medieval Learning and Literature: Essays Presented to Richard William Hunt. Ed. J. J. G. Alexander and M. T. Gibson. Oxford: Clarendon Press, 1976.

Medieval Lives and the Historian: Studies in Medieval Prosopography. Ed. Neithard Bulst and Jean-Philippe Genet. Kalamazoo: Medieval Institute Publications, 1986.

Medieval Scribes, Manuscripts and Libraries: Essays Presented to N. R. Ker. London: Scolar Press, 1978.

Medieval Trade in the Mediterranean World. Ed. and trans. Robert S. Lopez and Irving W. Raymond. Records of Civilization, Sources and Studies, vol. 51. New York: Columbia University Press, 1955. Repr., W. W. Norton, n.d..

The Medieval World. Ed. Peter Linehan and Janet L. Nelson. London: Routledge, 2001.

Meijers, Eduard. M. *Études d'histoire du droit.* 4 vols. Leiden: Universitaire Pers Leiden, 1956–73.

———. "L'Université d'Orléans au XIIIe siècle." In his *Études d'histoire du droit* 3:3–148.

———. "L'università di Napoli nel secolo XIII." In his *Études d'histoire du droit* 3:149–66.

Mélanges offerts à André Colmer. Paris: Litec, 1993.

Mélanges offerts à Étienne Gilson. Toronto: Pontifical Institute of Mediaeval Studies; Paris: J. Vrin, 1959.

Mélanges Roger Aubenas. Montpellier: Faculté de droit et des sciences économiques de Montpellier, 1974.

La mémoire perdue: À la recherche des archives oubliées publiques et privées de la Rome antique. Ed. Ségolène Demaugin. Publications de la Sorbonne, Série histoire ancienne et médiévale, no. 30. Paris: Publications de la Sorbonne, 1994.

La mémoire perdue: Recherches sur l'administration romaine. Ed. Claude Moatti. Collection de l'École française de Rome, vol. 243. Rome: École française de Rome, 1998.

Merello Altea, Maria Grazia. *Scienza e professione legale nel secolo XI: Ricerche e appunti.* Milan: A. Giuffrè, 1979.

Merzbacher, Friedrich. "Die Parömie 'Legista sine canonibus parum valet, canonista sine legibus nihil'" *SG* 13 (1967) 273–82 [= *Collectanea Stephan Kuttner*, vol. 3].

Mesini, Carlo. "Postille sulla biografia del 'Magister Gratianus' padre del diritto canonico." *Apollinaris* 54 (1981) 509–37.

Metzger, Ernest. *Litigation in Roman Law.* Oxford: Oxford University Press, 2005.

———. *A New Outline of the Roman Civil Trial.* Oxford: Clarendon Press, 1997.

———. "Roman Judges, Case Law, and Principles of Procedure." *Law and History Review* 22 (2004) 243–75.

Meyer, Andreas. *Felix et inclitus notarius: Studien zum italienischen Notariat vom 7. bis zum 13. Jahrhundert.* Bibliothek des Deutschen Historischen Instituts in Rom, vol. 92. Tübingen: Max Niemeyer, 2000.

Meyer, Christoph H. F. *Die Distinktionstechnik in der Kanonistik des 12. Jahrhunderts: Ein Beitrag zur wissenschaftsgeschichte des Hochmittelalters.* Mediaevalia Lovaniensia, Studia, vol. 29. Leuven: Leuven University Press, 2000.

Meyer-Holz, Ulrich. "Die Collegia iudicum und ihre Bedeutung für die Professionalisierung der Juristen." *Zeitschrift des historisches Forschung* 28 (2001) 359–84.
Meynial, Edouard. "Remarques sur la réaction populaire contre l'invasion du droit romain en France aux XIIe et XIIIe siècles." *Romanische Forschungen* 23 (1907) 558–84.
Michaud-Quantin, Pierre. *Universitas: Expression du mouvement communautaire dans le moyen-âge Latin*. L'église et l'état au moyen-âge, vol. 14. Paris: J. Vrin, 1970.
Migliorino, Francesco. *Fama e infamia: Problemi della società medievale nel pensiero giuridico nei secoli XII e XIII*. Catania: Giannotta, 1985.
Mikucki, Sylwiusz. "Remarques sur les origines du notariat public en Pologne: Étude diplomatique." *RHDF*, 4th ser., 16 (1937) 333–50.
The Military Orders: Fighting for the Faith and Caring for the Sick. Ed. Malcolm Barber. Aldershot: Variorum, 1994.
Millénaire monastique du Mont Saint-Michel. Ed. J. Laporte and Raymonde Foreville. 2 vols. Paris: P. Lethielleux, 1966–67.
Miller, Edward. *The Abbey and Bishopric of Ely: The Social History of an Ecclesiastical Estate from the Tenth Century to the Early Fourteenth Century*. Cambridge: Cambridge University Press, 1951. Repr., 1969.
Miller, William Ian. *Bloodtaking and Peacemaking: Feud, Law, and Society in Saga Iceland*. Chicago: University of Chicago Press, 1990.
Minnucci, Giovanni. *La capacità processuale della donna nel pensiero canonistico classico da Graziano a Uguccione da Pisa*. Quaderni di "Studi senesi," vol. 68. Milan: A. Giuffrè, 1989.
Minorities and Barbarians in Medieval Life and Thought. Ed. Susan J. Ridyard and Robert G. Benson. Sewanee Mediaeval Studies, no. 7. Sewanee: University of the South, 1996.
Miscellanea Francesco Ehrle. 6 vols. Studi e testi, vols. 37–42. Vatican City: BAV, 1924.
Miscellanea Rolando Bandinelli, Papa Alessandro III. Ed. Filippo Liotta. Siena: Accademia senese degli intronati, 1986.
Mitchell, Richard E. "Roman History, Roman Law, and Roman Priests: The Common Ground." *University of Illinois Law Review*, 1984, 541–60.
Mitchell, Rosamund J. "English Students at Padua, 1460–75." *Transactions of the Royal Historical Society*, 4th ser., 19 (1936) 101–17.
Momigliano, Arnaldo. "La caduta senza rumore di un impero nel 476 d. C." *Rivista storica italiana* 85 (1973) 5–21.
Moorhead, John. *Justinian*. London: Longman, 1994.
Moorman, J. R. H. *Church Life in England in the Thirteenth Century*. Cambridge: Cambridge University Press, 1945.
Mor, Carlo Guido. "Un ipotesi sulle scuole superiori dell'alto medioevo." *Studi e memorie per la storia dell'Università di Bologna* 16 (1943) 61–78.
———. "Legis doctor." In *Atti del Convegno internazionale di studi Accursiani* 1:193–201.
———. *Storia dell'Università di Modena*. Modena: Società Tipografica Modenese, 1952.
The Moral World of the Law. Ed. Peter Coss. Cambridge: Cambridge University Press, 2000.

Moraw, Peter. "Careers of Graduates." In *HUE* 1:244–79.

———. "Die gelehrten Juristen im Dienst der deutschen Könige im späten Mittelalter (1237–1493)." In *Die Rolle der Juristen bei der Entstehung des modernen Staates*, 77–147.

Mordek, Hubert. *Kirchenrecht und Reform im Frankreich: Die Collectio Vetus Gallica, die älteste systematische Kanonessammlung des Fränkischen Gallien*. Beiträge zur Geschichte und Quellenkunde des Mittelalters, vol. 1. Berlin: Walter de Gruyter, 1975.

Morey, Adrian. *Bartholomew of Exeter, Bishop and Canonist: A Study in the Twelfth Century*. Cambridge: Cambridge University Press, 1937.

Moriarty, Eugene J. *Oaths in Ecclesiastical Courts: An Historical Synopsis and Commentary*. Canon Law Studies, no. 110. Washington, DC: Catholic University of America, 1937.

Morin, Germain. "Le discours d'ouverture du Concile général de Latran (1179) et l'oeuvre littéraire de maître Rufin, évêque d'Assise." *Atti della Pontificia Accademia Romana di Archeologia*, 3rd ser., 2 (1928) 113–33.

Mornet, Elisabeth. "Pauperes scolares: Essai sur la condition matérielle des étudiants scandinaves dans les universités aux XIVe et XVe siècles." *Le moyen âge* 84 (1978) 53–107.

Morris, Colin. "The Commissary of the Bishop in the Diocese of Lincoln." *JEH* 10 (1959) 50–65.

———. "A Consistory Court in the Middle Ages." *JEH* 14 (1963) 150–59.

———. *The Discovery of the Individual, 1050–1200*. New York: Harper & Row, 1973.

———. "From Synod to Consistory: The Bishops' Courts in England, 1150–1250." *JEH* 22 (1971) 115–23.

Morrison, Karl F. "The Church as Play: Gerhoch of Reichersberg's Call for Reform." In *Popes, Teachers, and Canon Law*, 114–44.

Morrissey, Thomas E. "The Art of Teaching and Learning Law: A Late Medieval Tractate." *History of Universities* 8 (1989) 27–74.

Müller, Harald. *Päpstliche Delegationsgerichtsbarkeit in der Normandie (12. und frühes 13. Jahrhundert)*. 2 vols. Studien und Dokumente zur Gallia Pontificia, vol. 4. Bonn: Bouvier, 1997.

———. "Streitwert und Kosten in Prozessen vor dem päpstliche Gericht—eine Skizze," *ZRG*, KA 118 (2001) 138–64.

Müller, Wolfgang P. *Huguccio: The Life, Works, and Thought of a Twelfth-Century Jurist*. Studies in Medieval and Early Modern Canon Law, vol. 3. Washington, DC: Catholic University of America Press, 1994.

———. "The Recovery of Justinian's Digest in the Middle Ages." *BMCL* 20 (1990) 1–29.

Muldoon, James. "Boniface VIII's Forty Years of Experience in the Law." *Jurist* 31 (1971) 49–77.

Mundy, John H. *Society and Government at Toulouse in the Age of the Cathars*. Studies and Texts, vol. 129. Toronto: Pontifical Institute of Mediaeval Studies, 1997.

Munier, Charles. *L'église dans l'empire romain (IIe-IIIe siècle): Église et cité*. Histoire du droit et des institutions de l'église en Occident, vol. 2, pt. 3. Paris: Éditions Cujas, 1979.

Murphy, James J. *Rhetoric in the Middle Ages: A History of Rhetorical Theory from Saint Augustine to the Renaissance*. Berkeley and Los Angeles: University of California Press, 1974.

Murray, Alexander. "Pope Gregory VII and His Letters." *Traditio* 22 (1966) 149–202.

Murray, Alexander Callender. *Germanic Kinship Structure: Studies in Law and Society in Antiquity and the Early Middle Ages.* Studies and Texts, vol. 65. Toronto: Pontifical Institute of Mediaeval Studies, 1983.

———. "'Pax et disciplina': Roman Public Law and the Merovingian State." In *Proceedings X* (Syracuse), 269–85.

Murray, James M. "Failure of Corporation: Notaries Public in Medieval Bruges." *JMH* 12 (1986) 155–66.

Nardi, Paolo. "Relations with Authority." In *HUE* 1:77–107.

Naz, R. "Réginon de Prüm." In *DDC* 7:533–36.

Nelson, Janet L. "Dispute Settlement in Carolingian West Francia." In *The Settlement of Disputes in Early Medieval Europe*, 45–64.

———. "Kingship and Empire." In *The Cambridge History of Medieval Political Thought*, 211–51.

Neue Deutsche Biographie. Ed. Historischen Kommission of the Bayerische Akademie der Wissenschaften. 20 vols. to date. Berlin: Duncker & Humblot, 1953–.

Neuhauser, Walter. *Patronus und Orator: Eine Geschichte der Begriffe von ihren Anfänge bis an die augustische Zeit.* Commentationes Aenipontanae, no. 14. Innsbruck: Wagner, 1958.

The New Cambridge Medieval History. 7 vols. in 8. Cambridge: Cambridge University Press, 1995–2005. [*NCMH*]

Niccolò Tedeschi (Abbas Panormitanus) e i suoi Commentaria in Decretales. Ed. Orazio Condorelli. Rome: Il Cigno Galileo Galilei, 2000.

Nicholas, David. *The Evolution of the Medieval World: Society, Government and Thought in Europe, 312–1500.* London: Longman, 1992.

Noble, Thomas F. X. "Literacy and the Papal Government in Late Antiquity and the Early Middle Ages." In *The Uses of Literacy in Early Mediaeval Europe*, 82–108.

———. "The Papacy in the Eighth and Ninth Centuries." In *NCMH* 2:563–86.

———. *The Republic of St. Peter: The Birth of the Papal State, 680–825.* Philadelphia: University of Pennsylvania Press, 1984.

Nörr, Dieter. "Pomponius oder 'Zum Geschichtsverständnis der römischen Juristen.'" In *ANRW*, pt. 2, 15:497–604.

Nörr, Knut Wolfgang. "À propos du *Speculum iudiciale* de Guillaume Durand." In *Guillaume Durand, Évêque de Mende*, 63–71.

———. "Institutional Foundations of the New Jurisprudence." In *Renaissance and Renewal in the Twelfth Century*, 324–38.

———. "Der Kanonist und sein Werk im Selbstverständnis zweier mittelalterlicher Juristen: Eine Exegese der Proemien des Hostiensis und Durandi." In *Ex ipsis rerum documentis*, 373–80.

———. "Die Literatur zum gemeinen Zivilprozess." In Coing, *Handbuch* 1:383–97.

———. "Rechtsgeschichtliche Apostillen zur Clementine 'Saepe.'" In *"Panta rei"* 4:225–38.

———. "Reihenfolgeprinzip, Terminsequenz und 'Schriftlichkeit.'" *Zeitschrift für Zivilprozeß* 85 (1972) 160–70.

———. "Die Summen 'De iure naturali' und 'De multiplici iuris divisione,'" *ZRG*, KA 48 (1962) 148–63.

———. "Von der Textrationalität zur Zweckrationalität: Das Beispiel des summarischen Prozesses." *ZRG*, KA 81 (1995) 1–25.

———. *Zur Stellung des Richters in gelehrten Prozess der Frühzeit: Iudex secundum allegata non secundum conscientiam iudicat*. Münchener Universitätsschriften, Reihe der Juristischen Fakultät, vol. 2. Munich: C. H. Beck, 1967.

Noonan, John T., Jr. *Bribes*. Berkeley and Los Angeles: University of California Press, 1984. Repr., 1987.

———. "From Social Engineering to Creative Charity." In *Knowledge and the Future of Man*, 179–98.

———. "Gratian Slept Here: The Changing Identity of the Father of the Systematic Study of Canon Law." *Traditio* 35 (1979) 145–72.

———. "Novel 22." In *The Bond of Marriage*, 41–90.

———. *Power to Dissolve: Lawyers and Marriages in the Courts of the Roman Curia*. Cambridge: Belknap Press of Harvard University Press, 1972.

———. "The True Paucapalea?" In *Proceedings V* (Salamanca), 157–86.

———. "Who Was Rolandus?" In *Law, Church, and Society*, 21–48.

La norma en el derecho canónico. 2 vols. Pamplona: EUNSA, 1979.

North, John A. "The Books of the Pontifices." In *La mémoire perdue*, ed. Moatti, 45–63.

O'Callaghan, Joseph F. *A History of Medieval Spain*. Ithaca: Cornell University Press, 1975. Repr., 1983.

———. *The Learned King: The Reign of Alfonso X of Castile*. The Middle Ages Series. Philadelphia: University of Pennsylvania Press, 1993.

Ó Corráin, Donnchadh. "Ireland, Scotland and Wales, ca. 700 to the Early Eleventh Century." In *NCMH* 2:43–63.

Ohler, Norbert. *The Medieval Traveler*. Trans. Caroline Hillier. Woodbridge, Suffolk: Boydell Press, 1998.

Ollivant, Simon. *The Court of the Official in Pre-Reformation Scotland, Based on the Surviving Records of the Officials of St. Andrews and Edinburgh*. Stair Society Publications, no. 34. Edinburgh: Stair Society, 1982.

On the Laws and Customs of England: Essays in Honor of Samuel E. Thorne. Ed. Morris S. Arnold, Thomas A. Green, Sally A. Scully, and Steven D. White. Chapel Hill: University of North Carolina Press, 1981.

Osler, Douglas J. "The Composition of Justinian's Digest." *ZRG*, RA 102 (1985) 129–84.

O'Sullivan, Jeremiah F., and Joseph Leahey. *Cistercians and Cluniacs: The Case for Cîteaux*. Cistercian Fathers Series, no. 33. Kalamazoo: Cistercian Publications, 1977.

Otis, Leah Lydia. *Prostitution in Medieval Society: The History of an Urban Institution in Languedoc*. Chicago: University of Chicago Press, 1985.

Ourliac, Paul. "Bernard de Parme ou de Botone." In *DDC* 2:781–82.

———. "La pratique et la loi (Note sur les actes français et catalans du Xème siècle)." In *Orlandis 70: Estudios de derecho privado y penal, romano, feudal y burgués*. Ed. M. J. Peláez. Boletin semestral de derecho privado especial, histórico y comparado de la

Biblioteca Ferran Valls i Taberner, vol. 1, pt. 2, 93–119. Barcelona: Promociones publicaciones universitaries, 1988.

———. "Troubadours et juristes." *Cahiers de civilisation médiévale* 8 (1965) 159–77.

Owen, Dorothy M. "Ecclesiastical Jurisdiction in England, 1300–1550: The Records and Their Interpretation." In *The Materials, Sources, and Methods of Ecclesiastical History*, 199–221.

———. "An Episcopal Audience Court." In *Legal Records and the Historian*, 140–49.

———. *The Medieval Canon Law: Teaching, Literature and Transmission*. Sandars Lectures in Bibliography, 1987–88. Cambridge: Cambridge University Press, 1990.

———. "The Records of the Bishop's Official at Ely: Specialization in the English Episcopal Chancery of the Later Middle Ages." In *The Study of Medieval Records*, 189–205.

Owen, Dorothy M., B. Ellis, and L. F. Salzman. "Religious Houses." In *VCH*, Cambs. 2:197–320.

Oxford Dictionary of National Biography (online ed.). Oxford: Oxford University Press, 2004–2005. www.oxforddnb.com.

Oxford Studies Presented to Daniel Callus. Oxford Historical Society Publications, 2nd ser., vol. 16. Oxford: Oxford Historical Society, 1964.

Pachter, Walter. *Medieval Canon Law and the Jews*. Münchener Universitätsschriften, Juristische Fakultät, Abhandlungen zur Rechtswissenschaftlichen Grundlagenforschung, vol. 68. Ebelsbach: Rolf Gremer, 1988.

Padovani, Andrea. "Un 'consilium sapientis magistri Iohannes decretorum doctoris et magistri Iacobi Capoani' (Bologna, 1218)." *RIDC* 8 (1997) 63–76.

———. "Il titulo De Summa Trinitate de fide catholica (C. 1.1) nell'esegesi dei glossatori fino ad Azzone, con tre interludi su Irnerio." In *Manoscritti, editoria et biblioteche* 2:1075–1104.

Paetow, Louis John. *Two Medieval Satires on the University of Paris*. Memoirs of the University of California, vol. 4, no. 1. Berkeley: University of California Press, 1972.

"Panta rei": Studi dedicati a Manlio Bellomo. Ed. Orazio Condorelli. 5 vols. Rome: Il Cigno, 2004.

Pantin, W. A. *Canterbury College Oxford*. 3 vols. Oxford Historical Society Publications, n.s., vols. 6–8. Oxford: Clarendon Press, 1947–50.

Paolini, Lorenzo. "L'evoluzione di una funzione ecclesiastica: L'arcidiacono e lo Studio a Bologna nel XIII secolo." *Studi medievali*, 3rd ser., vol. 29, fasc. 1 (1988) 129–72.

Paquet, Jacques. "Coût des études, pauvreté et labeur: Fonctions et métiers d'étudiants au moyen âge." *History of Universities* 2 (1982) 15–52.

———. "L'universitaire 'pauvre' au moyen âge: Problèmes, documentation, questions de méthode." In *The Universities in the Late Middle Ages*, 399–425.

Paragolas Sabaté, Laureà. "Notaris i auxiliars de la funció notarial a les escrivanies de la Barcelona medieval." *Lligall* 8 (1994) 53–72.

Paravicini Bagliani, Agostino. *Cardinali di curia e 'familiae' cardinalizie dal 1227 al 1254*. 2 vols. Italia sacra, vols. 18–19. Padua: Antenore, 1972.

———. "Le fondazione dello 'Studium Curiae.'" In *Luoghi e metodi*, 57–81.

Paré, G., A. Brunet, and P. Tremblay. *La renaissance du XIIe siècle: Les écoles et l'enseignement*. Publications de l'Institut d'Études Médiévales d'Ottawa, vol. 3. Paris: J. Vrin, 1933.

Parieu, Esquirou de. "Étude sur la pratique dorée de Pierre Jacobi, jurisconsulte du quatorzième siècle." *Revue de législation et de jurisprudence* 20 (1844) 417–52.

Parker, James. *The Early History of Oxford, 727–1100: Preceded by a Sketch of the Mythical Origin of the City and University*. Oxford Historical Society Publications, vol. 3. Oxford: Oxford Historical Society, 1885.

Parks, G. B. *The English Traveler to Italy*. Vol. 1, *The Middle Ages (to 1525)*. Stanford: Stanford University Press, 1954.

Palmer, Robert C. "The Origins of the Legal Profession in England." *Irish Jurist* 11 (1976) 126–46.

Pawlisch, Hans S. *Sir John Davies and the Conquest of Ireland: A Study in Legal Imperialism*. Cambridge: Cambridge University Press, 1985.

Paxton, Frederick S. "Gratian's Thirteenth Case and the Composition of the Decretum." Forthcoming in French translation in *RDC*. English version published online (http://www.conncoll.edu/academics/departments/history/paxtonpubs/Gratian 13thCase.doc.).

Pedersen, Frederik. *Marriage Disputes in Medieval England*. London: Hambledon Press, 2000.

Pedersen, Olaf. *The First Universities: Studium Generale and the Origins of University Education in Europe*. Cambridge: Cambridge University Press, 1997.

Pegues, Franklin J. "Ecclesiastical Provisions for the Support of Students in the Thirteenth Century." *Church History* 26 (1957) 307–18.

———. "Royal Support of Students in the Thirteenth Century." *Speculum* 31 (1956) 454–62.

Pennington, Kenneth. "Baldus de Ubaldis." *RIDC* 8 (1997) 35–61.

———. "The Formation of the Jurisprudence of the Feudal Oath of Fealty." *RIDC* 15 (2004) 57–76.

———. "Further Thoughts on Pope Innocent III's Knowledge of Law." *ZRG*, KA 72 (1986) 417–28. Repr. in his *Popes, Canonists and Texts*, no. II.

———. "Gratian, Causa 19, and the Birth of Canonical Jurisprudence." In *"Panta rei"* 4:339–55.

———. "Henricus de Segusio (Hostiensis)." In his *Popes, Canonists and Texts*, no. XVI.

———. "Innocent III and the Ius Commune." In *Grundlagen des Rechts*, 349–66.

———. "Learned Law, Droit Savant, Gelehrtes Recht: The Tyranny of a Concept." *RIDC* 5 (1994) 197–209.

———. "The Legal Education of Pope Innocent III." *BMCL* 4 (1974) 70–77. Repr. in his *Popes, Canonists and Texts*, no. I.

———. "Nicolaus de Tudeschis (Panormitanus)." In *Niccolò Tedeschi*, 9–36.

———. *Pope and Bishops: The Papal Monarchy in the Twelfth and Thirteenth Centuries*. Philadelphia: University of Pennsylvania Press, 1984.

———. *Popes, Canonists and Texts, 1150–1550*. Aldershot: Variorum, 1993.

———. *The Prince and the Law 1200–1600: Sovereignty and Rights in the Western Legal Tradition.* Berkeley and Los Angeles: University of California Press, 1993.

Per Francesco Calasso: Studi degli allievi. Rome: Bulzoni, 1978.

Perez Martín, Antonio. "Büchergeschäfte in Bolognese Regesten aus den Jahren 1265–1350." *Ius commune* 7 (1978) 7–49.

Pescani, Pietro. "Honorarium." *Bollettino della Scuola di perfezionamento e di specializzazione in diritto del lavoro e della sicurezza sociale dell'Università degli studi di Trieste* 21/22 (1961/1962) 12–19.

Peters, Edward M. "Wounded Names: The Medieval Doctrine of Infamy." In *Law in Mediaeval Life and Thought,* 43–89.

Petrucci, Enzo. "An clerici artem notariae possint exercere." In *Studi storici in onore di Ottorino Bertolini* 2:553–98.

Pfeiffer, Rudolf. *History of Classical Scholarship, 1300–1850.* Oxford: Clarendon Press, 1976. Repr., 1999.

Piana, Celestino. *Nuove ricerche su le università di Bologna e di Parma.* Spicilegium Bonaventurianum, vol. 2. Florence: Typographia Collegii S. Bonaventurae, 1966.

Pini, Antonio Ivan. "'Discere turba volens:' Studenti e vita studentesca a Bologna dalle origini dello studio alla metà del Trecento." *Studi e memorie per la storia dell'Università di Bologna,* n.s. 7 (1988) 45–136.

Pitz, Ernst. *Papstreskript und Kaiserreskript im Mittelalter.* Bibliothek des Deutschen Historischen Instituts in Rom, vol. 36. Tübingen: Niemeyer, 1971.

Planas Rosselló, Antonio. "Los abogados de Mallorca en el sistema juridico de la recepción del derecho común." In *L'assistance dans la résolution des conflits,* 115–43.

Planck, Joseph W. "Cicero, Pliny, and the Roman Bar." *Michigan State Bar Journal* 25 (1946) 65–76.

Polak, E. J. "Boncompagno of Signa." In *DMA* 2:320.

———. "Dictamen." In *DMA* 4:173–77.

Pollard, Graham. "Mediaeval Loan Chests at Cambridge." *Bulletin of the Institute of Historical Research* 17 (1939/1940) 113–29.

———. "The 'Pecia' System in the Medieval Universities." In *Medieval Scribes, Manuscripts and Libraries,* 134–61.

Pollock, Frederick, and Frederic William Maitland. *The History of English Law before the Time of Edward I.* 2nd ed. 2 vols. Cambridge: Cambridge University Press, 1898. Repr., 1968.

Poly, Jean-Pierre. "Les légistes provençaux et la diffusion du droit romain dans le Midi." In *Mélanges Roger Aubenas,* 613–35.

———. "Les maîtres de Saint-Ruf: Pratique et enseignement du droit dans la France méridionale au XIIème siècle." *Annales de la Faculté de droit de l'Université de Bordeaux* 2 (1978) 183–203.

Pommeray, Léon. *L'officialité archidiaconale de Paris aux XVe–XVIe siècle: Sa composition et sa compétence criminelle.* Paris: Sirey, 1933.

Poole, Austin Lane. *From Domesday Book to Magna Carta, 1087–1216.* 2nd ed. Oxford History of England, vol. 3. Oxford: Clarendon Press, 1955. Repr., 1964.

Popes, Teachers, and Canon Law in the Middle Ages. Ed. James Ross Sweeney and Stanley Chodorow. Ithaca: Cornell University Press, 1989.

Post, Gaines. "Alexander III, the *licentia docendi* and the Rise of the Universities." In *Anniversary Essays in Mediaeval History,* 255–77.

———. "Masters' Salaries and Student-fees in the Medieval University." *Speculum* 7 (1932) 181–98.

———. "Parisian Masters as a Corporation, 1200–1246." *Speculum* 9 (1934) 421–45. Repr. in his *Studies in Medieval Legal Thought,* 27–60.

———. *Studies in Medieval Legal Thought: Public Law and the State, 1100–1322.* Princeton: Princeton University Press, 1964.

Post, Gaines, Kimon Giocarinis, and Richard Kay. "The Medieval Heritage of a Humanistic Ideal: 'Scientia donum Dei est, unde vendi non potest.'" *Traditio* 11 (1955) 195–234.

Postan, Michael M. *Medieval Economy and Society: An Economic History of Britain in the Middle Ages.* Harmondsworth: Penguin, 1975.

Pound, Roscoe. *The Lawyer from Antiquity to Modern Times, with Particular Reference to the Development of Bar Associations in the United States.* St. Paul: West, 1953.

Powell, Edward. "Arbitration and the Law in England in the Late Middle Ages." *Transactions of the Royal Historical Society,* 5th ser., 33 (1983) 49–67.

Power Elites and State Building. Ed. Wolfgang Reinhard. Oxford: Clarendon Press, 1996.

Powicke, F. M. *The Medieval Books of Merton College.* Oxford: Clarendon Press, 1931.

Pratiques de la culture écrite en France au XVe siècle. Ed. Monique Ornato and Nicole Pons. Louvain-la-Neuve: Leuven University Press, 1995.

Prawer, Joshua. *Crusader Institutions.* Oxford: Clarendon Press, 1980.

La Preuve. 4 vols. Recueils de la Société Jean Bodin. vols. 16–19. Brussels: Éditions de la Librairie encyclopédique, 1963–65.

Proceedings of the Second International Congress of Medieval Canon Law. Ed. Stephan Kuttner and J. Joseph Ryan. MIC, Subsidia, vol. 1. Vatican City: S. Congregatio de seminariis et studiorum universitatibus, 1965. [*Proceedings II* (Boston)]

Proceedings of the Third International Congress of Medieval Canon Law. Ed. Stephan Kuttner. MIC, Subsidia, vol. 4. Vatican City: BAV, 1971. [*Proceedings III* (Strasbourg)]

Proceedings of the Fourth International Congress of Medieval Canon Law. Ed. Stephan Kuttner. MIC, Subsidia, vol. 5. Vatican City: BAV, 1976. [*Proceedings IV* (Toronto)]

Proceedings of the Fifth International Congress of Medieval Canon Law. Ed. Stephan Kuttner and Kenneth Pennington. MIC, Subsidia, vol. 6. Vatican City: BAV, 1980. [*Proceedings V* (Salamanca)]

Proceedings of the Sixth International Congress of Medieval Canon Law. Ed. Stephan Kuttner and Kenneth Pennington. MIC, Subsidia, vol. 7. Vatican City: BAV, 1985. [*Proceedings VI* (Berkeley)]

Proceedings of the Seventh International Congress of Medieval Canon Law. Ed. Peter Linehan. MIC, Subsidia, vol. 8. Vatican City: BAV, 1988. [*Proceedings VII* (Cambridge)]

Proceedings of the Eighth International Congress of Medieval Canon Law. Ed. Stanley Chodorow. MIC, Subsidia, vol. 9. Vatican City: BAV, 1992. [*Proceedings VIII* (San Diego)]

Proceedings of the Ninth International Congress of Medieval Canon Law. Ed. Peter Landau and Jörg Müller. MIC, Subsidia, vol. 10. Vatican City: BAV, 1997. [*Proceedings IX (Munich)*]

Proceedings of the Tenth International Congress of Medieval Canon Law. Ed. Kenneth Pennington, Stanley Chodorow, and Keith H. Kendall. MIC, Subsidia, vol. 11. Vatican City: BAV, 2001. [*Proceedings X (Syracuse)*]

La production du livre universitaire au Moyen Age: Exemplar et pecia. Ed. Louis J. Bataillon, Bertrand G. Guyot, and Richard H. Rouse. Paris: Éditions du Centre National de la Recherche Scientifique, 1988.

Professions and Professionalization. Ed. J. A. Jackson. Cambridge: Cambridge University Press, 1970.

Professions in Theory and History: Rethinking the Study of Professions. Ed. Michael Burrage and Rolf Torstendahl. London: Sage Publications, 1990.

Pryds, Darleen. "*Studia* as Royal Offices: Mediterranean Universities of Medieval Europe." In *Universities and Schooling in Medieval Society*, 83–99.

Purvis, J. S. "Ecclesiastical Courts of York." *Archives: Journal of the British Records Association* 3 (1957) 18–27.

———. *Notarial Signs from the York Archiepiscopal Records*. London and York: St. Anthony's Press, 1957.

Queller, Donald E. *The Office of Ambassador in the Middle Ages*. Princeton: Princeton University Press, 1967.

Radding, Charles M. *The Origins of Medieval Jurisprudence: Pavia and Bologna, 850–1150*. New Haven: Yale University Press, 1988.

Radin, Max. "The Privilege of Confidential Communication between Lawyer and Client." *California Law Review* 16 (1927/1928) 487–97.

Rambaud-Buhot, Jacqueline. "Denys le Petit." In *DDC* 4:1131–52.

Ramsay, Nigel. "Retained Legal Counsel, c. 1275–c.1475." *Transactions of the Royal Historical Society*, 5th ser., 35 (1985) 95–112.

Rashdall, Hastings. *The Universities of Europe in the Middle Ages*. 2nd ed. Ed. F. M. Powicke and A. B. Emden. 3 vols. London: Oxford University Press, 1936. Repr., 1942.

Rathbone, Eleanor. "Roman Law in the Anglo-Norman Realm." *SG* 11 (1967) 253–71 [= *Collectanea Stephan Kuttner*, vol. 1].

Recht im Dienste des Menchen: Festgabe für Hugo Schwendenwein zum 60. Geburtstag. Ed. Klaus Lüdike, Hans Paarhammer, and Dieter A. Binder. Graz: Styria, 1986.

Rechtsgeschichte als Kulturgeschichte: Festschrift für Adalbert Erler zum 70. Geburtstag. Aalen: Scientia, 1976.

The Records of the Medieval Ecclesiastical Courts. Ed. Charles Donahue, Jr. 2 vols. Comparative Studies in Continental and Anglo-American Legal History, vols. 6–7. Berlin: Duncker & Humblot, 1989–94.

Redon, Odile. "Quatre notaires et leurs clientèles à Sienne et dans la campagne siennoise au milieu du XIIIe siècle (1221–1271)." *Mélanges de l'École française de Rome: moyen âge et temps modernes* 85 (1973) 79–141.

Reformata reformanda: Festgabe für Hubert Jedin zum 17. June 1965. Ed. Erwin Iserloh and Konrad Repgen. 2 vols. Reformationsgeschichtliche Studien und Texte, Supplementband, vol. 1. Münster i/Westf.: Aschendorf, 1965.

Reid, Charles, Jr. "The Canonistic Contribution to the Western Rights Inquiry." *Boston College Law Review* 33 (1971) 37–91.

Renaissance and Renewal in the Twelfth Century. Ed. Robert L. Benson and Giles Constable. Cambridge: Harvard University Press, 1982.

Renardy, Christine. *Les maîtres universitaires dans le diocèse de Liège: Répertoire biographique (1140–1350)*. Bibliothèque de la Faculté de Philosophie et Lettres de l'Université de Liège, fasc. 232. Paris: Les Belles Lettres, 1981.

———. *Le monde des maîtres universitaires du diocèse de Liège, 1140–1350: Recherches sur sa composition et ses activités*. Bibliothèque de la Faculté de philosophie et lettres de l'Université de Liège, fasc. 227. Paris: Les Belles Lettres, 1979.

The Responsible Judge: Readings in Judicial Ethics. Ed. John T. Noonan, Jr., and Kenneth I. Winston. Westport: Praeger, 1993.

Reynolds, Robert L. *Europe Emerges: Transition toward an Industrial World-Wide Society, 600–1750*. Madison: University of Wisconsin Press, 1961.

Reynolds, Roger E. "The Organisation, Law and Liturgy of the Western Church." In *NCMH* 2:587–621.

Reynolds, Susan. "The Emergence of Professional Law in the Long Twelfth Century." *Law and History Review* 21 (2003) 346–66.

———. *Fiefs and Vassals: The Medieval Evidence Reinterpreted*. Oxford: Oxford University Press, 1994.

———. "Medieval Law." In *The Medieval World*, 485–502.

Richard, Jean. "Bernard de Clairvaux, arbitre et médiateur." *Séance publique annuelle des cinq Académies*, 1990, 13–18.

Richardson, H. G., and G. O. Sayles. *The Governance of Mediaeval England from the Conquest to Magna Carta*. Edinburgh: Edinburgh University Press, 1963.

Riché, Pierre. "Les écoles en Italie avant les universités." In *Luoghi e metodi*, 1–17.

———. *Écoles et enseignement dans la haut moyen âge, fin du Ve–milieu du XIe siècle*. Paris: Picard, 1989.

———. *Éducation et culture dans l'Occident barbare, VIe–VIIIe siècle*. 4th ed. Paris: Éditions du Seuil, 1995.

———. *Enseignement du droit en Gaule du VIe au XIe siècle*. IRMÆ, vol. 1, pt. 5b, sect. bb. Milan: A. Giuffrè, 1965.

Ridder-Symoens, Hilde de. "Training and Professionalization." In *Power Elites and State Building*, 149–72.

Rieck, Annette. *Der Heilige Ivo von Hélory (1247–1303): Advocatus pauperum und Patron der Juristen*. Rechtshistorische Reihe, vol. 178. Frankfurt a/M: Peter Lang, 1998.

Riley-Smith, Jonathan. *The Feudal Nobility and the Kingdom of Jerusalem, 1174–1277*. London: Macmillan, 1973.

Ritchie, Carson I. A. *The Ecclesiastical Courts of York*. Abroath: Herald Press, 1956.

Roach, J. P. C. "The University of Cambridge." In *VCH*, Cambs. 3:150–312.

Roberg, Burkhard. *Das Zweite Konzil von Lyon [1274]*. Konziliengeschichte, Reihe A: Darstellungen. Paderborn: Ferdinand Schöningh, 1990.

Robinson, Ian S. "Church and Papacy." In *The Cambridge History of Medieval Political Thought*, 252–305.

———. *The Papacy, 1073–1198: Continuity and Innovation.* Cambridge: Cambridge University Press, 1990.
Robinson, Olivia F. *The Criminal Law of Ancient Rome.* Baltimore: Johns Hopkins University Press, 1995.
———. *The Sources of Roman Law: Problems and Methods for Ancient Historians.* London: Routledge, 1997.
Robinson, Olivia F., T. D. Fergus, and William M. Gordon. *European Legal History: Sources and Institutions.* 2nd ed. London: Butterworths, 1994.
Die Rolle der Juristen bei der Entstehung des modernen Staates. Ed. Roman Schnur. Berlin: Duncker & Humblot, 1983.
Rose, Jonathan. "The Ambidextrous Lawyer: Conflict of Interest and the Medieval Legal Profession." *University of Chicago Law School Roundtable* 7 (2000) 137–203.
Rossi, Guido. *Consilium sapientis iudiciale: Studi e ricerche per la storia del processo romano-canonico.* Università di Bologna, Seminario Giuridico, Pubblicazzione, vol. 18. Milan: A Giuffrè, 1958.
———. "Contributi alla biografia del canonista Giovanni d'Andrea." *Rivista trimestrale de diritto e procedure civile* 11 (1957) 1452–1502.
Roumy, Franck. "Le développement du système de l'avocat commis d'office dans la procédure romano-canonique (XIIe–XIVe siècle)." *TRG* 71 (2003) 359–86.
Rouse, Mary A., and Richard H. Rouse. *Authentic Witnesses: Approaches to Medieval Texts and Manuscripts.* Publications in Medieval Studies, vol. 17. Notre Dame: University of Notre Dame Press, 1991.
Rouse, Richard H., and Mary A. Rouse. *Manuscripts and Their Makers: Commercial Book Producers in Medieval Paris 1200–1500.* 2 vols. Turnhout: Harvey Miller, 2000.
Royal Commission on Legal Services. *Final Report.* 2 vols. Command Papers 7648. London: Her Majesty's Stationery Office, 1979.
Royden, Halsey L. *The Magistrates of the Roman Professional Collegia in Italy from the First to the Third Century A.D.* Biblioteca di studi antichi, vol. 61. Pisa: Giardini, 1988.
Rüegg, Walter. "Themes." In *HUE* 1:3–34.
Russell, G. W. E. *Collections and Recollections by One Who Has Kept a Diary.* 4th ed. London: Smith, Elder & Co., 1898.
Russell, Josiah Cox. *Late Ancient and Medieval Population.* Transactions of the American Philosophical Society, n.s., vol. 48, pt. 3. Philadelphia: American Philosophical Society, 1958.
Ryan, J. Joseph. *Saint Peter Damiani and His Canonical Sources: A Preliminary Study in the Antecedents of the Gregorian Reform.* Studies and Texts, vol. 2. Toronto: Pontifical Institute of Mediaeval Studies, 1956.
Ryerson, Katherine L. "Urbanism, Western European." In *DMA* 12:311–20.
Saint Bernard théologien. Analecta Sacri Ordinis Cisterciensis, vol. 9, fasc. 3–4. Rome: Apud Curiam Generalem Sacri Ordinis Cisterciensis, 1953.
Sambin, Paolo. "Giuristi padovani del quattrocento tra attività universitaria e attività publica: I. Paolo d'Arezzo († 1443) e i suoi libri." In *Università e società,* 367–97.
Sanderlin, David. *The Mediaeval Statutes of the College of Autun at the University of Paris.*

Texts and Studies in the History of Mediaeval Education, no. 13. Notre Dame: Mediaeval Institute, 1971.

Santini, Giovanni. "'Legis doctores' e 'sapientes civitatis' di età preireneriana: Ricerche preliminari (con speciale referimento al territorio della Romagna nel sec. XI)." *Archivio giuridico Fil. Serafini*, 7th ser., 38 (1965) 114–71.

Santini, Pietro. *Studi sull'antica costituzione di Firenze: La città e le classi sociali in Firenze nel periodo del primo popolo*. Florence: Tipografia Galileiana, 1903.

Sarti, Mauro, and Mauro Fattorini. *De claris archigymnasii Bononiensis professoribus a saeculo XI usque ad saeculum XIV*. Ed. C. Albacino and C. Malagola. 2 vols. Bologna: Merlani, 1888–96. Repr., Turin: Bottega d'Erasmo, 1962. [Sarti-Fattorini]

Sarti, Nicoletta. *Un giurista tra Azzone e Accursio: Iacopo di Balduino (1210–1235) e il suo "Libellus instructionis advocatorum."* Seminario giuridico della Università di Bologna, Pubblicazione, vol. 137. Milan: A. Giuffrè, 1990.

Satura Roberto Feenstra sexagesimum quintum annum aetatis complenti ab alumnis, collegis, amicis oblata. Ed. J. A. Ankum, J. E. Spruit, and F. G. J. Wubbe. Fribourg: Éditions universitaires, 1985.

Savigny, Friedrich Carl von. *Die Geschichte des römischen Rechts im Mittelalter*. 5th ed. 7 vols. Heidelberg: J. C. B. Mohr, 1834–51. Repr., Aalen: Scientia, 1986.

Sayers, Jane E. "Canterbury Proctors at the Court of 'Audientia litterarum contradictarum.'" *Traditio* 22 (1966) 311–44. Repr. in her *Law and Records in Medieval England*, no. III.

———. "Centre and Locality: Aspects of Papal Administration in England in the Later Thirteenth Century." In *Authority and Power*, 115–26. Repr. in her *Law and Records in Medieval England*, no. I.

———. "The Court of 'Audientia Litterarum Contradictarum' Revisited." In *Forschungen zur Reichs-, Papst- und Landesgeschichte* 1:411–26.

———. *Law and Records in Medieval England: Studies on the Medieval Papacy, Monasteries and Records*. London: Variorum, 1988.

———. "Monastic Archdeacons." In *Church and Government in the Middle Ages*, 177–203. Repr. in her *Law and Records in Medieval England*, no. VI.

———. *Papal Government and England during the Pontificate of Honorius III (1216–1227)*. Cambridge Studies in Medieval Life and Thought, 3rd ser., vol. 21. Cambridge: Cambridge University Press, 1984.

———. *Papal Judges Delegate in the Province of Canterbury, 1198–1254: A Study in Ecclesiastical Jurisdiction and Administration*. Oxford Historical Monographs. London: Oxford University Press, 1971.

———. "Proctors Representing British Interests at the Papal Court, 1198–1415." In *Proceedings III* (Strasbourg), 143–63. Repr. in her *Law and Records in Medieval England*, no. IV.

Sbriccoli, Mario. *L'interpretazione dello statuto: Contributo allo studio della funzione dei giuristi nell'età comunale*. Università di Macerata, Pubblicazioni della facoltà di giurisprudenza, ser. 2, vol. 1. Milan: A. Giuffrè, 1969.

Schieffer, Rudolf. "'The Papal Revolution in Law?' Rückfragen an Harold J. Berman." *BMCL* 22 (1998) 19–30.

Schmale, F.-J. "Synodus—synodale concilium—concilium." *Annuarium Historiae Conciliorum* 8 (1976) 80–102.

Schmidt, Tilmann. "Die Rezeption des Liber Sextus und der Extravaganten Papst Bonifaz' VIII." In *Stagnation oder Fortbildung?* 51–64.

Schmugge, Ludwig. "'Codicis Iustiniani et Institutionum baiulus'—eine neue Quelle zu Magister Pepo von Bologna." *Ius Commune* 6 (1977) 1–9.

Schrader, Gerhard. "Die bischöflichen Offiziale Hildesheims und ihre Urkunden im späten Mittelalter." *Archiv für Urkundenforschung* 13 (1935) 91–176.

Schulen und Studium im sozialen Wandel des hohen und späten Mittelalters. Ed. Johannes Fried. Vorträge und Forschungen, vol. 30. Sigmaringen: Jan Thorbecke, 1986.

Schulte, Johann Friedrich von. *Die Geschichte der Quellen und Literatur des canonischen Rechts.* 3 vols. Stuttgart: Ferdinand Enke, 1875–80. Repr., Graz: Akademische Druck- u. Verlagsanstalt, 1956.

Schulz, Fritz. *Classical Roman Law.* Oxford: Clarendon Press, 1951.

———. *History of Roman Legal Science.* Oxford: Clarendon Press, 1946.

Schwarz, Brigide. *Die Organisation kurialer Schreiberkollegien von ihrer Entstehung bis zur Mitte des 15. Jahrhunderts.* Bibliothek des Deutschen historischen Instituts in Rom, vol. 37. Tübingen: Max Niemeyer, 1972.

Schwinges, Rainer Christoph. "On Recruitment in German Universities from the Fourteenth to Sixteenth Centuries." In *Universities and Schooling in Medieval Society*, 32–48.

———. "Student Education, Student Life." In *HUE* 1:195–243.

La scuola nell'occidente latino dell'alto medioevo. 2 vols. Settimane di studio del Centro italiano di studi sull'alto medioevo, vol. 19. Spoleto: Presso la sede del Centro, 1972.

Il secolo XI: Una svolta? Ed. Cinzio Violante and Johannes Fried. Bologna: Il Mulino, 1993.

The Second Crusade and the Cistercians. Ed. Michael Gervers. New York: St. Martin's Press, 1992.

Select Essays in Anglo-American Legal History. 3 vols. Boston: Little, Brown, 1907–9.

The Settlement of Disputes in Early Medieval Europe. Ed. Wendy Davies and Paul Fouracre. Cambridge: Cambridge University Press, 1986. Repr., 1992.

Seven Studies in Medieval English History and Other Historical Essays Presented to Harold S. Snellgrove. Ed. Richard H. Bowers. Jackson: University Press of Mississippi, 1983.

Shapiro, Susan P. *Tangled Loyalties: Conflict of Interest in Legal Practice.* Ann Arbor: University of Michigan Press, 2002.

Sheehan, Michael M. "The Religious Orders, 1220–1370." In *HUO* 1:193–212.

———. *The Will in Medieval England from the Conversion of the Anglo-Saxons to the End of the Thirteenth Century.* Studies and Texts, vol. 6. Toronto: Pontifical Institute of Mediaeval Studies, 1963.

Sheehy, Maurice. "Influences of Ancient Irish Law on the Collectio canonum Hibernensis." In *Proceedings III* (Strasbourg), 31–41.

Shennan, J. H. *The Parlement of Paris.* 2nd ed. Stroud: Sutton, 1998.

Shifting Frontiers in Late Antiquity. Ed. Ralph W. Mathiesen and Hagith S. Sivan. Aldershot: Variorum, 1996.

Silano, Giulio. "Raymond of Peñafort." In *DMA* 10:266–67.

Simms, Katherine. "The Brehons of Later Medieval Ireland." In *Brehons, Serjeants and Attorneys*, 51–76.

Sivan, Hagith S. "Why Not Marry a Barbarian? Marital Frontiers in Late Antiquity (The Example of NTh 3.14.1)." In *Shifting Frontiers in Late Antiquity*, 136–45.

Smail, Daniel Lord. *The Consumption of Justice: Emotions, Publicity, and Legal Culture in Marseille, 1264–1423*. Ithaca: Cornell University Press, 2003.

Smalley, Beryl. *The Becket Conflict and the Schools: A Study of Intellectuals in Politics*. Oxford: Basil Blackwell, 1973.

———. *The Study of the Bible in the Middle Ages*. Oxford: Basil Blackwell, 1952. Repr., Notre Dame: Notre Dame University Press, 1964.

Smith, Cyril E. *The University of Toulouse in the Middle Ages*. Milwaukee: Marquette University Press, 1958.

Smith, David M. "The 'Officialis' of the Bishop in Twelfth- and Thirteenth-Century England: Problems of Terminology." In *Medieval Ecclesiastical Studies*, 201–20.

Soetermeer, Frank. *Livres et juristes au moyen âge*. Goldbach: Keip, 1999.

———. "La proportion entre civilistes et canonistes à l'Université de Bologne vers 1270." In his *Livres et juristes au moyen âge*, 273–88.

———. *Utrumque ius in peciis: Aspetti della produzione libraria a Bologna fra due e trecento*. Trans. Giancarlo Errico. Orbis academicus, vol. 7. Milan: A. Giuffrè, 1997.

Somerville, Robert. "The Beginning of Alexander III's Pontificate: *Aeterna et incommutabilis* and Scotland." In *Miscellanea Rolando Bandinelli*, 357–68.

———. "The Canons of Reims (1131)." *BMCL* 5 (1975) 122–30.

———. "The Council of Pisa, 1135: A Re-examination of the Evidence for the Canons." *Speculum* 45 (1970) 98–114.

———. "Pope Innocent II and the Study of Roman Law." *Revue des études Islamiques* 14 (1976) 105–14.

———. *Pope Urban II, the Collectio Britannica and the Council of Melfi (1089)*. Oxford: Clarendon Press, 1996.

Sommar, Mary. "Gratian's Causa VII and the Multiple Recension Theories." *BMCL* 24 (2000) 79–97.

Sorbelli, Albino. *Storia dell'Università di Bologna*. I: *Il Medioevo, sec. XI–XV*. Bologna: Nicole Zanichelli, 1940.

Southern, Richard W. "The Changing Roles of the University in Medieval Europe." *Historical Research* 60 (1987) 133–46.

———. "From Schools to University." In *HUO* 1:1–36.

———. "Master Vacarius and the Beginning of an English Academic Tradition." In *Medieval Learning and Literature*, 257–86.

———. *Medieval Humanism and Other Studies*. New York: Harper & Row, 1970.

———. *Scholastic Humanism and the Unification of Europe*. 2 vols. Oxford: Basil Blackwell, 1995–2001.

———. "The Schools of Paris and the School of Chartres." In *Renaissance and Renewal in the Twelfth Century*, 113–37.

Spagnesi, Enrico. *Wernerius Bononiensis iudex: La figura storica d'Irnerio*. Accademia Toscana di Scienze e Lettere "La Columbaria," Studi, vol. 16. Florence: Leo S. Olschki, 1970.

Spatz, Nancy. "Evidence of Inception Ceremonies in the Twelfth-Century Schools of Paris." *History of Universities* 13 (1994) 3–19.

Sprandel, Rolf. *Ivo von Chartres und seine Stellung in der Kirchengeschichte*. Pariser historische Studien, vol. 1. Stuttgart: Anton Hiersemann, 1962.

Spufford, Peter. *Handbook of Medieval Exchange*. Royal Historical Society, Guides and Handbooks, no. 13. London: Royal Historical Society, 1986.

Squibb, G. D. *Doctors' Commons: A History of the College of Advocates and Doctors of Law*. Oxford: Clarendon Press, 1977.

Stagnation oder Fortbildung? Aspekte des allgemeinen Kirchenrechts im 14. und 15. Jahrhundert. Ed. Martin Bertram. Bibliothek des Deutschen Historischen Instituts in Rom, vol. 108. Tübingen: Max Niemeyer, 2005.

Steffen, Walter. *Die studentische Autonomie im mittelalterlichen Bologna: Eine Untersuchung über die Stellung der Studenten und ihrer Universitas gegenüber Professoren und Stadtregierung im 13./14. Jahrhundert*. Geist und Werk der Zeiten, no. 58. Bern: Peter Lang, 1981.

Stein, Peter G. *The Character and Influence of Roman Law: Historical Essays*. London: Hambledon Press, 1988.

———. "The College of Judges at Pavia." *Juridical Review* 61 (1960) 204–13.

———. "Judge and Jurist in the Civil Law: A Historical Interpretation." *Louisiana Law Review* 46 (1985) 241–57. Repr. in his *Character and Influence of Roman Law*, 131–47.

———. "Labeo's Reasoning on Arbitration." *South African Law Journal* 91 (1974) 135–45.

———. *Legal Institutions: The Development of Dispute Settlement*. London: Butterworths, 1984.

———. *Regulae iuris, from Juristic Rules to Legal Maxims*. Edinburgh: Edinburgh University Press, 1966.

———. *Roman Law in European History*. Cambridge: Cambridge University Press, 1999.

———. "The Two Schools of Jurists in the Early Roman Principate." *Cambridge Law Journal* 31 (1972) 8–31.

———. "Vacarius and the Civil Law." In *Church and Government in the Middle Ages*, 119–37. Repr. in his *Character and Influence of Roman Law*, 167–85.

———. "Vacarius and the Civil Law in England." Introduction to Zulueta and Stein, *The Teaching of Roman Law in England*, xxii–xxvii.

Steins, Achim. "Der ordentliche Zivilprozeß nach den Offizialatsstatuten: Ein Beitrag zur Geschichte des gelehrten Prozeßes in Deutschland im Spätmittelalter." *ZRG*, KA 59 (1973) 191–262.

Stelling-Michaud, Sven. "Jean d'André." In *DDC* 6:89–92.

———. "Jean de Legnano." In *DDC* 6:111–12.

———. "Jean le Teutonique." In *DDC* 6:120–22.

———. *L'Université de Bologne et la pénétration des droits romains et canoniques en Suisse aux XIIIe et XIVe siècles*. Travaux d'humanisme et renaissance, no. 17. Geneva: E. Droz, 1955.

Stelling-Michaud, Sven, and Suzanne Stelling-Michaud. *Les juristes Suisses à Bologne (1255–1230): Notices biographiques et regestes des actes bolonais*. Geneva: E. Droz, 1960.
Stelzer, Winfried. "Aus der päpstlichen Kanzlei des 13. Jahrhunderts: Magister Johannes de Sancto Germano, Kurienprokurator und päpstlichen Notar." *Römische historische Mitteilungen* 11 (1969) 219–21.
———. "Beiträge zur Geschichte der Kurienprokuratoren im 13. Jahrhundert." *Archivum historiae pontificiae* 8 (1970) 113–38.
———. "Eilbert von Bremen." *Österreichisches Archiv für Kirchenrecht* 27 (1976) 60–69.
———. *Gelehrtes Recht in Österreich von den Anfängen bis zum frühen 14. Jahrhundert*. Vienna: H. Böhlaus, 1982.
———. "Niederaltaicher Prokuratoren: Zur Geschichte der Impetrationsvollmachten für die päpstliche Kurie im 13. Jahrhundert." *Mitteilungen des Instituts für österreichische Geschichtsforschung* 77 (1969) 291–313.
———. "Zum Scholarenprivileg Friedrich Barbarossas (Authentica 'Habita')." *DA* 34 (1978) 123–65.
Stickler, Alfons Maria. *Historia iuris canonici Latini: Institutiones academicae*. Turin: Pontificium Athenaeum Salesianum, 1950.
———. "Zum Apparat 'Animal est substantia.'" *BMCL* 1 (1971) 74–75.
Storti Storchi, Claudia. *Intorno ai Costituti Pisani della legge e dell'uso (secolo XII)*. Europeo mediterranea, no. 11. Naples: Liguori, 1998.
Straub, Heinrich. *Die geistliche Gerichtsbarkeit des Domdekans im alten Bistum Bamberg von den Anfängen bis zum Ende des 16. Jahrhunderts: Eine rechtsgeschichtliche Untersuchung*. Münchener theologische Studien, kanonistische Abteilung, vol. 9. Munich: Karl Zink, 1957.
Strayer, Joseph R. *Les gens de justice du Languedoc sous Philippe le Bel*. Cahiers de l'Association Marc Bloch de Toulouse, Études d'histoire méridionale, no. 5. Toulouse: Association Marc Bloch, 1970.
———. *Western Europe in the Middle Ages, a Short History*. New York: Appleton-Century-Crofts, 1955.
Stürner, Wolfgang. *Friedrich II*. 2 vols. Darmstadt: Primus Verlag, 2003.
Studi storici in onore di Ottorino Bertolini. 2 vols. Pisa: Pacini, 1972.
Studia in honorem Eminentissimi Cardinalis Alphonsi M. Stickler. Ed. Rosalio Castillo Lara. Studia et textus historiae iuris canonici, vol. 7. Rome: Libreria Ateneo Salesiano, 1992.
Studien zur europäischen Rechtsgeschichte: Helmut Coing zum 28. Februar 1972 von seinen Schülern und Mitarbeitern. Ed. Walter Wilhelm. Frankfurt a/M: Vittorio Klostermann, 1972.
The Study of Medieval Records: Essays in Honour of Kathleen Major. Ed. D. A. Bullough and R. L. Storey. Oxford: Clarendon Press, 1971.
Stutz, Ulrich. "Die Cistercienser wider Gratians Dekret." *ZRG, KA* 9 (1919) 63–98.
———. "Gratian und die Eigenkirchen." *ZRG, KA* 1 (1911) 1–32.
Sullivan, Thomas. *Benedictine Monks at the University of Paris, AD 1229–1500: A Biographical Register*. Education and Society in the Middle Ages and Renaissance, vol. 4. Leiden: E. J. Brill, 1995.

Summe—Glosse—Kommentar: Juristisches und Rhetorisches in Kanonistik und Legistik. Ed. Frank Theisen and Wulf Eckhart Voss. Osnabrücker Schriften zur Rechtsgeschichte, vol. 2. Osnabrück: Universitätsverlag Rasch, 2000.

Sumption, Jonathan. *Pilgrimage: An Image of Mediaeval Religion.* London: Faber & Faber, 1975. Repr., 2002.

Swanson, R. N. *Religion and Devotion in Europe, c. 1215–c. 1515.* Cambridge: Cambridge University Press, 1995.

———. *A Calendar of the Register of Richard Scrope, Archbishop of York, 1398–1405.* 2 vols. University of York, Borthwick Texts and Calendars, Records of the Northern Province, vols. 8, 11. York: Borthwick Institute, 1981–85.

Sweeney, James Ross. "Innocent III, Canon Law, and Papal Judges Delegate in Hungary." In *Popes, Teachers, and Canon Law*, 26–52.

Sydow, Jürgen von. "Il 'consistorium' dopo lo schisma del 1130." *Rivista di storia della chiesa in Italia* 9 (1955) 165–76.

———. "Untersuchungen zur kurialen Verwaltungsgeschichte im Zeitalter des Reformpapsttums." *DA* 11 (1954/1955) 18–73.

Tamba, Giorgio. *La società dei notai di Bologna.* Pubblicazioni degli Archivi di Stato, Strumenti, vol. 103. Rome: Ufficio Centrale per Beni Archivistici, 1988.

Taubenschlag, R. "The Legal Profession in Graeco-Roman Egypt." In *Festschrift für Fritz Schulz* 1:188–92.

Taylor, Nathaniel L. "Testamentary Publication and Proof and the Afterlife of Ancient Probate Procedure in Carolingian Septimania." In *Proceedings X* (Syracuse), 767–80.

Tellegen-Couperous, Olga E. "Quintilian and Roman Law." *Revue internationale des droits d'antiquité*, 3rd ser., 47 (2000) 167–77.

———. "The Role of the Judge in the Formulary Procedure." *Journal of Legal History* 22 (2001) 1–13.

Tellenbach, Gerd. *The Church in Western Europe from the Tenth to the Early Twelfth Century.* Trans. Timothy Reuter. Cambridge: Cambridge University Press, 1993.

Tervoort, Ad. *The Iter Italicum and the Northern Netherlands: Dutch Students at Italian Universities and Their Role in the Netherlands' Society (1426–1575).* Education and Society in the Middle Ages and Renaissance, vol. 21. Leiden: Brill, 2005.

The Theodosian Code. Ed. Jill Harries and Ian Wood. Ithaca: Cornell University Press, 1993.

Thieme, Hans. "Le rôle des doctores legum dans la société allémande du XVIe siècle." *Recueil des mémoires et travaux publié par la Société d'histoire et du droit des institutions des anciens pays de droit écrit* 6 (1967) 45–49.

Thomas, J. A. C. *Textbook of Roman Law.* Amsterdam: North-Holland, 1976.

Thompson, A. Hamilton. "Diocesan Organization in the Middle Ages: Archdeacons and Rural Deans." *Proceedings of the British Academy* 29 (1943) 153–94.

———. *The English Clergy and Their Organization in the Later Middle Ages.* Oxford: Clarendon Press, 1947.

———. "The Will of Master William Doune, Archdeacon of Leicester." *Archaeological Journal* 72 (1915) 233–84.

Thorndike, Lynn. "Law Advertising in Medieval Manuscripts." *Political Science Quarterly* 51 (1936) 270–72.

Thornton, Dora. *The Scholar in His Study: Ownership and Experience in Renaissance Italy.* New Haven: Yale University Press, 1997.

Tierney, Brian. *The Crisis of Church and State, 1050–1300.* Englewood Cliffs, NJ: Prentice-Hall, 1964.

———. *Foundations of the Conciliar Theory: The Contribution of the Medieval Canonists from Gratian to the Great Schism.* 2nd ed. Studies in the History of Christian Thought, vol. 81. Leiden: E. J. Brill, 1998.

———. *Medieval Poor Law: A Sketch of Canonical Theory and Its Application in England.* Berkeley and Los Angeles: University of California Press, 1959.

———. *Religion, Law, and the Growth of Constitutional Thought, 1150–1650.* Cambridge: Cambridge University Pres, 1982.

———. "Two Anglo-Norman Summae." *Traditio* 15 (1959) 483–91.

Todd, S. C. "The Language of Law in Classical Athens." In *The Moral World of the Law*, 17–36.

———. *The Shape of Athenian Law.* Oxford: Clarendon Press, 1993.

Torelli, Pietro. *Scritti di storia del diritto Italiano.* Ed. Giovanni di Vergottini. Università di Bologna, Seminario giuridico, Pubblicazione, vol. 21. Milan: A. Giuffrè, 1959.

Torelli, Pietro, and E. P. Vicini. "Documenti su Guido da Suzzara." In Torelli, *Scritti di storia*, 317–48.

Tout, T. F. "Bowet, Henry (d. 1423)." Rev. by J. J. N. Palmer. *Oxford Dictionary of National Biography* (online ed.).

Trabajos de derecho historico Europeo: Estudios interdisciplinares en homenaje a Ferran Valls i Taberner con occasion del centenaio de su nacimiento. Ed. J. J. Pelaez. Barcelona: Promociones Publicaciones Universitarias, 1992.

Travers, Maurice. *Les corporations d'avocats sous l'empire romain envisagées au point de vue de l'administration judiciaire.* Paris: V. Giard & E. Brière, 1891.

Trexler, Richard C. *Synodal Law in Florence and Fiesole, 1306–1518.* Studi e testi, vol. 268. Vatican City: BAV, 1971.

Trifone, Romualdo. *Diritto romano comune e diritti particolari nell'Italia meridionale.* IRMÆ, V.2.d. Milan: A. Giuffrè, 1962.

Trio, Paul. "Financing of University Students in the Middle Ages: A New Orientation." *History of Universities* 4 (1984) 1–24.

Trusen, Winfried. "Advocatus—zu den Anfängen der gelehrten Anwaltschaft in Deutschland und ihren rechtlichen Grundlagen." In *Um Recht und Freiheit* 2:1235–48.

———. "Die Gelehrte Gerichtsbarkeit der Kirche." In Coing, *Handbuch* 1:467–504.

Turner, C., and M. N. Hodge. "Occupations and Professions." In *Professions and Professionalization*, 17–50.

Turner, Ralph V. *The English Judiciary in the Age of Glanvill and Bracton, c. 1176–1239.* Cambridge Studies in English Legal History. Cambridge: Cambridge University Press, 1985.

———. *Men Raised from the Dust: Administrative Service and Upward Mobility in Angevin England*. Philadelphia: University of Pennsylvania Press, 1988.

———. "Richard Barre and Michael Belet: Two Angevin Civil Servants." *Medieval Prosopography* 6 (1985) 25–49.

Twelfth-Century Europe and the Foundations of Modern Society. Ed. Marshall Clagget, Gaines Post, and Robert L. Reynolds. Madison: University of Wisconsin Press, 1961.

Ullmann, Walter. *The Growth of Papal Government in the Middle Ages: A Study of the Ideological Relation of Clerical to Lay Power*. 2nd ed. London: Methuen, 1962.

———. *The Medieval Idea of Law as Represented by Lucas de Penna: A Study in Fourteenth-Century Legal Scholarship*. London: Methuen, 1946. Repr., New York: Barnes & Noble, 1969.

Um Recht und Freiheit: Festschrift für Friedrich August Freiherr von der Heydte. Ed. Heinrich Kipp, Franz Mayer, and Armin Steinkamm. 2 vols. Berlin: Duncker & Humblot, 1977.

Università e società nelle secoli XII–XVI. Pistoia: Centro italiano di studi di storia e d'arte, 1982.

Università in Europa: Le istituzioni universitarie dal Medio Evo ai nostri giorni, strutture, organizzazione, funzionamento. Ed. Andrea Romano. Soveria Mannelli: Rubbettino, 1995.

Les universités à la fin du Moyen Age. Ed. Jozef Ijswijn and Jacques Pacaut. Publications de l'Institut d'études médiévales, 2nd ser., vol. 2. Louvain: Leuven University Press, 1978.

Universities and Schooling in Medieval Society. Ed. William J. Courtenay and Jürgen Miethke. Education and Society in the Middle Ages and Renaissance, vol. 10. Leiden: E. J. Brill, 2000.

The Universities in the Late Middle Ages. Ed. Jozef Ijswijn and Jacques Paquet. Mediaevalia Lovaniensia, ser. 1, vol. 6. Louvain: Leuven University Press, 1978.

The University and the City, from Medieval Origins to the Present. Ed. Thomas Bender. New York: Oxford University Press, 1988.

The Uses of Literacy in Early Mediaeval Europe. Ed. Rosamond McKitterick. Cambridge: Cambridge University Press, 1990. Repr., 1992.

Vaccari, Pietro. *Diritto longobardo e letteratura longobardistica intorno al diritto Italiano*. IRMÆ, vol. 1, pt. 4b, sect. ee. Milan: A Giuffrè, 1966.

Valls-Taberner, Ferran. *San Ramón de Penyafort*. Madrid and Barcelona: Consejo Superior de Investigaciones Científicas, 1953.

Van Engen, John H. "Observations on 'De consecratione.'" In *Proceedings VI* (Berkeley), 309–20.

Verdon, Jean. *Travel in the Middle Ages*. Trans. George Holoch. Notre Dame: University of Notre Dame Press, 2003.

Verger, Jacques. "À propos de la naissance de l'université de Paris: Contexte social, enjeu politique, portée intellectuelle." In *Schulen und Studium*, 69–96. Repr. in his *Universités françaises au moyen âge*, 1–36.

———. "Le chancelier et l'université à Paris à la fin du XIIIe siècle." In his *Universités françaises au moyen âge*, 68–102.

---. "*Examen privatum, examen publicum:* Aux origines médiévales de la thèse." In *Éléments pour une histoire de la thèse*, 15–43.

---. "The First French Universities and the Institutionalization of Learning: Faculties, Curricula, Degrees." In *Learning Institutionalized*, 5–19.

---. "Le livre dans les universités du Midi de la France à la fin du moyen âge." In *Pratiques de la culture écrite en France*, 403–30.

---. "*Nova et vetera* dans le vocabulaire des premiers statuts et privilèges universitaires français." In *Vocabulaire des écoles et des méthodes d'enseignement au Moyen Age*, 191–205. Repr. in his *Universités françaises au moyen âge*, 37–52.

---. "Patterns." In *HUE* 1:35–67.

---. "Peut-on faire une prosopographie des professeurs des universités françaises à la fin du moyen-âge?" *Mélanges de l'École français de Rome* 100 (1988) 55–62.

---. "Les professeurs des universités françaises à la fin du moyen âge." In his *Universités françaises au moyen âge*, 174–98.

---. "Prosopographie et cursus universitaires." In *Medieval Lives and the Historian*, 313–31.

---. "Le recrutement géographique des universités françaises au début du XVe siècle d'après les Suppliques de 1403." *Mélanges d'archéologie et d'histoire* 82 (1970) 855–902. Repr. in his *Universités françaises au moyen âge*, 122–73.

---. "Teachers." In *HUE* 1:144–68.

---. *Les universités françaises au moyen âge*. Education and Society in the Middle Ages and Renaissance, vol. 7. Leiden: E. J. Brill, 1995.

Vetulani, Adam. "Le Décret de Gratien et les premiers décrétistes à la lumière d'une source nouvelle." *SG* 7 (1959) 275–353. Repr. in his *Sur Gratien et les décrétales*, no. VIII.

---. "Die Einführung der Offiziale in Polen: Ein Beitrag zur Verbreitungsgeschichte des bischöflichen Offizialats im Mittelalter." *Collectanea theologica* 15 (1934) 277–322.

---. "Encore un mot sur le droit romain dans le Décret de Gratien." *Apollinaris* 21 (1948) 129–34. Repr. in his *Sur Gratien et les décrétales*, no. IV.

---. "Gratien et le droit romain." *RHDF* 24/25 (1945/1947) 11–48. Repr. in his *Sur Gratien et les décrétales*, no. III.

---. *Sur Gratian et les décrétales*. Ed. Wacław Uruszczak. Aldershot: Variorum, 1990.

The Victoria History of the County of Cambridgeshire and the Isle of Ely. Ed. L. F. Salzman et al. 10 vols. to date. London: Institute of Historical Research [imprint varies], 1938–. [*VCH*, Cambs.]

Viejo-Ximénez, José M. "'Concordia' y 'Decretum' del maestro Graciano. In memoriam Rudolf Weigand." *Ius canonicum* 39 (1999) 333–57.

---. "La redacción original de C. 29 del Decreto de Graciano." *Ius ecclesiae* 10 (1998) 148–85.

Vinogradoff, Paul Gavrilovitch. *Roman Law in Medieval Europe*. Oxford: Clarendon Press, 1929. Repr., Cambridge: Speculum Historiale, 1968.

Visky, Károly. "Retribuzioni per il lavoro giuridico nelle fonti del diritto Romano." *Iura* 15 (1964) 1–31.

Vismara, Giulio. "Leggi e dottrina nella prassi notarile italiana dell'alto medioevo." In *Confluence des droits savants*, 313–40.

———. *Edictum Theoderici*. IRMÆ, vol. 1, pt. 2b, sect. aa α. Milan: A. Giuffrè, 1967.

Vleeschouwers-Van Melkebeek, Monique. *De officialiteit van Doornik: Oorsprong en vroege ontwikkeling (1192–1300)*. Verhandelingen van de Koninklijke Academie voor Wettenschappen, Letteren en Schone Kunsten van België, Klasse der Letteren, vol. 47, no. 17. Brussels: Paleis de Academiën, 1985.

Vocabulaire des écoles et des méthodes d'enseignement au Moyen Age. Ed. Olga Weijers. Études sur le vocabulaire intellectual du Moyen Age, vol. 5. Turnhout: Brepols, 1992.

Vodola, Elisabeth. *Excommunication in the Middle Ages*. Berkeley and Los Angeles: University of California Press, 1986.

Volterra, Edoardo. "Western Postclassical Schools." *Cambridge Law Journal* 10 (1949) 196–207.

Waldstein, W. "Tribonianus." *ZRG*, RA 98 (1980) 232–35.

Waley, Daniel. *The Italian City Republics*. New York: McGraw-Hill, 1969.

———. *Siena and the Sienese in the Thirteenth Century*. Cambridge: Cambridge University Press, 1991.

Wallace-Hadrill, J. M. *The Barbarian West: The Early Middle Ages, A.D. 400–1000*. New York: Harper & Row, 1962.

Walters, D. B. "Roman and Romano-Canonical Law and Procedure in Wales." *Recueil de mémoires et travaux publié par la Société d'histoire et des institutions des anciens pays de droit écrit* 15 (1991) 67–102.

Walther, Helmut G. "Anfänge des Rechtsstudiums und die kommunale Welt Italiens im Hochmittelalter." In *Schulen und Studium*, 121–62.

———. "Learned Jurists and Their Profit for Society—Some Aspects of the Development of Legal Studies at Italian and German Universities in the Late Middle Ages." In *Universities and Schooling in Medieval Society*, 100–26.

Watson, Alan. *Rome of the XII Tables: Persons and Property*. Princeton: Princeton University Press, 1975.

———. *The State, Law and Religion: Pagan Rome*. Athens: University of Georgia Press, 1992.

———. "Tricks of Advocacy in the Libri disputationum." *TRG* 30 (1962) 226–42.

Wattenbach, Wilhelm, and Wilhelm Levison. *Deutschlands Geschichtsquellen im Mittelalter: Vorzeit und Karolinger*. Weimar: Böhlaus, 1952–57.

Wege zur Globalisierung des Rechts: Festschrift für Rolf A. Schütze zum 65. Geburtstag. Munich: C. H. Beck, 1999.

Weigand, Rudolf. "Die Anglo-Normannische Kanonistik in den letzten Jahrzehnten des 12. Jahrhunderts." In *Proceedings VII* (Cambridge), 249–63.

———. "Bemerkungen über die Schriften und Lehren des Magister Honorius." In *Proceedings V* (Salamanca), 195–212.

———. "Chancen und Probleme einer baldigen kritischen Edition der ersten Redaktion des Dekrets Gratians." *BMCL* 22 (1998) 53–75.

———. "Frühe Kanonisten und ihre Karriere in der Kirche." *ZRG*, KA 76 (1990) 135–55. Repr. in his *Glossatoren des Dekrets Gratians*, 403*–423*.

———. "Gandulphusglossen zum Dekret Gratians." *BMCL* 7 (1977) 15–38. Repr. in his *Glossatoren des Dekrets Gratians*, 181*–214*.

———. *Glossatoren des Dekrets Gratians*. Goldbach: Keip, 1997.

———. "Die Glossen des Cardinalis (Magister Hubald?) zum Dekret Gratians, besonders zu C. 27 q. 2." *BMCL* 3 (1973) 73–94.

———. "Die Glossen des Cardinalis—Raimundus de (H)arenis—zu C. 16." In *Recht im Dienste des Menchen*, 267–83. Repr. in his *Glossatoren des Dekrets Gratians*, 149*–165*.

———. *Die Glossen zum Dekret Gratians: Studien zu den frühen Glossen und Glossenkompositionen*. 2 vols. SG, vols. 25–26. Rome: Libreria Ateneo Salesiano, 1991.

———. "Magister Rolandus und Papst Alexander III." *AKKR* 149 (1980) 3–44. Repr. in his *Glossatoren des Dekrets Gratian*, 73*–114*.

———. "Paucapalea und die frühe Kanonistik." *AKKR* 150 (1981) 137–57. Repr. in his *Glossatoren des Dekrets Gratians*, 1*–21*.

———. "Romanisierungstendenzen im frühen kanonischen Recht." *ZRG*, KA 69 (1983) 200–249. Repr. in his *Glossatoren des Dekrets Gratians*, 23*–72*.

———. "Studien zum kanonistischen Werk Stephans von Tournai." *ZRG*, KA 72 (1986) 349–61. Repr. in his *Glossatoren des Dekrets Gratians*, 167*–179*.

———. "Unbekannte (Überlieferungen von) Dekretalen zur Kardinalskollegium." In *Studia in honorem Eminentissimi Cardinalis Alphonsi M. Stickler*, 599–616.

———. "Versuch einer neuen, differenzierten Liste der Paleae und Dubletten im Dekret Gratians." *BMCL* 23 (1999) 113–28.

Weimar, Peter. "Corpus iuris civilis." In *Lexikon des Mittelalters* 3:270–77. Repr. in his *Zur Renaissance der Rechtswissenschaft*, 117*–125*

———. "Die legistische Literatur der Glossatorenzeit." In Coing, *Handbuch* 1:129–260.

———. "Die legistische Literatur und die Methode des Rechtsunterrichts der Glossatorenzeit." *Ius commune* 2 (1969) 43–83. Repr. in his *Zur Renaissance der Rechtswissenschaft*, 3*–43*.

———. "Zur Entstehung des sogennanten Tübinger Rechtsbuchs und der Exceptiones legum Romanarum des Petrus." In *Studien zur europäischen Rechtsgeschichte*, 1–24. Repr. in his *Zur Renaissance der Rechtswissenschaft*, 81*–104*.

———. "Zur Doktorwürde der Bologeneser Legisten." In *Aspekte europäischer Rechtsgeschichte*, 421–43. Repr. in his *Zur Renaissance der Rechtswissenschaft*, 307*–329*.

———. *Zur Renaissance der Rechtswissenschaft im Mittelalter*. Goldbach: Keip, 1997.

Wenskus, Reinhard. *Stammesbildung und Verfassung: Das Werden der frühmittelalterlichen Gentes*. 2nd ed. Cologne: Böhlau, 1977.

Westbrook, Raymond. "The Nature and Origins of the Twelve Tables." *ZRG*, RA 105 (1988) 74–121.

Wheeler, Mortimer. *Rome beyond the Imperial Frontiers*. London: Penguin, 1955.

White, Steven D. "'Pactum . . . legem vincit et amor judicium': The Settlement of Disputes by Compromise in Eleventh-Century Western France." *American Journal of Legal History* 22 (1979) 281–308.

———. "Proposing the Ordeal and Avoiding It: Strategy and Power in Western French Litigation, 1050–1110." In *Cultures of Power*, 89–123.

Whitwell, Robert Jowitt. "The Libraries of a Civilian and Canonist and of a Common Lawyer, An. 1294." *Law Quarterly Review* 21 (1905) 393–400.

Wickham, Chris. *Early Medieval Italy: Central Power and Local Society, 400–1000*. Ann Arbor: University of Michigan Press, 1989.

———. "*Fama* and the Law in Twelfth-Century Tuscany." In *Fama: The Politics of Talk and Reputation*, 15–26.

———. *Legge, pratiche e conflitti: Tribunali e risoluzione delle dispute nella Toscana del XII secolo*. Rome: Viella, 2001.

Wieacker, Franz. *Allgemeine Zustände und Rechtszustände gegen Ende des Weströmischen Reichs*. IRMÆ, vol. 1, part. 2a. Milan: A Giuffrè, 1963.

———. *A History of Private Law in Europe*. Trans. Tony Weir. Oxford: Clarendon Press, 1995.

Wilkins, Ernest Hatch. *Life of Petrarch*. Chicago: University of Chicago Press, 1961. Repr., 1963.

Williams, John R. "The Cathedral School of Reims in the Time of Master Alberic, 1118–1136." *Traditio* 20 (1964) 93–114.

Williams, Schafer. *Codices Pseudo-Isidoriani: A Palaeographico-Historical Study*. MIC, Subsidia, vol. 3. New York: Fordham University Press, 1971.

Williamson [Owen], Dorothy M. "Some Aspects of the Legation of Cardinal Otto in England, 1237–41." *English Historical Review* 64 (1949) 145–73.

Williman, Daniel. "Summary Justice in the Avignonese Camera." In *Proceedings VI* (Berkeley), 437–49.

Winroth, Anders. "Le Décret de Gratien et le manuscrit florentin: Une critique des travaux de Carlos Larrainzar sur Gratien, I." *Revue de droit canonique* 51/2 (2001) 211-31. Online publication, http://pantheon.yale.edu/-haw6/Critique1.htm.

———. "Les deux Gratiens et le droit Romain." *RDC* 48 (1988) 285–99.

———. "Gratian's Decretum and the Transformation of Sankt Gallen." Online translation of "Une critique des travaux de Carlos Larrainzar sur Gratien, II." http://pantheon.yale.edu/-haw6/Critique2.htm.

———. *The Making of Gratian's Decretum*. Cambridge Studies in Medieval Life and Thought, 4th ser., vol. 49. Cambridge: Cambridge University Press, 2000.

———. "Recent Work on the Making of Gratian's Decretum." Paper delivered at the Twelfth International Congress of Medieval Canon Law, Washington, DC, August 5, 2004. http://pantheon.yale.edu/-haw6/Recent%20work.pdf.

———. "The Two Recensions of Gratian's Decretum." *ZRG*, KA 83 (1996) 22–31.

Witt, Ronald G. *Hercules at the Crossroads: The Life, Works, and Thought of Coluccio Salutati*. Durham: Duke University Press, 1983.

Wojtyła, Karol [Pope John Paul II]. "Le traité 'de penitentia' de Gratien dans l'abrégé de Gdansk Mar. F. 275." *SG* 7 (1959) 355–90.

Wolf, Armin. "Das öffentliche Notariat." In Coing, *Handbuch* 1:505–14.

Wood, Ian. "Administration, Law and Culture in Merovingian Gaul." In *The Uses of Literacy in Early Medieval Europe*, 63–81.

———. "Disputes in Late Fifth- and Sixth-Century Gaul: Some Problems." In *The Settlement of Disputes in Early Medieval Europe*, 7–22.

Woodcock, Brian L. *Medieval Ecclesiastical Courts in the Diocese of Canterbury*. London: Oxford University Press, 1952.

The World of John of Salisbury. Ed. Michael Wilks. Studies in Church History, Subsidia, vol. 3. Oxford: Basil Blackwell, 1984. Repr., 1994.

Wormald, Patrick. *The Making of English Law: King Alfred to the Twelfth Century*. Vol. 1, *Legislation and Its Limits*. Oxford: Basil Blackwell, 1999. Repr., 2001.

Wretschko, Alfred von. *De usu Breviarii Alariciani forensi et scholastico*. In *Codex Theodosianus*, ed. Krueger and Mommsen, vol. 1, *Prolegomena*, cccvii–ccclxxvii.

Wunderli, Richard M. *London Church Courts and Society on the Eve of the Reformation*. Speculum Anniversary Monographs, no. 7. Cambridge: Medieval Academy of America, 1981.

Yunck, John A. *The Lineage of Lady Meed: The Development of Mediaeval Venality Satire*. University of Notre Dame, Publications in Mediaeval Studies, vol. 17. Notre Dame: University of Notre Dame Press, 1963.

Zaccagnini, Guido. "L'insegnamento privato a Bologna e altrove nei sec. XIII e XIV." *Atti e memorie della R. Deputazione di storia patria per le provincie di Romagna*, ser. 4, vol. 14 (1923/1924) 254–301.

———. *Vita dei maestri e degli scolari nello studio di Bologna nei secoli XIII e XIV*. Biblioteca dell'Archivum romanicum, ser. 1, vol. 5. Geneva: Leo S. Olschki, 1926.

Zanetti, Dante. "À l'université de Pavie au XV siècle: Les salaires des professeurs." *Annales: Économies, sociétés, civilisations* 17 (1962) 421–33.

Zimmermann, Harald. "Römische und kanonische Rechtskentnis und Rechtsschulung im früheren Mittelalter." In *La scuola nell'occidente latino dell'alto medioevo* 2:767–94.

Zimmermann, Reinhard. *The Law of Obligations: Roman Foundations of the Civilian Tradition*. Oxford: Clarendon Press, 1996.

Zingerle, I. "Bericht über die Sterzinger Miscellaneen-Handschrift." *Sitzungsberichte der Akademie der Wissenschaften zu Wien*, Phil.-hist. Kl. 54 (1866) 293–340.

Zulueta, Francis de. *The Roman Law of Sale*. Oxford: Clarendon Press, 1945.

Zulueta, Francis de, and Peter Stein. *The Teaching of Roman Law in England around 1200*. Selden Society, suppl. ser., vol. 8. London: Selden Society, 1990.

Zutshi, P. N. R. "The Office of Notary in the Papal Chancery in the Mid-Fourteenth Century." In *Forschungen zur Reichs-, Papst- und Landesgeschichte* 2: 665–83.

———. "Proctors Acting for English Petitioners in the Chancery of the Avignon Popes (1305–1378)." *JEH* 35 (1984) 15–29.

Index

Abbas antiquus. *See* Bernard of Montemirato
Abbo, 59
Abbots, jurisdiction, 150–51
Accursius, 119, 258; enforcement of agreements, 335. See also *Glossa ordinaria*: to Roman law
Actio in factum, 317–18
Adam (abbot of Perseigne), on moral shortcomings of lawyers, 482
Adam Usk, 330, 393
Addo (master), 113n148, 274
Admont (monastery), 100
Adrian I (pope), 64
Adrian IV (pope), 132, 181. *See also* Saint-Ruf
Advocates: access to their services, 471; admissions examination, 292; admissions oath, 285–86, 295–305; admissions procedure, 292; admissions registers, 305–6; admission to practice, 7, 218, 284, 285–90; advertising, 409; advice and counsel, 456; *advocati fisci*, 323; agreements with clients, 332–35; *allegationes*, 160, 352, 441–42; as angels, 476; appeals, 453–55; as arbitrators, 460; *articuli*, 434; attendance at court, 410; banned from chancellor's court, 448; barred from testifying, 325–26; betrayal of client, 318–20, 340; as bishops' officials, 141; and bloodshed, 175–78; body language, 310, 426; canonical, 44–45; careers, 344–49, 472–73; *causidici*, 130; chambers, 116, 352, 410–11; in civil litigation, 170–71, 182–84, 415–19, 428–29; clerical, 39, 165, 174–79, 194–98, 321, 469–71; clerks of, 411–12; client interviews, 314, 412–14; confidentiality, 185–88, 315; conflict of interest, 30, 189, 315, 317, 319, 320–25; *consilia*, 456–59; contingent fees, 198–200, 331–32; court appointed, 410; court attendance, 352; courtroom decorum, 429–30; criticism of, 165–66, 477–87; in *Decretum Gratiani*, 169–70; defined, 170; demand for services of, 167, 466; as diplomats, 463–65; disbarment, 189, 339, 410; disciplinary mechanisms, 218, 317–19, 338–42; discovering opponents' secrets, 326–27; dress, 310–11; duties to clients, 165, 183–88, 308–9, 314–28; duties to court, 165, 183, 308–14, 316; education, 7, 173, 287–90, 349, 490; ennobled by knowledge, 475; entering exceptions, 431–32, 438–39; entitled to fees, 191–92; es-

Advocates (*cont.*)
sential in litigation, 171; establishing a practice, 408–10; exemptions from civic obligations, 475; *exordium*, 440; fees, 165, 191–203, 302–3, 328–36, 414, 453–54, 456–58, 468; formal requirements for admission, 286–87; and former clients, 324; functions, 203–8; gatekeepers of court, 314; instructions, 414; intellectual freedom, 467; interrogatories, 436–37; investments, 340, 468–69; as *iurisperiti*, 350; joint practice, 412; as judicial assessors, 350–51; limits on fees, 202, 468; litigation costs, 201–2, 210–11; loyalty to client, 184–87, 315; meanings, 4, 61–62; mollifying judges, 426–27; moral aspirations, 476–77, 491–92; moral shortcomings, 477–87; negligence, 340; noncontentious matters, 455; not angels, 193; numbers of, 167–68, 171–73, 306–8; officers of court, 188–89, 313, 409–10; opportunities for advancement, 166; oral argument, 351–52, 440–41; out-of-court tasks, 411; at papal curia, 346–47, 454; partnerships, 352, 412; personal conduct, 313; petition for judgment, 442; as pleaders, 351–52; *positiones*, 352, 434; preparation for litigation, 416; preparation of *libellus*, 430–31; as priests of the law, 310, 475–76; private practice, 348–49; and proctors, 203–4, 207–8, 283n1; professional etiquette, 309, 310–11, 313, 424–30; professionalization of, 7, 488–92; professional networks, 409; professional organizations, 365–70; qualifications of, 173–74; redaction of case record, 446; relationship with colleagues, 427–28; right of audience, 284, 339, 410, 490; ritual impurity, 175, 178; scope of practice, 407; selling justice, 192; sins of, 483–84; social mobility, 350; social origins, 349–50; sources of income, 468–71; synonyms, 61; taxation of costs, 210–11, 334, 336–38, 444; tongue a flaming sword, 476; as warriors, 327; wealth, 467–72; as witness examiners, 147; zealous advocacy, 327–28. *See also* Calumny oath; Clients; *Iurisperiti*; Judicial assessors; Jurists; Law teachers; Lawyers; Legal ethics; Legal fees; Legal profession; Orators; *Praevaricatio*; Proctors; *Scholastici*

Advocates, Athenian, 10
Advocates, Icelandic, 72–73
Advocates, Irish, 71–72
Advocates, Welsh, 72
Advocates, Roman: admissions records, 26; advice for, 34–35; in bishops' courts, 42; bureaucratized, 27; client interviews, 31–32; conflict of interest, 30, 187–88, 189, 198; criticism of, 33–34; disciplinary procedures, 30; distribution of counsel, 33; ethics of, 28–33; fees, 35–38, 165, 191–203; irrelevant arguments, 29–30; legal aid for the poor, 190–91; as *milites*, 27; non-monetary rewards, 35; numbers limited, 27n87; professional organizations of, 26–27; requirements for admission to practice, 25–27; social status of, 25, 27; sons of, 27; testimony by, 31

Aegidius de Fuscarariis, 403
Æthelbert, king of Kent, 61
Agustín, Antonio, 97n90
Alaric II, king of the Visigoths, 56
Albericus de Rosate, 384
Albert of Mora. *See* Gregory VIII (pope)
Alciato, Andrea, 290
Alexander III (pope), 106n120, 110, 116, 132, 135n36, 165n1, 211; decretals of, 156; on discovering opponents' secrets, 326; on notarial documents, 212–13; and University of Bologna, 223; use of judges-delegate, 137
Alfonso III, king of Aragon, 292

Alfonso VIII, king of Castile, 242
Alfonso IX, king of Leon, 242
Alfonso X el Sabio, king of Castile and Leon, 242; *Siete partidas*, 319n111
Alfred, king of England, 222
Allthing, 73
Ambassadors, 463–65
Ambidexterity. *See* Legal ethics; *Praevaricatio*
Ambrose (master), 172
Ambrose, Saint, 44, 103, 222
Ammianus Marcellinus, criticism of advocates, 34
Anastasius IV (pope), 131
Anastasius, Roman emperor, 27
Angers, University of, 241. *See also* Councils and Synods
Anselm (bishop of Lucca), 104
Anselm, Saint (archbishop of Canterbury), 80
Anthemius, Roman emperor, 26
Antonio de Butrio, 325
Apostolic Camera, 393
Apparatus *Militant siquidem patroni*, 110n133
Apparitors, 148–49, 151, 372, 417
Appius Claudius Caecus, 13
Apuleius, criticism of advocates, 33
Aquitaine, 393
Arbiters: and arbitrators compared, 460–62; in recusal of judges, 386
Arbitration, 407, 445; as an alternative to litigation, 458; Athenian law, 459; early Middle Ages, 459–60; Germanic law, 55–56; not a cure-all, 462–63; procedure, 460–62; and professional lawyers, 460; Roman law, 17, 459
Archdeacons: courts, 150; jurisdiction, 149–50; monastic, 150n87; registrars, 151, 416–17
Archives, papal, 127
Archpriests, 150
Arezzo, 171; University of, 228. *See also* Bonaguida de Arezzo

Arles, 50
Arnulf of Séez (bishop of Lisieux), 88
Arras, 303. *See also* Councils and synods
Ars dictaminis, 169
Athalaric, Ostrogothic king, 57
Athens, and practice of law, 9–10
Audientia episcopalis, 42
Audientia litterarum contradictarum, 291, 346–47, 361, 371
Audientia sacri palatii. *See* Rota Romana
Auditors. *See* Judges, Judicial assessors
Augustine, Saint (archbishop of Canterbury), 92
Augustine, Saint (bishop of Hippo), 44, 97, 103, 168, 190; on legal fees, 192–93
Augustinian friars, 279
Augustus, Roman emperor, 15, 18, 23, 35
Austin canons, 280
Authentica "Habita." See Frederick I, Barbarossa
Avignon, 472; University of, 268. *See also* Councils and synods
Azo, 112, 190; as ambassador, 465n181; on contingent fees, 199; on *nuntii*, 464; and student universities, 225

Bagarottus, 308n74
Baldus de Ubaldis, 119
Bamberg, examination board, 292
Barbarians, Germanic: and the church, 49; courts and legal procedures, 53–55; kingdoms, 48–50; laws of, 50–53; migrations and settlement, 47–48; and Western Roman Empire, 47–48. *See also* Bavarians; Burgundians; Franks; Lombards; Visigoths
Barbentane, 472
Barcelona, 100; University of, 242
Barnwell Priory, 239, 240
Bartholomew of Brescia, 119n167
Bartolus, nobility of lawyers, 475
Bath and Wells, bishop of, 393. *See also* Councils and synods
Bavarians, 50; laws, 52

582 * INDEX

Bec, abbey of, 92
Bede, Venerable, 59, 60–61
Beirut, law school, 23, 57
Bencivenne of Siena, on notarial documents, 213
Benedict XII (pope), *Decens et necessarium*, 303–4, 312, 316n100, 331n151, 340nn183–84, 360, 421n46, 441n109, 448n129
Benedictine monks, 280
Benefices, 123, 164, 223, 271, 322, 391, 468
Berman, Harold J., 78–79
Bernard of Clairvaux, Saint, 91, 215; as arbitrator, 460; on lawyers at the papal curia, 133–35
Bernard of Montemirato, on recusal of judges, 390
Bernard of Parma, 119; on clerical lawyers, 469; on conflict of interest, 321; on judicial decisions, 378
Bernard of Pavia, 117, 124n182, 142n54; advocates needed in litigation, 192; on calumny oath, 294; on qualifications of advocates, 173
Bertram of Metz, 109, 121
Bertrandus, curial advocate, 201n120
Bishops: courts of, 137–49, 352; households of, 140–41; legal skills, 69–70. *See also* Consistory: bishop's; Court of Arches; Official; Officialities
Blackstone, William, 374
Blondel, David, 66
Bologna, 6, 104, 110, 111, 118, 131, 279, 409, 454; archdeacon of, 259, 261; Four Doctors of, 82, 85–89, 221, 488; law schools, 75, 88, 92, 112, 117, 223, 373, 488; lawyers' guilds, 366–67; legal fees, 330; St. Peter's Cathedral, 259. *See also* Decretists, Bolognese school
Bologna, University of, 221; alleged founder, 222; Cismontane University, 223, 224–25; College of Avignon, 275; college of doctors, 225–227; examinations, 226, 246, 257–62; law degrees, 226, 258–61, 264–65; migrations from, 228; municipal funding, 229–30; nations, 224; notaries, 401–3; numbers of students, 223n15; origins, 223–27; population, 403–4; *puncta*, 251–52; rector, 224, 227; Spanish College, 275; statutes of, 226–27; student fees, 229; student power, 227–28, 229; teaching staff, 264–65; Ultramontane University, 224. *See also* Alexander III; Honorius III; Innocent III
Bonaguida de Arezzo, 308n74, 309, 313, 326, 327, 412, 446, 471
Boncompagno of Signa, *Rhetorica antiqua*, 226
Boniface VIII (pope), 250, 303; *Cum ex eo*, 278–79; on gifts to judges, 390; on summary procedure, 449
Bordeaux, 393. *See also* Councils and Synods
Breviarium Alaricianum. *See* Visigoths: laws
Breviarium extravagantium. *See Quinque compilationes antiquae*
Bruges, notaries, 402, 406
Bulgarus de Bulgarinis (master), 82–83, 85–89, 90, 131, 132, 170; on calumny oath, 182; on conflict of interest, 188; *Excerpta legum*, 154–55; as papal judge-delegate, 136
Burchard (bishop of Worms), *Decretum Burchardi*, 67, 95, 104
Burchard III von Werberge (bishop of Halberstadt), 290
Burchard of Würzburg, 83
Burgundians: kingdom, 50; laws, 52, 56
Bury St. Edmunds, 239
Byzantine Empire, 59. *See also Corpus iuris civilis*; Justin I; Justinian I; Roman Empire, Eastern; Tribonian

Cahors, University of, 268
Caius glosses, 112–13, 119
Caligula, Roman emperor, 18

Calumnia, 318. *See also* Calumny oath
Calumny oath, 28–29, 182, 286; and medieval admissions oaths, 292–95; contents, 296, 433–34; revival of, 293–94, 296. *See also* Romano-canonical procedure
Cambrai, 198n109, 442
Cambridge, 6, 113, 392; church courts, 239–40
Cambridge, University of, 241, 268, 346; advocates banned from chancellor's court, 448; alleged founder, 222; chancellor, 248; law faculty, 248; origins, 239; Peterhouse, 276, 277; structure, 240–41; theology faculty, 248
Canon law: collections, 44, 63–68; curriculum, 250–51, 262–65; disputations, 120–21, 255–57; in the early church, 40–42; examinations, 246, 257–62; lectures, 118–20, 121, 249–50, 251–52, 253–54; and Roman civil law, 42–43, 58, 75, 124, 125, 233–34; sources, 43–44, 97–104, 250–51; teaching, 118–25; and theology, 67, 105, 125. *See also* Decretists; Law faculties; Law schools; Universities
Canon lawyers. *See* Advocates; *Iurisperiti*; Jurists; Proctors
Canons-regular, 131; and practice of law, 470; forbidden to study law, 180–81
Cantaber (mythical Spanish prince), 222
Canterbury: audience court, 410; court of, 172, 201, 307, 376, 451. *See also* Anselm; Augustine; Councils and synods; Court of Arches; Hubert Walter; John Pecham; Lanfranc; Robert Kilwardby; Robert Winchelsey; Stephen Langton; Theobald; Thomas Arundel; Thomas Becket
Capitularies, 97
Cardinalis. See Raymond des Arènes
Cardinals: college of, 127, 129, 164–65; functions, 129; as judicial assessors, 153–54; as legates, 129; as papal electors, 129 Carfania, 26

Carlo (Bolognese advocate), 409
Carmelite friars, 279
Casimir III the Great, king of Poland, 243
Castile, 202. *See also* Alfonso VIII; Alfonso X
Catalunya, 118
Cathedra, 123, 424
Cathedrals, and teaching of canon law, 121–22
Cato, 24n73
Causidicus. See Advocates
Chancellor, papal, 127
Charlemagne, 222
Charles V, German emperor, 243
Charles the Good, count of Flanders, 211
Chaucer, Geoffrey, 149
Chichester Cathedral, 113. *See also* Councils and synods; Seffrid II
Church reform movement: and *Decretum Gratiani*, 99; and Matilda of Tuscany, 84; and twelfth-century legal revival, 78–80
Cicero, 6, 10, 12, 19, 23, 24, 25, 60; advocates corrupt judges, 33; earnings from advocacy, 35; jurists as oracles, 17
Cino da Pistoia, 119
Cistercians, and study of law, 180n44, 280
Civilians, 123–24, 135
Claudius, Roman emperor, 23; on advocates' fees, 36
Clement V (pope): Clementine Constitutions, 251; on cost of degrees, 261–62; on summary procedure, 449–50
Clerics: and bloodshed, 177–78; celibacy, 80; defined, 179; knowledge of law, 63; as officials of the law, 73–74; and the practice of law, 39, 174–79, 194–98, 208–9, 321, 469–71; ritual impurity, 177–78
Clermont, 110. *See also* Councils and synods
Clients: identifying, 320–21, 323; recourse against advocates, 317–18. *See also* Advocates; *Iurisperiti*; Legal ethics; Proctors

Clos Brunel, 246, 254
Clovis, king of the Franks, 52
Cloyne, 71
Codex Euricianus. See Visigoths: laws
Codex Gregorianus, 21
Codex Hermogenianus, 21
Codex Justinianus, compilation of, 58. *See also the citations index*
Codex Theodosianus. See Theodosian Code
Codi, 91–92
Cognitio extra ordinem. See Roman civil procedure
Coimbra, University of, 242
Collectio Britannica, 95; *III librorum*, 104; *Dionysiana*, 64; *Dionysio-Hadriana*, 64; *Hispana*, 64; *Lanfranci*, 92, 94; *Polycarpi*, 104; *Tanner*, 178n39; *Tripartita*, 94–95, 104; *Vetus Gallica*, 66
Collegia. See Advocates, Roman: professional organizations of
Cologne, 109, 121; University of, 243
Coluccio Salutati, 400
Comes of Casate (cardinal), 274n198
Concordia discordantium canonum. See Decretum Gratiani
Consilia, 6, 350, 379, 407, 456–59; faulty, 340; fees for, 200, 457–58
Consilium principis, 24
Consistory: bishops', 140–43, 145–49, 352; calendar, 419–21; on circuit, 423–24; courtrooms, 421–24; holidays, 420; imperial, 129n14; jurisdiction, 146; papal, 129–35, 174, 312; registrars, 147, 416–17; scheduling cases, 420; seals, 147; witness examiners, 147. *See also* Officialities; Officials
Constantine I, Roman emperor, 26, 79; conversion to Christianity, 41–42
Constantinople, 58; law school, 57
Constitutio Antoniana, 14n23
Corbie, abbey of, 64
Cordoba, 50
Cork, Ireland, 71
Cornacervina, 84

Corporations, and conflict of interest, 323
Corpus iuris civilis, 59, 77, 107, 119, 153, 156. See also *Codex Justinianus*; Digest; Institutes; Novels
Councils and synods, 43, 66–67; Angers (1269), 470n11; Arras (ca. 1280–90), 303, 303n59; Avignon (1209), 177n35; Avignon (1282), 361n55; Bayonne (1300), 328n141; Bordeaux (1234), 191, 449n134, 470n11; 1 Canterbury (ca. 1213–14), 177n35; 1 Carthage (345–48), 208n143; 4 Carthage (419), 208n143; 5 Carthage (401), 187n69; Carthage (525), 67n80; Chalcedon (451), 61n62, 67n80, 176n32, 190, 194, 208n143; Champagne (1238), 470n11; Château Gontier (1231), 286n7, 296, 297–98; 1 Chichester (ca. 1245–52), 300n52; Clermont (1130), 124n182, 180, 231n47; Compostella (1114), 190; Cracow (1369), 303n110; 2 Durham (ca. 1241–49), 300n52; 1 Exeter (ca. 1225–27), 341n186; 2 Exeter (1287), 303, 303n59, 449n134; Lambeth (1281), 287–88; Langeais (1255), 287, 391n52; 2 Lateran (1139), 124n182; 3 Lateran (1179), 121, 122n175, 177n35, 178n39, 180, 196, 236n68, 287n12; 4 Lateran (1215), 121–22, 122n175, 138, 147, 213–14, 287n12, 390, 396, 449n134, 452n142, 453; Liège (1287), 306n68; London (1237), 147n76, 149n80, 299–300; London (1268), 300n52, 305n64, 375; London (1282), 303, 304n59; 1 Lyons (1245), 378, 379; 2 Lyons (1274), 301–5, 327, 360, 448, 468, 476n30; Mainz (847), 68nn80–81; Melun (1216), 296; Montpellier (1195), 180n46; Montpellier (1214), 180n46; Narbonne, (1227), 470n11; 1 Nicaea (325); 2 Nicaea (787), 67n80; Nîmes, 470n11; Noyon (1344), 361n56; Oxford (1222), 316n98, 316n100, 445n124, 459n163; Padua (1350), 404n110; Paris (1212), 198, 295; Paris (1222), 328n141; 4

Ravenna (1317), 404n110; Reims (1110), 85; Reims (1131), 124n182, 180, 231n47; Roffiac (1258), 423n50, 470n11; Rome (828), 68n84; Rouen (1216), 395; Rouen (1231), 286n7, 296–97; 1 Salisbury (ca. 1217–19), 177n35; 2 Salisbury (ca. 1238–44), 300n52, 449n134; Salmur (1253), 423n50; Serdica (343), 68n83, 175; Sisteron (1249), 470n11; Tarragona (516), 68n82, 176n32, 180n45, 194; 11 Toledo (675), 177n36; Toulouse (1229), 191; Tournai, 303, 303n59; Tours (1163), 124n182, 180n46, 231n47; Tours (1236), 287, 375, 402n105; Tréguier (1372), 304n52, 403n106; Trier (1277), 306n68; Verno (755), 68n80; Vienne (1311–12), 449; Wells (ca. 1258), 449n134; Westminster (1138), 236n68, 257n140; Westminster (1175), 142; Westminster (1247), 157n112; Worcester III (1240), 149n80, 300n52; York (1195), 142; York (ca. 1241–55), 147n73, 300n52
Court of Arches, 147, 288, 307, 312, 360, 369
Courts: calendars, 352; canonical, bloodshed prohibited, 178. *See also* Consistory; Court of Arches; Rota Romana
Coventry, consistory court, 307
Coventry and Lichfield, bishop of, 392
Cracow, 142; University of, 243. *See also* Councils and synods
Cremona, 130n16
Cresconius, *Concordia canonum*, 97n90
Crook, John, 34
Crusader States, 92
Curia, papal, 126, 195, 201, 209, 433; advocates at, 292; and career advancement, 346, 394, 409; and Roman economy, 133; University of the, 233
Custom, as source of law, 194–95
Cyprian, Saint, 67
Cyprus, 92

Dante Alighieri, criticizes lawyers, 485
David of London (master), 110–11

Deans, of chapters, 150
Decemviri, 11–12
Decretal collections, 114–18. *See also* *Quinque compilationes antiquae*
Decretales Gregorii IX. *See* Liber Extra
Decretals, 43, 115; counterfeit, 115–16
Decretists, 123; Anglo-Norman school, 110–14; Bolognese school, 106–7, 181–82; French schools, 107–9; Rhineland school, 109–10
Decretum Gratiani, 75, 87, 96–103, 114–15, 117, 118, 125, 173; on advocates and proctors, 204–5; and church reform movement, 99; recensions, 99–102; Roman law in, 104; sources, 97, 103–104; structure, 98; as teaching tool, 105; *Tractatus de legibus*, 102–3; use of distinctions, 98. *See also* Decretists; *the citations index*
Didache, 40
Didascalia apostolorum, 40
Digest, 132; compilation of, 58; importance of, 77; medieval divisions of, 77–78n10; recovery of in Western Europe, 77–78. *See also the citations index*
Diocletian, 21, 41
Dionysius Exiguus, 64, 64n67
Diplomacy, 407, 463–65
Disraeli, Benjamin, 310
Distinctiones "Si mulier eadem hora" (Distinctiones Monacenses), 110n133, 195
Distribution of counsel, 188–90. *See also* *Miserabiles personae*: legal aid for
Doctor of laws or decrees, 219–20, 223, 226, 227, 264; as counts, 267; degree requirements, 257–63; as knights, 267
Doctors' Commons, 369–70
Doctrine of the Twelve Apostles. *See Didache*
Dolezalek, Gero, 84
Dominate, the, 27, 38
Dominican friars, 279
Donation of Constantine, 65
Due process of law, 450
Durand, Guilielmus. *See* William Durand

Ecclesia vivit lege Romana, 155
Edict of Milan, 41
Egypt, Roman courts in, 29n97, 29n100
Eilbert of Bremen, 109
Ely, consistory court, 240, 307, 376
Emo (abbot of Bloemhof), 113n148
Erfurt, University of, 243
Etherius (bishop of Lyons), 66
Ethics, and professions, 2, 28, 165, 284. See also Legal ethics
Etienne Aufréri, 313
Eugene III (pope), 132, 137, 153, 172, 174n27; clerics not to represent laymen, 108n144
Euric, king of the Visigoths, 52
Everard d'Ypres, 108
Evesham, Abbey of, 112, 155, 201, 454, 455
Exceptiones Petri, 91
Exceptions: dilatory, 431; to documentary evidence, 439; mixed, 432; peremptory, 431–32; rulings on, 432; to witnesses, 438–39
Exeter, 112, 472. See also Councils and synods; John Grandisson

Fama, 381n34
Federico di Gionta (notary), 405
Fiefs, 322
Flanders, 154, 376, 402. See also Bruges; Ghent, notaries; Tournai; Ypres
Florence, 100; lawyers' guilds, 367; notaries, 403
Forgery, 185, 319. See also Pseudo-Isidorian Decretals
Fortescue, John, 376
Francesco Lando (cardinal), 274
Francesco Petrarca, 400
Franciscan friars, 279
Franciscus de Vercelli, 330
Franks, 50; laws, 52
Frederick I Barbarossa, German emperor, *Authentica "Habita,"* 88–89, 223
Frederick II, German emperor, 241; on advocates, 285; *Liber Augustalis*, 292;

oath of admission to practice in his Sicilian courts, 298–99, 300
Frisia, 113n148, 237. See also Addo; Emo
Fulbert (bishop of Chartres), 184n56

Gaius (Roman jurist), 20, 22, 58
Galbert of Bruges, 211
Galen, 80
Gandulphus (master), advocates should not take fees, 195
Gautier de Coinci, lawyers duplicitous, 480–81
Gelasius I (pope), 68
Gellius, Aulus, 6
Geneva: consistory court statutes, 213, 320; court calendar, 419–20; courtroom, 424; notarial fees, 403–4
Genoa, 138n45
Gerald of Wales, 123, 278; canon law lectures at Paris, 235; law stifles literature, 484
Gerard Pucelle, 97n90, 108, 109
Gerhoch of Reichersberg, 135
Ghent, notaries, 402
Gil Albornoz (cardinal), 275
Gilbert Foliot (bishop of London), 110
Gilles de Bellemère, 400
Glossa ordinaria: to Clementine Constitutions, 119, 249; to *Decretum Gratiani*, 119; to Liber Extra, 119; to Liber Sextus, 119; to Roman law, 83–84, 119. See also Accursius; Bartholomew of Brescia; Bernard of Parma; Johannes Andreae; Johannes Teutonicus
Grammarians, use of legal texts, 60, 82
Gratian (master), 83, 86, 94, 125; identity of, 99. See also *Decretum Gratiani*
Gratianus (cardinal), 212
Gregory I (pope), 50, 77
Gregory VII (pope), 77, 81, 128, 129
Gregory VIII (pope), 85, 132, 165n1
Gregory IX (pope), 118, 165n1, 335
Gregory X (pope): decretal collection, 250; and Second Council of Lyons, 301

Gregory XI, 448
Guala Bicchieri, 114n153, 238
Guibert of Tournai, 130n15
Guido de Baysio, 261
Guido de Cumis, 258
Guido de Suzzara, 230n42
Guillaume du Breuil, 313
Guiot de Provins, 315
Gundobad, king of the Burgundians, 52
Gwynedd, 72

Hadrian, Roman emperor, 24
Haimeric (cardinal), 86, 130–32, 153, 154, 155–56
Hainault, 143n57, 151n89
Halberstadt, consistory court statutes, 313
Hariulf (abbot of Oudenburg), 131–32, 153–55
Haskins, Charles Homer, 76
Heidelberg, University of, 243; students, 269–70
Heinrich von Stein (canon of Regensburg), 269
Henricus de Segusio. *See* Hostiensis
Henry II, king of England, 111, 211
Henry III, king of England, 374
Henry IV, German king and emperor, 81
Henry IV, king of England, 392, 393
Henry V, German king and emperor, 84, 85
Henry VI, German king and emperor, 205
Henry Bowett (archbishop of York), 393–94
Henry Burghersh (bishop of Lincoln), 288, 291, 307, 312
Henry Despenser (bishop of Norwich), 393
Henry de Staunton (official of the Court of Arches), 146–47
Henry the Poet, 346
Hereford, bishop's consistory court, 307
Hermes, 40
Hildesheim, 109

Hilduin (master), criticizes lawyers, 484–85
Homer, *Iliad*, 9
Honorarium: advocates' fee as, 36, 193, 457–58; beneficial interest in, 36; defined, 24
Honorius (master), 111–13, 141
Honorius II (pope), 171, 293
Honorius III (pope), 188, 191, 198n109; forbids teaching of civil law at Paris, 231–32; priests not to practice as paid advocates, 196; *Super specula*, 231–33, 277–78; and University of Bologna, 224, 257–58. *See also* Paris, University of
Honorius IV (pope), 233
Horace, 33
Hortenisius (Roman orator), 23
Hostiensis (cardinal), 230, 347; as ambassador, 465n181; on conflict of interest, 321–22; on education of judges, 375; on judicial decisions, 378; on sins of law teachers, 483–84
Hubert Walter (archbishop of Canterbury), 113n149, 114, 141, 172
Hugh Balsham (bishop of Ely), 276
Hugh Candlesby, 342
Hugh of Avalon, Saint (bishop of Lincoln), 113n149, 114
Hugh of St. Cher, criticizes lawyers, 484
Hugh of St. Victor, 221
Hugo da Porta Ravennate (master), 82–83, 85–89; on contingent fees, 199n113
Hugo von Trimberg, 384
Huguccio, 107, 176; on advocates and proctors, 204–5; on amount of legal fees, 200, 330n146; on arbiters and arbitrators, 461; on choosing cases, 182–83; on contingent fees, 199–200; on judges and advocates, 381; on payment of legal fees, 193
Hungary, 113, 237. *See also* Luke of Hungary; Nicholas of Hungary
Hywel Dda, Welsh king, 72

Iceland, legal system, 72–73
Inception, 258
Index librorum prohibitorum, 66n74
Infamia, 185, 299, 339; consequences, 30, 318, 340, 387, 417–18; defined, 318
Innocent I (pope), 175, 176
Innocent II (pope), 130, 131, 132, 293
Innocent III (pope), 138, 202, 205, 213, 328; and advocates' deficiencies, 381; on availability of advocates, 172; on corruption of judges, 389; on functions of advocates and proctors, 204; legal education of, 165n1; and University of Bologna, 225–26; and University of Paris, 235–36
Innocent IV (pope), 143; founds the University of the Roman Curia, 241; decretals of, 156, 250; on conflict of interest, 321; on negligent law students, 279; and study of civil law, 233
Inns of Chancery, 368
Inns of Court, 368
Institutes: of Gaius, 58; of Justinian, 58
Ireland: advocates, 71–72; Brehon law, 70, 72; law schools, 71; law tracts, 70–71
Irnerius (master), 81–85
Isidore Mercator, 65
Isidore, Saint (bishop of Seville), 62
Iudex. *See* Judges
Iurisperiti, 17, 123, 350; in arbitration, 463; availability of, 171, 172; conflict of interest, 187–88, 198; *consilia*, 456–59; consultation by judges, 442, 456–57; contingent fees, 198–200; in *Decretum Gratiani*, 169–70; demand for services of, 167, 466; as diplomats, 463–65; duty to client, 182; fees, 191–203; selling justice, 192. *See also* Advocates; Jurists
Iurisprudentes, 22
Ius commune, 3, 5, 7, 76, 156, 161n130, 210, 285, 373, 378, 407, 487, 488, 489, 492. *See also* Roman civil procedure; Romano-canonical procedure
Ius proprium, 161n130

Ius respondendi, 17
Ivo of Brittany, Saint, patron saint of lawyers, 477
Ivo, Saint (bishop of Chartres): canonical collections, 94–96, 97, 104, 216; patron saint of lawyers, 477n33

Jacobus (master), 82–83, 85–89
Jacques de Revigny, on judges, 374–75
Jacques de Vitry, 122–23, 138n45, 279n215
Jan Cremme (notary), 406
Jason de Mayno, on evasion of fee limits, 329
Jean Corsier (official of the archbishop of Toulouse), 380
Jean de Roaix, 274
Jerome, Saint, 44, 97, 103
Jocelin de Bohun (bishop of Salisbury), 208n144
Johannes Andreae, 119; as ambassador, 465n181; on conflict of interest, 324; on consulting fees, 458; layman, 469; on summary procedure, 450
Johannes Balduini, 258
Johannes Bassianus, 200n116; on advocates and proctors, 205; on arbiters and arbitrators, 461
Johannes Bazianus, 205n134
Johannes de Deo, 308n74, 313, 315, 414, 428; on arbiters and arbitrators, 461
Johannes de Dulmen, 282
Johannes de Legnano, as ambassador, 465n181; layman, 469
Johannes Monachus, as ambassador, 465n181
Johannes Teutonicus, 119, 200; on costs, 210–11; on education of judges, 374–75; judicial decisions, 378; on legal retainers, 203. *See also Glossa ordinaria*: to *Decretum Gratiani*
John VIII (pope), 127
John XXII (pope), 138n45; Clementine Constitutions, 251; Extravagantes, 251; *Ratio iuris*, 421–22

John Bromyard, on moral shortcomings of lawyers, 447, 481–82
John Comyn (archbishop of Dublin), 141
John Derby, 281
John Grandisson (bishop of Exeter), 472
John Grim, master of the schools of Oxford, 238, 239
John Lydford, 281–82
John of Fribourg, on lawyers' sins, 484
John of Kent, 112
John of Salisbury, 93, 137, 144n62, 216; on calumny oath, 294; criticism of lawyers, 216; on legal jargon, 481
John of Tynemouth, 111–14, 141, 168, 237
John Pecham (archbishop of Canterbury), on ignorant lawyers, 287
Judges: bias, 387, 388; bishops as, 129–40; careers, 391; in church courts, 7; clerical, 470; commissary, 146–47, 391; compensation, 391–92; conflict of interest, 325; and deficiencies of advocates, 380–81, 440–41; definitive judgments, 442–43; discipline, 384, 390–91; education of, 374–77; ethics, 382–84; gifts and bribes, 388–90; ignorant, 33; impartiality, 383; liability for error, 456–57; meanings of, 61–62; must disregard private information, 381–82; numbers of, 391; ordinary, 143, 371, 451; palatine, 128; professionalization of, 283–84, 372–74, 489; qualifications, 143; professional organizations, 365–70; recusal of, 126, 382, 384–91; ritual impurity, 175; Roman, 15, 16, 33. *See also* Judicial assessors; Judicial decisions; Jurisdiction; Officials; Romano-canonical procedure
Judges-delegate, papal, 126, 135–37, 154, 371; casualty losses, 389–90; compensation for expenses, 389; legal knowledge of, 136, 376; recusal of, 387–89; selection of, 136
Judgment by peers, 487

Judicial assessors, 44, 130, 136, 175, 350–51; conflict of interest, 188
Judicial decisions, 377–82, 442–43; definitive, 442–43; interlocutory, 161, 432; reasoned, 378–80
Julian, Roman emperor, 42
Jurisdiction: ordinary, 142, 143, 371; peculiar, 150–51
Jurists, 123; as advocates, 123; as judicial assessors, 16, 17; as legal advisers, 141; as priests, 13–14, 475–76. *See also Iurisperiti*
Justin I, Byzantine emperor, 176
Justinian I, Byzantine emperor: codification of Roman law, 57–59; on conflict of interest, 325; forbade pagans to teach law, 39; on law schools, 57; on legal education, 22
Juvenal: on advocates' fees, 37; criticism of advocates, 33

Kantorowicz, Hermann, 83
Kent, 113. *See also* John of Kent
Knowledge, a gift from God, 192

Lanfranc, 80, 92
Languedoc, 55, 242. *See also* Midi
Laon, 147n75
Larrainzar, Carlos, 101
Lateran Palace, 127, 128, 129, 135, 153
Law, and religion, 10–11, 13–14
Law, personality of, 50–51
Law faculties: calendar, 252; and certification of skill, 285; compared with law schools, 220, 244–45; curriculum, 245–46, 250–51, 262–65; deans of, 247; degrees, 258–65; disputations, 255–57; enrollment fluctuations, 486; examinations, 246, 257–62; lectures, 249–50, 252–53, 264–65; and professionalization of lawyers, 282, 489; *puncta*, 251–52; *repetitiones*, 254; *scientia lucrativa*, 467; seal, 247; statutes, 246; teaching practices, 248–49, 255–57; teaching staff, 264–67

Law of Citations, 22
Law of the Twelve Tables. *See* Twelve Tables
Law school, Roman, 19–20, 22–23, 59–60; at Beirut, 23; Proculian, 19; Sabinian, 19; at Smyrna, 23. *See also* Law teachers
Law schools, medieval: classrooms, 122–23; compared with law faculties, 220–21; financial support, 121; structure, 105–14, 121. *See also* Bologna; Law faculties; Universities
Law students: benefices, 277–79; canons-regular, 279–80; clerics, 270–71; *collecta*, 121, 229–30; college fellowships for, 276–77; cost of law books, 272–73; criminal charges against, 270n187; employment of, 281–82; expenses, 271–73; financial support, 121–22, 271–72, 274–82; flying grants, 280–81; friars, 279–80; loans to, 281; memorization, 254; monks, 279–80; negligent, 279; note-taking, 118–19; numbers of, 267–68; servants of, 269; socio-economic status, 269; study leaves, 277–79. *See also* Bologna, University of; Paris, University of; Heidelberg, University of
Law teachers, 264–67; absenteeism, 265; arrogance, 266; clerics, 122; disputations, 255–57; laymen, 122; lectures, 118–20, 249–54; *repetitiones*, 254; sources of income, 265–66. *See also* Canon law: teaching; Law faculties; Law schools; Universities
Lawyers: access to their services, 471; admissions registers, 305–6; admission to practice, 218, 284, 295–305; ambitious, 135; among cardinals, 132, 347; among popes, 347n13; amorality of, 215; as angels, 476; as arbitrators, 460; as bishops, 346; body language, 310, 426; canons-regular as, 80, 181, 470; careers, 2–3, 344–49, 472–73; clerical, 39, 165, 174–79, 194–98, 208–9, 321, 344–49; 469–71; compared to knights, 185, 474–75; compensation of, 345–46; competition, 345–46; courtroom decorum, 429–30; criticism of, 125, 215, 216–17; demand for their services, 167, 466; denigrated, 477–87; as diplomats, 463–65; ennobled by knowledge, 475; exemptions from civic obligations, 475; fear of, 485–86; greed, 192, 215, 328–29; guides to conduct, 285; guilds, 218, 365–70; intellectual freedom, 467; investments, 468–69; legal aid for the poor, 190–91; legalism, 473; libraries, 5; litigation tactics, 428–29; mollifying judges, 426–27; monks as, 470; moral aspirations, 476–77, 491–92; moral shortcomings, 478–87; in municipal administration, 348; noncontentious matters, 455–65; no room for them in heaven, 477; numbers of, 345; oaths of admission, 285–86, 304–5; opportunities for advancement, 164, 166–67, 214–15; at papal curia, 132–35, 171, 346–47; patron saints, 477; in positions of power, 472–74; pre-professional, 164–65; as priests of the law, 310, 475–76; private practice, 348–49; privileges, 474–75; professional etiquette, 309, 310–11, 313, 424–30; professionalization, 217–18, 282, 283–86, 342–43, 488–92; professional organizations, 365–70; reactions to criticisms, 486–87; relationship with colleagues, 427–28; resentment of, 125; as royal servants, 348; scope of practice, 407–8; seen as threatening, 217; selling justice, 192; sins of, 483–84; as a social group, 125, 188, 217, 300, 490; social mobility, 350, 475–76; and theologians, 215–16; wealth, 467–72. *See also* Advocates; Judges; Jurists; Legal fees; Legal profession; Notaries; Proctors
Legal ethics, 2, 7, 165, 181–91, 218; and admissions oath, 284, 295–305; and Bolognese writers, 181, 308n74; confidential-

ity, 31, 182; conflict of interest, 182, 189, 198; disciplinary sanctions, 218, 317–18, 340–42; duties to client, 165, 183, 308–9, 314–28; duties to court, 165, 183, 308–14, 316; excessive fees, 286; forceful advocacy, 182–84, 191–203; honesty, 286; legal aid for the poor, 190–91; loyalty to client, 181, 184–87; morality of aspiration, 313n91, 343, 476–77, 491–92; and north European decretists, 181, 308n74; personal integrity, 286; and professionalization, 342–43, 490–91; prolonging litigation, 286. *See also* Calumny oath; Legal fees; *Praevaricatio*

Legal fees, 119n113, 165, 191–203, 210, 214, 286, 302–3; 328–36; basis for determining, 330–31, 332; contingent fees, 38, 198–200, 286, 331–33; evading limits, 329–30; limits on, 202, 329; modern guidelines, 330n146; securing payment, 333–34; suits to recover, 334–36; taxation of costs, 334, 336–37, 444; variable, 332; when negotiated, 332–33; when not permitted, 328. *See also* Advocates; *Miserabiles personae*; Notaries; *Palmarium*; Proctors

Legal profession development of, 488–92

Legal profession, medieval: common culture of, 282; professional organizations, 365–70. *See also* Advocates; Judges; Lawyers; Legal ethics; Notaries; Proctors

Legal profession, Roman, 6, 9–45; ethics, 28–33, 300; fees, 35–38; training, 19. *See also* Advocates; Judges; Jurists; Lawyers; Notaries; Proctors

Leges Iuliae iudiciorum, 15

Legis actiones. *See* Roman civil procedure

Legists. *See* Civilians

Leicester, 472

Leipzig, University of, 243

Lenherr, Titus, 101

Leo I, Roman emperor, 26, 27, 351

Leo IX (pope), 128

Lérida, University of, 242

Lérins, 130n16

Lex Acilia. *See Lex de repetundis*

Lex Aebutia, 15

Lex Cincia, 35

Lex de repetundis, 31n111

Lex Irnitana, 16n30

Lex Iulia de civitate, 14n23

Lex Plautia Papiria de civitate, 14n23

Lex Romana Burgundionum. *See* Burgundians, laws

Lex Romana Visigothorum. *See* Visigoths, laws

Libellus: articulated, 434n86; in *cognitio extra ordinem*, 18. *See also* Romano-canonical procedure

Liber Augustalis. *See* Frederick II

Liber Extra, 118, 264. *See also the citations index*

Liber pauperum, 93–94. *See also* Vacarius

Liber Sextus, 250, 264, 303. *See also the citations index*

Libri duo de synodalibus causis. *See* Regino

Lichfield, bishops' consistory court, 307, 376

Liège, 147n77, 303; bishop's official, 307, 376. *See also* Councils and synods

Lincoln: archdeacon of, 151n89; bishop of, 172; cathedral, 113; consistory court, 449; diocese, 143n57, 146; lawyers' attire, 425; official-principal, 472. *See also* Henry Burghersh; Hugh of Avalon

Litigants, engaging an advocate, 408–10. *See also* Advocates; Legal ethics; Proctors; Romano-canonical procedure

Litigation: compromise encouraged, 430, 445; costs of, 201–2, 336–38, 445, 454–55; deficit financing, 362–63; delays in, 29; hazards of, 170–71; a last resort, 455; length of, 447–49; monastic pastime, 443–44; motives for, 444; at papal court, 126–31; as a pressure tactic, 445–46, 455; taxation of costs, 336–38; volume of, 126–27. *See also* Romano-canonical procedure

Livre tournois, 272n192, 302, 360
Llewellyn, Karl, 73, 216, 485
Lo Codi. See *Codi*
Lombard of Piacenza (master), 88
Lombards, laws of, 52
London: bishop of, 369; municipal courts, 305; St. Paul's Cathedral, 269
Lopez, Robert Sabatino, 77
Lorenzo Valla, 66
Louis IX, Saint, king of France, 373–74
Louvain (Leuven), University of, 243
Lucas de Penna, 400
Lucca: lawyers' guild, 367, notaries, 402
Lucius III (pope), on conflict of interest, 325
Lucius Licinius Crassus, 19–20
Luke of Hungary, 108n127
Lyons, 272n192, 376. *See also* Councils and synods; Etherius

Mabel de Francheville, 201, 209
Maine, county of, 296
Mainz, 109, 110. *See also* Councils and synods
Maitland, Frederic William, 61, 92; on importance of the Digest, 78
Mandate, 205–6, 210, 359. *See also* Proctors
Manfred of Antibes, 130n16
Mantua, 89, 228
Marcus Antonius (Roman advocate), 19
Marseilles, 50, 311, 449
Martial, on advocates' fees, 37
Martin V (pope): *In apostolica dignitatis*, 291, 312, 376–77; *Romani pontificis providentia*, 319–20
Martinus de Fano, on inadequately prepared advocates, 289
Martinus Gosia (master), 82, 85–89, 92; on conflict of interest, 188; on contingent fees, 199n113, 332
Matheolus: lawyers as prostitutes, 480; questions judicial integrity, 390
Matilda, countess of Tuscany, 81, 84
Merandus (Spanish advocate), 210n120

Midi, 91. *See also* Languedoc; Provence
Miserabiles personae, 40, 68; legal aid for, 190–91, 196–97, 410, 468
Modena, lawyers' guild, 367
Modestinus, Roman jurist, 20, 22
Monks: forbidden to study law, 180–81; and practice of law, 469
Montpellier, 90; availability of trained lawyers, 172; lawyers' guild, 367; University of, 228. *See also* Councils and synods
Montso, Cortes of (1289), 292
Morale de Toro, 362
Morris, Colin, 166
Moysis (master), 99n94

Naples, University of, 241
Narbonne, 302. *See also* Councils and synods
Negotiation, 407, 455, 456, 457, 459–63
Nero, 41
Nicholas I (pope), 66
Nicholas II (pope), 129
Nicholas III (pope), decretal collection, 250
Nicholas Breakspear. *See* Adrian IV, pope
Nicholas de l'Aigle, 112–13, 120
Nicholas de Romanis (cardinal legate), 238
Nicholas de Tudeschis. *See* Panormitanus
Nicholas of Hungary, 113n148
Nigel Wireker (Longchamps), criticizes lawyers, 484
Nîmes, 172, 349. *See also* Councils and synods
Normandy, 120, 141, 296. *See also* Decretists: Anglo-Norman school
Norwich, 360
Notaries, 4, 116, 407; admissions examinations, 401, 402–4; career prospects, 397; creation of, 399–400; demand for services of, 167; employment and functions, 394–97; fees, 214, 403–4; greed of, 202; income, 404–5; numbers of, 167–68, 306–8, 397–98, 401–2; papal, 127, 211–12; at the papal curia, 127, 395;

and proctors, 168–69; professional organizations, 365–70, 403; record court proceedings, 147, 396–97, 437; registers, 398–99; Roman, 38–39; scarce in northern Europe, 214; social status, 211–12, 400–401; training of, 62, 169, 400; types of, 394–95; workplaces, 405

Notaries, public, 4, 7, 169; appointment of, 398; become proctors, 290; documents presumed reliable, 212–13, 398; in officialities, 372; origin, 212

Notorium, 381n34, 386n50

Novels, of Justinian, 58–59. *See also* the citations index

Nuntius, defined, 464

Oaths, exculpatory, 69. *See also* Calumny oath

Odo (abbot of Battle), 139n48, 172

Odo (abbot of Cluny), 59

Odofredus de Denariis, 83, 225n22, 267; on dodging unpaid assignments, 198; on examinations, 258; on student budgets, 272

Odo of Dover, 108

Officials: archdeacons', 143n57, 151, 391; bishops', 139–45, 371, 391; critics of, 144–45. *See also* Consistory: bishops'; Judges

Officialities: apparitors, 148, 372, 417; calendars, 419–20; commissary judges, 146–47, 372; courtrooms, 421–24; defined, 371–72; geographical distribution, 141–42; holidays, 420; origins, 141–42; procurator fiscal, 372; registrar, 148, 416–17; scheduling cases, 421; structure, 145–46; treasurer, 148; witness examiners, 147. *See also* Consistory: bishops'

Olavus Johannis, 282

Olomüz, 142

Orators, Athenian, 10

Orators, Roman, 9, 16; knowledge of law, 17; rewards, 35

Ordeals, 54–55, 68

Ordinationes. *See* Law students: note-taking

Orléans, 107, 119, 121, 172

Orléans, University of, 241; as civil law faculty of Paris, 232–33; origins, 232; rivals Bologna, 233

Orphans. *See Miserabiles personae*

Otto (bishop of Freising), 89

Otto IV, German king and emperor, 205

Otto da Tenengo (cardinal legate), 299–300, 375

Otto of Pavia, 182; on advocates and proctors, 205

Ovid, 33

Oxford, 6, 119, 120, 279, 454; canon law schools, 111–14, 141; church courts, 237; lawyers in, 237. *See also* Councils and synods; John Grim; John of Tynemouth; Walter Map

Oxford, University of, 268, 346; alleged founder, 222; law faculty, 248; Merton College, 276, 277; migration to Cambridge and Reading, 238; origins, 237–39; *suspensio studiorum*, 238

Padua: lawyers' guild, 367; notaries, 402; University, 228, 241. *See also* Councils and synods

Palencia, University of, 242

Palermo, 382

Palmarium, 37, 199, 302, 329

Pandekta. *See* Digest

Panormia, 95, 96, 104. *See also* Ivo, Saint (bishop of Chartres)

Panormitanus, 271, 290, 325–26

Papinian (Roman jurist), 20, 22

Paris, 88, 100, 112, 119, 121, 279; archdeacon's court, 449; availability of trained lawyers, 172; cathedral of Notre Dame, 235; Communauté des procureurs, 368; Confraternity of St. Nicholas, 368; law schools, 90, 108, 110, 122; Order of Advocates, 368; St. Denis, 235; Sainte-Geneviève, 235; St. Victor, 235; Treaty of, 242. *See also* Councils and synods; Gerald of Wales; Honorius III; Innocent III; Orleans

Paris, University of, 221; alleged founder, 222; and the bishops' chancellor, 237; and the church, 234; Collège des dix-huit, 275; College of Autun, 277; College of the Treasurer, 277; dispensations from ban on civil law, 233; and Innocent III, 235–36, 237; law faculty, 231, 246–47; law students a minority, 232; migrations from, 231n44; origins, 230–31, 235–36; Sorbonne, 275; statutes, 236; structure, 230–31; students, 269; teaching licenses, 236–37; teaching of civil law forbidden, 231–32; theological faculty, 231–32. *See also* Robert Courson; Robert de Sorbon
Parlement de Paris, 304, 367–68, 374; clerical advocates, 470
Paschal II (pope), 86, 130, 136
Passaguera (imperial judge), 105
Paucapalea, 101, 106
Paul, Saint, 67
Paul the Deacon, 59
Paulus (Roman jurist), 20, 22
Pavia, 50, 92; law schools, 89, 124, 162n132; lawyers' guild, 367
Pays de droit écrit, 400
Pecia, 273
Peculium castrense, 36
Pepo (master), 80–82
Pérez, Suero (bishop of Zamora), 362
Perugia, University of, 228–29
Peter Abelard, 120, 221, 234
Peter Lombard, 105, 221
Peter of Blois, the elder, 108
Peter of Blois, the younger (archdeacon of Bath), 144
Peter the Chanter, 173n23, 182n50, 216n173; on lawyers' greed, 480
Peter the Venerable (abbot of Cluny), 172; on lawyers' faulty Latin, 484
Peters, Edward, 318
Petrus Beneventanus (cardinal), 201n120
Philip (archbishop of Milan), 205
Philip II, Augustus, king of France, 107n122

Philip III, king of France, 304
Philip IV, the Fair, king of France, 368
Philip VI, king of France, 368
Philippe de Beaumanoir, 313
Piacenza, law schools, 89
Pierre Bertrand (cardinal), 277
Pierre de Belleperche, and conflict of interest, 324
Pilgrimage, 138n45
Pillius, 90
Pisa, admission of advocates, 295
Placentinus, 90, 182, 228, 381
Plebeians, 11, 12
Pliny the Younger, 6, 31; rejects fees, 37
Poitiers, 196
Polycarp (cardinal), 104
Pontiffs, college of, 10–11, 13
Pope: appellate jurisdiction, 135; first instance jurisdiction, 135; legal advisers of, 128; ordinary judge of everyone, 135, 137–38
Practice rules, 309, 312, 313, 319–20. *See also* Legal ethics
Praetor, 16, 17, 25
Praetorian edict, 36, 188, 190
Praevaricatio: death penalty for, 319n111; defined, 30–31, 185–86, 318–19. *See also* Legal ethics
Prague, 142; University of, 243, 282
Prebends, 140–41, 164, 223, 321, 391. *See also* Benefices
Premonstratensians, 109
Principate, 23, 24, 38
Procedural law, 140; and professionalization of lawyers, 151–52, 489. See also *Libellus*; Roman civil procedure; Romano-canonical procedure
Proctors: abandonment of client, 317; access to their services, 471; admissions examination, 282; admissions oath, 301; admissions procedure, 292; admissions registers, 305–6; admission to practice, 218; and advocates, 204–5, 207–8, 283n1, 307, 354–55, 356–57, 359–60, 407; agreements with

clients, 334–35; betrayal of client, 30–31, 185–86, 318–20, 340; career opportunities, 344–39; clerical, 39, 165, 174–79, 194–98, 208–9, 321, 469–71; in *cognitio extra ordinem*, 17; conflict of interest, 30, 189, 315, 317, 319, 320–25; courtroom decorum, 429–30; criticized, 477–87; in *Decretum Gratiani*, 169–70; defined, 4, 167n6; delivery of *libellus*, 419, 430–31; demand for services of, 167, 466; in diplomacy, 464; disciplinary mechanisms, 218, 317–19, 338–42; *dominus litis*, 354, 356; duties to client, 316; duties to court, 316; entering exceptions, 431–32; ethical obligations, 354–55; expenses, 210–11, 337–38, 361–63; fees, 210, 302, 359–60; in formulary procedure, 15; functions, 353–54; gatekeepers of court, 414; -general, 354; hearing dates, 420; income, 364; in litigation, 354–64, 416–17; mandate, 205–6, 359; negligence, 340; and notaries, 169, 290; numbers of, 167–68, 306–8, 357–58; oath of admission, 285–86; occasional, 209–10; officer of court, 188–89, 313; open *litis contestatio*, 433; opportunity costs, 337; at papal curia, 281, 346; partnerships, 358; personal conduct, 313; plenipotentiary powers, 464; prestige, 364; private practice, 348–49; professional, 7; professionalization of, 217–18, 342–43, 488–92; professional organizations, 365–70; retainers, 361; scope of practice, 407–8; social origins, 363–64; standards of conduct, 308–28; standing, 291, 358; and syndics, 353n31; taxation of costs, 334, 336–38; training of, 168–69, 290–91, 355–56; travel, 363; as witness examiners, 147; workplaces, 358–59. *See also* Advocates; Lawyers; Legal ethics; Legal fees; Legal profession; *Praevaricatio*
Profession, meanings of, 1–2, 490–91
Properandum: implementation of, 303–4; influence on civil courts, 304–5; legal fees, 303–5, 360; length of law suits, 448; omitted from Liber Sextus, 303; provisions, 301–3; reaction against, 303; on zealous advocacy, 327
Provence, 92, 172. *See also* Midi
Pseudo-Isidorian Decretals, 64–66, 92
Pythagoras, school of, 287

Quaestiones Londonenses, 112, 120
Questiones Oxoniensis, 157n110
Quinque compilationes antiquae, 117–18
Quintilian, 6, 24; on advocates' fees, 37; on client interviews, 32; criticism of advocates, 33–34; on legal education, 20, 22

Rachymburgi, 54
Rahewin, 89
Ralph Niger, 81
Ralph of Diceto, 172
Ralph of Ford, 141, 209
Ravenna, 50, 57, 81; law schools, 89. *See also* Councils and synods
Raymond VII, count of Toulouse, 242
Raymond des Arènes (Cardinalis), 107n125, 195
Raymond of Penyafort, Saint, 118, 347; on gifts to judges, 390; patron saint of lawyers, 477n32; on sins of lawyers, 483
Raymond von Wiener-Neustadt, 316
Recceswinth, king of the Visigoths, 52
Regensburg, 269
Reggio Emilia, lawyers' guild, 367
Regino (abbot of Prüm), 66, 69
Reims, consistory court, 64, 148–49, 313; calendar, 419. *See also* Councils and synods
Renarius (canon of St. Andreas), 109
Reportationes. *See* Law students: note-taking
Responsa, 11, 17
Rhetoric, use of legal texts, 60
Rhetorica ecclesiastica, 109
Rhineland, 141

Richard I, king of England, 113n148
Richard II, king of England, 392, 393
Richard Barre, 344, 372
Richard de Anstey: litigation costs, 201–2; represented by proctor, 209
Richard de Leycestria (Wetheringsette), 246
Richard of Bury (bishop of Durham), lawyers as enemies of God, 481
Richard Scrope (archbishop of York), 392–93
Robert Courson (cardinal), 182n50, 198; and ethics of advocates, 295–96; and University of Paris, 236
Robert de Camera, 183, 315
Robert de Sorbon, 275
Robert Kilwardby (archbishop of Canterbury), 312, 369
Robert of Flamborough, on lawyers' sins, 483
Robert Winchelsey (archbishop of Canterbury), 288, 312
Rochester, bishops' consistory court, 307, 376
Roffredus Beneventanus, as ambassador, 465n181
Roger de Pont l'Évêque (archbishop of York), 92
Roger of Gloucester (bishop of Worcester), 212
Rogerius (master), 90
Rolandus (master), 106; on clerical proctors, 208–9
Rolandus Bandinelli. *See* Alexander III (pope)
Roman civil procedure, 152; in *audientia episcopalis*, 42; *Cognitio extra ordinem*, 17–19, 53; Formulary system, 15–18; *Legis actiones*, 11, 14–15; *ordines iudiciorum*, 161–62; in *Pseudo-Isidorian Decretals*, 153. *See also* Romano-canonical procedure
Roman Empire, Eastern, 46. *See also* Byzantine Empire
Roman Empire, Western: and barbarians, 47–48; and the church, 47; fall of, 46–47; frontiers of, 47
Roman law: and canon law, 75–76; classical period of, 24; codification of, 21–22; essential for canonists, 124, 233–34; and professionalization of medieval lawyers, 285–86, 490–92; study by clerics prohibited, 124
Roman Republic, 9n1, 10–11, 24, 28; expansion of, 14
Romano-canonical procedure, 5, 7, 125, 126; *allegationes*, 160, 352, 441–42; *apostoli*, 452; appeals, 160–61, 451–55; articulated *libellus*, 434n86; *articuli*, 158, 434; calumny oath, 157, 433–34; complaint, 157, 416–18; contumacy, 417–18; cost-shifting rule, 444; costs orders, 443–44; criminal procedure, 157n110, 415n23, 418n35; denial and counterclaim, 419, 431; depositions, 160; development of, 156; documentary evidence, 159–60, 439; due process, 450; exceptions, 157, 158, 431–32; execution of judgments, 443; full proof, 435; hearsay rule, 436; *Imperator Justinianus*, 162n132; interlocutory judgments, 161, 432; interrogatories, 158, 436–37; *libellus*, 157–58, 418–19, 430–31; *litis contestatio*, 158, 182, 193, 433–34; notice of appeal, 452; oral argument, 160, 440–41; *ordines iudiciarii*, 161–62, 285, 308–9; origin in paradise, 152; *positiones*, 158, 434; privilege against self incrimination, 435; production of witnesses, 435–36; and professionalization of lawyers, 156, 163, 488–89; publication of testimony, 159, 438; redaction of case record, 446; *replicatio*, 157, 431; *sententia*, 160; summary judgment, 432, 434; summary procedure, 157n110, 449–51; summons, 157, 417; suspect documents, 439; taxation of costs, 210–11, 334, 336–38, 444; variations in, 161; witnesses, 158, 435–39. *See also* Judicial decisions

Romans, avarice of, 132
Rome, 50, 57, 136, 454; population of, 171–72. *See also* Curia; Councils and synods
Romeo (Bolognese advocate), 409
Roncaglia, Diet of, 89
Rostock, University of, 282
Rota Romana, 312, 371; auditors of, 376–77, 391–92; courtroom, 421–22; dean, 379; *Decisiones Rotae*, 379–80; *ponens*, 379–80; rotal advocates, 346; scheduling cases, 421
Rothair, Lombard king, 52
Rudolf IV, duke of Austria, 243
Rufinus (master), 106–7; fees of clerical advocates, 194–95; on students with benefices, 277; *Summa*, 111, 175–76
Rupert of Deutz, 215
Rutebeuf, 274

St. Albans, Abbey of, 172
Sainte-Geneviève, 107n122, 121
St. Euverte, 107n122, 121
St. Gall, Abbey of, 101–2
St. Radegund, priory, 239
Saint-Ruf, canons-regular of, 90, 181
St. Swithun, priory, 335
St. Victor, Abbey of (Marseilles), 124
Salamanca, University of, 242, 268, 279
Salic law. *See* Franks: laws
Samius, 31
Samson (abbot of Bury St. Edmunds), 138n45; as papal judge-delegate, 136–37
Sanchez, Tomás: on conflict of interest, 325n129; on discovering opponents' secrets, 326
San Gimigniano, 382
Santa Maria di Reno, 131
Saturnalia, 36n133
Schöffen (scabini), 54, 55
Scholastici, 44, 122. *See also* Advocates; Law teachers
Seffrid II (bishop of Chichester), 141, 209

Senatus (monk of Worcester), 237
Senatusconsultum Claudianum, 36
Senchas Már, 71
Seneca, 23–24
Sepenumero in iudiciis, 109
Serjeants Inn, 368
Seville, 50
Sicard of Cremona (master), 108, 109–10, 409
Sicily, 241, 298. *See also* Frederick II
Siena, 171, 406; lawyers' guild, 367
Siete Partidas. *See* Alfonso X, *el Sabio*
Simone da Borsano, 267
Simon of Sywell (master), 111–13, 141
Simony, 79, 183n52, 195, 277, 389
Simplex canonista, 262
Slane, Ireland, 71
Smyrna, 23
Socrates, 10
Soissons, 147n75
Souviçille, 405
Spain, 176. *See also* Castile; Catalunya
Speculum iuris canonici. *See* Peter of Blois, the elder
Sportula, 37
Statute of Westminster I (1275), 304–5
Stephen (bishop of Tournai), 107, 108, 121, 180, 216n173; fees of clerical advocates, 195; on officialities, 372; *Summa*, 110
Stephen, king of England, 93
Stephen (Sicilian chancellor), 202
Stephen Langton (archbishop of Canterbury), 235; compares lawyers to Philistines, 484
Stourbridge Fair, 240
Studium generale. *See* Universities
Stylus curiae, 289, 415, 454
Suetonius, 18
Suillius, 31
Summa "Antiquitate et tempore," 105n115, 110n133
Summa "De iure naturali," 110
Summa "De multiplici iuris diuisione," 110
Summa "Ecce vicit leo," fees of clerical advocates, 197–98

Summa "Elegantius in iure diuino" (Summa Coloniensis), 109, 152, 191; on advocates and proctors, 204; on calumny oath, 294; on legal fees, 195–96
Summa "Omnis qui iuste iudicat" (Summa Lipsiensis), 111
Summa Parisiensis, 175–76, 195; on contingent fees, 199
Summa "Prima primi," legal fees for beneficed clerics, 197
Summa "Quoniam omissis," 110n144
Summoners. *See* Apparitors
Susanna and the Elders, 437
Syndics, 353n31
Synods, as courts, 68–69, 126n2, 139; papal, 128; procedures, 69. *See also* Councils and synods; Regino of Prüm

Tabelliones. *See* Notaries
Tacitus, 6, 31; on advocates' fees, 35–36; *Germania*, 51n15
Tancred (master, archdeacon of Bologna), 117n160, 171, 335; as ambassador, 465n181; on arbiters and arbitrators, 461; *Ordo iudiciarius*, 155, 162, 285, 461
Tarragona, 50. *See also* Councils and synods
Theobald (archbishop of Canterbury), 92, 215
Theodoric II, Ostrogothic king, 52
Theodosian Code, 21–22, 56, 58, 60, 104. *See also the citations index*
Theodosius I, Roman emperor, 42
Theodosius II, Roman emperor, 21, 58, 222
Theologians, rivalry with lawyers, 215–16, 231–32
Thomas Aquinas, Saint, 384
Thomas Arundel (archbishop of Canterbury), 392–93
Thomas Becket, Saint (archbishop of Canterbury), 88, 111, 211–12, 224
Thomas Kent, 369
Thomas More, Saint, 477n32
Thomas of Marlborough (abbot of Evesham), 112, 180, 204, 205; lawsuit against bishop of Worcester, 155, 171n14, 201, 454–55
Thomas of Sauteyrargues, 349
Tiberius Coruncanius, 13
Toledo, 50. *See also* Councils and synods
Toulouse, 50, 279; University of, 242, 268. *See also* Councils and synods; Jean Coursier; Raymond VII
Tournai, 147n75, 303, 376. *See also* Councils and synods; Flanders; Guibert of Tournai; Stephen (bishop of Tournai)
Tours, 120. *See also under* Councils and synods
Traditio apostolica, 40
Travel, hardships of, 138
Treviso, lawyers' guild, 367
Tribonian, and codification of Roman law, 57–58
Trier, 68n85; bishops' consistory, 424. *See also under* Councils and synods
Tübingen Law Book, 91
Tuscany, 81, 84. *See also* Florence
Twelfth century: commercial revival, 77; legal revival, 77–78; renaissance, 76
Twelve Tables, 11–13, 57

Ubertus de Bobbio, 308n74
Ulpian, 13–14, 20, 22, 311; on advocates' functions, 25; on advocates' shortcomings, 34; criteria for advocates' fees, 37; discourages taking fees, 37; jurists as priests, 475–76
Universitas, meaning of, 221n9
Universities, 6; colleges, 275–77; as corporate bodies, 219; disputations, 255–57; examinations, 257–62; foundation fables, 222; founded by public authorities, 241–43; as guilds, 221; law degrees, 219–20, 258–65; law faculties, 244–48; lectures, 249–50; mother of professions, 219; origins, 221–22; *repetitiones*, 254; and society, 243–44; stationers, 272–73; theology faculties, 244.

See also Arezzo; Avignon; Barcelona; Bologna, University of; Cahors; Cambridge, University of; Coimbra; Cracow; Curia, papal; Erfurt; Heidelberg; Law faculties; Law schools; Law teaching; Leipzig; Lérida; Louvain; Montpellier; Naples; Orléans, University of; Oxford, University of; Padua; Palencia; Paris, University of; Perugia; Prague; Salamanca; Toulouse; Vercelli; Vicenza; Vienna; Würzburg
Urban II (pope), 95–96, 128, 129
Urban V (pope), 243
Urban VI (pope), 392

Vacarius, (master), 92–94
Valens, Roman emperor, 69n85
Valentinian III, Roman emperor, 21, 56–57
Vanialbo, 362
Vassals, 322
Vercelli, University of, 241
Vespasian, Roman emperor, 22–23
Vicar-general, 142, 142n56
Vicenza, University of, 228, 241
Vienna, University of, 243
Villa Mayor, 362
Vincennes, 374
Vincentius Hispanus, 192; on conflict of interest, 322
Vinogradoff, Sir Paul Gavrilovich, 76
Virgin Mary, as an advocate, 477
Visigoths, 50; laws, 52, 56
Visitations, episcopal, 66–67

Wales, customary law, 72
Walfredus, 99n94
Walter de Merton, 276, 277
Walter Map (archdeacon of Oxford), 108n127, 114n151
Walter of Châtillon, 144–45, 219; criticizes lawyers, 484
Widows. See *Miserabiles personae*
William (archbishop of Tyre), 88

William (bishop of Paris), priests not to practice as advocates, 196
William (curial advocate), 201n120
William, duke of Aquitaine, 184n56
William Doune: career, 472; on lawyers' sins, 484; on legal fees, 331; *Memoriale presbiterorum*, 472
William Durand (bishop of Mende), 301, 335, 446; advocates as angels, 476; on arbitration procedure, 461–62; on client interviews, 314; commentary on 2 Lyons, 303; on conflict of interest, 319, 321–22, 324; on consulting fees, 458–59; on courtroom attire, 425; on excessive fees, 330–31, 403; on fee negotiation, 333; on flattering judges, 426–27; on *libelli*, 418–19; on litigation tactics, 428–29; on securing payment of fees, 333–34; *Speculum iudiciale*, 309, 310; on taxation of costs, 336–37
William Elphinstone (bishop of Aberdeen), 467
William Langland, on greedy lawyers, 480
William Lyndwood, on advocates' legal learning, 288–89
William of Canterbury, 110
William of Drogheda: on arbiters and arbitrators, 461; engaging an advocate, 414–15; fee payments, 334; suspect judges, 385–86
William of Pagula, 327
William of Saône (treasurer of Rouen), 277
William Wickwane (archbishop of York), 303
Wiltshire, 143n57, 151n89
Winchester: bishop of, 201; cathedral, 335
Winroth, Anders, 100–101
Woodcock, Brian L., 451
Worcester: bishop of, 155, 201. *See also* Councils and synods; Roger of Gloucester; Thomas of Marlborough
Worms, cathedral school of, 67

Würzburg: examination board, 292; lawyers' guild, 367; university, 243
Wrocław, 142

York, 113; archbishop's court, 307–8, 376; dean and chapter's court, 420; Minster, 148. *See also* Councils and synods; Henry Bowett; Richard Scrope; Roger de Pont l'Évêque; Thomas Arundel; William Wickwane
Ypres, notaries, 402

Zamora, 362
Zeno, 10
Zoen Tencarari, 275

Citations Index

Biblical

OLD TESTAMENT

Gen. 3:24, 476
Exod. 23:6, 190n79
Exod. 40:12–15, 475
Deut. 1:16, 384n41
Deut. 16:18, 384n42, 388
Deut. 16:19, 384n42, 388
Deut. 16:20, 384n42
Deut. 17:6, 435n88
Deut. 24:14, 190n79
Job 36:17–19, 384n42
Ps. 23 (Vulgate 22), 132n24
Ps. 36:6 (Vulgate 35:7), 427n61
Ps. 50:6 (Vulgate 49), 384n42
Ps. 104:4 (Vulgate 103), 476n29
Ps. 119:103–105 (Vulgate 118), 427n61
Prov. 10:23, 310n80
Prov. 14:21, 190n79
Prov. 31:9, 190, n79
Eccles. 4:10, 412n13
Jer. 23:1–5, 132n24
Jer. 25:34–38, 132n24
Jer. 31:10, 132n24
Dan. 12:3, 267
Dan. 13:42–63, 437

NEW TESTAMENT

Matt. 10:16, 428n68
Matt. 20:1–2, 278n210
Matt. 22:35, 40n149
Matt. 23:23, 40n149
Matt. 26:11, 190
Luke 7:30, 40n149
Luke 10:7, 278n210
Luke 10:25, 40n149
Luke 11:45–46, 40n149
Luke 14:1–6, 40n149
John 8:17, 435n88
John 10:1–16, 132n24
Acts 25:16, 190n79
Rom. 4:15, 40n149
1 Cor. 6:1–8, 459
1 Cor. 9:7, 193n90, 328n140, 474n23
2 Cor. 13:1, 435n88
Gal. 3:10–13, 40n149
Heb. 10:28, 435n88
1 Tim. 1:8–10, 40n149
2 Tim. 2:4, 39n148, 208, 470n11
James 1:19, 287
2 Peter 2:20, 470n11

Canon Law

DECRETUM GRATIANI

D. 2 c. 5, 459n163
D. 4 d.p.c. 2, 383n37
D. 10 c. 3, 139n48
D. 10 d.p.c. 6, 139n48
D. 10 c. 7, 139n48
D. 19 d.a.c. 7, 116n155
D. 20 pr., 116n155, 375n11
D. 21 c. 1, 179n42
D. 21 c. 9, 378n21
D. 23 c. 1, 129n11
D. 23 c. 22, 149n84
D. 24 c. 2, 257n139
D. 24 d.p.c. 4, 257n239
D. 25 c. 1, 149n84, 150n87
D. 26 c. 3, 316n97
D. 27 c. 8, 179n43
D. 36 d.p.c. 2, 373n6
D. 36 c. 3, 40n149, 122n176
D. 36 d.p.c. 15, 373n6
D. 37 d.p.c. 8, 271n191

D. 37 c. 12, 121n172, 121n174, 226n25, 236n68
D. 37 c. 14, 254n130
D. 38 c. 1, 257n140
D. 38 c. 4, 40n149, 122n176, 139n48, 174n28
D. 38 c. 6, 346n6
D. 38 c. 7, 139n48
D. 38 c. 12, 266n175
D. 39 c. 1, 139n48
D. 43 d.p.c. 5, 312n87
D. 45 c. 9, 187n70, 315n94
D. 45 c. 10, 170n11
D. 49 c. 1, 312n87
D. 50 c. 36, 178n38
D. 50 c. 64, 150n87
D. 51 pr., 170n13, 175n29
D. 51 c. 1, 175n29, 178n38
D. 53 c. 1, 177n37
D. 54 c. 3, 177n37
D. 61 c. 10, 175n30
D. 63 c. 3, 266n175
D. 68 c. 5, 316n97
D. 84 pr., 177n34
D. 84 c. 1, 68n82
D. 86 c. 26, 176n32, 194n94, 469n10
D. 87 pr., 177n34
D. 87 c. 1, 177n34
D. 87 c. 2, 68n82, 177n34
D. 87 c. 5, 184n56, 186n64
D. 88 c. 1, 197n106, 209n145
D. 88 c. 4, 68n80, 171n14
D. 88 c. 10, 177n37
D. 89 c. 5, 170n41
D. 93 c. 6, 149n83
D. 94 d.a.c. 3, 149n84
D. 94 c. 3, 149n84
D. 96 c. 7, 179n41
D. 96 c. 11, 203n127, 321n118
C. 1 q. 1 c. 8, 389n60
C. 1 q. 2 c. 11, 236n64 and n65
C. 1 q. 3 c. 8, 233n54

C. 1 q. 3 c. 10, 170n13, 183n52, 338n175, 389n60
C. 1 q. 3 c. 11, 333n158
C. 2 q. 1 c. 7, 384n43
C. 2 q. 1 c. 19, 325n230
C. 2 q. 3 d.p.c. 7, 315n96
C. 2 q. 3 c. 8, 186n64, 186n66
C. 2 q. 3 d.p.c. 8, 185n60, 186n63, 318n109
C. 2 q. 4 pr., 435n88
C. 2 q. 6 c. 28, 204n130
C. 2 q. 6 c. 29, 204n130
C. 2 q. 6 c. 33, 461n169
C. 2 q. 6 d.p.c. 33, 170n11, 445n124, 459n163
C. 2 q. 6 d.p.c. 36, 170n11
C. 2 q. 6 c. 38, 187n69, 325n131, 382n36
C. 2 q. 6 d.p.c. 39, 445n124
C. 2 q. 7 d.p.c. 9, 387n51
C. 2 q. 7 c. 10–15, 387n51
C. 2 q. 7 d.p.c. 27, 387n51
C. 2 q. 7 d.p.c. 52, 99n95
C. 3 q. 3 c. 1–4, 416n26
C. 3 q. 5 c. 15, 126n2, 179n40, 197n107, 385n44
C. 3 q. 7 pr., 204n131
C. 3 q. 7 c. 1, 173n22, 204n130, 206n138, 318n106, 387n51
C. 3 q. 7 d.p.c. 1, 143n58, 271n191, 286n8, 287n11, 324n127, 387n51
C. 3 q. 7 c. 2, 3n4, 170n12, 173n22, 191n85, 193nn91–92, 199n112, 113, 115, 200n117, 204n130, 205nn131–32, 286nn8–9, 309n78, 318n106, 323n125, 324n125, 327n137, 329n143, 330n146, 332nn156–57, 333n258, 339n178, 340nn182–83,

341n185, 351n24, 459n163, 471n16
C. 3 q. 7 c. 4, 325n130, 383n38
C. 3 q. 9 c. 18, 204n130, 207n141
C. 4 q. 2 c. 3, 187n69
C. 4 q. 4 c. 1, 325n129
C. 5 q. 3 pr., 178n39, 204n130, 207n141
C. 5 q. 3 c. 2, 207n141
C. 5 q. 3 c. 3, 176n33, 204n130 and n131, 207n141, 470n12
C. 5 q. 4 c. 3, 184n58, 207n141
C. 6 q. 1 c. 17, 318n106
C. 6 q. 1 c. 18, 318n106
C. 6 q. 1 c. 19, 318n106
C. 6 q. 4 c. 7, 68n83
C. 9 q. 3 c. 2, 373n5
C. 9 q. 3 c. 17, 68n83, 135n35
C. 10 q. 2 c. 4, 193n90
C. 11 q. 1 c. 29, 470n12
C. 11 q. 1 d.p.c. 30, 139n48
C. 11 q. 1 c. 38, 170n11, 179n43
C. 11 q. 1 c. 39, 459n163
C. 11 q. 1 c. 46, 170n11, 459n163
C. 11 q. 3 c. 3, 254n130
C. 11 q. 3 c. 66, 389n60
C. 11 q. 3 c. 71, 191n85, 193n92, 333n158, 383n38, 389n60, 458n158
C. 12 q. 2 c. 66, 335n167
C. 12 q. 3 c. 71, 177n34, 183n52, 193n90, 200n119
C. 13 q. 1 c. 1, 193n90
C. 13 q. 3 c. 11, 191n85
C. 14 q. 2 pr., 325n131
C. 14 q. 2 d.p.c.1, 325n131
C. 14 q. 5 c. 2, 178n38
C. 14 q. 5 c. 10, 177n34, 203n127, 321n118

C. 14 q. 5 c. 15, 187n70,
  191n85, 193n90, 198n108,
  389n60
C. 15 q. 1 c. 1, 178n39
C. 15 q. 2 pr., 179n40,
  198n108
C. 15 q. 2 c. 1, 176n32,
  177n36, 197n105,
  469n10, 470n12
C. 15 q. 2 d.p.c. 1, 194n95,
  328n140
C. 15 q. 3 pr., 143n58
C. 15 q. 3 c. 1–3, 217n177
C. 15 q. 4 c. 1–2, 420n42
C. 15 q. 7 c. 6, 373n5
C. 16 q. 1 c. 6, 179n42,
  197n106
C. 16 q. 1 c. 8, 197n106
C. 16 q. 1 c. 40, 179n43
C. 16 q. 1 d.p.c. 40, 179n42,
  257n140
C. 16 q. 1 c. 61, 99n95
C. 16 q. 1 c. 115, 99n95
C. 16 q. 1 c. 181, 99n95
C. 16 q. 2 c. 20, 287n11
C. 16 q. 2 c. 25, 287n11
C. 16 q. 6 d.p.c. 7, 204n130
C. 16 q. 7 c. 12, 179n42
C. 17 q. 4 c. 27, 179n43
C. 17 q. 4 c. 28, 179n43
C. 17 q. 4 c. 29, 179n43
C. 21 q. 2 c. 9, 314n94
C. 21 q. 3 c. 1, 176n33,
  177n34, 194n94, 469n10
C. 21 q. 3 c. 2, 177n37,
  209n145
C. 21 q. 3 c. 4, 209n145
C. 21 q. 3 c. 4, 177n37,
  209n145
C. 21 q. 3 c. 5, 177n37
C. 21 q. 3 c. 6, 177n37
C. 21 q. 3 c. 7, 177n37,
  178n38
C. 22 q. 4 c. 23, 203n126
C. 22 q. 5 c. 17, 420n43

C. 22 q. 5 c. 18, 18n56
C. 23 q. 1 c. 5, 185n59
C. 23 q. 2 c. 2, 327n136
C. 23 q. 5 c. 8, 170n13,
  188n71
C. 23 q. 8 c. 4, 178n38
C. 23 q. 8 c. 6, 178n38
C. 23 q. 8 c. 29, 270n187
C. 23 q. 8 c. 30, 177n36,
  178n37, 198n108,
  270n187
C. 24 q. 3 c. 1, 316n97
C. 24 q. 3 c. 19, 187n70
C. 27 q. 1 c. 40, 179n43
C. 27 q. 3 pr., 177n37,
  209n145
C. 28 q. 1 c. 8, 193n90
C. 30 q. 5 c. 11, 381nn31–33
C. 31 q. 7 d.p.c. 1, 339n178
D. 3 de pen. c. 35, 314n94
D. 6 de pen. c. 1, 315n94,
  375n11
C. 33 q. 5 c. 17, 143n58

DECRETALES
GREGORII IX

Proem., *Rex pacificus*,
  118n162
1.2.1, 383n37
1.2.11, 236n65, 418n34
1.3.28, 138n45, 206n137,
  449n134
1.5.3, 381n32
1.6.1, 156n41
1.6.19, 387n52
1.6.47, 353n31
1.9.6, 378n22
1.11.17, 318n106
1.14.11, 270n186
1.14.15, 373n6
1.16.1, 338n176
1.23.1, 149n84
1.23.7, 149nn83–84,
  150n87, 373n5
1.23.9, 149n84, 257n141

1.24.1–4, 150n87
1.29.5, 135n36
1.29.16, 135n36
1.29.17, 325n129, 383n38
1.29.19, 144n60
1.29.28, 452n145
1.29.33, 219n110
1.31.13, 325n130
1.32.1, 188n73, 191n83,
  198n110, 309n77,
  340n182, 374n13, 410n6
1.35.1, 335nn167–68
1.35.3, 335n167
1.36.2, 470n12
1.37 pr., 290n21
1.37.1, 173n25, 196n104,
  198n108, 231n47, 287n12,
  333n161, 469n10,
  470n12, 471n14
1.37.2, 287n12, 469n10,
  471n14
1.37.3, 321n119, 327n137,
  471n14, 483n54
1.38.1, 206n137, 359n50
1.38.2, 359n51, 418n34
1.38.3, 206n136
1.38.4, 356n40, 359n49
1.38.6, 211n150, 325n132,
  359n51, 363n62
1.38.7, 236n66
1.38.9, 353n31
1.38.14, 358n47
1.39.1, 353n31
1.41.2, 340n184
1.43.2, 326n132
2.1.7, 435n90
2.1.14, 341n186
2.2.17, 336n172, 387n52
2.3.2, 419n38
2.5.1, 433nn83–84
2.6.2, 386n50
2.7.1, 293n33, 294n37,
  434n85, 480n40
2.7.2, 293n33
2.14.5, 336n172, 448n131

2.15.3, 211n150
2.17.1, 336n172, 338n175
2.18.1, 318n106, 384n43
2.19.11, 214n161, 396n85, 399n92, 437n97
2.20.14, 179n41
2.20.37, 435n89
2.20.40, 325n130, 383n38
2.20.52, 436n95
2.21.1–3, 435n89
2.21.4, 326n134
2.22.2, 213n156, 398n92, 439n102
2.22.3, 439n103
2.22.6, 439nn102–3
2.22.9, 439n102
2.22.10, 439n102
2.24.16, 461n169
2.25.5, 383n40
2.25.12, 432n81
2.26.16, 193n90
2.27.16, 378n21, 378n22
2.28.11, 452n145
2.28.36, 325n129
2.28.59, 453n146
2.28.60, 386n49
2.28.61, 385n44, 386n47, 386n49, 390n67
3.1.7, 226n25
3.1.10, 332n156, 359n51, 383n38, 389nn61–62, 390n64, 392n71
3.1.15, 217n177
3.3.2, 270n188
3.5.4, 170n13, 197n106
3.35.8, 450n136
3.39.21, 328n140
3.50.2, 208n144
3.50.3, 124n182, 177n37, 197n106, 231n47, 233n53
3.50.4, 208n144, 231n47
3.50.5, 177n37
4.1.6, 315n94
4.14.1, 375n11
5.1.17, 324n127

5.1.21, 318n106
5.1.26, 450n136
5.5.1, 121n172, 122n175, 236n68
5.5.2, 236n68
5.5.3, 236n68, 257n140, 266n175
5.5.4, 122n175
5.5.5, 267n176, 278n210
5.7.10, 287n12
5.7.11, 384n43
5.7.13, 287n12
5.12.19, 314n94
5.20.5, 440n104
5.33.24, 452n142
5.33.28, 231n46
5.34.16, 383n38, 389n62
5.38.12, 314n94
5.38.13, 314n94

LIBER SEXTUS

1.3.3, 478n34
1.3.11, 383n38, 390nn65–66, 435n90
1.6.43, 449n135, 450n136
1.19.1, 356n40
2.2.1, 448n131, 478n34
2.10.3, 325n131
2.14.1, 383n37, 383n38
2.15.1, 378n22
3.2.1, 270n186
5.2.20, 449n135, 450n136
5.7.2, 233n53
5.11.1, 279n23
5 RJ 12, 383n39

CONSTITUTIONES
CLEMENTINAE

2.1.2, 449n135, 450n136
5.11.2, 418n36, 419n40, 449n135, 450n138

EXTRAVAGANTES
COMMUNES

2.1.1, 138n45

Roman Law

INSTITUTES

1.20.7, 206n135
2.23.12, 293n31
4.10, 17n35
4.16.1, 28n93, 293n31

CODE

1.1.1, 42n156
1.1.2, 42n156
1.2.21, 310n83, 311n83
1.3.25, 338n176
1.3.40(41), 176n32, 287n11
1.4.15, 39n147, 287n11
1.11.10, 39n147
1.19.8, 312n87
1.51.14, 26n83, 30n102, 188n71, 325n129
2.1.4 153n96
2.4.15, 315n94
2.6.1, 339n178
2.6.2, 324n125
2.6.3, 37n137, 200n119, 329n144, 330n146, 335n168
2.6.4, 29n99
2.6.5, 3n4, 29n99, 38n141, 199n111, 332n154 and n155, 335n168
2.6.6, 30n102, 38n141, 188n71, 194n92, 310n78, 314n93, 325nn129–30, 329n143, 333n161, 426n59
2.6.7, 33n116, 188n72, 198n110, 339n178, 340n182
2.6.8, 3n4, 26n83, 39n147, 173n24, 287n11, 310n82, 311n82, 475n26
2.7.1, 30n107, 186n63 and n65, n66, 187n67, 318n106, 318n109, 324n128

CITATIONS INDEX * 605

2.7.3, 3n4, 26n84, 328n139
2.7.4, 3n4, 36n135, 193n92, 365n67
2.7.6, 26n84, 364n66, 475n25
2.7.9, 27n90
2.7.11, 26n84 and n86, 27n87 and n88, 289n18, 290n21, 292n27, 306n64, 475n25
2.7.13, 24n73, 26n82 and n85, 27n87 and n88, 285n6, 306n64
2.7.14, 3n4, 27n90, 170n13, 185n59, 198n108, 351n25, 474nn22–23
2.7.15, 27n88
2.7.17, 27n87
2.7.18, 3n4
2.7.20, 3n4
2.7.22, 26n86, 27n89, 174n26
2.7.23, 364n66
2.7.24, 3n4, 174n26, 288n15, 307n72, 365n70, 374n12
2.7.26, 307n72
2.7.29, 306n64
2.8(9).1, 30n102, 324n125
2.8(9).2, 323n125, 324n125
2.9(10).1, 187n57
2.9(10).2, 187n57
2.10(11).1, 184n57, 381n30
2.12(13).12, 365n67
2.12(13).22, 354n33, 356n40
2.12(13).23, 354n33, 356n40
2.12(13).25, 207n141
2.27.24, 288
2.52(53).6, 29n99
2.55(56).3, 461n169
2.58(59).2, 28n93, 296n44
3.1.7, 288
3.1.9, 381n33
3.1.13, 29n99, 36n134, 192n89, 317n104,

336n171, 338n177, 444n119, 447n127
3.1.14, 28n94, 294n36, 294n38, 327n137
3.1.15, 337n173, 338n177
3.1.16, 385n44, 386n48
3.1.17, 289n17
3.2.4, 318n106
3.5.1, 385n44
3.13.4, 371n1
3.13.7, 225n22
3.28.33, 450n136
4.6.11, 193n91
4.20.11, 435n90
4.21.17, 39n143
4.28.5, 272n192
4.34.4, 211n150
7.6.1, 14n23
7.14.3, 416n26
7.45.4, 153n96
7.45.13, 383n37
7.49.1, 186n62, 186n64, 318nn107–8
7.62.39, 312n87
7.65.5, 453n146
7.65.7, 375n14
9.22.21, 39n144
9.22.22, 450n136
9.43.3, 185n61
10.32(31).10, 364n67
10.32(31).15, 39n146
10.52(53).7, 266n175
10.59(57).1, 365n67
10.61(59).1, 30n105
10.65(63).2, 37n137, 329n144
11.9.1, 23n65
11.48(47).20, 29n99
11.74(73).2, 371n1
12.1.2, 26n79
12.15.1, 23n64, 267n177
12.61(62).2, 37n137, 329nn143–44

DIGEST

Const. *Omnem*, 57n39, 174n26, 375n12
1.1.1, 161n130, 311n83, 384n41, 476n28
1.1.6, 81n27
1.1.9, 161n130
1.2.2, 81n27
1.2.4, 457n155
1.12.1, 30n104, 266n173
1.16.1, 310n78
1.16.2, 310n78
1.16.6, 191n85, 389n58
1.16.9, 24n73, 25n74, 30n104, 33n116, 34n125, 189n72
1.22.1, 24n70
2.1.5, 371n1
2.1.6, 371n1
2.1.17, 188n71, 325n129
2.13.10, 311n86
2.14.2, 464n178
2.14.53, 38n141, 199n115, 332n155
3.1.1, 25nn74–75, 26nn79–80, 170n12; 173n23, 186n66, 189n72; 191n81, 286n8, 327n137, 351n24, 364n66, 410n6
3.1.3, 173n24
3.1.6, 285n6
3.1.7, 285n6, 339n178
3.1.9, 285n6
3.1.11, 30n102
3.1.12, 324n125
3.2.4, 30n106, 185n60, 186n63, 186n66, 318n109
3.2.20, 326n133
3.3.1, 17n35
3.3.8, 30nn103–4
3.3.22, 30n103
3.3.31, 354n33
3.3.41, 26n80
3.4.1, 26n81

4.3.1, 318n109
4.3.7, 30n107
4.3.33, 318n109
4.4.18, 31n110, 186n65, 318n105
4.8.25, 326n133
4.8.27, 461n169
4.8.31, 31n108, 186n65, 318n109, 319n110
4.8.32, 309n76
4.18.1, 186n63
5.1.12, 286n8
5.1.15, 383n37
5.2.1, 316n97
5.2.32, 30n102
9.2.52, 315n94
10.2.39, 211n150, 338n176
11.6.1, 36n134
12.2.28, 315n94
12.2.42, 315n94
12.3.4, 338n177
12.3.5, 337n173
12.21(22).8, 39n145
12.29(30).3, 39n145
17.1.2, 326n133
17.1.7, 193n92
17.1.26, 144n60
17.1.27, 144n60
17.2.6, 461n169
17.2.76, 461n167, 461n169
18.1.1, 464n178
19.2.38, 36nn134–35
21.1.31, 475n27
22.3.2, 153n96
22.5.3, 173n23
22.5.25, 31n111, 187n68, 325n131
22.6.2, 315n94
26.7.12, 271n191
27.1.6, 23n64
27.13.1, 474n22
29.7.14, 315n94
34.2.32, 312n87
35.2.5, 312n87

39.2.39, 211n150
43.5.3, 39n143
44.1.3, 432n80
46.7.5, 211n150
47.15.1, 30n106, 185n61, 186n62, 318n109
47.15.2, 185nn60–61
47.15.3, 31n110, 318n109
47.15.4, 30n107
47.15.5, 30n107, 108n109, 185n61, 186n66
47.15.7, 185n61
47.22.3, 26n81
48.2.8, 173n23
48.10.1, 31n108, 186n66, 319n110
48.10.13, 29n95
48.16.1, 30n106, 185n61, 186n62, 318n109
48.16.6, 185n61
48.16.7, 185n61
48.19.9, 24n70, 30nn104–5
48.19.38, 31n108, 319n110
49.1.1, 453n146
49.1.6, 178n38
49.16.6, 185n60
50.2.3, 30n105
50.13.1, 23n64, 24n70, 25n75, 36nn135–36, 37n137, 37n139, 38nn140–41, 191nn84–85, 193n92, 202n123, 271n191, 288n15, 329nn143–44, 330n146, 332n158, 333n159, 334n166, 457, 467n4, 476n28
50.13.4, 24n71, 36n134, 193n92
50.13.6, 318n105, 383n37
50.16.88, 311n86
50.16.233, 28n93
50.17.2, 26n80

NOVELLAE LEGES

1 epilogue, 191n84
22.10, 338n177
44.1.1, 39n146
44.1.4, 39n145
44.2, 39n144
53.1, 336n171
53.3, 386n50
82.10, 336n171
86.2, 384n44, 461n167
96.2, 386n50
123.6, 39n148
124.1, 296n44

THEODOSIAN CODE
Codex Theodosianus

1.1.5, 58n43
1.5.12, 371n1
1.5.13, 371n1
1.27.1, 42n157
1.29.1, 170n13
2.6.6, 30n102
2.7.2, 29n99
2.10.1, 27n87, 307n72
2.10.2, 26n85, 29n96, 306n64, 317n104
2.10.3, 29n99
2.10.6, 3n4, 36n135, 170n13
2.11.1, 29n100
2.12.7, 17n35
2.18.1, 381n33
6.21.1, 23n64
8.10.2, 37n137, 329n144
9.1.3, 32n114
9.19.1, 39n144
12.1.3, 39n146
12.1.152, 26n81, 26n84
14.9.3, 23n65
14.10.2–4, 48n5
16.1.2, 42n156
16.2.23, 69n85
16.5.6, 42n156

Constitutiones Sirmondianae

1, 42n158
3, 68n84

Novellae Theodosii

10.1.4, 26n84
10.2, 27n87

Novellae Valentiniani

2.2.4, 27n87, 170n13
10.2, 27n87
32.1.6, 57n37